TOM

TOM

The Unknown

TENNESSEE WILLIAMS

Lyle Leverich

CROWN PUBLISHERS, INC.

NEW YORK

Grateful acknowledgment is made to the following for permission to reprint previously published material.

NEW DIRECTIONS PUBLISHING CORPORATION: Excerpted material from *Collected Stories* by Tennessee Williams. Copyright © 1939, 1945, 1950, 1954, 1966, 1982 by Tennessee Williams. Excerpted material from *The Glass Menagerie* by Tennessee Williams. Copyright © 1945 by Tennessee Williams and Edwina D. Williams. Excerpted material from *In the Winter of Cities* by Tennessee Williams. Copyright © 1956, 1964 by Tennessee Williams. Excerpted material from *Orpheus Descending/Battle of Angels*. Copyright © 1955, 1958 by Tennessee Williams. Excerpted material from *27 Wagons Full of Cotton and Other One-Act Plays*. Copyright © 1945, 1953 by Tennessee Williams. Excerpted material from *Vieux Carré*. Copyright © 1977, 1979 by Tennessee Williams. Excerpted material from *Where I Live: Selected Essays*. Copyright © 1944, 1947, 1978. Reprinted by permission of New Directions Publishing Corporation.

MARGUERITE COURTNEY: Excerpted material from *Laurette* by Marguerite Courtney. Copyright © 1968 by Marguerite Courtney. Reprinted by permission.

WILLIAM JAY SMITH: Excerpted material from *Army Brat: A Memoir* by William Jay Smith, published in 1980 by Persea Books, copyright © 1980 by William Jay Smith. Excerpts reprinted by permission.

THE NEW YORK POST: Excerpted material from "A Man Named Tennessee" by Robert Rice (articles in the *New York Post*). Copyright © 1958 by the *New York Post*. Reprinted by permission.

All previously unpublished material of Tennessee Williams © John L. Eastman, Trustee under the Will of Tennessee Williams, 1995.

Published by Crown Publishers, Inc., 201 East 50th Street,
New York, New York 10022.
Member of the Crown Publishing Group.
Random House, Inc. New York, London, Toronto, Sydney, Auckland
CROWN is a trademark of Crown Publishers, Inc.

Manufactured in the United States of America

Design by Lenny Henderson

Library of Congress Cataloging-in-Publication Data
Leverich, Lyle.
Tom : the unknown Tennessee Williams / Lyle Leverich.—1st ed.
Includes index.
1. Williams, Tennessee, 1911–1983—Biography. 2. Dramatists, American—20th century—Biography. 3. Leverich, Lyle—Friends and associates. I. Title.
PS3545.I5365Z736   1995
812'.54—dc20   95-6038
[B]

ISBN 0-517-70225-8
10 9 8 7 6 5 4 3 2 1
First Edition

For Tennessee,
who asked me to report,
in truth,
his cause aright.

Contents

PART I   LODESTAR   1900–1929

PART II   MOONWARD   1929–1937

PART III   OUTER SPACE   1937–1939

PART IV   WANDERINGS   1940–1943

PART V   NEW HARBORS   1943–1945

GENEALOGY OF
Tennessee Williams

John Lanier, French Huguenot, immigrated to England, and to the USA in 1658

The Williamses came of an ancient Welsh family of Langallen

John and Mary Williams from Wales in 1738

Half-brothers

Sampson Lanier
m.
Elizabeth
Washington

Nicholas
Lanier

Nathaniel
Williams
Hanover County,
Va

Williams

Orig. Daykin
Norman-English,
1066

James Lanier
c. 1724–1786
m.
Mary Cooke
d. 1774

Thomas Lanier
b. 1722
m. 1744
Elizabeth
Hicks
b. 1722

Timothy Dakin
b. 1723
A Quaker from NY
m.
Lydia Fish
b. 1725

Col. Joseph "Duke of
Surrey" Williams
1748–1827
m.
Rebekah Lanier
1757–1832

John Williams
1745–1799
m.
Elizabeth
Williamson

Preserved Fish
Dakin
1749–1835
m.
Deborah Akin
1755–1804

Sampson
Lanier II
1770–1823
m.
Elizabeth
Massey
1770–1834

Betty Lanier
m.
Maj. Joseph
W. Winston

Daykin

James Dakin
1790–1857
Judge of
Common Pleas
m.
Mary Ann
Sabin

Sterling Lanier
1794–1870
m.
Sarah Fulwood
1803–1868

"Prince John" Williams,
1778–1837
U.S. Senator and
Minister to Guatemala
m.
Melinda White
1789–1838

Thomas Lanier
Williams I
1786–1856
Senator, Judge
m.
Polly L. McClung

Brothers from
Hamburg, Germany
immigrated
1857   1863

William   Frank Henry
Otte   Otte
m.
Elizabeth
von Albertzart

Robert Sampson
Lanier
1819–1893
of Macon, Georgia
m.
Mary Jane
Anderson
1822–1865

Dr. Edwin
Francis
Dakin
1819–1892
m.
Hannah Bellar
1825–1886

Col. John
Williams II
1818–1881
m.
Rhoda Campbell
Morgan
1819–1867

Margaret
Williams
m.
Richard Pearson
Chief Justice,
North Carolina

Estelle, Clemence,
and Frank
Otte

Sidney Clopton
Lanier
1842–1881
"America's Sweet
Singer of Songs"

Thomas Lanier
Williams II
1849–1908
Tennessee
Commissioner
of Railroads
m.
Isabella Coffin
1853–1884

John Williams III
1847–1933
m.
Lizzie Nelson
1852–1885

Mary Williams
m.
David Meriwether

The Rev. Walter
Edwin Dakin
1857–1954
m.
Rosina
Maria Francesca
von Albertzart-
Otte ("Grand")
1863–1944

Ella Williams
1875–1958

Cornelius Coffin
Williams
1879–1957
m.
Edwina Estelle
Dakin
1884–1980

Isabel Williams
1883–1938
m.
William G. Brownlow II
(Grandson of William
"Parson" Gannaway
Brownlow,
Gov. of Tennessee,
1885)

Lanier

Rose Isabel
Williams
1909–

Thomas Lanier Williams III
"TENNESSEE"
1911–1983

Walter Dakin
Williams
1919–
m.
Joyce Crost
1921–

STRIKE DAKYN   IN THE HEMPE
THE DEVIL'S

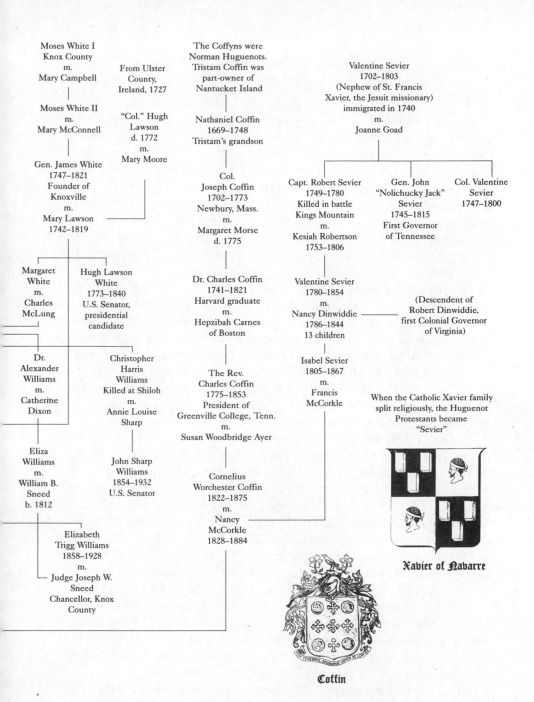

Moses White I
Knox County
m.
Mary Campbell
|
Moses White II
m.
Mary McConnell
|
Gen. James White
1747–1821
Founder of
Knoxville
m.
Mary Lawson
1742–1819

From Ulster
County,
Ireland, 1727

"Col." Hugh
Lawson
d. 1772
m.
Mary Moore

The Coffyns were
Norman Huguenots.
Tristam Coffin was
part-owner of
Nantucket Island

Nathaniel Coffin
1669–1748
Tristam's grandson

Col.
Joseph Coffin
1702–1773
Newbury, Mass.
m.
Margaret Morse
d. 1775

Valentine Sevier
1702–1803
(Nephew of St. Francis
Xavier, the Jesuit missionary)
immigrated in 1740
m.
Joanne Goad

Capt. Robert Sevier
1749–1780
Killed in battle
Kings Mountain
m.
Kesiah Robertson
1753–1806

Gen. John
"Nolichucky Jack"
Sevier
1745–1815
First Governor
of Tennessee

Col. Valentine
Sevier
1747–1800

Margaret
White
m.
Charles
McLung

Hugh Lawson
White
1773–1840
U.S. Senator,
presidential
candidate

Dr. Charles Coffin
1741–1821
Harvard graduate
m.
Hepzibah Carnes
of Boston

Valentine Sevier
1780–1854
m.
Nancy Dinwiddie
1786–1844
13 children

(Descendent of
Robert Dinwiddie,
first Colonial Governor
of Virginia)

Dr.
Alexander
Williams
m.
Catherine
Dixon

Christopher
Harris
Williams
Killed at Shiloh
m.
Annie Louise
Sharp

The Rev.
Charles Coffin
1775–1853
President of
Greenville College, Tenn.
m.
Susan Woodbridge Ayer

Isabel Sevier
1805–1867
m.
Francis
McCorkle

When the Catholic Xavier family
split religiously, the Huguenot
Protestants became
"Sevier"

Eliza
Williams
m.
William B.
Sneed
b. 1812

John Sharp
Williams
1854–1932
U.S. Senator

Cornelius
Worchester Coffin
1822–1875
m.
Nancy
McCorkle
1828–1884

Elizabeth
Trigg Williams
1858–1928
m.
Judge Joseph W.
Sneed
Chancellor, Knox
County

Xabier of Nabarre

Coffin

Tennessee Williams wrote that he was composed of "a little Welsh wildness, a lot of puritan English and a big chunk of German sentiment," and that he had " a combination of Puritan and Cavalier strains which may be accountable for the conflicting impulses" he wrote about. His pedigree included one bona fide saint, Huguenots and Quakers persecuted for their religious beliefs, ruthless Indian fighters and militarists, a few madmen, and a string of politicians along with two American "first families"—the adventurous Seviers, who carved out the state of Tennessee, and the intellectual New England Coffins, one of whom was the poet Tristam Coffin. The Laniers stemmed from a line of Elizabethan court musicians that led to the poet Sidney Lanier. It was a heredity of which Williams was justly proud.

Chart © 1995 by Richard Freeman Leavitt. Research assistance by Allean Hale.

Notes to the Genealogy

While it is true that Tennessee Williams was descended from ancestors who were distinguished in the history and founding of the state of Tennessee, the facts were somewhat confused and often dramatized by the dramatist. Nevertheless, as Steve Cotham, Librarian of the McClung Historical Collection in Knoxville, says, "In investigating his ancestry, I find that Tennessee Williams is connected in multiple ways to many of the leading families of East Tennessee, especially the McClungs, the Whites, and the Coffins. Through the intricate web of intermarriages of these families, he is nominally related to an even wider circle of the leading families of the state and region." [Cotham to LL, letter dated 18 June 1985]

Col. Joseph Williams (1748–1827) and Rebekah Lanier (1757–1832) were married in 1772 and settled at Panther Creek in Surry County, North Carolina. He was a colonel in the Colonial Army, but when war was declared against Great Britain, he resigned his commission and became a colonel in the Continental Army. Her family were French Huguenots who left France after the revocation of the Edict of Nantes. (In 1963, the Oxford historian A. L. Rowse uncovered evidence that he felt identified Shakespeare's "Dark Lady of the Sonnets" as Emilia Bassano Lanier, the wife of a court musician, who was, Rowse claimed, an ancestor of Tennessee Williams.)

Among Joseph and Rebekah's ten children, Thomas Lanier Williams (born 1786) became an early state senator, judge, and chancellor, a legal office of the East Tennessee district. His brother, John Williams (1778–1837), fought in the War of 1812 but not, as Tennessee Williams believed, at King's Mountain, a battle that took place during the American Revolution. John was a United States senator in 1815. He married Melinda White (1789–1837), daughter of Gen. James White (1747–1821), a pioneer and frontiersman and the founder of Knoxville; their son, John, Jr. (1818–1881), became the father of the second Thomas Lanier Williams (1849–1908), whose wife was Isabella ("Belle") Coffin (1853–1884), daughter of Nancy and Cornelius C. Coffin.

Isabella, Tennessee Williams's paternal grandmother, was descended from Valentine Sevier (Xavier), who came to America about 1740 and among whose children were Gen. John ("Nolichucky Jack") Sevier (1745–1815); Col. Valentine Sevier (1747–1800); and Capt. Robert Sevier (1749–1780), who was killed at King's Mountain.

Cornelius Coffin Williams's descent is traced in the family Bible of Ella Williams, his sister, and in her records taken from Historical Families of Tennessee, Lawson McGhee Library, Knoxville. Williams, White, Sevier, and Coffin biographies are from *The French Broad-Holston Country: A History of Knox County, Tennessee*, Mary Rothrock, ed. (Knoxville: East Tennessee Historical Society, 1946. No. 58, "Tennessee Williams's Family Books," in Special Collections, Washington University Library, St. Louis.) See also Dr. William J. MacArthur, Jr., "Knoxville: Crossroads of the New South,

1890–1918" (McClung Historical Collection, Knox County Library System.)
Robert Sevier also had a son named Valentine (1780–1854), who became a railroad commissioner. His granddaughter, Nancy, married Cornelius C. Coffin, whose daughter, Isabel, married Tennessee Williams's grandfather, Thomas Lanier Williams, also a railroad commissioner. (It should be noted that Gen. John Sevier, who at one time resided along the Nolichucky River—hence his nickname—was a famed Indian fighter who led 240 men across the Smokies to a decisive victory over the British at King's Mountain and who became the first governor of Tennessee. He did not fight a duel with Andrew Jackson, as legend has it, although theirs became a celebrated feud. Tennessee Williams took pride in being descended from the Seviers and often referred to their fighting spirit as a characteristic of the Williams line.)
Genealogies have traced the Seviers to the Xaviers in the kingdom of Navarre, one of whom became a ward of the Bourbon monarch. Subsequently the family was divided religiously. At the time of the St. Bartholomew's Day Massacre, the Roman Catholics kept the name of Xavier while the other side, the Huguenot Protestants, changed theirs to Sevier and fled to England. The original Valentine Xavier was a Basque and brother of Saint Francis Xavier. The fact that the great Jesuit missionary was evidently an ancestor did not especially impress the Protestant wing of the family, although Tennessee Williams allowed that possibly he was related and that this was "the family's nearest claim to world renown." (See "Sevier Family History" by Cora Bales Sevier & Nancy Madden, 1961, pp. 13, 418, 437, 441–442.)

The spelling of Daykin was an adaptation of the Norman-English "Dakyn" as it appears on the family coat of arms. As far as the genealogy has been traced, the first American Dakin lived in Concord, Massachusetts, before 1650, after which members of the family moved to New York State. During the American Revolution, a branch of the family emigrated to Canada as Tories, or King's Loyalists, and settled in Digby, Nova Scotia.

William Otte was born in Hanover and sailed to America in 1857. He first lived in Cincinnati and after that in Richmond, Indiana, finally settling in Marysville, where in 1871 he and his brother began a family business that continued until 1976. (See *Marysville Journal-Tribune*, 2 July 1976, p. 1.)

Edwina Dakin Williams maintained that a relative, Elijah Sabin, was disqualified as acceptable lineage because he was a Quaker and would not have fought in the Revolution. While it is true that Quakers did not take up arms, the DAR ruled that, if they had furnished food and other comfort to the Colonial Army, they qualified as proper reference. Sabin is in fact in the DAR lineage books.

Acknowledgments

It is especially difficult to single out among a biographer's acknowledgments those who have given indispensable support. A grueling effort has been made to document the contents of this book, involving long hours in travel, in examining papers and correspondence, and in interviewing many of Tennessee's friends and associates. As it is in the production of a play, the writing of a biography is dependent upon the close collaboration of many good people. For reasons that can only be called discreet, they are listed alphabetically and are accompanied by a fervent hope that no deserving soul has been inadvertently omitted.

Herman Arrow, the closest and most loyal of friends, was the first to insist that I meet with Tennessee to propose a book about the playwright in the theatre. A first-rate photographer, Herm provided not only impetus but superb photographs of Tennessee.

Bill Barnes, as my representative, gave of himself in ways that no writer could reasonably expect of an agent. He was there at the beginning of this adventure and provided at Tennessee's urging access to an important variety of documents, journals, and correspondence in his keeping. He never for a moment let go his faith and support.

I was also given indispensable and inordinate support from Tennessee's great friend, the "legendary" Paul Bigelow, who in turn became my own treasured friend. Tennessee's letters to Paul and those of Paul to his companion of many years, Jordan Massee, have provided both pertinent information and keen insight. Paul's close friend and executor, Henry (Hank) Schwartz, has also given unstinting and valued support.

Andreas Brown, Tennessee's bibliographer and archivist and proprietor of New York's famed Gotham Book Mart, met with me in 1979 when Tennessee asked him to give me his full cooperation. As critic and catalyst, he has been of inestimable help in continuing the tradition of the Gotham's founder, Frances Steloff. He has given generously of himself as a friend, opening the way for me to many who knew and worked with Tennessee Williams, for which I will always be grateful.

Jackson Bryer, professor at the University of Maryland and loyal supporter, gave many hours to a scrupulous line reading of the manuscript and in addition sought out other important avenues of assistance, for which I am most thankful.

Charles V. Carroll, Jr., formerly Personal Representative of the Tennessee Williams Estate and Vice President of Private Banking and Trust at Southeast Bank of Miami, contributed immeasurably by being among the first to recognize Tennessee's wish that I be his chosen biographer and, as the original executor, by giving me permission to quote from Tennessee's unpublished writings.

Louise M. Childs, leading cheerleader and dearest of friends, gave unwavering help and encouragement year after year through the countless ups and downs of writing this first volume. Her daughter, Leslie Anne Childs, has been a constant source of joy and comfort.

Thomas R. Congdon, publisher-editor and challenger, at the outset threw down the gauntlet and called out strengths that seemed beyond my reach.

Marguerite Courtney kindly gave permission to quote from *Laurette*, her fine biography of her mother, Laurette Taylor.

Brian Fitzgerald's devoted friendship and force of personality exemplify what is meant by New Orleans hospitality.

I am most thankful to Lucy Freeman for her friendship and for having given me access to her correspondence with Tennessee. I found her book *Remember Me to Tom* extraordinary for its consistency with the facts as Edwina Dakin Williams remembered them and as my research has largely verified them.

Allean Hale, a foremost Tennessee Williams authority, did much to enlighten me about Tennessee's life in St. Louis and at the University of Missouri. A gifted and dogged scholar in writing her own book about the playwright's later plays, Allean has provided insight into his work taken as a whole. And in the preparation of this book, I am grateful to her for her editorial and research assistance.

Mary C. Henderson, eminent theatre historian and biographer of Jo Mielziner, designer of most of Tennessee's major plays, made many helpful suggestions and has become a valued friend.

John Lahr, drama critic for *The New Yorker*, gave support well beyond his call of duty, opening doors and minds in his devotion to Tennessee's place in the theatre and literary worlds.

James Laughlin, esteemed editor-publisher at New Directions, was among the first to offer encouragement. I am especially indebted to Peggy Fox for her invaluable help and kindness.

Richard Freeman Leavitt, author of *The World of Tennessee Williams* and *Ave Atque Vale!*, the memorial tribute on Tennessee's death, researched and assembled the photographs for this book while offering both valued advice and his own recollections of Tennessee.

Clark Mills McBurney, poet and scholar, with humor and intellect cast a special light on the life of the young Tom Williams and on that of anyone fortunate enough to call him friend.

Ghity Penney's constancy, affection, and generosity afforded moral support during the years when it was most needed.

Edmund J. Perret II, to whom I will always be grateful, gave unwavering love and support from the time in New Orleans when Tennessee first introduced him to me.

Russell Rocke opened the door to New Orleans, retaining me as production consultant to his production of *One Mo' Time* and giving me access to Tennessee's world in the Vieux Carré.

Skip Rognlien provided a refuge in the wilds of New York City, a snug and comfortable shelter in which to labor without distraction day and night, and proved himself through every crisis a true and valued friend.

Jane Lawrence Smith, whom Tennessee called his other Rose, imparted a gentle strength throughout the ordeal of trying to get this first book published.

Dakin Williams generously gave me access to his family's photographs and papers and the exclusive right to quote from them, and met with me for many hours of interviews in St. Louis and New York. As Tennessee's "kid brother," Dakin had the firsthand experience of growing up under the same parental roof, and his recollections lent important authentication.

I must also include among this hierarchy those friends and associates who have my gratitude for their valuable and kind contributions:

Charlotte Abramson; Wesley Addy; Professor Thomas P. Adler at Purdue University; Robert Anderson and the Authors League of America; Aaron Asher; Jack Barefield; Joanna Barnes; Chair and Professor Milly S. Barranger at the University of North Carolina; Barbara Baxley; Camille Bernardi Schwartz; Lawrence Bernfeld, Esq.; Jeanne (Mrs. Fritz) Bultman; Professor Robert H. Butman at Haverford College; Lehman Byck; Justin E. Caldwell; Sandy Campbell; Chair and Professor Virginia Spencer Carr at the University of Georgia; Anne Cole; Nancy Coleman; Phyllis Colon; Jay Leo Colt; Dennis E. Cook; Cheryl Crawford; Jay Dillon; Harriette K. Dorsen, Esq.; Horton Foote; Ruth Ford; James Frasher; Cathy and Scott Fuerman; Larry Fuerman; Lillian Gish; Phil Gordon; Professor William S. Gray at Randolph-Macon University; Preston Greer; Joseph Gross, M.D.; Helen Hayes; Joseph Hazan; Celeste Holm; Lawrence Hughes; William Hughes; Dan Isaacs; Nancy Johnson at the American Academy & Institute of Arts & Letters; Frank Krause; Floria Lasky, Esq.; Kenneth Lohf, Director at Butler Library, Columbia University; Claire Luce; Philip Lyman, Molly Gee, Flip Matthew, Gina Guy, and the staff of the Gotham Book Mart; Remy (Mrs. Clark Mills) McBurney; Inez Metzl; Sylvia Miles; Arthur Miller; Charlotte Moore; Professor Kenneth Moore at the University of Notre Dame; Julie Haydon Nathan; Roy G. Nelson; John Nicholson; Frederick Nicklaus; David Peterson; Jean Porter; Joseph and Anne (Bretzfelder) Post; James Purdy; Louis Sheaffer; Michele Slung; Donald Spoto; Stephen S. Stanton, professor emeritus at the University of Michigan and founding editor of the *Tennessee Williams Review;* Elaine (Mrs. John) Steinbeck; Richard Stoddard at Performing Arts Books; Richard Sugarman, Esq.; David Summers; Dorothy Swerdlove, Paul Myers, and Lacy McDearmon at the New York Public Library Performing Arts Research Center in Lincoln Center; Catherine Tatge and Dominique Lasseur at International Cultural Programming; John Uecker; Michael Valenti; Debbie Velez; Vassilis Voglis; Miles White; Max Wilk; Donald Windham; Henry Wyatt; and Shela Xoregos.

In New Orleans: James Bailey; Dorian Major Bennett; Lillian Boutté; Granger Carr; George Dureau; Jack N. Fricks; Robert L. Hines; Professor W. Kenneth Holditch, founding editor of the *Tennessee Williams Literary Journal;* Lily Hood; Don Lee Keith; André de La Barre; the Reverend Sidney Lanier; Marcel de Nièvre; Eric Paulsen; the Reverend Robert Pawell O.F.M.; David Richmond; Pancho and Juan Rodriguez; Clifford R. Scott; Martin C. Shambra, Jr.; Professor Alan Shapiro at Tulane University; Ronald Sher, Esq.; Tony Solar at the Howard-Tilton Memorial Library, Tulane University; Florence Sumonville at the New Orleans Historical Collection; George deVille; Jules Weiss; Timothy Wilson; and Leon Zainey.

In St. Louis: Harriett Holland Brandt; Jane W. Bruce; Inez Hall Clark; Jeanne Favre; Wesley and Lucellea Gore; Samuel F. Halley, Jr.; Mrs. N. J. Law; Herb Macklin; William Jay Smith; Jane Wonders Stewart; Marjorie Punch Stuart; and Esmeralda Mayes Treen. At Washington University: Professor Herbert E. Metz and Valerie Safron; Timothy D. Murray, Curator of Manuscripts; Jean Gaines, Registrar; and Joyce (Mrs. Dakin) Williams.

In San Francisco, California: Alexis Arrow; David Arrow; Lois Arrow; Sue Binder; Ina Claire; Judith Hersh Clark; Michael DeMoss; Stanley Eichelbaum; A. J. Esta; Peter Gabel; Dean Goodman; Bill Kruse; Andrew Lyndon; Bruce Blair Miller; Olwen Morgan; Elsa Peters Morse; Rolly Mulvey; Brian Mulvey; Martin Ponch; James Summers; and Joy Waterman. In Los Angeles: Bill Alexander; A. Scott Berg; Joanne Carson; Lois Chiles; Tony Goldwyn; David Greggory; Michael Hopkins; Kim Stanley; Dan Sullivan at the *Los Angeles Times;* and Pat and Michael York.

In Key West: Robert Carroll; Charles House; Leoncia McGee; Kate Schweppe Moldawer; William Prosser; Gary Tucker; and Schuyler Wyatt.

In Austin, Texas: Virginia and Elsworth P. Conkle and George Franklin; at the Harry Ransom Humanities Research Center, University of Texas: Dr. Thomas F. Staley, Cathy Henderson, Kenneth Craven, Patrice S. Fox, and John R. Payne. In San Antonio: Fred Todd.

In Columbia, Missouri: Professor Albert J. Devlin and Larry Clark at the University of Missouri; Jeanne Singleton Beynon; Harold A. Mitchell; and Edna Don Carlos Watson.

In Iowa City: Charles Calmer and Edmond Williams at the University of Iowa; Jean Fitzpatrick Arnstein; Milton Lomask; Dr. Thomas D. Pawley; Robert Leo Quinn; Truman G. Slitor; and P. A. M. Stewart.

In Westport, Connecticut: Eloise Sheldon Armen. In New London: Lois E. McDonald, Assistant Curator, Eugene O'Neill Theatre Center. In Hamden: Helen Sheehy.

In Cambridge, Massachusetts: Dr. Jeanne Newlin, curator of the Harvard Theatre Collection. In Nantucket: Joseph M. ("Mac") Dixon and Linda Loring. In Provincetown: Ruth Hebert.

In Columbus, Mississippi: Chehie A. Bateman, director, Lowndes County Library System; James Hardy; Davis Patty; and Katherine Searcy. In Port Gibson: the Reverend James Chambers of Saint James's Episcopal Church and Elizabeth S. McLendon. In Vicksburg: Gayle Magness. In Clarksdale: Pauline Alston Clark; Alida Clark Heidelberg; and the Reverend John Clark Smith.

In Nashville, Tennessee: Louise Davis at *The Tennessean* and Anne W. Magruder and Eliza Warren Magruder. In Knoxville: Margaret Brownlow; Helen Brownlow Fritts; Steve Cotham, Librarian, and Linda Posey at the Calvin McClung Historical Collection, Knox County Public Library System; and Dr. Harry C. Rutledge and John Dobson at the University of Tennessee.

In Marysville, Ohio: Mary Ann Garcia at the Marysville *Journal-Tribune;* Robert Otte Hamilton, Esq.; and Mrs. William Otte. In Waynesville: Dennis E. Dalton, Community Historian at the Mary L. Cook Public Library, and Inara Turkopuls. In Gambier: Meryem Ersoz and Thomas B. Greenslade, archivist at Kenyon College.

In Tuscaloosa, Alabama: Rachel Dureet at the *Tuscaloosa News* and Professor George Crandell at the University of Alabama.

In Washington, D.C.: Richard L. Coe and David Richards at the *Washington Post.*

Finally, grateful attention must be paid to Peter L. Ginsberg, my loyal, energetic representative at Curtis Brown Ltd. I am especially grateful for the guidance at Crown Publishers of Ann Patty, my editor Michael Denneny and his assistant John Clark, Camille Smith, Laurie Stark, Carol Edwards, Andrew Martin, and Hilary Bass. At the time the manuscript was held at Grove Weidenfeld, I had the great good fortune to find in Mark Polizzotti an extraordinarily gifted editor. I am also grateful to Walter Bode, John Herman, Alan D. Williams, Pam Lyons, Margo D. Shearman, and Mary Flower, among the talented staff at Grove. For his generosity and astute advice, I am indebted to my accountant, Bernard P. Rosenberg, CPA. Warm gratitude is extended to the family of photographer William Viggiano and to Bill's kind and generous friends Tavo Serina and Bob Melbourne.

Although I should stress that this is not an estate "authorized" biography, I was gratified to learn in November 1994 that trustee John Eastman and the estate's attorney, Michael Remer, had kindly cleared the way for publication.

I must add a caveat: that no biographer should ever paddle his way through the perilous seas of the publishing world without the enlightening direction of counsel, and I am most beholden unto my attorney R. Stephen Goldstein, with special thanks to his assistant Gwen Dangerfield, and to Gale Elston and Lana Halliday for their invaluable legal assistance.

The Shattered Mirror:
Origins of a Biography

In January of 1976, Tennessee Williams was in San Francisco to attend the final rehearsals of his new play, *THIS IS (An Entertainment)*. At a press conference held prior to a highly publicized opening sponsored by the American Conservatory Theatre (ACT), I spoke to Tennessee's agent, Bill Barnes, concerning a possible production of one of the playwright's later plays, *Out Cry*. Barnes said that Tennessee had revised and renamed it *The Two-Character Play*, its original 1967 title, and that he would mail the galleys as soon as he returned to New York.

Instead of an experimental tryout, *THIS IS* was given an extravagant New York–style premiere and received devastating reviews. Subsequently, Tennessee came to the theatre I managed, The Showcase, and we made plans for an opening in October of *The Two-Character Play*, which I proposed to produce in tandem with *The Glass Menagerie*. Although he was preoccupied with various other productions in Los Angeles, New York, and Vienna, Tennessee made three transcontinental trips back to San Francisco to supervise the direction and casting of a play that he described to the producer as being probably the most difficult he had ever written, "the interior landscape of the most terrible period of my life." He chose the director and worked with the actors, Fred Ward and Patricia Boyette. He came to the opening night and sat with venerable actress Ina Claire, and he was pleased at the audience's reception. Although as *Out Cry* the play had been poorly reviewed in New York, as *The Two-Character Play* it received respectable notices in San Francisco from the same critics who had rejected *THIS IS*, and he left in a cheerful frame of mind. I had made a friend.

During the next two years, Tennessee and I would meet when he came to the West Coast or when we both happened to be in New York. We would often go to a film (for him a lifelong escape) or have dinner together. In San Francisco, I remember the enjoyment he had in cooking grits and bacon as his contribution to a potluck supper at the home of an actress friend of mine, Olwen Morgan, who had played Amanda to acclaim in *The Glass Menagerie*.

Whenever Tennessee and I were alone, he would frequently talk about incidents in his life or aspects of his career. Although I was not then entertaining the notion of anything so romantic as becoming a Boswell to his Johnson, I was impelled to write a criticism of Robert Brustein's review of *Tennessee Williams' Letters to Donald Windham* as being factually inaccurate and critically gratuitous. In a letter dated December 11, 1977, Tennessee asserted, "No one has ever written a more powerful and eloquent defense of my work and character." His conclusion that it was "so marvelously good" inspired me to go on writing about him.

In January 1978 in Atlanta, over dinner with Tennessee, I said that I felt *Memoirs* had done him a disservice, if only because it failed to reflect his stature as a man of the theatre, the person I knew and worked with. I said that there should really be a publication about Tennessee Williams at work in the theatre, and he said, "Baby, you write it!" When at lunch the next day Bill Barnes offered to handle the book, I returned to my home and devoted the next few months to writing a biographical section, meant to *precede* the viewpoints of Tennessee's theatre associates as they saw and worked with him in the production of his plays. That seemed a formidable enough task, and I would have been quite content to let it go at that.

Bill quickly found a publisher for the work, and Tennessee read the first drafts. However, on the basis of that initial effort, he decided that I should write a full biography and chose to announce this on the night of the 1979 Kennedy Center Honors award when he introduced me to his brother, Dakin, as his "authorized biographer." Because the publisher subsequently decided that it did not want an authorized biography, Tennessee gave me a letter of authorization, urging me to find another publisher so that we could continue to work together.

During the final months before he died, when I saw him in New Orleans and when he called from Key West, Tennessee asked me pointedly about my progress toward completion of the book. The biography had taken on a sudden urgency in his view, and I reassured him repeatedly that I was keeping my end of our agreement. Despite several years of research and numerous interviews with him and those friends and associates he singled out, as well as the writing of initial drafts, I confided to a friend that I found writing the biography of someone as sensitive and volatile as Tennessee Williams not a little like performing an autopsy on a living person. I told Tennessee that I was concerned about writing truthfully and reporting divergent views of his character, and he remarked, "You can always say that the ol' hound dog could be a son of a bitch and not shoot wide of the mark!"

Bill Barnes told me how hesitant he had been to take on Tennessee as a client, having heard how difficult and demanding he could be. Add to that the onus of his succeeding Audrey Wood, Tennessee's agent for over thirty-two years. Both Bill and the dauntless Miss Wood were employed at International Famous Agency, later ICM (International Creative Management). She and Tennessee had parted company acrimoniously in the summer of 1971 when he accused her of no longer caring about his career, of being interested not in his new plays but only those with commercial potential. It was a tragic ending to an extraordinarily close and productive association. Barnes, a young and handsome southerner, "charming Billy," as his friends called him, first met with his mercurial client at New York's popular St. Regis hotel bar, where Tennessee told him that, having somehow survived his decline both professionally and physically during the sixties, he wanted once again to see his name up in lights on Broadway. After Audrey assured Bill she would guide him through the shoals, he gave seven years of hard labor to the task of being, as Tennessee insisted, his "representative," not his agent.

In my conversations with him, Tennessee readily admitted that he was given to paranoid rages, often out of foundless suspicions, that were as quick to flare as they were to subside, and he was concerned that many of his actions would be misconstrued after his death and exploited unfairly. Since then, it has become apparent to me that he wanted to choose his own biographer during his lifetime for evidently much the same reason his friend Gore Vidal has chosen his. The truth is that Tennessee saw his own faults more clearly than did any of his detractors. Normally, he was gentle with those who were gentle toward him, but he was all too painfully conscious of what evidence could be turned against him if his biographers were to dwell mainly on his peccadilloes, addictions, and "failed promise." He apparently felt that I would not, at one extreme, indulge in the hagiography his idolaters would like, nor, at the other extreme, exploit him personally at the expense of his place as an artist.

On the day he left New Orleans for the last time, he phoned me at a theatre where I was working to ask if I had delved into his archives at the University of Texas in Austin. I said, yes I had, the previous year, but not as extensively as I would have liked. He asked me about my progress on the biography, adding that en route to the airport he would drop off a letter for me. This second authorization, dated January 25, 1983, gave me "full access" to his papers, journals, and correspondence. One month later to the day, I received a phone call from Bill Barnes giving me the terrible news of Tennessee's death. His letter was still open on my desk. I could only look upon it as his mandate to continue our work, and I left immediately for New York to give the biography my full attention.

As Tennessee Williams's chosen biographer and as a theatre person writing about a theatre genius, I have been quite naturally drawn to what was dramatic in his life and what in his character determined his becoming a preeminent American playwright. He not only wrote of dramatis personae, he was one among them, the chief protagonist. Although the theatre forged our bond I, like many who knew him personally, would find myself on occasion baffled by Tennessee's contradictory behavior. His eccentricities, his quickly shifting moods, his shrieks of laughter intermingled with his despondencies— all made him somewhat puzzling. His was the most enigmatic personality I had ever encountered in or out of the theatre. Accessible as Tom, elusive as Tennessee, he could be candid and deceptive, kind and cruel, generous and penurious, shy and aggressive, trusting and suspicious, lucid and manic. Often purposely evasive, he seemed composed of several personalities. Playwrights, like actors, are artists of many parts and play many roles, and so Tennessee was many things to many people, including those intimates who pridefully staked their claim to knowing the "real" person. His letters were frequently slanted to the pleasure or expectations of the recipients, whose reminiscences are too often colored by a one-sided picture of their friend.

Memoirs and his antic public behavior, in contrast with those quiet occasions I shared with him at rehearsals or in a darkened theatre or in walks or over meals, made it clear that behind the persona of Tennessee Williams there also existed someone frightened, leery, and diffident, someone called Tom. At other times, I would be witness to the oddest balance between sanity and madness, conduct that would mystify and often antagonize those in and out of his favor, especially those who thought of themselves as confidants but whom he, in fact, suffered or tried to avoid.

What I remember most was the warm generosity he brought to our meetings and his extraordinary sense of humor, which was always ready to relieve seriousness when it became excessive. He could turn a simple dinner party into a hilarious carouse, then, bedeviled by the dread of loneliness, suddenly disappear into the night—"the enormous night"—in pursuit of an anonymous companion. "Old men go mad at night," he wrote. From its outset, I can say that I very much enjoyed his friendship, while increasingly I became determined to justify his faith in me as his biographer. Despite all that he had told me and all the information I had accumulated about him, after his death in 1983 I was still confronted by the mystery of the person—the labyrinthine nature of his personality—the unknown Tennessee Williams.

As I began to examine the important early papers of the Dakin and Williams families, it was Tom Williams who more and more caught my interest. Here in his troubled childhood, his youth and young manhood—all that I was able to reassemble from the shards of the shattered mirror he left behind— there existed the insight I was seeking. From those myriad reflections of his childhood experiences, those deeply fissured, painful, and powerfully rooted impressions, emerged the man and his art.

I started my explorations into Tom's early life never suspecting that his flight from his family into the refuge called "success" would at length compose the contents of the first volume of my biography, posing what was causative against what would become symptomatic in Tennessee's later life. The material simply mandated its form, and so the book, like the play it celebrates, became memory. For the first thirty years of his life, he was living *The Glass Menagerie*, and it was from that traumatic experience that his masterpiece—this "little play," as he disdainfully called it—evolved.

In producing *The Glass Menagerie* together with *The Two-Character Play*, I felt that there was a psychic line passing through the characters of the brother and sister that connected both plays. Tennessee was conveying with the power of illusion what in life is so often inexpressible: the tragic failure to communicate one's true feelings not only to others but also to oneself in an interior dialogue. Through that failure, there emerges a theme underlying almost all of his writings: the terrifying isolation of loneliness.

While it has been argued that his later work suffered from a conscious effort to create art, I believe that on close examination it can be shown that his struggle to fuse the poetic with the dramatic is as much in evidence in these so-called minor works as it was in his major plays. He was as much concerned as ever in his final efforts with the depths and origins of human feelings and motivations, the difference being that he had gone into a deeper, more obscure realm, which of course put the poet in him to the fore, not the playwright with his concern for audience and critical reaction. In the 1960s, he became acutely aware that he was in competition with himself—the self he had created as Tennessee Williams. He was confronted with what everyone had come to regard as "a Tennessee Williams play," and in the midst of a radically changing theatre, he found himself cut off and in danger of becoming an anachronism.

Trying to move from what he saw as his "operas" to his "chamber pieces," Tom, the poet, was attempting to divorce himself from Tennessee, the playwright. Because of the changes taking place after President Kennedy's assassination and throughout the nightmare years of the Vietnam War, the Broadway theatre was rapidly becoming some kind of relic, and Tennessee was in dread of becoming a relic with it. And so he wrote plays that clearly reflected his own tensions and those of the times in which he was living. He was not, certainly in my experience with him, one whose talent or professionalism had failed him. On the contrary: He was, first to last, our foremost poet-playwright, a man who drove himself unrelentingly as an artist despite personal and career reversals. He gave up only when death intervened.

The provenance of much of Williams's writings is of necessity a perplexing mystery, at best a matter for scholarly conjectures. In his short stories and plays, Williams exists in myriad ways and speaks through almost every character. Although I have made an effort, wherever an incident, letter, or journal entry gave clear evidence of the origin of a work, to cite it, the speculations I have let go. Since Tennessee was always the arch observer, as any true artist must be, he selected from an enormous store of impressions of people and events to forge the synthesis of his art. One ponders: Is this character or that setting or that scene related to this actual person or that place or that real happening? Largely, it is anybody's guess.

Tennessee was a fabricator—*that* was his profession—and often, too, that was what he was personally. Actors, directors, and playwrights often have this trait in common, and as someone schooled in theatre and film, I have tried to keep to the narrative line of a *scenario*, to tell the dramatic *story* of Tom Williams's life as he lived it and to resist falling prey to the digressive details of his literary life.

In my quest for an always-elusive truth, I have often been confounded by questions giving rise to questions. Invariably, the biographer must forgo or at least temper the fallibility and prejudicial memory of friends and enemies in favor of what clear evidence is revealed in the form of letters and journals and, in Williams's case, even in many of his candid interviews, which have been aptly characterized as confessionals, the dramatist dramatizing himself. I have also been confronted with surprises encountered in the most unlikely places. In Clarksdale, Mississippi, the "Rosebud" in young Tom's life was a real menagerie of little glass animals sparkling in the front window of Mrs. Maggie Wingfield's home. Examining Rose Williams's medical history and other documentation, I determined that the infamous lobotomy did not take place in 1937, but years later, and that hers was not, in fact, among the first such operations.

However, I feel the most important revelation, as detailed in the first half of this volume, was the discovery of two major formative influences in Tom Williams's development as a poet and a playwright: Clark Mills, the "brilliantly talented and handsome poet," and Willard Holland, the equally brilliant and dynamic theatre director. Personally, Tennessee Williams was never able to reconcile the diametric pull in being both a poet *and* a playwright, but he did manage to draw on these alien roles as creative forces, and in the final analysis, it was the fusion of poet *with* playwright that gave him his uniqueness in the American theatre.

Once he arrived in New York in 1940 to confront the Broadway theatre, there were other influences: the intrepid Audrey Wood; his mentor, the theatre historian John Gassner; the actor-director Hume Cronyn, who subsequently optioned his one-act plays at a time when Tennessee was in dire straits; and his remarkable friend, "the legendary," as he was called, Paul Bigelow. In the same year, his early friendship with Donald Windham and Fred Melton sparked a desire to duplicate what he saw in them as an ideal bonding and what he vainly sought to duplicate in his relationship with Kip Kiernan, the most romantic of his attachments.

I have not attempted to psychoanalyze his paradoxical character. As Ned Rorem has said, "Motivation is in the eye of the beholder." On the other hand, I have also eschewed a purely objective approach. Knowing Tennessee for the years I did, I have offered both viewpoint and interpretation. I have, for example, come to a conclusion forced by events documented in Tom's

home life and in his writings that it was his "hated" father who *most* influenced him personally. I believe that subconsciously in manifold ways, the
Williams side in Tennessee was acquired directly from C. C. Williams, manifested in his sudden irrational bursts of temper, his strange attitudes toward
money, his great pleasure in a game of poker, his need to win and dominate,
his addiction to alcohol, his sensuality, his pride in his heritage, and in his
dedication to work. Trivial as it may seem, even C.C.'s devotion to a Boston
terrier, Jiggs, was duplicated in Tennessee's favorite pet, Gigi.

Certainly none of these characteristics appear to have come from the gentler Dakin side of his nature, inherited from his mother and her parents. Edwina Dakin, as she emerges from her voluminous correspondence, was a
woman of remarkable strengths and complexity: a "mother-wife" to her son
Tom until their "divorce" was occasioned by Tennessee's success. Like her
son, she had the artist's talent for observation, and both her secret diary and
her correspondence reveal a southern lady gifted in reporting with a controlled sensitivity, often misunderstood as insensitivity. She was, in fact, an
ace reporter. She had not just a gift of gab but, along with Tom, a literary
talent of her own. At the same time she could be kind, she could also be cruel,
generous and stinting, affectionate and distant, trusting and possessive. She
has been blamed for just about everything, from her daughter's lobotomy to
her son's homosexuality. But as much as she lent herself to caricature, she was
finally a heroic figure of a woman, her every trait and facet of character embedded in the persona she called her "alias," Amanda Wingfield.

Moreover, something as deeply embedded as one's psychosexuality cannot
be simplistically attributed to any single influence or trauma in a child's life.
Still, I can think of nothing that injures more the developing manhood of a
young boy, nothing that can be more intensely felt, than the unrequited love
of a son for his father. And no mother's or sister's love can replace or compensate for that rupture. It was a loss that Tennessee felt to his dying day, a loss
that he projected into the act of creation. The missing ideal of a son in the
loving image of his father became instead the identity of the artist in revolt. It
was why Tom chose the name Tennessee, deeply impressed as he was with the
fighting spirit of his father's Tennessean forebears.

Oscar Wilde saw biography as "adding to death a new terror." He might
have added, a terror for the biographer, as well. Like the actor moving into his
role, the biographer is in danger of identifying too closely with his subject,
taking on his blemishes and, he hopes, some of his virtues. It is an intimacy, a
double life, which at times can terrify someone caught up so intensely in the
déjà vu of feelings and events similar to those of his own life. But I was reminded over and over again that, with all his sins remembered, Tennessee's
overriding virtue was his fervent involvement with life, in living it and in writing about it with *passion*. It has been his example more than any other influence that has kept me at my desk.

Finally, since these are prefatory observations, I would also like to mention the fact that in Chicago in early 1945, when I was in the navy, I had occasion to witness Laurette Taylor's magnificent performance in *The Glass Menagerie*. Although I had seen her previously in 1938 in *Outward Bound*, I still was not prepared for an experience so indelibly memorable. More than the stunning impact of her performance, however, there was my lasting fascination with the play itself, evolving into my later production of *The Glass Menagerie*, my friendship with its author, and the writing of a first volume that can best be described as the story of the actual menagerie and of how his early life led to the phenomenon known to the world as the poet-playwright Tennessee Williams.

Lyle Leverich
San Francisco
27 May 1995

My greatest affliction . . . is perhaps
the major theme of my writings,
the affliction of loneliness
that follows me like a shadow,
a very ponderous shadow too heavy to
drag after me all of my days and nights.

—Tennessee Williams, 1979

Tennessee Williams:

The Man and the Artist versus His Image

Throughout his life, Tennessee Williams had two overriding devotions: his career as a writer and his sister, Rose. He had said he would want to die if he could no longer write. Following a sudden debilitating loss of energy, that is what happened in New York early on the morning of Friday, February 25, 1983, a month before his seventy-second birthday.

In the days preceding his death, Williams had hoped to return to his home in the French Quarter of New Orleans, his first refuge in a lifelong flight from a family he could never escape. His strength was fast ebbing. Like Eugene O'Neill at the last, the torment he felt was not just the disabling effect of his illness but also the fact that he was no longer able to sustain any effort at writing.

The last month of his life was spent traveling by himself in panic and desperation, as if in taking flight he could outdistance death. Whenever he felt cornered by friends and associates or blocked in his writing, he would suddenly move on to new environs. But his last journey was an aimless flight from New Orleans to New York to London, then to Rome and Taormina, and finally back to his favorite New York hotel, the Elysée. By then, he was in a state of total exhaustion and had asked his friend the theatre director John Uecker to stay with him. Uecker had been with him during his last trip to New Orleans, and Williams felt that if he was about to die, he wanted it to be in his apartment in the French Quarter, in a big brass bed, the site of "some of the happiest hours of my life." But Uecker said that Williams could not possibly have summoned the energy to return to New Orleans, and death, when it came, was in truth as much a surrender to the inevitable as it was evidently an accident.

Elysée translates as "mythical paradise of the dead," and there on the thirteenth floor in the hotel's Sunset Suite on that cold Friday morning, Uecker discovered the playwright's body slumped at the side of his bed. Near him was an empty prescription bottle that had contained thirty Seconal tablets, many of them scattered about the bedroom. There were other prescribed medicines on the night table and two partly emptied wine bottles that had been in the room since his return from Italy. And on his bed, there was a photocopy of "Some of These Days," a short story by his friend James Purdy, across the top of which Purdy had written the lines of the young and ill-fated eighteenth-century poet Thomas Chatterton:

> *Water witches crowned with reeds*
> *bear me to your lethal tides.*

Williams had apparently died of the one thing he feared most: suffocation. As a child stricken with diphtheria, he nearly strangled to death, and the trauma left him terrified at the symptoms of heart and respiratory ailments, whether real or imagined. During the last night of his life, he swallowed, along with the barbiturate secobarbital, a plastic medicinal overcap, which the chief medical examiner said had become lodged in his glottis, shutting off air to his lungs and causing asphyxia.[1] Michael Valenti, composer of the original music for Williams's last Broadway play, *Clothes for a Summer Hotel*, said that on several occasions he had seen Williams unscrew an eyedrop bottle and, holding the cap in his teeth, his head leaning back, apply the lubricant to his eyes. Valenti always feared that a sudden intake of breath might lodge the cap in his throat. In a last split second of consciousness, he may have felt that he was suffering a heart attack. It was a sudden, tragic, and ironic end to a career that spanned four decades, a bizarre death he might have written for a character in one of his plays.

During Tennessee's final weeks, few among those closest to him recognized that his life was nearly over. Those who did see him were struck by his quiet, almost deliberate manner and by the way he was methodically tying up loose ends. He closed his house in Key West with the intention of never returning and bid good-bye to Leoncia McGee, his faithful housekeeper of more than thirty years: "Lee, I don't know if I'll ever see you again."[2] In New Orleans, during the late winter of 1982, renovations were begun on his apartment complex, and in a meeting with real estate agents, he made known his plan to sell the property with a leaseback provision for his own second-story flat. While in New York, he participated in negotiations for a revival Off-Broadway of his play *Vieux Carré*, asking that Sylvia Miles be engaged to repeat her London award-winning performance. He also discussed a refilming of *A Streetcar Named Desire*, hoping that Meryl Streep would play Blanche DuBois, but, on learning of Streep's unavailability, he gave his approval to a television production starring Ann-Margret. He wanted to attend the National Arts Club presentation of its 1983 medal to James Laughlin, his great friend and publisher at New Directions, but, unable to summon the energy, he sent a written homage instead:

> By nature I was meant more for the quieter and purer world of poetry than for the theatre into which necessity drew me.
>
> And now as a time for reckoning seems near, I know that it is the poetry that distinguishes the writing when it is distinguished, that of the plays and of the stories, yes, that is what I had primarily to offer you.[3]

Those words, "now as a time for reckoning seems near," read as they were only hours after the world had learned of Tennessee Williams's death, made a strong emotional impact upon the audience and moved Laughlin to tears.

John Uecker and a close friend of Tennessee's, actress Jane Lawrence Smith, were the last persons with him. Previously, he had startled his agent, Luis Sanjurjo, by informing him that he was dying and wanted to put his affairs in order. He had also told another friend, Edmund Perret, "I think I might be cashing in," but Perret, like Sanjurjo, tended to discount this, believing it to be a self-dramatization he had heard before.

On the other hand, Uecker was at a loss: "I called Tennessee's doctor and described his condition. I asked, 'What if he should take all those Seconals?' But the doctor thought I was an alarmist and said, 'If there's no liquor there, just don't worry about it. His system is accustomed to the medication. He can't do any damage without alcohol.' I answered, 'But he hasn't eaten enough to sustain himself.' He said not to worry."[4]

Uecker then conferred with another of Williams's longtime friends, Vassilis Voglis, who agreed that Tennessee must be hospitalized. The two conspired to have him admitted, but, ironically, this was scheduled to take place on the morning of his death. "Of course Tennessee knew what was going on," Uecker said. "The kind of contact he and I were making was on a level beyond all our communication during the years before. He was reading my mind. *His* mind was sharp and alert; he knew everything that was going on.

"He would turn to me, crystal clear, eye-to-eye, and say, 'I'm dying.' He wasn't acting. I could only hang my head. I thought if I could claim some moment when he wasn't so lucid, if he passed into some exhausted state of mind, near coma, then I could easily get him into the hospital. But he read my thoughts, and if the medics had come in on him suddenly, he would have affected the same attitude as before. He would have *appeared* fine and sent them away—and never have spoken to me again," Uecker said.

Three days before his death, Tennessee called Jane Smith to suggest that they have dinner together. She and her husband, the sculptor Tony Smith, had first met Tennessee some forty years before. Trying to renew his energy, he went off almost all medication, which served only to depress him further. On the strength of Seconal, from a new prescription, and black coffee, buoying his spirits, he dressed immaculately for the occasion and shaved his beard, prompting Jane to remark that he looked younger than he had in years. They dined across the street from the Elysée, and Jane recalled, "We had a wonderful time. John told me he hadn't heard Tennessee laugh like that in months. Afterward we went up to his suite and watched television and talked." Taking her aside, however, Tennessee confided, "Jane, I have faced the facts."[5]

Uecker felt that there were those who were always trying to orchestrate Tennessee's life and that his dread of going into a hospital was that he might be hooked up to life-sustaining equipment or would die surrounded and all but suffocated by possessive friends. Williams had often declared that his strongest instinct was to be free, to take off when life closed in on him. Now his greatest fear was that he would end up comatose and bedridden like Audrey Wood, his agent of thirty-two years.

His doctor in Key West had recently told him he could not continue much longer without prolonged hospitalization. "He just wouldn't have it," Uecker remarked. "A man like that you do not treat like a regular person, as I would my mother or my father. He must choose his own way. Life *and* death. Who can presume to know what is best for genius, much less force the presumption? You couldn't tell him anything. He would do only what *he* wanted to do.

"But I was not going to let him commit suicide. If he had sent for a bottle of liquor, I would have balked. That would have been the sign. But he was drinking only a glass or two of wine a day. In his studio in Key West, when he was writing, the whole house became like an unrecognizable set, he so charged the air around himself. But now, in his suite at the Elysée, it was much more than that. The energy in those rooms—I could never describe it. It was as though we were 75,000 feet above New York City. It wasn't Death. It wasn't God. I don't know. I'd go to bed in my room and lie down, hold on to what strength I had, then go back to him. I was on automatic pilot. We both were. It was overpowering. I would have understood if he had been searching for some kind of renewal or if he had been turning to his friends for the source of it, as he had many times before, but friends or familiar places, nothing worked."

The scene inside and outside the Hotel Elysée that Friday morning was pandemonium. Uecker called Williams's attorney John Eastman and agent Luis Sanjurjo, both of whom rushed to the suite. He also summoned the hotel manager, and shortly after, the police and a medical team arrived; then detectives and the coroner crowded the suite. Later, when the police statement was read to the press at the precinct, a reporter twisted an account attributed to Uecker that "about 11 P.M. Thursday he heard a noise from Williams's room, but did not investigate."[6] Uecker strongly denied this, insisting that he heard Williams moving about and at one point did what he had been forbidden to do: opened the bedroom door slightly, to see Tennessee sitting on the edge of his bed. Subsequently, he was advised not to try to make a correction, and as a result, an erroneous impression of willful neglect continues, to John Uecker's professional detriment. "Discovering him as I did, crouched between his bed and the night table, he looked like a man who had given everything there was to give and had slumped exhausted to the floor. I had never seen or felt anything in my life so shocking and sad."[7]

At first, the medics and police, without realizing who the hotel guest was, dismissed what they took to be the all-too-familiar sight of an addict who had overdosed. It was an antic scene, as Uecker described it, until the arrival of Jane Smith. Grief-stricken, crying aloud, she grasped the coroner's black bag in her arms while morgue attendants were attempting to remove Williams's body from the hotel. Suddenly, except for Jane's sobbing, there was a stillness and the realization of a great man's passing.

By noon, only a few hours after the announcement of Williams's death, a huge crowd had gathered outside the Elysée, blocking traffic. People from all walks of life—executives, hard-hat workers, delivery boys, theatre folk, friends, and outcasts—stood silently waiting. Linda Winer described the scene in *USA Today:* "When told Tennessee Williams had just died upstairs, no one needed to ask who he was. . . . Celebrity, of course, is no proof of greatness. Yet it is impossible to name another modern playwright who has broken into America's consciousness with Williams's complex, vivid force. Despite publicity about drugs, alcoholism, homosexuality, and failures of his later plays, it is the award-winning playwright's work—the knives and poetry of flawed humanity—that remains."[8]

Radio and television news programs covered the story at noon, while the *New York Post* was the first to publish it that evening in three-inch front-page headlines: "TENNESSEE WILLIAMS DEAD! Empty pill and wine bottles near playwright's body in N.Y." The following morning, the *Daily News* also reserved its full front page to proclaim: "TENNESSEE WILLIAMS DIES. Playwright, 71, found in hotel." On the first page of the *New York Times*, a heading over a large picture of the playwright announced: "TENNESSEE WILLIAMS IS DEAD HERE AT 71," followed by critic Mel Gussow's long, eloquent account: "Though his images were often violent, he was a poet of the human heart."[9]

That same evening, the *Post* once again gave over its front page: "TORMENT OF TENNESSEE WILLIAMS. Playwright dies alone—by drugs, despair. Broadway mourns a genius." The next day, the Sunday *Daily News* published still another front-page headline: "Williams' autopsy: TENNESSEE CHOKED TO DEATH." Both *Time* magazine and *Newsweek* reserved a full page in recognition. *Time*'s Ted Kalem, who in 1962 reversed the periodical's antagonistic policy toward Williams's life and career with a cover story, headed his paean "The Laureate of the Outcast."[10]

All three New York papers devoted their inside pages to a detailed summary of the playwright's career and to a profusion of photographs from his plays: the legendary Laurette Taylor in *The Glass Menagerie;* Jessica Tandy and Marlon Brando in *A Streetcar Named Desire;* Geraldine Page in *Summer and Smoke* and with Paul Newman in *Sweet Bird of Youth;* Maureen Stapleton and Eli Wallach in *The Rose Tattoo;* Burl Ives, Barbara Bel Geddes, and

Ben Gazzara in *Cat on a Hot Tin Roof;* Katharine Hepburn and Elizabeth Taylor in the film version of *Suddenly Last Summer;* Stapleton and Cliff Robertson in *Orpheus Descending;* and Bette Davis and Margaret Leighton in *The Night of the Iguana.*

Accolades from his colleagues in the theatre were many and deeply felt. Actor Marlon Brando spoke of Tennessee as a compatriot: "He told the truth as best he perceived it and never turned away from things that beset or frightened him. We are all diminished by his death."[11] Playwright Arthur Miller, who saw him as a mentor, said, "He came into the theatre bringing his poetry, his hardened edge of romantic adoration of the lost and the beautiful. For a while, the theatre loved him, and then it went back to searching in its pockets for its soul. He chose a hard life that requires the skin of an alligator and the heart of a poet. To his everlasting honor, he persevered and bore all of us toward glory."[12]

His friend and the producer of four of his plays, Cheryl Crawford, cried out: "Oh, God Almighty, I hope it's not true. I loved him very much. He's our greatest playwright without question."[13] Critic Walter Kerr concurred, saying that he was indeed the greatest American playwright, period. And Elia Kazan, who had directed several of his plays, chiefly *A Streetcar Named Desire* and *Cat on a Hot Tin Roof,* said, "He lived a very good life, with the most profound pleasures, and lived it as he chose. . . . Imagine yourself being in his skin the mornings he wrote some of those speeches or watching them performed . . . of seeing his family transmuted into art. . . . Let's do what the Indians in the East do at funerals of distinguished persons. Let's celebrate his life."[14]

Although Tennessee Williams may be regarded as a distinctly American dramatist, the response to his death was global. By 1983, he had become an international figure with an enormous following abroad. His work reached people all over the planet and on every level of life. Other than Chekhov, he was the most popular playwright in the Soviet theatre, and at the time of his death, several of his plays were being presented at once in the repertories of Moscow theatres alone, the most performed being *Orpheus Descending,* then in its seventh year. Now, more than ten years after his death, Williams's popularity endures undiminished in the free Russian theatre, as it does in most of the theatres of the world. No American playwright has ever been more universally recognized and admired. There is scarcely a literate person who does not recognize the name of Tennessee Williams, even if unfamiliar with his writings. Often a celebrity's reputation is eclipsed by his death, but Williams's fame remains as worldwide as ever.

While he had his detractors, those who did not appreciate his work or disliked him personally, there were few he deliberately alienated. His "galloping paranoia," as he characterized it, would rise one day in fury and subside as quickly the next. Generally, he not only aroused an affectionate regard among his friends but could depend upon the impulsive "kindness of strangers." Frequently, he was recognized and stopped on the street by some admirer in awe of him, as if he were some revered film star. Although he met and knew a wide range of celebrities, he was more at ease in the company of the young and unsophisticated; some were society's outcasts and alienated, but largely they were youthful admirers eager to help him in ways his older and more preoccupied friends were unable to. He particularly enjoyed being with those who made him laugh. Much in life, and even in his plays, that most people take seriously was, from his Olympian perspective, a laughing matter.

On Friday, March 8, 1983, at 8:00 P.M., the marquees over twenty Broadway theatres were darkened for a minute in his memory. All during that week, homage was paid and services were held throughout the country. In New York, at the Frank E. Campbell Funeral Home, hundreds came and passed by the open casket or stood silently to one side. "Some were weeping," the *New York Times* reported, "some fought back tears. Others stood silently for long periods looking at Tennessee Williams's coffin." Tennessee was lying in the same mortuary where twenty years before, in 1963, he had viewed for the last time the body of Frank Merlo, his longtime lover and friend, whose loss left a vacancy in his feelings that no one else was ever able to fill.

At the Actors Studio, friends gathered to honor him, and at Saint Malachy's in the Theatre District, a special memorial Mass was held. In New Orleans, within the cathedral that for nearly two centuries has stood in the heart of the French Quarter, a large crowd of people from all walks of life gathered to pay tribute. Then to celebrate his birthday on March 26, a special program open to the public was presented at the Shubert Theatre. Lines began forming at 7:00 A.M., and at noon, when the doors opened, the fifteen-hundred-seat theatre quickly filled, with Maureen Stapleton commenting to resounding applause, "I think Tenn would be glad to know that he had a full house."[15]

Shunning a microphone, Jessica Tandy performed a speech by Blanche DuBois from *A Streetcar Named Desire*. For ten minutes, the audience was held spellbound, and after an ovation, the actress said, "I'm so glad I reminded you that he wrote the words." Others appearing on the program were Lady St. Just, Kim Hunter, Elizabeth Ashley, Anne Jackson, and Geraldine Fitzgerald, who sang his favorite, "Danny Boy."

But the most mesmerizing and moving moment came at the very end, when the playwright's own voice was heard reading the opening monologue from *The Glass Menagerie*, concluding with the description of the fictitious father, who had deserted his family:

> He was a telephone man who fell in love with long distances. He gave up his job with the company and skipped the light fantastic out of town. Last we heard of him was a picture postcard from Mazatlan, a message of two words. Hello-goodbye, and no address.

This was a stage idealization of Williams's actual father, who never abandoned the family and who was, perhaps because he lacked the courage to leave, the most profound disappointment in his son's life. The play itself is a depiction of what *might* have happened if his mother had been left to care for her daughter and depend upon her son. In the end, Tom Wingfield marshals the courage to leave his family to follow in his father's footsteps.

In 1979, the playwright attended a Tennessee Williams Festival at Lynchburg College in Virginia. His appearance came as the climax of a two-week celebration. An occasion that he first approached with misgivings turned out instead to be a happy event, heightened by his wild sense of humor and famed shrieks of laughter. Seated on the apron of a stage surrounded by the setting for *Summer and Smoke*, with a looming representation of the stone Angel of Eternity upstage to his right, Williams entertained an audience of 2,300 with his wit and charm. It was a performance, the projection of an image, what he referred to as "my public self, that artifice of mirrors."[16] Here was the renowned celebrity, the Pulitzer Prize–winning playwright, very much onstage, as he was at press conferences and in interviews and at social gatherings. He has been described anonymously as "his own greatest work of fiction" and "a tragicomic genius on and off stage, a lyric poet whose wry, sad protagonists lived life through each sweaty nuance, in much the same way as he chose to live. He was often impossibly demanding, purposefully irrational, egocentric, vulnerably generous, and hilariously funny, all within the same 60 seconds."[17]

Drama critic David Richards once wrote that "those who knew him were aware that there was a craftiness behind his apparent willingness to divulge the squalor and agony of his life. He liked to give a good show, being something of an actor as well as a playwright."[18] And here at the Lynchburg College festival, he was giving a good show, enjoying the plaudits of the faculty and the company of young and attractive students at various banquets given in his honor, as much as he was relishing the laughter and applause of the thousands in his audience.

When he was asked about the one thing he might wish to change in his life had he the power, he quipped, "One thing? Well, I have *two* of most things you're supposed to have two of . . . but one thing? Well, I don't want to change my sex." Then his manner became serious: "One thing?" After a long silence, Tennessee removed his mask and Tom Williams confessed, "I would have won my father's affection. He wanted to win mine. But I . . . my mother turned us [my sister and me] against my father, and I regret that the most, I think."[19] On that note, he ended his appearance at the festival.

During the years of his success, Tennessee Williams had sedulously avoided any contact with the father whom he told everyone he hated: "I loved him only after he was dead."[20] By 1947, Cornelius Coffin Williams had retired from his position as sales manager at a St. Louis shoe company and had separated from his wife, Edwina, who ordered him out of their home. Cantankerous and drinking heavily, he spent years desultorily wandering about, seeing only his younger son, Dakin, but rarely Tom. In 1957, at the age of seventy-seven, he died; Tennessee immediately plunged into a clinical depression and entered analysis. But it was too late to "restore his father's lost pride and manhood"[21] or his own.

As children, both Tom Williams and his sister, Rose, vainly sought their father's love. Tom defensively took refuge in his writing, but for Rose, the shock of outright rejection compounded by her disappointments in love gradually eroded her sanity, until finally she was diagnosed as schizophrenic and in 1937 admitted to a state asylum. On the occasions after Tennessee's death when Jane Smith and John Uecker would visit Rose at Stony Lodge sanitarium in upstate New York or take her shopping in Manhattan or to a musical, Jane might compliment her on the dress or a ring she was wearing. Her answer would be a proud: "My father gave it to me." Once she identified her brother's picture as that of Cornelius and sometimes volunteered that she was going to St. Louis to visit him. She seldom, if ever, mentioned or talked about her mother.

In 1979, Edwina Dakin Williams was in her ninety-fourth and last year, and she, like her famous son, had attained a consummate skill in role-playing. While Tom Williams always had ambivalent feelings toward her, it was only after Cornelius's death, and after his analyst convinced him that the "hate" he felt toward his father was in fact a sublimated love, that he expressed feelings of malice toward his mother. He began ridiculing her as "a little Prussian officer in drag,"[22] and referred to her as "psychotic," while at the same time he sent her gifts and letters of concern urging her to spend winters with him at his home in Key West. "I must say," he admitted, "she contributed a lot to my writing—her forms of expression, for example. And that underlying hysteria gave her great eloquence. I still find her totally mystifying—and frightening. It's best we stay away from our mothers."[23]

Edwina's domineering influence left her son with a susceptibility and an attraction toward women of tensile strength. She was not the only woman in his life who sought to possess him. He roused the maternal in many of his women friends. As a child, he had had no escape, but as an adult, when such a love became too oppressive, he simply boarded a plane. He often described himself as "a moving target." His clarion cry was *En Avant!* In one way or another, he was always in flight from confinement in all its guises, which he described as the greatest dread of his life.

Even in death, he wanted somehow to be free of the symbolic confinement of a coffin and repeatedly said he wished to be "sewn up in a clean white sack and borne out to sea in an inexpensive little vessel, perhaps a shrimping boat. I suggest it put out from my island home at Key West, and when this small craft has arrived at the point most nearly determined as the point at which

Hart Crane gave himself to the sea, there, at that nearest point that can be determined by any existing records, I wish to be given back to the sea from which life is said to have come."[24]

He had said that he wanted his bones to intermingle with those of the poet who had long been his favorite, who inspired him as Shelley inspired Crane. Instead, at the last, his body was transported from New York, "a rock from which no roses spring," to be buried in St. Louis, the city he hated more than any other. The irony of this caused a furor, especially among Williams's young and more romantic friends, who threatened to kidnap his corpse and take it out to sea. It was his brother Dakin who had decided that his brother would be buried in the family plot next to his mother, in St. Louis's historic Calvary Cemetery. Describing Tennessee Williams as the greatest poet-dramatist since William Shakespeare, he said, "I feel very strongly against disposing of the body of a person who had the giant literary stature of my brother. His remains should be placed in a readily accessible place."*[25]

On Saturday, March 5, a large group of family and friends, many of whom were not speaking to one another, gathered for a requiem Mass at the huge St. Louis Cathedral. And although there were those still trying to take possession of him even in death, they had only the lifeless shell of the man to bicker over, not Tom Williams, that most elusive of human spirits. Dakin's parish priest, the Reverend Jerome Wilkerson, intoned, "I bless the body of Thomas Lanier Williams with the holy water that recalls his baptism," while an Episcopal priest, the Reverend Sidney Lanier, a cousin of the playwright, read from the Old Testament.

Williams characterized himself as a "rebellious puritan." Very early in his life, he came under the religious influence of his beloved grandfather, the Reverend Walter Dakin; he was reared an Episcopalian but in 1969 became a Roman Catholic "only for one day," as he later said, through the persuasion of his brother, who was a convert. He maintained that he had always been very religious and asserted, "Of course, God exists. I don't understand how. But He exists. How can there be creation without a creator? Still, I don't think there is an afterlife. At least I'm afraid there isn't."[26] As for the Ten Commandments, he commented, "I don't steal. I don't covet my neighbor's wife or his ass. . . . Maybe I should correct that. I honor the Lord. I don't kill. I don't bear false witness. Ha! I bear excessively true witness for most people."[27]

He had written, "Death is one moment, and life is so many of them."[28] The attendance at the ornate Byzantine cathedral swelled to a congregation of

---

*Severely criticized for his decision, Dakin Williams said that it was not his alone. "When I arrived in New York on February 26, my brother's body was already placed in a very handsome 'Orthodox Jewish' casket. The decision to bury him had already been made by trustees Maria St. Just and attorney John Eastman. The funeral director, Frank Campbell, took me aside and said, 'We are planning to ship the remains to Waynesville, Ohio, to be buried alongside his grandparents.' I then selected St. Louis, where visitors could come to pay their respects, rather than inaccessible Waynesville" (WDW to LL).

over twelve hundred. And after the services, clusters of spectators standing in a light rain or in the doorways of their homes watched a long cortege wind its way through neighborhoods in University City and Clayton, where young Tom Williams had grown up and started his career. At 1:00 P.M., family and friends arrived at Calvary Cemetery and crowded before his coffin under a green canvas tent. Nearby, glistening in the rain, a handsome stone marked the grave of Edwina Dakin Williams.

In due time, the mourners wept and went away, leaving Tom and his mother alone.

PART I

Lodestar
1900–1929

———

"the idea of life as a nothing—withholding
submission of self to flame"

I

The Family

1900–1907

In the fall of 1900, Edwina Estelle Dakin was commencing her third year at Harcourt Place Seminary, an Episcopal finishing school in Gambier, Ohio. She had turned sixteen on August 19 and was the only child of the Reverend Walter Edwin Dakin and Rosina Otte Dakin, who lived in the vicinity of Springfield, Ohio. Small, pert, and vivacious, she had a habit, passed on to her "writin' son" in later years, of lifting her chin defiantly when challenged or crossed. It fostered an illusion of height, a way of "standing tall."

In these early years, though, she was seldom out of sorts. She was pretty and popular, and her beaux and girlfriends saw her as happy—to a degree bordering on hysteria. Her diaries[1] chronicled an endless swirl of entertainments at dinners, dances, sports events, and weekend outings. Although she was a good student and wrote well, her consuming, almost exclusive, interest was in the young men attending school at nearby Kenyon Military Academy. Her favorite cadet, revealed among the first entries in her diary, was Frederick Raiff Stott, to whom she attached the word *love*.

Almost all of the girls at Harcourt were from wealthy families and were preparing either for entrance to eastern colleges or for a "suitable" marriage, but Edwina was not really intent on such goals. It was enough that she was accepted socially by her girlfriends and by her beaux at Kenyon, most of whom mistook her for a lively southern girl because of her southern accent.

She had, in fact, been born in Marysville, in central Ohio, but spent the early years of her childhood in southern Tennessee. Her father entered the ministry after studying at the University of the South at Sewanee, but neither he nor his wife expected to stay in the South. Although they readily adapted themselves to what they observed as the southerners' gentle and appealing way of life, they regarded themselves as Ohioans. But their daughter thought of herself as southern and consummately played the role for the rest of her life.

She quickly took on all the customs and mannerisms of the southern belle, and even when she was in her nineties, living out her life in St. Louis, her drawl was described by an interviewer as still lazy and elongated and capable of making the shortest sentences "roll on and on like Ol' Man River." When she was younger and her speech ran swiftly at flood tide, she had much the same story to tell of her girlhood in the South as she told to the interviewer:

> Mah fathuh was a very beloved clergyman in each parish, and of course that made me very populuh. Ah had a very gay time. Ah think I had about the gayest youth of any person imaginable. We'd have elaborate parties. Ah don't know of any place in the world that was gayer than the South, even after that terrible war. Of course, that was a *terrible* war. The boys volunteered to fight for the South when they were only fifteen years old. It's very sad, Ah think, that fifteen year-olds would be called into the war.[2]

Except for Christmas holidays and summer vacations with her parents, Edwina stayed at Harcourt Seminary, attending various school functions and making occasional weekend trips with her girlfriends to their luxurious homes in neighboring towns. Because of the sizable number of young men at the military academy, she received invitations to many social and sports events, all recorded in Edwina's diaries in considerable detail.

> Thanksgiving! Nov. 29, 1900.
> What a jolly day we had, in the morning we went to church, did not last very long, after luncheon we went upstairs and danced so as to make the floor smooth for the dance. When I came down I found a ticket [to the football game] from Mr. Stott. At 2:30 we all started for the game and nearly froze before we had been there ten minutes. . . . As we had an eight course dinner it was nearly half-past eight when we left the table and the boys arrived soon after. I had the best time at the dance that I [ever] had at Harcourt. I had my first dance of course with *Mr. Stott*, when he gave me his K.M.A. pin. I had all my dances taken but I can't remember all of the boys' names I danced with. . . . The dance ended at twelve o'clock and seemed entirely too short.

On December 12, Edwina appeared in a play called *Six Cups of Chocolate*. "I distinguished myself in the role of actress," she told her diary, "Ahem!!" She had been cast as a southern girl, and the one line that she never forgot and described as her "parting shot" was: "If he had been down South, my pa would have fixed him!" After that, whenever she encountered a certain young man on the Harcourt campus, she said, "He would call out teasingly, 'What *would* your pa do to me if I were down South, Miss Dakin?' "

At the dance that followed her dramatic debut, she noted, "Poor Frederick was ill and had to go home," adding that among others, she met a Mr. Balph and "had some dances with him." "Poor Frederick" Stott apparently did not survive the holidays in her affections. She never mentioned him again, but she placed Rowland Pollock Balph, "the dearest boy at KMA," at the head of her evaluation chart and mentioned him frequently in her diary—for a time.

By the end of the spring term, Edwina had excellent grades, and happily, she confided to her diary, "Rowland and I took a walk around the 'hedge.' How romantic! We went home escorted by the boys at ten o'clock. They left us [at the] door. Rowland shook hands with me three times."

Edwina had expected to return to Harcourt in the fall for her final year, but the Dakins were now in the midst of plans to leave Springfield and return to the South. On June 19, she noted that this was "Good-bye to Gambier!!! Packed all morning." Later, she added, "Rowland went as far as Columbus [Ohio] with me." And so it was also good-bye to "the dearest boy" of them all.

While Edwina would miss her many friends at Harcourt and the distinction of being their only "Southern girl from Ohio," the prospect of returning to the South could only be a matter for jubilation. She enjoyed traveling and cheerfully adapted to new surroundings, and in this she had much in common with her father, a trait she would ultimately pass on to Tom.

"Stryke Dakyns, Ye Devils in Ye Hempe"

Restless and missionary in spirit, Walter Edwin Dakin was the kind of minister who liked moving about and meeting the challenge of rebuilding foundering parishes. He was born in Harveysburg, near Waynesville, in southwest Ohio, on April 23, 1857, the son of Dr. Edwin Francis Dakin, a kindly, though somewhat impractical, country physician. Dr. Dakin practiced medicine in the Harveysburg-Waynesville region from the mid-nineteenth century until after the Civil War and eventually moved his practice to Waynesville itself, a charming Quaker village. Walter, one among six sons, was confirmed in Waynesville's Saint Mary's Episcopal Church, and he later served there as a deacon.

Although attracted to the ministry, Walter realized this was no more practical a calling than that of a country doctor. Following his graduation from high school, he left for Poughkeepsie, in upstate New York, to study at the Eastman Business College. There, in Dutchess County, Walter was in contact with the branch of the Dakin family who spelled their name *Daykin* and whose ancestors had emigrated to the New World from England in the 1600s.[3]

Edwina was always proud to say, "The Dakins could trace themselves back to the Normans. One of our ancestors was the captain of a ship that sailed to England at the time of the invasion under William the Conqueror. When the wind wreaked havoc with his sails, he climbed up to untangle sail from rope.

Our coat-of-arms bears the motto: *Stryke Dakyns, Ye Devils in Ye Hempe*, referring to the wind tangling the rope that was strangling the sails. The coat-of-arms also holds the words, *Sir Baldwyn Dakeny, Knt.*, and the picture of a knight's breastplate with four lions, one in each corner, and his helmet. Above the latter, a crown contains a hand stretching out of it with a spear, poised as though ready to strike."[4]

Among the Dakins who moved west was Edwina's great-great-grandfather, Preserved Fish Dakin. Of English Quaker ancestry, Preserved Fish was born in Vermont, a descendant of Thomas Dakin of Concord and Sudbury, Massachusetts. Around 1814, he settled in New Burlington, Ohio, and then finally moved his family to Waynesville, where he acquired a large parcel of land later known as Dakin's Corners.

After young Walter had completed his studies at business school, he returned to Ohio and found work as an accountant in Marysville. He then met and fell in love with Rosina Otte, whom he first saw proudly riding through the streets on her own horse. She was fourteen and the daughter of German-American parents, and her full baptismal name was an imposing Rosina Maria Francesca von Albertzart-Otte. A lovely girl, she was called, appropriately, Rose.

Edwina's maternal grandfather, Frank Henry Otte, had come to the United States from Hanover, Germany, in 1853, at the age of seventeen, and had traveled extensively about the country. Eight years later, he married Elizabeth von Albertzart. After further travels through New Orleans, St. Louis, and Cincinnati, the couple settled briefly in Buffalo, New York, where in 1863 Mrs. Otte gave birth to Rose. Finally, the Ottes moved to Marysville, a village with a population of fewer than two thousand. Here in 1871, Frank and his brother, William, who had emigrated from Hanover in 1857, established F. H. & W. Otte, merchant tailors, a successful business that remained in the family for over one hundred years.[5]

Frank and Elizabeth Otte became the parents of four children, two boys and two girls. A proud, aristocratic woman, Mrs. Otte tended to look down upon the other German families in Marysville for what in fact they largely were: immigrant farmers. Although the Ottes were strict Lutherans, they, like many well-to-do Protestant families, felt their children could be better educated in Roman Catholic schools, and so Rose was sent to a Catholic boarding school up north, in Youngstown, Ohio. There the Ursuline nuns reinforced the severe upbringing she had received from her parents. Along with the other disciplines that every cultured young girl was taught in those times, she also studied music. After Youngstown, she was enrolled in Cincinnati's famous Conservatory of Music, and a love and mastery of music was instilled that would last all of her life. Upon her return to Marysville, she became engaged to Walter Dakin. On October 10, 1883, when Rose was twenty and he twenty-six, Edwina's mother and father were married. Frank Otte, whose speculations had depleted the family fortune, was at first disappointed by his daughter's marriage. He had hoped that Rose would wed someone from a more affluent family, but the Ottes nevertheless accepted the couple into their home. On August 19, 1884, Edwina Estelle Dakin was born: named Edwina after her paternal grandfather, Dr. Edwin Dakin, and Estelle after Rose's sister.[6]

Because Rose's mother was both unhappy in Marysville and afflicted with a bronchial ailment, both the Otte and Dakin families moved to the mountain ridges of southern Tennessee, east of Chattanooga, where Frank Otte had purchased a few hundred acres of farmland. For a time, the Ottes, the three Dakins, and Rose's two brothers and her sister all settled in the same house. But the farm itself was starkly isolated, a considerable distance from any neighboring community, and it was not long before the brothers left for Texas, disappeared, and were believed to have been murdered.

Walter, who was unable to find work as an accountant, was teaching locally when he was offered the position of superintendent in charge of the Shelby-ville Female Institute. At last, the Dakins were able to move away from the farm and into quarters of their own on the institute's campus, which was located midway between Chattanooga and Nashville. Although often sepa-rated from children of her own age, Edwina was growing up a gregarious, affable little girl. Pampered by her father and guided by her mother, she would be the Dakins' only child.[7]

While Walter attended to the institute's administration, Rose took charge of the school's music department. She had become an excellent pianist and appeared there in concert. Among Edwina's earliest memories were those of her mother "looking regal as she swept across the stage to seat herself at the piano. . . . To look at Mother, you'd think she was the Queen of Sheba, al-though she might often be wearing old dresses she had made over."[8]

The institute would have proved an ideal situation for the Dakins had it not become financially encumbered by a new and inexperienced owner. Follow-ing a year without pay, Walter was compelled to accept the position of super-intendent of public schools in Shelbyville. The family boarded at a rambling old mansion owned by the Singleton family. Their daughter, Claire, was to become Edwina's lifelong friend, and their eight-year-old son, John, her first sweetheart. He first proposed the following year, when he and Walter Dakin were driving to Nashville: "In all seriousness, Mr. Dakin, I'd like to ask Ed-wina's hand in marriage."[9]

Edwina's father laughingly told her of John's proposal, and she said that from then on they were embarrassed in each other's company: "He even stopped carrying my books to school." Among Edwina's effects, discovered after her death, was a tiny book, *The Fairy Bride of Croton Lake*,[10] inscribed, "To Edwina from John Singleton, Xmas 1892," and inlaid within its covers was a four-leaf clover. It concerns a "wondrously beautiful maiden" named Blanche, the captive of a wrathful tyrant. Its worn pages suggest long use and the possibility that Edwina read it to her son Tom when he was a youngster.

Eventually, Walter Dakin accepted a teaching post at Woolwine, a college for young men in Tullahoma, Tennessee. A forceful and interesting speaker, he was frequently a lay reader in the local Episcopal church. The Right Reverend Charles Todd Quintard happened to hear him and was sufficiently impressed to persuade him to take up the ministry. Walter did not require much persuasion. Becoming a minister of God was something he had desired for some time; but, because of its impracticality, he had kept the idea a secret from Rose. But she was, as she always would be, fully committed to what had become Walter's main purpose in life. She gave music lessons, became an expert seamstress, and took on other chores to earn money for the family so that her husband could concentrate on his studies for the ministry.

On March 23, 1895, after attending the Episcopal Theological School at the University of the South, founded in 1857 high atop a Tennessee mountain, Walter Edwin Dakin was ordained to the Episcopal diaconate. A year later, he entered the priesthood, with the distinction of having completed the course in less time than anyone before him.

Episcopalianism was not the leading faith in the South; it was considered elitist and too close to Roman Catholicism. As a result, there were many parishes struggling for existence and in need of an energetic reformer. In Walter Dakin, his congregations would find not only a strong motivating force toward the love of God but also a love and concern for them as individuals. More significant was his sense of the high drama of the Episcopal Mass, an attraction that he imparted to Edwina and to a grandson who would eventually devote his life to the theatre.

Although he never neglected the poor and humble among his flock, it was obvious that Walter was attracted by the superficially sumptuous living of the wealthier Episcopalians. He felt in common with them a delight in travel, changes of scene, excellent food and wine, and making and cultivating a host of friends. Much of his affection for the South stemmed, in fact, from an open enjoyment of the good life; not just Episcopalians but many high-living southerners in general were scarcely burdened by a sense of original sin or by any of the self-immolating Calvinist traits that weighed leadenly at that time on the Protestant faithful in the North.

While the festivities of the wealthy delighted Walter, Rose was often shocked by her husband's eager participation. Edwina at first thought it was lucky that "Episcopalians do not think it a sin to dance and have a good time."[11] But, confronted by their indulgences and her father's part in them, this was an opinion that she would eventually modify, inclined as she was toward her mother's puritanism. Love her father as she did during these early years, she was her mother's daughter.

Rose Dakin had become an Episcopal convert, but there remained much in her makeup that reflected the German Lutheran faith of her parents. Although kindly and often referred to as "a saint," she was at the same time stern and firmly self-disciplined. By comparison, Walter was the bon vivant, and ultimately both Rose and Edwina would disapprove of the Reverend Dakin's participation in the affluent life among Episcopal ladies and gentlemen of leisure.

In 1897, Walter Dakin and his family left Tennessee and returned to Ohio. He had accepted the ministry of a troubled parish near Springfield at a time when Bishop Quintard had journeyed to England in quest of grants for his hard-pressed church. Walter realized that the bishop would be disappointed at his leaving Tennessee, but the decision was occasioned by financial necessity. Edwina was first sent to Wittenberg College, "a junior college which accepted younger girls." As her grades were exceptional, she was soon offered a scholarship to Harcourt Place Seminary. She remarked that it was the only way she could have attended such a school, "because Father could not afford to send me there."[12]

A Social Butterfly and a Bachelor's Dream

After her three years at Harcourt, Edwina returned once again to the South to begin the five happiest years she would ever know, a period of time that would become forever engraved in her memory and in her heart and about which she would never stop reminiscing.

Bishop Quintard had lured the Reverend Dakin away from Ohio by offering him a beautiful old church in Cleveland, Tennessee, northeast of Chattanooga. Edwina was enrolled for her senior year of high school at the Tennessee Female College. Ever since her debut in *Six Cups of Chocolate*, she had been harboring a secret desire to be an actress on the musical stage, and now, in Cleveland, her amateur theatrical career "blazoned." Among several plays in which she appeared was one called *A Bachelor's Dream*, and the role she enacted was, in fact, typecasting: that of the bachelor's first sweetheart.

After her graduation, Edwina and the Dakins were on the move again, this time to the Deep South. The bishop had asked Walter to take over a ministry at Church Hill, near Natchez, Mississippi. At that time, there was no deeper South than the area around Natchez, with its many magnificent antebellum homes. By the turn of the century, the wounds of the Civil War, if not entirely healed, were looked upon with commiseration for both the gray and blue sides. The turbulence and upheaval of the twentieth century were not to be felt for another decade. In Natchez, Edwina was to discover to her delight that Mississippians still held to all of the Old South's genteel codes and customs— the receptions and cotillions, the courtly manners and reverence for home and family. Except for the industrialized cities of the New South like Knoxville, the postwar era in Mississippi was more reversion than Reconstruction.

Walter and his family spent little more than a year at Church Hill before moving on to Port Gibson, a plantation center that Gen. Ulysses S. Grant had declared "too pretty to burn." Located near the Mississippi River between Vicksburg to the north and Natchez to the south, Port Gibson was famous for two landmarks: the Presbyterian church, its steeple being an enormous gold hand with its forefinger pointing up to heaven, and the ruins of what had been the finest plantation in the South, with only the twenty-two four-story-high Corinthian columns of the Windsor mansion left standing. Though merely local attractions to his mother, they would become symbols to Tennessee Williams.

Edwina said she spent the happiest years of her life in Port Gibson. She was by then a young lady of eighteen, properly educated and of marriageable age and finally freed from a school's rules and regulations. Occasionally, she would help her mother with the housework in the rectory that had recently been built for the Dakins, and she would teach Sunday school, but, as she savored her newfound freedom, her main preoccupation was with the rounds of card parties, elaborate dinners and dances, and the attentions of her new gentlemen friends.

Mr. and Mrs. Dakin were well liked in Port Gibson, and Walter's standing as rector of Saint James's Episcopal Church gave his daughter a respectability that opened doors at the homes of their more prosperous neighbors. Edwina recalled how the prominent families on the large plantations held endless garden parties, where they would dance on the huge verandas or stroll around the wide lawns lit in rainbow colors by Japanese lanterns. She admitted to having been something of a social butterfly but said:

> Many of the girls were belles in those days, with Southern men spending half their time making sure we enjoyed ourselves. Most of the families were wealthy and could pass on estates and money to their children without inheritance taxes slicing it away. Sons knew they would be planters like their fathers before them. Cotton was everything. The young men had little to do but get up on a horse and ride around the plantation, watching overseers parcel out work, or else spend their time hunting quail or deer. My beaus had so much leisure, they would even take me for buggy rides in the morning.[13]

By the fall of 1902, Edwina's popularity was so great among Port Gibson's young men that they not only hand-delivered their cards but used the mails to woo her. For Miss Dakin to be "at home" to callers, it was customary for them either to deliver personally or to mail a small note requesting the pleasure of her company. These formal invitations to anything from a dance to a casual afternoon ride in some young gentleman's carriage were considered de rigueur.

She even received a proposal of sorts in the mail in the form of a poem entitled "A Toast to Beauty." It was carefully placed in her diary but elicited no comment.

Sweet Little, Pretty Little, Coy Miss Dakin,
The one, you know, who sets hearts aching.
With face so sweet—Her eyes are too—
She sets you wild when she glances at you. . . .
With light brown hair, and dark brown eyes,
You see therein, where her power lies.
We'll pledge ourselves to the pretty Miss Dakin,
The one, you know, with ways so taking.
So here's a toast, to our feminine host,
May she ever be so fascinating!
From your two most devoted, Warren and Harry,
Either one of whom, with you would marry.

The Reverend Dakin's modest salary, augmented by the income from his wife's music lessons and dressmaking, was adequate enough so that they seldom found it necessary to deny Edwina her many pleasures. Not only did she enjoy the society of old Mississippi families in Port Gibson, Natchez, and Vicksburg but she also visited in cities as distant as Montgomery, Alabama, and Baton Rouge, Louisiana. Her diary reads like one long social calendar of card and garden parties, dances and cotillions, music and theatre events.

In those years, the American theatre was largely a hodgepodge of wild melodrama, silly operetta, and bowdlerized Shakespeare, all taken with utmost seriousness, especially when the attraction emanated from New York. Miss Dakin, aspiring musical actress, attended these events. And in years to come, she would impress her love of theatre upon her son Tom.

The program for the touring play *Two Little Waifs*, appearing at the Port Gibson Opera House on November 25, 1903, failed to list the playwright but gave a prominent place to the director. Over the play's title, a notice admonished: "Ladies will please remove their hats"—hardly the great help one would suppose, since most ladies wore their hair in towering pompadours. The play had five acts and equally as many scene changes, and the program was careful to direct attention to "the moving clouds and the rising moon effects." The next attraction was announced as *Her Only Sin*, and no doubt audiences could barely wait to see what *that* might be!

In 1904, Edwina would become twenty years old. Considering the anxiety that young ladies and their families began to feel about daughters in their twenties still unmarried, it may well have been at this time that Edwina changed her birthdate from 1884 to 1885, a little secret she kept until she was well into her nineties and proud of her advanced age. Since it would not be until August that she would actually turn twenty, now, in February, she was still nineteen, and, as far as anyone outside the family knew, she could just go on for another year being nineteen.

During the summer of 1904, the Dakin family journeyed from Port Gibson to the Louisiana Purchase Exposition in St. Louis. Edwina could hardly have expected that St. Louis would someday be her home for the rest of her life or that she and her son would spend many hours in Forest Park, on these same fairgrounds.

With the approach of the Christmas holidays, her diary for December 23 noted that she had returned from "a few days visit to Vicksburg where I helped receive at Clara Moore's debut. Had such a pleasant visit with her. Stayed to the dance given by the young men at the Carroll Hotel. Went with Mr. Reeve Deason. We had thirty some callers on Sunday!" Her father, though, managed to close his year on a more cerebral note when Port Gibson's Book Club presented him lecturing on "Shakespeare's Heroines." The like of Edwina was not among them.

The year 1905 brought about yet another change of scene and parish. In mid-June, the Dakins moved to Columbus, an old Mississippi town situated on the Tombigbee River a few miles from the Alabama border, where Walter Dakin became rector of Saint Paul's Church. Edwina, who was visiting in Natchez at the time of the move, wrote her parents, "Mr. Chamberlain says that Columbus is a twin the size of Natchez and very like it and plenty of boys!!" On her arrival, she found there were indeed many young gentlemen eager to call. She soon announced she was off to her first dance with Mr. Gaius Whitfield, Jr., taking a drive with him the next day behind his spirited horse Ku Klux.

Walter had a quite different view of their new location, albeit equally enthusiastic. In an account he wrote later in the year for his hometown Waynesville newspaper, he described Columbus as "a beautiful little city, with still many of the 'before the war' homes . . . having suffered less from the devastation of war than the towns around. You may recall that it was at this place that the women first placed flowers upon both Federal and Confederate graves alike."[14] He said he was happy with the church on South Second Street and the old Southern Gothic rectory.

The Reverend Dakin was not only vigorous in the pulpit, giving his congregation much to think about from Sunday to Sunday, but he and his wife moved in manifold ways and performed wonders in the community. At home, Walter read a great deal from a large library of the classics, while Rose busied herself with household chores, civic projects, and her music. Edwina, although always respectful and rather in awe of her parents' gentle but firm authority, created an air of excitement in the home that was more often a disturbance. The local newspaper reported, "Miss Dakin will be quite an acquisition to our younger social set," and years later a neighbor, Melissa Whyte, commented, "I remember watching her as her skirts flounced about her ankles, thinking to myself that as soon as I was eighteen I would have long skirts too. She never knew me, but she was the minister's daughter and known to many that she did not know."[15]

Finally, Edwina had to admit to being twenty years old, although actually she was twenty-one. Her gaiety had become edged with anxiety and the fear of spinsterhood, and her prattle about her social life was incessant. Many of her former schoolmates and girlfriends had married and were young mothers, and she found herself invited to their homes often with the ill-concealed intent of introducing her to a prospective mate.

The question why one so pretty, vivacious, and popular had not readily found a husband is perhaps related to a characteristic also attributed to Edwina's daughter in later years: Her nervous chatter bordered on hysteria and created panic in any would-be suitor. She was the kind whom a young man would like to conquer but not marry. And she was the kind who might have become a reluctant virgin had not fate intervened and had she not persisted in her determination to get married. Her social calendar was becoming more and more like a battle plan and her home like campaign headquarters. Mr. Dakin's reading must have led him to identify with Jane Austen's Mr. Bennet, and he must also have thanked God that he had only one and not five such daughters.

On the surface, Edwina was the actress playing the role of coquette. Underneath, she was the resolute puritan, ensuring that her behavior would always be above reproach. Any overzealous young man with excited ideas would quickly be reminded that Miss Dakin was very much the minister's and her mother's daughter. The "Sweet Little, Pretty Little, Coy Miss Dakin" disguised another contradictory side of her nature: a rockbound Christian conscience that would be brought to bear with shattering impact on her husband and children, something she was never able to see or understand in herself.

Edwina believed in God and original sin, went to church regularly, if not religiously, and rode out her full share of life's vicissitudes with the same grim vigor she pursued its many trifling pleasures. The transcendent experience was beyond her reach, nor was she able to comprehend the mortal extremes of the tragic and the absurd as anything but God's will, and as a result, she would maintain to the very end a doggedly clear conscience. As far as *social* conscience was concerned, sin by association never entered Edwina's mind; she simply adjusted herself to the mores and prejudices of the times.

In 1905, Edwina was invited to join the Columbus chapter of the Daughters of the American Revolution, and to her at the time, as it would be all of her life, this was a singular honor. There was a problem, though: Her father's ancestors before the Revolution were both Quakers and Tories who held grants of land from the English throne. Fortunately, a librarian in Columbus, who coincidentally was a Dakin, revealed that there had been a farmer also named Dakin who had discarded his plow for a Colonial musket. And so it was that he had the qualifications, and Edwina met the DAR requirement in order to become a Daughter and later in life a regent.[16]

<0e17>26</0e17>

Among Edwina's beaux, a likely suitor appeared in the person of one Franklin O. Harris, a young lawyer and her most persistent caller.

> Miss Edwina Dakin
>   at Home.
>
> Dear Miss Dakin—
> In pursuance of our little chat last Sunday, I hereby notify you that the writer would like the best in the world to call tomorrow night—and he hopes with your sweet permission to be with you at such time.
>   He indicts himself as
>
>   Yours sincerely,
>   Franklin O. Harris

As an attorney-at-law in Columbus, a gentleman of an esteemed profession, Mr. Harris was certain to meet with the Dakins' approval. Although Edwina did not exactly refer to him as a suitor, her diaries indicate that he was the most constant of her gentleman callers. He sent her numerous such lawyerlike missives, and in her diary on December 18, she declared, "At last have gotten our own phone after so many months. No more engagements by *note*!!!" Conventions die hard, however. The following day, she received yet another note from Mr. Harris.

> Miss Edwina Dakin
>   At Home
>
> My dear Miss Dakin—
> May I talk to you Thursday night? The temptation is to ask you for an earlier date, but I am somewhat afraid you'd say me nay.
>   I started to call Sunday afternoon but I was not acquainted with His Honor's ruling on that point, and so denied my self.

On Christmas morning, Edwina attended her father's services, and upon returning home, she found "a beautiful book of Rileys hanging to door knob. Sender unknown, but I have suspicions." After dining with friends of the family and going for a drive with a Mr. Hester, at nine that evening she attended a dance: "Wore my white chiffon—blue sash—blue gloves—blue slippers." Blue was not only her favorite color, as she would say over and over again, but it would become her son's, too, and would appear throughout his writings.

Three days later, she was off to Tuscaloosa, Alabama, arriving in time to dress for the LTF ball. A newspaper account, dated Saturday, December 20, 1905, said that "Miss Edith Lodge was the sweet and gracious hostess Saturday evening at one of the prettiest and most attractive parties given in some time. The affair was in honor of her windsome [*sic*] guest, Miss Edwina Dakin of Columbus." The entry in her diary, though, was brief:

Dec. 31st Sun. Went to Church. Took dinner with Marilou Alston who invited four girls besides Edith and me. Came home at half-past three and had twenty-five callers before supper. All *men*.

For Edwina, this was an appropriate way to end one year and begin what would prove the fateful year of 1906. By spring, a new name would appear in her diary—a Mr. Williams.

A Gentleman Caller from Knoxville

During this last year of Edwina's unmarried life, the bliss of being single and free had begun to cloud over. She appeared to have all the necessary prerequisites for married life, including intellectual pretensions, if not preoccupations. She took French and German lessons, the latter because her mother felt that she should learn the language of her grandparents' homeland, and although she was not at that time an avid reader, she joined the local book club, one of whose members must have bewildered her with his ostensible erudition.

My dear Miss Dakin:
It is aphoristic; I'll admit almost bordering on the trite, to say that 'tis better late than never—but even so here is the fulfillment of a promise which has been neglected by reason of manifold duties, the enumeration of which I shall spare you.
    I hope you will enjoy [the books] and find them interesting—Maria Stuart, for instance. I can envy you the time to indulge in German and wish exceedingly I could join your little class. But I fear me the time is some days off when I shall again follow the peregrinations of Peter Schlemil, shadowless, or commiserate with the beautiful ill-starred Queen of the Scots.
    With kindest regards to all—and the hope of seeing you again soon, I am

Very sincerely yours,
Chas. Hartwell Cocke

Mr. Cocke's letter was simply placed in her diary with no further comment about it or, for that matter, him.

Spring in the South, particularly in small towns like Columbus, always brought with it the feeling of rebirth. The sudden red flash of cardinals swooping from oak to cedar to pine trees and down into fields of jonquils, with mixes of jasmine and honey locust and moon vine with its glowing white bloom, gave people a feeling of slight intoxication, especially the young, for whom love and its pursuit took on a particular urgency.

Thurs. afternoon (May 10th) Had engagement to go driving but had to attend card party. Mr. Harris and Mr. Williams called.
Friday—11th—Card party in the morning at Mrs. Sanders. Drive in the afternoon with Mr. Williams.
Sat. Night May 12th Mr. Williams again!

The young gentleman who called with Mr. Harris was Cornelius Coffin Williams, a visitor on business from Memphis, where he worked for the Cumberland Telephone and Telegraph Company in what would now be regarded as a paralegal position. He had journeyed to Columbus for a court case involving his company, and Franklin Harris, Esq. was apparently consulted in the matter. In the evening, Mr. Harris took Mr. Williams to a rehearsal of *The Mikado* to see the object of his attentions, Miss Edwina, enacting one of the Three Little Maids from School. A few days later, Mr. Harris and Mr. Williams called on her at home. Prior to that, however, the appropriate formalities had been observed. Mr. Harris gave his assurance to the Dakins that Mr. Williams was a young gentleman whose family was among the Four Hundred of Knoxville.

By the turn of the century, Knoxville had become a sooty industrial center and, unlike Columbus, no longer a part of the Old South.[17] It represented, in fact, the epitome of the New South, calling itself the "Queen City of the Mountains" and moving rapidly into the twentieth century. It measured its progress not in the distinction and preservation of its residential districts but in the number of its factories. Although Knoxville was legally dry, there was no lack of liquor in the clubs and homes of those with money and an educated thirst.

Cornelius's education in this respect was completed by the time he met Edwina, although it was a facet of his behavior that she would not see for some time. Twenty-seven years old, of erect military bearing and rather serious mien, he must have struck her as an imposing figure. At this early stage of their acquaintanceship, the most she was able to learn about him was that he came from a prominent Tennessee family and that he had worked himself into a managerial position with the telephone company. He was proud of the fact that he had served as a second lieutenant in the army during the Spanish-American War. Unfortunately, as a consequence, he had suffered typhoid fever and lost most of his hair, but being slim and youthful, he was nonetheless a good-looking suitor. Edwina was never to say that she fell in love with him, only that he swept her off her feet.

It soon became obvious that Mr. Harris and Mr. Williams were rivals for Miss Edwina's attention. She noted in her diary that Mr. Williams showed her the local telephone headquarters, of which he was regional manager, and called on her frequently. Undoubtedly, the clergyman's daughter appealed to Cornelius as a pretty and charming little chatterbox, the ideal "toy wife."

Cornelius began calling on Edwina daily. Together, they attended parties and card games and took a ride on the new electric streetcar. The Dakins, if not concerned, were certainly curious about their daughter's ardent new beau and were making their own inquiries. While it was too early to ask his intentions, it was fitting to pose discreet questions. Cornelius, though, was reticent about his family history. He was fond of saying, "Bragging about ancestors is like bragging about potatoes: The best part is underground."[18] Still, his was undeniably a distinguished lineage, leading to the founding of the state of Tennessee and of the nation itself, and Miss Edwina was duly impressed, as her first son, Tom, would be openly proud of the Williams heritage, if not his imposing name, Thomas Lanier Williams III.

At the time of the American Revolution, Col. Joseph Williams married Rebekah Lanier, and they had a son, the first Thomas Lanier Williams. The second was Cornelius's father, who had had a long career in public service but who had waged several unsuccessful campaigns for governor. In his last years, he held the office of state railroad commissioner. By 1906, he was ill and had retired to the imposing family home in Knoxville of his brother-in-law and sister, Judge and Mrs. Joseph W. Sneed.

Cornelius's mother had died in 1884 of tuberculosis, when she was only thirty-one, leaving her husband to raise a five-year-old son and two daughters, Isabel and Ella. In the year of his mother's death, the boy fell out of a second-story window onto a brick pavement and suffered a partial loss of sight in his left eye. The greatest loss to him, though, was a mother's caring love at an age when he needed it most. Her maiden name was Isabella Coffin, and her father was Cornelius Coffin, a direct descendant of the Nantucket Coffins. Although militarists and statesmen were pointed to among the Williamses with pride, very little was made, particularly by Cornelius, of the fact that two illustrious American poets, Tristram Coffin and Sidney Lanier, were also family ancestors.

Outwardly, the relationship of Cornelius to his father seemed agreeable enough, but as a child growing up without the softening influence of his mother, Cornelius had had his emotions sealed off, and any expression of love was difficult, if not impossible. Shunted from one aunt to another, he was sent first to Rogersville Synodical College, a Tennessee seminary he found stifling, and finally to Bell Buckle Military Academy, which he would later refer to as "a school for bad boys." The effect was so restraining that it served only to deepen his resentment and incite rebellion against any form of authority. The disciplines and the punishments he received for defying them formed in him a hard and masculine attitude toward the outside world. He ran away so often and spent so much time in the brig that eventually it was agreed by all concerned that he should leave the academy.

After two years spent studying law at the University of Tennessee, where he became a member of Pi Kappa Alpha fraternity, Cornelius joined the army at the outbreak of war with Spain and emerged with a passion for the itinerant life: hard drink, loose women, and all-night poker games. Everyone who knew him in Knoxville as a fun-loving young bachelor saw a different person from the sedate one he presented in Columbus.

Cornelius's father, no paragon, also had a reputation for his pursuit of manly pleasures. After his wife died, he not only failed in politics but also seriously diminished the family fortune by spending freely and making imprudent business deals. As a result, the father had placed Cornelius in a position where he had to make it on his own, instilling in him a niggardly attitude toward money. Neither Edwina nor her parents were aware of any of this. What they saw was Cornelius on his best behavior, a young swain apparently well brought up and well-off.

Although the lawyer Franklin Harris was still calling on Edwina, it was Cornelius, she noted, who accompanied her for a drive in the afternoon and escorted her to a theatre party. Also, she told her diary, "Took supper with him at 'Bell' Cafe (our shadow was there). Mr. Williams spent evening with me." The next day, Cornelius and Mr. Harris saw her off on the twelve o'clock train for Tuscaloosa to attend the university commencement and an SAE dance. She wrote that on the afternoon of her arrival, she had "thirty some callers, young men of town and University—at night more callers!" By midweek, Mr. Harris, presumably Edwina's "shadow," had come to Tuscaloosa to escort her home.

On June 16, Cornelius, who had gone to Memphis, returned and took Edwina driving. She said they "stopped at his boarding house on the way home to get a box of Floyd's candy he had brought me. All the boarders stared so, I believe they thought he was going to bring me in." Cornelius soon had to leave again on business for the telephone company, but by mid-July he sent Edwina a postal telegram from Yazoo City, Mississippi:

> WILL ARRIVE COLUMBUS NOON TOMORROW. WILL REMAIN UNTIL NIGHT TRAIN. C. C. WILLIAMS

C. C. Williams was the signature Cornelius used all of his life, even when writing to his children. By now, Edwina was using her nickname for him, "Neil," which could not have amused him much, since she also had a pet fox terrier by that name, whose distinction was that he caught rats during the night and in the morning presented them on the front porch.

The following Tuesday, it was Cornelius's father who wired:

> CORNELIUS ARRIVED AT KNOXVILLE THIS MORNING. HE GOES BACK TO MEMPHIS SUNDAY NIGHT. WROTE TO YOU TODAY. WRITE ME HERE. THOMAS L. WILLIAMS

It was clear from this that the two families were now in touch with each other and that Cornelius's intentions were serious. But since he and Edwina were not as yet officially engaged, they both felt free to enjoy separate social lives. The day after he departed on the night train, Edwina went for a drive with Mr. Harris and later in the week took part in what the local newspaper called "one of the most successful entertainments ever given by amateurs . . .":

> . . . The first number was the Ping Pong chorus by twenty young ladies in native costume assisted by six young men in Japanese attire. . . . The Butterfly Song and Dance by Miss Dakin was an artistic success. Miss Dakin has an exceptionally sweet voice and sings with much feeling which occasioned enthusiastic encores.

Mainly because of her vacation plans and his work, Edwina and Cornelius would not see each other again for a few months. As serious as his intentions seemed, he may have had second thoughts, and as much as she was impressed by his pursuit of her, she was in no sense promised to him. Apparently, they were both feeling ambivalence about making an irrevocable commitment. He had stopped writing to her, and she kept silent.

In August, Edwina left Columbus to visit her childhood schoolmate and lifelong friend Claire Singleton, who was now living in Fairfield, Tennessee, near Shelbyville. During this time, she also became reacquainted with Claire's brother, John, whom she had not seen since he "proposed" at the age of nine. Although it was a confession that Edwina would not make until years after Cornelius had died, she would tell her sons that it was the handsome young John Singleton whom she had wanted to marry. Her younger son, Dakin, said, "John Singleton was the one Mother really loved."[19] If there was, as she claimed years later, a rekindling of their affection, she made no mention of it in her diary.

Instead, she told of going on to visit her mother's sister, Aunt Estelle, who had married and was living in south Pittsburg. Estelle commented that, after the Dakin family had left the Otte farm, she had become so lonely in that vast mountain country that she had stood on the front porch and shouted "hello" in order that a friendly echo would come back to her from an opposite ridge.

Edwina's vacation ended abruptly when, stricken with fever, she was brought home on a cot in a baggage car. It was then mid-September, and in later years she recalled that she had come down with "typhoid fever and malaria both at once. I lost half my hair. The young lawyer who introduced me to Cornelius was so concerned lest I lose all of it that he brought over a special hair tonic, claiming that it would save what remained. Thus I owe him both my husband and my hair!" After she emerged from the delirium of fever, Edwina discovered that Cornelius had been sending her bouquets of roses every day. "His thoughtfulness impressed me, as did the telephone calls every night," she said. "Since he was a telephone company employee, they didn't cost him anything, but the roses that still arrived every day did."[20]

By October, Cornelius had become manager of three southern "telephone exchanges" headquartered in Gulfport, a pleasant Mississippi beachfront town on the Gulf Coast. And he had replaced the roses with an engagement ring. Edwina's parents were "sold on" Cornelius. When he asked the Reverend Dakin for her hand, Walter, while accepting the proposal, cautioned him that his daughter was hardly the ideal homemaker: She could neither cook nor sew. Cornelius was said to have replied, "Mr. Dakin, I am not looking for a cook," words that he would live to regret.

It was becoming clear that Edwina's fiancé was, in her words, "the kind of man who never took no for an answer." She would soon learn that persistence was a long-standing Williams trait. Rejection became simply a further challenge: "He showered me with attention, and even though I refused his proposal several times, he kept persevering in the tradition of his family motto, *Cognoscy-Occasionrn*, 'Know Your Opportunity—Seize It.' " While Cornelius was to discover that Edwina was not easily "seized," she now found him hard to resist. As a descendant of several fighting strains—the Williamses, Seviers, and Laniers—Cornelius took on in her eyes the hard metal of a knight in armor.

During the Christmas holidays, it was decided that there would be a large church wedding at Saint Paul's in June, with members and friends of both families in attendance and with the Reverend Dakin officiating. But the plans went awry. Thomas Lanier Williams, who was to have been his son's best man, was taken seriously ill during the following spring, and Cornelius had to spend as much time in Knoxville as his work would permit.

Edwina did not hear from him for some time. She recalled, "I had about given up the idea of marrying him and accepted an invitation to a college house party, intending to go with the sister of the man who asked me. As I was leaving the house, the telephone rang. It was Cornelius. 'I'm coming down with the wedding ring' he announced."[21]

Neither the desperately ill Thomas Lanier Williams nor his daughters, Isabel and Ella, who were nursing him, were able to attend the wedding.

On the first of June, Cornelius arrived in Columbus, and on the same date Edwina made a final entry in her diary in a curiously uncertain handwriting:

> Many men have said, "I love you."
> Only three said, "Will you marry me!"
> I will marry him, next Monday.
> Have cancelled visit to Edith.
> Rosalie will go—alone.
>   "Finis"
> Good-bye

On Monday, June 3, 1907, at ten o'clock in the morning, Edwina Estelle Dakin married Cornelius Coffin Williams, and the couple left immediately for a honeymoon and a home in Gulfport, Mississippi.

2

A Mother Is Born

1907–1918

The young couple spent their honeymoon happily in Gulfport and lived as paying guests in a handsome antebellum home facing directly on the Gulf. Cornelius in his important management position "had the world by the tail," Edwina said. "When he came home at night he would be carrying a parcel—a large hat or a new pair of shoes—for me. Every night we would take a stroll down by the pier and watch the gulf waters. For eighteen months we were childless, and Cornelius was delighted."

Throughout their marriage, they would often speak of Gulfport nostalgically and would plan trips there together. The town was small, and Edwina quickly made friends. They soon had an active social life, as she described it, "sometimes going out to dance, sometimes playing cards, sometimes chaperoning young couples on moonlit parties to Ship Island."[1]

Of the letters she received, the two that Edwina kept were from her father and her father-in-law:

July 3, 1907

Dearest Daughter—
A month ago you left us and it seems ages and we are trying hard to adjust ourselves to the thought you belong *in part* to another.

It seemed at first like you were away or visiting but little by little the truth is borne in upon us—you are now *Mrs.* W.... We are so happy you are well and getting rid of the malaria. So many send love to you and inquire about you regularly.... Your mother bathed Neil recently and did not fasten his collar securely so it came off. Oh, he does have the fleas!

The first signs of Yellow Fever you must flee—unless you won't leave Cornelius.... Mother joins me in dear love to our children.

Lovingly,
Dad

Knoxville, Tenn. Dec. 30, 1907

My dear Edwina:
Your valued letter of the 22nd inst. has been received and both the girls and myself thought it was very sweet and lovely of you to think of and

write me. My greatest wish, now, is to know you for I feel that I and Ella & Isabel will love you very much.

My long and painful illness has so frustrated me in strength and financially that I am unable to get far from home. Otherwise I would gladly visit you and Cornelius at Gulfport. . . . I received a letter from [him] for the first time in many months. I am so glad you are both well and happy. Cornelius has always been very close to me. His mother died when he was five years old and after that, for many years, he clung to me tenaciously. Of course that made him very close and dear to me and now that I am growing old my heart goes out to him every day. May God bless you both in every good way. . . .

With best wishes and much love—I am affectionately,

Thos. L. Williams

On the twenty-third of September the following year, Thomas Lanier Williams died and was buried in the family plot in Knoxville's Old Gray Cemetery. For Cornelius, his father's death left a deep wound, and afterward neither Edwina nor their children could ever get him to talk about his parents or his early years. What they learned, they learned from his sisters. In all matters involving his innermost feelings, he remained beyond reach and outwardly taciturn.

Before the death of their father, Cornelius's favorite sister, Isabel, had married Will Brownlow, a member of a renowned Knoxville family. Ella, the eldest of the three children, would remain unmarried during a long and active life in Knoxville. Although the sisters would communicate by letter with Edwina and her children, they seldom saw their brother's family. Cornelius, however, made regular trips each year to visit with relatives and friends in his favorite city. Ultimately, he would die there and be buried near his father in Old Gray.

The work of manager for the Gulfport telephone company became Cornelius's first experience of being tied down to a desk, and the constraint soon proved more than his restless spirit could bear. Whether he left his position or was let go—there were rumors of a scandal—he would never say. In all probability, the combination of management and marriage was more than he could handle. As she was to learn, Edwina could press for answers to her questions for only so long before he would either explode or lapse into glum silence.

Cornelius's break with the telephone company came shortly after Edwina's revelation that she was pregnant. "I can see it now," she said many years afterward, "just as it was that night full of joy we walked down to the pier. Then I broke the news and it was as though a thunderclap had broken."[2] Cornelius took the news as though it were a personal affront.

His next job was much more to his liking: selling men's apparel for Claiborne, Tate & Cowan, a Knoxville clothing manufacturer. The life of a travel-

ing salesman meant that he would often be away on the road and would return
to his wife only on occasion. Without having to account to her or his boss, he
was free to indulge in a night of poker or other diversions. Among personal
and business friends, C.C. was respected as both a high-liver and a top salesman. He truly liked his work, enjoying the aggression needed to convince his
customers that they wanted what he had to sell. Above all, he enjoyed being
free and on the road.

Suddenly, Edwina was enduring a lonely existence, "confined" as she was
according to the custom of the time. In contrast to her years as a social butterfly, her honeymoon days and nights as a newlywed became too painful. Early
in 1909, after a year and a half away, she returned home to the church rectory
in Columbus: "I was expecting my first baby and wanted to be with my parents, as my mother had been with hers when I was born."[3] Cornelius had no
objections—he was, in fact, indifferent—and the Dakins were as happy to
have their only child home again as they were at the prospect of a grandchild.

On November 19, 1909, Edwina gave birth to Rose Isabel Williams.
Named Rose for Edwina's mother and Isabel for Cornelius's, she was a lovely
and cheerful baby girl and a delight to the family—including her father, who
suddenly regarded his daughter as a personal accomplishment and something
to brag about on the road. It was like closing his first deal. Edwina remembered Cornelius at that time as an openly proud parent.

The church rectory was large enough to accommodate a sizable family.
Returning to visit on weekends, Cornelius was able to spend whatever time he
wanted with Edwina without his infant girl causing him much loss of sleep or
disposition. He contributed to the household regularly enough, but not as
generously as he might have, since he always had the excuse of various travel
expenses. All in all, this was a good arrangement for a beginning family, with
the inevitable familial strain between husband and wife kept to a minimum. It
was to last for nearly a decade.

Although no longer a fiancée or a bride, Edwina was still, in Cornelius's
eyes, the same pretty little magpie, and like so many southern women at that
time, she had also become the dutiful wife and mother. If she resisted his sexual advances, he could ascribe it to coyness and regard it as a challenge to his
masculinity. If she became quarrelsome or petulant, it took only a gift or an
evening at a dance or the theatre to placate her. The Dakins were ideal baby-
sitters, and in many different ways, Edwina was able once again to enjoy the
social life of Columbus. The salesman's life that Cornelius enjoyed on the
road was strictly his own business.

"I was born old."

In a southern town like Columbus during the first gentle years of the new
century, inconsequentials became the general preoccupation; the days were
long, but the years moved swiftly. A life could pass uneventfully, with little to

mark change within the family except birth and death and birth again. On Sunday, March 26, 1911, Thomas Lanier Williams III was born, the namesake of his paternal grandfather.

Only minutes before Tom's birth, Edwina and her mother arrived at their doctor's small hospital, while at the same time the Reverend Dakin was officiating at services. Now with the birth of a male child, there was the promise of carrying on the Williams family name. Cornelius's reaction to the birth of a son was both proud and suspicious. Although he made no accusations, he did take account of Edwina's old beaux. He could have suspected his former rival—"our shadow," Franklin Harris—except that the young lawyer had married soon after Edwina had left for Gulfport and now had a little son of his own, Frank Orr Harris, Jr.

Cornelius's jealousy was caused mainly by Edwina's doting affection for little Tommy. Edwina had become more the mother of a newborn than his wife. Rose, too, was jealous of the attentions paid her baby brother, whom she at first regarded as an intruder who had stolen love and devotion that rightfully belonged to her. Cornelius was said to have remarked to Rose, "We don't think much of that new baby, do we?" When, according to the story, he added the opinion that the infant was not good for much, she readily concurred.

Tom, though, from the moment he became aware of her, was delighted with his sister, and as he grew older, he became enchanted with her vivacity and her beauty. She *was* lovely—everyone remarked about that. Her head was covered with auburn curls, and her eyes were described by her mother as blue and by her brother as an "expressive gray-green." Not only pretty, Rose was quick to learn and took pride in imparting her superior knowledge to an obvious inferior who looked up to her in every way. As Tom grew older, she instructed him in their games and taught him his alphabet. There were, of course, the usual disputes over property rights, accompanied by screams of indignation and hair pulling, but at the same time there was a love taking root that would entwine them for all of their lives.

Once he could maintain an upright position, Tommy was as spirited in their play as his sister, and with only fourteen months' difference in their ages, they grew to look more and more alike, enough so to be mistaken for twins. While Rose's imagination was confined to her dolls and games of her own invention, from his first recognition of the world around him, Tommy was fascinated and curious about it. One of Edwina's favorite photographs depicts Tom at a year and a half, his back to the camera and his golden ringlets curling about his head. In his hand, he clutches a blue morning glory, which he studies intently.

With their father away a good deal of the time, Tommy and his sister were coming under the steady influence of their grandparents. To Rose, Walter Dakin was "Grandfads," a childhood sobriquet that she would continue to use as a term of endearment long after she was grown. In a sense, he was a surrogate father to them both. The kindly, aristocratic minister had a free-ranging mind and a love of books, inculcating in Tom his admiration for the written word. He also had a keen memory, which became a trait of his grandson, as well. Tennessee remembered the old gentleman reciting passages for him from Milton, the *Iliad*, and the melodramas of Shakespeare; he said, "Grandfather was crazy about Poe. He was interested in the macabre."[4] Melodrama and the macabre would especially leave their imprint upon his grandson's imagination. Staring at the lines of books on the shelves of the minister's library, Tommy began early in life to wonder about the magic existing within their different colored bindings.[5] Whether it was his grandfather or his mother who presided over the ritual of bedtime stories, it always meant going to those shelves and opening those covers to find wondrous tales to tell.

Shortly after Tom was born, someone with a gift for spinning yarns joined the household. She was Tom and Rose's beautiful black nurse, known only as Ozzie, and to them she was an absolute magician because she could spin spellbinding stories about all kinds of animals without ever once looking at the pages of their grandfather's books. Tom, particularly, became attached to Ozzie; she would assume an ongoing life in his memory and in his writings long after she had disappeared from the Dakins' home.

Ozzie's family were sharecroppers who lived on a plantation. When Edwina and the children went off for vacation at a summer resort, Ozzie would return home and be put to work by her brothers in the cotton fields. She was about sixteen when she first arrived at the Dakin household seeking work. Edwina said, "She had come to us clad in rags and we clothed her, gave her a good salary, taught her to read and write."[6]

Although the Dakins recognized the color line between whites and blacks and held the view of their southern neighbors that "colored folk" were a lesser race, theirs was a mute and benevolent attitude in contrast to that of the extremists symbolized by the Ku Klux Klan. While they might deplore the violent ends of segregation or the cruel means often used to enforce it, they would do little, if anything, to oppose it. Still, they were especially kind toward those blacks who knew "their place" and who were loved, if not as equals, then like Ozzie, as family.

Growing up in a rectory during his formative years and regularly attending church and Sunday school, Tom had instilled in him a love of God in heaven and a dread of Judgment. Edwina, reared under the same religious influences, added her own authority as the boy's mother, admonishing him when he misbehaved, "God will punish you."[7] He witnessed the examples of Christian tolerance, compassion, and duty in his grandmother's actions and heard them exalted in Grandfather's sermons.

Tom Williams was, in fact, growing up more a minister's son than the son of a traveling salesman, whom he scarcely recognized as a father. A puritan strain that would for all of his life become the gentle Dakin side of his nature came in direct conflict with a side born of the wild, cavalier disposition of the

Williams family. This dichotomy divided him against himself and was exhibited in contradictory behavior. As a child, he saw the brute, pioneer Williams
side personified in Cornelius, and it terrified him. "Often the voice of my
father was jovial or boisterous. But sometimes it was harsh. And sometimes it
sounded like thunder. To a small boy, he looked awfully big. And it was not
a benign bigness. You wanted to shrink away from it, hide yourself."[8] But
with time, Tom would see this trait as the origin of the strength he needed
to survive.

Tom's mother would also become increasingly caught up in this same clash
between her parents' gentility and her husband's bluntness. Nonetheless, in
the early years of their marriage, the sight and sound of the salesman returning like a warrior from the field of battle was often a source of excitement for
her, compared with the mundane life of a young married lady no longer
sought by innumerable gentlemen callers. She may not have been in love with
Cornelius, as she was still with John Singleton, but she was being regularly
swept off her feet, as she put it, by her husband's gallant behavior.

Since her travels had taken her only to southern towns and cities very much
like Columbus, Edwina had little concept of the outside world, the world that
C. C. Williams knew all too well. What she learned was mainly what Cornelius had to tell her: William Howard Taft was a relatively moderate presence
in the White House, having succeeded Theodore Roosevelt, who had been
C.C.'s kind of man and his leader in the Cuban invasion; the country was still
at peace except for those "anarchists" agitating in the big cities "up North";
Europe was a place you might visit "for the culture" once in a lifetime; and
Edwina's Columbus, Mississippi, was about as far removed from the reality of
that outside world as any place could be.

Whenever Cornelius made one of his infrequent visits, he would come
laden with small gifts and always bearing something especially nice for her.
Added to that were evenings out to dinner and dances and what Edwina liked
best, the theatre. Although her girlhood dreams of appearing on the musical
stage had been overshadowed by marriage and motherhood, she still attended
the touring attractions that had originated in a fabled district in New York
called Broadway. In December 1912, an event with particular portent for her
son was the triumphant appearance in New York of an actress named Laurette
Taylor in the play *Peg O' My Heart*. This single role, which she enacted in
over six hundred performances, would enshrine her in the minds of drama
critics and her peers and in the hearts of audiences as one of the truly great
performers of the American stage.

Tommy's only exposure to theatre at this early time in his life was witnessing the high drama of the Episcopal liturgy and the pyrotechnics of his grandfather at home and in the pulpit. It was generally conceded that the Reverend
Dakin was something of a performer himself, much admired not only by his
parishioners but also by a grandson who would someday exhibit a distinctly
theatrical flair on the lecture platform.

Walter Dakin had become so popular that he was approached several times to take over another parish. On one occasion, Bishop Bratton offered him the position of dean of the faculty of All Saints College in Vicksburg, a school recently established by the Episcopal church. Walter turned this down, as he had the previous offers, despite the fact that it would have meant a substantial increase over his yearly salary of twelve hundred dollars. But the bishop knew that a troubled parish posed a different and irresistible challenge to the Reverend Dakin's organizational skills. In December 1913, he accepted the ministry of the Church of the Advent in Nashville, and the family moved from Mississippi northward to Tennessee.

Now, whenever Cornelius visited his family, he could feel he was on home ground, for Nashville, like Knoxville, was a center of burgeoning industries, proud of its rapid growth and its dominant place in the New South. The Church of the Advent, though, was located in a pleasant neighborhood away from the busy downtown section, and the minister's family found pleasure and contentment living in the pale brick rectory next door.

A local paper praised the new minister, calling him "a man of magnetic personality [with] a wonderful power of conveying to his hearers the real meaning of his subject. He is a great worker and organizer and will carry out his theories on a strictly business plane." Rose Dakin was described as "an elegant woman, gifted with a talent for both literature and music and possessed of one of the sweetest and most amiable of dispositions." It predicted that she would be "a great addition and help in the charitable and educational work of the city."[9] Edwina was remembered as "a darling . . . who sang in the church choir [and] took an active part in church work. She, with her children . . . and Ozzie, the colored nurse they adored, made the rectory a center of idyllic adventures."[10]

August 1914

The peace of the world, all worlds, was about to be shattered. And a war to ignite all wars was about to send forth reverberating shock waves of death and violence, of human misery on a scale that would mark the twentieth as one of history's darkest centuries. Dismissing the outbreak of war as another one of the isolated and ancient European struggles for power, the new President, Woodrow Wilson, promised to keep our boys at home. Further assurance came in the form of a proclamation of neutrality. But there was a swell of excitement rising out of the daily headlines, a vicarious release from the workaday monotony and sameness of family life. And in the South, where it was manly discourse to talk of wars, one could hear faint echoes of the rebel yell.

Like many men with family responsibilities, Cornelius was bound to the care of his young wife and children. Also, at thirty-five and with the physical infirmity of being nearly blind in one eye, he was ineligible for military service. The most he could do was read the newspapers and, along with his salesmen cronies, cry a distant havoc. But 1914 brought change for Cornelius after all. He was offered a job as a traveling salesman for the International Shoe Company in St. Louis, and he left the wholesale clothing firm in Knoxville with a glowing reference.[11]

During this period of change in Nashville, when their mother and grandparents were living in a new and large city and their father was beginning a new job, the children drew especially close to Ozzie. Tom in particular was under her spell. Among her magical tales, Ozzie conjured an apparition of the devil and told of the dark labyrinthine snares within the kingdom of evil. A three-year-old boy, who was unaware and uncomprehending, could hardly have considered such talk as merely mythical yarns. Edwina discovered him one day in the backyard, under a hot summer sun, drenched with perspiration, feverishly digging a hole that was more like a minor excavation. Asked what he was doing, he paused just long enough in his labors to explain, "I'm diggin' to de debbil." Edwina later reflected, "You might say Tom went on 'diggin' to de debbil' the rest of his life, trying to discover where the devil lives inside all of us."[12]

As young as he was, the boy would often enthrall neighborhood children with *his* versions of Ozzie's fantasies. On an occasion when a group of vacationing adults was sitting in front of a fire telling adventure stories, he was encouraged to spin one of his own. To Edwina's surprise, he overcame his shyness to relate how he had become lost in the woods and was being chased by a variety of fierce animals. Finally, it became too much for him. He stopped and closed his eyes, then said, "It's getting scarier and scarier. It's just getting so scary, I'm scared myself."[13]

Tom's clearest memories were of Ozzie. When Edwina was preoccupied with church activities, "singing in the choir or serving at ice cream festivals to raise money, Ozzie would play with the children as one of them."[14] Tom absorbed many of his early ideas from her. He also absorbed her dialect: Repeating Edwina's caution, stemming from the current fad of "Fletcherizing," that the children should thoroughly masticate their food, Ozzie would say, "Chaw, honey, chaw," and Tom would assure her, "I chaw." Edwina said that whenever Ozzie would give him a bath, "he would chase little celluloid fishes around the tub, calling out excitedly, 'I kotch him, Ozzie. See? I kotch him.' I was afraid that child was never going to speak proper English."

Ozzie would often take Tom and Rose to Nashville's Centennial Park with its replica of the Parthenon. By now the children were so much alike that she called them "the couple." On summer days, the three of them would sit under the trees while Ozzie read ghost stories and made up others. "And then," Tom remembered, "I would go home at nap time and make up more stories while I was going to sleep."[15] An interviewer wrote that Williams told him "when he lay in bed with his eyes closed, he could see, moving across the backs of his eyelids, processions of colorful characters performing exciting deeds. And, cultivating this gift, he turned what he saw when his eyes were closed into games he could play, with Rose or alone, with open eyes."[16]

Tennessee Williams's memories of Nashville were among his fondest; he loved his new home. "I remember so many things about it—picking flowers in the park, little flowers . . . a terrible thunder storm that tore the awning off our porch . . ."[17] When his mother first took him to kindergarten, she stayed on for a while, watching him as he became absorbed in the various playthings. "I was enchanted," he recalled. "I loved all the ABC blocks and the modeling clay. Then all of a sudden I looked up and my mother wasn't there. I lay on the floor and kicked and screamed."[18] Edwina, half a block away, heard the commotion and hurried back to take him home.

A Mrs. J. F. Jenkins, who taught the kindergarten class in the church next door to the rectory, described Tom as "a clinging child—beautiful, round-faced, chubby and shy."[19] She said he always tagged along with Rose and "would not leave his sister for a moment." By contrast, Rose at this time was almost extroverted in her behavior and had a marked tendency toward self-dramatization. Once, she told a family friend a ridiculous story that her grandmother forced her to do all the hard housework and that she had to wash and iron her grandfather's shirts. There were other, more subtle bids for sympathy and attention, but no one thought anything about this other than that it was the overactive imagination of a little girl, perhaps trying to overshadow her brother's storytelling talents.

Clarksdale, Kindred Point of Heaven and Home

On December 31, 1915, the family left Nashville and returned to Mississippi, first to Canton, then after a few months to Clarksdale—on the northwest side of the state—a town bordered by the Sunflower River. By now even the restless clergyman, let alone the ladies of the house, would have preferred to settle down. But once again Bishop Bratton was grappling with the problem of a distressed parish, and once more he chose the Reverend Dakin as the rescuer. This time, though, except for a year spent troubleshooting in Bay St. Louis, Mississippi, Mr. and Mrs. Dakin would remain in Clarksdale* at St. George's Church for fourteen years, until his retirement in 1931.

A longtime resident recalled that Clarksdale, a rough river port in those early years, was "considerably east of Eden. There was much for any minister to do who came there. And Mr. and Mrs. Dakin got right to work."[20] As they had before, the industrious couple gradually won over the support of the congregation and began increasing its numbers.

---

*Before the Civil War, Clarksdale had been the plantation of John Clark. As a young man from Philadelphia, stranded in New Orleans when his father died of yellow fever, Clark "went up and down the Mississippi River like Huck Finn on flatboats and somehow put together enough cash to buy from the Governor land around Friar Point that had been abandoned by the Choctaw Indians. After the War, he saw to it that the railroad came through the town and he called it Clarksdale" (The Reverend John Clark Smith to LL, interview, 4 December 1986, New York).

Clarksdale was a typical flat Mississippi Delta city surrounded by cotton fields; its business district has been described as bare and treeless, with a number of stores, cotton gins, warehouses, and loading platforms relieved by silver maples and water oaks lining the quiet, secluded residential streets. Although it would take a while for Tom to accept this rural town as home after the excitement of a city like Nashville, Edwina was happy to be back in the Magnolia State, even though she found Clarksdale "quite different in spirit from Columbus [which] considered itself far more cultured and sophisticated."[21]

Her marriage remained much the same. "Cornelius was not around a lot those years when he turned from selling men's clothing to selling shoes," she wrote. "He never paid much attention to the children, anyhow; my father was more like a father to them. One summer, when we vacationed in Tennessee, I did not see my husband at all. Occasionally he would pick me up at the rectory and we would drive off in his car for the weekend."[22] Sometimes Cornelius would drive his wife and son north of Clarksdale to the Peabody Hotel in Memphis. Tennessee remembered his parents bouncing him on their knees while they sang about a steamboat comin' round the bend. For Tom, an excursion of this kind was filled with strange and exciting sights, and for Edwina, it became an enjoyable respite from her uneventful life in Clarksdale.

There seemed to be no question that Cornelius was still in love with the woman he saw as his charming little wife. But although C.C. always prided himself on his successful sales record, Edwina was one sale he was never able to close. She continued to resist his fumbling advances, leaving him frustrated and angry. As young as he was at the time, Tennessee remembered hearing his mother's crying protests in her bedroom. Enduring the boisterous salesman for short intervals was about as much as she could stand; any longer, she, like her parents, *suffered* him, as did the children, who could scarcely accept the fact that he was their father.

In the summer of 1916, Tom was stricken with diphtheria and almost died. Childhood illnesses were often fatal in those times of widespread epidemics, and diphtheria was particularly dreaded because of its serious aftereffects. Prompt vaccination with an antitoxin was the only known remedy. In a later day, Tom would have been hospitalized, but then, as Edwina recalled in her memoir, "all we could do was to care for him as best we could at home. I slept with him for nine nights, following the doctor's direction to keep his throat packed in ice, changing the ice all night, so he would not choke to death."[23] A harrowing disease, it left him with a growing fear of the suffocation that finally, ironically, took his life.

During the many weeks that Tom was bedridden, Edwina devoted herself entirely to him. She read from Dickens, Thackeray, and Shakespeare and from magazines like the *Literary Digest*, which he pronounced the *Little-ary Digest*. She also joined in games mostly of his invention, where bedcovers became hills and dales and his toys came to life.

When finally Tom was permitted to get up, it was discovered that he was unable to walk, the result of Bright's disease, an acute inflammation of the kidneys. Sitting on a little stool, he tried to push himself about. Later, Edwina bought him a toy called an Irish mail, which enabled him to move around without strain on his legs. He had to learn gradually how to walk again, with his mother and grandparents watching him as, in pain, he practiced walking up and down the sidewalk outside the rectory.

The ultimate effect of the ailment was to leave both Tom and Edwina emotionally entwined, and to turn Tom's childhood energies in upon himself, opening the way to an interior life that would become his own very private world. Looking back, Tennessee Williams declared that the illness had changed his nature as drastically as it had his health: "Prior to it, I had been a little boy with a robust, aggressive bullying nature." After it and because of it, he became "a decided hybrid, different from the family line of frontiersmen-heroes of east Tennessee."[24]

While the other members of the family gave Tom their loving support, it was his mother who doted upon him. She had saved his life during those first critical days, and she never let him forget it. The shock of nearly losing her "precious" boy aroused in her an overprotective concern that prompted Cornelius to complain that she was pampering Tom too much and making a sissy of him. From then on, the more attentive Edwina was to the child's symptoms, the more preoccupied Tom became with this and other of his illnesses that were to follow. The seeds of his lifelong hypochondria had been sown.

Tennessee Williams would look back on his two years of invalidism as the most joyously innocent of his life.

> My sister and I were gloriously happy. We sailed paper boats in washtubs of water, cut lovely paper dolls out of huge mail-order catalogs, kept two white rabbits under the back porch, baked mud pies in the sun upon the front walk, climbed up and slid down the big wood pile, collected from neighboring alleys and trash-piles bits of colored glass that were diamonds and rubies and sapphires and emeralds. And in the evenings, when the white moonlight streamed over our bed, before we were asleep, our Negro nurse Ozzie, as warm and black as a moonless Mississippi night, would lean over our bed, telling in a low, rich voice her amazing tales about foxes and bears and rabbits and wolves that behaved like human beings.[25]

As it happened, though, Ozzie unwittingly became the cause of still another trauma in Tom's life, and this would leave him with a lasting burden of guilt and shame. Shortly before she left on her annual trip home during the summer of 1916, Tom, in a fit of childish fury, had called her "a big black nigger." Ozzie never returned. Thereafter, Tom believed that she had left *him* because he had so deeply hurt her. Though his mother tried to reassure him, the incident was burned into his conscience. This handsome young woman with the bearing of an Indian princess remained fixed in his memory, as did the terrible plight she suffered only for being born black.

Edwina wrote that "Tom loved Ozzie and I'm sure she felt his love. I think the truth, rather, is that she came to some harm. It was not like Ozzie to leave without a reason." She had returned the year before deathly ill, her "eyes bloodshot, looking thin and acting nervous. She told us that her brothers had forced her to work in the cotton fields. The following fall she did not return at all. I think she met with foul play at the hands of her brutal brothers."[26]

There was one other event during the summer of 1916 that would bear significantly on Tom's future. In New York, the theatre was still offering plays with such titles as *Please Help Emily*, *Pollyanna*, and *Melody of Youth*. But farther north, on Cape Cod, in a seacoast settlement that would someday take on great importance in Tom's life, a small theatre group called the Provincetown Players was giving a boldly experimental twenty-seven-year-old playwright his first production. The play at the Wharf Theatre was *Bound East for Cardiff*, and the playwright was Eugene O'Neill.

The year 1917 brought about a change that was difficult for Tom to comprehend, one that affected his life and the lives of all Americans. He was slowly becoming aware of neighboring families whose grown, uniformed sons were now marching off to war and of homes that soon would have gold stars in their front windows as symbols of those who would not be coming back. Now President Wilson was promising "a war to end all wars," and patriotism was the order of the day.

In Knoxville, Tom's Aunty Ella had volunteered to drive a Red Cross truck in France. Unlike her dignified sister, Isabel, she had become an assertive, independent woman who shocked family and friends by smoking in public. But her patriotism prompted a distant relative, John Sharp Williams, the senator from Mississippi, to write to her in Paris: "I am proud that you are doing your part. We were an old family in Wales before we came to America and in the History of America and of the South we have hitherto done our part."[27]

Ella sent numerous cards to the children from France and in a letter wrote, "During this present big battle I saw lots of little French girls and boys going along this road with their Mother and a cart of household-goods fleeing from the Germans who had set fire to their homes. These children are called refugees and are most pitiful. I know you are thankful for a comfortable home and that your daddy has not been killed in the war."[28]

By January 1918, little Tom had recovered sufficiently to be able to walk about, although somewhat unsteadily. When his grandfather took him by the hand to visit the homes of church members, the boy saw firsthand the impact of war on grief-stricken families who had lost sons in the same foreign lands where Aunty Ella was serving. He also saw those parishioners who were seriously ill or dying. Years later, Tennessee claimed that he witnessed not only the sick but the dead. In the South, caskets are usually opened, with the deceased exhibited for family and friends to pay their last respects, and children are sometimes lifted and told to kiss the cold lips of the departed. The effect on little Tommy of seeing these funeral rites was traumatic and made death a lasting obsession.[29] It was always to the warmth and security of his grandparents' home that he would return, and this was the boy's fortress, his one great defense.

But it was a fortress and a defense soon to be shattered by the person he was told to call Father. Hardworking and hard-drinking, boisterous and coarse as ever, C.C. would still periodically storm the bastion of the Dakin household and as quickly leave it in peace. Now, all that was to change. The International Shoe Company was suddenly in need of replacements for those managers called to service, and just as suddenly the Delta drummer, as the regional salesmen were called, found his life and the lives of his wife and children about to undergo a profound change. Promoted to a managerial position in a branch of the shoe company, Cornelius was expected, of course, to transport his wife and children to St. Louis with him.

Since Rose and Tom were both of school age and would soon need separate rooms, even the Dakins had to admit that it was time for Edwina and the children to have a home of their own. Cornelius had gone ahead to St. Louis, a city—like all major cities in the throes of wartime activities—beset with a severe housing shortage. Despite the fact that Edwina had been ill with the flu, he would leave to her the chore of looking for a suitable place for the family to live. While it would have been too much of a burden to take both children with her, Edwina was not about to leave Clarksdale without Tommy, and the Dakins agreed that Rose should remain with them for the time being.

As Tom, amidst tears and brave smiles, boarded the train with his mother for St. Louis, he was enduring the painful experience of being separated for the first time from those he loved best in the world. He was excited about riding in a real train and told his mother he wanted to be a locomotive engineer when he grew up. But looking out the window as his car pulled out of the Clarksdale station and seeing his grandparents and Rose left behind, the tears he shed sprang from "the little frightened heart" in him.

3

Saint Louis

1918–1924

On a sweltering July day in 1918, two diminutive figures stepped off a train
into St. Louis's vast Union Station. As they hesitantly entered the crowded
waiting room, Edwina held seven-year-old Tom firmly to her side, as much
from her own apprehension as from maternal protection. Tom had not yet
fully recovered from his illness, and now his mother was fearful that he would
contract the flu, as she had recently. They were both in a visibly weakened
condition.

The weather was humid and stifling, and its effects were dangerous because
Spanish influenza had spread to epidemic proportions, compounding the
fatalities of a nation still at war. The symbols of death and disease were in
view, with the many coffins being unloaded from the train's baggage cars. In
this alien environment, Tom was shy and frightened, but what he was witnessing also fascinated him. Milling around in this one train station were more
people, it seemed, than in the entire town of Clarksdale. Everywhere he
looked, there were soldiers and sailors and war workers in a hurry, and there
were ladies in Red Cross uniforms, like his Aunt Ella overseas.

During their long trip north, Edwina had done her best to answer her son's
many questions and explain why they were relocating in such a big city as St.
Louis, at that time one of the largest in the United States. She was trying not
only to allay Tom's apprehensions but her own misgivings, as well. How
could she be sure she was doing the right thing? After their sheltered life in
Clarksdale, residing in the spacious two-story rectory in the neighborhood of
their friendly southern parishioners, the shock of suddenly arriving in St.
Louis was profound for both Tom and Edwina.

Also, there was the fact that she and Cornelius had never actually lived
together except for their brief time in Gulfport. Despite the many years of
their marriage, it was still as though she were a bride about to become a wife.
Her husband's life had completely changed now that he had been promoted
to assistant sales manager in the Friedman-Shelby branch of the largest shoe
manufacturing company in the world. And her life was about to change radically, too, since advancement in Cornelius's position was dependent upon
family responsibility and social respectability. Both Edwina and Cornelius
had good reason to look back at earlier times, she sentimentally and he rue-

fully. They both, for different reasons, had been content with the way things were. They had been leading separate lives. Now they were to learn the real meaning of marriage, and all they had in common was a determination to make the best of life in St. Louis. By the time he met his wife and son in Union Station, C.C. already looked the St. Louis businessman, sporting an expensive suit and a solid-gold watch, one of three he had won as a top salesman. Thirty-eight years old, he was now inclining toward overweight and was nearly bald. His left eye, which had been injured when he was a child, tended in times of anger to give him a fierce and threatening look.

As he led his family out of the huge stone station, they passed a fruit stand. Tom reached out and plucked a grape, and Cornelius delivered a stinging slap to the boy's hand. "Never let me catch you stealing again!" he bellowed. It was an incident that Tennessee Williams would never forget, and he was to say of his father, "A catalogue of unattractive aspects of his personality would be fairly extensive, but towering above them were, I think, two great virtues . . . total honesty and total truth, as he saw it in his dealings with others."[1]

C.C. dominated almost everyone who entered his limited sphere of influence, except his indomitable mate. And this fact left him totally unprepared now that they were taking up the unfamiliar roles of man and wife. Edwina was tiny in appearance; but small as she was, she stood up to her husband's bullying tantrums, and invariably this would set off a pitched battle. From the very beginning of their life in St. Louis, the two were bitterly at odds and equally miserable.

In August, Edwina would turn thirty-four. Although she was still a young woman, illness and the strain of the past few years had given her the look of middle age. The dark and conservative styles of the times only accentuated this image. Skirts were long—no more than six inches above the ankles—and tapered, restricting her gait to an almost Oriental daintiness. Her hats were large, brimless, and high and were fitted with plumes or discreet little veils nestled in the long hair she wore coiled up on her head. She powdered her face but never applied lipstick, which in those twilight days of America's Victorian era was something a lady would not do. Finally, a corset kept her erect and gave her a somewhat severe and dignified bearing overall.

As she gradually made her adjustment to St. Louis society, Mrs. Cornelius C. Williams was often looked upon as snobbish and haughty. Among those who came to know her intimately, however, she was always "Miss Edwina," a friendly and chatty woman. The quintessential southern lady was about to enter an environment and an era foreign to her way of life; both the mores of urban St. Louis and the coming Jazz Age of the 1920s were to constitute profound assaults upon her Christian sensibilities.

Militantly forthright and possessed of puritanical opinions, Edwina was frequently disliked for the very thing for which her son would become esteemed: a mastery of words. She not merely talked—and talked—she had the ability to overcome friend and adversary alike, usually leaving them limp and defenseless under the sheer weight of words. Later, Tennessee Williams would readily confess that his mother held him under her spell, and his friends would frequently remark on how silent he became in her presence, listening as if transfixed and then, clearly exhausted, desperate to find the nearest exit. As a child, however, Tom was barely able to comprehend what she was talking about a good deal of the time. The stories she told, seldom of any real significance, fascinated him simply because of the richness of language: the effusion, the cadences, the colloquialisms, the expressions "Merciful heavens!" and "Possess your soul in patience," all delivered in her acquired syrupy, southern drawl. In her running battles with Cornelius over money, alcohol, and poker nights, in that order, she used words as her weapons. Always the salesman, though, C.C., too, could talk up a storm. The result was her lightning and his thunder, which made Tom's new home, after his serene existence in a rectory, a terrifying place in which to live, and outside he found city life every bit as frightening.*

Being southerners gave Mr. and Mrs. Williams a certain distinction, and Miss Edwina played the role for all it was worth. Cornelius, though, soon shed his Tennessee accent and manners and assumed the blunt ways of the northerner. This further alienated Tom from his father and helped make this big man even more of a stranger in his own home. At seven years of age, the boy might have understood Cornelius's command that he must not steal, but there would be other bursts of temper and bombastic pronouncements toward which he could react only with fear or puzzled silence. Tom never talked back to his father. He would say nothing, and when it came to defending himself, he left it to his mother to do all the talking, which she did—endlessly.

During her first six months in St. Louis, Edwina was ill and homesick. First Tom and then she came down with the mumps. They were staying in a boardinghouse on Lindell Boulevard, and when finally she went to a doctor to find out why she continued to feel so poorly, he told her that she was pregnant. While Cornelius loved his wife despite their differences and the distance she tried to keep between them, now with another child on the way he felt threatened and cut off. When Edwina gave him the news, he exploded in a jealous rage, saying, "Then it isn't mine!"[2] To be accused of carrying someone else's child deeply shocked her. She never forgot his cruelty, or forgave him.

August heat in St. Louis is normally bad enough. Ill and pregnant, while at the same time looking for an apartment ample enough for a growing family,

---

*St. Louis, a hybrid city that had grown from a colony of French fur traders to over half a million inhabitants, was neither northern nor southern, Missouri having been a free state during the Civil War. Many of its citizens were émigrés from the South. Across the Mississippi River, East St. Louis, Illinois, with its large settlement of free Negroes, was more like a ghetto. Its stockyards and red-light district were kept separate from the preserve of the genteel, predominantly white St. Louisans.

Edwina looked upon the city as a place on the borderline of hell. The boardinghouse on Lindell was then a fashionable address on the outskirts of Forest Park, and to live in the western vicinity of the park, with its lakes, pagodas, classical buildings, and new natural-habitat zoo, became Edwina's goal. The farther west she was able to move, the greater her social status. To Edwina and Tom, the park represented the tranquil outdoors they had recently left behind, and they took refuge there as often as possible.

While Edwina was looking back nostalgically, she was at the same time looking ahead defiantly. The comparison of city life with her happy memories of less populous towns like Clarksdale, Columbus, and especially Port Gibson made the past an idyllic refuge. Even a simple picnic with Tom in Forest Park awakened recollections of a carefree time when, in 1904, she had visited the world's fair on these very grounds.

Over and over again, she would tell Tom about garden parties and cotillions and her gentlemen callers, until he could recite the stories by rote. She said that in those days she saw only "the charming, gallant, cheerful side"[3] of the smiling bridegroom who had been a telephone man "in love with long distance."[4] In Tom's mind, these images of his mother—once upon a time a young and pretty southern belle whose venturesome husband had deserted her to go on the road—eventually became entangled with perpetually dark apartments, with Rose's tragic turns, and with his own desperate attempt to free himself from the web of family. For years, these painful reflections lingered in his imagination, until at length they merged into "a memory play" he was to call *The Glass Menagerie*.

> **"Gone, gone, gone.**
> **All vestige of gracious living!**
> **Gone completely!"**

On the eleventh hour of the eleventh day of the eleventh month of 1918, the war in Europe ended. Everything changed, not only in Europe but the world over. Over 10 million soldiers were dead, and the social fabric of humankind was torn to shreds. Within a few months, an army of veterans would be returning to the United States and would be seeking work. C.C. and many family men like him were now up against the hordes of former heroes who would be desperately job hunting and looking upon those profiting on the home front as a new enemy they had to face. Ironically, Cornelius's managerial position offered him not just security but a first line of defense. It put him in the situation of hiring sales crews for a job noted as much for its glowing promise as its rapid turnover. Change was being forced upon the onetime traveling salesman, and, like his wife, he was reluctantly, unhappily moving into an unwanted future.

Outside his home, C.C. was generally good-humored and liked; always in command, he was popular among his sales crews. Since he kept his feelings to himself, it was difficult to recognize that he was in truth a desperately unhappy man. He felt chained to a desk that, as his son said later, deprived him of "the freedom and wildness on which his happiness depended."[5] Now all at once, he was a respectable St. Louis businessman with a family to house, clothe, feed, and educate. Having only his wife's support, never her love, he felt trapped in both his family and his work. Like many men of his time, goaded by the adventurous spirit of their forebears, he looked upon himself as diminished and imprisoned in a twentieth century where the limits of sales territories had replaced the pioneer's territorial horizons.

Edwina conceded that "because of us, he had to take this higher-paying job, one he really didn't want or like," and she theorized that this gave rise to a self-directed hate that he took out on his wife and children. But self-contempt in Cornelius and the Williams family was more deeply rooted than that, and it would perpetuate itself in his children, as well.

"He was a very restless man. . . . He would always want to be out doing something, although he also liked to be read to; one way to keep him home at night was to read a good novel,"[6] Edwina recalled. Another way was to be a willing and loving bed partner, but she simply did not allow such thoughts to enter her head. Sex was a man's pleasure and a woman's duty. Now she was pregnant with a child that he had denied was his. If he had not retracted this in his fashion, which always meant an assortment of flowers, gifts, and apologies, she would surely have left him. Her pregnancy and her illnesses became part of her strategy of withholding sex as often as she could. Since they were both accustomed to long separations, this, too, gave her an added edge, and she took it.

She might have come to understand him, but always at the core of their differences was the fact that she did not love her husband in the way he loved her, and he knew it. In her romantic view, it was John Singleton she had loved and still did. Increasingly, sometimes with the legitimate excuse of illness, she resisted her husband's sexual overtures. She tried to love him, in her way. But *his* way was fumbling and crude and instilled in her only fear and revulsion, a reaction to both his sexual desires and his extroverted behavior.

Since Edwina's culinary skills were limited to baking an angel food cake, the boardinghouse on Lindell Boulevard had its advantages. Also it gave her more free time to search for lodgings and to make the acquaintance of Cornelius's boss, Paul Jamison, and his wife, Ida. The Jamisons lived on Washington Boulevard, close to Forest Park, and they took an interest in the Williams family, giving them furniture and even passing on their son's carriage for the new baby. Living close to Cornelius's place of work downtown did not suit Edwina's social aspirations. At length, she found an apartment in Westminster Place, then one of the more exclusive residential districts, a space large enough to accommodate Rose and a newborn child. Despite the postwar housing crisis, she spotted an ad offering an apartment, with the proviso that the tenant also agree to buy its furnishings. And so, Mrs. Cornelius Williams made the first of nine westward moves, dragging her family behind her.

Westminster Place was a pleasant street lined with big trees and private homes, which made it almost southern in appearance. Theirs was an apartment building at the wrong end of the street, however, and undoubtedly Edwina and Cornelius were none too happy to add the name of Williams next to those of Cohen and Katzenstein on the mailbox. But only a block away was the fashionable Second Presbyterian Church and, across from it, the Wednesday Club, a prestigious civic and literary society run by ladies who most certainly would not *encourage* Jews to become members.

Although the apartment at 4633 Westminster did have six rooms, it was a dark center unit with windows only in the parlor, which faced the street, and in the kitchen and back bedroom, which overlooked an alleyway. "It was a gloomy place," Edwina commented, "so dark we had to leave the lights on most of the day, but it was no tenement."[7] To Tom, accustomed to the sunlit rooms of the rectory, it seemed even more gloomy. Although he had a tiny space off a side hall to call his own, he spent more time in his sister's room or sitting on the iron fire escape.

In September, Tom entered the first grade at the Eugene Field Elementary School on nearby Olive Street. A huge redbrick structure, to him it had the forbidding look of a prison, with its two watchtowers rising above the rooftop. For two years, his life here would be a waking nightmare. "I was scared to death of everyone on earth and particularly of public school boys and public school teachers and public school principals," he later recalled. "That name, public school, kept stabbing at my guts till I wanted, as old as I was, to sit down and cry."[8] When he was hesitant answering a question, his teacher remarked scornfully, "Anybody can tell you're from the South—you're slow as molasses in January."

The boys took pleasure in tormenting him because of his southern accent and manners and because he was unable to compete in their rough-and-tumble games. "I can remember gangs of kids following me home yelling 'Sissy!'—and home was not a very pleasant refuge. If I had been born to this situation I might not have resented it so deeply. But it was forced upon my consciousness at the most sensitive age of childhood."[9]

On February 21, 1919, Edwina gave birth to another son, Walter Dakin Williams, named after his grandfather; to avoid the confusion of two Walters, he was called Dakin. Grandmother Dakin had come to St. Louis to be with her daughter, bringing Rose with her, but Tom's joy at being reunited with his sister was tempered by their visit to Saint Anthony's Hospital to see their little brother. Rose thought "Sonny," as she dubbed him, was just wonderful; what Tom thought about this competition, he was not saying. Then, the Reverend Dakin arrived from Clarksdale to officiate at the baptism. And, although in time Cornelius would grow much closer to this child than to either Rose or Tom, the infant was now just one more weight to tie him down.

Once Rose was in St. Louis, she and Tom soon made friends on the block and had "an agreeable children's life among them," playing hide-and-seek and fly, sheep, fly and bathing under garden hoses with the return of summer. Williams remembered, "We were only a block from the Lorelei swimming pool and the West End Lyric movie and we had bicycle races about the block. Rose's closest friend was a pretty child whose mother was a snob who made catty remarks about Mother and Dad in front of us. I recall her once saying, 'Mrs. Williams always walks down the street like she was on the boardwalk at Atlantic City and Mr. Williams struts like the Prince of Wales.' "[10]

The "pretty child" was Mary Louise Aid, who attended Mary Institute, a private preparatory school for girls connected with Washington University; one had to be enrolled at the institute practically at birth. All of Rose's new friends went there, as did the Jamisons' daughter, while Rose and her brother went to Field. To send your daughter to Mary, your son to Country Day School, to belong to the Wednesday Club, the St. Louis Woman's Club, or the Bellerive Country Club—these became Edwina's criteria of social success, and because she could not afford them, in her frustration she developed a reverse snobbishness. She declared Rose's and Tom's friends unsuitable companions and St. Louis itself a city where only money and social position mattered. Still, it was a challenge to a Daughter of the American Revolution. If it was to be St. Louis, she would make the best of it, attracted as she was to the cultural life of the "Great River City": the symphony, the Art Institute, the Municipal Opera, the legitimate theatre, large libraries, and, important for Tom and Rose and now Dakin, an outstanding school system.

It didn't help that Tom and Rose felt snubbed by the children of wealthy families when, because there was no Episcopal church in the vicinity, they attended Sunday school down the block at the Second Presbyterian Church. Accustomed to attention as the rector's grandchildren, here they were nobodies. At length, they stopped going and spent their offering money at the soda fountain of the nearby Masserang Drug Store, until Edwina discovered their deception. At the same time, she, too, was being subjected to the snobbery of the more affluent churchgoers and the neighbors who owned their own homes and flashy cars like the Maxwell. This gave her greater reason to nurse her memories of the social distinction she had enjoyed in the South, where family was all-important and where it was considered nouveau riche to mention money or ostentatiously to exhibit one's wealth.

But Tom and Rose were quickly made to feel that there were two kinds of people in St. Louis, the rich and the poor, and that their family was poor. Tom, who always identified with his mother, absorbed and even exaggerated her resentment. Years after, when she had settled in St. Louis, wealthy and independent thanks to her son's having immortalized both her and the city, Tennessee Williams would still speak of St. Louisans as "cold, smug, complacent, intolerant, stupid and provincial."[11]

The words that Cornelius had spoken when Mr. Dakin admonished him that his fiancée could neither cook nor sew ("Mr. Dakin, I am not looking for a cook.") came home to roost. Where in former times Edwina had scarcely gone into the kitchen, now she was virtually living in it. Sometimes it took her an entire day to prepare dinner, and a great deal of fortitude in the evening for the family to consume it. But she was learning a few favorite dishes and waiting for the day when she could afford a servant.

As a ritual, she would arise at six o'clock to cook a big breakfast for Cornelius to ensure that he would be off to work on time, and in the evening, she made sure that he found a hearty meal on the table. Before she served dinner, she always took a bath and changed to a dainty dress, a gesture that could have given him only small comfort. In time, Cornelius grew increasingly resentful toward his family as his confinement behind a desk entrapped him more and more. The only release he found was in a game of golf or, on weekends, a poker night with the boys in a downtown hotel, where he could indulge in some hard drinking and an occasional dalliance with a lady of the evening. These peripheral nighttime escapades were hidden from Edwina at first. Then, as she put it, she discovered the "Mr. Hyde." She firmly disapproved of his drinking and constantly berated him for it. With the advent of Prohibition, which rose out of the Spartan restrictions of a wartime economy, Edwina had the moral support of a sweeping majority of American women. To add to C.C.'s misery, she would soon have the power of the vote, with its symbolic independence.

Money was the one weapon that Cornelius had at his command, and he often used it vengefully in his effort to control the uncontrollable in Edwina. Tightfisted in business, he became unreasonable at home, making his wife battle for small sums, grocery money, clothing, and schoolbooks for the children. The parents' confrontations were now more like open warfare, and in this, Cornelius would meet his match as the magpie turned to scold. Tiny as she was, Edwina would lift her chin in defiance and look up into his face, talking, talking, talking until sheer exhaustion would overtake them both. When money was not the issue, they would find other things to dispute: She upbraided him for his drinking and other un-Christian ways, and he complained about her spoiling the children by giving them the attention he wanted.

Tom's life at home was profoundly marred by their constant and bitter quarrels. His only escape from his parents' incessant bickering was to be alone as much as possible, sequestered in his room with his fanciful imaginings and his books, and with Rose, to whom he clung. From the beginning, Cornelius had always exhibited a strangely distant attitude toward Tom, until at length there was only the most perfunctory communication between them. He struck back at Edwina's domination by calling his son "Miss Nancy." The boy surely wanted his father's love and needed it, but instead the fear he felt toward him surfaced as hate. Years later, when it was too late for his father to know, Tom would write with compassion and pity that Cornelius had been trapped like a jungle animal in a cage.

Clarksdale Revisited

On March 11, 1920, Tom's school records noted that he "left city." Edwina was ill, the strain of living with Cornelius and raising three children proving too much for her to bear. As she would many times, Grandmother Dakin—"Grand," as she was called affectionately by the children—took the long train ride from Clarksdale to be with her daughter. Rose was of some help around the house, particularly in watching over her baby brother, but Tom, who still had not adjusted to his new existence in St. Louis, was doing poorly in school and was also feeling the pangs of sibling rivalry toward "King Dakin," as he referred to him. Tom Williams was an unhappy little boy.

It was decided that he would go to stay in Clarksdale with Grandfather Dakin and later with Grand, once she was able to return. Late in February, Tom left St. Louis, accompanied by a friend of the family, a Mr. Moss, and the moment he stepped off the train and into the arms of his grandfather, he knew he was home. He was about to experience one of the happiest and most formative periods of his life.

Now that Tom was nine years old and insatiably curious, he saw the little city of Clarksdale and its inhabitants from a different perspective. His mind came alive with new images and deeply stored impressions. With the end of World War I, Clarksdale had been enjoying an unprecedented, largely wartime prosperity. The evidence of new wealth was everywhere to be seen, an affluence that would last another year, until the collapse of the cotton market in 1921. Whether the times were good or bad, the Reverend Dakin and his wife characteristically moved with them, accepted the changes, and made the best of them. But Tom was not that malleable; he would never lose his love for the old and gentle ways and would all of his life decry the brutalization of the Romantic tradition. In this, it was like mother, like son. Years later, he would say that "the South once had a way of life I am just old enough to remember—a culture that had grace, elegance . . . an inbred culture . . . not a society based on money, as in the North. I write out of regret for that."[12]

Just as another southern writer, William Faulkner, had staked out nearby Sardis and Oxford, Mississippi, as his Yoknapatawpha County, so Tennessee Williams would claim a circle of some twenty miles around Clarksdale as his literary territory. Clarksdale would be renamed Blue Mountain, and a gambling club near Lula would be called the Moon Lake Casino. Actual names like the Alcazar Hotel, Friars Point, Lyon, Tutwiler, Coahoma County, the Sunflower River, and Moon Lake would figure in a number of his plays and stories.

One dwelling that particularly caught Tom's interest was the Cutrer mansion, located on a knoll overlooking the Sunflower River, and its beautiful gardens, stables, and the servants' quarters across the road. Built in 1916, it was a replica of an Italian villa and quickly became "one of the Delta's opulent showplaces and the backdrop for extravagant yard parties and masked balls with Japanese lanterns and full orchestras."[13]

But it was the interior of the mansion, decorated by Charles J. Duveen, that was unlike anything that Tom could have imagined. Florentine-styled, but with an elaborate mixture of eighteenth- and nineteenth-century Italian and English furnishings, it was presided over by a lady whom Williams would cite in later years as a true grande dame, Mrs. Blanche Cutrer.[14] He especially remembered Mrs. Cutrer, who was the daughter of Clarksdale's founder, John Clark, as one of those remarkable Delta matriarchs who lived in great style. She had a handsome son, John, who drowned in a boating accident on Moon Lake, an event Williams would adapt in *The Glass Menagerie*, and a beautiful daughter-in-law named Stella, a name he would use, like that of Blanche, in *A Streetcar Named Desire*.

Another lady whom Tom came to know was a friend of the Dakins, a Mrs. Maggie Wingfield, who ran two "de luxe" boardinghouses.[15] Alida Clark Heidelberg, a neighbor, remembered Mrs. Wingfield as having had "a collection of glass animals in her front window, tiny little glass animal figures. When the sun hit them, everyone would remark that they were just absolutely gorgeous!"[16] Mrs. Heidelberg's cousin, Phil Clark, was one of the few Clarksdale friends that Tom made in his own age group. He didn't get along all that well with other playmates, and Phil's aunt, Pauline Alston Clark, recalled that "down the street from the rectory where the Dakins lived there was a boy, Brick Gotcher, who couldn't stand sissies. Tom Williams just drove him crazy and he would beat up on him—and Tom would go home weeping either with a fat lip or his feelings hurt. But Tennessee Williams waited about thirty years until he wrote *Cat on a Hot Tin Roof* to get back at Brick, and he fixed him— made him a latent one."[17] The fictional character is said to have been a composite of Albert "Brick" Gotcher and John Wesley Clark, who broke his leg one night on the Elks Club lawn.

During his time away from St. Louis, Tom was deeply drawn to his grandfather, as was the old gentleman to him. On Sundays, the boy would hear the clergyman's sermons and observe how the parishioners would speak to him appreciatively after the service. Life in the rectory was church-centered and tolerantly moralistic, and Tom in his obvious adoration of Walter Dakin had unconsciously come to feel like a minister's son. A story Williams would write later, called "de preachuh's Boy," romanticized Tom as he saw himself in Clarksdale: a delicate boy of nine years, whose congenital weakness of the heart kept him from leading an active child's life. He described his alter ego as having features that were

spiritually beautiful, his skin transparently fine. Blue veins were visible around his throat and temples. His hair was a cloudy gold and his eyes were as introspectively still at times as blue pools in the middle of a forest and then as mobile as tongues of blue flame. The small boys of the town called him a sissy. His timidity, his gentle manners, formal language, and unearthly blue gaze set him oddly apart. . . . But the preacher's boy . . . never seemed to mind his loneliness. Unconsciously he was preparing to become a poet. He was the local child prodigy, and though all the members of the congregation praised him highly to his parents, they were thankful that their own children were developing along more normal lines.[18]

In Edwina's absence, Tom's grandmother became the maternal guardian who cooked his meals, saw that he was dressed properly, made it to Oakhurst Elementary School on time, and who gave him piano and violin lessons. As it had been with their daughter, Grand was the gentle disciplinarian and Grandfather the fascinating storyteller who indulged his grandson's whims and gratified his hunger for knowledge.

One of Walter Dakin's tales concerned an elderly lady in Columbus, Miss Julia Meek, who possessed a letter written by Lord Byron, which Tom supposed was a love letter addressed to her. Twenty years later, a one-act play emerged, *Lord Byron's Love Letter.* There are those who believe that a young woman named Maggie from Coahoma County became the prototype for Margaret in *Cat on a Hot Tin Roof.* The many experiences of members of the minister's congregation were stored like myriad pieces of mirror, only to reappear years afterward as vivid reflections in Tom's writings. But much of what the Reverend Dakin related was in the form of parables about the struggle between good and evil. Inculcated in Tom during this time was a deep moral sense of the consequences of evildoing, and the imponderable question of whether humankind is guided by free will or is powerless before God's will.

It was largely because of the superior St. Louis school system that in Clarksdale Tom skipped to the fourth grade, and it was not surprising that his grades were improved greatly, especially in reading. Now he was able to go to his grandfather's bookshelves and select for himself his favorites: Dickens, the adventure stories of Sir Walter Scott, and the great violent melodramas of Shakespeare. One that fascinated him in particular was *Titus Andronicus,* and he apparently found the cannibalism in this play so intriguing that later, in *Suddenly Last Summer,* he employed it as a metaphor to describe the way people in modern society consume one another. Williams never stressed this symbolism; he simply related a phantasmagoric incident of cannibalism as something that happened, as he also did in his short story "Desire and the Black Masseur."

During these few months he spent with his grandparents, Tom grew to love them more than ever. They accepted and embraced him. Of course, he missed his mother and his sister, but not his father. On the other hand, Rose, who yearned for her daddy's love, was, like Tom, rejected by Cornelius. On an occasion when she danced for him, his only response was to remark, "Just like a moo-cow." Although she did everything possible to win his affection, it was her grandfather who responded. For her birthday in November, Walter sent her a copy of the book *Daddy Long Legs* and a postcard picture of Saint George's Church and rectory, on which he wrote, "I thought you would like a glimpse of your old home. I hope you are doing fine in school and looking after Dakin." He signed it "Grand-Faddy."[19]

Cornelius's sisters, Isabel and Ella, were well aware of his troubled marriage and the strain on the children. Although they loved their brother and wrote to him frequently, they also understood how difficult he could be, and they made a point of keeping sympathetically in touch with Edwina, too. Unlike Isabel, who was regarded as a great beauty, Ella Williams was short and dark and tended toward overweight. After returning to Knoxville from overseas, she opened a gift shop, which subsequently became her residence, as well. At Christmas, while Tom was still in Clarksdale with his grandparents, Ella sent him five dollars, telling him, "When you get back to St. Louis I want you to get Daddy to take you downtown and I want you to buy a big globe of the world on a stand . . . they cost $4.50 which will leave 50 cents for you to spend any way you please."[20] He bought the globe, it became one of his treasures, and he vowed someday to go to all those places.

"Clothed as Sorrow Is"

At the end of the spring term, Tom returned home. Although he had disliked St. Louis from the outset, now he came truly to hate the city—and to hate his father—and to hate the Eugene Field Public School, which he reentered in September 1921. About this time, it was decided that Rose, too, would benefit from a year with the Dakins, particularly since she was neither getting along with her father nor doing well in school. From all evidence, however, her year in Clarksdale was not as happy as Tom's. She loved her grandparents and probably was better behaved than her brother and was not as inquisitive or demanding, but she clearly missed Tom and her mother—and the father she was unable to reach with her affection.

Twelve years old, she also missed playing "mother" to Sonny. Dakin would be three on February 21, 1922, and soon after that date, Rose wrote to her mother:

I have a canary bird Grand Fads bought it for me it is a fine singer but has a frightful temper. It tries to bight me everytime I come near the cage because I give him a bath every day. I put him in the tub and turn the water on him. He loves to be dirty and hates water. . . . Yesterday some woman came to the door and asked for Mrs. Dakin. Grand came down and stayed a long time and called me she had bough[t] a set of books for me very like the Knolege books only *better* 7 vol. $37.50 pay $3.00 month fine books and the things are easy to study fine school books *so* like the K.

books. Of course Grand Fads was mad as the duce but they are bought
and will arrive Saturday. Tom can use them.[21]

During the spring of 1922, Edwina and Cornelius moved in the same
neighborhood to a larger downstairs apartment on the corner of Taylor and
Laclede. C.C. had been promoted to full sales manager, which meant an increased salary and also that he would be able to travel occasionally in order to
supervise his salesmen in their various territories around the country. The
new apartment was in a different school district, so Tom transferred in March
to Stix School on nearby Euclid Street, where Rose would also go when she
returned.

In *Memoirs*, Williams attributed the move from the dark apartment on
Westminster Place to the fact that the rooms at 5 Taylor Street admitted
more sunlight and that Edwina, who was recuperating from inflammation of
her lungs, needed the change. "Anyway it was a radical step down the social
scale," he claimed, "a thing we'd never had to consider in Mississippi; and all
our former friends dropped us completely—St. Louis being a place where location of residence was of prime importance."[22] While it is true that the Taylor location, with a trolley line running down the center of Laclede, was not as
pleasant as the Westminster Place neighborhood, the ostracism that Tom felt
was likely more a product of paranoia than of reality.

It was at this time that he made the two best friends of his childhood, who
were themselves best friends, Hazel Kramer and Esmeralda Mayes. Hazel
lived around the corner from South Taylor in her grandparents' mansion on a
tree-lined thoroughfare called Forest Park Boulevard. Her friendship with
Tom began when some young ruffians were throwing rocks at her and he
came to her aid, both of them making a hasty retreat into her house, straightway up the stairs to a hiding place in her attic. "I was eleven and Hazel was
nine. We started spending every afternoon in her attic. Being imaginative
children, we invented many games, but the chief diversion that I recall was
illustrating stories that we made up. Hazel drew better than I and I made up
better stories." He described her as "a redhead with great liquid brown eyes
and a skin of pearly translucence."[23]

At first, Edwina did not pay too much attention to Tom's friendship with
Hazel. She had recently suffered a miscarriage, and her health was in a precarious state. Cornelius was disturbed by his wife's lingering infirmities, and he
didn't hesitate to spend whatever it cost to help her. Although this contradictory behavior was in all likelihood a reflection of his ambivalent feelings toward her, in sickness or in a crisis of any kind involving Edwina and the
children, he was always quick to respond. He would be there to do whatever
he could or should, a trait that Tom would grow up to assume himself. Despite Edwina's one-sided view of her husband, there was much, in fact, that he
did that was not solely for his own welfare but for the family's, as well.

Illness seemed to plague both the Williams and Dakin families; it was accepted more as a fact of their lives than as a matter of health. There was something distinctly hypochondriacal in their attitudes, and Cornelius was not the least self-concerned among them. Both he and Edwina complained that they must be among the city's foremost contributors to the medical profession—particularly to nearby Barnes Hospital.

Cornelius's employer, Paul Jamison, had become fond of Edwina and was worried about her. In the summer of 1922, he arranged a business-pleasure trip to California for both of them. Edwina had been diagnosed as having incipient tuberculosis, and it was hoped that the trip would improve her health—and the marriage. Bringing Rose with her, Grand came to stay at the Taylor Street apartment to care for all three children. A postcard addressed to Tom, picturing the excursion steamer *Avalon* en route to Catalina Island, off the Southern California coast, read:

> This is the boat that brought us to this lovely island. We were on the Pacific about two hours and a half and I did not get seasick! We will be here two days and then go to San Francisco. Hope to hear that you have not caused Grand any trouble!
>
> Lovingly, Mother[24]

When she returned from California, Edwina still had not fully recovered, and she remained under constant medical care. Neighbors remembered her as reclusive and thought perhaps she was snubbing them. Rose and Tom tended to keep to themselves. A family named Bruce lived in the same apartment building, and their daughter, Jane, recalled, "On Laclede, a long block from Taylor to Euclid, there were at least seventy children, if you included the toddlers, so it was very easy to have private age-gangs that could even exclude your own brother and sister. If you were small and shy, as was Tom Williams, you had a very hard time of it."[25]

Another family, the Shackelfords, lived across the street from the Williamses. Before they became good friends, Mrs. Shackelford considered Edwina distant and reserved, while C.C. seemed quite the opposite: the hearty, outgoing salesman who worked with her husband at the International Shoe Company. Pat Shackelford would become Cornelius's best friend and poker-playing crony. When Pat asked about the family, C.C. would complain that when he got home from work, he usually found his wife in the living room reading a book, Rose in her room reading a book, Tom out on the fire escape reading a book—and, thank God, Dakin too young to read!

Miss Edwina had great faith in the power of books. Her father, with his huge library, set the example for her and for Tom. To kindle the boy's interest, for Christmas 1923 she gave him a copy of James Whitcomb Riley's *Rhymes of Childhood*, and in her own library she kept an edition of Riley's *Love Lyrics*, inscribed "Christmas 1905." The love of poetry, it is said, begins early in life, even if the poetry isn't great or good.

The Paper Lantern

As the Jazz Age began to accelerate, Edwina found herself divided against not only Cornelius but her children, as well. It seemed to her as though revolution was everywhere, abroad and at home. Warren G. Harding was in the White House, but there was no return to normalcy, as had been promised; in fact, a scandal was about to break over the President's head. Reds were on the march, and radical talk had become social talk, especially in New York, where a revolution of another kind, called "serious theatre," was under way. The young Eugene O'Neill had come down from Provincetown, and after the Broadway premiere of his *Beyond the Horizon*, in 1920, the American theatre would never be the same.

Nor would the country. In the White House, President Harding had been inducted into the Ku Klux Klan, which by 1924 would have risen from a following of a few hundred in 1915 to nearly 4.5 million. The postwar American landscape was torn from one end to the other with labor and management strife. Gangsters, bootleg liquor, the Red scare, the radicalism of minorities, who were in turn persecuted by conservative power blocs, riddled the country with corruption. Worse, the world had not been made "safe for democracy," and it was already moving inexorably, as the dying ex-President Wilson warned, toward another world war.

As southerners, the Williams and Dakin families were Democrats, but they were hardly democratic. While they could view a Harding and then a Calvin Coolidge in the White House with disdain, they were in fact traditionally conservative. The influx of Negroes into the North and into St. Louis after the war brought with it race problems that were inconceivable in the South, and the Williams family simply carried on attitudes that were maddeningly patronizing. For Tom, though, the memory of Ozzie and what it meant to call someone a "black nigger" burned bright.

Edwina might have dismissed all this social change as being of no particular concern to her, except that Rose brought it home: She belonged to a new generation that was beyond her mother's comprehension. A vivacious and outgoing girl, warm and affectionate, Rose wanted peer recognition and to be accepted among her friends. More than that, she wanted her father's approbation. She was behaving naturally, as most girls do at puberty, quarreling with their mothers and seeking the affectionate intervention of their fathers. She did everything she could to reach her father with tender, ineffable little gifts of love and was met only with an insensate response. Occasionally, Cornelius would try to reciprocate her affection by going through the motions, in ways that seldom deceive children; and the more he rejected her, the more Rose tried to win his acceptance, until finally, she was left defenseless and vulnerable in a way that her brother was not. Tom was growing remote, taking refuge in his own interior life of memories and fantasies, creating resources, while she had none.

Edwina was well aware of her husband's indifference to their daughter, but ironically, at the same time she was never able to understand the destruction that came of withholding love, hers from Cornelius and his from Rose and Tom. Her way was to overcompensate, to substitute devotion and a martyrdom to duty. With her romantically unreal notions of what love should be, Edwina simply could not respond to the attack of a crude lover. Her miscarriage resulted in two subsequent operations and finally a hysterectomy. After that, she resisted Cornelius's sexual advances more and more. What began as Edwina's crying protests, Tennessee remembered, now became screams emanating from the bedroom; the impression he had was that of rape. Whether this was imagined or not, at length husband and wife occupied separate bedrooms, and they no longer had a sexual relationship. At best, the atmosphere in the home became a strained southern gentility; at worst, it was open warfare.

The effect upon Tom and, particularly, Rose—and eventually Dakin—was that of a deep and permanent injury. As Dakin said, "Mother was president of the anti-sex league."[26] Sex for Edwina had become a horror, and inevitably she conveyed this attitude to her children. She implied it was dirty and dangerous and something that should be confined to a marriage bed. Tom would be twenty-seven before he had his first sexual experience; Dakin would be inexperienced until his marriage, when he was in his late thirties; and Rose would remain a virgin all her life.

After she returned from Clarksdale in the fall of 1922, Rose entered Stix School, where she managed to complete the sixth and seventh grades, but she was not interested in study. Despite the fact that she obviously did not have any real talent for music, she took piano and violin lessons to please her grandmother, who paid for them. In December 1922, shortly after Rose's thirteenth birthday, the Elise Aehle School of Music presented a "Costume Violin Recital" at the North Side YMCA. Second on the program, Rose was to play Papini's "Romance," but it was a total embarrassment to everyone present, especially Rose. She stopped in midpassage, then went back and repeated it, and finally stopped altogether and left the stage in tears.

It was a crushing experience, but one that fueled her spirit of defiance. She was in revolt, like many girls of her age; and having to give a recital, especially of classical music, was something she hadn't wanted to do in the first place. The music she enjoyed was jazz and blues, and whenever she was alone, she tried dancing to their rhythms. Jane Bruce, Rose's neighbor, remembered her as being "very pretty and a bit standoffish. She used makeup, which, in those times, especially for a young girl, was rather shocking."[27] But that was the point: It was fun to shock one's parents, and nothing was *anything* in those times unless it was fun.

Tom's defiance and idea of fun, however, took an inward turn. It was then, at the age of twelve, that he said he had begun to find life unsatisfactory as an explanation in and of itself, and he was forced to adopt the method of the artist of not explaining but putting the blocks together in some other way that seemed more significant to him. And so he started to write. Among his early efforts, written during his year in Clarksdale, was a colorfully illustrated declaration: "I have just found the beginning of The Rainbow and I hope it['s] so interesting that you won't want me to find an end. You'll be so happy after you've read Rainbows Comic Paper that you will shine like a Rainbow." It was signed with a self-portrait, "The great finder of the end of The Rainbow. Thomas Lanier Williams."[28] Seeing this and other examples of his numerous compositions, Edwina spent ten dollars and bought him a secondhand typewriter.

During the late winter of 1924, the Williams family moved farther west to 5938 Cates Street. From Edwina's point of view, it was a move in the right direction, although the apartment itself was no improvement: It was smaller and on the top floor of a two-family house with a flat roof, which made summers unbearably hot and August vacations an imperative. The move was made mainly so that Rose could enter Soldan High School and Tom could graduate from Stix School to Ben Blewett Junior High.

Rose's change to Soldan, though, turned out to be a disastrous failure academically, and she dropped out after the first quarter. In September, a desperate Edwina and Grand, who paid the tuition, enrolled her in an exclusive private school for girls, Hosmer Hall, a finishing school emphasizing French, music, dances, bridge, and so forth. But her education, particularly her spelling, was not much improved. In her yearbook, she is pictured with bobbed hair, lipstick, a defiant thrust of her chin (not unlike her mother's), and a faraway look.

Although she loved Tom, there were times when she became distant and strangely aloof toward him, and these would be abrupt changes in her that he could not understand and that hurt him and made him resentful. Rose was suffering late menstrual periods, and at his age Tom was unable to comprehend the stress she was under emotionally. Nor could he accept the changes that ensued in such "silly" things as a new hairstyle and clothes that looked to him as though they should belong to his mother. But Rose was changing in other ways, too: Her good spirits were turning into a kind of hysteria; her laughter was more nervous than natural; she was moody and was developing a strange little hunch; and she often quarreled over inconsequential things with Tom and Mother and Daddy. Inclined toward self-dramatization, she would even imitate her mother's illnesses. Everything was, as she kept saying, "just tragic!"

Later, Tennessee would write about this time in their lives in a poignant account he entitled "The Resemblance Between a Violin Case and a Coffin." The story is more an elegy, in which he mourns the passing of their happy, isolated times as children, how they came tremulous and unprepared into "the broken terrain . . . the wilderness" of adolescence. "I saw that it was all over, put away in a box like a doll no longer cared for, the magical intimacy of our childhood together, the soap-bubble afternoons and the games with paper dolls cut out of dress catalogues and the breathless races here and there on our wheels. For the first time, yes, I saw her beauty. I consciously avowed it to myself, although it seems to me that I turned away from it, averted my look from the pride with which she strolled into the parlor and stood by the mantel mirror to be admired."

What puzzled Tom even more than his sister's rejection of him was the fact that she had forsaken him for Richard Miles, a handsome seventeen-year-old—a youth in the adult world perhaps, but a man in a little boy's view of him. Shyly and surreptitiously, Tom studied him: His gracefulness and untarnished beauty made him a young man unlike any the boy had ever seen, at least in such dazzling proximity. What was more, his sister had fallen in love with Richard, and so it followed that Tom would, too—differently, to be sure, since her love was infatuation and his was fascination.

In retrospect, Tennessee Williams would come to regard this as the first stirring of an attraction to his own sex that would take years to surface into consciousness:

> When I recall what a little puritan I was in those days, there must have been a shocking ambivalence in my thoughts and sensations as I gazed down upon him through the crack of the door. How on earth did I explain to myself, at that time, the fascination of his physical being without at the same time, confessing to myself that I was a little monster of sensuality? Or was that before I began to associate the sensual with the impure, an error that tortured me during and after pubescence, or did I, and this seems most likely now, say to myself, Yes, Tom, you're a monster![29]

Dakin recalled that there was indeed a Richard Miles and that this was the first of Rose's many disappointments in love. Whether or not Richard died of pneumonia, as Williams wrote in his story, he did evidently die while still a teenager. Tom was too young to understand what that meant to Rose, nor could he understand what had come between him and his sister.

Now Tom was on his own. The sister who had so suddenly grown up, the one who was older and wiser, the one whom he could trust and look up to, had become someone else. It represented another loss. Would she marry someone and go away and never return, just disappear like Ozzie? Whom could he turn to when he was puzzled or distressed? Who, then, would tell him what to do?

> *. . . At fifteen my sister*
> *no longer waited for me,*
> *impatiently at the White Star Pharmacy corner*
> *but plunged headlong*
> *into the discovery, Love!*

Then vanished completely—

for love's explosion, defined as early madness,
consumingly shone in her transparent heart for a season
and burned it out, a tissue-paper lantern.[30]

4

The Writin' Son

1924–1926

From the moment Edwina gave him a secondhand typewriter, large and up-right and with the explosive sound of an ancient Gatling gun, Tom never stopped typing. Eventually, he would take a typing course and become an ex-cellent high-speed typist, but for now it was hunt-and-peck. From that machine would issue a steady stream of stories, poems, letters, and such miscellany as contest entries, including "An Ode to Crisp Brown Muffins" for Jenny Wren Flour.

Tom was twelve and still in grade school when he wrote his first school composition; his teacher had asked the class to select a picture on the class-room wall and write about it. He was immediately struck by a print of a paint-ing inspired by Tennyson's heroine the Lady of Shalott, depicting her floating trancelike down a river. Called to read his paper before the class, Wil-liams remembered, "It had a very good reception. From that time on I knew I was going to be a writer."[1]

Junior high was a new educational concept in the United States, and Blew-ett, built only seven years before, was among the most innovative such schools in the country. Pupils were grouped on the basis of intelligence-test results, and according to ability, they were moved rapidly through grades seven to nine. Blewett was a huge school with a diverse ethnic mix, and there was con-siderable emphasis on citizenship, student government, and school activities. Organized like a small city, it had a bank, a good library, a large orchestra, baseball and basketball teams, and some thirty clubs, with students encour-aged to join at least one. Homerooms were microcosms of the whole, and they competed with intense rivalry for the bronze and silver medals awarded for achievement.

Tom, just turning thirteen, tested 114 on the Terman I.I. test and was as-signed to the Woodrow Wilson group. The Terman, an IQ adaptation of the

Stanford-Binet tests, chiefly reflected native endowment, but results were often tempered by environment, previous educational experience, and such psychological factors as anxiety. Tom, with some strikes against him on all these grounds, nonetheless ranked well above normal.

He chose as eighth-grade electives Latin and art and cited his planned curriculum in high school as "Classical"—undoubtedly the influence of his grandfather. From early childhood, when he would close his eyes and see pictures, Tom displayed an extraordinary visual imagination not only in his storytelling—a tiny landscape done when he was five prefigured what would become a lifelong interest in painting.

Tom was not a joiner, and in this mammoth school setting he might have been lost, but fortunately an important student activity was participation in publishing the biweekly newspaper, *The Junior Life*. Here he found his milieu, and here Thomas Lanier Williams was first published. Significantly, the piece was called "Isolated" and appeared in the November 7, 1924, issue.

It tells in the first person how, fishing on White Fan Island, the author falls asleep, to be awakened by the noise of the river at flood tide, a river that had "changed into a roaring torrent of brown eddies." With a penchant for melodrama even then, Tom wrote, "That night the flood was illumined from shore to shore by torches of searching parties who were reclaiming dead bodies, and salvaging half-inundated ground. After a long cold wait I was finally rescued by one of these searching parties. As we rowed back to the mainland, the waves washed over the last hillock of my erstwhile refuge."[2]

Writing was stressed at Blewett, and in all probability this was one of the "Class Exercises in Development of Paragraphs from Topical Sentences" required by Miss Connor's English class. A pennant was awarded for the best article, and Tom's chief rival for it was a handsome boy he had met at church, Scott Robertson, who would in a few years become a more serious competitor when they attended the same college.

The one thing that now meant most to Tom, his writing, became the one thing that Cornelius could least tolerate. As he saw it, everyone knew that writers and artists were a queer lot who never made any money, and this was the last thing in the world he wanted for a son of his—one named Thomas Lanier Williams III at that! Tennessee said later, "My father thought writing a lot of foolishness, especially poetry writing."[3] But regardless of Cornelius's (or anyone's) opinion, Tom had found an outlet, a door that let out into the world, and he went through it as often as he could.

While his grandparents gave him encouragement at every opportunity, his staunchest ally was his mother, the one who had given him a typewriter and who was soon referring to him as "mah writin' son." As Cornelius spurned Tom's efforts, Edwina doubled her support. Whether intentionally or not, she had fashioned a vengeful weapon that served as a permanent wedge between father and son. And it served to isolate Cornelius within his own family.

There was no way "the old man," as Tom referred to him when he was out of earshot, could articulate his loneliness. He could strike out only in a burst of temper or, sinking into a sullen mood, sit on the living room couch and glare. He might have tried to confide how he felt to his sisters, particularly Isabel, but from childhood he had learned to keep his feelings to himself. In Knoxville and in the company of cronies like Pat Shackelford, he was regarded as carefree and good-humored.

Now that he was a full-fledged manager, C.C. was expected to be a model of the behavior he wanted to see in his salesmen, and often he became a tyrant to field representatives who were on the road, where he wanted to be. *His* model was his employer, Paul Jamison, staid and disciplined, to whom Edwina would point as an example in every way. And since she and Jamison had become good friends, Edwina had fashioned another wedge that she could and did drive.

As a result, C.C. kept his happy hours within the precincts of a speakeasy or a downtown hotel room. The only liquor in Edwina's household was what he managed to stash away in some hiding place. During the week and at work, he conformed, and only when he went off on weekends with his buddies or traveled to sales territories could he relax and feel like one of them, once again a Mississippi drummer.

Whenever he returned from a business trip, Cornelius was generally in an agreeable mood; it was then he would take the family on outings and show them how generous he could be. From Edwina's point of view, her husband was generous when it included *his* pleasure. He spared no expense when it came to dressing himself properly or joining a country club to play golf, she complained, but he railed against the spending of money for the necessities of home and children. That fight was joined and would go on and on like the Hundred Years War.

Asked why she endured it, Edwina would say, "I suppose if I had been like the women of today, I would have left my husband after the first few years. The Episcopal Church is strict, though, about divorce. And if I had left him, there would have been no Rose, or Tom, or Dakin. So I just stood by and took it. I wanted my children to feel there was one parent in whom they could have faith."[4]

But there was more to it than family and religion. Edwina knew a few divorced ladies among her friends, and she knew, too, that their status was hardly enviable, even if a younger generation of women was making a place called Reno a portal to freedom. By 1925, Edwina, who was typical among many of her married middle-aged friends, was beginning to attain social recognition, being both a member of the DAR and the wife of a businessman in management. Also, there were other southern families at the shoe company, and this enhanced her image as Miss Edwina.

There was another image important to her—and to Cornelius, too, for that matter—and that was the one of Mr. and Mrs. Williams, respectable middle-class Saint Louisans. Even C.C. was concerned with keeping up appearances when the situation called for it. They regularly attended such company functions as the annual picnic and presented the semblance of a happily married couple. Paul Jamison not only liked Edwina; he also knew that she was her husband's ballast and that had he been a bachelor, Cornelius would never have made the grade at the shoe company.

So, to Edwina, religious scruples aside, divorce in her social circles would be a badge of shame and, in her forty-first year—well, really, most impractical! To go home to Clarksdale with three children to raise would place an impossible burden upon her parents, and as a divorcée, what would she do? What *could* she do, she asked Tom and Rose, sell real estate?

The fear she felt toward her husband was not for her own safety but for her children and their security. She was apprehensive that his drinking and poker nights might cause him to be fired. And if he *was* fired, where would she and the children be? She worried that he would take off on the road again, this time not to return, entranced as he was by far-off places. And hadn't he threatened to do just that! She constantly voiced her dread to the children, and it was a fear deeply embedded in both Tom and Rose.

Mrs. Cornelius Williams made up her mind that, outwardly at least, the marriage would appear conventionally proper. She joined Saint George's Episcopal Church, on the corner of Olive and Pendleton, which gave her entrée to a more elite stratum of St. Louis society. It was in this church that Tom was confirmed by no less than the Right Reverend Daniel S. Tuttle, who was presiding bishop of the Episcopal church in the United States. But try as she might, Edwina could not hope to reach the society pages, which were "dominated by old French names: Chouteaus, Desloges, Papins, making their debuts or serving as royalty at the Veiled Prophet's Ball and who stood aloof from the new-rich beer barons, the Anheusers and Busches with their hunt clubs and their Bavarian brides." Instead, she would have to settle for being one among the sedate southern families who "shopped at Vandervoort's, went to outdoor opera on summer nights and stopped afterwards for ice-cream at Dorr and Zeller's catering house. Saturday afternoon pop concerts were part of the pattern as were trips to the Art Institute, with its golden roof and the statue of Saint Louis surveying the city from the vantage point of Art Hill."[5]

This was the city that Edwina was determined to inhabit, but what Tom saw was something else: a downtown "canyon" of office buildings, railroads, river barges, factories, and cramped Negro tenements. In the postwar city, the gemütlichkeit of beer gardens and of Adolphus Busch's breweries was overshadowed by a growing number of factories belching clouds of grimy black coal dust.

In June, an entire glossy page of the school yearbook was devoted to "Demon Smoke" by Thomas Williams, ninth grade. The process of coking the coal used in factories had made smoke a serious problem in St. Louis, where some mornings the smog was a pea-soup green, so thick that it was impossible to see across the street and barely possible to drive a car. Tom's socially conscious poem ended:

> *For law alone and legislation*
> *Can banish from the air,*
> *Can make this Demon captive, and*
> *Consume him in his lair.*

At the end of the 1925 spring term, it was clear that something had to be done about Rose. Since Hosmer Hall was not bringing about the changes in her behavior that Edwina and Grand were hoping for, a decision was made that would further separate Tom from his sister. In September, Rose would be sent away to school, far away south to Vicksburg, Mississippi, and far away from the corrupting influences of a northern city. She would be enrolled in the fall at All Saints' College, an Episcopal diocesan school for girls. The school's yearbooks indicate that the requirements there were considerably lower than what Rose was used to, with emphasis on the arts, languages, Bible study, deportment, and (unfortunately for Rose) music. Classes were small, some frankly labeled "nonacademic," and students came almost entirely from the South. The school itself was geographically isolated, as Rose would be, too.

Of course, it was this remoteness and the fact that Vicksburg was still a part of the South with which Edwina was familiar that influenced the decision. Edwina could no longer cope with her daughter's rebellious and erratic conduct, and a school for young southern ladies seemed a sure solution. She kept saying that there was something wrong with the girl, and a school like the ones she herself had attended could straighten Rose out before she got into trouble with some boy. Cornelius agreed, if only because it would cost less to board and clothe her in Vicksburg than it would to indulge her wants at home. Also, her grandfather, who had once been offered the post of dean of faculty at All Saints, had secured a scholarship for her.

The more Rose reacted to her mother's prudish demands, the more Edwina tended to discipline her and force on her behavior Edwina thought was correct conduct for a girl of southern breeding. This, to Rose, was old-fashioned, and it *was*, for the customs and manners of Edwina's day were becoming anachronistic in the radically changing times of the twenties. Modern girls, Rose's girlfriends, were emulating their modern mothers: raising hemlines above the knees, making up with lipstick and mascara, bobbing their hair, smoking in one another's company, dancing fox-trots, and necking with their boyfriends. It was "flaming youth" and vo-de-o-do, and Edwina would have none of it.

By 1925, well into her lifelong role as a symbol of southern womanhood,

General John "Nolichucky Jack"
Sevier, the first governor of Tennessee,
an ancestor

The poet Sidney Lanier,
"America's Sweet Singer of Songs,"
an ancestor

Thomas Lanier Williams II, Tom's
grandfather and namesake

Isabella Coffin Williams,
Tom's grandmother

5

6

Tom's beloved "Grand,"
Rosina Otte Dakin

Dr. Walter Edwin Dakin,
an Episcopal minister, Tom's
grandfather

7

St. Paul's rectory in Columbus, Mississippi, Tom's first home

Mr. Robert Barclay Poague.

JUNIOR PROMENADE

JUNE 4th, 1902.

ADMIT ONE

Mr. H. Rowan Gaither

Richard L. Lodge

K. K. K. K.

Edwinna Dakin

YOU WILL BE CALLED FOR DANCE

NO. *2 - 3*

Mr. Harry Marks.

8

Edwina Estelle Dakin, the social butterfly, just prior to her marriage

9

Cornelius Coffin Williams, Tom's father

10

Thomas Lanier Williams III

Edwina with Tom and his sister, Rose Isabel

BELOW LEFT: "The couple," with their story-telling nurse, Ozzie

BELOW: Rose Isabel

Rose, age 7

Tom, age 5

The happiest years of their childhood were spent in Clarksdale living
with their grandparents in St. George's rectory.

Union Station in St. Louis

LEFT: Edwina with her youngest son, Dakin

BELOW: Tom, as "our literary boy" in Ben Blewett Jr. High School

Tom and Hazel Kramer with Edwina, c. 1923

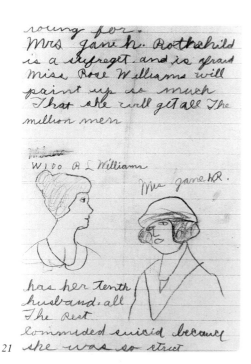

Nine-year-old Tom made Rose
the main character in a comic paper
he produced for her.

Tom at Italy's tomb of the Unknown
Soldier, summer 1928

23

Rose Williams in 1927 at the time of
her failed debut

24

Aunt Ella Williams

Tom and Hazel Kramer's high school
graduation photos

25

26

Miss Edwina had made up her mind that any daughter of hers was going to get a proper education, grow up a proper young lady, and make a proper marriage—not make the mistake she had! But, logically, Rose was just as determined to be a part of her own generation as, illogically, her mother expected Rose to be a part of *hers*. For one thing, it distressed Edwina that Rose was becoming boy crazy, and if this would suddenly bring up a reminder of her own girlhood, she could tell herself, Well, that was different; *that* was a time of graciousness and beauty—and morals. Not like *now*!

In many ways Edwina was right: It *was* different; the times and customs had all changed, and not, in her view, for the better. When she was a girl, she argued, there were no aeroplanes, auto*mo*biles, speakeasies, dance halls, and, above all, no loose behavior—except perhaps in cities like C.C.'s Knoxville or among "colored folk." While Tom's life was miserable enough in St. Louis, Edwina truly suffered the change; since she was an adult, there was so much more that she could remember wistfully and with longing, so much that was irretrievably gone and that had no reality except in memory. And not only memory isolated her—she also suffered a marriage made in hell and a husband to whom she could give every dutiful attention except love.

To make matters worse, her health was deteriorating. Despite the employment of a domestic, Edwina insisted on doing much of the work herself, the way she felt it should be done, and it made her ill. Above all, there was the aggravation that Rose was causing, their constant quarreling, and this, too, affected her. It would not be until September that Rose would be leaving for Vicksburg, and in the meantime, the two were constantly at odds.

Colds and flu had gone the rounds, and with the arrival of summer, everyone was just plain exhausted and ready for a vacation. Cornelius rented a house for the month of August at Elkmont, a resort in the Great Smoky Mountains, southeast of Knoxville. En route, he stopped to visit with his sisters. This had become a kind of ritual, one that Edwina did not especially relish because of Aunt Belle. Isabel Brownlow was prominent in Knoxville society because of her prestigious marriage and her church activities. Tom saw her as a formidable beauty, "probably the one woman in the world [by] whom my mother was intimidated." He likened these visits to "priestly tributes to a seat of holiness, for though my mother would certainly never make verbal acknowledgement of my aunt's superiority in matters of taste and definitions of quality, it was nevertheless apparent that she approached Knoxville and my father's younger sister in something very close to fear and trembling."[6] It was said that Isabel had virtually taken over the Knoxville Presbyterian Church and had had the minister fired because he was short on "fundamentals." Cornelius's cousin Margaret Brownlow remembered Isabel as "a very beautiful person, she had a great personality and a great many friends, but she was inclined to be a little over the edge religiously."

At the same time, Mrs. Brownlow's memory of Edwina was that she was rather austere: "She was always nagging at the children. In fact, the first time

I ever saw them, she kept fussing over Rose and Tom. She dressed them beautifully, I have to say that. But Edwina never lifted a finger to do something for herself. She wanted to be waited on. I don't know whether she was a sickly person or whether she just liked to think she was. She was a *star*; she thought there was nobody as good as she was, unless it was the Brownlows—she was perfectly willing to concede that we might be on the same level, but aside from that, nobody was as good as she was. I could never understand how Cornelius and Edwina ever got together."[7]

At Elkmont, the Brownlows belonged to the Appalachian Club, and there Tom learned to swim. "It was Aunt Belle who taught me, in the pool of fabulously cool, clear water formed by the dam, which offered a sparkling waterfall over bone-white rocks. Aunt Belle tried to support me with a hand under my belly in the pool, and when I said to her, 'Aunt Belle, I'd rather depend on myself,' she came out with this choice endorsement: 'Oh, Tom, dear Tom, when you depend on yourself you're depending on a broken reed.' Actually she was speaking of herself and her dependence on God."

Then, and for many years to come, Tennessee Williams was no less a dependent and as much a "true believer," though not as openly as Aunt Belle, nor as churchgoing as his mother. If pressed, Williams would unabashedly admit to belief in the existence of God and to the efficacy of prayer. He was quick, however, to disavow the claim laid upon God and His Son by multifarious church groups. But he admitted, "I am as much of an hysteric as Aunt Belle, you know. . . ."*[8]

"Deception, Deception, Deception"

For Edwina, the summer of 1925 was one unending torment. She was more seriously ill than even she realized, and as a result just about everything upset and annoyed her, especially Rose, who was at her most rebellious. Tom simply went along with his sister's various undercover schemes to have things her way. He didn't intend to deceive his mother—he just liked being with Rose and her friends and joining in their mischief.

Tennessee Williams's dimly diffused memories of that "wild jazz age summer" were variously of Dakin's (or "Dinky," as Tom called him) contracting "a serious distemper" and of Grand's making buttermilk in a churn, since that was all his brother could digest. He also remembered his pride in his first long pants and Rose's vanity in summer dresses bought for her by Aunt Belle. He said that his sister had boyfriends and that they danced the Charleston, and that he had become aware once again of something within him as magnetic in its pull as it was mysterious.

---

*When an irate Cornelius Williams read "The Resemblance Between a Violin Case and a Coffin" upon its publication in 1950, he called his son's agent, Audrey Wood, with the demand, "Tell Tom to keep my family out of his stories!"

"The Appalachian Club was full that summer of boys that I couldn't keep my eyes off, as they lay sunning themselves on the rocks in the stream," he remembered.[9] Williams recalled an afternoon when he and Rose, accompanied by two of her girlfriends and two adolescent youths, went hiking to nearby Gatlinburg. "On the way there was a great thundershower and it drenched us. The girls retired to change in one place and I went with the boys." And the boys, whom he described as devoted to one another, "stripped naked in front of me and I stayed in my wet clothes until they undressed me. Nothing happened of a scandalous nature, but their beauty is indelible in my prurient mind, and also their kindness to me."[10]

That was how Tennessee remembered what had happened to Tom, but in the fragment of a letter, written by an unknown correspondent to a Knoxville girlfriend, Margaret Tappan Thomas, a different account emerged:

> There is an adorable girl from St. Louis here. Rose Williams is her name. Ever since I arrived I have aided and abetted her in deceiving her mother! Isn't that wicked? But really we shouldn't be blamed; "No" is the principal word in Mrs. Williams' vocabulary. No matter what Rose asks to do—her Mother says no. Then Rose proceeds to do it and while she is busily engaged in disobeying her mother, her Grandmother soothes Mrs. Williams' wrath enough to make it safe for Rose to go home.
>
> One of Mrs. Williams' strictest rules is that Rose shall never spend the night anywhere except at home. So of course Rose has a perfect passion for spending the night out. Another aid to our deception is Tom, Rose's fourteen year old brother, who is her constant companion, as well as our colleague.

One morning, Rose's friend suggested they walk to Gatlinburg, seven miles away; as she explained, "even the most ambitious don't try it without horses. . . . Mrs. Williams was at a bridge party next door. Rose rushed over and asked her mother if she could—Her mother answered stormily, No! We couldn't bear missing a chance to deceive Mrs. Williams. So, taking the patient Tom, the long-suffering Arthur Tripp, two packages of chewing gum and several chocolate bars, we set out on the long dusty road to Gatlinburg afoot." When they finally got there, she said, "We defiantly mailed a postcard to Mrs. Williams, so it would be postmarked 'Gatlinburg'! There being no sights to see we immediately resumed the road. After three miles and being caught in a healthy young thunderstorm we got a pickup and rode home on a running board."[11]

The trip to Gatlinburg was evidently not as romantic as Tennessee remembered it; "the two adolescent youths, devoted to each other" were not two but, in fact, one of two brothers—the "long-suffering Arthur Tripp," who was enamored of Rose. Tennessee's memory of that summer made no reference to his mother's distress, nor to Rose's deceptions, nor to his role as accomplice. Clearly the distance of time had abstracted what was documented in the letter. Tom Williams was beginning to experience life through the eyes of a writer, transmuting memories into art. There would be other summers seen through the prism of memory, hazily golden and drifting timelessly, stilled and faded in his mind like old photographs.

Hazel

Walter Dakin arrived in Elkmont none too soon, with the intention that he and Grand would escort Rose to All Saints' College in Vicksburg. Edwina's patience with Rose was at an end. Her health had worsened, and the summer at Elkmont had done nothing to repair it. Walter had taken leave from Saint George's in Clarksdale for a year and would go on south from Vicksburg with his wife to Bay St. Louis on the Gulf to assume the pulpit of Christ Church. Many tears were shed at Rose's departure, but those that were most heartfelt were Tom's. Now he could no longer be her constant companion, as he had been all summer, and he would miss her very much. But there was someone else at home in St. Louis he could turn to.

Hazel Kramer was twelve and Tom was fourteen, and it followed that they would put aside their playthings and become involved in such grown-up pursuits as dating and dancing and going to the movies together. Tom was struck by Hazel's red hair and extraordinarily beautiful legs, and he noticed that her breasts were well developed for her age. Tennessee Williams was to write, "I suppose that I can honestly say, despite the homosexual loves which began years later, that she was the great extra-familial love of my life."[12]

Edwina, however, increasingly disapproved of Hazel, and, not recognizing it as jealousy, she fastened her objections on Hazel's mother, Miss Florence, an exuberant personality, loud of manner and dress, in keeping with the fashion of the twenties. Tom was very much taken with Miss Florence and described her as a sort of antic butterball. He believed that she loved him as a son and said she talked to him as an adult about her unhappy life with her tyrannical parents. But Esmeralda Mayes, Hazel's best friend, saw another side of Miss Florence, that of an intensely possessive mother whose nest was constructed of barbed wire: "Miss Florence drew Hazel's bath and put the toothpaste on her toothbrush—and in the morning the milk and sugar were already on her cereal—and Miss Florence would say, 'That's the least I can do to help Hazel!' "[13]

Hazel lived in a large, dark house with her mother and grandparents, a small couple who paid little or no attention to any of their granddaughter's friends. On one occasion, when she was recovering from an illness, Esmeralda was standing in the entry hall waiting for Hazel: "Old Mrs. Kramer came down and saw me. I said, 'Hello, Mrs. Kramer,' and she said icily, 'Oh, hello, dear! It is so nice to see you. You know, we never thought you would live!' "[14] Mrs. Kramer owned the family's "electric" automobile, and Tennessee's recollection was that "the pretentious old lady loved to sit in its square glass box tooling sedately among the more fashionable residential sections of the city."[15]

Hazel was not overly fond of her grandfather, and she remarked many times that she would never marry a German. Emil Kramer had been successful in real estate and subsequently assumed a managerial position at the International Shoe Company. Although Edwina was to say that Cornelius had a higher status in the company, Esmeralda remembered it as just the opposite; she also said that the Kramers enjoyed a social standing in St. Louis superior to the Williamses'.

Esmeralda said, "Hazel's parents were divorced when she was about six weeks old. Her name was actually White. She never knew her father. Her mother took back her maiden name, and for legal reasons Hazel's grandfather adopted her, and so she was legally her mother's sister!" Miss Florence declared she would rather be a divorcée than an old maid, but it was an outward manner, thinly disguising her disappointment in love. She had been hastily courted and as summarily dropped after her marriage to a socially prominent ne'er-do-well. Emil and Emma Kramer soon made it known that they were not about to support their daughter's husband in the fashion to which he was accustomed, and he departed unceremoniously.

Miss Florence was an unhappy woman who had fastened her thwarted love on her daughter, but this was belied by an air that fascinated Tom: "a great animation and gusto of manner when she was out. She played the piano by ear with great skill and considerable volume, and she had an excellent and lusty singing voice. Whenever she entered our apartment, she would seat herself at our upright piano and go into some popular song-hit of the day which was naturally quite unpopular with Miss Edwina."[16]

Although Hazel was always very proper and constrained in her behavior when in Tom's company, particularly compared with her fun-loving mother, Williams recalled that "it was at puberty that I first knew that I had a sexual desire for Hazel and it was in The West End Lyric, a movie house on Delmar Blvd. Sitting beside her before the movie began, I was suddenly conscious of her bare shoulders and I wanted to touch them and I felt a genital stirring."[17] While Tom undoubtedly missed his sister, having a girlfriend, and the status it was giving him as a young man, filled the vacuum Rose left.

Tom now was trying to write poetry in earnest, which did little to improve relations with his father. He was published again in the November 25 issue of *Junior Life*—a poem entitled "Nature's Thanksgiving," about the sadness of the waning year. His last poem, written while he was still at Blewett, had been published in the January 22, 1926, issue of *Junior Life* and was called "Old Things." More lyrical than the others, it concerned an old man alone "in the silence of the garret, midst things long ago," and it showed a gift for both poetic language and dramatic imagery, two distinct talents Tom would try to fuse when he began to write plays.

His grades during his final year at Blewett were what one might expect from a budding writer, marks of 80 to 84 out of 100 during the two terms of English I. The surprises in his transcript were 82 to 95 in Latin II and 85 to 90 in civics and economic vocations. To no one's surprise, first-year marks in algebra averaged 65 to 67. But perhaps his greatest triumph as he left Blewett was his characterization among thirty-six graduating classmates in the Woodrow Wilson group as "Tom Williams—Our literary boy."

By the end of 1925, Edwina's health had become so precarious that the family had grown alarmed. She hadn't said anything but admitted later that "before we left for Elkmont, I fainted one day trying to get lunch."[18] With the approach of the holidays, in order to avoid any more of the stress that Edwina had been under during the summer in Elkmont, it was decided that Rose would join her grandparents in Bay St. Louis on the Gulf and not go home. It was also decided that she would not be told of her mother's illness.

Tom was no problem. He had his writing, and he had Hazel. And their close companionship was ripening, as he was to say, into "that full emotional dependence which is popularly known as love."[19]

Poor Butterfly

At the beginning of 1926, Tom was enrolled for one term at Soldan High School before going on in September to University City High School. For Edwina, this was to be a year marked mainly by severe illness. "I was ill during most of Tom's high school days, first undergoing five minor operations and then a major one," she wrote. "I lingered between life and death for five days."[20] It was not until after the holidays that her illness required hospitalization and a difficult hysterectomy was performed.

Rose was in Bay St. Louis for Christmas with her grandparents, and when the Dakins learned of Edwina's condition, they went over to New Orleans. On the pretext of wanting to spend part of the holidays with her other grandchildren, Grand suddenly departed for St. Louis, leaving Rose and her grandfather to enjoy a brief stay in New Orleans, where Walter had many friends.

Rose, unaware of her mother's ailment, wrote home on January 4:

> Dear Family,
> Here I am on my way back to school. I had to leave on Sunday and we couldn't make train connections so Grand Fads and I are spending the night at Hotel Monteleone, which is large and beautiful. I certainly have had a fine Christmas and am going to work even harder when I get back to school. . . . Grand & Grand Father have been wonderful to me. Grand got me a beautiful henna satin in New Orleans with a flaring skirt. . . . New Orleans is great—sure wish Tom was here to see it with me.

She also mentioned that examinations would commence in two weeks— "Pray for me."[21]

Subsequently, Tom wrote his grandfather, "As Grand has informed you, Mother got through her very serious operation quite well according to the reports we have received. We haven't seen her yet. The doctor said it would be dangerous for us to visit her as she had to keep absolutely quiet. We feel, now that she has survived the operation and these first two days, she will surely get through allright. The morning of the operation was certainly an anxious one for us. We waited two hours while she was on the operating table."[22]

After Rose had returned to school, she wrote again to "Dear Family." She told about having had "the grandest time" when "six boys from C.H.A. [Chamberlain Hunt Academy, a military school] Port Gibson got on the train. . . . I got a letter from one of them yesterday." After expressing her hope of being able to spend Easter in Baton Rouge, she appended, "Tom, you ought to write me oftener. I haven't heard from any of you since the last time Daddy wrote and sent my checque."[23]

In another message, this time to "Dear Mother & Dad," she enclosed a letter she had received from the boy from CHA, Dan H. Buie.

> My dear Rose, I know that you will be some what surprised to hear from me for I bet you thought I was lying and fooling the other day, on the train when I got your address. Well you see I was not. I really ment that I wanted to correspond with you for you impressed me very much. I would like the best in the world to see you again and know more of you. Guess that would be impossible as long as you are in school, or rather in prison. . . . Hopping that I may hear from you real soon.[24]

Cadet Buie must also have heard from Miss Rose, since she told her parents that he was writing to her once a week and is "so nice." It was not likely Edwina would have said anything to C.C., but her memory of Rowland P. Balph of Kenyon Military Academy, "the dearest boy at K.M.A.," could hardly have escaped her, nor the realization that even as remote as Vicksburg was, the girls' main preoccupation would be with boys.

Dan Buie could not have known how right he was in his characterization of Rose, immured as she was at All Saints'. Isolated on its hilltop, the school in those days could only have seemed like a prison, with its bleak dormitory rooms furnished with iron cots. Vicksburg was a long way from Dan in Port Gibson, and Rose would have little opportunity to see her "nice" cadet again. Instead, she was surrounded by a chattering bevy of girls, girls, girls and a hard-of-hearing principal, Miss Newton, who disciplined her when she did not speak up loudly enough. Then there were her teachers, all women, and no gentlemen callers.

On January 23, still unaware of Edwina's illness, she wrote to her mother that she was petrified at the coming examinations. She said reassuringly that she had had her Bible exam and "know that I passed with a good grade." The fact that her grades proved uniformly high says more about the school than about her ability. The limited faculty, tiny classes, and subjects taken indicate easy standards. Rose was graded in English, French, history, piano, and even Sunday school, deportment, and neatness. The yearbook, *The Angel's Record*, shows few and pious activities: altar guild and glee club. In the glee club picture, Rose sits with folded hands, a faraway, almost pained look in her eyes.

Clothes would prove a lifelong enthusiasm, and in making plans for her Easter vacation, she asked her mother, "Please help Daddy select a nice pair of kid or calf skin pumps for me. Not heavy ones like I got last summer." She mentioned that Dan Buie was going to meet her train on her way to Baton Rouge for her vacation: "He certainly is nice." Another news item was included that could hardly have delighted Edwina: Her daughter said there was a lot of excitement on the third floor when "two large rats jumped out of one of the girls hat boxes."

Despite the cheerful tone of her letters, there were signs that Rose was beginning to feel bored and restive; she complained that everything was dull and sleepier than ever in Vicksburg and that she was not getting along with some of her teachers. She described one as "a regular pill," who had the face of a horse, who shimmied when she went from room to room and thought she ran the school. "I detest her thoroughly." She had seen Harold Lloyd in *The Freshman* and commented that it certainly was funny. She said that she needed something to cheer her up, that she got quite blue at times.

At length, when the family felt Edwina was sufficiently recovered, Rose was told that Edwina had been ill but not how seriously. In a letter to her mother in February, she wrote, "Certainly was sorry to hear about your being sick and am glad that you are able to be up again. The weeks seem to drag by here, it seems as if we are cogs in a big machine doing the same things at the same times and knowing what we are going to have each day before we come to the table."[25]

During the spring of 1926, she wrote many letters home, and while they were often determinedly cheerful, they also contained a number of complaints about school restrictions, sparse diet, and her lack of money. But Rose's main difficulty stemmed from her being forced to take music lessons, which triggered a serious nervous reaction and sent her to the infirmary. As she wrote in a desperate letter to Grand:

> I don't know what was the matter with me except that I was so nervous that I couldn't hold the glass to take my medicine in. I stayed in bed all day long and had a big dose of calomel and I feel better but still weak. I had just finished a music lesson, and Miss Butell nearly drove me wild. I simply can't stand to take another lesson from her or anyone else. It makes me as nervous as a cat. . . . I suppose you have paid for my music by the term but perhaps if you write Miss Newton she would refund half the money and I could have peace again. I can't do a thing any more and it is

making me lose time that I could put on my history and French. *Please*
please do let me drop it. I will practice on Saturday mornings if you wish.

Rose concluded her letter by saying that her mother's friends, the Joneses,
had invited her to visit them at Port Gibson after Easter. "Of course I accepted with great glee. They are so sweet and I hope will like me. They said I
looked and talked like Mother." Then, as reassurance, she added, "Tell
Mother that she can be sure I'll 'conduct myself properly' and be a 'Lady' as
far as I am able. . . ."[26]

For once, she could say that she had had "a marvelous time" at the Joneses'
and she wrote to tell her grandfather in Baton Rouge: "Every one was so nice
to me and I am happy to say I believe everyone liked me. I never had such a
good time before. I met so many nice boys and had a date Friday night with
Ed Stokes who goes to Tulane Univ New Orleans. He was home for the holidays and was dreadfully popular so I was pleased as punch when he asked me
for a date. I like him better than any other boy I ever met but he is so popular
that I suppose he has forgotten me already."[27] So much for Dan Buie.

With Edwina ill, Cornelius in his way was attempting to live up to the role
of dutiful parent. He doled out the money that Rose asked for; he also wrote
letters to her and sent her slippers. Shoe *samples*, sniffed Edwina. But Rose was
nonetheless grateful for any gesture he might make. "Dear Daddy," she
wrote, "The slippers are beautiful and that color of tan or creme is all the
rage. I had been admiring some down town just like them and was so surprised
and pleased to get them. They fit perfectly and I like the heels so well they
make me look an inch taller and I am still next to the smallest [girl here] which
nearly kills me since I always wanted to be tall and imposing."[28]

Rose was growing up petite like her mother, but unlike Edwina as a school-
girl, she was neither as vivacious nor as self-confident. Her gaiety was often
compounded of affectation and sometimes outright desperation. The fact was
that she only "looked and talked" like her mother and, unlike Edwina at her
age, was in desperate need of love and approbation.

Tragically and beyond Rose's comprehension, her father was one among
that species of American male who cannot appreciate women, however much
he may be attracted to them physically. Cornelius's was not a misogynous
attitude or habitual brutality; it was simply an insensitive response to a
woman's needs. If ever he had been able to reach Edwina with tenderness,
they might have had an amicable marriage and given Rose the parental love
she craved—and Tom needed.

It was Dakin, now a seven-year-old, to whom Cornelius could honestly
relate. He had long accepted Dakin as *his* son, but he looked upon Tom with a
mixture of disgust and disbelief as a mother's boy. C.C. believed in hard work,
the sports page, and military discipline and blamed Edwina for ruining Tom,
failing to understand that she was taking refuge from her husband in a deepening dependence on her "writin' son." Because Dakin was born in St. Louis

and was so much younger than his brother and sister, he had not experienced their shock when they moved from the security of their grandparents' home and saw their mother and father constantly quarreling. "I never knew anything *except* turmoil," Dakin remarked later. But he was growing tall and beginning to look like his father, and they got along well together. "Dad took me to ball games," he said, and as he grew older, he sat by his father's side and "listened for hours to the games on radio."[29] Occasionally, C.C. even let him watch as he played poker.

If Tom resented this, he didn't show it. Aside from teasing Dinky, Tom exhibited real and open affection for his brother. He felt that he hated his father, and so he could hardly have envied a love he believed he didn't want. It would take years for a depth of feeling for his father to surface and for a sibling rivalry to emerge. At this point, however, the last thing Tom wanted was what his father wanted. They had virtually nothing in common and nothing to say to each other that wasn't strained and artificial. But Tom was no longer isolated in his family as he had been, for now he had friends. There was Hazel and, above all, there was his writing. He could feel that he was moving in the right direction.

Rose, however, was stalemated, her life at a standstill. She was mainly interested in keeping up with the times; pretty clothes and being thought of as beautiful were her preoccupations. In a letter to her brother, she wrote, "Here I sit in agony my face covered with green beauty clay and I don't dare even smile. I don't need to tell you how striking the effect is. I think its lovely of you to write to me so often even though I don't answer them as often as I should. You know stamps amount up and I am so busy."[30] On the letter, Rose drew in colors a typical flapper: rolled hose, short skirt well above the knees, low sash, Cupid's bow mouth, tousled red hair. Captioned "Hazel E. Krammer" [sic], it was everything that Edwina feared and Rose longed to be.

Even as far away as Vicksburg, and certainly in Baton Rouge and New Orleans, the Jazz Age was in full flower. The question was, How far could a "good" girl go without being labeled "fast"? On all sides, she was surrounded by a world of "jazz, gin, prohibition, one piece bathing suits and the Charleston. Texas Guinan, F. Scott Fitzgerald, Rudolph Valentino, were the headliners in the newspapers. *Jada, How Dry I Am, We Won't Be Home Until Morning* were the songs which came through the earphones of their crystal sets."[31]

Prior to the time she left for All Saints', Rose and Tom loved to play the Victrola and dance, and she taught him all the new steps. Dancing together helped to dispel their shyness in the company of others. One song in particular struck Tom, and it stayed with him all his life. Friends recalled that suddenly, for no apparent reason, he would burst out with what he called his theme song, "Five-foot two, eyes of blue, has anybody seen my gal . . ." accompanied by fitting dance steps. Miss Edwina in her girlhood may have been a social butterfly but the events of the next year and the years to come would make Rose's song, appropriately, "Poor Butterfly."

5

University City

1926–1929

In June of 1926, after Tom had completed his one semester at Soldan High, the family moved to an apartment at 6554 Enright Avenue in University City, just over the city line from St. Louis. The move was made so that Tom could enter University City High School, and for Edwina, it was one more westward step. As it turned out, though, they were to remain in this dismal, over-crowded flat for nearly ten years.

Although it would prove an unhappy move in the life of Tom Williams, it would become the most important event in the career of Tennessee Williams. An ugly city apartment building of mustard-colored brick, since demolished, it became the "tenement" of *The Glass Menagerie* and the background for several fragments entitled "Apt. F, 3rd Flo. So.," "Carolers! Our Candle!" "If You Breathe, It Breaks" (subtitled "Portrait of a Girl in Glass"), "A Dramatic Portrait of an American Mother," and, finally, the setting of the first drafts of *Menagerie*, initially called *The Gentleman Caller*.

It was in this depressing apartment, located on the corner of Delmar, a busy street across from the Tivoli Theatre, that Tom could hear the alley sounds, mixed with streetcars clanging and strains from a nearby ballroom. An open alleyway ran alongside the building, but it was not a cul-de-sac where dogs could corner and slaughter cats, as Tennessee later claimed. Westminster Place, the family's first residence with its dark rooms, impressed itself on the seven-year-old mind of Tom, but it would be the hard experiences of life in the congested Enright complex from now through the Depression years that would be reflected in *The Glass Menagerie*.

Once again, the family spent its summer vacation in Elkmont, Tennessee, but on this occasion Edwina was still convalescing, and it would appear that Rose and Tom were more considerate of her nerves, even if that meant the constraint of unreasonable obedience. Miss Newton, the principal of All Saints' College, wrote to Rose in mid-July, sending "My dear love to your mother; I am so glad she seems to be better in the good mountain air. It sounds quite ideal there with you all together, and with horseback riding and swimming and everything else that fits a summer vacation."[1] She assured Rose she could have the roommate of her choice, and with the opening of school in September, Rose returned to Vicksburg for a final year.

Tom had transferred in midterm to University City High School, and it was there that he developed the habit of blushing whenever anyone looked him in the eyes, as though he was harboring some abominable secret. He said later, "My adolescent problems took their most violent form in a shyness of a pathological degree."[2] He was often rendered tongue-tied and practically immobilized by any direct confrontation, whether it was an encounter with one of his schoolmates or his teacher asking him to read in front of the class.

His English instructor, Margaret Cowan, recalled, "Tommy Williams was not socially inclined toward the group, he had too many thoughts of his own. His grades were average. There was no evidence of brilliance in his work. I fear he was not well adjusted. In the period I knew him he never was clear about tomorrow's lesson. Tommy belonged to another world."[3]

Indeed, it was a secret world, a bastion, his salvation, as he saw it, but it was also what set him apart, made him different, an oddity among his peers. The feelings of wonder, resentment, and guilt that he was trying to articulate could only be put in writing, but even then he was hampered by much that he did not understand about himself. It made him painfully self-conscious—and it made him blush.

"This blushing made me avoid the eyes of my dear friend Hazel," Williams declared. He said it happened "quite abruptly and both Hazel and her mother, Miss Florence, must have been shocked and puzzled by this new peculiarity of mine. Yet neither of them permitted me to observe their puzzlement. Once Hazel said to me on a crowded streetcar, after a little period of tense silence on my part, 'Tom, don't you know I'd never say anything to hurt you?' This was, indeed, the truth: Hazel never, never said a word to hurt me during the eleven years of our close companionship."[4]

With the new year of 1927, Tom was endeavoring to keep his attention on his schoolwork, but more and more his energies were being diverted to his writing. To be published meant recognition of his talent, and to be *paid* meant vindication in his father's eyes. Not only did he continue to write stories and poems in the hope of breaking into magazine markets but he also continued to enter competitions and ad contests.

In the spring, he received a third prize of five dollars in a *Smart Set* magazine contest for writing a letter, in the person of the divorced husband of a faithless wife, in answer to the question "Can a Good Wife Be a Good Sport?" His reply was a decided no!

It began:

Can a woman after marriage maintain the same attitude towards other men as she held before marriage? Can she drink, smoke, and pet with them? Can she do those things which are necessary to good sportsmanship, as the term generally applied to a girl? Those are questions of really great pertinence to modern married life.

In recounting my own unhappy marital experiences, perhaps I can present convincing answers.

One can imagine Cornelius's reaction to finding a marriage expert under his roof. Rose's response, however, was ecstatic: "Tom you are a wonder—simply wonderful and I'm proud to death of you."[5] Grandfather Dakin had his reservations: "I was proud of you gaining the 3rd prize (what *was* it?) in the 'Smart Set' but didn't admire the subject or the magazine which published it. *You* can beat that. Do you read biography and history any? *I* ruined my mind and memory by reading too much *trash*. My father and mother were too busy to oversee my reading and I have suffered all my days on account of it." Then he advised, "*If* you continue to write to such magazines use a nom-de-plume instead of your own name."[6]

This, Tom's first nationally published work, appeared in the May issue, among other "true confessions" such as "Hunted Lovers," described as a "Self-Told Romance of the Wild North," and "Forgive Me My Trespasses," the "Life Story of a Girl with a Siren Heart." Among twelve contestants, Tom was the only male. The editor commented, "Thomas Lanier Williams, of St. Louis, Mo., gave a rather dreary picture of the man's side of the problem. . . ."

Apparently, Tom's letter was convincing enough to persuade the editor that Mr. Williams's was a voice of experience. Edwina said, "Shortly after Tom received the prize, I noticed he kept coming into the house through the back door instead of the front as he usually did, looking anxiously into the living room before he would enter. I am sure he feared the magazine would send someone to the house to check up and discover this supposedly sophisticated divorced prizewinner was sixteen and had never even proposed to a woman."[7] *Smart Set*, after all, *was* subtitled "True Stories from Real Life."

Tom's next venture was into sheer melodrama: a short story, "The Vengeance of Nitocris," based on a section from the ancient histories of Herodotus. It told how Nitocris, an Egyptian queen, avenged her brother's murder by building along the banks of the Nile a vast underground chamber with sluice gates that, when opened, would drown his assassins. Inviting her disloyal subjects to a banquet, she leaves them to carouse, opens the gates, and seals them in a watery tomb. Realizing that she will be destroyed once it is discovered what she has done, "she resolved to meet her death in a way that befitted one of her rank."

Therefore upon her entrance into the palace she ordered her slaves to fill instantly her boudoir with hot and smoking ashes. When this had been done, she went to the room, entered it, closed the door and locked it securely, and then flung herself down upon a couch in the center of the room. In a short time the scorching heat and the suffocating thick fumes

of the smoke overpowered her. Only her beautiful dead body remained
for the hands of the mob.[8]

Although "The Vengeance of Nitocris" was accepted for publication in
Weird Tales, a pulp magazine devoted to the "Bizarre and Unusual," it would
not appear until a year later, in August 1928, at which time Tom was due to
receive the munificent sum of thirty-five dollars. Cornelius could not have
been other than impressed, if only because *Weird Tales* was a man's magazine—and because of the thirty-five dollars.

One thing that did *not* impress Cornelius was Tom's growing affection for
Hazel, an attachment he resented. Though at first he did not give voice to his
disapproval, for once he shared an opinion with Edwina, that a girl with a
flashy, eccentric divorcée for a mother was not good enough for a son of the
Williams family. According to Esmeralda Mayes, old Mr. Kramer, who was
listed in the St. Louis Blue Book among "the most prominent citizens," held
quite the opposite view: that Tom Williams was unworthy of his granddaughter.

Esme, as she was commonly called, remembered Cornelius at that time,
and said, "Tom and Hazel would make fun of him—they'd say Cornelius *Coffin* and then they'd go off into gales of laughter. I remember we were going
someplace, and Mr. Williams was driving, and I sat in the front seat next to
him, and I thought, Gee whiz, this is the horrible ogre they were always talking about, so I was very nice to him, talked to him all the way. He told Tom I
was the only sensible girl he'd ever brought around—that I would be much
better for him than Hazel."[9]

Tom, now in his sixteenth year, and Hazel, in her fourteenth, were extremely close and regularly went out to movies and dances together; it was
clear to everyone that they were going steady. A popular diversion in St. Louis
was to take moonlight excursions upriver to Alton, Illinois. Williams recalled,
"One evening I took Hazel on the river steamer 'J.S.'—and she wore a pale
green chiffon party dress with no sleeves, and we went up on the dark upper
deck and I put my arm about those delicious shoulders and I 'came' in my
white flannels. How embarrassed I was! No mention was made between us of
the telltale wet spot on my pants front but Hazel said, 'Let's stay up here and
walk around the deck, I don't think we ought to dance now. . . .' "[10]

Despite Tom's being published, Cornelius persisted in his belief that his
son was wasting his time and should be thinking of a more practical way of
making a living. He saw the energy that Tom devoted to his writing as unnatural for a boy his age. Even the relationship with Hazel was in Cornelius's
view unmanly, in that they seemed to behave more like girlfriends. Worse,
Tom did not have companions among boys of his own age, nor did he participate in sports. He was forever in the company of women—his mother, Grand,
Rose, Hazel, Miss Florence—and since C.C. was unable to get along with any

of them, save Mrs. Dakin, it was galling that Tom was the favorite, even of Cornelius's sisters in Knoxville.

Furthermore, Tom's way with women was not the cavalier Williams way. It was one thing to be courtly while in hot pursuit of the ladies, in the true southern gentleman's tradition, quite another to be gentle and caring. Tom thoroughly empathized with their feelings, even identified with them; and as a result, Tennessee Williams's work would be characterized by an uncanny understanding and genuine liking of women: Amanda and Laura Wingfield, Blanche DuBois, Alma Winemiller, Serafina Delle Rosa, Maggie Pollitt, Lady Torrance, Baby Doll, Catherine Holly and Violet Venable, Alexandra del Lago, Hannah Jelkes, Flora Goforth, the Woman Downtown, Mrs. Wire, Zelda Fitzgerald.

What perhaps baffled Cornelius still more was that Tom was in no manner an obvious sissy or, God forbid, a "queer." Although he was short and slight like Edwina and Rose, in voice and gait he appeared to be like any other boy his age. He was even able to hide his sensitivity through carefully cultivated masculine attitudes. Outwardly, he passed easily, as he would until success brought him freely to admit his homosexuality. And though Tom Williams may not have gone out for sports, he did have a steady girlfriend and, from the snickering viewpoint of his schoolmates, was probably "getting into her."

Hazel, certainly as much a virgin as Tom, never even permitted him to kiss her on the lips except on Christmas and her birthday. In later years, he speculated that she was perhaps frigid, but in all probability she simply did not feel as he did. His love for her was more adoration, and the shyness Tom felt stemmed instead from some deep fear that he could not identify. He also felt it in the company of other boys and was even more diffident among them, while conversely he was attracted by their howling adolescent antics. But instead of having a best friend, he had Hazel.

From the time he first referred to Tom as a "Miss Nancy," Cornelius was instrumental in creating the very thing in his son that he abhorred and feared most. It was a defense of his own masculinity as he wanted it manifest in his son: a father's self-fulfilling prophecy that became fixed in the child's mind. At the same time, Edwina was reinforcing Cornelius's prediction by pressing her claim upon "my boy" in the form of a love diverted, excessive, covetous. Where fathers have often sought to realize thwarted dreams through their sons' accomplishments, Edwina was now transferring her thwarted energy into Tom's quest of a writing career. It seemed to answer a hidden and vicarious need in her for expression as much as it strengthened her defiance of Cornelius. As a result, Tom became their battleground. Rose was cruelly excluded. And Dakin was Cornelius's only recourse other than the power of money. Muted though it was, the depth of pain Tom was feeling as an adolescent was excruciating, borne down deep within him and only beginning to find expression in his writings.

In a remarkable short story entitled "His Father's House" and signed Thomas Lanier Williams, Tom expressed a clear sensual *interest* in the opposite sex, unable as he was to break through the barriers to a sexual relationship.

> When it was April I met a young girl on the street. It was raining a little but the girl stood in front of a window and seemed not to mind the rain. She was looking at a dress that hung in the window. And all the while that she looked at the dress I looked at her, moving closer to her and feeling something inside of me that I had never felt until then. At last I was so close to her that my arm was against hers. Her arm was soft. I looked at her and thought that her body all over would be soft like her arm, or even softer.
>
> The girl turned toward me and smiled: "I would sure like to have that dress," she said. "I'd do anything for it! I'd even marry a man for a dress like that!"
>
> That evening I stole some money from my uncle's purse. I went to the house of the girl. I told her about this new thing that I felt inside of me and showed her the money I had taken. She counted the money and took half of it for herself. Then she turned on the victrola and said she would teach me to dance. She placed herself against me and told me to move with the music. Holding her in my arms was strange. It was like wanting to eat but having no mouth to put food in.
>
> "Don't you see?" she said, "You go this way, and this way, and this way!" All at once she stopped dancing and pushed me away. "Please go home," she whispered, "I don't want to see you again."
>
> After that I started looking around the city for death. Death is a thing that happens in the dark, I thought. So I became like a cat stealing at night through the city. But death was like everything else that I wanted. It couldn't be found. . . .[11]

Death, the fear of suffocation, and loneliness, the dread claustrophobic feeling of isolation, were beginning to close in on Tom. He wished that he could take flight, that there might be some escape from his sense of being cut off: estranged in Cornelius's hate and smothered in Edwina's love. Rage at his impotence was what he felt toward them, and it was being stored in him as if in some volcanic cauldron, waiting to erupt finally in his writings.

The Girl in Glass

The rage that Rose felt would be more and more turned in on herself. There was no other way for her to express it. In her letters, she generally put on a happy face: It was "dear Daddy" and "dearest Mother" and chitchat meant more to buoy their and her grandparents' spirits than to reflect her own. Underneath their effusiveness, though, her letters betrayed a growing anxiety about whether she was liked and whether she was thought of as pretty. In the 1927 *Angel's Record* yearbook, her portrait no longer shows a sweetly smiling face with flapper bangs: Her face is sober, the expression intense, and her shoulders slightly hunched.

No one was really close to her—except Tom, and then only in their correspondence. She had boyfriends, but none was special or, if he was, lasted for very long. From Port Gibson during her Easter vacation, Rose told her mother, "My beau hasn't arrived yet, he comes in the morning and stays until one o'clock every night. I'm so tired of him I could scream. Otherwise I'm having a good time."[12] After her return to Vicksburg, she wrote Edwina again to say that the aunt of her roommate, Katherine, had invited the two girls to spend a week with her at the close of school. This was to be her second visit with the family, and she said that "they all made such a fuss over me that I really felt like somebody." She added, "I do wish Tom were going to be with me. He would adore riding those horses and I'll bet would get good and fat."[13]

By the time Rose returned to University City, Cornelius and Edwina had decided that this would be her third and last year of high school at All Saints'. The decision was made not only because of the cost of further schooling but also because of the realization on Edwina's part that "for the past few years something unknown and fearful had been taking place in the mind of our spirited, imaginative Rose."[14] Others had failed to take notice—or, if they had, said nothing—but Edwina was the first to recognize Rose's behavior as occasionally abnormal. She was eighteen, and the family felt that a good marriage might be the answer to many problems—hers as well as Edwina's in having her at home—especially since Cornelius was in no way reconciled to the role of loving father. While spending his vacation in Knoxville, Cornelius consulted with his sisters and returned to announce that he, Isabel, and Ella had decided that Rose should make her debut in the fall instead of returning to school.

Although Edwina agreed, she no longer looked favorably on debuts, feeling that "for most girls they are hardly the happy experience you're led to believe in the society columns." Nonetheless, she knew that Cornelius's sisters, who were handling the arrangements, would give Rose the care and attention she longed for. But Rose was headed into "what proved a fiasco from the first, as everything in Rose's life seemed to be."[15] A tornado hit St. Louis at the end of September and killed eighty-seven people; it seemed like an omen. By November, Rose was eagerly assembling a wardrobe, her debut dresses having been bought by Grand and Aunt Belle. Nini, the senior Mrs. Brownlow, Isabel's mother-in-law and a prominent figure in Knoxville society, had made elaborate plans to present Rose at her debut. Then a telegram arrived with the news that Mrs. Brownlow had died suddenly, and that the debut, as a result, would have to be canceled.

Instead of a debut, it was decided Rose would be introduced at a number of small informal parties. Again, she put on a happy face to disguise her disappointment. Aunt Belle wrote to say that she was giving her niece an evening wrap as a birthday present: "Isn't it nice that we are to have you here for your birthday?" Isabel went on to describe the luncheons to be held in her honor, as well as "three big debut balls . . . all 'put' parties so you will be certain to go. Several other people have spoken of entertaining you. Let us know on what train to expect you."[16] During her stay in Knoxville, Rose kept a diary much like her mother's social calendar of card parties, luncheons, dinners, and dances:

> November 18, 1927
> Arrived Thursday evening after a delightful trip, no mishaps. . . . Aunt Belle and Uncle Will met me at the station and we stopped by the shop to see and take auntie [Ella] home to dinner with us. It was my nineteenth birthday dinner and Ida, the cook, had made me a beautiful birthday cake with nineteen candles. Auntie gave me some adorable pink panties and compact, and Aunt Belle a handsome evening coat. Went to bed early.[17]

The Sunday edition of the *Knoxville Journal* ran a large close-up picture of Rose with a somewhat wistful smile, her curly hair neatly bobbed, a little double string of pearls about her neck, and a shoulder corsage. The story predicted that she "will be the recipient of marked social attention." And that she was, almost daily for over a month.

Although Tom thought that there was some one boy in Knoxville with whom Rose had fallen in love and who rejected her, her diary gave no hint. Again, as in her mother's girlhood chronicle, many were mentioned but none at all seriously. A typical reaction to one of her escorts was that he was "a nice fellow who took *good* care of me. I was rather shakey [sic] since it was my first ball and I felt as Cinderella must have!" In entry after entry, she made succinct record of her dates: to a dinner-dance at the country club, she "went with John Lessums," and after that "went to supper and dance 6–8 ATO House with David Merriwether." The next day, it was to Polly Lawford's debut: "Went with Gordon Reid—ball at White Springs." The following Tuesday, it was another debutante's ball: "Went with Ed Thomas." The next night a dinner-dance: "Went with Baxter Ragsdale." December 4: "Sunday School— Presbyterian Church—St. John's. Dinner 1 o'clock—Sigma Nu House— went with Roy Hardison . . . William Chaple called Sun evening." But none seemed seriously interested.

She said that she "went with" others, such as "David McArthur (of varsity football team—1927)" and Alvin Tripp, the brother of her ardent beau Arthur at Elkmont, who escorted her to a fancy dress ball at the Girls Cotillion Club. "I went as a Christmas tree," she wrote, a costume that Edwina described as "a crown of stars on her head and a gown of green tarleton flounces covered with little tinkling glass ornaments, mostly animals."[18] Much of her remaining time in Knoxville was spent Christmas shopping, attending luncheons and dinners, going to movies, and saying her good-byes. Among the gifts and clothing she brought home with her was the costume with its glass trinkets. For Tom, they could only have been reminiscent of the menagerie in Mrs. Wingfield's window, each little animal so delicate, like Rose's hold on sanity would prove to be, that "if you breathe, it breaks."

The Vortex

Both Tom and Rose yearned to move out of the family orbit, he to go off adventuring on his own and she to go on the hand of someone who would take her away. For Tom, 1928 would provide the first of many journeys; for Rose, it was the beginning of a lifelong imprisonment.

On her return to St. Louis, Rose exhibited the first signs of serious depression. She was sullen and withdrawn and would not confide her feelings to anyone, even her brother. He could only suppose the problem was a disappointment in love, that she had become infatuated with someone in Knoxville who had not reciprocated. More likely, it was the fact that, of all the boys she "went with," not one had asked her for a date more than once.

Hazel's friend Esmeralda remembered Rose at the time as "a very, very pretty girl—who giggled a lot and who was so shy with boys she didn't know how to behave in their company."[19] Tom would later recall, "Rose was a popular girl in high school but only for a brief while. Her beauty was mainly in her expressive green-gray eyes and in her curly auburn hair. She was too narrow-shouldered and her state of anxiety when in male company inclined her to hunch them so they looked even narrower; this made her strong-featured, very Williams head seem too large for her thin, small-breasted body. She also, when she was on a date, would talk with an almost hysterical animation which few men knew how to take."[20]

If there was a decisive problem or one fatefully rooted in her personality, Tennessee said that she was never the same after her return from Knoxville. When Tom asked about her visit, she would merely remark, "Aunt Ella and Aunt Belle only like charming people and I'm not charming." He said, "A shadow had fallen over her that was to deepen steadily through the next four or five years."[21]

Soon Rose began experiencing severe stomach pains, and eventually she imagined that someone was trying to poison her. Most of the time, she was moody and spent long hours alone in her room, with its white furniture. Tom was practically her only companion. Esmeralda remembered that he was extremely solicitous of his sister, careful to include her on trips to the movies or Saturday nights at Esme's house, where they would dance or play bridge. In his company, Rose could relax and enjoy herself.

Esme recalled one incident: "We were all sitting around in the living room and then adjourned to the kitchen because we wanted to be by ourselves where we could drink dago red wine. And I told the story about the blue roses.

My father was a surgeon and a colleague was Dr. Gustav Moser, a dentist who had come from Germany and had married a nice German girl named Olga. Dr. Moser had a pronounced German accent and Olga called him 'Sweetie' and my father's nickname was 'Dodie.' One day, my mother got a call from Mrs. Moser and she was crying, 'Oh, Sweetie is so sick, so sick, and it's strange to see him.' Mother asked, 'What's the matter?' and she answered, 'Dodie says he's got blue roses!' My mother said, 'He's got *what*?' 'Blue roses!' My mother called my father, 'Joe, what in the world is wrong with Moser? Olga says he's very, very sick with a strange disease you diagnosed as blue roses.' Daddy went into hysterics, and he said he had told Moser he had pleurosis. Well, we all just roared and made jokes about blue roses."

Of course, Tennessee Williams co-opted it in *The Glass Menagerie*:

JIM *(The Gentleman Caller)*: I remember now. And I used to call you Blue Roses. How did I ever get started calling you a name like that?
LAURA: I was out of school for a little while with pleurosis. When I came back you asked what was the matter. I said I had pleurosis and you thought I said Blue Roses. So that's what you always called me after that!

While it was true that Tom made every effort to include his sister in anything he did socially, he was not always able to be with her, preoccupied as he was with his writing and his last term of high school. In another year, he would be going away to college. Occasionally, Rose would go out with Tom and Hazel to a movie or make dates as part of a short-lived romance, but in the main she was alone and at a loss to know what to do with herself.

Edwina, omitting any reference in her memoir to her own problems with Rose, maintained that it was about this time that the girl began to fight bitterly with Cornelius. There were scenes at the dinner table, from which Rose would flee, crying hysterically. Edwina would come to the girl's defense, and Cornelius would turn on her, ordering her to take Rose and Tom and leave. When on one occasion Edwina asked him why he threatened her constantly, he replied it was because he was unhappy with her. At the suggestion *he* leave *her* if he was so unhappy, Cornelius threw some clothes into a valise and stalked out of the house. At that, Edwina said Rose burst into tears and sobbed, saying, "Mother, he won't ever come back. What will we do?"[22]

Although Tom wished he *would* leave, C.C. always returned to his family. Now it was Tom who more and more wished *he* could leave home, for he, too, was fascinated with long distance, with all those faraway places on the globe that Aunty Ella had given him. And in 1928, his grandfather gave him his wish. A Waynesville, Ohio, newspaper told the story:

FORMER CITIZEN HIGHLY HONORED

Rev. W. E. Dakin, a former Waynesville boy, now rector of St. George's Episcopal church at Clarksdale, Miss., will sail July 6 for Europe, returning early in September. His grandson will accompany him. . . . Mr. Dakin's parishioners are giving them the trip. Celebrating his seventy-first birthday Mrs. Wingfield planned the party and was assisted by other members of the congregation.

As he had been once before, Walter Dakin was again chosen as the nominal leader of a church group, all of whom planned to rendezvous in New York and sail from there on the SS *Homeric*, a ship that had once been the pride of Kaiser Wilhelm's merchant fleet. Rose, happy as she must have been for her brother, could not have helped feeling left out, her only consolation being the presence of Grand during the long, hot St. Louis summer.

On their arrival at Grand Central Station, Tom and his grandfather made straightway for the nearest newsstand. And there it was!

WEIRD TALES

The Unique Magazine
August 1928

THE VENGEANCE OF NITOCRIS

Thomas Lanier Williams page 253
*Weird revenge was taken by
the sister of the Pharaoh on
those who had murdered him—
a true story of old Egypt*

Tom was published, no doubt about that, but he still had not received his thirty-five dollars. His father had given him a hundred dollars, a good deal of money even in the days of "prosperity," especially when given to a seventeen-year-old—and by C. C. Williams at that! It might better have been entrusted to the Reverend Dakin, for Tom was to claim that the money had been stolen by a pickpocket in Paris, at the Eiffel Tower. Benton Addey, a friend from Columbus among the tour group, was quoted as saying, "Tom just about ruined that trip for everybody bitching about that wallet he lost."[23] It would not be the last time that Tennessee Williams reported something stolen that in all likelihood he had lost. The only solace he felt was that he was not just a high school student absorbed among the touring adults but a bona fide published writer, for no doubt Grandfather Dakin made sure that everyone within reach was shown a copy of *Weird Tales*.

For the few days before embarkation, Tom and his grandfather stayed at

the Biltmore, the luxury hotel then located next to Grand Central Station. On
July 2, Tom wrote home:

Dear Mother,
I am dead tired! It is after eleven o'clock and this Biltmore bed looks as
seductive as Paradise to the damned. . . . We have just concluded dinner
with a multi-millionaire, one of Mrs. Watson's partners, in his seven
room suite at the end of the hall. Dinner served in princely style by the
foreign waiter!
    Grandfather is perfectly thrilled. And of course I am! This man is a
partner of *Wrigley*'s. The first thing he did was to offer us some chewing
gum. Tomorrow morning Grandfather and I are to have our breakfasts
served in our room. At noon we meet Mrs. Watson and motor out to her
magnificent country Estate. In the evening we attend a performance of
The Show Boat. . . .
    Also Mrs. Watson has assured Grandfather that if Gov. Al Smith, who
rooms at the Biltmore at present, comes here, she will give Grandfather
an introduction. Really, I wouldn't be a bit surprised if Mrs. W. K. Van-
derbilt didn't call at the door this next instant!
    What almost knocked me over during the dinner was when Mr. Cum-
mings told me that I was sitting at the same table, in his private suite,
where the Prince of Wales had sat during his stay at the Biltmore in
1921!! Did that kill me!
    Mrs. Watson is a lovely woman but I've never known anyone to talk
with the rapidity that she does. She can't seem to get the words out of her
mouth fast enough to suit her. . . . Well, we had a perfectly splendid trip
up here on the train. I wish I could tell you all the things we're going to
do here, but I don't know myself yet. Tomorrow morning Grandfather
and I are going to do a little excursioning on our own—around the Main
Blvds, on the buses, etc.
    In the meantime, the strongest smelling salts couldn't keep me awake.
                                                    Love to all,
                                                    Tom[24]

    Tom had not spent time alone with his grandfather like this since he was
nine years old in Clarksdale. They went everywhere together, and in a letter
to Grand, Walter told how they had dined at the "Westchester Biltmore
Club," saying, "It is the *largest* and finest country club in the *world*."[25] They
also visited Grant's Tomb and old Saint Paul's and Trinity churches. After
riding on the upper deck of a Fifth Avenue bus, they returned to the hotel and
found a note from Mrs. Watson containing a hundred-dollar bill and tickets
to the theatre. The likelihood was that Tom's wallet was lost in New York,
not Paris, and that Mrs. Watson had heard all about it, too.
    The tickets were to Florenz Ziegfeld, Jr.'s lavish production of *Show Boat*.

It was Tom Williams's first exposure to Broadway, a street he would cross and that would cross him many times in the future. That night, as he and his grandfather walked to the theatre, the marquees along the Great White Way were ablaze with the titles of a variety of hit shows: *The Royal Family, Burlesque, Porgy, Good News!, Paris Bound,* and Mae West's *Diamond Lil.* The doomsayers were foretelling the theatre's demise following the advent of "100% All Talking Motion Pictures," inaugurated the previous October with the not quite "100%" *Jazz Singer.* But the New York theatre was thriving. Two hundred and sixty shows were produced in the 1927 season in seventy theatres. By 1928, Broadway had become the cynosure for serious playwrights like Sidney Howard, Maxwell Anderson, Elmer Rice, George Kelly, S. N. Behrman, Philip Barry, and Robert E. Sherwood. Reigning over them all was Eugene O'Neill.

The 1928 Pulitzer Prize, O'Neill's third, had been awarded to *Strange Interlude* as produced by the prestigious Theatre Guild. Tom was not able to see the O'Neill play, but it did not escape his notice, for he was to tell his grandfather, "Its unusual feature is that all the actors speak their thoughts, showing the decided difference between what people *say* to others and what they *think* in reality. It is tremendously long—begins at 5:00 o'clock and lasts till 11:00, with only a short intermission for dinner."[26]

On July 6, the Dakin party sailed at midnight. It was a gala departure, with a brass band playing, paper ribbons and balloons, and much drinking and laughing. Tennessee Williams recalled that it was all very Scott and Zelda Fitzgerald, but Tom—imbibing a green crème de menthe—suffered the effect of its apparently turning *him* green. By their second day out to sea, he was able to confess to his mother that he was finally recovering from a "dreadful attack of seasickness. I will never again see anything humorous in people being sea-sick." Omitting the crème de menthe, he added, "I should not have eaten so much in N.Y. before embarking."[27]

Among the passengers was someone Tom would never forget, a Miss Pinkie Sykes. Her bobbed hair was dyed red, and she wore flapper skirts and spike-heeled shoes. He estimated her age at about fifty, which was belied by her "incredible animation," and despite his shyness, they became good shipboard friends. Pinkie was one of those middle-aged "girls" who clings to her youth in a "valiant minimization of her real age." Twenty years later, she was seen tottering down the streets of her native Aberdeen, Mississippi, clearly in her seventies but still sporting her dyed-red hair, her waistless chemise dresses, and her very high heels. Although Tom would see her only on this one occasion aboard ship, she would reappear in his writings among those female hysterics struggling against the ravages of age to whom he could give a gift of ongoing life.

In a letter to "Dear Family" written as the *Homeric* was approaching the British coast, Tom observed, "I begin to understand how Columbus felt when he came into sight of the West Indies . . . for six days we have seen nothing but the desolate vastness of the sea." He was struck by an immense flock of gulls, which, he said, had "the remarkable faculty of standing perfectly still in the air," and by the northern lights, which looked like "enormous search lights across the sky." Then he mentioned what he recalled as one of the happiest events of the crossing: "In our party there is a young widow who is studying theatrical dancing under the great Ned Wayburn in N.Y. I have had her for a partner and we have got along splendidly. We have become quite celebrated aboard the ship. She has taught me the finale hop—one of those stamping dances—and since I have quite a penchant for stamping anyway, as Rose knows, we do it very well."[28]

Years later, Williams recalled that the widow, who was about twenty-seven, had been conspicuously flirting with a Captain De Voe in the party, and he had become annoyed at her dancing with Tom. The captain and the widow had engaged in a "mysterious conversation," and Tom had found it disturbing. "The three of us were at a small table in the ship's bar one night, toward the end of the voyage, when Captain De Voe looked at me and said to the dancing teacher, 'You know his future, don't you?' She said, 'I don't think you can be sure about that at the age of seventeen.' "[29] It was one of those acid remarks that burn into consciousness, lasting until its meaning finally becomes clear.

Placing his grandfather in other than a pious light, Tom mischievously concluded his letter with a report that must have brought some frowns and pursed lips among the ladies at home—and a cynical snort from C.C.:

> There is a saloon aboard the ship which offers all kinds of alcoholic drinks and believe me, there is never a lack of customers. Every night there's at least half a dozen choruses of Sweet Adeline sung from the bar-rail troubadors. Grandfather, himself, keeps his tongue pretty slick with Manhattan cocktails and Rye gingerales. I have tried them all but prefer none to plain gingerale and coca-cola. So I'm afraid I'm not getting all the kick out of this boat that the others are getting.[30]

The Reverend Dakin's report was somewhat less incriminating: "Tom plays the piano, dances and seems to be having a great time. Every one is pleased with him. . . . Tom had the time of his life in New York: he sure did enjoy the hotel where we were entertained. . . . We will be in Paris on Thursday for lunch. . . ."[31]

Paris was still agog over Charles Lindbergh's lone transatlantic flight, underwritten by a group of St. Louis financiers, in a small single-engine plane, *The Spirit of St. Louis.* There was hardly a boy anywhere in the world at that time who, as a result, didn't have his private fantasies—why, it was like a trip to the moon! And it was probably the only thing that gave Tom pride in his own hometown.

Walter Dakin wrote to his wife to say that he and Tom had been out in the country to see Napoleon's home and also the Barbizon forest, where Millet had painted *The Angelus*. He said, "Paris is *so* beautiful—like a dream." In a letter to Hazel, Tom echoed the same ecstatic response: "Paris is simply sublime, Hazel. Absolutely nothing like it. . . . Saw the most charmingly wicked show last night—Les Folies Bergere. I will tell you all about it when I get home. We are doing more delightful things! Dining at the Ritz!" He signed his letter with "Je suis le votre. Avec un couer [*sic*] plein d'amour"—a bit of fractured French, but perhaps a more sophisticated and easier way for *him* to say, "I am yours. With a heart full of love."[32]

How it is that a letter written to Hazel was discovered many years later among Edwina's collection of family correspondence can only be conjectured. It may have been included in a letter Tom wrote to his mother, and Edwina may have decided not to deliver it.

Paris, le 19 Juillet

Dear Mother,
I have just imbibed a whole glass of french champagne and am feeling consequently very elated. It is our last evening in Paris which excuses the unusual indulgence. French champagne is the only drink that I like here. But it is really delicious.

We have certainly had an exciting time in Paris. We've done practically everything there is to do. Today we went to the Louvre and out to Versailles. . . . We stood upon the balcony upon which Marie Antoinette boldly faced the mob which came to threaten her life. We looked into the secret passageway through which she fled when the crowd of enraged citizens broke into her boudoir.

The palace is exquisite throughout. All the ceilings are covered with rich paintings—the walls inlaid with gold. We walked down the long hall of mirrors, with its resplendent chandeliers and windows opening out upon the beautifully landscaped garden. It is the room in which the peace treaty of the Great War was signed. We saw the very table it was signed upon.

What appealed to me the most was the park in which Marie Antoinette found retreat from the court life which she detested. It was in this park that she played milk-maid. We saw . . . the huge, gold carriages in which she rode on fete days.

He said he hadn't had "a real bath" and had had to use a sponge since his arrival in Paris, as baths were "considered a vanity." He had been to Paris's famous Opera House to see *Romeo and Juliet* and found the music very beautiful. Then, knowing the shock it would create, he confessed:

We have seen the two notorious Parisian shows—The Folies Bergere and the Moulin Rouge. They both completely live up to their reputation. No

American show would dare to put over the things that they did. It was, however, more artistic than it was immodest. Anyway, when you're in Paris, you might as well leave all dispensable conventions behind. I can easily see why some people look upon Paris as the whole world. It really is marvelous.[33]

"This Adversary of Fear"

While walking alone down a Paris boulevard, Tom experienced what Tennessee Williams would describe many years later as "the most dreadful, the most nearly psychotic, crisis" of his early life. In *Memoirs*, he wrote:

I will try to describe it a little, for it has significance in my psychological make-up. Abruptly, it occurred to me that the process of thought was a terrifyingly complex mystery of human life.

I felt myself walking faster and faster as if trying to outpace this idea. It was already turning into a phobia. As I walked faster I began to sweat and my heart began to accelerate, and by the time I reached the Hotel Rochambeau, where our party was staying, I was a trembling, sweat-drenched wreck of a boy.

He said nothing to his grandfather. This was the first of two similar episodes: "At least a month of the tour was enveloped for me by this phobia about the processes of thought, and the phobia grew and grew till I think I was within a hairsbreadth of going quite mad from it."[34] For Tom, the experience of thinking about thought itself had an effect similar to that of seeing the myriad reflections of himself in a hall of mirrors.

On July 20, the party left Paris by train for Marseilles, going on to Nice and Monte Carlo, then down to Naples, Rome, and Milan, a city Tom considered "next to Paris in beauty" and in which he saw Leonardo da Vinci's *The Last Supper*. The party toured through Florence, then Venice, where he sent a postcard: "Dear Dad, Yesterday we went all through the old Doge's palace, seeing the dismal dungeons where prisoners were tortured, etc."[35] Proceeding to Switzerland, Tom wrote his mother from Chillon:

Today we went by motor boat up the lake shore to the romantic old Castle of Chillon . . . not at all dismal as we had expected but really quite attractive with its court-yard filled with flowers and its large bushes. If captivity for life were imposed upon me, I should prefer the Castle of Chillon to any other prison. We were shown the places where Byron, Shelley, Dickens and H. Beecher Stowe had scratched their names on the wall; the stone pillars and iron rings to which the famous prisoner of Chillon and his six comrades were strapped; also the deep pit into which

the condemned were tossed to suffer slow death by starvation. I volunteered to go down in the hole to see what it looked like—but when informed that there would be no way out, I withdrew the offer quite hastily!

It is not likely that his mother took much comfort when Tom reassured
her, "You do not need to feel the least bit concerned over my safety as long as
I am with Grandfather. He is the most apprehensive person imaginable and is
perfectly terrified if I step off the train for a second during a thirty minute
stop, and at the dinner-table whenever fish is served, he hollers down the
table, as if he had discovered dynamite, that there are bones in the fish."[36] The
problem was that Grandfather could not always be present, and in a later letter, Tom detailed an adventure that in Edwina's mind could only have demolished the previous assurances he had given her:

> There was a cave in [a] glacier, carved right through the solid ice. It was
> most interesting, although rather chilling and dampening to walk
> through the ice-walled tunnel. It was dazzling bright from the intense
> reflection of the sun and a clear, beautiful blue in color. In our eagerness
> to get some good camera pictures, Benton and I clambered considerably
> beyond the danger line on the top of the glacier and the Swiss guide be-
> came almost frantic, since the day was unusually warm and the ice slip-
> pery. Fortunately Grandfather was not present. If he were, he would
> surely have collapsed. We got down quickly enough, as soon as we real-
> ized that we were the cause of all that wild excitement below.[37]

Doubtless he caused some excitement in St. Louis, as well.

After Switzerland and a trip down the Rhine, they reached Cologne. It was
here that his "phobia" reached a climax. Tom and the other travelers were
visiting the cathedral, "the interior of which was flooded with beautifully colored light coming through the great stained-glass windows." Suddenly overtaken with panic, he knelt and began praying, remaining there after everyone
in his group had left. "Then a truly phenomenal thing happened," he later
wrote. "It was as if an impalpable hand were placed upon my head, and at the
instant of that touch, the phobia was lifted away as lightly as a snowflake
though it had weighed on my head like a skull-breaking block of iron. At seventeen, I had no doubt at all that the hand of our Lord Jesus had touched my
head with mercy and had exorcised from it the phobia that was driving me
into madness."[38]

In Amsterdam, before the group went on to London, Tom's phobia re-
curred, although less forcefully. He was extremely unsettled, having believed
that the evil had been expelled in the Cologne cathedral:

> That night I went out alone on the streets of Amsterdam and this time a
> second "miracle" occurred to lift the terror away. It occurred through

the composition of a little poem. It was not a good poem, except perhaps
for the last two lines . . .

> *Strangers pass me on the street*
> *in endless throngs: their marching feet,*
> *sound with a sameness in my ears*
> *that dulls my senses, soothes my fears,*
> *I hear their laughter and their sighs,*
> *I look into their myriad eyes:*
> *then all at once my hot woe*
> *cools like a cinder dropped on snow.*[39]

Long after that night in Amsterdam, Tennessee Williams wrote, "That
little bit of verse with its recognition of being one among many of my kind—a
most important recognition, perhaps the most important of all, at least in the
quest for balance of mind—that recognition of being a member of multiple
humanity with its multiple needs, problems and emotions, not a unique creature but one, only one among the multitude of its fellows, yes, I suspect it's the
most important recognition for all of us to reach now, under all circumstances
but especially those of the present. The moment of recognition that my existence and my fate could dissolve as lightly as the cinder dropped in a great fall
of snow restored to me, in quite a different fashion, the experience in the
cathedral of Cologne."[40]

Following the trip to Europe, a restlessness was stirring in Tom, a passion,
the need to change scenes, to move on. The mystical experience in Cologne
may well have been, as he said, of a religious nature, or, in Amsterdam, he may
have released temporarily a mounting tension by the simple act of writing
down his innermost feelings. But whichever it was, just moving to new environs on impulse, often for no particular reason, and as quickly leaving them,
was to become an obsessive pattern in his life as a writer, his only way to
defuse the unnameable terrors that rose out of too closely examining not only
the processes of thought but those of life itself.

On Tom's return to University City High School as a published writer and
a world traveler, he was something of a celebrity among his peers. A check for
thirty-five dollars, as payment for "The Vengeance of Nitocris," was waiting
for him, and he was feeling more confident, his ambition to write now more
focused than ever. In his senior year, he joined the staff of *Pep*, the school
paper, and wrote a series of travel features based on his trip diary. They were
so successful that he was asked to continue writing them after his graduation.

There seemed little doubt that Thomas Lanier Williams could write, but
there was a nagging question in his mind. On the one hand, even Cornelius

could see his son making a respectable living as a magazine and newspaper writer, and if Tom was to continue his education, the consensus was that he should enter a school of journalism. On the other hand, there was in him the poet's quest, a smoldering desire to give expression to the undefined and mysterious in life.

On October 15, Edwina penned a note on her personal stationery, excusing Tom for a school absence. Evidently, it was not delivered. In keeping with his lifelong practice of using any available scrap of paper, Tom used the reverse side of his mother's note to begin a short story—hardly the kind of news reporting his father had in mind:

> The wild and haggard face of a woman was pressed against the bars. Her eyes half blind by the lightlessness of her confinement stared hungrily at the dim glow of my lantern. Twenty years ago she had been the greatest beauty of the court. But through her association with some intrigue she had incurred the displeasure enmity of the Doge. He had condemned her to his dungeons for the rest of her life.

Perhaps he was thinking of a sequel to "The Vengeance of Nitocris," to be submitted again to *Weird Tales*. Judging from this scrap of evidence and from his tale of the vengeful Egyptian queen, it would appear that the keynote was set for much of the work that was to follow, the violence born of fear. As he later remarked: ". . . this adversary of fear, which was sometimes terror, gave me a certain tendency toward an atmosphere of hysteria and violence in my writing, an atmosphere that has existed in it since the beginning."[41]

Now, with the new year of 1929, Tom could look forward to another important change of scene in his life, and he wrote enthusiastically to the one person in his family who, too, was an adventurer.

> Dear Grandfather,
> I suppose you have already received news of that momentous event in my career—my graduation from high-school! I received my report card this Monday. I had passed all my exams very creditably.
> In a few days I am going to register in one of the two fine business schools here. I think I will take a course in short hand and typewriting. I am also going to continue my course in Latin at the High-School so that when I enter the University in Sept. I will have had a complete 4 years of Latin and also an extra credit to my account.
> I have bought the Tuxedo which you gave me money for. It is very handsome, satin lapels and trouser stripes and a silk, brocaded vest. It fits very nicely. The Prom will take place in just a week now. . . . The editor of the school paper, who is in my Latin class, wants me to continue writ-

ing for the paper. I have just concluded an article on Pompeii this evening which I will send to you as soon as it is published.

With much love to you and Grand,

Tom[42]

The letter was postmarked January 31, 1929, and may have been written earlier, when he *thought* he was to graduate on January 24. Previously, during the Thanksgiving holidays, Tom wrote his grandfather that, with graduation "getting very close," he had received his class ring and said that, with the school emblem engraved on it, it was "quite handsome. . . . Mother and I have decided that I should wait until the beginning of the school year, in September, to enter [as planned then, St. Louis's Washington University]. It is much simpler and easier than entering in January. Besides, to jump directly from high-school into college would be rather breath-taking."[43]

In January, however, there were twenty-four graduates, and Tom was not among them. In fact, he did not graduate until June 13, 1929, the Certificate of High School Credits listing him as ranking fifty-third among a graduating class of eighty-three, with a grade point average of 65. In March, Tom wrote to his grandfather again, saying, "I've never been busier in my life than I am at present, attending two schools, three subjects in one, two in the other, and a goodly amount of homework to be prepared in the evening."[44] His transcript lists two possible incompletes in economics and sociology; evidently, he spent the spring months making them up while at the same time attending a business school.

Park Austin, who was Rose's best friend, became secretary to the principal on her graduation in January. She signed Tom's diploma, and she told Allean Hale that she remembered Edwina arriving at the school on the afternoon of June 13 to attend a ceremony that had already taken place that morning. Tom had misinformed his irate mother and gone downtown to the St. Louis Public Library, not bothering either to attend the graduation or to pick up his diploma.[45] His indifference to punctuality and formalities was a pattern he would maintain through his years at three universities and into his life thereafter.

What primarily engaged his thoughts now was the prospect of entering the University of Missouri at Columbia in September. With his regularly published travel pieces in the school paper and two magazine articles to his credit, Tom was giving serious thought to a career in journalism, and Missouri had an excellent program in the field. This would be his first real opportunity to get away from the increasingly oppressive atmosphere of his home and of St. Louis itself. Originally, the family had talked about his attending the University of the South, his grandfather's alma mater, but because Sewanee was too far away, it was now considered impractical. On the other hand, Cornelius felt that Washington University, in St. Louis, was too close to home. Columbia was distant enough for Tom to feel liberated and near enough for Edwina to make occasional trips to look after her boy.

During the remaining months, the poet Williams immersed himself in a biography of "Mad Shelley" and was "fascinated that the poet had been wild, passionate and dissolute."[46] Also, there were the women in Shelley's life—Harriet, Mary, and Claire—and the one in Tom's life to whom he had written from Paris "with a heart full of love." Hazel and her best friend, Esme Mayes, still had one more year at Mary Institute, after which they planned to attend the University of Missouri together. Tom took this to mean that Hazel wanted to be near him. Although as friends they were as close as they had ever been, Hazel steadfastly resisted any overt gesture of love. Looking back, Williams speculated on the possibility that she might have been leading him on or else reacting puritanically to the embarrassingly immodest behavior of her mother.

But the truth was that there was someone else, although Tom would not know it for some time to come. It had begun on an evening when Hazel and Tom were at Esme's house and they needed a fourth for bridge. Esme called Dr. Meisenbach's son, Ed. "He was a very tall, good-looking young man," she said, "and he and Hazel took one look at each other—and it was just like that! Tom had no idea of what was going on. He was getting ready to leave for Columbia and would be gone all the time Ed and Hazel were going steady."[47] Vengeance takes many forms and identities. Tennessee took his in *The Glass Menagerie* by changing Ed to Emily Meisenbach and referring to him/her as "that kraut-head!"

Tom subsequently told his grandfather that "for the first time in our dramatic social history, one of us is going to attend the V.P. [Veiled Prophet's] Ball—in the dress circle! It's Rose, of course. She has been invited by a Mr. Matthewson who works down at Dad's office and with whom Rose has had several dates of late. He is a very nice, attractive fellow, and Rose is as excited over going with him as the ball itself."[48] He and Edwina had been given seats "way up in the peanut gallery. I suppose we shall be able to see Rose dance, however." Later, Tom told of Rose and Mr. Matthewson having "just returned from the picture show and all the family [having] retired to the back of the house to give them undisputed sway. Last Saturday they went out to the Country Club's Thanksgiving dance."[49]

After the holidays, Rose saw Mr. Matthewson infrequently and found herself at home and with little to do. She had gone to the family doctor several times to be examined for her stomach trouble. Diagnosing the problem as nervous indigestion, the doctor was of the opinion that there was nothing seriously wrong with her. She had been put on a strict diet, which Tom felt was too bad, since she was about to leave for a visit with Aunt Belle in Knoxville, where her aunt would be feting her with lavish dinners and rich foods. Everyone believed the change would do her good, except Edwina, who was apprehensive about Rose's peculiar behavior. If anyone else in the family regarded her conduct as anything but normal nervousness for an unmarried young lady in her twenty-first year, they were not saying anything. They *would* say that Rose was just a high-strung girl and always had been, as everyone knew.

At the end of April, Rose wrote her mother from Knoxville about a Bill Chable, whom she had met during her last visit: "Bill is perfectly lovely, so handsome and nice, but hasn't any money. His girl Polly Sanford is in Europe and is supposed to return home Sunday. She has been gone for almost a year and he told Aunt Belle that he felt that she was almost a stranger. I wish she was. Isn't that mean? She has worlds of money and is supposed to be very attractive." Rose also said that she planned to have dinner with Aunty Ella that evening and to see a Mary Pickford film afterward, then commented, "I feel it is about time for me to come home. I have had a perfectly marvelous visit. But have eaten the richest kinds of food the whole time. I am almost well, but think a plain diet would be better for me. I haven't had lunch at home but about twice since I've been here. Please ask Dad when he thinks it best for me to leave."[50]

Tom wrote to his grandfather, "I suppose you have already received letters from Rose describing her marvelous times in Knoxville. We received one containing her picture published on the society page of a Knoxville paper." He said that she seemed to be going out as often as she had when she last visited there, but that "Mother feels anxious, somewhat, about her having enough endurance for such an active life as she is leading."[51] During these years, Rose's letters were increasingly concerned with clothes, food, money, and boys: the search for props and strengths outside herself, a frantic preoccupation that her doctors were able to diagnose only as a nervous stomach. All that Edwina could do was watch and worry while Cornelius, demonstrating concern in the only way he understood, kept his daughter supplied with pretty shoes.

As for Tom, at the moment he was excitedly making preparations to leave for college. For a time, though, it looked as if he might not be able to go, since Cornelius suddenly decided that he could not afford the expense. In the end, he underwrote the tuition, maintaining later that he had to borrow the funds; but for everything else Tom needed, the Dakins would have to dig into their savings. Cornelius knew he could depend upon them, having housed his family and his responsibilities with them for years. Not just Cornelius but, over and over, Edwina, too, would continue to call for help, and as always Grand would send money or make the long trip to St. Louis to come to the rescue. Dakin has described his grandmother as "a much stronger person than my grandfather by far. She was a perfect person—not a selfish cell in her body— and she was a very beautiful woman, too. With all those problems we had, Grandfather would pray over them and Grand would get to work and come up with the solutions."[52]

It would appear that Cornelius's real motive in stalling Tom's leaving for school was to intervene in Hazel's plan to attend the University of Missouri the following year. C.C. maintained that Tom at eighteen was much too young to be thinking of marriage and that Hazel's presence at the university would interfere with his studies. Edwina contended that her husband "went to unbelievable lengths to destroy Tom's morale." According to her, Cornelius handed down an ultimatum to Hazel's grandfather that "he would not allow Tom to attend the university if Hazel did. The grandfather, no doubt feeling his job in jeopardy, enrolled Hazel in the University of Wisconsin and thereafter Hazel and Tom saw each other only during vacation."[53]

Esme Mayes's memory of the incident was quite the reverse—that it was Grandpa Kramer who objected. In all probability, there was total agreement between Cornelius and the old man. It would be a long time before Tom learned about the interference of Emil Kramer, whom he would represent sympathetically in the short story "Sand," but later as two unpleasant characters: Mr. Krupper in "Hard Candy" and Emiel Kroger in "The Mysteries of the Joy Rio."

In late September, Tom wrote to his grandfather, "I'm leaving for school exactly one week from today and I am awfully busy making the final preparations, going to the dentist's, getting clothes and all other necessary equipment." He added that he was trying to get a lot of exercise this last week, playing golf and going swimming, to be in better condition. "Mother is going up with me to spend one day to see that I am properly settled. She acts as though I were leaving for war instead of college."[54] In truth, Tom was moving out of the war zone, and for him at least the next three years would be a blessed truce.

PART II

Moonward
1929–1937

———

"Of rimless floods, unfettered leewardings . . ."

6

The New Terrain

1929–1932

Unable to conceive of himself as a fraternity member, Tom neglected to leave for the university in time for rush week. But Cornelius, having been a Pi Kappa Alpha at the University of Tennessee, had other ideas, and so with father pulling levers at home and mother accompanying her "boy" to school, Tom was on his way to Columbia and away from St. Louis—for a time.

The University of Missouri was less than a three-hour drive away, but it took most of the day by rail. All during September, trainloads of students were arriving on the Cannonball, and once again Edwina had Tom in hand, if not *by* the hand, as the two arrived in the busy Wabash Depot. Located midway between St. Louis to the east and Kansas City to the west, Columbia[1] was at that time a small college town built around the university, southern in atmosphere, and Tom would always remember it as "charming" and the university as "a giant country club" that provided some of the happiest days of his life.

By 1929, the university had become famous for having the oldest and foremost school of journalism in the United States. Journalism was the field that Tom intended to enter in his junior year, not only because newspaper work would make his other interests in writing avocationally possible but also because Cornelius saw this as the only way his son could write and be paid for it. Although Columbia's labor force was predominantly professional and white-collar, Tom would find a touch of irony in the fact that the city's blue-collar workers were mainly employed in a factory branch of the Hamilton-Brown Shoe Company, his father's company's chief competitor.

On their arrival, Tom and his mother spent their first night at a hotel. Edwina undoubtedly was aware of the scandal surrounding a university "sex questionnaire"; it had been making headlines in St. Louis and may well have determined her chaperoning Tom to Columbia. In a sociology course on

"The Family," a voluntary quiz on social, sexual, and moral attitudes of women resulted in two professors being fired and created a national controversy over the issue of academic freedom. Question number three, addressed to girls, sent shock waves throughout the state: "Are your own relations with men restrained most by religious convictions, fear of social disapproval, physical repugnance, fear of pregnancy, lack of opportunity, fear of venereal diseases, or pride in your own ability to resist temptation?" Worse, it asked, "Have you ever engaged in specific sexual relations?"[2] Columbia by now was labeled "Sin City," and during their train ride, Edwina may well have given Tom an admonishing lecture.

Tennessee recalled that the next day his mother "selected for me what she regarded as a suitable boardinghouse." It was segregated sexually in two frame houses at 1002 and 1004 University Avenue run by "a very lively middle-aged landlady," Effie Graham, "a widow with a bright red Buick convertible. The boys and girls met only at meals."[3]

With Edwina's departure, Tom was finally alone. This time, when his mother left him at school, he did not kick and scream, as he had in kindergarten. Doubtless, he felt great relief, having at least the *illusion* of independence. The first night in the boardinghouse, he wrote to Hazel proposing marriage, but this prospective union was also to prove an illusion. Within a week, he received Hazel's reply, which said that they were much too young to be considering marriage. No doubt, Hazel had been made fully aware of her grandfather's disapproval, and possibly, too, of his father's view that Tom at eighteen was not old enough. Also, there was Ed Meisenbach for her to consider.

In all likelihood, Tom knew nothing of C.C.'s and Emil Kramer's conspiracy to separate them. All he knew was that for the first time in their relationship, he and his father were on common ground: A compromise had been reached on Cornelius's part with regard to his son's writing and he was taking an active interest in Tom's education. In the three years Tom was at Missouri, he wrote respectfully, if not affectionately, to "Dear Dad." It appeared that father and son were at last becoming friends. Tom's first letter home, dated October 4, was written to Cornelius. He thanked him for a set of golf clubs and said they were being put to good use, since his roommate at the boardinghouse, Harold Carroll, was teaching him about the game.[4]

Not long after Tom's arrival on campus, a local paper ran an interview headed "Shy Freshman Writes Romantic Love Tales for Many Magazines." It reported that Tom intended to enter the school of journalism, had had a "number" of stories published in *Weird Tales* and *Smart Set* magazines, and had received twenty-five dollars for an article on "The Type of Woman a Man Wants to Marry." Obviously, the title was invented, implying that the shy freshman had written out of "my own unhappy marital experiences." Tom had already learned that reporters, like dramatists, tend to exaggerate. A further description of him, however, was accurate:

It bothers Mr. Williams to have anyone ask him questions about himself. He is little more than five feet tall. He has clean cut features and smooth brown hair. His eyes, which have a look that seems thousands of miles away, add to the unapproachable and reserved appearance which he presents. He is equally as reticent and shy as he appears and feels that having his stories published is nothing out of the ordinary.[5]

The article also said that, while he liked to write love stories, he admitted that his inspiration rose not so much from actual experience as "from reading a wide variety of authors" including his favorite writer, Louis Bromfield.

Although Tom and everyone who knew him in college spoke of his extreme shyness, he seldom gave account of how it manifested itself. Many things that Tennessee would recall in *Memoirs* as having happened during his years at the University of Missouri were in fact the wishful imaginings of a painfully shy Tom. One occurrence that Tennessee recalled at the boarding-house concerned a blond adolescent farm boy, a somnambulist, who clambered into his bed one night. When Tom cried out in surprise, the boy mumbled incoherently and returned to his own bed. "For several nights, I waited for this fit of somnambulism to come upon him again and hoped that it would lead him in the same direction. Well, it only happened that one time"—if it happened at all, outside his imagination.

While undeniably Tom was experiencing a growing attraction to members of his own sex, it was evident in the journals he began several years later that even then he could not understand this in himself. Like many another sensitive youth, particularly with strong religious and societal restraints, he refused to give quarter to feelings he would only come to comprehend and accept in time. For most of his three years at the university, Tom was troubled by the problem of sexual identity, his homoerotic impulses countered by a strong sensual response to girls, who were constantly in his company. He had come to the borderline of a new terrain of love but would be unable to cross it for years.

Tom had not been living long at Miss Effie's when he received a visit from a select committee of Alpha Tau Omega fraternity brothers, the result of his father's maneuverings. Cornelius had a pair of young cousins in ATO at the University of Tennessee; he had prevailed upon them to write the Columbia chapter that "the son of an executive in the International Shoe Company was 'hiding out' in a boardinghouse and that this would not do, since he was descended from the Williamses and Seviers of East Tennessee, was a published writer and a traveler of the world."[6]

In a letter home, Tom said that he had some very big news for them: "I have just pledged the Alpha Tau Omega. They invited me to supper last night and afterwards took me up to the council chamber where I was asked to join the Frat. and offered a pledge pin. I have never accepted anything with more alacrity. . . . They are just completing a new chapter house—one of the finest on the campus. I don't think I could have made a better Frat." He added that, on entering the parlor wearing his pledge pin, he was surrounded by members congratulating him. "I had never felt so important."

As further bait for Cornelius, he added, "From what I hear, living in a Frat is more expensive than boarding out. However, the social advantages of being a fraternity man are certainly great enough to warrant the extra expense. A non-frat man is practically 'out of it' in Columbia, as I have found out in the past month. In business and social life after you are out of the University, belonging to a fraternity is still a very big asset."[7] C.C. could only say, Damn the expense—full speed ahead!

As a result, he made trips to Columbia and met several of Tom's fraternity brothers. Now that Tom was away from his mother's constant fussing over him, Cornelius was determined to make a man out of his son. Being in a fraternity under the guidance and example of older men, going out for sports, and taking ROTC (the required Reserve Officers' Training course) was, he felt, just what his son needed. C.C. put up the fifteen-dollar deposit for a uniform, while Tom, appalled, read the list of mandatory equipment for infantry drill: .30-caliber Springfield rifles, Colt's automatic pistols, Browning machine guns, trench mortars, gun carts, field packs, and shelter tents. To his grandparents, Tom wrote to say that for the first time he had taken part in competitive athletics: "I was one of the five ATO fellows representing the frat in the cross-country races. We had to run 2½ miles—to my surprise, I was right there at the finish."[8]

Tom had expressed concern to his parents about Rose, who had been in and out of Barnes Hospital in an attempt to determine what precisely was causing her stomach ailment. But at the same time, Rose and Tom wrote to each other in a determinedly lighter vein. He responded to a letter of hers, saying, "I was greatly amused by your letter describing Hazel's party. After such a wild revel, I wonder that you are even in a condition to write letters." He also mentioned that "I spent all yesterday—from 9:00 in the morning 'til 4:00 in the afternoon—working at the frat house. . . . I had to get down on my knees and apply wax with a cloth over the whole surface of the floor; then get a polishing brush to rub over it until it glistens. I think in a month or two I will qualify as a male house-servant."[9]

"The Fiery Braille Alphabet of a Dissolving Economy"

In September, a trading slump gave clear indication that the stock market, which could survive only by constant rises, had reached the limits of its climb. On October 29, the United States trembled from what was felt more as an implosion than an explosion. Among the nation's newspapers, none could have put it more succinctly than the show-business weekly *Variety:* WALL ST. LAYS AN EGG. The story went on to say, "The most dramatic event in the financial history of America is the collapse of the New York Stock Market. The stage was Wall Street, but the onlookers covered the country. Estimates are that 20,000,000 people were in the market at the time."

Before long, the word was all over campus; many students from formerly well-to-do families would soon be forced to leave universities throughout the country, and Tom could not help but wonder what effect this would have on his father and on his being able to continue at school. The Great Depression gave Cornelius an irrefutable argument about the spending of "tight" money and a sharpened weapon with which to threaten his family. According to Dakin, he had a golden rule of his own: "Them's that's got the gold makes the rules!"

If Edwina was aware of a crash, it could only have been C.C.'s fist on the dining room table when at dinner he learned that his wife's reaction to the national calamity had been to trade in their upright for a small grand piano. Some thirty years later, her justification was simply that the piano, after all, was still standing in her living room.

Modest middle-class though his family was, Tom could stay in school because Cornelius was comparatively well-off; he owned stock in his company, and as far as is known, these were his only holdings. He had always been willing to gamble at poker but not on the market. He had, in fact, been as shrewd in handling his assets as he had been penurious. Also, he had the security of his position at the shoe company, where he was valued by his boss as an excellent sales manager. There was another reason he was valued, of which he evidently was not aware—namely, that Paul Jamison had for some time been attracted to his wife. Miss Edwina, still the coquette, flirted with him in turn. In all likelihood, it was harmless enough, but when Grand overheard two women in a department store discussing the "affair," she returned home to give her daughter the kind of lecture that Edwina had reserved for *her* daughter.

Toward the end of January, after spending the holidays at home, Tom wrote to his grandparents, saying that this would be his last weekend in Miss Graham's boardinghouse before he moved into the newly built ATO house. He also said that his mother was planning to come up to look over his quarters, "supervise moving," and meet his fraternity brothers.

Although his first term at Missouri was spent as earnestly and industriously as Tom knew how, his transcripts and other records show that his grades were only slightly above average. He made a conspicuous effort to adapt to the university's academic requirements and social activities, particularly those of his fraternity. But however serious his intentions were, he was fast becoming a campus character. His fraternity brothers frankly didn't know what to make of him. Certainly he was an enthusiastic enough pledge, but often what he did was wrong or at best singular. As a result, he was frequently brought under discipline to explain, for example, why he "borrowed" a brother's clean white shirt without permission in order to be properly dressed for dinner. His response was that he would otherwise have missed a meal; like all of his rationalizations, it had a certain logic.

And there were other infractions of the rules, such as "kiting" checks against insufficient funds, because, as Tom explained it, he didn't know what balance, if any, he had in his account. Also, instead of dating one of the sorority girls whom pledges were instructed to bring to chapter dances, he would, as he recalled, "bring some girl who was either not even a member of any sorority or was from a sorority that was considered of no consequence, such as Phi Mu or Alpha Delta Pi, which owned the dreadful, sub-rosa sobriquet of 'After Dinner Pussy.' " One girl he described as "an hysterical nympho: and very, very pretty," and although considered "a social disgrace," she nonetheless accommodated a goodly number of his brethren.

Clearly, the cordiality with which Tom had at first been received at the ATO chapter soon became dismay, and finally despair. He later wrote:

> Once a week at midnight there was held what was called a "kangaroo court." At this court, conducted with great solemnity, the transgressions of each pledge were read aloud to the gathering and punishment was meted out in the form of paddling. The paddling was light in some cases, and heavy in others. A brother would stand poised with a paddle at the end of the long front room. The pledge to be punished would be instructed to bend over, presenting his backside to the brother with the paddle, and to hold up his balls, since the brother did not want to include castration in the punishment. Then the brother with the paddle would come dashing across the great chamber and swat the pledge's backside.[10]

Ten such swats were the maximum allowed, and Tom often received the limit, leaving him barely able to make his way upstairs to bed. That he helped himself to a brother's clean white shirts, Tom usually explained, was due to the meagerness of his father's monthly allowance. But the facts, as borne out in numerous letters to his mother, are that he frequently acknowledged receipt of a box of laundered shirts, while he just as often confessed to having forgotten to send home a soiled batch.

For those who were forever picking up after him, or, like his roommates, organizing around him, his absentmindedness was hardly endearing. In fact, it could be damned exasperating. Tom's skipping classes or missing exams wasn't so much deliberate as that he simply forgot them. If this neglect had been willful laziness, it would never have been tolerated. But he had an air of sheer helplessness, even desperation at times, that made all but the hardened want to help him. He was a dependent, and while he hated it, he also relied upon it—which is to say, discovering its power, he was not above using it. And in this, he would never change.

Allean Hale, who attended the University of Missouri a few years later, did extensive research into Tennessee Williams's undergraduate period. "His

Columbia years were perhaps the most normal in his life," she wrote. "He went jellying and juking at campus joints, attended dances at Christian College and went on double dates with close friends like Elmer Lower, who usually had to find him the girl. He bought riding breeches and took Equitation, which must have seemed more romantic than 'Phys Ed.' "

Lower told Hale that Tom was "untidy, absent-minded, an oddball." The boys made fun of him because he just didn't fit in. For example, the required ROTC uniform for the weekly march around Francis Quadrangle was a blue jacket with white trousers. "Out of 1,000 people, 999 would have on white pants," Lower remembered. "Then there would be one pair of legs wearing blue. That was Tom."[11] Williams said on reflection, "I despised R.O.T.C., flunked it three times. It was ridiculous. Perspiring and weary I would just park myself down on the curb, unload my gear and dodge the parade. No one missed me. There were one thousand cadets."[12] Among Lower's other recollections was one concerning Tom's short-lived career in wrestling:

> The fraternity, despairing of his ever gaining the required points for other sports activities, forced him to enter the intramural competition as a 120-pound fly-weight. [Actually, he fit the requirements for a good wrestler who, according to Coach Fisher, should be "clever, fast, and a quick thinker . . . also well developed physically, although it is not necessary for him to be a circus strong man."] Ignorant but wiry, Tom embarked with great zest, defeated two farm boys and put a sign on the bulletin board, "Williams Ultimatum: Liquor! Liquor! Must have liquor for my bout with the aggressive agrarians." His brothers obliged, Tom got into the finals and thus earned more points for the ATO house than they won on basketball.[13]

There were conflicting accounts as to whether he won or took two falls, but he did acquire the tag of "Tiger" Williams. Tiger also demonstrated prowess on the dance floor, and he showed a great interest in girls as partners, as they did in him. He loved to dance—as he did all of his life—and was a welcome stag at sorority parties. Years later, he very nearly wrecked a restaurant demonstrating the gyrations of The Fish, which he said he had learned at "Ol Mizzou": "It's stand still and rooooo-tate. Stand still and rooooo-tate."[14] The rotation, of course, was what caused the mayhem.

Tom may have been regarded among his brothers as a bit quirky, but no one thought of him as or even suspected him of being a "fairy." That was the unthinkable disgrace, particularly within the confines of a fraternity house. Inevitably, it would result in the brother's not only being drummed out of the fraternity but in his being run off campus and out of town, as well.[15] The caveat was simple: You had to be caught. Men could be "inseparable friends," even more devoted to one another than they often were to their girls; and men could joke around in locker rooms or wrestle on their beds in their shorts, goose one another, and thinly disguise their erections—that was considered perfectly normal, but it was also where the line was drawn.

Because this was his first exposure to a segregated male society, Tom exerted every effort to think and act as the others did. What made him accepted as "normal" was the fact that he obviously liked girls and, once he knew them, was not at all shy in their company. They liked him, as well, no doubt to the envy of some of his less popular brothers. He did not make passes, because in those days you were not supposed to do that with "good girls." He dated and danced with them, picnicked and went on hayrides and read poetry to them, and gossiped about them to his brothers—but that, too, was all perfectly normal.

Though Tom could feel relaxed in the company of girls, he could look upon his fraternity brothers only in awe and wonder. In his memoirs, Tennessee Williams gives a somewhat scrambled account about someone who seems to have been his first roommate. Since a fire in the 1950s destroyed most of the fraternity's records, and since, according to Lower, roommates were rotated as often as monthly, the roommate cannot be identified. The brother, whom Williams chose to call Smitty, was pictured as a youth who made playfully sexual overtures toward him. Although he wrote that their attachment had begun to trouble the brothers, the romantic events he describes, which portray him in various escapades with Smitty on and off campus, appear to be fanciful, a wishful feeling in the recesses of Tom's mind and a figment of Tennessee's imagination. In truth, many of the adventurous memories Williams later envisaged were the fantasies of a troubled youth.[16]

What those like Elmer Lower recalled more than anything about Tom Williams was his reticence and isolation. Since journalism was Tom's intended career, nothing was made of the fact that he remained in his room to write a good deal of the time. As would prove true all of his life, his social being existed on a level very different from that of his artistic self. Outwardly, there was Tom, who in conversation or correspondence with friends and family seemed a rather ingenuous, plainly middle-class young man. But in the recesses of his personality, there existed another maturing identity that would someday emerge as Tennessee Williams.

One would hardly have noticed him had it not been for his sudden, uncontrollable laugh, which had the strangled sound of an asthmatic duck, the more startling because it erupted on wholly inappropriate occasions. Williams would come to refer to his laugh as his "mad cackle," and indeed it was frequently maddening for those in his company, who, when accompanying him to a restaurant or the theatre, felt as though they would like to slide under their seats. In a sense, the laugh could be taken as a trait of the artist: a different perspective, as though from his Olympian post he could enjoy a privilege of the gods, seeing humor in the folly, even the tragedy, of mortals. But in a fraternity house, the reaction to Tom's improbable shriek was simply to circle a forefinger at one's temple. Those with any memory of him at all said that they tended to regard him as the house thick wit. They teased him a great deal, which he took in good humor, and more or less wrote him off as forgettable. In later years they admitted to profound shock when they discovered that this same Tom was Tennessee Williams.

At the same time, and unbeknownst to his scoffing frat brothers, Tom was constantly observing those around him, scrutinizing and disguising them in his writings. Unusual names of classmates fascinated him, like Goforth, Bachelder, Moise, Venable, Jimmy Dobyne, Mitch, Pollitt, Stallcup, and Hertha. Usually, he gave them different physical attributes, but one of them, Jim Connor, a handsome Irishman from St. Louis, became the actual prototype of Jim O'Connor, the gentleman caller in *The Glass Menagerie*.

Tom enjoyed a kind of insulation, mainly because no one took him very seriously as a writer—that is, except for one professor on campus, Robert Ramsay, who taught modern drama and recognized something promising in Tom Williams. Though Tom chose not to take the course for credit, he did audit the class and, at Ramsay's urging, entered the Eighth Annual One-Act Play Contest sponsored by the Missouri Workshop, the university's dramatic organization.*

As far as is known, Tom's 1930 entry, *Beauty Is the Word*, is the earliest play written by Tennessee Williams. It is perhaps significant not only because its Shelleyan fervor reflects Tom's own enthusiasm for the poet but also because the theme, while not a restatement of Shelley's atheism, was Tom's first attack upon the inhibitions of puritanism and its persecution of the artist, and, incidentally, upon his own religious upbringing. He had begun to feel that "nearly all religions were based on a concept of guilt."[17] The impact of his reading Shelley's life and writings was both to open his own mind and, in *Beauty Is the Word*, to depict the heroism of a freethinker.

Set in the South Seas, the play tells of a New England missionary and his wife and their reproving attitude toward her honeymooning niece, Esther, a dancer, and Esther's husband, an artist. Denouncing the restrictive doctrines of her aunt and uncle and their repressive impact upon the island's natives, Esther exclaims, "The fear of God! Always, the fear of God. It's amazing, isn't it, that any one could be so stupid that he couldn't see that fear and God are the most utterly incompatible things under the sun. Fear is ugliness. God—at least *my* God—is Beauty." Esther delivers another message when she upholds the physical beauty and sexual freedom, the "shameless nakedness," of the island's natives.

---

*Professor Ramsay's course in modern drama was based on the famed George Pierce Baker 47 Workshop at Harvard, which gave impetus to a number of prominent American playwrights, including Eugene O'Neill. By 1930, O'Neill had brought a high degree of innovation to the one-act play. It was the ideal form in which to exhibit the work of developing dramatists, and Ramsay's approach was unique in its time for the creation of a kind of tryout theatre and critical laboratory.

This was a Shelleyan belief, but coincidentally it was also a belief of a writer who would have a more profound and lasting influence on Tom. Early in March, it was widely publicized that D. H. Lawrence had died, and it is possible that Tom would have been privy to discussion of Lawrence's view of the sensual as spiritual, which is precisely what he has Esther saying. This same theme, compounded with the role of guilt and the quest for God, would pervade the major works of Tennessee Williams and ultimately make Lawrence a primary influence on them.

Beauty Is the Word was not performed, but it was reviewed in the student newspaper, the *Daily Missourian*, in mid-April. The paper reported that the play had taken sixth place in the contest and that, although it espoused an original and constructive idea, the handling was "too didactic and the dialog often too moralistic." But, it added, "Mr. Williams is the first freshman to win honorable mention in the Dramatic Arts Contest." Of course, Tom would have preferred the fifty-dollar first prize and a workshop production. Anything less gave him small comfort. Winning was what mattered and always would.

In the May 1930 issue of *The Columns*, the student literary magazine, there also appeared a short-short story by Thomas Lanier Williams, "A Lady's Beaded Bag," an ironic study of the contrasting attitudes between a trash picker and a wealthy woman. Tom received no money for this, either, and since earning a livelihood from his more esoteric writing was his main bent, for the moment he saw a career in journalism as his only practical alternative.

Also in May, ATO held its annual Mother's Day, when the mothers of the brothers descended en masse on the Gamma Rho chapter. Mrs. Cornelius Williams would not have missed it for the world—miss a chance to talk about her boy? Tom's was not the only pained expression as the mothers brought out snapshots and contested among themselves with regard to their sons' virtues. No sooner had the ladies left than the true colors were raised over Gamma Rho. Virtues were quickly shed, and pandemonium returned to its normal pitch. Tom woke up next morning to a problem that occasioned yet another of the apologies for which he was already achieving a certain fame. He wrote to his mother:

> I suppose you were justly wrathful when you arrived in Saint Louis and found that I had forgotten to 'phone Dad to meet you. I was quite ashamed of myself when I remembered the next morning. There were some mitigating circumstances, however. My roommate and several others in the house started drinking beer as soon as all the Mothers got out of the house Sunday afternoon. They went to a restaurant and got so hilariously drunk that the proprietor had to call out the police. Warned that the police were coming, they went to another restaurant to continue the carouse. The police finally overtook them in the Davis tearoom. There was quite a brawl in which Anderson one of the men in the house was hit

over the head with a police club. Of course the whole house was in a furor over it; we had to stay up all night cajoling the drunkards. The Dean of Men, Mr. Heckel, found out about it and I'm afraid some of them will be kicked out of school.

Tom also mentioned that the photographs taken on Mother's Day turned out "pretty good—particularly the ones of you," then added artfully, "Bill Reese, a boy from Saint Louis, said you must have had 'a very carefree life' to be looking so 'young and pretty.' " The letter was signed, "Very lovingly, Tom."[18] Even recognized for what they were, such crafty endearments always had the effect of softening Edwina's indignation.

Tom had turned nineteen by the end of the school term, and his grades were B- for the fall semester and C+ for the spring, which despite eighteen absences made him a better-than-average student. He returned home for the long, hot St. Louis summer, only to be met with Cornelius's edict that he find work to help with his expenses if he was to return to school in the fall. What he found was door-to-door magazine sales, about the only job opening available and, given his temperament, about the worst. That he was able to find work at all would have been surprising had it not been for the fact that St. Louis, with its widely diversified industries, did not suffer the Great Depression as devastatingly as did one-industry cities such as Detroit and Pittsburgh. Still, there were breadlines and people down on the riverfront foraging out of trash cans.

On June 16, Tom wrote to his grandfather:

This job of selling *Pictorial Review* subscriptions is extremely strenuous and not at all suited to my personality, as you can easily imagine. It is a good experience, however, and the salary of 21.00 a week comes in handy. It is house to house canvassing from 9:00 in the morning til 8:30 at night. It is quite exhausting at the end of each day and I wonder if I will be able to endure another day of it. There is so much unemployment and poverty that selling magazine subscriptions is difficult even for experienced salesmen.

He went on to say that Rose had had a clinical examination at Barnes Hospital, that her problems were solely nervous, and that she was under the care of a nerve specialist, although she had suffered a virtual nervous breakdown. "Of course she is very nervous and unreasonable. She had a quarrel with Dad last night and became so furious that she left the house and spent the night with Miss Florence who happened to be visiting with us." He added that she was certainly a great worry to his mother and Grand and himself. "I think the doctor will be able to get her out of it. He has given her a schedule to live by which should be effective in relieving her nerves."[19]

Edwina hastened to reassure her father, "I know you must have been worried after Mother's letter. We have had a hectic time! Cornelius wasn't himself when he ran Rose out of this house last Sunday night and was very sorry afterward." Rose's doctor had reassured Edwina that the girl would be all right, that she just needed a goal, something to work toward in order to get out of herself. Tom had given up on magazines and had gone downtown to Rubicam's Business School to investigate an intensive ten-week course; it was decided that Rose would attend, too, and that Tom would help her with her work. Edwina explained, "Rose is selling two of her shares of stock to 'Grand' to pay for her business course. Tom is selling his to pay for his course, as Cornelius said he could not do anything to-ward it."[20]

Rose could not cope with the workload; her Gregg shorthand manuals contained underlined entries like "Learn this by *Friday.*" Her instructor subjected her to scathing comments, and as a result, she stopped going to school, without telling her mother. She simply wandered about the city and Forest Park. Later, in *The Glass Menagerie*, Tennessee would have Laura say:

> . . . I went in the art museum and the bird-houses at the Zoo. I visited the penguins every day! Sometimes I did without lunch and went to the movies. Lately I've been spending most of my afternoons in the Jewel-box, that big glass house where they raise the tropical flowers.

During the two weeks Tom worked with a field crew, he was paired off with someone who was an even more unlikely salesman than he, a young fellow from Tulsa, Oklahoma. Tennessee Williams remembered "Tulsa" as "blond and rather pretty," but someone who interested him at first "only as a funny companion at a very tedious job." The oppressive summer heat and door-slamming rejections were made more endurable by having an antic partner who took it all as a joke.

Tom suggested that they go on a double date with Hazel and a girlfriend named Lucy. When they arrived at Hazel's door, her manner was distinctly cool. As Williams later told the story:

> It seemed to me that the night air had made my partner a bit wacky with exhilaration. He kept repeating the name "Lucy" and going into soprano howls of amusement. The howls had an hysterical note. I believe that Hazel was much wiser about the sex scene than I was at that time. When she admitted him to the Kramer residence, she looked at the Oklahoma kid with a touch of dismay in her great brown eyes. All during the evening he kept chattering like a bird and putting special emphasis on the name "Lucy." . . . But my partner's behavior was really quite overboard and the "double date" ended upon a somewhat ambiguous note. Hazel seemed more than a bit put off with me for the first time in our long relationship.[21]

The "Oklahoma kid" stayed around St. Louis throughout the summer, despite the intense heat. Tom was relieved when he finally went home. Later, Tulsa sent him a written declaration of love, but Tom regarded it as just one more example of his outrageous behavior.

There was another reason for Hazel's coolness, as Tom was to find out on encountering Esme Mayes outside Rubicam's. She recalled:

> It was there I told Tom about Hazel and Ed Meisenbach. He was waiting for a trolley to go back to University City. Tom said something about when he and Hazel would be married, and I exclaimed, "But, Tom, don't you know?—about Ed and Hazel?—don't you know they're going steady?" Never in my whole life have I seen such a stricken expression as that on Tom's face. He made no comment, just boarded a trolley and went on. I remember berating Hazel for leading him on. But she was furious at me for telling him! She liked Tom and his puppy-dog affection, but that's where it ended for her.[22]

In his fashion, Tom hid his feelings and saw Hazel occasionally during the time she was getting ready to leave for the University of Wisconsin.

The summer's only accomplishment for him was the improvement in his skill as a typist. Edwina later discovered a page on which he had typed the same exercise five times: "There is a difference between talent and genius. Talent does what it can. Genius what it must. But it is the little more that makes the difference."* Whatever helped Tom to become a good writer was all that mattered, for as he was to say, "Writing is ideal reality and living is not ideal."[23]

"He liked me and so I loved him"

Tennessee Williams felt that life was "an incomplete experience without its expression in art,"[24] and in these early years at the University of Missouri, he gradually began to infuse actual people and events into his writings, seeing them through a prism that filtered his truth from reality. On his return to school in the fall of 1930, there were friendships that had greater meaning for him than his friends realized at the time or, for that matter, than he understood himself.

Esmeralda Mayes, who had entered her freshman year at Missouri, became a constant confidante. Since they both intended to major in journalism, they talked of their interest in writing as a career. The two would be seen spending

---

*As Donald Spoto pointed out in *The Kindness of Strangers* (Boston: Little, Brown and Co., 1985), p. 30, Mrs. Williams may have thought this "an extraordinary insight," while not recognizing it as "an excerpt from Bulwer-Lytton's 'Last Words of a Sensitive Second-Rate Poet.'"

many afternoons on the steps outside the Chi Omega sorority house, reading poetry or deep in discussions about art and literature. They also went on hay-rides together and to movies and to dances, which prompted Esme in later years to say, "Tom was the best dancer I ever danced with. It was the custom for each girl in a sorority to invite her date for a dance and to submit three names for the stag line. This made for a fun evening because everyone was always being cut in on. I wouldn't have left Tom off the list for the world."[25] Still smarting at Hazel's rejection, Tom resorted to his writing for solace and to the companionship of a friendly youth named Harold A. Mitchell.

About the same age as Tom, with dark hair and blue eyes, Mitch came from a rural farming community in Missouri. He became a pledge at the ATO fraternity and roomed with Tom for one semester. As Mitchell remembered him, Tom looked and acted as if he had come from a small southern town, in contrast to the sharp Kansas City boys who composed most of the fraternity. "He was shy and a loner and kept pretty busy with his writing."[26] Mitch also saw him as compassionate. "I remember one time when I went through the hazing bit, they whacked the hell out of me, and after we'd gone to bed, Tom said, 'I'm sorry for what the fellows did to you.' He was a second-year man, an active, but said, 'I don't do things like that.' I also remember he was sloppy, terribly sloppy, but then I was, too, and we got along just fine."[27] Although Mitch enjoyed ribbing his bashful roommate, he was kind and gentle toward Tom and stirred in him feelings that were mute and tender and beyond his understanding.

There was much about Harold Mitchell that Tom could admire and envy, including his buoyant and outgoing nature and the fact that he had a father he idolized, who had sacrificed his dental practice for his son's education. On one occasion, Mitch traveled with Tom to St. Louis for a weekend and met his parents. He remembered that Cornelius was "cordial" and Edwina "friendly," but he did not recall meeting either his brother or sister. "For excitement that Saturday night," Mitch said, "Tom suggested we go across the river to East St. Louis and visit the red light district. We talked to a lot of gals but didn't do any 'business.' It was Depression time and neither of us could afford the pleasure."[28]

On occasion, Tom would join Mitch and his attractive girlfriend, Edna ("Donnie") Don Carlos, at Jimmy's College Inn for Cokes and conversation. She recalled, "Tom was Mitch's best friend, and my memory is that he was a lot of fun and not particularly shy when he joined us for an evening."[29] Much of their talk had to do with the Depression and what was happening in the nation. By the new year of 1931, pessimism was settling over the land like a giant dust cloud. Young people facing an uncertain future became drawn to one another; they took their inexpensive pleasures together, danced together, and went to movies together. When Tom was not studying or writing, he would go off campus to be with Mitch and Donnie. This was the beginning of a lifelong attraction to couples in love, in which he would be always the third member, the one who shared vicariously in their affection for each other.

Because at the end of the term Mitch lost his job as cashier in a campus drugstore, he could no longer afford to live at the ATO house. In order to continue his studies, he stayed in town with friends of his father, and with that, the fraternity meant no more to Tom than a place to room and board and write. He thought of Mitch as his best friend and saw him as often as he could. Years later, he would reflect on the spring of 1931 as perhaps the happiest period he had ever known. Mitch recalled, "I knew he was different, and I knew he was a hell of a lot better writer than I was. He had quite an imagination and had gotten a pay check from *Weird Tales* magazine—$35! That really impressed me. He had worlds and worlds of talent, but I would never have predicted his success. It wasn't until after he died I realized this same Tom Williams had become a famous playwright."[30]

Tom, in fact, showed little interest in playwriting that spring, but he was listed among fifty contestants in the First Annual Mahan University Essay Contest. The first prize of fifty dollars was won by Harold Vincent Boyle for "Confessions of a Well Read Man." Hal Boyle would become the syndicated columnist and journalist Williams never became, but for someone who read as much as Tom did in those days, the piece must have irked him—not to mention missing out on the fifty dollars. Instead, he received honorable mention for a short story, "Something by Tolstoi," but that, too, was small consolation, for in first place he would have won both the top honor *and* one hundred dollars.

"Something by Tolstoi" tells of a Jewish bookstore owner whose Gentile wife deserts him for fame as a singer and for all that money can buy. Realizing that success is empty without the love that they shared from childhood, she returns many years later to the bookshop, to find that his grief has left him withdrawn and unable to recognize her. He asks her, "Do you want a book?" She can't remember its name, she says, but tells him the plot, which is their own story, and he replies that he finds it familiar: "It seems to me that it is something by Tolstoi."

Unexpressed, unrequited love and the pain of loss was something that Tom was enduring now, an awakening of the heart, about which he had only read in books. With the end of the spring term, Mitch would be moving out of his life and going on to the University of Iowa. Forty-five years later, Tennessee wrote in *Memoirs* of his one-sided attraction to Mitch as "a fantastically aborted but crazily sweet love-affair." He was remembering what Tom felt but was unable to voice. Mitchell himself recalled, "I liked Tom—he was a very nice guy—but there never was anything between us but a good friendship. I didn't know he was gay, and I don't really believe he knew he was, either."[31]

Tennessee Williams would grace Mitch with a touch of immortality by naming a sensitive, caring character in *A Streetcar Named Desire* Harold Mitchell.

The Diary of a Resolute Woman

In January 1931, the Reverend Walter Dakin, at seventy-three years of age, had retired from Saint George's Episcopal Church in Clarksdale after fourteen years' service and began moving out of the rectory. Before they went to live in a house they owned in Memphis, the Dakins were saddened by the death of their great benefactor, Mrs. Maggie Wingfield. Funeral services were held at her home, with Mr. Dakin officiating. Mrs. Blanche Cutrer was among those attending.

At that time, Tom wrote Rose a brief note, mentioning that he had been living a life of virtual retirement in order to complete numerous papers and had written about six thousand words the previous night: "I have really gotten my fill of over-stuffed courses and am going to act with much more caution in my next semester's enrollment."[32] Rose had initially decided to attend an ATO dance, but this plan, like many others, seems to have gone awry. She was showing only intermittent improvement. Although she was going out on occasion with various young men, none seemed to have any serious interest in her.

Her relations with her father were also deteriorating. Edwina told of an instance when Rose had invited a young man to the house: "Cornelius refused to leave the living room so she could entertain her caller. He stayed stretched out on the sofa, listening to the radio, although he could have gone into his bedroom. She phoned the young man and told him not to come over. Then she walked into the living room and evidently said something her father considered saucy. He slapped her."[33] She fled the house, then returned as she had before, refusing to speak to him for days.

On his return to St. Louis for the summer, Tom was met with a disgruntled father, angry that his grades were down from the previous year. Cornelius promptly put Tom to work in the typing pool at the Continental Shoe Company, a division of International Shoe. It was a tedious job that would last until mid-September.

By summer's end, Tom was anxious to get back to Columbia, not only to get free of his job but also to get away from his parents, whose battles were now at their worst. Edwina kept a diary of this time, discovered many years later among her letters and memorabilia.*

Sep. 4th 1931 (very embarrassing)
    I receive notice through the mail that our charge accounts at the Dry Goods stores have been discontinued.

---

*In her memoir, *Remember Me to Tom*, Edwina Williams wrote, "I kept a diary which I later destroyed when I read it and realized the horror of things happening in my daily life. But at the time, I had to write of my husband's brutality or I could not have endured it" (p. 59). The diary was found in the Dakin Williams collection.

Sat. Sep. 5th

I took Tom to town to buy his shirts, socks, etc. as he leaves for College next Wednesday. We bought most of his things in Boyd's basement to get them as cheaply as possible, had them sent C.O.D.

In the after-noon I did my marketing, carrying everything home as I now have no charge account at the Grocery store. Cornelius generally comes home late for his supper on Sat. evenings as he goes out to a country club on that after-noon ostensibly for golf, but mainly for drinking. For supper I made some Chili-con-carne of which he is very fond and it is something that can easily be kept hot. Tom and Rose leave early for a card party. Cornelius does not show up for supper or even telephone. I wait up for the children. They come in at 2 o'clock. Cornelius, not til 3 o'clock, stayed for the dinner-dance at the Club. He became angry because I reproached him for not letting me know he would not be home for supper. He has had too much to drink, tells me in a voice loud enough to wake the neighborhood that I make "life a hell" for him and can leave.

When Tom returned to the university for what would prove to be his third and last year there, he began his courses in journalism. But things were different, and his spirits were low. He had an older roommate, Guy Tourney, who was often away on band gigs and whom he didn't particularly like. As was his wont, Tom retreated into his writing, even to the neglect of his studies.

Another cause of neglect was that he had become infatuated with Anna Jean O'Donnell, a friend of Esmeralda and also a Chi Omega. He was entranced by her Irish beauty, her dark hair, and deep blue eyes. Anna Jean, who was active in the drama workshop and a candidate for Queen of the St. Pat's Ball, doubtless had beaux more handsome than Tom, but theirs became a special relationship. Williams described it as "a poignant and innocent little affair. My feeling for her was romantic."[34] He wrote poems to her; one beginning "A kiss brings pain" was published in the 1932 yearbook. Another was written more out of pique than affection:

To Anna Jean

> *You Damned Blockheaded Irishman—*
> *You Blue-eyed, Darling little fool—*
> *Your only use in life is making men your Tool—*
> *You precious, lying, loving cheat*
> *Your playing, praying, I repeat*
> *is just a pose, a rouse [sic], a Scene—*
> *A well-staged play, with lights and screens,*
> *Oh, well—At that you're mighty Damned Sweet!*

During the school year, Tom saw Anna Jean frequently, and although she did not take this as seriously as he did, she provided solace for the sense of loss he was feeling in the absence of both Hazel and Mitch.

In October, an event occurred that sent reverberations into theatre companies throughout the country: the Theatre Guild's production of Eugene O'Neill's *Mourning Becomes Electra*, a modern adaptation of the *Oresteia* trilogy of Aeschylus, starring the incomparable Russian actress Alla Nazimova.* The critical response was unprecedented. *Time* magazine, calling him "a mature genius at 43," placed the dark, brooding image of O'Neill on its cover. This could not have escaped Tom's attention. Inevitably, there was renewed discussion of O'Neill on campus, particularly by Donovan Rhynsburger and those studying theatre. Professor Ramsay's list of "Fifty Best Plays" for students to read included O'Neill's *Ile*, *Bound East for Cardiff*, and *In the Zone*. As a result, an expressionist production of O'Neill's *The Hairy Ape* was planned by the workshop for the spring.

Whether Tom was mindful of O'Neill or simply reflecting upon the times, he was preparing to enter his second play (following *Beauty Is the Word*) in the annual Dramatic Arts Club One-Act Play Contest. He named it *Hot Milk at Three in the Morning*, and it was notable for its similarity to O'Neill's one-act *Before Breakfast* in its depiction of a desperate Depression-era laborer and his sickly, whining wife. The subject of a man trapped in marriage with his home a veritable prison—an archetype of the caged animal and the symbol of his own father—was one that Tennessee Williams would use repeatedly.

In the heat of their argument, the wife says, "You know that before you married me you was just a common tramp, that's all you was!" Angered, he replies:

Yeah, you bet I was. An' I was satisfied, I was happy! You bet I was. I tramped from Massachusetts to Oregon, and I tramped from Oregon to Alaska. An' I stayed one place just as long as I liked it and when I got tired of it I went on to another place. I was free! Yeah, I was a real man then, before I married you. I wasn't afraid of no one. And now what kind of thing have I turned into? A mill hand! A wage slave! A chained animal! An' I work for a little grey weasel that I'd like to tear the guts out of, but I gotta say "Yes, sir" to him, cause if I lost my job I couldn't just hit the road again like I used to, and go on to another town and another job,

---

*Francis Donahue in *The Dramatic World of Tennessee Williams* (New York: Frederick Ungar, 1964), p. 7, and Donald Spoto in *The Kindness of Strangers* (pp. 37–38) maintain erroneously that Williams saw Nazimova on the Missouri campus in a touring company of Ibsen's *Ghosts*. In fact, she never appeared at the university, and he saw the actress in *Ghosts* only when she came to St. Louis on tour in February 1936. Professor Ramsay did not include Ibsen as required reading in his lectures, but he did include Strindberg. However, in Stockholm during the summer of 1955, Williams specifically denied the influence of Strindberg.

'cause I got a sick wife and a bawling baby a-hanging on to me. That's what I got when I got hitched up with you![35]

Tom would later revise *Hot Milk* and rename it *Moony's Kid Don't Cry*, perhaps thinking of the O'Neill title *The Dreamy Kid*. Along with two other one-act plays, it would win recognition years later in a contest sponsored by the Group Theatre.

At the moment, though, Tom's concern centered on the journalism courses he was taking, what they would mean in establishing him as an independent writer and in liberating him from a home where there was nothing but strife. In early November, C.C. had just returned from one of his regional sales tours, while Edwina continued to record everything in her diary.

We've had two terrible scenes since Cornelius' return. In both of them he says he is going to "quit" me. A nice sense of security that gives to the children. No wonder they are both nervous. I receive a letter from the school doctor saying Dakin is "nineteen pounds under-weight" and I've been trying so hard to build him up giving him hot malted milk every night, etc. . . . I had to hand him a bill . . . from Barnes hospital for the "Shadow pictures" Dr. Alexander had made of Rose last spring. This occasioned another tempest and when I very mildly reminded him it wasn't my fault or Rose's either, he interpreted me as giving him a "dirty crack" and said, "One more and I leave you"! . . . I'm wondering how much longer I can endure this. I had awakened feeling so gay. It was a beautiful morning, the sun shining so brightly, and though I was tired from the strenuous Sunday (we motored to Columbia the day before and had a nice visit with Tom at the fraternity house) I got up as usual at six-thirty to make Cornelius' breakfast and was happy in thinking how well Tom looked and to find that he had been doing well in his journalistic work. Then the thunder-bolt!

She was afraid to point out that she had had to get Tom's glasses mended—they were tied together by a piece of string—and ended up paying for them herself out of her household fund. In her diary, Edwina then told how Tom had returned home for the Thanksgiving holiday, only to be confronted with still another family crisis:

Nov. 29th 1931
    Quite the biggest up-heavel we've had yet was staged to-day, Sunday. It was the new girl's pay-day and Cornelius became infuriated because I had not obtained her cheaper. . . . Such a torrent of abuse he heaped upon me! The children were present and he said, "I'm leaving you. I'll pack my grip and go to the hotel." Both Dakin and Rose became hysterical. Cornelius then turned on Rose berating her for everything imaginable.

"Dakin is the only one of you worth a d————" said he, as he flung himself out of the room. Tom was packing his grip in his little room preparing to leave for Columbia on the two o'clock train. "Mother," said he,
"tell him to get the h———— out of here" the first time I've ever heard
Tom be profane. I went quietly back to the sun-room and gave Cornelius
his grip and told him I was tired of these scenes and he could go whenever he [wanted], that I couldn't have Dakin a nervous wreck, as he has
made Rose. He announced he would go when he got ready.
Next day—
    Tom stayed until the mid-night train as he didn't want to leave me
with such a storm brewing. Cornelius has calmed down and evidently
decided to remain. Poor Rose was ill all night and couldn't sleep. I feel
as weak as if I'd gotten up from a sick bed. How much longer am I to
endure this? Tom said, as far as he was concerned, he'd rather go to
work and live in the cheapest part of the city than see me go through
this any more.

    After his return to school, Tom wrote to Rose, saying, "As you can readily
understand, I am very anxious to hear from you concerning the situation on
the home front. Has the spirit of Quiet Night now descended?"[36]
    It had not, either at home or abroad. The year 1932, from its outset,
augured important changes in Tom's life and in a nation gone almost overnight from an affluent Jazz Age to an epoch of despair and defeat unlike any in
its history. The White House was still occupied by a much-despised Herbert
Hoover, but it would in a year's time be occupied by a wealthy autocrat named
Franklin Delano Roosevelt. He was proposing sweeping reforms, and now, in
the year before he was to take office, there was a wisp of optimism in the air.
And Tom, too, was looking forward confidently, taking it for granted that he
would continue at the university until graduation the following year. His
mood was up, if not his grades—he was passing, if barely, in everything except
ROTC. That, he felt, was beneath his concern. Cornelius would have a different opinion.
    Toward the end of January, Tom wrote a somewhat formal letter to his
father, a respectful request for money. Whenever he received a return check,
he would run through the hall, waving it and shouting, "The Red Goose flies
again!" Referring to a special line of shoes that C.C. promoted, he concluded
his letter with the hope that "the Red Goose is now flying out of the black
clouds of depression," and he signed it, "Lovingly, Tom."[37]
    These petitions were always received with either a bellow or a grunt, and
now with St. Louis in the grips of the Depression, Cornelius could point to
the fact that in Columbia the Hamilton-Brown Shoe Company had gone
under and he might find himself out of a job, too. In any event, he was convinced that, after his family had bled him of his last cent, he would end up
alone in a poorhouse or in a potter's field.

The truth was, Cornelius did not cut corners when it came to his own pleasures, and he continued to indulge in country club golf and weekend binges. He knew that he could always depend on the Dakins, and that, even with their meager resources, Grand would continue to send Edwina money for the children. Apparently, Cornelius reneged on the tuition, prompting Tom to ask his mother, "How the devil did Grand scrape together $250 in these times of famine? I almost suspect her of embezzling church funds!"[38]

In January, Tom had joined the Missouri Chapter of the College Poetry Society. Esmeralda was one of twenty-five female members and he one among seven males. It is not likely that anyone who knew—*really* knew—Tom Williams at that time would have voted him treasurer, but somehow he got hold of the Poetry Society's ledger, with its title page written in a fine feminine hand: "Treasurer's Book—Missouri Chapter of the College Poetry Society of America." The first three pages were given over to "1931–1932 Expenditures and Receipts," with Tom's dues of "2.50" noted and, under expenditures, the treasurer "book & folder .65." Enticingly, the remainder of the book contained nearly two hundred blank pages, and in 1936, he would put the sixty-five-cent book to more practical use as his journal.

Tom now had a new roommate, Bill Bell, who, although not a member of the poetry group, had something of a poetic flair, spiced with a raffish sense of humor. Many years later, when he, like many others, was startled to learn that Tennessee Williams was none other than Tom, he inquired:

> Are you the T.L.W. that attended the Univ. of Missouri 1931–32?
> Are you the T.L.W. that was ATO?
> Are you the T.L.W. whose home was in St. Louis?
> Are you the T.L.W. that dated Esmeralda Mayes?
> Are you the T.L.W. that made me very mad by calling my Chi Omega Sweetheart "Bouncing Bubbles"?
> Are you the TLW that drank $4 per gallon creek likker, puked on the floor of our room and then covered it (the puke, not the room) with newspapers?
> Are you the TLW that never gave me a single lick during the two years I was a pledge?
> Are you the TLW that looked so lousy in your R.O.T.C. uniform?[39]

Almost all who attended the journalism school were under the impression that this was where they were going to learn to write. They didn't understand that they were expected to master a craft, a trade involving the whole range of newspaper functions, from layout to advertising to reporting. Tom was becoming disenchanted when he wrote to his mother, saying that he had recently been given a highly unsatisfactory "beat" in his journalism class. He averred that he would prefer to remain "un-honored" rather than have the burden each day of reporting the costs of local produce and listing the prices of light and heavy hens, sour cream, eggs, and geese, all of which left him no time for creative writing.

But the next "beat" was even worse, when Tom was told to write an obituary. "Well, I went to the house where the death had occurred," he later said. "There was all this squalling going on, and it was not a pleasant place to be. Quite obviously a death had occurred. I reported that the professor had died. Actually, his wife had died, not he. But it came out in the paper that *he* was dead. So, they immediately fired me, of course. . . . I couldn't take journalism seriously."[40]

Tom's grades in journalism and other courses were sliding, and not telling his mother that he had failed ROTC, he reassured her, "Although I did not make any poor grades, the fact that I was taking such a large course, 22 hours, which is 5 in excess of the number that can be taken with credit, I could not put very much time in upon individual courses, and suffered accordingly, in the grades that I received."[41] Tom also made mention of trouble he was having with a series of sties on his left eye, a developing cataract, as it turned out, that would cause him great distress in the immediate years to come.

On March 26, Tom turned twenty-one, that symbolic age of certifiable manhood. He was filled with visions of leaving the university—and his home—the following year for a position on a newspaper or a magazine. Then he would enjoy the luxury of writing for a living and also writing "on the side" for his own pleasure, or so he thought.

In that same spring of 1932, a tragic event was taking place about three hundred miles north of Havana, aboard the liner *Orizaba*. On Wednesday, April 27, shortly before noon, the American poet Hart Crane came on deck dressed in pajamas covered by an overcoat. In the words of one report: "He walked rapidly aft, threw the coat on the deck, climbed up on the rail, and jumped over the side. Life preservers were thrown at once, the ship was manoeuvred and a boat put over the side, but no trace of Crane was found. He had been seen once after his body struck the water and apparently he made no effort to reach the life preservers thrown him."[42] Among the passengers who had witnessed Crane's leap overboard, there was conflicting opinion whether the hand that had shot to the surface had been grasping for a life preserver or simply making a gesture of good-bye. Hart Crane would become the poet Tom idolized above all, and it was Tennessee's wish upon his death that his body be sewn up in a simple white sack and borne out to sea to rest as close as possible to Crane's remains.

Tom was only beginning to experience the disappointments, the rejections, the isolation that make up the lives of artists such as Hart Crane. His play *Hot Milk at Three in the Morning* took only thirteenth place in the Dramatic Arts Club One-Act Play Contest and failed to get the workshop production he would have liked. It would be several years before his interest in writing plays would be rekindled. But there was some slight solace in the fact that a short story, "Big Black: A Mississippi Idyll,"[43] had won an honorable mention in fifth place.

It was his earliest known story about the South. For the past year, the famed Scottsboro case had been making headlines, and Tom was aware, as he would be all his life, of the plight of the Negro in America. The narrative of a black man on a road gang and his imagined relationship with a white woman was startling for its time, and the work notable for its dialogue and mature treatment of a sophisticated and controversial subject. It anticipated the milieu of future plays and stories regarded as classic Tennessee Williams, and it would be Tom's last effort at the university to gain recognition for his work as a writer.

Tom went home for the Easter holiday, and on his return to school, Rose wrote a letter to "Dearest Brother" that seemed tinged with hysteria and jealousy. She told him that she had a date with a beau named Carter, who was concerned about her making a favorable impression on his family. She also mentioned the mother of her closest girlfriend, Park Austin, as being "very much worried at present about my spiritual development. . . . She thinks Dr. Block's Sunday School [where Rose was teaching] has gone to rack and ruin with Carter and me in there. Smoking, Dancing, Card Playing Sunday School teachers!"

Park and Mrs. Austin lived across the street from the Williamses on Enright. Rose visited them frequently and alarmed Mrs. Austin with behavior that was often erratic. Dakin said that his sister didn't really like Carter, although he was her only boyfriend at the time.

With apparent mixed feelings, Rose in her letter asked Tom, "How is my biggest love? I didn't see much of you during the holidays but you are still the 'salt in my stew' that is, unless Anna Jean has taken my place in your heart."[44] Tom was seeing a good deal of Anna Jean O'Donnell during those spring months. He hoped to win her over to take Hazel's place, and among the poems he wrote to her, there was one that Tennessee Williams could always quote from memory:

> *Can I forget*
> *the night you waited*
> *beside your door—*
> *could it have been more*
> *plainly stated?—*
> *for something more.*

> *You spoke a rhyme*
> *about young love*

while we stood
breathing the rain-sweet
fragrance
of the wood.

I was a fool, not
knowing what
you waited for.
And then you smiled
and quietly
shut the door.[45]

7

The Celotex Interior

1932–1935

On arriving home for the summer, Tom was surprised to learn that his grades had been sent earlier than expected and were already in his father's hands. His marks would have enabled him to return to begin his senior year in the fall, but what enraged Cornelius was Tom's F in ROTC. To him, it was obvious that Tom was deliberately flunking military training; this was inexcusable, a reflection on the Williams name. He hadn't sent his son to the University of Missouri to bring disgrace upon a family whose ancestors were distinguished for their patriotism and military accomplishments.

Cornelius took this as a personal insult. A year later, Edwina recorded in her diary: "He made Tom leave the University and go to work on a small salary in the Vitality branch of the International Shoe Co. and it has taken all of his salary to pay for the accident he had last summer and his clothing, lunch money, etc. He would have received his degree in Journalism this Spring which is the kind of work he loves to do."[1] The accident to which Edwina referred occurred when Tom went for a swim at the Westborough Country Club; on diving into the pool, he smashed into its concrete side, requiring protracted dental work.

In her memoir, Edwina maintained that Cornelius was not about "to put out one more cent for Tom's education," although "Tom wanted with all his heart to get a degree, to keep learning, to be able to write more effectively. I think he would have given anything to remain in college. But he did not defy his father." C.C. got him a job at sixty-five dollars a month, and so "Tom entered a world of dusting shoes, typing out factory orders and hauling around packing cases stuffed with sample shoes, the world of his father."

The Great Depression was Cornelius's crowning argument. He was hardly going to throw good money after bad—he was not going to borrow more to finance an education for a son whose only ambition was to become an improvident writer. Learning what it took to make a living, especially in these times, he contended, would provide the kind of education Tom really needed to wake up to reality.

C.C. Williams was certainly witnessing firsthand the effects of the Depression as hordes of job seekers applied for nonexistent work at the doors of his company. Nearly one-fourth of the American labor force was unemployed. Only persons with pull, like Tom, were getting jobs at International Shoe, and even those were often on a daily cash basis. That being the case, C.C. felt that Tom should be damned grateful to have a job at all, however menial. In her diary, Edwina commented:

> June 27, 1932
> . . . We really hear less about our "poverty" than we did during all those years the rest of the world were enjoying their prosperity. With the exception of one evening about three weeks ago, when Cornelius said he was going to have to take Tom out of school and that Rose would have to "clerk," things have been quite peaceful. Rose cried all the next day because she still is not well.

With "peace" in the Williams household being always a lull between battles, C.C. for the moment had the advantage, constantly citing "world conditions" as an excuse for his niggardliness. But Edwina had her wait-and-see strategy: Her method was always to wait for an opening. Theirs was no longer a marriage, but a contest between a patriarchy challenged by a matriarchy, and it was just a question of holding power to see who would eventually win. The difference between the two was her driving ambition both for herself socially and for her "writin' son" posed against Cornelius's status quo, content as he was with his business position, golf at the country club, the poker nights, and, above all, the power of his purse.

C.C. contended that Tom, at twenty-one, and Rose, twenty-two, should be earning their livings and contributing to the household as long as they were living under *his* roof. Moreover, there was his pride and joy, Dakin, to think about and his education: *He* was a true Williams. Damn it, he could say, it was bad enough having a nagging wife always crying for more and more money, but having the whole family on his back was just too much!

Edwina saw her husband as penny-wise and penny-pinching, except for his own pleasures. She claimed that Cornelius "wasn't poor, but felt poor," and added, "I imagine my husband could have become rich if he had been wise enough to know when to invest money in the stock market. All the executives of the shoe company became millionaires over-night, buying stocks which they sold before the crash. They built handsome houses far out in the country, launched their daughters in society, and from then on, although they had been our friends, found no time for us."[2] There were those who became paupers overnight, too, but Edwina would not have taken notice of this, since it would have destroyed her argument.

Tom's job was hellishly repetitious: riding into work with his father every morning, unable to think of anything to say; C.C. making no effort at conversation at all; the mundane chores of repeatedly dusting shoe samples and typing order forms. But ultimately, vengeance was his. A coworker endures, but an artist co-opts. Although he was faced with three years of drudgery within "the celotex interior under fluorescent tubes," in time Tom was able to say that the work may have been "indescribable torment to me as an individual but of immense value to me as a writer." It gave him, he said, "first-hand knowledge of what it means to be a small wage earner in a hopelessly routine job.[3]

"Still," as Williams said on reflection, "I learned a lot there about the comradeship between co-workers at minimal salary, and I made some very good friends, especially a Polish fellow," whom in *Memoirs* he called Eddie but who, it appears, was actually a worker named Stanley Kowalski. There was also a spinster named Nora at the desk next to his, with whom he "carried on whispered conversations about the good movies and stage shows in town and radio shows such as 'Amos and Andy.' "[4]

Tom—along with an entire nation trying to escape the Depression—was becoming a regular filmgoer. The Fox downtown was an ornate movie palace that showed both talking pictures and stage shows. Among the films that Tom could likely have seen was *Faithless* starring Tallulah Bankhead, an actress who would someday play an important role in his life and career. In this film, which was like many with a social message, Bankhead portrayed a young, dependent American woman who is unemployed and constantly confronted by NO HELP WANTED—THIS MEANS YOU! signs and who ends up selling herself in order to survive, a prototype that in life would linger in Tom's mind.

Apart from going to the movies or swimming, there was not much in the way of recreation for Tom. Rose would sometimes accompany him, but generally he was alone. He was still in love with Hazel, and his lingering hope was that, when she returned from school, they would marry. He confided his despair and loneliness in a poem to his friend at Missouri, Anna Jean O'Donnell, with its intimate reference to Hazel:

MADRIGAL
(to A. J.)

Today, I am dull, I am dull!
The light has gone out of me:
My hungering soul is a gull
That circles an empty sea.

. . .

Hand in hand with the Spring you came—
Her's your sweetness, her's your flame!
Her beauty with yours indivisibly blent,
Hand in hand with the Spring you went![5]

Anna Jean responded, "Please accept my deepest condolence upon hearing of Hazel's absence this summer. I'm sure though, Tom, that there are many other auburn-haired gals in St. Louis, so don't pine your nights away but be up and stirring!"[6]

In an attempt to unburden his feelings, Tom wrote to his grandfather, complaining of his not having time for writing, except at night, when he had energy only for his poetry. "I am, of course, very much disappointed that I cannot return to the University this Fall. . . . I am trying to save some money toward going to Columbia—which is the country's very best school of journalism."[7] Grand and Walter for once were unable to come to the rescue, preoccupied as they were with the cost of moving to Memphis and discouraged, too, as they were by Cornelius's refusal to give any financial assistance at all to Tom.

In mid-August, Tom received a letter that could only have pained him, lighthearted though his reply was. The editor of his fraternity's newsletter, *The Link*, unaware that he would not be returning to school in the fall, "delegated the job of fashion tips to the one and only T.L. 'Red Goose' Williams." A different source of pain came from the fact that he was being fitted with a temporary bridge as a result of his swimming accident. Tom answered:

Having been laid up the past few weeks with a crack[ed] upper jaw and a number of semi-detached molars, I was truly grateful for the heartening tribute of a letter from my journalistic colleague. Also, for the overwhelming compliment of being asked to contribute an article to the LINK. But, why, my dear Oscar, of all subjects from the mating instincts of the walrus to the latest inside dope on the Alpha Chi's and why Ezzie can't go swimming did you select me to write on sartorial hints? Is it possible that the honorable editor, whose memory has always equalled that of the proverbial elephant, has forgotten those occasions during the past year when, within the sacred temple of friendship, before the bros. assembled, I was reprimanded by ye worthy master with all the severity at his command, for having entered the dining salon of an evening in such a state of disarray—sans socks and with vest unbuttoned—that I seemed to be giving an impression or impersonation of the mad genius?

I think that it would have been far more suitable if I had been asked to expound in Jules Laverne [*sic*] style, From Shower to Dinner Table in Three Seconds, and the question of proper dress delivered into the more competent hands of our esthetic pedagogue, Pottsy Batchelder, now sojourning in the cultural center of Boston, who could design as a rush week uniform, I presume, some very charming ballet costumes of black silk sprinkled with pink and blue and yellow dots, in which we might embrace our prospective—shall I say victims—to the airily symphonic strains of Narcissus.

But since you have in your superior wisdom seen fit to impose this office upon me of Worthy Arbiter of Fashion, I have done my best in the following. No seersuckers (oh those nasty, vile things) and leave the flannels with the loud stripes at home . . . and emerald studded belts are not in this year . . . but tab shirts are . . . and look nice, too . . . and don't forget your white flannels . . . but no diamond rings . . . nor any trick a la Bell hats . . . nor any Tahitian sunrise motifs in the neckwear . . . and Homburg hats will be good this fall . . . and bring along your white shoes . . . and summer ties . . . and linen suits . . . and I don't have to chew beer . . . I can just smell it and pass out together with R. S. C.[?].

> Yours fraternally,
> The Red Goose,
> Worthy Arbiter of
> Fashion[8]

As long as Tom was earning his sixty-five dollars a month and was off the paternal dole, Cornelius had little to say about his son's determination to become a writer. He had by now lost all faith in Tom and centered his hopes on Dakin, who was thirteen and doing very well in school. The boy earned his own pin money, which of course impressed his father. Dakin admired and looked up to Tom, who liked playing the role of older and wiser brother. In *Memoirs*, Tennessee described Dakin as "always an indomitable enthusiast at whatever he got into—being a Williams, you see," and said that his brother had at one time "turned our little patch of green behind the apartment on Enright into quite an astonishing little vegetable garden. If there were flowers in it, they were, alas, obscured by the profuse growth of squash, pumpkins, and other edible flora."[9] As far as C.C. was concerned, in these depressed times, *this* made sense, because you can't eat flowers.

Dakin's recollection of his life in the cramped Enright Avenue apartment was that "Dad slept in my room—the back 'sun-porch' had twin beds—and he snored very loudly from heavy drinking on weekends. He took me to Cardinals baseball games and to Ruggieri's Steak House for a 75-cent T-bone steak and cussed out the waiter very loudly when it was too tough. He smoked Chesterfield cigarettes constantly, so it was downright bad for my health spending every Sunday afternoon in the small front sun-room listening to Dizzy Dean and the Cards on the radio."[10]

Another program that Cornelius listened to regularly and accepted as a different kind of gospel was that of the "fighting priest" Father Coughlin, who would go from local muckraking broadcasts in 1926 to weekly radio sermons on the CBS network. Until 1940, when the government and the Catholic church itself moved to silence him, the Reverend Charles E. Coughlin became famed for his attacks on the denizens of Wall Street, whom he blamed for the Depression, and finally on the Wall Street Jews, whom he considered the cause of world war. His rampant anti-Semitism was met with approval in St. Louis, especially among many of the German families. Actually, C.C. was not violently anti-Semitic; he just accepted Jews the same way he did Negroes—as inferiors.

"He was a sort of 'hail and well-met' fellow," Dakin said.

> Every once in a while I would come into the shoe company . . . and his desk was right up front. He was sales manager, one of about three, and he would have his little secretary sitting right in front of him while he was dictating a letter to one of his salesmen. Now, if anyone else were dictating such a letter, he'd say, "Dear Jack, I must tell you your sales record has been very disappointing this month, and you're going to have to do something about it, or we'll have to make some changes." But does C.C. do that? No! He bellows, "God-damn it, Jack! If your sales don't go up next month, you're going to be fired!" You'd think the salesman was sitting right there. Dad could be heard all over the room, and his secretary would write it all down exactly the way he dictated it.

Dakin saw his father as a deeply frustrated man. "He got no sex from Mother, so he was not averse to picking up a discreet female companion whenever the opportunity beckoned—but did not go around 'chasing.' Actually he had a very big nature and didn't hold grudges or resentments for very long—his only bad habit was excessive drinking." Of course, Edwina was aware that her husband had women friends—as did many of his married cronies—and so she could and did use this as reason enough to lock him out of her bedroom. Dakin acknowledged, "Mother had a lot of faults—in that she overdid the puritan business—and she considered sex to be dirty, I'm sure. And the fact that my Dad was running around with other women was welcomed as an excuse to cut him off from sex."[11]

Furthermore, Edwina wasn't about to contract a venereal disease, as one of the salesmen did, passing it on to his wife. She knew why Paul Jamison fired the salesman, and it horrified her to imagine such a thing happening to her and Cornelius. The one thing she did not approve of, though, and took a strong stand against, was his staying out overnight. She was always fearful that he would fail to turn up at work the next day. Getting up at six in the morning, making breakfast, and seeing that he and Tom got off to the shoe company on time—this, she felt, was her responsibility. Otherwise, the less she saw of Cornelius, the better. And whenever he would take off on occasional business trips, the only sigh that was more audible than hers was his. For him, being away was like the good old days on the road; for her, it was respite from hell.

> Sunday—Aug. 29th
> Cornelius is angry because I charged a bill of $4 or thereabouts [for] a few things at Scrugg's—around $8—things I needed for Dakin. He says I'll have to buy everything for the house, food, clothing for my-self, Dakin, etc. out of that $135 I am now getting. I tell him I cannot do it so he says "We will talk it over with Mr. Jamison, and then you can get out." Alright, I've done the best I could. My conscience is clear. My poor little children. What will become of them? I've had such a struggle trying to build strong bodies for them. . . . My knees and hands are trembling so I cannot write more. What-ever comes God is my strength and my refuge.

Whenever Dakin asked his mother why she married his father, she would reply, " 'I don't know'—but she posed the question more than anyone." Amanda Wingfield in *The Glass Menagerie* was perhaps more insightful.

> AMANDA: Oh, I don't know how he did it, but that face fooled everybody. All he had to do was grin and the world was bewitched. I don't know of anything more tragic than a young girl just putting herself at the mercy of a handsome appearance. . . .

If Edwina had been deceived by appearances, now it was *she* who had to keep them up, which in time became obvious, especially to someone like Paul Jamison, upon whom Edwina relied. More than C.C.'s employer, he was her confidant and close personal friend. Since they were attracted to each other, the friendship might have become more than that, had they not been constrained by the mores of the time and their own morals. As it was, Jamison not only helped Edwina to keep up appearances; he indirectly provided the source of security that she needed to maintain her home and a respectable place in the community. In other words, he kept C.C. on a short rein.

Throughout her illnesses, her struggles to raise the three children and to withstand her embattled marriage, Edwina acquired a kind of tensile strength. More than simply endure the city, she grew to like St. Louis. During her long life, she held steadfastly to the role of "Miss Edwina," keeping up her southern accent and ways, for she realized this gave her a certain distinction in St. Louis society. Also, being a member of the DAR and a frequent guest of the Wednesday Club elevated her position.

But her main concern—and topic of conversation—was her family and always would be: her "precious" children, her "dear" parents, and even her husband's "thoughtful and kind" sisters. Strangely, they created a bond between Edwina and Cornelius. It was this kinship that created a curious ambivalence in C.C.'s attitude toward his family and toward Tom. His older son was a Williams, after all, even if he didn't behave like one. He was also a Dakin, as Edwina would be quick to remind Cornelius. Finally, pride in family was all that bound them in marriage.

Actually, unlike her gregarious husband, Edwina had few interests outside her family. Whenever she stopped talking *about* them, she wrote letters *to* them. For many years, until enfeebled by age, she used a voluminous correspondence as a means of binding her family to her: It was an ingrained, old-fashioned habit, one that her children, notably Tom, carried on. During his lifetime, prolific as he was as a writer, Tennessee Williams was also a prodigious correspondent.

Stairs to the Roof

Once Tom realized that he would not be returning to the university in the fall, he became more determined than ever in his writing. Edwina recalled, "Every evening when he came home from the shoe company, Tom would go to his room with black coffee and cigarettes and I could hear the typewriter clicking away at night in the silent house. Some mornings when I walked in to wake him for work, I would find him sprawled fully dressed across the bed, too tired to remove his clothes as he fell off to sleep at heaven knows what hour."[12]

Instilled in Tom during those trying times was a discipline, an incredible capacity for work, that remained undiminished throughout most of his life. It was an application, a dedication, to his writing that staggered often younger, certainly healthier, friends and associates. He would write, oblivious to his surroundings or to anyone even in the same room. Those who were witness to this all attested to an ability in him to concentrate that seemed almost inhuman.

By now, any illusions Tom had of pursuing journalism as a career were gone. "I wrote not with any hope of making a living at it, but because I found no other means of expressing things that seemed to demand expression. There was never a moment when I did not find life to be immeasurably exciting to witness, however difficult it was to sustain."[13] Tennessee Williams might have said that on reflection, but there were times, many times, when Tom Williams earnestly doubted that his life was worth living.

Tom was alone as never before, no longer a precocious child, but a young adult confined to the same prison as C.C., his jailer. Confinement was what he most feared, the feeling of suffocation, and the agony he was suffering was the worst he had ever known. The long, seemingly unending hours in the warehouse and the time spent in his little room by himself gave him no relief from self-doubt and worry. Some nights, he would go out with Rose, who, fueled by failures to find employment and someone to court her, was enduring her own private hell. On occasions when Tom would see Miss Florence, she would tell him of Hazel's success singing on the radio up in Madison. He seldom heard from her. The loneliness he felt, though, did not relate solely to Hazel. It rose out of his isolation, the need to be alone, to write, versus the need for companionship, someone to love, to love him. His smoking and coffee drinking inevitably affected his health. His left eye continued to trouble him; he was becoming an insomniac and obsessed with specters of insanity and death. As a little boy, he had been afraid to go to sleep at night because he feared that he might not wake up in the morning. Sleep and death had become equated and entangled in his mind.

By November, Tom Williams was regarded as a worker among workers, and while he had definite convictions about the many facets of his fellowman as a social being, his primary interest was in individual human nature. He listened attentively and he observed, but he didn't talk or write about overtly political issues. In those days, you were not supposed to talk in genteel company about politics, religion, or sex, pretty much in that order, lest you wreck the peace in the front parlor.

But the summer of 1932 had erupted into a time of tumult: The desperation of masses of Americans was no longer quiet desperation. Across the nation, protest and violence had been exploding in thousands of incidents, from the breaking of food-store windows at night to the looting of delivery trucks. Jobless men in groups of as many as thirty to forty were entering chain stores demanding food for their families, and the store managers acquiesced out of fear of retaliation and the ensuing publicity. Urban mass actions were taking place in industrial centers, with demonstrators being fired upon, murdered, and maimed by hired police. In Washington, Gen. Douglas MacArthur, ignoring President Hoover's instructions, ordered his soldiers to fire upon unarmed veterans in an effort to drive the so-called Bonus Army out of the capital. Farmers in the drought-stricken Midwest were witnessing the loss of life savings and foreclosures on their land. Families were even going so far as to store months' worth of food supplies in their cellars. Contrary to Hoover's rosy prognostication, it was revolution, not prosperity, that was "just around the corner."

A sales tax had been proposed in Congress as a remedy for a deficit approaching 60 percent of spending. A cynical substitute to replace upper-income and corporate taxation, the bill prompted Socialist party candidate Norman Thomas to remark, "It's a wonder they don't put a tax on tickets to the breadline."* Tom considered himself a socialist and believed all his life

*It was, in fact, comparable to a more recent proposal to tax unemployment benefits. Those who were literally counting pennies and selling off everything they owned, like people in boats jettisoning cargo to stay afloat, were outraged at the very idea.

that capitalism must inevitably give way to some form of enlightened social-ism. Although a worker, he was not among those at the shoe company who were actively campaigning for the Democratic candidate, Franklin Roosevelt, or among those avowed Communists who supported William Zebulon Fos-ter. The Socialists, particularly the somewhat quixotic but humane Norman Thomas, appealed to Tom, whereas he instinctively distrusted the cold didac-ticism of the Communist leadership—he had had enough of that at home under his father's direction. Now at twenty-one, he cast his first—and last—vote for Thomas, a lost cause if ever there was one. The Williamses, being southern, were Democrats, and on election day they voted for Roosevelt, who promised "social justice through social action."

Also arriving in November, doubtless of far more interest to Tom, was a letter from Cardinal Le Gros, the editor of *Neophyte*, a St. Louis poetry jour-nal: "Thank you for letting us see the exceptionally good poems. We are filled up for the next month, after which we shall be happy to receive these, or others."[14] Since Tom was turning out a steady stream of poetry submissions, he was encouraged to receive a note from a well-known editor, even if it was in effect a rejection slip.

Another letter, which arrived in mid-December, was from Professor Ram-say at the University of Missouri, an affirmation that was desperately needed at this time. It began:

> My dear Mr. Williams:
> Your absence from the University this year has been a matter for real regret to all of us who knew the excellent work you did here the last few years, especially in the field of creative writing. I hope very much you will be able before long to return and finish your course. . . .

Ramsay added that his letter was concerned specifically "with the fine story 'Big Black' which you submitted in the Mahan Story Contest last year. I should like to see that story published somewhere."[15]

What pained Tom now were the recollections of his all-too-recent days in school, memories that Ramsay's letter called up of those who had encouraged and befriended him: Elmer Lower, Jim Connor, Esmeralda, Anna Jean, and, most especially, Mitch. In the years to come, Tom would incorporate in his writings the names of at least twenty-five people and places he had known at Ol' Mizzou.

In January, the entire nation was looking hopefully to the new president. His inaugural words—"The only thing we have to fear is fear itself"—sounded a message that held a special meaning for Tom as well as for millions of others. And when, after thirteen years, national Prohibition came to an end, Cornelius was able to join in the chorus of "Happy Days Are Here Again." There was no celebration on the family battlefront, however; the marriage of

Edwina and Cornelius Williams had hit rock bottom. As Edwina recorded it in her diary:

> New Years Day 1933 will be long remembered by the children and me. Cornelius stayed out all night, came home at seven while I was preparing breakfast. I made the mistake of protesting, not realizing how much under the influence of liquor he was. . . . He flew into a rage and threatened me. I locked my door and tried to reason with him through the closed door. "Open that door or I'll bust it in!" Before I could obey the command he had suited the action to the word, the lock broke, the door flew open striking me in the nose and knocking me to the floor where I lay dazed. Meanwhile Rose wakens, hears the commotion, sees me lying on the floor with nose bleeding and rushes into the hall screaming "Help, he is killing her!" I come to my senses, find Cornelius bending over me and a strange man in the hall, had a nervous chill—the children send for a doctor.

Rose, hysterical, had fled from the house and brought in a stranger from the street. Edwina wrote in her diary: "When I regained my senses, I heard Rose screaming and a strange man's voice in the hall, and Cornelius telling him to go away, that I was alright. I'll not write more except to say I was sick after-ward and the children sent for Dr. Falk."

Dakin's recollection was that she attempted to slam the door in his father's face and that he gave it a sudden shove:

> It flew inward, striking mother on the bridge of her still-perfect aquiline nose. Mother gave a bloodcurdling second scream, falling backward on her bed in what I believe was a genuine faint. Blood trickled from her nose in a volume sufficient to convince C. C. that he had done all the damage he could safely do. He snorted a couple of times and went out the kitchen door to the garage, where he furiously backed out the Studebaker, striking a fender in his rage.
>
> "This time he can't blame the dented fender on Tom," I thought, as I witnessed the scene of his departure through the sun room curtains. I went to the icebox and got a towelful of ice to revive mother. She was in an angry mood when she came to and discovered the injury to her once beautiful nose. "Well," she said, "I will call Paul Jamison first thing [this] morning. If your father thinks he can divorce me, he will have another think coming."

Dakin said that his father did not come home that night and that Rose stayed over with a friend. "I remember falling asleep with my eyes full of tears." Cornelius "sheepishly" returned to the apartment the following evening, and Edwina prepared her "famous pork chops with bow-tie macaroni, all just as though nothing had happened."[16] While the fighting would continue, the confrontations always loud and bitter, the dialogue of C.C. and Edwina had become empty and repetitious. In August, she would turn forty-nine; he, in the same month, fifty-four. Life had gone on without them, and such dreams as they each might have harbored were now transferred, hers to Tom and his to Dakin.

What was awakened in Edwina was a reinforced need to rule the roost. Having lost this last fight, Cornelius had become a humiliated cock of the walk. Gradually, very gradually, the dominant roles were reversed, until finally C.C.'s threats and roars became meaningless echoes. More than anything, it was his attack upon her children that divided them. He was plainly jealous of the affection and attention his wife lavished upon them, particularly Rose and Tom. Envy of his own children and resentment of his wife led to brutish behavior toward his family that was nowhere in evidence in his behavior toward his friends. A fundamental weakness in his character had been revealed: the unfulfilled love of the child in him for a mother who tragically had died when he was barely able to remember her.

Now that he had struck her, the immediate role that Edwina, with her bandaged, broken nose, was able to assume was that of "a Christian martyr." In her middle age, she was more churchgoing than ever, which added to a holier-than-thou attitude she assumed toward a husband who, as Dakin said, was "definitely *not* a church-goer" and who became "for a while an Episcopalian only to please her. But when he got tired of pleasing her, he lost all interest in what he called 'Pisky-Palians.' Dad was nominally a Presbyterian. Once in mid-life crisis, he joined a St. Louis Presbyterian Bible Study Group called Caravan Class, but religion was never his thing. Booze was his main 'opiate.' "[17]

Having Saturday afternoons off from work enabled Tom, now twenty-two, to set up, as he said, "an unvarying regime for those lovely times of release. I would go to the Mercantile Library, far downtown in St. Louis, and read voraciously there; I would have a thirty-five-cent lunch at a pleasant little restaurant. And I would go home in a 'service car'—to concentrate upon the week's short story. Of course all of Sunday was devoted to the story's completion. . . . During the weekdays I would work on verse: quite undistinguished, I fear."[18] Regardless, he pressed his poetry on any number of editors, one of whom was Harriet Monroe of the prestigious *Poetry* magazine. He wrote what proved to be an irresistible plea to her: "Will you do a total stranger the kindness of reading his verse? Thank you! Thomas Lanier Williams."[19]

On August 5, Edwina Williams made a brief entry in her diary: "Twice this month Cornelius has remained out all night." After that, she would have less and less to add before she tucked the tiny notebook away, later believing she had destroyed it. C.C., having lost more ground than he realized, would in his frustration turn his rage on Rose, insisting she find work, and on Tom, threatening to charge him rent.

After a year of laboring at the shoe company, Tom took a vacation at Lake Taneycomo, in the Ozarks, with his mother and Dakin. On his return, he received a letter from William A. Martin, editor of *Inspiration*, a poetry magazine, saying, "Dear Sir, Your poem 'Under the April Rain' has been awarded first prize in our 'Spring Number' contest. Congratulations!"[20] There was no money, but it was a *first* prize at last. Tom answered by recommending to Martin two young poets he had known at the University of Missouri, and by sending some more poems. As a result, he received another first prize from the same publication for one of the poems he enclosed, "Her Heart Was a Delicate Silver Lyre."

His poetry was soon recognized by the reputable Writers Guild of St. Louis, and more poems were published: "Modus Vivendi" in the July issue of *Counterpoint* and "Ave Atque Vale" in the October issue of *L'Alouette*, a magazine of verse, whose editor, C. A. A. Parker, advised him with congratulations that the poem would also appear in their anthology, *Chanson L'Alouette*, volume four. These lyric poems owe much to the inspiration of not only Keats and Shelley but also Emily Dickinson, Edna St. Vincent Millay, and especially the St. Louis poet Sara Teasdale, whose suicide earlier in the year had deeply affected Tom. His sudden acceptance in poetry circles prompted him to write his grandparents, saying that although his verses were being published in "a couple of Eastern newspapers," it amounted to recognition but no money. "It is as hard to get rich on poetry as fat on vinegar, you know."

On a more practical note, he added, "I am going to night-school now at one of the high-schools, and am trying to get in a short-hand class, as Dad says if I become pretty good at it, it might be possible for me to get a stenographic job at the office with higher salary than I am now receiving." Tom concluded his letter saying, "Rose and I are going to a costume dance tonight. Rose is going as a gold-digger."[21] A New Year's party was the occasion and Rose's inspiration was *Gold Diggers of 1933*, a hit movie musical, giddily mindless in its optimism at a time when the Depression had reached its lowest depths. Still, everyone wanted to believe that the worst was over, and no one had greater reason to hope than Rose, who was trying, as much as her family, to understand her illness.

It helped Rose to have Tom at home, and because of the unending stress in the family, the two were drawn to each other in a way they had not been since they were children. Dakin, too, was now old enough to enjoy their company, and the three would often go out riding in C.C.'s Studebaker or traveling by streetcar to the movies. Tom heard nothing from Hazel, only *about* her from Miss Florence. And, although Rose would go out on dates once in a while, these were more often disappointing or sometimes disastrous.

One who was not romantically interested in Rose but was an occasional companion was David Merriwether, the cousin whom she knew from her visits to Knoxville and who was being sponsored by C.C. at the company. Dakin recalled: "I remember him comforting me one night when I was crying after one of my father and mother's violent fights. And if they affected me that way, I'm sure they disturbed my sister even more. She'd lock herself in her room to escape their wrath, and Tom would hole himself up in a tiny little room behind the dining room and write until three or four in the morning and smoked like a furnace—so that, when Mother opened up his door in the morning, trilling 'Rise and shine! Rise and shine!' a cloud of stale smoke would come out."[22]

The year 1934 began auspiciously for Tom. Although he was still writing poetry, he had begun to send out a number of short stories, and a letter he received on January 31 from J. Louis Stoll, editor of *A Year Magazine*, concerned "A Tale of Two Writers," which Stoll hoped to publish. Tom had sent him a dollar for a subscription to the Philadelphia-based magazine, along with a revised manuscript. The editor wrote, "I think you have done a fine job. It really has retained its power about which I was much afraid. I do agree with you that it has gained strength."[23]

Meanwhile, Rose's frequent erratic behavior was becoming a concern within the family. Edwina could not bring herself to believe there was anything the matter with her, other than a "high-strung" temperament. There were long spells when mother and daughter got along agreeably, but underneath there was seething resentment in Rose, and when it surfaced, her temper was unbridled. In a rage, she would often pack her things and storm out of the apartment, vowing never to return. Except to stay a day or two with a sympathetic friend, like the daughter-fixated Miss Florence, she had no place to go, no wherewithal, no job skills. And, for her, to leave home was to enter a world mired in the cruel reality of the Great Depression. After a short while, she would return to her "prison," sullen and defeated, and stay for hours on end in her "cell," alone and utterly miserable. Then a solicitous Edwina or a gentle Tom would coax her back into the family fold.

The jobs that Rose sought during the thirties, she would fail to get because of a lack of self-confidence—a timidity diagnosed by the psychiatrist whom she had begun seeing at Barnes Hospital as a fear of sex, stemming from her mother's own puritanical abhorrence. In time, Rose would come to look upon her mother as much a jailer as her father. Edwina, of course, dismissed talk of sex as Freudian nonsense. She didn't want to hear it. There was, in fact, never *any* discussion of sex in the Williams household. But the family physician, Dr. Alexander, concurred with the psychiatrist's belief that Rose, being dominated by her mother's archaic attitudes, needed an outlet, even if it had to be arranged. Edwina's reaction to the very suggestion of "a therapeutic relationship" was readily predictable. She simply wouldn't discuss it. She felt it was monstrous, something a young lady of breeding simply would not do.

Then Edwina came up with her own solution. It amounted to something more like a campaign. Rose should have gentlemen callers, as she herself had had, and should marry the right man, as she had not. Tom should bring home some young friend.

> AMANDA: Down at the warehouse, aren't there some nice young men? . . . Find out one that's clean-living—doesn't drink and—ask him out for sister! . . . For Sister! To meet! Get acquainted!

But Tom was at a loss; he didn't have that many friends. There was his pal at the warehouse, Stanley Kowalski, but he was going steady, and there was his fraternity brother Jim Connor, who lived in St. Louis. Apparently, Connor did call—but only once. He had "strings" on him.

At twenty-four, Rose was still a virgin and still strangely hysterical in the company of young men. Dakin remembered an incident when Tom and Rose and a salesman at the shoe company named Colin went out together. Tom overheard his sister proposition the young man, and afterward Tom berated her, saying in effect, "Rose, I heard you offer yourself to Colin, and I want you to know that you disgusted me."

Tom was, of course, as much a virgin as his sister at that time, and at twenty-two he still had not consummated a sexual experience. He could only imagine what it would be like but could not picture himself doing such a thing—well, furtively perhaps, but not with a girl he loved. His reaction to Rose's sad little overture was every bit as puritanical as their mother's: He was, in truth, as sexually frustrated as Rose. What exacerbated the problem even more was the fact that Tom had idolized his sister since he was an infant and had delighted at the very sight of her. As he later came to see it, his was a deeply instilled love that was—except possibly for some innocent byplay when they were very young children, some incident that would long have been buried among other guilt feelings—"a close relationship, quite unsullied by any carnal knowledge."

He added that "as a matter of fact, we were rather shy of each other, physically, there was no casual intimacy of the sort one observes among the Mediterranean people in their family relations." He had noted that "some perceptive critic" had once made the observation that the true theme of his work was "incest." In time, it became apparent that Tom's and Rose's love for each other was the deepest in their lives and, as Tennessee said, "perhaps, very pertinent to our withdrawal from extrafamilial attachments."[24]

Force of circumstance also played its role during the mid-1930s. Both Tom and Rose had been unable to complete their educations and were confined within their parents' home at the very time when they should have been venturing out on their own to meet and marry and have children of their own. Instead, they were bound together, and the only real comfort they knew was in each other's company. They went for long walks in the business district of University City, window-shopping, with Rose especially interested, as she would be all her life, in the latest styles of women's clothes and accessories. She had a pitifully small wardrobe. Cornelius was perfectly content to let Grand buy or make her dresses, but of course she did have a good selection of shoe samples. Tennessee later recalled that their evening walks along Delmar—"that long, long street which probably began near the Mississippi River in downtown St. Louis and continued through University City and on out into the country"—became a ritual.

It was Rose who taught Tom to dance "to the almost aboriginal standing (non-horned) Victrola that had been acquired in Mississippi and shipped to St. Louis at the time of the disastrous family move there."[25] Rose and Tom would go to dances together, and on other occasions they would go off in the stifling heat of summer or in the bitter cold of winter seeking refuge in downtown movie palaces like the Fox or the St. Louis, where for twenty-five cents there would be a moving picture, vaudeville acts, and an organ concert on the giant Wurlitzer. Dakin remembered how devoted Rose and Tom were to each other and said that, while Rose was always affectionate toward him, it was Tom she truly loved.

Something or someone that Tom could laugh at could at the same time cause him anguish: There was always that ambiguity he would perceive as he looked into the faces of the desperate, the lonely, the hungry, and the homeless. It was in the *character* of these rootless people, the pariahs, that he took interest and about whom he had begun to write. There was no need to indulge in polemics (he made no comment; he simply explored); it was what was implied in the mean existence of these hapless creatures that made the strongest possible social statement—and the deepest possible impression upon him.

Having decided that poetry, as he told his grandparents, was more preoccupation than occupation insofar as monetary rewards were concerned, Tom started putting greater effort into marketing his short stories, concentrating on one market in particular, the prestigious *Story* magazine. Submitting what he said was his second offering, "Stella for Star," he went on to say:

> I am now twenty-two, and have not had a story published since I was seventeen, when I sold a story about an Egyptian queen to WEIRD TALES magazine, an achievement which I never tried to repeat. Lately I have been trying The Little Magazines and have received a number of very polite letters and warned against the influence of Erskine Caldwell. STORY magazine is my particular star, of course.[26]

It would take him five years to break the *Story* market. "I would write and complete one story a week and mail it, as soon as I finished, to . . . *Story*. It was the time when the young Saroyan had made a sensation in that magazine with

'The Daring Young Man on the Flying Trapeze.' At first the editors encouraged me with little personal notes of criticism. But soon I began to receive those dreadful 'form' rejections."[27]

Despite Tom's low opinion of his poems, in 1934 a short verse, "After a Visit," was published in *Voices*, a reputable poetry magazine, and also in the *Literary Digest*, a national publication of some literary merit, if not distinction. Although he was still working at "a job designed for insanity . . . a living death," he could send his grandfather a cheerful letter in early June, during the first week of his vacation, which he said he was enjoying "quietly and economically at home." He mentioned that he was using the time off to catch up on his correspondence and was devoting the mornings to his writing. "I am sending a good many stories out, and hope to have some acceptances before long." He added on a somewhat prophetic note, "I am glad that you are thinking of renting your house and going to Florida. It would be great for you. And if I become a successful writer one of these days, I will take the first airplane down there myself and we'll have a cottage on the beach."*[28] The big news he had to report, though, was that he had acquired, for twenty-nine dollars, a little roadster to drive around in. Having a car of his own meant that he would not have to borrow his father's; he dubbed the vehicle "Scatterbolt" because you could always hear it before you saw it.

The second week of Tom's vacation was in August. Cornelius had joined the Woodlawn Country Club in nearby Webster Groves, a suburb of St. Louis where wealthy relatives Ned and Agnes Harford had made their home available for a few weeks to the Williams clan. Rose played golf with Dakin and tennis with Tom. And Tom, who was by now addicted to swimming, spent a large part of his week in the pool. Always amiable and gregarious company outside his home, Cornelius was off playing golf most of the time. And Edwina would have been at peace had it not been for Tom and an episode involving Scatterbolt.

Dakin's memory of the affair was that it occurred on a Saturday night when Tom phoned to say that he was stuck out on Sappington Road because he had run out of gas. Normally, his having forgotten to fill the tank would not have surprised anyone who knew him, least of all his mother. His father, who more than once had gone to the rescue by managing to solve some complicated problem, like changing a tire, was not at home. And so Edwina's solution was for Rose and Dakin to take a taxi to the stranded driver, picking up a can of gas en route.

This all took considerable time, as such a mission usually provides an excuse to stay out late. When finally Scatterbolt and its laughing occupants made a noisy entrance into the driveway, Miss Edwina was fuming in a manner that she herself would describe only as "fit to be tied." She knew better

---

*Tennessee and his grandfather would have to wait another twelve years before they could enjoy just such a retreat together in Key West.

than to ask Tom how he could have forgotten something as basic as gas and oil, but instead, she went straight to a matter of growing curiosity: Where had he been? Where did he go at night by himself? "To the movies," was his standard reply, but this time in her fury, Edwina exclaimed, "I don't believe that lie!" Whereupon gentle, docile Tom, for once and to the astonishment of all, blurted out, "Well, you can go to hell then!"

Dakin recalled, "Mother's eyes shot up in their sockets toward the ceiling. She staggered back as if struck by a physical blow. Cunningly she glanced behind her to be sure there was an overstuffed chair in the correct position, and proceeded to fall backward in a well-planned and frequently performed faint." She was duly revived, as she was on other occasions, since she "pulled this on a monthly basis when arguing with Dad over bills."[29] Revived, yes, but recovered from the shock of hearing such a thing from her precious boy?

The Underground Rebellion

The year 1935 brought change. For Tom, it was for the better, but for Rose the change was for the worse.

A drive to Columbia and Rose's attendance at a Sunday school convention was part of Edwina's strategy to get Rose involved in church work, to help her meet a nice young Christian man, and to take her mind off sex. Every Sunday, the family, with Cornelius occasionally in tow, attended Saint Michael's and Saint George's Church, on Wydown Boulevard; these two Episcopal parishes had been combined as one. Rose and Tom sang in the choir and Dakin was an altar boy. Miss Edwina made herself conspicuous among the staid Episcopalians by sporting an odd display of Sunday finery and by singing lustily. She was matched, if not outdone, by the minister, the Reverend Dr. Karl Morgan Block, whose sermons were famed for being more dramatic than pious, mixing Shakespearean passages with excerpts from the Scriptures and consequently playing to packed houses. Dakin said Sunday attendance was excellent because Dr. Block "never disturbed anyone's conscience by his sermons."

Being a minister's granddaughter made Rose well qualified for teaching Sunday school, and she had the satisfaction of doing something successfully at last—that is, until she became involved in an unfortunate incident of anti-Semitism, a virus that was spreading beyond the borders of Hitler's Third Reich, notably to communities like St. Louis where there were large settlements of German-American families. The Jewish population, particularly the Orthodox Jews, were set apart by the rigors of their religion and by their own tendency to segregate themselves and to hold Gentiles suspect, if not in contempt. Many of the more pious Christians, in turn, held Jews up to ridicule, if not outright vilification. The seeds of genocide were not being sown in Germany alone.

University City had a sizable settlement of Jewish families and was frequently referred to as "Jew City," a variant of its more popular diminutive,

"U-City." Prominent Jews such as Morton May, founder of the May Company, were generally respected, but even they could be excluded, like blacks, from membership in exclusive clubs and from invitations to social affairs. Rose had overheard some gossip about Dr. Block having "Jewish blood," and without any malicious intent, she repeated this to a member of the congregation, her friend the portrait painter Florence Ver Steeg. Word of what Rose had said traveled with the usual speed of such rumors, and Dr. Block confronted her, saying that even if it was true, he would not be ashamed to admit it, but adding that there was no room in his flock for rumormongers. Of course, he said, she could attend services, but she could no longer teach Sunday school.

Rose was so humiliated and unnerved that she returned to Barnes Hospital for further treatment. When Edwina remonstrated with the minister, impressing upon him the severity of Rose's reaction, Dr. Block expressed his regret, but his apology had negligible effect upon Rose's crumbling self-esteem. After that, Tom could be persuaded to return to church only on occasion.

Late in January, Tom received a note from Winifred Irwin of the St. Louis Writers Guild, congratulating him and wishing him continued success. He had won first prize among seventy-six entries for his revised story "Stella for Star," and as important, he also won ten dollars—important not only for the money but because now possibly he could make his talent for storytelling profitable.

His happiness was short-lived, though, for in February, on an occasion when Miss Florence was giving one of her impromptu recitals at Edwina's piano, she suddenly stopped and announced that Hazel was engaged to be married in September to someone she had met in Wisconsin. His name was Terrence McCabe. Characteristically, Tom gave no outward sign of his feelings. Years later, however, Tennessee admitted that Terry was "a personable young Irishman of fantastic humor, and we hit it off well. I recall an hilarious evening the three of us spent together, after getting quite drunk—at least I did at the Saint Louis Athletic Club. We drove around town, singing and exchanging mad jokes."[30] But such "an hilarious evening" must always end sadly when "the three of us" becomes the two of them and the one of him. Regarding Hazel, he confessed, "I never loved anyone as I loved her,"[31] and long after she married McCabe, Tennessee told his mother that the beautiful redhead was very much the deepest love of his life.

There *was* something he loved more, though, and would all his life. Tom's reaction was to plunge into work; Edwina and Dakin remembered his typewriter clicking away until they thought it would fall apart. The story he had begun to write—called "The Accent of a Coming Foot," after a line from Emily Dickinson—was plainly a catharsis. It tells of a young poet, Bud, twenty-three years old, who has become a virtual hermit in his own home, isolated, beyond the reach of his sister—and of Catharine, whom he knew and loved when they were boy and girl together. After a long separation, Catharine has come to visit, but Bud is unable to face her again. He is wandering around outside in a driving rain, and his sister, Cecilia, complains that he has become strange: "Most of the time he's up there in the attic by himself, pounding away on that old typewriter of his that he got from the junk-shop. . . ." When Catharine asks what he is working on, Cecilia replies, "God only knows! He has poetry published in the little magazines, you know, but they never pay him a cent for it!"

At length, Catharine sees Bud's "tall shadow drawn against the streaming oval glass of the door" and feels herself "impaled upon the semidarkness of the staircase" on which she is standing:

> The door swept all the way open and banged against the hatrack. And there he stood, dripping with rain, his tousled head bare, his shoulders hunched, his face lifted intuitively toward the dark staircase. And all that Catharine could see of him plainly was his eyes: arrowbright: unable to move from her own till some sign set them free, eyes like a possum's glaring at night from a torch-lit tree with the hounds and the men forming their fatal circle around it. . . .
>
> The moment gathered intensity. Still neither moved. Then it ended with a noiseless splintering like a tree lightning-struck seen falling through a storm. Bud bowed slightly from the waist . . . stiffly, and with averted eyes he backed noiselessly out of the door and closed it behind him. . . .
>
> But Catharine was already flying up the rest of the stairs, her heart beating like a captured bird against the very top of her throat. She plunged into the misty white bedroom and flung herself down on the bed, crying terribly, achingly, knowing that she could never find him again.

Years later, Tennessee described the impact that writing this narrative had on him:

> It was immediately after the conclusion of this story [which he previously had said was written in March 1935] that I suffered my first heart-attack. . . . I found that my heart was pounding and skipping beats. Something more than cups of black coffee, something too close to myself in the character of Bud and the tension of Catharine triggered this first cardiac seizure. . . . I rushed down the back fire escape and I went wildly along the midnight street, quickening my pace as my pulse quickened. I must have rushed for miles, all the way from the suburb to Union Boulevard deep into St. Louis. It was March: the trees along the streets were beginning to bud. With characteristic ro-

manticism, I kept looking up at those green bits of life emerging again and somehow it was this that quieted my panic. . . .

Later that week, after work, I went secretly to a doctor who informed me that I did, indeed, have a defective heart. Shortly afterwards a second attack occurred which hospitalized me for a week and which had one great compensation—it released me from the shoe-business in which I'd been trapped for three years. . . .[32]

Tennessee believed all his life, despite repeated diagnoses to the contrary, that his "defective heart" was an organic condition rather than one subject to "functional episodes" intermittently precipitated by emotional and physical stress—an excessive demand he continually made upon himself.

Now one event followed close on another. First, Hazel and Terry returned to Madison to be married. What followed was described by Edwina as a "rebellion." On the eve of Tom's twenty-fourth birthday, he and Rose went downtown to Loew's State Theatre to see Leslie Howard in the movie classic *The Scarlet Pimpernel*. It was meant to be a respite, but instead, Tennessee recalled, "I was too tense to pay much attention to the film. Afterwards, we took a service car home, a phenomenon of city transportation in the depression era. It cost fifteen cents a passenger from downtown St. Louis to suburban University City."[33]

As they traveled along Delmar Boulevard, Tom became increasingly tense and lost sensation in his hands. Approaching Saint Luke's Episcopal Hospital, he asked the driver to pull into the emergency entrance, convinced that he was having a heart attack. He experienced difficulties in breathing and was immediately taken upstairs for examination and admission to a ward.

Dakin's recollection was of Rose returning home, only to be met with Edwina's hysterical report that Tom had had a heart attack and that she feared he was dying. On the other hand, Edwina's memory was of Rose calling from the hospital to say that Tom had had a stroke. In fact, it was neither. Tom remained in the hospital for nearly a week, and his doctor diagnosed him as suffering from total exhaustion and underweight and said he needed a complete rest.

"Rose sailed magnificently through the crisis," Edwina said, referring to her behavior at the hospital. "But that night at home, she broke. She lost control of her senses, wandering from one room to another in panic. She woke up her father screaming in terror, 'You're going to be murdered! We're all going to be murdered!' It was as though Tom's slight breakdown had destroyed the slender thread by which she had been hanging on to a reality she could no longer grasp."[34]

While still in Saint Luke's, Tom received a letter from Hazel. "Dearest Tommie—I just found out from Mother that you have been in the hospital with High Blood pressure. That's awfully bad news and I'm sorry to hear it. How are your nurses? Pretty? When are you getting out? Do you feel like writing? Anything I can do for you? Now that I've asked you enough questions I'll tell you a couple of things. I'm trying to arrange a little visit at home sometime this Spring. It's not at all definite but if I can get off work for a few days I'm coming. The Irishman, I hope to inveigle into coming with me—so's we can have another rousing evening."[35]

Not only had Hazel gone out of his life; Tom had suffered the recent loss of the protective friendship of Stanley Kowalski, who had married and left the shoe company. Like Harold Mitchell, he would be immortalized in *A Streetcar Named Desire*, but whether the Stanley Kowalski Tom knew bore any resemblance to his stage counterpart can only be conjectured. Evidently, there was some physical likeness, and it appears the two friends had a relationship of idol to hero-worshiper. Kowalski died about ten years later, and his family remained in St. Louis for some considerable time afterward, but little else is known about him.

After Tom returned home from the hospital, he was made aware that his sister's mental state was obviously disturbed. He remembered her wandering into his small room and saying, "Let's all die together." He added that the suggestion didn't appeal to him in the least. Rose's behavior had taken some bizarre turns, such as collecting the labels from Campbell's tomato soup cans for no other reason than that it was the only soup she would eat. Although the family had become accustomed to Rose's periodic fits of hysteria or depression, Cornelius was now forced to consider Tom's health as well, and he was alarmed. Dakin said that for once he was not objecting to the medical expense. In fact, Dr. Falk, at Edwina's behest, made house calls to assure her and C.C. that Tom was not suffering from a heart ailment but, rather, sheer nervous exhaustion. It was agreed that he should spend the summer in Memphis with his grandparents.

"Within a week, I had submitted my resignation to Dad's friend, Mr. Fletcher of Continental Shoemakers and had received a politely phrased acknowledgement of it: 'Best wishes for an early return to health. We have all appreciated your *many sterling qualities.*'" Tennessee added that the italics were his and wished that he had had that letter framed in silver. "And so, as a twenty-fourth birthday gift I received a permanent release from the wholesale shoe business in St. Louis."[36] More significantly, it was a release from—or at least a relaxation of—the iron grip his father had on him. For all of Cornelius's trumpeted desire to "make a man" of his son and his sneering criticism of Edwina's possessiveness, the irony was that he was far more domineering and destructive in his control over Tom. And to Tom, his father was always a mysterious figure, contradictory, unfathomable, unpredictable, and someone he openly feared. Dakin remembered that his brother would often go out the back door as soon as he saw his father coming in the front. Tennessee wrote, "He always enters the house as though he were entering it with the intention of tearing it down from inside."[37]

As for his father's antagonism toward Hazel, he added, "I still haven't the faintest idea why my father opposed our attending the same university but then there was never any communication or understanding between us, since even being under the same roof with him was acutely uncomfortable for me." When he later learned of his father's intervention, his reaction was one of "desolation—not fury. I guess I had begun to regard Dad's edicts as being—as far as I was concerned—too incomprehensibly and incontestably Jovian to feel about them anything but what a dead-tired animal feels when it's whipped on further. Of course, under this hopeless nonresistance there must have been an unconscious rage, not just at Dad but my own cowardice and impotent submission. This I realize because as I have grown older I have discovered a big underground rebellion was there all along, just waiting for a way out."[38]

After Tom left for Memphis, he received a letter from his father that could only have perplexed him the more for its uncharacteristic concern. Was it guilt? A matter of obligation? Or underneath was he struggling to say something else? Something more?

Dear Tom,
I arrived back in St. Louis Sunday morning and was very sorry, indeed, to find that you had been back and had another attack but hope you are gradually improving.

Your insurance is paid up until June 1st . . . this should be converted between now and June 1st to some other policy and not be allowed to expire. . . . This costs I believe $14.65 every six months. I will pay the first six months for you and, no doubt, by the end of that time you will be well enough to be at work again and carry on the insurance. . . .

I hope you are going to improve right along and will be able to come back home some time soon. If there is anything you want, don't hesitate to write me.

With love from us all, affectionately your father,

C. C. Williams[39]

Tom, who was once again enfolded within the love and affection of his grandparents, must have felt as he did when as a nine-year-old he returned to Clarksdale. Now he would be able to write when he wanted to—in the mornings—and he would have the gentle encouragement of the two people in the world he most revered. Although his grandfather had been retired for the past four years, he was as active as ever amid friends whom Dakin described as "very cultured and polite, very friendly and sincere—typical Episcopalians!"[40] Among them was Peyton Rhodes, a professor at nearby Southwestern University, and his wife, whom Tennessee described as "Virginians of the first rank. Later on Professor Rhodes became the president of the university: in the summer of 1935 he was, I believe, head of the English Department. He got me access to the library of the university and I spent most of the summer afternoons reading there, or at the downtown library on Main Street."[41]

It was during those quiet afternoons that he discovered the short stories of Anton Chekhov, which introduced him to "a literary sensibility to which I felt a very close affinity at that time." In later years, Williams would always claim that Chekhov influenced him more than any other figure, nonetheless adding that, for his taste, the great Russian writer held too much in reserve. But considering the years of repression Tom was enduring in St. Louis, it is not difficult to imagine him identifying with characters who suffer stifled and frustrated passions.

His repressed attraction to members of his own sex—homoerotic impulses that surfaced briefly in his friendships with Harold Mitchell and Stanley Kowalski—might have been openly expressed had there been any reciprocal gestures. But Tom's friends were aggressively interested only in the opposite sex, as he thought he was. More than that, there was his religious restraint, which prevented self-confrontation. Effeminate or openly gay youths were largely avoided as weird. There were minor encounters, though, and one in particular in Memphis that summer, which Tennessee later described in *Memoirs*.

He had gone swimming with two university students—friends of his grandfather—who in retrospect he realized must have been lovers. "They were exceptionally handsome: one was dark, the other a shining blond." It was the blond whom he found attractive and who apparently had more specific intentions in mind, since he invited Tom to dine alone with him in the Peabody Hotel's dining room. "We had beers; I doubt that the beer was the true cause of the palpitations that suddenly began to occur in my excitable heart. I went into panic and so did the blond. A doctor was summoned. The doctor was a lady, and an extremely bad doctor. She gave me a sedative tablet of some kind but informed me, gloomily, that my symptoms were, indeed, of a serious nature." She warned him that he must do everything carefully and slowly, counseling that only if he kept to that regimen could he live to forty. The blond boy's response was that Tom should heed her advice because "he walked much too fast for someone with a cardiac condition." Tennessee referred to the incident as "a return of the cardiac neurosis."[42]

Another incident that summer struck at the one fear that Grand had always concealed, that of becoming destitute and dependent in her old age. Tennessee wrote:

> Through the years, through the miracles of her providence, her kitchen drudgery, her privations and music pupils and so forth, she had managed to save out of their tiny income enough to purchase what finally amounted to $7500 in government bonds.
>
> One morning that memorable summer a pair of nameless con men came to call upon my fantastically unworldly grandfather. They talked to him for a while on the porch in excited undertones. He was already getting deaf, although he was then a relatively spry youth of eighty, and I saw

him leaning toward them cupping his ear and giving quick nods of mysterious excitement. After a while they disappeared from the porch and he
was gone from the house nearly all of that fierce yellow day.

That evening, a crestfallen and bewildered old man returned home and
confessed that he had sold their bonds and given five thousand dollars in cash
to "this pair of carrion birds." When Grand repeatedly asked, "Why, Walter,
why?" he replied at length, "Rose, don't question me any more because if you
do, I will go away by myself and you'll never hear of me again!" Whatever the
reason, Dakin said that it was all kept very hush-hush between Mother and
Grand and that presumably Cornelius knew nothing about it. Nobody knew
the truth of the situation, Tennessee wrote, except his grandfather and "those
rusty-feathered birds of prey who have gone wherever they came from—
which I hope to be hell, and believe so."*[43]

A Jewish family lived next door to the Dakins, and their daughter, Bernice
Dorothy Shapiro, was a member of a small theatre group called, appropriately, the Garden Players, since their productions were staged outdoors on a
large, sloping back lawn. Tom found Dorothy to be a friendly and lively girl,
and she persuaded him to collaborate with her on a play that they would then
submit to the Players. By mid-June, in response to a letter from Dakin, Tom
said that he and Dorothy had fitted out a studio/solarium in their backyards in
which to work on their play and that they had completed it. "I wrote the play
and Miss Shapiro wrote the prologue and epilogue. It has been accepted by
the Garden players and is now being rehearsed almost every night at the
Shapiros'. The leading lady bawls her lines so loudly that she sounds like she is
selling fish. I am intending to take a part in the first act, a street scene, in
which all kinds of pedestrians cross the stage. I will probably be the blindman
with the tin cup and dog. Not a very difficult part but quite sufficient for my
dramatic capabilities."[44] He added that he was getting along quite well, resting a good deal but feeling stronger.

On the evening of July 12, 1935, Tom Williams saw the first production of
a play he had written, entitled *Cairo! Shanghai! Bombay!* Set in a seaport town
and presented in four scenes, it is, as he described it, "a farcical but rather
touching little comedy about two sailors on a date with a couple of 'light ladies.' " What he recalled most was "the laughter, genuine and loud" at the

---

*It is possible that the two "birds of prey" were the two university students with whom Williams
had gone swimming and who he said were friends of his grandfather. Possibly, too, one or both of
the students were the victims of blackmailers, who Dakin said were particularly active in Memphis during the Depression, preying upon the elderly. In later years, Williams would tell friends
that the Reverend Dakin was gay, although closeted because of his profession and naïveté. He was
an open and friendly old gentleman and, in 1935, when he was living in retirement, would have
been vulnerable to the stratagems of blackmailers.

comedy he had written—and the applause. He was enchanted.

At last he had found a way to break through the poet's four-wall silence. He had discovered a means of communication with built-in reciprocation: that of a live audience's response. It was a thrill and enticement that from then on would prove irresistible and would make the theatre the lodestar of his life. As he wrote in his memoirs, "Then and there the theatre and I found each other for better and for worse."[45]

8

Blue Devils

September 1935–August 1936

Returning home to University City from his summer in Memphis, Tom entered a handsome two-story house at 6634 Pershing Avenue that Cornelius had leased for two years. Edwina argued, and Cornelius finally agreed, that leaving the cluttered Enright Avenue apartment for a house in a quieter neighborhood had become a matter of necessity. Rose's hysterical reaction to Tom's nervous relapse prompted the family doctor to urge a change of scene, where the children, particularly Rose, might be happier. Her moods had been fluctuating between extremes of depression and euphoria, and Edwina said that after they moved she would sit in the yard looking at the flowers and listening to the birds and gradually began to come back to herself.

Before their move, Rose had been reluctant to go anywhere, but now she was eager to travel with her parents to Memphis to accompany Tom home. She missed and needed her brother's company. In a letter to his grandparents, Tom depicted the return trip as one during which he and Rose enjoyed stopping at Cape Girardeau and walking together "down by the water-front which was very old and quaint." He went on to describe their new home:

> The house is perfectly lovely, even prettier than I expected. It is Colonial style throughout. The living-room is gorgeous. It has a big crystal chandelier and crystal candelabrums on the long white mantal [sic], built-in bookcases on either side of the fireplace . . . the most charming small home I've ever seen. We found everything in perfect order, the grape arbor loaded with ripe grapes and the rose garden in full bloom. The place seems so quiet and spacious and dignified after our sordid apart-

ment-dwelling that it doesn't seem like we are the same people. I'm sure you'd be just crazy about it if you were here. The street is quiet as the country. But only a half block from the campus and city car-lines.[1]

Despite his newfound generosity, Cornelius still adamantly refused to finance Tom's return to college. With Washington University so close to his home, however, Tom at least had the opportunity to audit a few classes and to take advantage of the school library. Mainly, he was occupied with his writing, an opportunity he seized, since there was no suggestion at this time that he return to work. Because Cornelius was troubled by what the doctors had told him and by the fact that it was common knowledge why Tom had left the shoe company, he put on a transient show of paternal concern and affability.

But the new peace and quiet soon became as charged with internecine bickering and recriminations as ever, except that Cornelius was now on the losing side, slowly but steadily surrendering to Edwina's will. A two-story house being obviously too much for her to manage alone, Edwina employed a "colored" servant, Susie Sanders, who was remarkably durable; she remained with Edwina for nearly all of the following thirty years. Susie had not only to withstand "Miz Williams's" eternal fussing and fuming over household chores but also had to bring some semblance of order to the chaos that was left in the trail of "Mister Tom," no small job by itself.

With the change to a new environment, Tom was beginning to socialize more, as was Rose. He was not then aware of how emotionally disturbed his sister actually was; she *seemed* so much better. Edwina and Cornelius, in fact, were careful to keep their fears between themselves, alarmed that both Rose and Tom had been on the verge of nervous collapse and mental illness. As much as they were apprehensive about the disgrace this could bring upon the family, as parents they were also genuinely distressed, especially Edwina, who began making every effort she could to help Rose and Tom through what she saw as their emotional difficulties, a temporary upset that she blamed on Cornelius. Neither parent ever seemed to understand the extent of the damage that had been done and was still being done by their unending war of nerves. Ironically, to them this was either unrelated or it was the other's fault.

As for Rose, her mother was still convinced that some Prince Charming in the guise of a gentleman caller would alleviate all her daughter's problems. No one was aware, not even Rose's doctors, that an event begun in London during the past summer at the Second International Congress of Neurology would hold such dreadful portent for her. A Portuguese neurologist, Egas Moniz, inspired by an entire day's discussion devoted to the frontal lobes of the human brain, would in November supervise the first lobotomy, which he called a leukotomy: the drilling of two holes through a patient's skull and the injection of alcohol into both sides of the forehead. It was an event, a lurking horror, that would affect the lives of thousands of helpless Americans, like Rose, within less than a decade.

As for Tom, auditing classes after a three-year hiatus was both an exhilarating and a frightening prospect. He was conscious of being older than most of his new friends on campus, despite the advantage he had of *appearing* the youngest among them. His feelings of insecurity were rooted, however, in more intense concerns than simply the vanity of age: What they mirrored was loss of time and, with it, the deepening of self-doubt and dependency. In Columbia, there had been at least geographical distance from home, but here at Washington University, he lived only half a block away. It was a dread distance. He had simply moved from one prison in University City to another, albeit on nicer grounds, with gardens and two huge oak trees on either side of a well-tended front lawn.

In other respects, too, Washington University was in no way comparable to Ol' Mizzou, at least not in Tom's view and approach to campus life. He had no intention of becoming involved in the broad scope of school and fraternity activities; now his sole academic goal was to take nighttime extension courses and accumulate credits enough to enter his senior year and then finally graduate. His only other, greater interest was in his writing and in meeting fellow writers. One, in particular, Clark Mills McBurney, who was taking postgraduate courses at Washington in the fall of 1935, was destined to become one of the most important influences in Tom Williams's life and in the career of Tennessee Williams. Although Tom was still working in the shoe factory when he first met Clark, their friendship now began to take on a new vigor, and in 1938 Tom was to write a tribute he called "Return to Dust" to the poet and scholar, who published as Clark Mills:

It was at a literary meeting about five years ago. An electric victrola was playing a symphony by Brahms, the parlor was lighted by candles, twenty young writers were making a conscientious study of the ceiling and the chandelier.

Somebody turned off the music.

"Is everybody here?"

"Everybody but Clark Mills."

"Who is Clark Mills?" I asked.

"Oh, don't you know?" said the young lady in black. "He's the boy that writes crazy modern verse nobody understands but God and himself!"

Now I'm convinced that the best assurance of a brilliant future in writing is to have somebody describe you in that way—as the boy that writes "crazy modern" verse! Because today the boy so described, Clark Mills McBurney of Clayton, is recognized as one of America's most promising younger poets. He has had things in such periodicals as *Poetry, The Nation, Forum, The New Republic, American Mercury, Voices, The Partisan Review*. Last year he was awarded fifty dollars as the year's most "promising" contributor to *College Verse* and shortly before some of his work appeared in *Trial Balances*, a cross-section of the lyrical tomorrow, published by Macmillan. Now he has finished a book-length manuscript called "January Crossing" which has an intensity and breadth of conception which caused some critics to compare it with works like *The Bridge* by Hart Crane.[2]

Tom found in Mills a mentor, one who awakened in him an intellectual hunger and who, without being aware of his role, gave new direction to Tom's poetic talent. Tennessee Williams recalled, "Clark's admiration for my verse was tempered by a more technical approach than my other admirers'. He was usually given to owlish nods and bronchial noises when I showed him my verse."[3] More exemplar than teacher, Mills was a voracious reader; he always had a stack of books with him that had been checked out of the university library. When Tom began auditing classes in September, he and Mills would meet regularly on campus to discuss the work of writers who were at that time either new or controversial.

From his earliest years, Mills made books a mainstay in his daily life, and he recalled having taken the streetcar downtown to the main library at age eleven: "I was interested in Aldous Huxley and wanted to take out his *Antic Hay*, and they wouldn't let me. I recall creating quite a scene. I guess you'd say I was precocious, and by the time I met Tom, I not only carted all kinds of books out of the library but had acquired quite a few of my own."[4] He explained that, although his father had contributed almost nothing to his education and, like Tom's father, felt that "book learning" was a waste of time, Clark had developed a small personal income. He was expert on the violin and gave lessons, and he used the money to buy books.

Tennessee noted, "It was Clark who warned me of the existence of people like Hart Crane and Rimbaud and Rilke, and my deep and sustained admiration for Clark's writing gently but firmly removed my attention from the more obvious to the purer voices in poetry. About this time I acquired my copy of Hart Crane's collected poems which I began to read with gradual comprehension."[5] The volume he had "acquired" was in actuality appropriated from the university library, and he carried it with him for many years afterward. The reasoning behind his pilferage was simply that the book "had been taken out almost no times at all, and I felt it wasn't being properly valued."[6] "What I remember," Mills said, "was the impact Hart Crane had upon him. That struck him like lightning. I was amazed at his reaction. I was impressed by Crane; I thought he was pretty damned good, but I didn't regard him as highly as Tom did. He just sort of went haywire over him."*[7]

Although Tom made other friends on campus, among them the poet William Jay Smith, it was Mills who was closest to him at that time. In fact, Smith

---

*Hart Crane has been described by poet Robert Lowell as the Shelley of this age. The interaction between Shelley's appeal to Crane and Crane's to Williams is clearly evidenced in their poetry.

held Mills in the same regard as Tom did. While Clark eschewed the Romantic poets, he did cut a rather romantic figure himself, if not in his poetry, then in his person. This was not only Tom's and Bill Smith's view of him but also that of the girls in their group, tall and handsome as he was.

In contrast to his life at the University of Missouri, Tom chose now to become identified as a writer among writers. It was within a small circle, eclectic in their views and distinctly singular, that he began to move. "At Washington U. in those years," Mills recalled, "there was one group, a kind of bohemian element—an intellectual underground. They didn't *look* it; in fact, they were good students, but they rejected fraternities, football, basketball, the rah-rah games, and campus social life. The group was a pretty wild bunch: I mean, there was drinking and a good deal of sexual activity. That was about the only social set that Tom frequented, or that I knew of. It was the crowd I was in.

"His mother—rather pitifully, I think—organized social occasions, to raise the tone of the family in their new home and to elevate Rose to eligibility. And there was one time—I don't think she ever knew what was going on. We had a fellow in our group named Willie Wharton, and he was really the wildest of all. He came to one of her parties and he had a quart of cheap whiskey, which we hid on the back porch. Mrs. Williams served tea in pink glass cups and saucers—so, Tom and Willie and I would go out in the kitchen to refill our own tea, but instead, of course, we put in whiskey and ice cubes—and I remember Mrs. Williams remarking on it being so unusual to put ice cubes in one's hot tea. And Tom said it was the best way—and of course it was straight whiskey. So, these parties collapsed into nonintellectual chaos, leaving Mrs. Williams pretty unhappy."

Early in the summer, Tom received the heartening news that *Manuscript*, a national bimonthly magazine headquartered in Athens, Ohio, had accepted one of his stories written when he was in Memphis. The subject also left Miss Edwina "pretty unhappy," and, for that matter, Miss Rose. Mills's recollection was that in those days, "Tom was attracted, peculiarly, to very large, fat girls, and in fact, at one party, he surprised the whole group. There was a fat girl there, and he didn't say very much to her—actually, there was nothing we heard him say to her—except that he went over and sat down beside her and held her hand all evening.

"One day he came to my house with this piece he had written—it was a kind of prose poem rather than a short story—and in it was a very, very fat wife of the owner of a plantation. And the foreman was an *exact* duplicate of Tom himself: I mean, he described himself physically, just absolutely perfectly. She was sitting on a porch swing and swinging back and forth, and he was standing near her with a black snake whip, one that you snap. Her refrain was, 'God, ain't it hot? God, Jesus, ain't it hot?' His refrain was, 'Let's go inside where it's cool and quiet,' and then, snap, the whip would go at her heels and she jumped. And this went on over and over again, and finally it led up to the line where Tom and I simply collapsed with laughter. Picture Tom reading, 'Oh, c'mon—I love you 'cause you're as big as America' and her replying, 'All right, I'll go in, but you must promise me, you won't hurt me.' Well, we just fell on the floor laughing—the picture of this enormous fat woman and little skinny Tom—because in those days he was very thin and small."[8]

In an early draft of the story, Tom had written a sensitive and perceptive description of the plantation owner's wife: "Those excess pounds were so well disposed of that only the most discerning and critical of her fellow females ever hissed that ugly and cruel word 'Fat' about Georgia. No single part of her fair, creamy body had received more than its share of those pounds. If the most discriminate artist or beauty parlor expert had to direct the distribution of them, they would not have been placed more judiciously."

John Rood, the editor of *Manuscript*, wrote to say that he would like to publish the story Tom had entitled "Twenty-Seven Wagons Full of Cotton." Acknowledging it as "a fine piece of work," he said it was "perhaps a bit strong in the sex business, but still too fine to pass up."[9] When the story was subsequently published the following year in August, Tom told his grandparents, "Mother and Rose are not used to modern writing and were very displeased with the subject, which is an affair between a crude Arkansas couple, and so Mother forbids me to send the magazine to anybody. She thinks it is too shocking. It is supposed to be humorous but she and Rose don't take it that way."[10]

In his letter, Rood added a familiar refrain: "You understand, I suppose, that we do not pay for stories." It didn't matter that consumers consumed them—and also consumed many promising writers in the process—this was just the way it was: no money. But the government took a different, egalitarian view. And as ridiculous as it sounded to millions of Americans—especially to conservative business leaders, who readily accepted government aid and then voted Republican—the Roosevelt administration had adopted the unprecedented position that qualified writers should be paid to write.

January 1936 heralded an election year, and the radio in the Williams household was ringing with speeches, ranging from the demagoguery of Father Coughlin and the Reverend Gerald L. K. Smith to President Roosevelt's clarion call summoning the nation to "wage increasing warfare" against "the forces of privilege and greed." For the first time in the country's history, there was federal support for the arts. With the failure of the private sector to give any but trifling sums, and then only to elitist arts organizations, the government now had sufficient reason to employ artists in various work programs, the objective being to secure the arts as an integral force in American democracy. It was at best a good start and one that would be evolving long after the Depression, but a noble beginning it was.

A comparatively small appropriation from the administration's work relief program instituted Federal One. Under Federal One, the Works Progress

Administration (WPA) established four programs: (1) the Federal Art Project (FAP), which hired painters, sculptors, and other fine artists to create murals, sculptures, tapestries, and so on, mainly for public buildings; (2) the Federal Music Project (FMP), which put some fifteen thousand unemployed musicians and composers to work; (3) the Federal Theatre Project (FTP), which employed theatre artists across the nation, notably Arthur Miller, Orson Welles, John Huston, Lehman Engel, Howard Da Silva, John Houseman, and others, with the result that upward of 30 million Americans saw live theatre, most of them for the first time; and (4) the agency that most interested Tom, the Federal Writers' Project (FWP), which was actually paying writers to write, among whom were Richard Wright, Saul Bellow, John Cheever, Margaret Walker, Conrad Aiken, and Ralph Ellison. Because in the administrators' view Tom was mired in "middle-class respectability," he was unqualified to join the WPA Writers' Project, but he felt "a fine thing was created for St. Louis writers. For many of them it was 'rain from heaven.' For the first time in their lives they had enough to eat, enough to wear, a reasonable certainty of where they would sleep the night after next. . . . But it all broke up in a tragic, useless 'strike.' "[11]

Solitary and introverted and competitively suspicious of one another, writers were the most resistant to organized, collaborative effort. Even when they set out on their own initiative to institute projects and publications, such efforts usually came a cropper of vanity. The League of St. Louis Artists and Writers, with which Tom and Clark Mills were associated, was one such attempt. One other short-lived effort dissolved for more arcane reasons. Tom and Mills had organized a chapter of the College Poetry Society of America. Tom recalled:

> Ours was an ideal chapter. It was composed of Clark Mills, Wm. Jay Smith, and myself who wrote poetry and an exactly equal number of girls who served refreshments. Refreshments were usually cocoa and cookies. But once somebody brought a case of beer. That was the last meeting of our poetry club. Writers are notoriously bad drinkers (or good, if you will) and upon this occasion something like a riot occurred with one male member chasing one female member round and round a fifty-dollar "vahse" which resulted finally in that ornament's complete demolition. Following this incident the girls went on strike—it was spring, anyway, and our meetings disintegrated into weekly picnics around the Meramec or Wild Horse Creek.[12]

It would seem the youths' preoccupation with the Muses led to a Dionysian spring festival.

Ghosts

In January, Tom decided to enroll in an English extension course at Washington University. Clark Mills was taking postgraduate courses there at the time, and they were able to meet on campus to discuss their readings. Once again it was Grand who was making it possible for Tom to go back to school, drawing from pension funds and the slight income she derived from teaching piano. Not only was there her support; the time he had recently spent in Memphis had other reverberations, too, for Tom's mind was still alive with the lingering excitement he had experienced there of seeing a play of his, even if a shared credit, on a stage, with actors interpreting his characters and reading his lines. He wasn't quite sure what it meant or how it would relate to him, but he was thinking more and more about writing plays. Then, during the first week of February, an event took place at the American Theatre in downtown St. Louis; suddenly he was made aware of a glimmering light on the horizon, the eastern harbor of the New York theatre.

The American was the city's main legitimate house. Touring productions would book the theatre, and St. Louisans were afforded the opportunity to see prominent actors in Broadway plays. Most were single, independent attractions, although the formidable Theatre Guild also offered subscribers a series each season. Except for the works of O'Neill and Shakespeare, most audiences went not to see plays but actors: stars such as John and Ethel Barrymore, Alfred Lunt and Lynn Fontanne, Helen Hayes, Fredric March, Ina Claire, Walter Huston, Judith Anderson, Eva Le Gallienne, Melvyn Douglas, Tallulah Bankhead, Leslie Howard, Ruth Gordon, Laurette Taylor, and the acknowledged "first lady," Katharine Cornell, whom Tom had recently seen in her most successful vehicle, *The Barretts of Wimpole Street*.

But what electrified Tom Williams was the acting of the great Russian actress Alla Nazimova, who was touring in Henrik Ibsen's *Ghosts*.[13] Her magical performance as Mrs. Alving had been acclaimed by New York critics as her finest achievement, surpassing even her portrayal of Christine in O'Neill's *Mourning Becomes Electra*. As he did with other road company shows, Tom saw *Ghosts* from the third balcony of the American, the "peanut gallery," as it was called, where seats cost as little as fifty cents and where one had an excellent view of the top of actors' heads—that is, when they were playing downstage; it didn't matter, because in those days they had magnificent, unmiked voices that carried to the reaches of the upper balconies. Tennessee remembered Nazimova's playing as "so fabulous, so terrifyingly exciting" that he was unable to stay in his seat: "It was so moving that I had to go and walk in the lobby during the last act. I'd stand in the door and look in, then I'd rush back to the lobby again." He said that it was "one of the things that made me want to write for the theatre."[14]

A coincidence that happens only in life was cited in Louis Sheaffer's definitive two-volume biography of Eugene O'Neill: "In the spring of 1907 O'Neill saw his first Ibsen performance, *Hedda Gabler*, with Nazimova. Though it was not until six years later that he decided to write for the stage, a submerged part of him was already looking in that direction, evidently, for he saw the play ten times. Only an apprentice, an acolyte who has had the call, would have been so fascinated." The performance, he said, opened a new world of the drama for O'Neill. " 'It gave me my first conception of a modern theatre where truth might live.' "[15]

What struck Tom as deeply as Nazimova's performance was the figure of Mrs. Alving's dying son, Oswald, a victim of syphilis, inherited from his dissolute and diseased father. Ibsen's depiction of the character's encroaching madness climaxes with the mother giving her son an overdose of a drug that causes his death. *Ghosts* has been described as Ibsen's greatest play, invested with the intensity and fatalism of a Greek drama and the first to deal with both euthanasia and a clinical comprehension of heredity. Its impact upon Tom was truly profound for the very reason that his nervous instability and Rose's increasingly eccentric behavior raised the possibility of insanity in his own family and the question of whether his father might have had the same venereal disease when he married his mother.

Sur l'Autre Côté de la Lune

Becoming more and more aware of what was happening on the New York stage, Tom now was reading with fascination the accounts and articles in *Theatre Arts* and was engrossed in the plays of O'Neill, Ibsen, Strindberg, and Shakespeare. The violent plays, he said, were the ones that particularly interested him. Violence not only interested him; it was contained *within* him: the nightmare side of his life that no one saw or suspected until gradually it became reflected in his writings. Not in his letters or in his conversations, nor even to his one confidant, Clark Mills, did he reveal the inner turmoil he was suffering. This he set forth only in his journals,[16] which he would refer to as "an emotional record" and which he began in March of his twenty-fifth year. Across the title page of the College Poetry Society's account book, "acquired" while he was at the University of Missouri, he wrote, "Dead Planet, The Moon, I salute you! (A Writer's Journal)" and then made his initial entries:

March 6—Friday—Saw first robin today—two in fact—pains in the chest all morning but okay tonite. Went swimming—mailed verse to Liberty [magazine] Amateur Contest at Miss Flo's suggestion. Now have 4 manuscripts in the mail not counting plays & poems in St. Louis contest. Returned case of empty bottles—collected $1.00—felt rather stupid all day but will write tomorrow.

March 7—Sat.—Nice day—went swimming in a.m.—wrote story "Cut Out"—pretty cheap but well-done—I feel rather guilty writing such stuff—so far from what I really want to do.

I am writing this Sunday morning—pinkish green buds all over the elm tree outside my window—first buds I have seen.

March 9—Monday . . . Mr. Kanter dead—Mr. Wells dying—Mr. Kramer afraid of dying. Me? Damned glad to be alive!

Although Cornelius remained steadfast in his determination not to finance his son's further education, Tom started making his own inquiries with a letter to the registrar at the University of Missouri:

I would like to have a list of my credits in the Arts and Science and Journalism schools of the University, as I am continuing my education at the Washington University night and summer schools and hope to obtain either a B.J. or B.A. degree. I would like to know how many more credits I would have to obtain for both degrees.[17]

Returning to a classroom after the interim of three years made Tom Williams acutely self-aware. He was competing with many students who were younger, taking the extension course as a prerequisite for college entrance, and he felt removed from them, if only because he was their senior and was expected in a sense to be superior. At the other extreme, there were also older, more experienced writers in Professor Frank Webster's short-story class, and this only exacerbated in Tom a painful self-consciousness. He said that in his short-story class there were two professional writers, one writing for *Story* and the other for *Manuscript*. They both had been offered contracts by book publishers and were working on novels.

March 10—Tuesday . . . I was sick tonight—attack of nervous heart, in short. Story class—got worked up over Prof. reading my story aloud. Why, I don't know—I must learn to control my nerves—didn't last long. I took a pill—still it is always very depressing—makes you feel cut off from the world and just at a time when I am so eager to be a part—still— things like this prove one's spirit—ignore it I say—go on as if nothing happened—the only way—besides I'm no longer a coward about it—I was actually *not* afraid—just embarrassed because I felt my nervous agitation was so obvious. Class criticizes my story very harshly. Only one girl liked it and she didn't get the point. Prof. Webster seemed pleased with it however and told me to write more soon. But I was disappointed in story and feel discouraged about my whole prospect as a writer.

March 11—Weds. Evening closes down and I turn to my journal for lack of anything else to do. Felt remarkably well today. Even swam my usual 15 lengths. But how stupid! Looked thru some old stories and made half-hearted effort to straighten out my desk. That's all—feel as tho my writing is all a lot of trash—except the one story "Gift of an Apple."[18] Maybe it will turn out to be the same when "Story" sends it back. How I fool myself about my writing! . . . Moons do not have corners except in the early evening—new moons do *not* rise. . . . I have taken a sleeping pill as I was feeling terribly nervous. Now better. A cool and beautiful night. Wind. Or is it rain? I will turn out the light and see.

About this time, he sent off one of his deceptively cheerful letters to his grandparents, saying that his mother and Susie were in the throes of spring housecleaning in preparation for a DAR tea. "I'm getting along fine with my university subjects. Lately I've been thinking of getting my degree, if possible, and then applying for a teaching job in some small town high-school. I believe a B.A. degree would be sufficient for that. And I know I could teach high-school English. I don't believe I would have to acquire many more credits."[19]

Tom had now begun in earnest the habit of swimming nearly every day, regardless of the obstacles of snow-covered streets or his studies at school or the lack of a fifteen-cent carfare. It was a habit that would in time become as ingrained as writing every day and one he would maintain for the rest of his life wherever in the world he might be or whatever the conditions he might encounter. Edwina declared, "I marvel that he ever learned to swim because when he was a boy, one summer at a resort on the [Meramec], his father tried to teach him by throwing him into the river and Tom nearly drowned. Later I sent him to the Lorelei, a pool in St. Louis, where he learned to swim."[20] More than simply a pleasure, this one exercise over the years enabled Tennessee Williams to develop a remarkable physique and withstand many illnesses and forms of self-abuse that otherwise could easily have killed him. He seemed to understand instinctively that it was this regimen more than anything that kept him alive.

Through his journal, Tom was able to externalize his anxieties and work through various of the crises that Rose, mute in her torment, was unable to articulate.

Thursday Morn—March 19—Let us not speak of it. This agony. Forget it. Find strength somehow to go on. Work to be done. Feel sometimes as though I could relinquish this life easily. Last night I saw the Little Theater play Ode To Liberty. Very amusing. Between acts I stood at an open window and saw the revolving electric cross over a Union Ave. Church. Same one when I first became ill that Sat. night last March (an anniversary?) when I walked miles and miles with my heart nearly jumping out of my chest. That cross helped me that night. The cross and the money I gave the street beggar, and finally those new star-shaped leaves. A strange night. But I've had many since then.

Thursday night—Oh my, what blissful exhaustion! I haven't felt quite like this since that night in Cologne or Amsterdam—when the crowds on the street were like cool snow to the cinder of individual "woe." Over seven years ago. A state in which the damndest seems to have happened and you can't be any more completely damned—and the tired brain and body has simply got to rest for a while. I am positively limp in every muscle. Feel deliciously warm and fuzzy. Tomorrow? There *is* no tomorrow! Ah, but there *is:* and I'll have to face it somehow. . . . This afternoon Am[erican] Prefaces ret'd "Bottle of Brass" with letter saying story was "told" rather than "lived." I agree—in part.

With the number of manuscripts Tom had in the mail, coming and going, it was inevitable that at least one editor would recognize the worth in much that he was writing, rough-hewn though it might have been. John Rood at *Manuscript* was among the first. In an unmailed letter of gratitude, Tom acknowledged Rood's "helpful criticism," saying, "Like most young writers, I lack the ability to criticize my own work and even my best friends can't tell me. Sympathetically critical letters are a courtesy I have received only from Martha Foley [*Story* magazine] and the Little Magazine editors. Yours was particularly helpful. I am glad you rejected the stories, as I certainly don't want to publish inferior stuff."

The letter was typewritten at the top of the page, but in the white space below he wrote:

> *Tonight I stay at the Summit Temple,*
> *Here I could pluck the stars with my hand,*
> *I dare not speak aloud in the silence,*
> *For fear of disturbing the dwellers of heaven.*
> *Chang Chow in dream became a butterfly,*
> *And the butterfly became Chang Chow at waking.*
> *Which was the real—the butterfly or the man?*[21]

On his twenty-fifth birthday, Tom noted in his journal that he had completed revising his one-act play *Moony's Kid Don't Cry,* adapted from *Hot Milk at Three in the Morning,* written when he was at the University of Missouri. Saying that he intended to submit it to Professor Webster, he looked upon it as "a little bit windy I'm afraid—but I think it would be effective on the stage. Wish I could have a play produced."

What he described as "another piece of good luck" happened the day before: "While I was out swimming lady from Wed. Club called up and told Mother I had been awarded the $25 prize for 'Sonnets for the Spring.' Will get it at meeting tomorrow." The sonnet was among 420 poems submitted by 123 entrants, and Tom found himself the subject of articles and captioned photographs in all the St. Louis papers. The award ceremony at the Wednes-day Club was not as grueling as he had anticipated. He said that it could not have been made easier for him. "No stage. No speech. Just a room full of tired, elegant old ladies, a couple of priests and some very young poets. Lovely sunny place. Nevertheless palpitations for about five minutes. Afterwards tea and talk—nervous but felt okay." The competition itself had been originated a decade before by Sara Teasdale, which gave Tom a special reason for pride in the award.

His aunt Belle, who always believed his poetic gift had been inherited from her ancestor Sidney Lanier, sent him an effusive but touching letter:

> Dearest Tom:
> I scarcely know how to write to you about your beautiful sonnets. I deeply appreciated your mother's sending them to me. Oh, son, I do so rejoice in this gift of your's and I know you will hold it inviolate—Never cheapen it—make it count for all that is noble and fine and for that which contrib-utes to the very best. . . . Tom, I am so eager for you to get a place in some great Publishing House—some place where you can be with kindred spirits in the great world of literature.
>
> Oh, I so long for you to go on and on—and son, never let anyone discourage you by attempting to measure your success by the money you make. The poor world has sordid ways of counting things—but take the high way, Tom, and never mind the world.
>
> With dearest love to my dear singer—
> Aunt Belle

Always the missionary, she added "II Cor—9:8."[22]

As further cause for celebrating his twenty-fifth birthday, a poem Tom had entitled "My Love Was Light" had been chosen for publication in *Po-etry*. In a letter to the esteemed editor, Harriet Monroe, Tom said that he was surprised and delighted at the selection: "It is the kind of poem which I write most naturally but am always afraid editors will find too much in the traditional style."[23] He enclosed three dollars, and in his journal he commented: "The Wednesday Club's twenty-five dollar poetry prize . . . affords me the luxury of a subscription. Hurt to put out that much money but will be worth it." Here there emerged a trait that would become char-acteristic of almost every success he ever achieved. *Poetry* was and remains *the* magazine of modern poetry, publishing over the years such major poets as Eliot, Pound, Frost, and Sandburg. The fact that Tom made no other comment in his journal about being published in so reputable a magazine and spoke only of the cost of a subscription was not an affected insou-ciance, for success, when it came, was something he would always take for granted; it was failure of any kind that caused him to cry out.

Tom's sudden notoriety prompted an officer of the St. Louis Writers

Guild to suggest that he become a member. He noted in his journal that Clark Mills belonged, but he added that he "probably won't be invited and am not sure I would want to belong. I'm hardly well enough for that sort of thing. Or am I?" He spoke of feeling extremely nervous and not getting any sleep. "Horrible now, but will try to pull myself together. Ghastly dinner. Snapped at everyone, even the old man, but then he was particularly awful about the Kramers where I spent last night."

This led to his writing a short story, "Sand," and Tom said that he was "rather pleased with it—about old Mr. & Mrs. Kramer."[24] By now, Hazel's grandfather had retired from the shoe company and had apparently suffered a stroke. The once socially active Mrs. Kramer was, as a result, burdened with the care of him. Tom had reason to feel pleased with "Sand." He had written a poignant character study of the plight of an elderly couple who can look in only one direction: back to their early years together. He noted that he had mailed "Sand" to *Story* and that he was trying that elusive market once again. He also mentioned that the latest issue of the magazine had just arrived and that he thought it was deteriorating. "I believe [editors Martha] Foley and [Whit] Burnett are becoming regular Babbitts. Prosperity doesn't agree with literary folk." At the same time, he wrote an unmailed letter to "Dear STORY Publishers":

> As I am obviously not one of your favorite contributors (the score so far is twenty-two to nothing in your favor), I have no reason to suppose that you might be interested in my comments on the short story situation, but am going to make some just the same.
>
> I have been a contributor and subscriber for the past two years and my many personal rebuffs (all of which were more or less deserved) have neither discouraged nor soured my spirit—I still think STORY is unsurpassed in its field. There is just one thing that troubles me: what has become of your once-vaunted interest in the experimental short story? . . . I know the position that you are in. The magazine BUY-ING public is not—(alas)—interested in experimentation! Of course there's still another angle to the situation. Successful writers (with the brilliant exception of Saroyan and one or two others) are AFRAID of writing experimental stories. They have too much to lose. For the most part they have quit hoboing, dish-washing, Etc. . . . They depend on their writing for their living. So they don't dare write anything but what they're pretty sure the public wants. The result is that most literary experimentation is now being done by incompetent young nobodies like myself who have absolutely nothing to lose, no money, no reputation, no public or editorial favor, by writing any way they damned please! Of course our experimental stories don't get into print—I've even given up submitting mine to editors—and I don't

contend that American letters are suffering great injury on that account. . . .[25]

Like painters who paint themselves into a corner, writers can also box themselves in, and in this instance Tom's lofty harangue finally lost its way— which may explain why it wasn't mailed. Or he might not have had the postage. Or he might have *thought* he had mailed it and become irate when it failed to elicit an answer. Or he might simply have misplaced it, discarding it among a multitude of other sheets of paper scattered about his room. Edwina had by now begun the practice of saving everything of his she could get her hands on, fearful that he might be throwing away something that might eventually be of value, even unmailed letters.

The complaint to *Story*, though, has more significance than an author's indignation at the slings and arrows of rejection. More than that familiar grievance, it pointed at a problem that would plague him for the rest of his life. Long after he had attained success and recognition, Tennessee Williams would fight for his right to experiment—and suffer both the critics' and the public's rebuff. It would become a bête noire.

Tom was struggling to achieve recognition on his own terms, not to slant his work to the needs or style of a particular periodical. The result was a collection of rejection slips. Still, there were a few, like John Rood, who saw promise in Tom's writing. Another was Wilbur L. Schramm. As the editor of *American Prefaces*—described as "A Journal of Critical and Imaginative Writing"—Schramm wrote to Tom: "I think this story ought to be published, but my associate editors will not agree that it should be published in PREFACES. Send it around. You can write. I hope to see one of your stories in our magazine before long, and I hope you will let us see more of your manuscripts soon. Good luck to you!"[26]

Early in April, Edwina departed for the gentler clime of Memphis and the ministrations of her mother in order to recuperate from an attack of influenza. But before she left, she noticed an item in the newspaper regarding a one-act play contest sponsored by the Webster Groves Theatre Guild, an amateur group located in a fashionable suburb of St. Louis. She urged Tom to enter the contest. The deadline did not give him much time, but as those closest to him had repeatedly observed, he worked with incredible concentration and swiftness. Before long, he had completed and submitted a play he entitled *The Magic Tower*, and then he thought no more of it—just one more iron in the fire.

Writing poems, short stories, and now plays in an almost feverish outpouring would normally by itself be prodigious enough, but underlying this effort was a driving desire not simply to have his work published or produced but to break out and away from his home, and over and over in his journal entries he cried out to be free.

Wednes. (April 15) . . . This house frightens me again. I feel trapped—
shut in. The radio is on—that awful ball-game—it will be going every
afternoon now and hearing it makes me sick. I'm too tired to write—can
do nothing . . . I wish I could write something decent, strong—but everything about me is weak and silly. Terrible to feel like this. I have been so
well the past two weeks—like a different person. Now I guess it's starting
again. Well, I must learn to take things on the chin because nothing will
be easy for me—nothing has ever been easy . . . this rather hopeless situation—I hardly dare to say hopeless but in my heart I know very well that
it is. I would like to get away some where. . . . Oh, God, I'm so miserable
and lonely and so afraid of *people*! This reminds me of how I used to feel
that first spring at college—afraid to go out on the street!

Clark Mills, recalling Tom as he was at that time, observed: "One of the
things that puzzled me about him: I thought he was oddly docile. I couldn't
imagine how he was able to tolerate his situation at home. In that respect, he
was very decent. He hardly spoke of it at all, except to say that it was difficult
to write there. He didn't complain, but I felt that a lot was quite apparent. All
you had to do was go to his home to see what the situation was. The impression I got was that he was an insoluble problem to the family, and the problem
was his writing.

"They gave him nothing, not even a decent suit of clothes. He always wore
the same suit, and it was absolutely threadbare. I guess his family thought to
buy him anything like that would be a ridiculous, a symbolic waste: It might
encourage him in his foolish ways. I remember one awful rainy night when
he was visiting me and I gave him fifteen cents to get home. And he said
nothing!"

But, Mills added, "He would open up socially in our antisocial group—he
would become quite lively and wasn't so docile then."[27]

After Edwina returned from Memphis toward the end of April, Tom received a letter from the contest chairman of the Webster Groves Theatre
Guild. His play *The Magic Tower* had been awarded the prize: "The decision
of the judges was unanimous. My warmest congratulations to you, and may
your pen continue to flow freely!"[28] Although Tom made no mention of the
award in his journal or in correspondence, Edwina got off word to her parents
posthaste: "Last night Tom and I went to the 'Little Theatre' to see The
Cherry Orchard by the Russian author, Tchekov. It was too much for amateurs to handle but we enjoyed it. At the end of the second act, the prize was
awarded to Tom over the footlights. It is a sterling silver plate for cakes or
sandwiches with the inscription, 'Prize, one act play contest Webster Theatre
Guild—1936.'" It was to be expected that Tom would find a no-money
award disappointing, but, as he sat in the car on the way home—Edwina
proudly clutching the silver plate—the real award he had to look forward to in
the fall was a promised production.

Edwina had other news for the Dakins, as well. "Thursday I had two callers from the board of Jefferson Chap., D.A.R. who informed me I had been selected from the chapter to be the next Regent." She said that she had apparently met the requirements of the hard-to-please older members. "They approved of my 'minutes' and the 'way I read them,' my 'tact,' 'charm,' 'graciousness,' etc. . . . There's no telling what I've let myself in for and I am quaking in my boots!"[29] Edwina would turn fifty-two in August, and as regent of the Jefferson chapter, she had at last achieved a social status that was, in her view, a vindication for the ignominy she had suffered during her first years in St. Louis. Cornelius even offered to pay her way to the DAR September conference in Washington. The boost to her self-confidence was such that she began talking again about possibly beginning a career in real estate.

Still another letter at this time from Wilbur Schramm of *American Prefaces* reaffirmed his belief in Tom's "potential achievement." Regretting the fact that again his letter was in effect a rejection slip, Schramm wrote, "Some of these days you are going to burst out and write some fine stuff."[30] If, like the Theatre Guild's silver platter, the editor's letter was meant to encourage a young writer, it in fact served only to deepen Tom's doubts and depression. Rejection in any form disturbed him; it was defeat. Winning, with its monetary rewards, was all that mattered.

> May 8—It is a lovely fresh May morning—but I am tortured by thoughts. The last three days a steady crescendo—my head aches—I pound the bed with my fists and make horrible faces. Such a helpless, frustrated feeling—and all so silly! Like being scared of my own shadow and that's what it is. I must somehow overcome this idea of defeat—overcome it permanently—completely—or it will drive me mad. . . .

By this time in Tom Williams's life, his focus had become almost totally on *self:* He was suffering an inverted hysteria with a full range of neurological symptoms: nervous exhaustion, arrhythmic heartbeat, immobilizing indecision, self-conscious blushing, shyness, and a gamut of unnameable fears. Used as a method of self-examination, his journal gave vent to his terror of encroaching madness. He was taking pills to sleep and drinking black coffee to keep awake. Twenty-five years old, he was still without any sexual experience. Although he was often in the company of young friends like Clark Mills and Bill Smith who had intimate girlfriends, his personal relationships were kept on a surface, if not a superficial, level, in no way reflective of what he actually felt. In his journal, he wrote, "If only I could realize I am not 2 persons. I am only one. There is no sense in this division. An enemy inside myself!"

There were no further entries in the journal until the end of May, when Tom reflected upon what he had previously written and confessed that "it is really when feeling worst that I feel the need to express it." The journal had the added advantage, he told himself, of proving that nothing lasts, not even pain and despair. In other words, he had had a good month.

Among the writers who especially engaged his interest during this period was D. H. Lawrence.[31] Steeped as he was in Lawrence's novels, Tom could not have failed to identify with the mother-fixated Paul Morel in *Sons and Lovers*, nor, for that matter, to recognize counterparts in Edwina and Cornelius to Morel's mother and father. Chekhov may have been a "dramaturgic mentor," as Tennessee Williams would come to idealize the Russian playwright, but now it was Lawrence's depiction of the isolation and loneliness of the artist as well as his passionate belief in sensual freedom that fascinated and challenged Tom. Everything Lawrence represented was what Tom wished he had the courage to emulate in his personal life, let alone invest in his writings. Of his other idol, Tom went on to say, "I've been reading a lot of Hart Crane's poetry—like it—but hardly understand a single line—of course the individual lines aren't supposed to be intelligible. The message, if there actually is one, comes from the total effect—much of it has at least the atmosphere of great poetry—it is a lot of raw material, all significant and moving but not chiseled into any communicative shape." On June 7, he reported: "Summer school starts the 12th. I plan to take a course in the technique of drama for one."

Instead, he took off for Chicago with Mills to attend the Mid West Writers Conference, his first such symposium. Afterward, he wrote in his journal that the event itself was a flop for him and the whole trip in fact "a ghastly fiasco. Went up on night bus with Clark Mills and Will Wharton. Sleepless night. Horrible humor. Sitting next to a negro on bus with Clark & Will across the aisle. Clark and I both very glum." He said that Mills, however, was excited over a trip he would be making in August to California, where he would be writing a master's thesis on Jules Romains; Mills had won a scholarship for a six-week session in California with the eminent French writer and scholar.

Visiting the offices of *Poetry*, they found that, ironically, editor Harriet Monroe had gone on to St. Louis. "We had a pleasant talk with Geraldine Uddell who is Harriet's business mgr.," Tom wrote. "She had us sign [a] visitor's book. Clark was quite rude. Introduced himself to the girl and left his name on card but *ignored* me—apparently did not wish to injure his prestige by having his exalted name associated with mine. At the close of the interview however I managed to introduce myself which probably displeased him considerably."

The conference itself Tom described as "dreadful" and in a letter to Wilbur Schramm said that the editor was wise to have stayed away. "As might be expected," he told Schramm, the meeting "seemed more concerned with politics than literature and was so exhaustingly dull that I left immediately after the morning session and did not return. I found the Chicago lake front much more edifying. All this hullabaloo about Fascist repression seems like so much shadow-boxing to me at the present time. The fiercest of our revolutionary writers are now receiving monthly checks of well over a hundred dollars from the Government for activities which they themselves describe as mainly 'boondoggling'—so I cannot feel that the Fascist peril is very imminent at this moment!"[32] He did manage to shake hands with his other partisan editor, John Rood, but found little else to make the trip worth the time and money.

Out of feelings of envy and his own insecurity, Tom was even beginning to exhibit ambivalent attitudes toward Clark Mills, who was oblivious to his friend's moods.

> Clark and I went to a horribly cheap restaurant. I could eat nothing. Clark ate a hamburger and egg sandwich, black coffee and a piece of apple pie. I was so sick that I nearly passed out watching him eat. We were completely estranged by this time. At last when he had finished eating—with the greatest deliberation—he remarked "I bet you thought I would never get through." I said, "It did seem rather drawn out." He seemed to relish my discomfiture. . . . Impression of Clark Mills, *poet:* Very talented, even *brilliant*—Clark Mills, *person:* Very conceited, spoiled, bigoted, childish and painfully lacking in a sense of humor.

Not long after, Tom was confessing to his journal, "I'm a swell one to accuse anybody of lacking a sense of humor. Apparently I've completely lost my own." Beyond that, he sent a letter of apology to Clark, and to Schramm he wrote that he thought Clark Mills was probably the most distinguished among the young poets. Doubting that he would ever hear from Clark again, Tom did receive a friendly postcard reply and reflected, "I'm sometimes ashamed of myself for being such a *worm.*" Tom's was seldom a lasting pique but, like bad weather, always subject to change.

On his return from Chicago, he complained about brooding and whining to himself.

> Fancy myself sick and refuse to do any work. Of course it is exhaustingly hot and this house—this domestic life—is quite fiendish. The old man like a dormant volcano, mother nagging a great deal, Rose and Dakin in continual quarrels. Even I cannot keep my temper and act childishly. How stupid we all are! It is impossible to think of such fools as we are having immortal souls—we have plenty to eat but actually squabble over food sometimes as though we were starving. We say petty, annoying things to each other. Today I feel as though I dislike them all and could feel no sorrow if they all were gone. Dreadful to hate everyone as I do sometimes. And yet I have such a profound capacity for love and happiness.

The thing really troubling him was the belief that "I can't force myself to do anything." He had been thinking of rewriting *Moony's Kid Don't Cry* as a verse drama but had abandoned the idea. "No use. If I don't want to write I *can't* write."

Early in July, Cornelius drove Edwina and Rose to Washington, and, concerned that Tom was on the verge of another nervous collapse, his grandparents came to St. Louis to stay with him. He wrote, "These are the two persons I do love and always shall—more than anyone else in the world. My Grandmother's got more of God in her than anything or anybody else I've yet discovered on earth! When I think of God I think of her. But it is hard to think of God these days except with a feeling of sorrowful perplexity. *How strange this life is!!!!*"

Tom might also have been referring to the "sorrowful perplexity" of the world outside his, a world irrevocably slipping into the tides of war. On July 17, in Spain, the fascist Generalissimo Francisco Franco, aided by "volunteers" from Germany and Italy, ignited the civil war that would spread across continents around the globe like a raging fire, destroying the lives of innocent millions then living in the delusion of peace.

In the early morning of August 19, a squad of Falangist soldiers ushered the poet-playwright Federico García Lorca into the fields of his native Granada and executed him. He was thirty-eight, the creator of a dozen of the twentieth century's finest plays and recognized even then as Spain's foremost dramatist. Tom and Clark Mills and their politically conscious circle were shocked and vocal in their outrage and support of the Spanish forces fighting fascism, and in time, Lorca would make a deep and lasting impression on Tennessee Williams.

After his grandparents had come and gone, Tom remarked, "Their visit was lovely. Like a dream now. The life here so quiet and perfect just like it was in Memphis when I was with them. Now that is over. The family has returned." Tom felt as though the members of his family were looking at him and wondering what he was going to do with himself. "I wish that I knew. I woke at three o'clock. It is now light enough outside for me to write without the lamp. The world looks tired this morning. It needs rain. The wind sounds fretful and dry like a person squirming in a fever." Still unable to write, he felt that his confinement within the home was responsible. "I am furious with the whole family. I have to take insults from them all. Can do nothing about it. How stupid. We all are in this house and yet how full of pride and conceit! I suppose it is the same way in most other houses, and yet people are afraid to die. Especially myself. I hate the thought of ever dying. . . . I feel as though I will go mad in this house tonight."

Tom's omnipresent feeling now was separation, not only in his ambition to be a successful writer but in his isolation within his family, as well. Even he and Rose were estranged. Neither Tom nor Edwina made mention of a sudden recurrence of Rose's "old mental state," as her mother had been referring to her eccentric demeanor. Tom had become so absorbed with his own emotional problems and so preoccupied with his writing that he looked upon Rose's behavior as putting on an act. In truth, she was mentally ill, but no one wanted to face it—no one in the family, not Tom, not her doctor, and least of all Rose herself.

On their return from their summer trip to Washington, the family brought with them a new member, a gregarious Boston terrier named Jiggs, who won everyone's affection, especially Cornelius's. Now, as Edwina remarked, there were two things in the world Cornelius loved—Dakin and Jiggs. When the dog died twelve years later, Edwina said it was the only time she had ever seen Cornelius cry.

At this point in the summer, Tom was hoping to enter his senior year at Washington University in September but hadn't the slightest idea how it would be possible. Cornelius was sounding the usual claps of thunder about his idle son, prompting Tom to write in his journal, "I hate this house and today I hate everyone in it and they all look at me and wonder what the hell I'm doing here and despise me too. Yes, I heard Dad saying last night that *he* wanted to know when I was going back to work and it had better be soon because soon I'd be too old (!!) and nobody would want me and Dakin said he didn't tell him I was planning to go back to school this Fall and heaven knows what he'd say about that!"

Cornelius was about to take his annual vacation in Knoxville, and Edwina, concerned about Tom's depressed state, pressured Cornelius to let her send Tom and Dakin to Lake Taneycomo and leave her alone with Rose. Despite temperatures reaching 120 degrees, Rose in a letter to the Dakins said that she and her mother were reveling in the peace and quiet.

On his return from the lake at the end of August, Tom wrote his grandparents that he had received a letter from the publishers Simon and Schuster, inquiring about his writing a novel. "So I think that I will try to write one during my spare time—just a short one. It is easier to sell a good novel than a good short story."[33] It wasn't easier, though, and not long afterward he wrote in his journal, "My novel has acquired a first chapter—but dreadfully cheap—I don't want to write that kind of stuff."

Edwina gave Tom the good news that the Dakins had decided to pay his tuition, enabling him to enroll at the university in the fall, and she wrote her parents, "I doubt if Tom could get his degree by next Spring as the requirements are so much more than at Missouri and very little of his journalistic course could be applied on the B.A. However, I'll find out all about it and let you know. If it takes longer, would you still want to give the year's tuition? By that time, he might be making enough money on the side to finish it. The publishers write him very encouraging letters, so I think in time his writings will pay. I'll send you the story ("Twenty-Seven Wagons Full of Cotton"] in 'Manuscript.' I didn't like the subject, though it is well written."[34]

Earlier in the summer, Tom had made his own inquiry to Washington

University and had received a letter from the registrar: "Inasmuch as you have not completed the Physical Education requirement in the Freshman and Sophomore years, you are admitted for the present as a Student Not a Candidate for a Degree. You will be given regular classification as soon as you have completed three semesters of Physical Education."[35] Tom was not able, as he had hoped, to get out of physical education, but, given his previous illness and a recent diagnosis of high blood pressure, swimming, as it turned out happily enough, was acceptable in place of more vigorous forms of exercise. But whether he deliberately chose not to tell his family that he was entering as a student ineligible for a degree or did not understand this stipulation, he would go through an entire school year indifferent or unaware that he would not be able to graduate.

Once Tom had returned to the enclosure of his room and the resumption of his various writing projects, he set down in his journal a philosophy, or, more exactly, a prospective modus vivendi that he would pursue for the rest of his life.

> Sunday Aug. 30 . . . Now I'm back "home," which isn't quite true. The whole world is really my home—not any single cramped unhappy place. But just the same I've got to stay here or so it seems and being here is very miserable. I hate brick and concrete and the hissing of garden hoses. I hate streets with demure or sedate little trees and the awful screech of trolley wheels and polite, constrained city voices. I want hills and valleys and lakes and forests around me! I want to lie dreaming and naked in the sun! I want to be free and have freedom all around me. I don't want anything tight or limiting or strained.
>
> Here's the old life again with all its old problems. Maybe if I look hard enough into this fog I'll begin to see God's face and can manage to find my way out.

The following day, he addressed the "enemy inside myself"—an essential division in his personality that would plague him and manifest itself in patterns of contradictory behavior throughout the years to come. It would divide him not only against himself but often against those closest to him, leading him to characterize himself as "half-mad."

> Monday Aug. 31—A little crazy blue devil has been with me all day. I wish I could shake him off and walk alone and free in the sunlight once more. There is one part of me that could always be very happy and brave and even *good* if the other part was not so damned "pixilated." I see so much beauty and feel so much that there is no reason why I should make myself miserable. . . .

But as Tom would discover, the "blue devils"[36] were beyond his control. They had fastened on him and would appear and reappear again in his journals and reveries. As a symptom of schizophrenia, "seeing" angels and devils has often been regarded as a characteristic of a poetic genius of a tortured and compulsive kind. Tennessee said, "Of that demon, I think invariably of Hart Crane, at the very center of whose life it exploded, and destroyed."[37][38]

Having just returned from his two weeks in the Ozarks, it is quite possible that Tom overheard a familiar Ozark expression, "He's blue-deviled." Blue devils appear to have had their origin in ancient Britain and France. In the nineteenth century, the painter and journalist John James Audubon cited blue devils—*"les diables bleus"*—writing, "I . . . have had the horrors all around me. . . . I walk the streets it is true, but neither hear nor see any thing but my fancies dancing about through the atmosphere like so many winged Imps resembling in shapes, colour, & capers all the *beau ideal* of the Infernal regions!"[38]

In the psychic life of Tennessee Williams, the blue devils become a matter for speculation. Blue was his and his mother's favorite color. The infant imprisoned in his cradle looked up in both rage and affection into his mother's blue eyes. As a child in Nashville, his little pail and shovel in hand, he was discovered "diggin' to de debbil," and in the sermons of his grandfather and in the somber tales of his black nurse, Ozzie, the Devil was all too real. Not until he was thirty-two did he finally confide in a friend the torment of the blue devils and the fact that he had first become conscious of the specter when he was ten years old.

Now he was beset with the fear of encroaching madness, along with the misery of sexual repression that he was still suffering at age twenty-five. Tennessee later asserted that he had not even masturbated by then but remembered only an incident of lying on his stomach and thinking about the physique of a swimmer, which caused an ejaculation. With strong religious restraints binding him, the thought that he might be homosexual remained forbidden and inadmissible, literally unthinkable. What clearly was building was a tidal wave within him that would eventually be released in uncontrollable, addictive sexual behavior.

As a result, a terrible passion was borne in upon him and sublimated, to become a powerful energy channeled into his writing. As he would someday say about O'Neill, "To be passionate and to be lonely isn't the easiest of things in the world."[39] It was, in fact, torture. The only real solace he found was in the blue devils' adversary.

> . . . I do believe in God. I know that I do. There are times like this when I feel God is sitting right at my side with one hand on my shoulder. Then I feel warm and safe and the universe is not a cold mysterious immensity but a nice comfortable little house for me to live in. That is putting it a little too prettily but I do have such feelings once in a while and though cruel reason tells me that I am hopelessly adrift on a shoreless sea full of hungry sharks there is a small trusting little boy in me that won't believe it and still thinks there's a rudder on the boat and a good wind blowing.

9

Blue Roses

September–December 1936

During the few remaining months of 1936, a change would come into Tom's life, and it would save him from the insanity that was finally, irrevocably destroying his sister's mind. As he wrote in his journal, he could not believe that he was "hopelessly adrift" but thought, rather, that there was a rudder on his boat and "a good wind blowing." Word was quickly getting around St. Louis of a promising writer named Tom Williams, and by this time it had reached Willard Holland, organizer and director of a first-rate nonprofessional acting company called the Mummers. The wind was indeed blowing in the right direction, and Tom was setting sail toward the home port of theatre.

Holland had phoned him at home, and Williams remembered Willard's voice as high-pitched and nervous. "He said I hear you go to college and I hear you can write. I admitted some justice in both of these charges. Then he asked me: How do you feel about compulsory training? I then assured him that I had left the University of Missouri because I could not get a passing grade in ROTC. Swell! said Holland, you are just the guy I am looking for. How would you like to write something against militarism?"[1]

Holland was staging the St. Louis premiere of a play that had created a sensation in New York in 1936 called *Bury the Dead*, launching the career of a young writer named Irwin Shaw. The play was not a full-length one, and what Holland wanted was a curtain-raiser to set the antimilitaristic tone of the evening. Recalling C.C.'s fury at his having failed ROTC, Tom readily agreed and set to work.

Bury the Dead was not scheduled to open until November 11, Armistice Day, but now Tom found himself in the midst of rehearsals for his play *The Magic Tower*, which was set to premiere on October 13 at the Webster Groves Theatre Guild. In addition, he was at work on a long play that he said he intended to enter in a theatre contest or give to Holland once he had finished it. He noted in his journal that it was "improving but slowly," and he also mentioned that his "sainted Grandparents sent me a check for $125. To pay my tuition at Washington University. So now it is definitely decided that I am to go there. I want to make every day of it *count*—since my lovely grandparents have sacrificed so much to send me."

On September 21, he was admitted to Washington University in the College of Liberal Arts as a student but not as a candidate for a degree. Going back to college at the age of twenty-five gave schooling a different meaning and purpose. For one thing, Tom no longer believed a degree in journalism was necessarily the means to a writing career, and for another, here was an excellent way to keep out of the shoe factory. But by far the most important thing was the fact that he would not only have the time to write but was becoming recognized as a writer.

By mid-September, Tom had completed the short play for Willard Holland and named it *Headlines.* Plays had become his focal interest. In a letter to his grandfather, he commented, "I am still working on the coal-miner play and expect to submit it in the Little Theatre Contest this year. I want to visit some real coal-mines in Illinois before doing so."[2] He would eventually name this—his first full-length play—*Candles to the Sun;* he would submit it to Willard Holland and the Mummers, and it would identify him once and for all not simply as a writer but as a playwright.

Sadly, though, even as Tom was gaining confidence in himself, that same ground was fast slipping out from under Rose. She was beyond his reach. This was also true of everyone else in the family, involved as they were in their own activities. Edwina was excitedly making plans for a trip to Washington to attend a DAR convention. Cornelius was preparing to leave on a business trip. Dakin was busy socializing and excelling in his last year of high school. And Tom was taken up with his new theatre associates. But Rose's life was at a virtual standstill. While she did have girlfriends whom she saw occasionally, at twenty-six she still was without a gentleman caller seriously interested in her, and not being desired romantically, she had become excessively self-conscious. Like Tom, she was suffering the stress of sexual repression, and like him, she hid her private anguish and desperation behind "appearances," to be kept up at all costs among friends and relatives.

Edwina told her parents about C.C.'s being away on business and said that she would enjoy her trip to the DAR convention, "especially since Cornelius offered to pay my way." She also mentioned, "He called me up the night after he left home from Chicago, to tell me he had caught a cold and to ask how 'Jiggs' is! Tom broke his new glasses and owes his dentist nine dollars and Dr. Alexander ten. Isn't it the limit!!!" Then she added, "I'm sorry I can't take Rose but it would be too expensive for us both to go."[3]

Everything now in Rose's life was going awry. A plan she had nurtured to visit her cousin Rose Comfort in Memphis, and at the same time see her grandparents, was canceled when it appeared that her aunt Isabel might be coming to St. Louis. But then Isabel, busy with her church activities, decided not to go. Rose wrote again to Rose Comfort in the vain hope of going to Memphis to see her in October.

Tom, on the other hand, buoyed by a widening circle of friends, wrote in his journal: "I want to have a party this week or go to one. I am lonely. I need people around me. That is because I am feeling good. I want to raise hell and make love and maybe get a little drunk." To combat his restlessness, his mother had given him a dollar to see *The Great Ziegfeld*, the film biography of the producer of *Show Boat*, the musical Tom and his grandfather had seen in New York in 1928. He found the movie "very entertaining—you really had the feeling of a man's whole life unfolding before you—a rare achievement on the screen." The next day, he still found his existence "smooth and unannoying," but also felt "the need for company—and no one calls! I wonder if I shall see anyone this weekend?"

On the last day of September, Rose wrote to assure her grandfather, "We are getting along nicely without Dad or Mother," but commented, "Tom has become a little too sociable. He is having company to-night and I am so tired I am afraid I shan't be very agreeable. There is so much to do around here even with Susie."[4] In the final account, Tom's party may have done much to alleviate his loneliness, but it also created havoc that would unnerve Rose and result in repercussions like shock waves to last for months, even years, to come.

Clark Mills's memory of the evening was fragmented, influenced as it was by the surfeit of alcohol and the resultant social mayhem. Tom had invited the poets and sundry other members of his literary circle, anticipating a convivial, if not exactly high-minded, gathering. As it turned out, the festivities were indeed more bacchanalian than cerebral in spirit. In Mrs. Williams's absence, the immaculate living room and kitchen were reduced to picnic grounds, while the noise of shouting and laughter penetrated the night air. Rose, who was not present, although upstairs, listening to everything, was shocked by the goings-on, especially at one point when someone went to the telephone located on the landing of the stairway and started making obscene phone calls. The next day, Tom lamented:

> Oct. 1. The first morning in October will have to go on record as one of the world's worst. I am disgraced at home and disgusted with the world— especially literary people. Sick at my stomach. Never spent such a nauseous night. I no longer have any trust in human nature. Honestly I had better live the life of an Anchorite than go with such people—selfish, egotistical, vulgar, absurd. All that I said of McBurney following the Chicago trip was true. He is really an ass. Poor Wharton is simply nuts. And I am a damn fool to tolerate such a bunch.

Miss Edwina could not have agreed more, for on her return that day from her sojourn among the Daughters of the American Revolution, exhilarated but exhausted, she encountered Rose in a highly agitated state—sickened and distraught that her brother could have such uncouth friends and could permit such disgusting behavior in their home; above all, she was horrified that he drank alcohol like her father. Edwina, acting out the role of outraged parent, only exacerbated Rose's hysteria.

At the same time, the fact that Rose would betray Tom and become an informer served to anger him more than his own self-recriminations. More traumatic than the party was an incident that took place afterward, when Tom was going down the stairs and Rose was coming up. Tennessee recalled, "We passed each other on the landing and I turned upon her like a wildcat and I hissed at her: 'I hate the sight of your ugly old face!' Wordless, stricken, and crouching, she stood there motionless in a corner of the landing as I rushed out of the house."[5] He was to consider this the cruelest thing he had ever done and something for which he could never properly atone: something that separated them and drove his guilt into the deeper realm of a *shame* burdening him for the remainder of his life.

At first, though, Tom was able to understand his reaction only as a justifiable resentment toward what amounted to familial treason. There was an erosion and resentment now in his relationship with his family: not only with his father but also with his mother and her fussing and nagging, with Dakin and his social activities, and, tragically, with Rose, as well, torn from him as she was. Since she had always been prone to dramatize herself, he regarded her weird behavior as "some kind of an act." His own pain was so acute, so embedded, that he was unable to empathize with her suffering, and in this sense they had lost contact with each other. Because he felt desperately trapped in his home—*their* home, as he saw it—his only escape was into his writing and, through it, to the outside world. But for Rose, there was no escape, no channel, and for much the same reasons she became increasingly insensitive to Tom, as well, even to his writing, which she did not understand. Theirs was an alienation that isolated them from each other and led to heartbreak for them both.

> Oct. 7 . . . The house is wretched. Rose is on one of her neurotic sprees— fancies herself an invalid—talks in a silly dying-off way—trails around the house in negligees. Disgusting.*
>
> They are still hounding me for the party Tuesday night. But I am getting tough. I can take it.
>
> Friday Oct. 9 . . . Poor Rose is worse than ever today. We must pray. That is all there is to do. One very indecent thing about me is my indifference. I do not worry about her nearly as much as I should. But life is all so confused and mad—it is no wonder that I behave in a mad fashion.

In a letter to her parents, Edwina said, "Rose went back to her old mental state of last Spring this week, so I haven't known what to do about sending her down to Memphis. She has a letter from Rose Comfort inviting her there.

---

*Three years later, in reviewing his journal, Tom encountered this entry and did not delete or change it, simply appended, "God forgive me for this!"

To-day, she seems more her-self again."[6] Once again, Rose abruptly acted as though nothing at all had occurred. Whenever she behaved irrationally, she could see alarm mirrored in the faces of her family, and the realization frightened her as much as it did them. It was then that she would bring herself up sharp, leading them to believe what they wanted to believe: that these episodes were just temperamental outbursts. But she was aware more than anyone that there was something wrong with her.

Tennessee recalled a drive in the country with some companions. "We started, the young friends and I, to laugh at the outrageous behavior of an acquaintance who was losing his mind. Miss Rose turned very grave and stiff in the back seat of the car. 'You must never make fun of insanity,' she reproved us. 'It's worse than death.' "[7]

What Edwina and her parents knew was a closely guarded secret—and it is unlikely that even Cornelius and his sisters were aware of it—but there was a history of "alarming incidences of mental and nervous breakdowns" in both the Dakin and Otte families.[8] Ironically, Cornelius knew—and probably his sisters knew, too—that there were members of the Williams clan who had spent time in the Lyon's View Asylum in Knoxville. Grand was not reassured at being told that Rose seemed to be more herself again, and she decided to leave for St. Louis as soon as possible. While the Reverend Dakin prayed, Grand marshaled the energy to return once more to the Williamses' embattled home to be with her granddaughter.

Doctors and family members alike concurred that Rose's main difficulty was the lack of something to do. Edwina certainly agreed. Keeping her busy with housework had become as much a prescription as a household duty, but the problem was that mother and daughter quarreled constantly over trivia and managed only to increase Susie's already-heavy burden. Keeping Rose occupied with housekeeping clearly was not enough. The girl clung to her illusion that she would get a job, move into her own apartment, and meet some eligible young man who would want to marry her.

Edwina had bought Rose a typewriter of her own, and although she spent hours trying to master the keyboard, she was clearly inept. The one occasion when she did find employment resulted in a catastrophe. She had managed to secure a position as a secretary-typist in the offices of two doctors and a dentist. While the typing was light, there were other chores as well in taking care of the offices, such as washing bowls in the dentist's office. Edwina remembered her returning home tired but proud that she was being paid for her efforts. But it was not long before she was told that the work was obviously too difficult for her and was dismissed. Rose reacted hysterically, locking herself in the office lavatory and crying uncontrollably until finally Edwina and the boys had to go downtown and persuade her to unlock the door. This had been her last hope for gainful employment, and she was inconsolable.

Since she was clearly unable to find or keep work of any kind and became extremely upset at the suggestion that she look for a job, Edwina's strategy was to keep her busy with "wifely" chores and to renew her campaign of encouraging gentlemen callers. Above all, she was determined that Rose would have a Christian, *not* a companionate, marriage! She felt that Dakin's friends were, of course, too young, but surely, she insisted, Tom knew some eligible bachelors among his friends. Clark Mills was one of them: "I did see Rose on occasion, but my exchanges with her were very brief. I may have been only one of several gentlemen callers. It was a very pitiful affair: the way a nightmare resembles reality. Rose, despite her photographs, I recall as being much more beautiful. She was a very beautiful girl, at least she was to me."[9]

Everyone remarked on her exquisite appearance. Edwina wrote, "They say a flowering tree is most beautiful the year before it dies and it seemed the last year Rose spent at home, dying spiritually . . . she never looked more beautiful. Her face held a faraway expression as she sat on the ground for hours, her lovely eyes reflecting the blue of the sky, that cloud of auburn hair falling softly around her shoulders."[10]

Physically, she was indeed lovely, but Mills was appalled at what she wore. He remembered: "She was dressed in the most god-awful ankle-length, shapeless chiffon-type dress that looked like it dated from 1922. Very awkward, I remember her standing in the shadow in the dining room, unable or unwilling to come in—and, as I recall—she never spoke at all. One reason I don't have any memory of her saying anything: From the moment I walked through that door, Mrs. Williams *never stopped talking*. It was a nightmare, just yammer, yammer, yammer, to the point you were ready to go through the ceiling. From a distance, it had a comical aspect, but close up, watch out: It was absolutely destructive. . . . Mrs. Williams as a social figure had an element of lunacy about it—it had no connection with reality except in a grotesque way—all that talk about her elegant past and their southern gentility. I couldn't find any redeeming quality in her at all. To me, the word *nightmare* is strictly applicable, because she *was* a nightmare."[11]

In his memoir, the poet William Jay Smith had a similar view of Miss Edwina, although not quite as caustic. He said that the College Poetry Society usually met at the Williams home:

> . . . first in the living room where Mrs. Williams received us, and afterward on the sun-porch, where we sat for hours criticizing one another's poems. The house, with its Oriental rugs, silver, and comfortable if not luxurious furniture, was located in an affluent neighborhood and was higher on the social ladder than Clark Mills's modest home in Clayton. [Edwina] presided over it as if it were an antebellum mansion. A busy little woman, she never stopped talking, although there was little inflection or warmth in the steady flow of her speech. One topic, no matter how trivial, received the same emphasis as the next, which might be ut-

terly tragic. I had the impression listening to her that the words she pronounced were like the red balls in a game of Chinese checkers, all suddenly released and clicking quickly and aimlessly about the board.

In contrast Tom was the shyest, quietest person I had ever met. His stony-faced silence often put people off: he appeared disdainful of what was going on around him, never joining in the quick give-and-take of a conversation but rather listening carefully and taking it all in. He would sit quietly in a gathering for long periods of time until suddenly like a volcano erupting he would burst out with a high cackle and then with resounding and uncontrollable laughter. Those who knew him well found this trait delightful, but to others it seemed rude and disconcerting. He was certainly quick and ready with words when we discussed our poetry. With one another's efforts we were nothing if not severe. Tom's great god was D. H. Lawrence, and some of his lyrical Laurentian outpourings got cut back in our sessions.[12]

Smith said that Rose was rarely mentioned when the poetry group congregated on the sunporch, but they knew she was probably in her room or on the stairs, listening to them.

Roger Moore, a good-looking and brilliant young man, lived across the street from the Williamses and had called to ask Rose to go with him to a Democratic rally. A Rhodes scholar, he had received his Ph.D. in political science at Yale and was running for mayor of University City, but unfortunately he had pitted himself against a powerful incumbent, a cog in a political machine, and to make matters worse, he tried to use logic and ethics as a rationale to win over the voter. It was like using the blade of a finely honed sword to cut through concrete; to his disillusionment, he was to discover the hard rock of American politics.

Moore liked Rose, and probably, as much out of sympathy as attraction, he took her out occasionally. Tom and Dakin did some pamphleteering for him, but Tom's principal interest was in Roger's sister, Virginia Moore. A lovely and charming woman, she was also a polished poet and the author of *Virginia Is a State of Mind*. Tennessee Williams recalled, "That summer I showed my juvenile poems to Virginia Moore, and how very gracious she was in giving one of them tactful praise."[13]

William Jay Smith remembered meeting her at Tom's home:

Virginia Moore, who had been married to Louis Untermeyer, had left him after only a few years of marriage and returned to her home in St. Louis with her small son. . . . [She] had published one or two volumes of poetry, and her work had appeared in Louis Untermeyer's anthology. She was a strikingly beautiful woman, but, along with her beauty, we admired her connection with the literary world. She had met all the important people and was a breath of fresh air, from the great outer world. Mrs. Williams thought her impressive, and found reassurance in her approval of Tom's work. This approval from someone so acceptable socially seemed to make her feel that Tom was doing very well, although I don't think she had any real idea what he was up to in his work. What mattered most to her was that he was at the university and appeared to be on his way toward getting a degree.[14]

In truth, what mattered most to Edwina at this time was Rose. She said nothing to Tom about her fears, nor did she tell him that Grand was on her way to give what help she could.

Not knowing Grand was en route, Tom sent his grandparents a report of his progress at the university: "I have three courses which require a tremen- dous amount of outside reading. For one course I am having to read all of O'Neill's plays to make a term paper on his work." The paper, entitled "Some Representative Plays of O'Neill and a Discussion of His Art," was something less than laudatory in characterizing O'Neill as "first, last, and always the born showman."[15] Many of his points were well taken, but they prompted his professor to comment, "Not quite in accord with your earlier estimate. Your style is a bit too truculent." Nevertheless, he graded the paper an AB. Tom added that he had also to read all of Sophocles's tragedies and in his French course was "kept busy reading Voltaire, Etc."[16] During the days that followed his ill-fated party, Tom found himself drawn increasingly toward theatre ac- tivities and away from his more accustomed literary pursuits. When he first began his classes in English literature, he was very enthusiastic, but now he was writing in his journal that he felt "dull and disinterested in the literary line. Dr. Heller bores me with all his erudite discussion of literature. Writing is just *writing!* Why all the fuss about it?"

Otto Heller, widely respected as a distinguished professor of literature, was a rigid, Teutonic academic with a thick German accent. He was then in his seventies and spending his final year at Washington University. Although Tom's notebooks attest to the fact that he was well read, and in spite of the fact that Tom received an A in Heller's course, he became increasingly an- noyed by the professor's intellectual posturings.

At the time he was sounding a sour note about Dr. Heller's course, Tom was also reporting, "Willard Holland just called up. Wants me to see him tomorrow. He has read my long play." In these initial meetings with Holland, Tom was encountering his first dedicated man of the theatre. In need of a haircut, always wearing a baggy and shining blue suit and often a scarf in place of a shirt, Holland was playing out the role of the eccentric director. Williams observed, "This was not what made him a great director, but a great director he was. Everything that he touched he charged with electricity. Was it my youth that made it seem that way? Possibly, but not probably. In fact not even possibly: you judge theatre, really, by its effect on audiences, and Holland's work never failed to deliver, and when I say deliver I mean a sock!" As for his company, the Mummers, Williams wrote:

> There was about them that kind of excessive romanticism which is youth and which is the best and purest part of life. . . . Most of them worked at other jobs besides theatre. They had to, because The Mummers were not a paying proposition. . . . Many of them were fine actors. Many of them were not. Some of them could not act at all, but what they lacked in ability, Holland inspired them with in the way of enthusiasm. I guess it was all run by a kind of beautiful witchcraft! It was like a definition of what I think theatre is. Something wild, something exciting, something you are not used to.[17]

Tom's one-act *Headlines* was set for mid-November production, but Holland said his long play needed reworking. He held out the promise of an early spring production, provided Tom could make suitable revisions. Here, to Holland's surprise, was a fledgling playwright willing not only to make changes but to make them even when the director didn't need or want them. "You could talk out any point with him about his plays. He had no temperament about his work," Holland later said. "Right from the beginning I thought of him as a professional. I thought to myself when I read his first plays: here is something; nothing like this has hit the American theatre since the early O'Neill stuff."[18]

After the meeting with Willard Holland, Tom and Clark Mills—their friendship having once again survived Tom's fits of disillusionment—attended a rehearsal of *The Magic Tower*. Tom said:

> [They had] a pleasant evening. Met [director David] Gibson in café. . . . Drank a couple of beers and felt rather desperately gay—recited Ernest Dawson [Dowson] on the way home. Wet streets and lamps. Disappointed in the play. Too sugary. But I don't feel like doing anything better. I am in one of my defeatist moods about writing. If only I could always love my work—then I would be a great artist. But I would never be vain. That is the one very decent thing about me. I have no inclination toward vanity. Another decent thing about me is my tolerance and my love of people and my gentleness toward them. I think I have acquired that through suffering and loneliness.

> Monday. Oct. 12 . . . Grand is here, an unexpected visit. Tomorrow night my play—feel absolutely no interest. Isn't that silly? Nothing to say tonight—except I feel in excellent shape physically—no nerves—just depression.

The following night, Grand, Edwina, and Tom attended a program of three one-act plays presented by the Webster Groves Theatre Guild in the local high school auditorium. The third was Tom's first-prize winner, *The Magic Tower*, which had the added distinction of garnering his first review— and a favorable one, at that. In part, the reviewer described the prizewinning play as "a poignant little tragedy with a touch of warm fantasy. It treats of the love of a very young, not too talented artist and his ex-actress wife, a love which their youthful idealism has translated into a thing of exquisite white beauty. They call the garret in which they live their 'magic tower' and are happy there until the artist's belief in his star fails. Then the magic tower becomes a drab garret once more; and tragedy, like a gray woman, glides in to remain."

The review continued: "Exquisitely written by its poet author and beautifully directed by David Gibson, this play evoked the emphatic response of the audience throughout, in spite of the fact that Elizabeth Rush should *not* have been cast in the role of the heroine. Her nervous acting and hurried speeches failed to convince, largely, we believe, because hysterical parts are her métier."[19] Apparently, as acted, the character was the prototype of numerous Tennessee Williams heroines to come, and what he regarded as "too sugary" would soon become astringent in the plays taking shape in his mind. Despite other glowing reviews, he despaired of his situation, entreating, "Oh, God, help me to do what I should do—be brave and live a free life."

With Grand's firm hand and gentle presence again pervading the Williams household, a serenity seemed gradually to settle over everything, Tom and Rose both becoming quiet of mind, at least for the time Grand could be away from her own home. Edwina, too, was brought under control, and even Cornelius became civil in Mrs. Dakin's company—though out of her presence, he was drinking heavily and still indulging in his poker nights with the boys.

"A Rendezvous with Destiny"

Although Tom had recently heard the Socialist candidate, Norman Thomas, speak and had "found it impressive," he did not bother to vote for him as he had in 1932. The outcome of the election was predictable. The Republicans had nominated Alfred M. Landon, the governor of Kansas, and proudly referred to him as the "Kansas Coolidge." President Coolidge may have been taciturn, but he at least had a dry wit, befitting a New Englander. But Alf Landon was no match for either Coolidge or, certainly, FDR when it came to rhetoric; his one great oft-quoted line was: "Wherever I have gone in this country, I have found Americans."[20]

Roosevelt's aim was at the jugular of the "economic royalists," calling them "the enemy within our gates" and saying that private enterprise had become privileged enterprise, not free enterprise. He attacked a breed of capitalist, "the Wall Street neanderthal," without discrediting capitalism itself, and in the process undercut the effectiveness of both Communists and fascists with the same double-edged sword. He was returned to office in an unprecedented popular and electoral vote, prompting *New York Herald-Tribune* columnist Dorothy Thompson to declare, "If Landon had given one more speech, Roosevelt would have carried Canada too."

Although Tom was often in the company of Communists on and off campus, he was avowedly no sympathizer. It was not so much the goals of communism that soured him as it was the grim and rabid fellow travelers innominate in their appropriately named "cells" that he found repugnant. He simply had no wish to join the masses; he felt he was suffering anonymity enough in his own one-room cell at home.

One of Tom's acquaintances was an outspoken advocate of the Communist Manifesto, USA-style, if not a Party member. He was also something of a self-styled drama critic, and Tom set forth in his journal not just an opinion of this gentleman but also a view he would carry into the theatre with him: "There's just a natural uncongeniality between me and that bunch. They are professional 'againsters'! I don't believe in that stuff. It's not necessary to be against everything else in order to be for Communism. They seem to think it is." Calumnious social or dramatic criticism, with a few exceptions, all amounted to the same thing in his view: the venom of underlings.

As for socialism, Tom continued to believe in the quixotic Norman Thomas as a sincere, if not a viable, candidate. Tennessee Williams and Thomas would, in fact, become personal friends, but now, in 1936, the plain truth was that President Roosevelt had already instituted many of the reforms that were being branded "socialism" by his adversaries. When asked what it was that caused the Left to lose its momentum, Thomas replied, "In a word, Roosevelt."

As a result, Tom Williams, like many other middle-class Americans who were comparatively well-off, simply did not feel the urgency to be a part of any egalitarian movement. Cornelius and Miss Edwina—DAR or not—were southern Democrats and again voted for Roosevelt. She could be justly shocked at fourteen thousand jobless St. Louisans being thrown off relief, but such things had virtually no reality for the Williams family. Clark Mills said that Tom and their friends were conscious of problems like these only when campus radicals and insurgent poets made them aware. Then it became noblesse oblige to second the motion and recite the cant.

While Tom was steeped in his own personal struggle against puritan constraint, he was at the same time artist enough to recognize that a play, as a work of art, must exist in an undefined realm somewhere between the extremes of soap opera and soapbox. Although his early work did have a distinct dramatic flair, his choice of subject matter reflected the social consciousness of the times and the influence of liberals like Willard Holland and the more radical members among the Mummers.

On November 11, Armistice Day, at 5:00 A.M., Tom wrote in his journal that he had not been able to get a wink of sleep all night. "My prologue 'Headlines' will be given this evening. Holland has made something very clever out of it. He's a genius, I think—a real genius—though I can't say I like him especially as a person. He's too slippery. I enjoy working with 'the Mummers'—a delightful bunch of young people. Nothing snooty or St. Louis 'social' about them."

When Tom returned home, his opinion was that *Bury the Dead* had been "very forcefully done" but that his prologue, however, was "rather botched." He regarded it as a "stupid, pointless thing anyway—a piece of hack work." Though the Washington University student paper was noncommittal as to artistic merit, it at least did take notice of the curtain-raiser, if only because its author was anonymous and sounded suspiciously like someone on campus:

> "Bury the Dead," the story of tomorrow's war, was presented by the Mummer's last Friday at the Wednesday Club Auditorium. . . . A large group of students attended. Before the opening . . . a short skit was given called "Headlines," in which a senator gives an armistice day address, interspersing it with scenes of how Americans are behaving about the war problem. One of these scenes, called "Allison's C.M.E.O. Activities Result in Dismissal from University," was a direct take-off on the recent [Don] Ellinger case on this campus.[21]

Writing her parents, Edwina commented, "Tom received two tickets to the 'Mummers' Play for which he wrote the 'Headlines.' I went with him, and it was good. They wanted to sign his name but he couldn't let them do so as there has been a big Campus rumpus over the Students working against the R.O.T.C. and one boy lost his scholarship thereby."[22]

Ten years after that night, Tennessee Williams referred to Irwin Shaw's opus as

> one of the greatest lyric plays America has produced . . . a solid piece of flame. Actors and script, under Holland's dynamic hand, were one piece of vibrant living-tissue. Now St. Louis is not a town that is easily impressed. . . . They certainly were not used to the sort of hot lead which the Mummers pumped into their bellies that night of Shaw's play . . . it paralyzed them. There wasn't a cough or creak in the house, and nobody left . . . without a disturbing kink in their nerves or guts, and I doubt if any of them have forgotten it to this day.[23]

What gave the play its special impact in St. Louis, as in New York, was not only Holland's staging or Shaw's writing but also the omens of war, the mounting apprehension over what was happening in Europe. Those dark horizons gave mothers with sons, like Edwina, a feeling of an increasing undercurrent of anxiety. *Bury the Dead* was a pacifist's outcry. It was a vivid reminder of the tragic waste of World War I, and now in 1936 there were millions of Americans demanding that Roosevelt keep them out of another such conflagration. But, in Spain, peace was already succumbing to war. The President's words, delivered in his speech accepting renomination, had taken on a deeply portentous meaning: "This generation of Americans has a rendezvous with destiny."

The fact that *Bury the Dead* was written by a twenty-three-year-old playwright from Brooklyn proved more than an inspiration for Tom Williams; at age twenty-five and stuck in St. Louis, he took it as an oblique challenge. Tom was not yet orbiting in the world of the theatre, but its spheres and those of his world were touching. Now everything, it seemed, served to remind him of the theatre. The day after the opening of *Bury the Dead*, the newspapers announced that O'Neill, at forty-eight, had won the Nobel Prize for literature, the citation reading: "To Eugene O'Neill in recognition of his dramatic art, imbued with strength, honesty and deep feeling, as well as by a personal and original concept of tragedy."

Except for a charming, somewhat whimsical autobiographical comedy, *Ah, Wilderness!*—staged with great success in 1933—and another, unsuccessful, play in 1934, *Days Without End*, O'Neill had been conspicuously absent from the theatre and would remain so for several years to come. When he was awarded the Nobel Prize, he was at work on a cycle of plays covering five generations of an American family. He was also in a hospital in Oakland, California, and unable to travel to Sweden for the presentation, but he paid full tribute to his mentor, "that greatest genius of all modern dramatists, your August Strindberg."[24] Even in his most fanciful imaginings, Tom Williams could not have envisaged that he, as Tennessee Williams, would within a decade take his place beside Eugene O'Neill.

> Sunday, Nov. 15—My, how this Fall is going by. It's perhaps the happiest season I've had since the spring of '31—or was that really as happy as it seems in retrospect? Nostalgia for an old love—it does strange things. What I need now is love—life *is* empty without it. I need a great love for someone beside myself. That would keep me from being morbid and silly—I would like to lose myself in some great love or great noble cause. I am not happy now. I am just busy and fairly comfortable. I have few grand moments of exaltation, but some. Nature affects me a great deal lately—the clear beauty of autumn mornings—smoke of burning leaves. Oh, but I want something *real* in my life. When will it happen? When will it come? Never?

If this was Tom's "happiest season," it was Rose's most abysmal. She, too, wanted something *real* in a life that was becoming progressively unreal. She could have asked the same questions as Tom: When will it happen? When will it come? She, too, desperately wanted to leave home and, like Tom, needed someone's love. She was turning around and around in a room without doors or even windows, only mirrors—and to confront her image in this way was to see a hope without hope. In her frustration, rage would overflow into hysteria and gradually subside into a trance: the refuge of fantasies. It was then, as Edwina and the family believed, "Rose was her old self again."

Edwina sent letters to her parents and Cornelius to his sisters. It had become a refrain that Rose needed something to occupy herself. Ella wrote to her brother, "Your letter came Saturday, and I am awfully distressed about Rose. I do wish she had an interest of some kind. She has nothing to do, and no doubt broods about herself. I wish I knew something to suggest. If she had a light job of some kind it would be good for her. However, jobs are not to be had for the asking."[25] Edwina's letter said Rose had gone to church by herself on Sunday. "I had to stay at home as she said she wouldn't go if I went. It did her good, though she talks all the time about wanting to go away from the family, especially me! . . . She is very pitiful. I try to excuse all in her, but she *is* a trial."[26]

On November 19, 1936, Rose turned twenty-seven. She received a new dress that had been exclusively made by a seamstress in Memphis and other gifts from her grandparents. In her letter of thanks, Rose made no mention of Tom but commented that she and Dakin were going out to supper to celebrate her birthday and to a movie afterward. She apologized for having been "so mean" to Grand when she was visiting. "Things look a little brighter now. My head doesn't feel quite so thick and I am able to get around."[27]

By now, a distance measured in silence had grown between Rose and Tom. He made no mention of her birthday, nor, apparently, did he observe it in any way. More than the incident following his party, it was this estrangement from her at a time when she needed him most that precipitated her tragedy, the immensity of which neither was able to understand. The "twins" had been separated, and each was struggling alone against the threat of madness. In his journal, Tom in anguish asked, "I want to get away. But where?"

Monday—Nov. 23—10:20 P.M. Just passed through dreadful nervous crisis. Can hardly write so shaken. Fear. Had been working on play all evening. Got too tired I suppose. . . . I took a mebral and 5 teaspoon[s] of sodium bromide elixir—enough to tame a wild horse. I must get my mind off my body and onto other things. I must not worry anymore. I am praying tonight. After all prayer is quite a necessary thing. There are times when you simply can't help yourself. And that won't do.

With the approach of the holidays, Tom kept to his room, trying to cope with his studies and further his writing, which had first priority. His persistence was beginning to show results, even on campus. The managing editor of Washington University's *The Eliot* was prompted to single out "THOMAS LANIER WILLIAMS. We have been looking for poetry like his for some time."[28] At the moment, though, his main focus was on writing his first full-length play in hopes that the Mummers would produce it.

December was to prove a climactic month for Rose, one from which there would be no turning back. Edwina admitted to her parents that she was at a loss to know what precisely to do and that Rose needed to get away from the family. She had refused to go back to Dr. Alexander, and Edwina complained, "If I could just get Rose into her right senses, we would be 'sitting pretty'!" After another of Rose's irrational "spells," Edwina managed to put her in Barnes Hospital. Cornelius objected to the expense and wanted Rose removed, but, following a discussion with a new psychiatrist, Edwina reported, "He has only said she had to get into a cheaper room! He has been very quiet without much to say so I imagine he is doing some thinking." Edwina had some thinking of her own to do after the psychiatrist gave her what she called "the third degree."[29]

At the hospital, Rose had initially been placed under sedation, and then gradually she was drawn into analytical discussions relating mainly to her unhappy home life, that she had at first resisted. Analysis was the only apparent remedy for an illness that her doctor might have been inclined to diagnose as dementia praecox, or schizophrenia, for which there was no known cure. With Cornelius at work or out drinking, Dakin preoccupied with his social life and schoolwork, and Tom alone in his room, Edwina was left to face an irreversible catastrophe.

> Dear Mother and Father,
> We brought Rose home from the hospital this morning after being there nine days. I had a good deal of trouble getting her home. I went over after her yesterday after-noon, and she carried on so, said she'd never put her foot in this house again, etc. that I didn't think I could get her away, but she came very peaceably this morning, and has seemed very well to-day. She still says crazy things but I think she is better. The doctor will be over to see her to-morrow morning. . . . The only thing I can see that the doctor has done for her is to start her smoking. "He is so sweet to me," says Rose, "brings me a package of cigarettes each time he comes." He says (which we already knew) that she needs to be busy!![30]

Both Tennessee and Dakin recalled that another dimension to Rose's problems during this time was a caller, whom she fancied to be her beau. Tennessee described him as a junior executive at the shoe company, "a young man of very personable appearance, social grace and apparently of great and unscrupulous ambition. For a few months he was quite attentive to Rose." They dated frequently and were almost going steady, according to Tennessee.

> Rose would tremble when the telephone rang, desperately hoping the call was for her and that it was from him. This was while Dad's position as sales manager at Friedman-Shelby branch of International was still, if not ascendant, at least one of apparent permanence and continued promise.
>
> But Dad was playing fast and loose with his position. He was continually alarming the "establishment" and International by his weekend habits. Significantly, he had not been elected to the "Board of Executives," despite the fact that he was the best and most popular sales manager of International, and the only one who delivered speeches. His speeches were eloquent—and pungent. He did not talk much about his success at oratory but I think it pleased him enormously. He got up there on the platform before the assembled salesmen much in the style of his political forebears running for high offices in East Tennessee.[31]

Cornelius was plainly becoming as much a law unto himself at the company as he was in his home. Rose's mental illness posed the possibility of a scandal; Cornelius's behavior precipitated it. It was at this time that he wrecked his career at the shoe company, and it was also at this time that the upwardly mobile junior executive ceased to have anything to do with the Williams family, including, of course, Rose.

> Dec. 11 It is 3 A. M. Mother just received a call from Barnes' saying Dad had had an accident. Didn't say what kind. Frightened. Can't sleep. A terribly still night. I have taken a sleeping tablet and will read Ibsen. Hadn't enough things happened to us already? Apparently not. One thing and then another and another.

The next day, Edwina wrote to Grand, "This has been a very hectic week for me. Last week I was busy visiting Rose at Barnes. *This* week I'm visiting Cornelius, also at Barnes! A perfectly terrible thing happened to him!" She went on to tell what had occurred once she had been permitted to see her husband, Paul Jamison having persuaded her to wait until morning.

> We rushed down as soon as we could, found Cornelius with head all bound up. He had been in a card game with one of the International salesmen (not his) who had been drinking heavily. They quarreled over the game, he cursed and hit Cornelius and C. knocked him down (a man who was big as Hatcher). This infuriated him so that he bit a piece of Cornelius's ear off! We've been afraid of blood poisoning but so far he seems to be alright in that respect. Mr. Jamison has been so fine about it.

He phoned me not to worry, that he was keeping it from being known, all the men concerned sworn to secrecy and it has been given out to the men that he is at home with an infected ear.

Edwina went on to say that the incident was most unfortunate because Cornelius had intended to make a special trip to Knoxville in order to persuade his sister Ella to take Rose for a time: The psychiatrist had told him that his daughter needed a change of scene. How Rose would adapt to being with her aunt, though, was hard to predict, although Edwina told her mother that Rose was sufficiently herself to go to the symphony with the mother of Dakin's best friend and to enjoy it thoroughly. "Sometimes she seems alright and, at others, all off, and I hardly know what to do about her, going about." She added that "Cornelius seems quite chastened by the recent events of the past two weeks, so it may not be all in vain."[32]

C. C. Williams had, in fact, much to think about as he lay in the hospital. While he knew that it was unlikely he would be fired, that he was a valued sales manager at the shoe company, he also knew that he had gone about as far as he would go in the hierarchy and that he would never become an executive of the company. One other thing he could depend upon: Edwina would never let him hear the end of it, the fact that socially his behavior inhibited her, too. Not only his family but others like the Jamisons were affected, as well, and more than anyone, his best friend, Warren Hatcher. Dakin recalled, "Hatch was a big man, very much like my father, and they were poker-playing—and drinking—buddies. Finally, Hatch killed himself. Shot himself. Why? Liquor ended his future at the company, too."[33]

Cornelius was not just a hard drinker, as he liked to think of himself, but in truth a clinical alcoholic. He was resorting to what were open secrets within the family: the familiar, but what he thought to be clever, deceptions, such as hiding a bottle behind the bathtub or in other dark corners. He was on an irreversible course toward self-destruction. No one knew why. It would be too facile to say, Well, with a wife like that . . . Edwina in her defense contended that it was because he was a bridled aristocrat. His sisters felt it was because of their mother's early death. Dakin said it was because he liked gin.

Tennessee Williams might have been speaking of himself when he said that his father's nature could not conform to conventional social molds and patterns and that his restlessness would have driven him mad without the release of liquor and poker and wild weekends. Self-destructiveness is more profound than that. Increasingly, it is thought that there is a causal tie to alcoholism: genetic links on a molecular level tying one generation of alcoholics to another. The behavioral patterns are clear. Thomas Lanier Williams II was also "a hard drinker," who begot one in Cornelius C. Williams, who also had a son, Thomas Lanier Williams III, who would earn a reputation as a confirmed alcoholic. The reasons a person destroys himself are as elusive as they are manifold, and more than anyone they elude and bedevil the person himself. Cornelius and his son were both "blue-deviled." For Cornelius's daughter, within her "enclosed garden," the roses were flowering blue.

During the holiday season, Rose was once again her "old self," but now the family proceeded with caution. She was not told why her father had been hospitalized. Although she was trying to resume her social life as best she could, there was no word from either Roger Moore, busy with his mayoral campaign, or from the junior executive at Friedman-Shelby. Despite Paul Jamison's efforts to conceal Cornelius's "secret," once the junior executive heard the rumors of what had happened to "Mr. Williams," it marked the end, as Tennessee said, "of Rose's dates with her handsome and unscrupulously ambitious 'beau,' who no longer was a potential husband." But this Rose would not learn until after the holidays.

Shortly before Christmas, Edwina wrote to her parents to say that she had just gotten a wire from Ella asking her to send Rose on to Knoxville. Edwina was also assured that there would be considerable effort by both Aunty Ella and Aunt Belle to see that Rose had the happiest possible holidays. At first, Rose refused to go, but finally she was persuaded that the trip would be good for her. Edwina said, "She will leave to-morrow night. It will be best for her, I'm sure, as Cornelius has been at home and she has been getting on his nerves. I'm also glad to get her away from the Psychologist. While of course he has helped her, I don't trust them."[34] She was to say that she didn't believe, as Freud did, that sex was everything, but held with others like Jung—likely without having read either.

After her arrival, Rose wrote to Grand, explaining, "I decided to come to Knoxville on the spur of the moment; got packed in one morning, went down town to get some shoes, mules and a blouse and left on the 10:30 train. We had our first snow the night before I left. The train was three or four hours late in arriving." She told of luncheons and parties and a reunion with family members and old friends. She received gifts from her aunts, from her grandparents, and from the family at home, all of which, of course, Edwina had selected, labeled, wrapped, packed, and shipped. In her letter, Rose mentioned that Aunt Belle's nephew, John Brownlow, home for the holidays from West Point, was "something to look at in his uniform." She had gone to a tea dance at the Cherokee Country Club, saying, "The orchestra was good. I had an enjoyable afternoon, danced with three or four nice married men and saw two girls I knew." She also said that cousin Rose Comfort in Memphis had sent her "an attractive scarf. It is the most becoming one I have. I am planning to visit her on the way home if it will be convenient for her to have me."[35] On Christmas Eve, she wrote home from Ella's home on Locust Street:

My dearest Mother:

I am writing this on Aunty's little table. There is very little room so excuse the scribbling.

I am having a lovely time doing just what I want to do. Annette Thomas took me to a movie yesterday. I had dinner with the Jack Brownlows the night before. Miss Margaret is as pretty as a picture, looks like a young girl and her daughter is darling. She is taking me to the mid-night service to-night. So you see I am having a lovely time.

I do hope you are well and are not wearing yourself out with Christmas shopping.

I am broke, have one dollar left and I want to take Helen Brownlow to lunch. Tell Tom I think he would like her. She says she is interested in writing. She has her mother's lovely complexion and is so sweet.

Please send me my other five dollars.

With much love to you all, especially Dakin.

Rose Isabel[36]

The holiday season of 1936 would have to have been the unhappiest in Edwina Williams's life. She was, as Tennessee said, a woman who cried all of her tears alone and, tiny as she was, could be depended upon to rebound defiantly, lifting her chin to adversity. In the years to come, with her sons away from home and her husband a deteriorating alcoholic, she would wage a valiant and lonely, and finally futile, struggle to reclaim her daughter's sanity. Indestructible as her hope was, she now at this moment had every reason to feel terror at the prospect of a new year.

December 27 was another morning after the night before, Tom having been among the poets again, this time at one of *their* parties: "Oh, Lord, what a night and what a morning. My head is splitting. The next time I get lonely and want a party I'll remember last night and be grateful for solitude. Possibly each individual at the party was—taken individually—a fairly decent person—but put together they become absolute asses and make me despise them. I was miserable and acted it. In one of my anti-social conditions. It is a wonder anyone ever likes me at all. Maybe no one does. And yet I'm not a bad guy at heart, am I? I just can't get along with 'people'!"

He had expressed a conflict and reservation about himself and his sociability that would trouble Tennessee Williams the rest of his life.

10

Elegy for Rose

Winter–Spring 1937

With the new year, Tom's disposition toward "people," namely his friends, and toward his writing, particularly his work in the theatre, was undergoing a distinct change for the better.

> Sun. Jan 3 . . . School begins tomorrow. Too bad. My play is practically done and I have almost complete assurance that it will be produced this season. Willard Holland has such a swell sense of the incongruous. At our last meeting we discussed the play's ending and both agreed that there should be mingled sadness and exaltation. Willard suggested that we have the triumphant singing of the workers interspersed with the screams of a woman in childbirth.

By 1937, with a Wall Street stock market decline signaling a further recession, a play without social consciousness was immediately dismissed as trivial and, in the Communist press, as treason to the cause. Pulitzer Prizes had been awarded to a comedy and a farce, *Idiot's Delight* and *You Can't Take It With You*, both of which had pointed social messages. To get a production of a full-length play, Tom by this time would have interspersed the Communist Manifesto in rhyming couplets.

Willard Holland found Tom Williams also had a "sense of the incongruous." Appearances so often conceal an opposite side, and Holland's view of the young playwright "in residence" was that of never "being run-down, of needing food or sleep. He always looked perfectly healthy, not someone who was abusing himself staying up late and writing all night long. As far as I know he always got to school on time. He wore good conservative tweeds and always wore a shirt and tie. As a matter of fact he always looked like a young bank teller to me." One can only assume that Holland was laboring a comparison with his own sartorial dereliction and with the look of his company of players.

He noted, "I couldn't get warmed up to Tom as a friend. There was something of an iron curtain . . . he drew between himself and other people and it was hard to get through to him." What confused and ultimately hurt Holland, along with many who knew Tennessee Williams professionally, was that he could be so bold in artistry and so removed of person; the "iron curtain" was in truth his "affliction of shyness."

What impressed the troupe's director most, however, was Tom's immersion in his work. "I must say this for Tom: he was amenable and easy to work with once you explained what the problem was. He was sensitive to criticism only when a play was in its produced form, after it had opened. One of Tom's most likeable traits when he started writing was that he would listen to people who knew more than he did. If you tell the average playwright that his play is unproduceable you crush him . . . but to Tom it just represented some type-written pages. In anyone else this kind of speed writing would have seemed feverish, but Tom seemed able to do it without any apparent effort."[1] As was true of Clark Mills as mentor and arbiter, Willard Holland became a catalytic force, and what he saw as Tom's impervious resilience was as deceptive as his calm outward mien; underneath was a desperate dependency and desire to meet the director's expectations. Holland was the first among other dominant theatre figures in Tennessee Williams's career.

After their meeting in January, Tom wrote in his journal, "I have been pursued by the little blue devil of defeat all week but it is such a bright morning and I feel so clean and well after my shower perhaps he will abandon the chase. I'm planning to deliver my play now complete (?) to Mr. Holland. Will he approve or is it all just a—one of those things!"

> Tuesday—Jan. 12 . . . I am very quiet tonight and superficially peaceful. I am reading the letters of Van Gogh, the artist, to his friend (Amice) Rappard. I know I would have liked him. We would have understood each other. He went mad & killed himself. Why? His letters are so full of rich, confident life. The bare branches of the trees were full of black birds making sounds like the ripping of coarse cloth.

> Wed. Jan. 13—Disgust! Drank coffee to write. Got the jitters so bad had to stop. Took a sleeping pill and then a mebral. Felt like I was blowing up. Read over plays. All seemed utter trash.

With the diversion of the holidays gone and once again *her* stark reality reasserting itself, Rose wrote to Dakin from Knoxville.

> My dearest little brother:
> Your picture is on Aunty's table near my bed and I have been wondering how you and Jiggs are, not to mention the other members of the family. I know that you were all glad to ship me down here. . . . I am going to look for a job Saturday. I envy Aunt Belle's vim and vitality. She seems to accomplish so much that I feel like crawling into a hole and never reappearing. She gave me some exquisite solid gold earrings which belonged to my Grandmother. . . .

Tell Dad I will write to him to-morrow.
With a heart full of love,

Your sister
Rose Isabel[2]

The search for a job also figured in a letter written to her parents the next day. "*If* I get it I shall have to get up about six o'clock to report to work." Neither she nor her aunts mentioned a job again. The letter, though, went into considerable detail describing receptions given her by various friends and family members, her wish to reciprocate by taking them to luncheons, and her preoccupation with the accoutrements, color, and size of her dresses. And finally, she said, "I hope you are not exhausted after the many trials you have had, Mother. Aunty and I have a very peaceful time. We have a fire almost every night. I love to watch it, it makes a room so cosy and inviting."[3]

Ella's report to Cornelius reflected guarded optimism, a cautious attitude shared by her sister, Isabel.

> Rose seems perfectly well. Her mind is as clear as yours or mine, and I feel that all that is wrong with her is that she is bored to death with no interests. Last week I was so busy I couldn't show her anything, so she rarely came into the shop . . . said she would only stay two weeks and go home. I have talked her out of that, so now she says she would like to stay in the shop part of the day. I am going to let her do as she pleases. Her friends here are all married with babies, but I hope they will come to see her and ask her out. I don't know any suitable men for her, which I am sorry about.[4]

Isabel was clearly at a loss. She agreed that Rose needed a new outlook and had tried to persuade her not to drink so much coffee. "Five and six cups a day are enough to make her intensely nervous. She insists they do not hurt her as she sleeps so well—all night—every night—but of course so much of it does affect her nerves. I must confess she does not even seem nervous." As if to convince herself, Isabel maintained, "Certainly there is absolutely nothing the matter with her mentally or physically. Her mind is not in the very least 'bewildered' and she is not sick. I simply cannot account for her 'breakdown' at home, unless it is nervous hysteria."[5]

No one in the family—or, apparently, the medical profession—except Edwina understood the full portent of Rose's behavior, and she felt more and more powerless to do anything about it. In a letter to her parents, enclosing Ella's and Isabel's comments, she wrote, "They can't seem to realize the nature of Rose's trouble. Of course she was practically normal when I sent her to them or I couldn't have allowed her to travel alone. As it was, I felt uneasy about it."

Cornelius was the main cause of Rose's problem, as Edwina saw it. Without being able or willing to accept her share of the responsibility, she maintained, "I attribute Rose's and Tom's nervous break-downs to the eternal friction that Cornelius has made in the home. If you study Psychology you find out what that does to the nervous system and of course they had inherited poor ones to begin with."[6]

Rose's letters from Knoxville were brief and chatty, if not cheerful. She made a point of the fact that it had been raining steadily, that she was quite well, had gained thirteen pounds, and was planning to leave for home in about ten days. She was still hiding behind "the happy face," and so, too, was Ella in writing her report to Edwina:

> This is just a line to let you know that Rose is fine. I never saw her look better or prettier. In fact she seems in better health than I ever saw her. She says she has gained 13 pounds, but I think she is mistaken. She weighed 105 the other day. She has probably gained about five pounds. She eats 7 or 8 times a day. At first I protested as I thought so much eating between meals was not good for her, but she said she did it at home all the time, and when I saw she ate heartily at meals I let it go. It doesn't seem to hurt her and she says she is hungry all the time. . . . [She] seems anxious to get home. I am afraid she has had a stupid visit. . . . I wish she would study something. She needs to use her mind very badly. She has just plenty of sense and there is nothing the matter with her mind but lack of use. . . . She doesn't use her head about anything. I hope you don't mind my writing you this. I love you and Cornelius and all your children. You might talk to this Dr. Alexander Rose is always talking about. I'm sure he will tell you what I have—Rose needs an object in life and she hasn't got it. She is going to have to exercise her brain. You can't just stop thinking.[7]

Shortly thereafter, though, Ella wrote to her brother, admitting, "I think Rose's condition is grave, and it makes me sick to think about it. She is so pretty." Cornelius had sent her a check for Rose's room and board, and Ella acknowledged it gratefully:

> I hate to take it, especially as the trip did Rose very little good. For the first three weeks she improved so much physically and seemed all right, but the last ten or twelve days I saw a change in her, and it troubled me very much, and frightened me too. Sometimes I would speak to her three or four times before she would hear me, and she couldn't remember anything. I feel very troubled about her—I don't believe she could possibly hold a job. She tires very easily and is obliged to lie down every afternoon. If she could find an easy job for half a day it would be great but such jobs are all but impossible to find.[8]

On the day Rose departed from Knoxville, it was raining incessantly. In Washington on Wednesday, January 20, President Franklin D. Roosevelt took the oath of office for a second term, promising to end the tragedy of "one-third of a nation ill-housed, ill-clad and ill-nourished." Crowds of on-lookers at the inauguration stood in a downpour that was fast turning into a deluge and precipitating the great Ohio River flood. Thousands of muddy rivulets were coursing down hillsides, flooding, among vast farm and many urban areas, the city of Louisville.

Writing to Cornelius, Isabel recounted Rose's ordeal:

> Brother, we were so unhappy about Rose's experience of spending the night in the Louisville station. Of course we knew nothing of the water rising to any extent in Louisville. That is, that it would in any way hin-der travel. That night—the one Rose left—Sister heard an announce-ment concerning it over the radio and we were both so worried about Rose. . . . Sister had insisted that Rose wait over until Tuesday of the following week, but Rose elected to leave on Friday, and we found we had no influence with her as soon as she arrived.
>
> I was not surprised, dear, when you and Tom both wrote Rose's prin-ciple [sic] trouble was that "she was down on everybody"—We found that out right away, and we were distressed that she no longer cared anything for us. Sister really tried so hard—but the visit I fear was not a success, excepting in the one way, which was the main reason for Sister's sending for Rose at that time of year—that Edwina could have a little rest—for from her letters she was in really desperate need of one.

Isabel also expressed concern and found it "incredible" that neither Ed-wina nor Rose had written to Ella—"I cannot believe that Edwina would let herself be prejudiced in the light of all that she knows"—and she added, "The whole family tried to be sweet to Rose, but she was not interested." Isabel said that she had begged Rose to write to her grandmother but that she seemed "to have lost all love for her and I simply could not understand it for Mrs. Dakin has always been an angel of goodness to those children." Finally, Isabel told Cornelius, "I am so very sorry, but I love you so much and I do not want you to be in any doubt about this. We can only construe Edwina's silence to be thru some misapprehension about Rose's visit."[9]

Edwina was indeed piqued at what she mistakenly felt was a failure to help Rose. She wrote to her parents instead:

> I'm facing my biggest problem again. What to do with Rose! She re-turned through this awful flood and is lucky to be here. . . . As soon as she crossed the threshold I saw she was all off and no wonder for she had sat up all night in the station at Louisville with refugees. She began to rave as soon as she got inside. Cornelius is nervous at best and since this trouble with his ear he is worse, so he lost his temper, told her she was crazy and that he was going to put her in the State Asylum. He will do this too, if I

don't do something else with her. I can't take her back to those doctors—I can't see that either Dr. Alexander or Dr. Saterfield helped her
any. . . . The last time she went to Dr. Alexander he told her that what was
the matter with her was "that she needed to get married." She has been
raving on the subject of "sex" ever since and I was ashamed for Dakin and
Tom to hear her the other night. It made them so nervous that I feared
for the "finals" that both of them are taking. They each have five hard
ones they are taking this week.

Dr. Saterfield sent Cornelius a bill for ninety dollars and Cornelius
said she couldn't go back there. Neither Ella nor Isabel seemed able to do
any thing for her. They don't want to believe the truth. I think they could
have saved her. I suppose it is a good thing that I have this D.A.R. work
that I've had to do. It has made me think of something else. Living in the
house with Cornelius is bad enough. With the two of them it is terrible
and there is liable to be a fatal tragedy. Now, father, is there not a Church
home somewhere that I could take Rose to? Will you enquire around
among the clergy? Things can't go on like this. I'm sorry to trouble you
but there is no one else to whom I can turn for advice.[10]

At the same time, Tom wrote in his journals:

Monday Jan. 25 Tragedy. I write that word knowing the full meaning of
it. We have had no deaths in our family but slowly by degrees something
was happening much uglier and more terrible than death. Now we are
forced to see it, know it. The thought is an aching numbness—a horror!

I am having final exams but can't study. Her presence in the house
is a—

Clearly, he was unable to continue; from this time on, he would live not
only in the horror of what was happening to his sister but in terror that it
might also happen to him. Confronted as he was with Rose's insanity, Tom
began a desperate struggle to keep his emotional life on as even a course as
possible.

These were to be the last weeks that Rose would spend at home. By
now, there was no one in the immediate family who doubted that her condition was indeed grave. There were brief periods when she would behave
quite normally, others when her behavior was embarrassingly erratic, and
times when something—usually something her father would say or do—
caused a violent reaction. Now she exhibited open hatred toward him, and
her doctors warned Edwina that she was a threat to Cornelius's life. Much
of the time, however, Rose spent alone in her room, sorting her clothes
and playing incessantly with Jiggs.

Recalling those final days and weeks, Tennessee was later to comment,
"It's not very pleasant to look back on that year and to know that Rose

knew she was going mad and to know, also, that I was not too kind to my sister. . . . Little eccentricities had begun to appear in her behavior. She was now very quiet in the house and I think she was suffering from insomnia. She had the peculiar habit of setting a pitcher of ice-water outside her door, each night when she retired."[11]

Early in February, Edwina wrote to her parents,

> I have Rose in the hospital again for observation and under a new psychiatrist suggested by Dr. Bunting to whom I took her this after-noon after she refused "to stay at home another night" and had packed her grip to go to the "Y." I'm quite worn out with it all. Dr. Bunting thinks she needs to go to a sanitarium and I went out and looked at it to-day. It is fifty dollars a week and I don't believe any better than the State one would be, so I don't know what to do. A pity the Church hasn't a place for girls like Rose.[12]

On her return home, Rose seemed "a hundred percent better," although Edwina admitted there was no way of knowing for how long. About Isabel and Ella, she felt "they must have taken Rose to task. She won't write to either of them and says she'll never go back there. She was raving crazy when she got here and I didn't think I'd be able to do a thing with her for several days. She takes spells of being mean now, and I never know what to expect of her. I think if we could send her away somewhere it would be the best thing for her. To be in the house with Cornelius is bad for her as he has no patience with her."

Candles to the Sun

Sat. Jan. 30th Though it is still mid-winter I feel this morning a presentiment of spring. Maybe because I saw a lovely blue jay perched in the fork of the elm right outside my window, trying to keep dry from the slow, soft spring-like rain.

Last night I saw two lovely pictures, Elisabeth Bergner in "As You Like It" with Laurence Olivier and Maxwell Anderson's "Winterset"* with Burgess Meredith, an exquisitely fine actor. I have never been strongly impressed by Anderson's poetry but this cinema was certainly full of poetry. There were some shots of Brooklyn Bridge that were fairly

---

*Later in the year, Tom saw a local stage production of *Winterset* and said that it lacked the "poetry" of the film and labored too much of Anderson's poetry. Because the Pulitzer Prize had been awarded to an unworthy competitor, the New York Drama Critics Circle was founded and gave its first annual award to *Winterset*. The influence of Anderson's play, or, more exactly, the film version, became readily apparent in Williams's final drafts of his first full-length play, *Candles to the Sun*, and, more prominently, later in 1937, in his second play, *Fugitive Kind*.

breath-taking. I can well understand Hart Crane's inspiration by this thing—probably the most exciting piece of architecture in America.

He spoke of Clark Mills's *Proem* being published in *Forum* and thought it exceptionally fine: "the usual effect of restrained careful power." He said he had been with Holland all afternoon making changes in his play. "He is a master. Could get work out of an oyster." He felt the play showed promise but "of course it may fall completely flat."

Despite his growing boredom with his studies and his increasing interest in writing plays, Tom managed to pass five subjects, including Greek. He and Dakin were being paid five dollars each to deliver circulars in Roger Moore's campaign for mayor. By day, he was attending rehearsals of his play, named *Candles to the Sun* after several title changes, and felt encouraged. But late at night, alone in his room, he awakened suddenly and recorded in his journal: "Just had a horrible surrealistic dream about the fear of death and taking pills to prevent it. Felt the need of a warm, friendly light and someone to talk to."

When not attending classes, he would fill that need in the company of Clark Mills or among the Mummers. Holland recalled Tom's presence at rehearsals: "He had the most inane laugh I ever heard. It was a high squeaky cackle, a shriek and a cackle. We would be desperately working on something. The blood could be flowing all over the floor: we could be butchering his brain child on the stage, and he would come out with his cackle because something struck him funny. It would drive me mad."[13] No one, in fact, who has ever been in a rehearsal of one of Williams's plays and heard his laugh could describe the experience as anything less than paralyzing. Actresses would put a hand to their mouth and actors would check to see if their pants were unzipped. Stage managers would look frantically to see what had gone wrong. Directors would just freeze. Others sitting in the orchestra watching the rehearsal would take the shriek as a cue and emit a kind of dry, puzzled laugh. And Tennessee Williams would be totally unaware or happily oblivious of them all.

Toward the end of February, Tom made a casual entry in his journal, even accepting a rejection without the usual attendant despair: "Days pass quietly, pleasantly and with disturbing celerity. Sonnet accepted by *American Prefaces*, story rejected with criticism 'fairly undistinguished treatment of a common thing'—'The Treadmill'—somewhat discouraging as I had liked the story. My new play goes badly. I feel not especially bright these days—but peace is nothing to be valued lightly." He then said, "I have accepted—of all things—a part in a French play [on] April 16. Heaven knows how that will turn out. Still it is amusing."

Even more casually, he mentioned that Hazel was in town and that he had spent the previous Monday evening with her. "Strange how completely dead all that is now. Barely a flicker of interest. Just a friendly feeling. It could be revived however pretty easily as I still see in her all the old qualities that I once adored." A while later, he wrote:

Letter to an Old Love

I sold you playthings, very little more
Though greater things for less I might have given:
You only lock such small things from my store
As a cup of wine or a penny's worth of ribbon!

I sold you silly trinkets to amuse
You for an idle summer's hour or two:
Upon my higher shelves were things to use
More earnestly, but these escaped your view.

Or if you noticed them you gave no sign,
And I somehow lacked courage to display
Such precious things. You drank the cup of wine
And tucked the bit of silken goods away
And nonchalantly went on graceful feet
To spend your gold across the shallow street.[14]

"How things slip by—!! so quietly, so imperceptibly," he wrote. "Someday we will wake up and find that everything has gone. Youth like a bright distant dream nearly forgotten." In this same plaintive vein, he observed, "It is nearly a year since I started this journal—such a strange, rapid year. The next? The pages are still unwritten. Their blankness is an exciting and rather intimidating challenge."

The pages of 1937 and the last years of the decade were to be filled to overflowing with events not just in the life of Tom and his family but in the history of the nation and indeed the world, as well. An economic recession was fueling Cornelius's eternal clamor over domestic finances, while it was also firing up labor strife and Republican vilification of Roosevelt as a "traitor to his class." The American view of international crises centered not on the slaughter by German planes of more than eight hundred men, women, and children in a Basque village called Guernica, but on the abdication of an English king in 1936 and his subsequent marriage with "the woman I love." Largely ignored or little understood were such catastrophic incidents as the diplomatic appeasement of Adolf Hitler, or Poland's suicidal defiance of the Nazis, or the Moscow purge trials, or Japan's invasion of China, or the Catholic church's support of Franco's fascists in Spain—thus dooming the last hope for "peace in our time."

The futile opposition on the part of the United States to involvement in foreign wars had been symbolized by Roosevelt's signing of the U.S. Neutrality Act in 1935, thus encouraging masses of Americans to avert their gaze from harsh reality toward a variety of diversions, such as the "Brown Bomber" Joe Louis's ascendancy to the heavyweight crown of the world in 1937. Ventriloquist Edgar Bergen and friend Charlie McCarthy captivated radio listeners. Film fans escaped with Ronald Colman into the never-never land of Shangri-la in *Lost Horizon* and into the dreamland of Jeanette MacDonald and Nelson Eddy in *Maytime*.

On Broadway, the gradual wartime move away from plays of national social significance to sheer entertainment had begun. Lillian Gish and Burgess Meredith escaped on *The Star Wagon*, John Garfield was *Having a Wonderful Time*, and, in critic John Mason Brown's words, Tallulah Bankhead as Cleopatra "sailed down the Nile . . . and sank." Katharine Cornell revived Shaw's *Candida*. Ruth Gordon slammed the door on *A Doll's House*. O'Neill continued his long silence, and only Clifford Odets introduced a serious, successful new play with the Group Theatre's production of *Golden Boy*. Margaret Webster's shrewd direction of Maurice Evans in Shakespeare's *Richard II* introduced the contemporary note of an English king's abdication. More than this, the one ringing denunciation of fascist dictatorship came with yet another of Shakespeare's historical plays: Orson Welles's stunning modern-dress production of *Julius Caesar*. The Bard even stole the musical stage with Rodgers and Hart's *The Boys from Syracuse*.

The distant sounds of war were also drowned out by Benny Goodman, the "King of Swing," and the era of the big bands was in full swing. Bobby-soxers, attired in long skirts and saddle shoes, and their jitterbug boyfriends in double-breasted, padded-shouldered suits danced a new craze called the Big Apple. Tom, though, was distantly removed from it all:

Feb. 24—Downstairs the radio is playing "Mood Indigo." That's just about how I feel—pretty low—tired of myself—nervous and sad—not for any particular reason and not to any crucial extent—so I should give myself a good kick in the pants and quit slobbering! Went over to gym to swim and watch a wrestling match. Not much energy for swimming.

Dad leaving for week's trip tonight. Maybe the car will be available for party some evening. That's what I need. That and to write something worth while!

Rose talks wildly again. I guess there'll be no end to that. It comes slowly. That's the way with most awful things. Perhaps a great mercy. We couldn't stand them all at once.

March 2—Tuesday . . . Busy day. Went to Holland—then to the Star [*St. Louis Star-Times*] to be interviewed. Very stupid. I felt like a fool talking so much about myself. . . . Virginia Moore will visit the Poetry Club Friday night. A charming person.

March 3—Wed.—The same only more so. A headache. Must not go on like this. After all, one's sanity is worth something. R. makes the house tragic, haunted. Must be put away I suppose. An incredible horror to face. "No one is to blame," Mother admitted. How true! But why do such things happen? There is no answer.

To be "put away" in those times held as much terror for the family as it did for those who were mentally ill. State asylums were called "snake pits," and for good cause. The administration of them was only a little improved from the horrendous conditions that had prevailed throughout previous centuries. The problem was not only medical ignorance but professional irresolution, as well. Freud was still alive in 1937 and was regarded by many in the medical profession as a heretic; as a result, the methods of psychiatry and psychoanalysis were at odds, although both were crude and often cruel. Cornelius had threatened Rose with the state asylum, which would have been viewed as a disgrace in the eyes of both friends and family, and Edwina in desperation appealed to his sisters.

They responded immediately. Isabel wrote, "I want you to know that I feel just exactly as you do about placing Rose in an asylum. In the first place she is not *deranged*, but would certainly become so in an institution of that kind. *It simply must not be*, and I am writing Brother by this mail along the same line. What a tragedy that he and Rose affect each other as they do—and what a trial for you." She added, "My heart aches for you until it hurts. When I think of lovely little Rose as she was, and then how warped her nature has become a great pity takes possession of me—but I feel, as you do, that this can be overcome in her. I *know* that God alone can do it. I also *know* that He uses human instrumentality more often than not and I *believe* that. He will answer our earnest prayers for Rose—tho' we must be submissive to the Divine will."

Isabel finally admitted that Rose was sick, "there is no doubt about that." But at the same time, her wish was that she might be committed "to a sanitarium for nervous people—in no wise an institution for the insane. *She is not insane*. I believe she has a strong instinct for dramatizing herself and that she has a *very bad state of nerves*. Part of this is accentuated by the constant, really terrible coffee-drinking." She recommended "Sanka coffee at 45 cents a pound."[15]

Ella, for her part, maintained that there was nothing the matter with Rose's mind and that it would be "an outrage" to put her in an asylum. She felt that her brother would not consider such a move, and she wrote, "I am much more worried about you than I am over Rose or Cornelius. . . . The only thing I am afraid of is that she will kill you, for she certainly is trying. I don't see how you stand it. Of course I will write to Cornelius, though I have no influence with him, for Rose is certainly not crazy."[16]

Of Rebellion's Self

When Tom's poem "The New Poet" appeared in the February issue of *American Prefaces*, it was evident that he was not losing interest in writing poetry, nor would he ever. Preoccupied though he was with Holland and the rehearsals of his play, he nevertheless had joined the staff of the university's *The Eliot** and was still meeting on occasion with members of the Poetry Society, particularly with Clark Mills and William Jay Smith. Although Mills urged modern poets such as "T. S. Eliot and the young English poets, Auden, Spender, Day Lewis, and MacNeice" upon Bill Smith,[17] Tom clung mainly to the works of Hart Crane and D. H. Lawrence but found a new interest in Rainer Maria Rilke.

Even at this early stage, Mills saw Tom struggling to effect an amalgam of poetry with his playwriting. "I think he has more poetry in his plays than in his poetry. And, in fact, I would say there is a quality that I think is unique to him. It has to do with the *flow* of his language and dialogue: It has some kind of a poetic quality to it. I don't know of any other American playwright, living or dead, who has it. That quality was present even in the early days when he would come to my house and write, banging out page after page and throwing them on the floor. I'd pick up and read what he'd discarded, and there still would be this magic quality in the dialogue—it wasn't the language or the words or the sentences or the way they were put together; it was the 'sound' of the voice that came through somehow. He seemed to 'hear' the voice as much as he heard the words. And I think when you hear the voice like that, you're in the realm of poetry."†

Mills saw Williams's spontaneous transmission of mind onto paper as a "phenomenon," wholly lacking in the deliberation that usually characterizes the writing process. "I could never have imagined anyone writing as he did.

---

*John M. Pickering, who became managing editor of *The Eliot* in 1937, recalled that Williams contributed twenty poems to *The Eliot*, Washington University's undergraduate magazine, between November 1936 and February 1938. He said that Tom's poems were "perfectly crafted, deeply felt (in a late adolescent way), conventionally designed, and yet subtly revealing of the themes he was to develop in his plays." He remembered Tom to be the model contributor, "reliable, neat, careful and literate," and he met his deadlines with "impeccably typed poems, each ready for the typesetter without correcting spelling or usage and without mentioning meter, rhyme, or tense."

†Mills recollected that he had called Tom's attention to a book that particularly impressed him; it was written by Edward D. Snyder, an associate professor of English at Haverford College—*Hypnotic Poetry, A Study of Trance-Inducing Technique in Certain Poems and Its Literary Significance* (Philadelphia: University Press, 1930). Although Snyder did not cite Hart Crane directly, he did single out Crane's mentor, Shelley, for both his spell weaving and intellectualist poems.

He would do, say, a half page or two pages, and it was fast—he was fast on the typewriter—he would be operating as if blindly. He was never sure if he knew where he was going, but when he got there—when he finished that passage and it might not be right—he'd toss it aside and start all over again. While he would do the whole business over, it would go in a different direction. It was as if he was throwing dice—as if he was working toward a combination or some kind of result and wouldn't have *any* idea what the result might be but would recognize it when he got there. You know, usually one sits down and writes page one, two, three, four, and so on—but he would write and rewrite and even in the middle of a passage, he'd start over again and slant it another way."

Although Willard Holland had the impression of Tom as being strong, organized, and punctual, Mills and others close to him saw him as vulnerable. The "iron curtain" that Holland perceived was in fact protective. Tom said very little to anyone unless he felt confidence in the person whose company he kept. With Mills, he was often voluble. But he spoke of his family and particularly of the problem with Rose in scant terms, so that Mills at the time had no idea she was so extremely ill, let alone that she would soon be confined to a sanitarium. All that Mills observed in Tom was a fanatical dedication to his writing. "I never saw anybody work in a more maniacal way on his manuscripts. It was fantastic the way he labored. Until his first play with Holland's Mummers, I don't think Tom ever had a clue how he was going to succeed. I couldn't help feeling sorry for him."[18]

The Mummers production of Tom's *Candles to the Sun* became his "baptism of fire," an indoctrination into the workings of professional theatre. It was a challenge and a test that he met headlong. Though many of the actors and crew were, strictly speaking, nonprofessionals, under Willard Holland's astute and demanding direction, they rose considerably above the stigma of amateur. As a result, Tom put in a prodigious amount of labor. Holland recalled, "Writing always came easier to Tom than it does to most people. His original manuscripts were the length of three full plays, and you could throw out heaps of typewritten pages and still have more than enough left over for a full-length play."[19] There remain, in fact, well over four hundred pages of *Candles to the Sun* at the Humanities Research Center in Austin, Texas. These original drafts are largely unnumbered; Tom would always leave the collating of his work to the last or, if he could, to others. These versions also bear a number of titles, such as *The Lamp, Place in the Sun*, and *Candles* in *the Sun*.

The combination of Willard Holland and Thomas Lanier Williams proved to be an auspicious team for the times: the one concerned with a theatre of social protest and the other with a dramatic depiction of violence in society, both believing the individual ineffectual except as a member of the collective consciousness. One critic, Reed Hynds of the *St. Louis Star-Times*, observed that "lobby critics" immediately characterized *Candles to the Sun* as "a propaganda play," although Hynds himself called it "an earnest and searching examination of a particular social reality set out in human and dramatic terms. Only the fact that it is concerned with coal miners who strike gives it the tone of a propaganda play."[20] Tom, interviewed in the same paper, said that *Candles to the Sun* was first conceived during the summer of 1935, when he was visiting his grandparents in Memphis. "It deals with group welfare as opposed to individual welfare and [is] set against a background of southern miners." He explained, "The candles in the [title of the] play represent the individual lives of the people. The sun represents group consciousness. The play ends as a tragedy for the individuals, for in the end they realize they cannot achieve success and happiness apart from the group but must sacrifice for the common good."[21]

The play opened on Thursday, March 18, and received rave notices in all three St. Louis papers. Colvin McPherson of the *St. Louis Post-Dispatch*, and later a supportive friend of Tom's, described *Candles* as one of the strongest plays the Mummers had ever attempted and as a drama of social content:

> Williams, 25-year-old Washington University senior, is revealed not only as a writer of unusual promise but one of considerable technical skill right now. His theme is spread in realistic, swift strokes, with sound knowledge of locale and a mature appreciation of human affairs. If, impatient with time-honored dramatic technique, he employs two acts and 10 scenes, he still has devised effective curtains for all divisions.
>
> "Candles to the Sun," set in the Red Hills mining section of Alabama, dramatizes the yearning of the laboring population, especially of the mothers in that class, for something better. It has poverty, degeneracy, accidents on the fifth level below ground, a strike and a brutal murder, ending with beans for everybody, hope and the singing of "Solidarity Forever." Our author, in a phrase, shoots the works.
>
> Yet although he has been beguiled by his many colorful opportunities, his writing is rarely unsteady and his play has an emotional unity and robustness. It stands on its own feet. Its characters are genuine, its dialogue of a type that must have been uttered in the author's presence, its appeal in the theater widespread.[22]

McPherson, like Hynds, was unaware that Williams had never been in Alabama's Red Hill mining country, nor had he listened to the talk of its miners. He had instead the "ear" and the "eye" of an arch observer, and it is likely that somewhere along the line he had found a role model. Holland remarked:

> Tom's earlier plays were about sad people with problems . . . strong on characters and dialogue. There was this amazing thing about Tom: he

could sit down at a typewriter and write a characterization and dialogue for a character that wasn't part of any play. I'm sure any writer would give his arm to be able to do that, or to write the way Tom could write reams of dialogue. He had no sense, in those days, of plot construction or story line whatsoever. But his people were really fantastic. You could take a page or pages of dialogue he wrote, give them to an actor, and just put a spotlight on him, and anyone who just happened to walk into the theater couldn't turn away from the strength of it.[23]

Dakin recalled having been present on opening night, along with his mother and father, who attended together. He said that Tom was alone in an aisle seat—something that Tennessee Williams would always insist upon, no matter what the occasion. Enthusiastic first-nighters greeted the play with shouts and cheers and foot stomping, while "the pink-faced author took his first bow among the grey-faced coalminers that he had created out of an imagination never stimulated by the sight of an actual coal mine."[24]

Tom, however, was not all that pleased with the play itself. When it was repeated again on Saturday, the twentieth, Clark Mills was present: "I don't remember the play especially. That's because our underground crew, the poets, were all there, and we were as busy drinking as we were watching, I think. That night was the only occasion when I saw Tom really staggering drunk. He drank, of course, but not to get drunk—and when he was writing, it was just sip and type, sip and type. But that night, he disappeared. He was there at the beginning of the show, but at the intermission Tom was gone—nobody could find him. Finally, I found him outside. It was a cold night—he was sitting on the curbstone in front of the theatre with a bottle of whiskey—and he was drunk as a skunk and in total despair. Apparently, something had gone wrong, or he imagined it. I know he was intensely concerned with the reaction of audiences, and now suddenly he saw the play as hopeless, and he was drinking himself into oblivion. He refused to go back in—he saw it as just a total disaster. That was the only time I ever saw him really drunk."[25]

Among the many congratulatory messages Tom received, there was one he kept that had special meaning:

Congratulations on your success! Mother sent me the grand clipping about your play. I don't remember when I've read such a favorable write-up. Mother wrote that she enjoyed seeing it so much and believe me Terry and I were awfully sorry that we didn't get the opportunity to see it, too.

At any rate we both want you to know that we think it's pretty swell, and we're quite proud of you. . . .

Mother tells me that Rose has been ill. Is she feeling better now? I do hope so. She certainly has had a tough time of it and we both were sorry to hear that once again, she is having bad luck.

Please write when you have time. We'd like awfully much to hear
from you.

Love,
Hazel[26]

One can imagine his mixed feelings on receiving a letter from Mrs. Terrence McCabe. In his journal, he wrote simply: "Very weak and tired this
morning. Got drunk twice last week. Yes, I'm a social success but I don't like it
especially. It means and matters so little. Love is the thing and that I haven't
got. No wonder I find life tiresome now."

On March 26, Tom turned twenty-six, and his aunt Belle wrote to him,
saying, "I was so proud of you and read with intense interest the clippings
your dear mother sent to me about the production of your play. It must have
been a thrilling evening for you. . . ." She concluded her letter, "My heart is
aching because of Rose's condition. To have a sick mind is very sad—but we
must not think of it differently from having a sick body—and we must *know*
that God is just as able to heal one as the other. Poor little child—my heart
yearns over her."[27] In his journal, Tom noted simply, "R. in psychopathic
ward at Missouri-Baptist. I belong in one myself. Tomorrow see Miss Florence and Holland. Life will go on, I suppose."

Walter Dakin had made inquiries about a hospital in North Carolina, and
for a time the family considered moving Rose there. Tom commented in his
journal with some bitterness, "R. will probably go to Sanitarium in Asheville,
N.C. The Williams family originated in N.C. So now the triumphal return!"
Edwina objected to the distance, and it was decided instead that Rose would
be moved nearby to Saint Vincent's, a Catholic convalescent home, and
placed under the custodial care of nuns. Not just Rose was committed to a
sanitarium; so, too, was Roger Moore. He had suffered a crushing defeat in his
bid for mayor, and the effect upon him was devastating. It would be many
weeks, however, before the Williams family would learn what the Moore family was suffering in silence. As far as anyone knew, Roger had simply gone
away to recuperate from the rigors of the campaign.

On July 4, 1937, Tom wrote in his journal, "Wed. the French play. How
can I get through it—Je ne sais pas!" But get through it he did. The play was a
French-language production of Molière's *Les Fourberies de Scapin*, presented
by the university's French department. William Jay Smith wrote of Tom's
acting debut:

[He was] persuaded to take the part of the old father. He read his French
lines with a kind of hound-dog ferocity and deliberation, as if he were
chewing on a large section of the Mississippi delta. When he moved
woodenly across the stage with absolute seriousness pounding the floor
with his cane, small and square in his satin suit, an enormous blond wig

flopping about his shoulders, he gave a performance that a more sophisticated audience would have taken as high camp. As it was, our local audience had not the remotest idea of when to laugh since it had not a clue as to what was going on.[28]

At the time, Tom held his performance in higher regard. Writing to Willard Holland, he said, "I made my stage debut last week in the Molière. I was not at all nervous—actually enjoyed myself on the stage—which surprised me tremendously as I had always fancied myself a hopeless victim of stage-fright. Instead of being frightened by the full-house I was stimulated and found myself ad-libbing both lines and action—so now I am a full-fledged Thespian!"[29] Molière was, alas, defenseless, but one wonders what the young playwright would have thought of an actor "ad-libbing both lines and action" in *his* play.

On Saturday night, April 17, Tom went to a cast party for members of the French play. On Sunday morning, he recorded the results: "Just finished vomiting for the 5th time. Sick as a dog from last night's French play dinner, etc.—Also sick of that crowd. Smith and Marsh are nice but the others are silly." By Tuesday, he lamented, "What a hang-over that was! Okay Sunday night. Went over to Clark's and spent evening with him and Marsh so I must retract that unkind remark about my intellectual friends. I am never quite sure what I think of anyone."

He told Holland he had written some new one-acts under the overall title of *American Blues*, and among them he intended to include *Escape*, which was actually the title he gave to two plays: one about a seventeen-year-old youth, his mother, and their servant; and the other, set in a bunkhouse, about the escape of three convicts. He was also working on a long play called *April Is the Cruelest Month*, which, he informed Holland, "is potentially better than 'Candles' as the subject is one which I can handle better—it is purely characterization. Of course the dialogue is pretty crude at this stage—the first draft—but I may bring it over early next week to let you have a look at it."[30]

Tom could feel uncertainty about his plays, and always would, but what he felt toward those who rejected his work was amply illustrated when on April 20 he wrote:

It looks like I got eliminated from the Webster Groves Play Contest. Tonight they make the announcement and I haven't heard a word about it. Feel quite sore and depressed . . . I thought the play I submitted was pretty good—"Death of Pierrot" a fantasy—was I as badly mistaken as this would seem to indicate? The thought is disturbing. I would like (almost) to put a stick of dynamite under their damned old play tonight. Yes, I'm still very touchy about such things. They hit me where it hurts most. Well, if there's been any dirty work I'll get back at the sons of bitches some way! With this tender little sentiment I may as well close.

Here was an attitude that Tennessee Williams would strike repeatedly during the rest of his life, except that in time it would become more open than this confession made to his journal.

A kind of desperation attached to his work, to which both Clark Mills and Willard Holland were witness. Tom, like Tennessee, could, and more often did, keep several major works in progress at once, constantly under revision, submitted, withdrawn, revised again, and resubmitted. As a result, there were always several versions extant, few of which ever became the final script. During these last months of his life at home in St. Louis, Tom had numerous plays, short stories, and poems both in progress and in circulation.

Despite his periods of depression and self-doubt, his reliance alternately on black coffee and sleeping sedatives, and on alcohol to stimulate his writing, Tom could nevertheless take satisfaction in his accomplishments. His writings were published and his plays produced, and he was being publicized and recognized as a promising new writer. Edwina wrote to her parents to say, "I've gotten Tom, at last, to apply for a copy-right of his play and he has sent it on to the agent in New York [Olga Becker]. Poems he wrote are to be published in the next [June] issue of 'Poetry' magazine.³¹ He will be paid for them. He also has two in this month's school magazine, 'The Eliot.' "

She also told her parents, "Tom and I went out to see Rose Sunday. She sent word that she didn't want to see us but I insisted upon going in, as I wanted to see for myself just what condition she was in. Her face looked so yellow and bloated and she was so full of delusions about people and things that I see she has not improved. . . . The visit made Tom ill so I can't take him to see her again. I can't have two of them there!"³²

For Tom, the fear of madness, intermixed with shame and guilt, would elicit a transmuted love and devotion for his sister that ultimately would exclude all else. Very often Rose used the expression "It's tragic—it's just tragic" to describe whatever it was that disturbed her. And now the harsh, pitiful reality of seeing her confined within Saint Vincent's sanitarium, and of realizing how tragic indeed her life had become, was fully and lastingly impressed upon her brother.

Elegy for Rose

She is a metal forged by love
too volatile, too fiery thin
so that her substance will be lost
as sudden lightning or as wind.

And yet the ghost of her remains
reflected with the metal gone,
a shadow as of shifting leaves
at moonrise or at early dawn.

A kind of rapture never quite
possessed again, however long
the heart lays siege upon a ghost
recaptured in a web of song.[33]

11

The Literary Factory

Spring–Summer 1937

Tom did not return to see his sister at Saint Vincent's for some time. While he was visibly shaken by the experience, it also left a dread imprint on his imagination—one of several nightmare memories of Rose's incarcerations that would surface years later when Tennessee, having submitted himself to analysis, wrote a play called *Suddenly Last Summer*.

A week after going with Tom to the sanitarium, Edwina wrote to her parents:

> I went into St. Vincent's to see Rose again last Sunday over her protests. She seemed glad to see Dakin and me, after we got in, and talked very rationally, also looked quite normal this time. They have gotten her away from cigaret smoking and she doesn't even mention them. She said she was learning to crochet and liked it. She asked for some music to play as they have a piano in their sitting room. I went into her bedroom also. There is a lovely view of the front grounds from it. Altogether she is as nicely situated as possible in such a place. It *should* be at five dollars a day! We also got a nineteen dollar dental bill for her![1]

Edwina was satisfied to have Tom sequestered in his room and removed from Rose's torment. But it was borne in upon him again. In a May 27 journal entry, he wrote, "Thursday—Roger Moore killed himself yesterday morning. Jumped in front of a truck near sanatorium. Ghastly! I doubt that I shall ever do that."

Edwina wrote immediately to the Dakins, "The boys have just returned from across the street where they saw Virginia Moore. Another tragedy for that family! We haven't seen Roger since the election and I surmised something was wrong. He has been in the sanitarium to which I took Rose that dreadful Sunday afternoon. Does that not seem strange!"[2] On the afternoon of the funeral in the Moore home, Tom wrote that "Virginia made a speech and read one of her poems. Very beautiful and touching. She wears sorrow very becomingly."

By month's end, Tom was becoming restive, confiding to his journal feelings of self-loathing and apprehension, confronted as he was with failure in school and having to disappoint his mother and especially his grandparents. He had only to look back in his journal to remind himself of the pledge he had made when he entered the university: "I want to make every day of it *count*— since my lovely grandparents have sacrificed so much to send me." What he wrote now was a reproach: "Having no self-respect one doesn't have the pain of losing it. I am so used to being a worm that the condition seldom troubles me. Now I face the problem of the summer—What will I do? Heaven knows."

He had taken two "easy" exams—"Problems of Philosophy" and "The American System of Government"—but received D's in both. He did get a B in English 16, given by Professor William G. B. ("Pop") Carson, a course described as Technique of Modern Drama. A practical approach to playwriting, it involved students in writing and reading aloud one-act plays that at the end of the term would then be entered in an annual contest. An independent jury would subsequently select three plays, which were then given workshop productions. One of the three would finally receive the distinction of "best" and the playwright awarded fifty dollars. Tom's only interest in the course was centered on the outcome of the contest. Bitterly disappointed in the failure of *Death of Pierrot* to garner even an honorable mention in the Webster Groves contest, Tom submitted another play—*Me, Vashya!*—expecting that it would compensate for the loss. "Play announcement—when? Horrible if I were eliminated!"

His final examination was to be in Greek, but he was not studying for it. The weather had turned suddenly "oppressively hot—yellow sunlight," and his concentration became focused on other outside diversions: "I need relaxation badly." On May 30, he wrote:

> Sunday—Last night I went out with Clark Mills and B.J. [Blandford Jennings, a high school teacher] to Black Forest Beer Garden—met two other teachers—very dull—at least I was. In one of my horribly taciturn humors from drinking beer—must remember never to drink beer again when I want to have a good time. Clark saw a man tapping rhythm on beer steins and remarked, "That is the same thing we do with our poetry, only a more elemental form." He says very clever things at times. I felt like an awful bore—positively tongue-tied.
>
> Blue devils all this morning. I'm going to live this thing down—not

dodge it but charge straight through it. I know that I can beat it all right. Tomorrow Greek final which I will undoubtedly flunk.

Monday. Never woke in more misery in all my life. Intolerable. The brilliant earth mocks my fear. Children and birds sing. People speak in casual voices. The poplar leaves shine. Yet I up here in this narrow room endure torture. God help me! Please! I've got to have help or I'll go mad. What is this a punishment for? What? Or is it all blind, blind without meaning!

Flunking Greek was nothing compared to the distress Tom felt when his play for English 16 was given fourth place and rejected for presentation. "Never a more ignominious failure!" he recorded in his journal.

Went to Carson's office this morning and he gave me the news—without any apparent compunction. But why should I expect sympathy from anyone—especially a Washington University professor—the stronghold of the Reactionaries! Still it does hurt to get a direct kick in the face like that and if there is any guts left in me I'll make up for it some way. It looks like I'm on the way down—hitting the toboggan—but maybe not—

Thirty years later, Tennessee Williams told Robert Rice of the *New York Post*, "It was a terrible shock and humiliation to me. It was a crushing blow to me. I had always thought I was shy, but I discarded all humility. I stormed into Carson's office. (He was a good professor.) I screamed at him. I forget what my parting shot was, but I remember it was quite a shot. I surprised myself."[3] It was an incident of which Carson had no recollection, but, like the parting shot that comes to mind *after* the opportunity to deliver it has passed, Tennessee may have remembered only what Tom *wished* he had said.

Professor Carson's comments on the event were written in 1961 to Andreas Brown, Williams's bibliographer: "I can recall no hint of the resentment which rightly or wrongly he evidently was feeling at the time."[4] Carson thought that the chief reason for their differences was Tom's choice of a subject for his play *Me, Vashya!*—based as it was on the notorious munitions manufacturer Sir Basil Zaharoff. There is no record of why Tom chose so remote a subject except that possibly he had heard a recent "March of Time" radio broadcast, a dramatized obituary of the munitions tycoon as played by Orson Welles, a characterization that had much in common in its biodramatic treatment with Welles's masterpiece a few years later, *Citizen Kane*.

One of Tom's classmates was Wayne Arnold, whose *First Edition* had been chosen for production among the top three. Arnold had occasion to read Tom's play and said that the plot concerned a peasant youth who had fallen in love with a child princess and later, having acquired a fortune in munitions sales, married her. Arnold summarized:

As the curtain rises, Mrs. Vashya is in a bad mental state. It seems that she
has a deep friendship with a young poet who had managed to arouse the
jealousy of her husband, who saw to it that said poet was shipped off to
the front lines in some war or other and got it in the head. The princess is
distraught and has been having visions of her friend standing at the front
of her bed urging her to kill her husband for what he has done to man-
kind. A psychiatrist is brought in, the princess has a tirade against her
husband and finally shoots him dead. Dying, he kisses the hem of her
garment.[5]

Another student winner, with his one-act *Who's Aunt Tillie?*, was Aaron
(A. E.) Hotchner, who became a prominent St. Louis divorce lawyer and, ultimately, Ernest Hemingway's friend and biographer; he remembered *Me,
Vashya!* being read aloud in class and there being stifled laughter. He said that
on the last day in class, Professor Carson announced the contest winners and
that Tom "rose slowly from his seat, suffused with anger, and left the room.
None of us ever saw him again."[6]

Classmate Martyl Schweig recalled, "In 1937, I was nineteen and Tom
Williams seemed ages older. He did not sit with the class but to the left of
Professor Carson facing us. I remember him vividly because of his sallow
complexion, nasal voice and the fact that he wore the very same brown suit all
year, so worn that it was purply and shiny at the elbows and seat. My recollection of his droning voice and boring play [is that they] prompted me to do my
next class' homework during the reading."[7] In the June issue of *The Eliot*,
Martyl Schweig illustrated an anonymous article entitled "What College Has
Not Done For Me"—a thinly disguised characterization of a distinctly disenchanted graduate student.

Tom maintained that his play was intended as a melodramatic fantasy and
not meant to be realistic, but it would seem the very controversial nature of
the story called for a more polemical treatment. In the late thirties, munitions
makers like the vilified St. Louis du Ponts were openly despised as society's
war-makers and were allegedly members of international cartels who sold ar-
maments to either or both sides in a war. By 1937, antiwar sentiment was at
such a pitch that a subject of this sort demanded a more contentious playwright than Tom Williams. What interested him was not political significance but the mad princess.

One could, in fact, trace the nature of the princess's illness to the influence
and symptoms of Rose's mental breakdown, what Tom was directly experiencing, and to the omnipresence in his own life of a persistent blue devil.
William Jay Smith remembered *Me, Vashya!* and, in particular, the munitions
maker's mad wife as "the first of Tom's many splendid, wild heroines. I
thought at the time that the play was superb, but my opinion was not shared
by the judges of the competition." He said that, in actuality, "those of us

around Tom were outraged. This rejection had much to do with souring him on Washington University."[8]

Something else, something as traumatic as the rejection of his play, also took place at this time. Clark Mills had a distinct memory of seeing a letter that Tom had written to Professor Otto Heller, whom he despised. Whether it was ever mailed or not, Mills characterized it as "an explosive denunciation—total warfare." Dr. Heller, who was seventy-three in May of 1937, had been a distinguished full professor at Washington for forty-five years and had gained a reputation as an Ibsen scholar with the publication in 1912 of *Henrik Ibsen, Plays and Problems.* He had given Tom an A at the end of the fall term in his course Principles and Problems of Literature but now saw fit to grade him a D. What could well have prompted Tom's letter was a term paper he had written entitled "Birth of an Art (Anton Chekhov and the New Theater) by T. L. Williams," which reflected more of an interest in theatre than General Literature III.

Dr. Heller made two notations, either one of which would have been strong enough to inflame Tom's anger: "This paper in no way fulfills the requirements of a term paper as indicated repeatedly," and "All of this, or nearly all, was written without reference or relation to literary standards and criteria as studied in the course.—O.H." For a self-proclaimed writer to receive a D in philosophy and American government might be understood, but to get a D in General Literature III could evoke only a sneer from Tom's father—that, and the fact that he had gone from a B to a C in advanced physical education. He had been humiliated, and it was all that Cornelius needed to reopen his campaign to get him back to work in the shoe factory.

Evidently, Tom had not told his family of a notice he had received on April 20 from the registrar's office informing him that he would not graduate in June and that he had been placed on scholastic probation, with the caveat that he "must consult Dean before reregistering 6-8-37: may register in summer session."[9] In other words, Thomas Williams was still classified as a student, but not as a candidate for a degree, and would remain so until he passed Greek and took another term of physical education.

To make matters worse, all this had to be explained to his mother and grandparents. And so, undecided what to do, he put off reregistering until it was too late. The fact that he was not to graduate and had forfeited an entire year of credits toward a degree did not bother him nearly as much as the failure of his play to win and win unqualifiedly. Throughout his life, the failure of his plays would mean more than their success.

Tom had suffered a reversal, as he saw it, and for days afterward it rankled him.

Saturday P.M. [June 19] That was a week ago and is all but forgotten—at least the sting is removed. I suppose the psychological shock still remains—among countless others. Did some fair writing this afternoon, but after reading new play—laid in a flop-house—felt thoroughly disgusted. Will I ever produce another full length play that's worth producing? Maybe.

Sunday: Had a delightful evening with Miss Florence. . . . Walked up to the Muny Opera [an eight-thousand-seat amphitheater in Forest Park]. Laughed and acted like kids. The Bell Trail. Miss Flo is really a grand old trouper. Pretended to flirt with all the men passing in cars—flaunting her tremendous pearl necklace.

One strange interlude—saw Jim Connor [his classmate at University of Missouri] at opera. He also saw me I'm sure but neither of us spoke. How silly! My shyness is a never-ending affliction. I know it was only shyness in Jim too. He is not the type that would deliberately snub anyone. There is something mysterious and touching about him. He looks so wise and sad—as sad as I am and very much wiser. For that reason I should like to renew our acquaintance.

Today wanted to go swimming but the old women prevented because of my bruised nose. Angry and bored. Wonder if I shall end up like Rose? God forbid!

The Time of the Solstice

Early in the summer, Edwina and Cornelius began searching in earnest for another place for the family to live. The lease on the Pershing Avenue house was about to expire, and soon there would be the upheaval of Edwina at the fore, packing and moving. Initially, it was thought that Tom, who would certainly be more in the way than any real help, might spend the time with his grandparents in Memphis. Instead, late in June, Walter Dakin came up to St. Louis to look over a small old house on Watermann Avenue as a place where he and Grand could live and be closer to the family. There were other reasons why a relocation seemed advisable—primarily Grand's health and the fact that her many trips from Memphis to St. Louis were obviously wearing on her. Tom wrote, "Grandfather is here and I enjoy his company—today we visited Rose—she seemed better." He also mentioned that he had completed the first two acts of his new play, that they were "fairly presentable," and that he was about to try writing the third. That same evening, he said, "Wrote some good stuff—all but last scene of first draft finished. Took a long walk, clear up to Clayton Pool and back, composing dialogue—some of it quite good."

Willard Holland called and asked to meet him, and Tom received the disquieting news of his friend's imminent departure: "He's going to take a Paramount screen test in Hollywood. I don't wish him bad luck—but if he should get in the movies, what chance would I have of producing a play next season?"

Just before Holland's departure, Tom gave him the completed script; he "seemed fairly pleased though much rewriting is necessary."

Sunday—July 4 . . . This morning had odd experience—wakened by a bird call—gave me a strange, delightful sensation—an atavistic emotion from my early childhood. So clear and pure—the delight of an early morning in childhood—pure, spiritual delight—made me realize what a muddy stream my adult life has become. If only I could regain that lost clarity and purity of spirit!

Tuesday—July 6—Yesterday spent a swell afternoon at Tree Court [with Esmeralda Mayes and others]. Discussed Tallulah Bankhead's alleged perversion and promiscuity—"Gable is good but Garbo is better"—an obvious lie. So much filth nowadays. No one is left untouched. Or is it filth? Perhaps it is only robust, natural life boiling up to the surface. It is all in the way you look at it. But I want something clean—something that is pure without being false or squeamish—is there such a thing?

Weds. [July 7] Suffering torments of the damned with an awful burning skin eruption on face and arms. Also blue devils. No sleep tonight. Am I losing my mind? Recent entries sound so chaotic—like the product of a diseased mind. No delusions but certainly not a normal state of mind— feel trapped tonight—frightened—have taken a sleeping pill but little effect. . . . My life is entirely too internal. I need action on the outside—in the world! Tonight I would gladly enlist in the Loyalist Army in Spain— and might even relish the sounds of an aerial bombardment. Wish I were going somewhere new and exciting. I wish that something would happen. And something *will*—I can feel it coming!

The Dakins returned home once Grand had come to look over the house on Watermann, and shortly afterward Edwina and Cornelius decided to lease a larger but less attractive house at 42 Aberdeen Place in nearby Clayton, a fashionable suburb of St. Louis. For Edwina, it was a step up socially and a last move before buying a house. She immediately wrote her parents, saying that Cornelius "doesn't think it wise for you to own two houses," adding that their new house was "plenty large enough for you . . . and any furniture you want me to keep for you."[10] Edwina admitted that Aberdeen Place was not everything she had hoped for, but rentals were scarce, and it was situated quite near the church and near enough to Washington University for both Tom and Dakin to walk there.

Cornelius's letter was addressed to "Dear Mrs. Dakin" and typewritten on Friedman-Shelby stationery, with its inevitable slogan, "Red Goose Shoes are half the fun of having feet." It was a two-page missive detailing the problems with the house on Watermann and singing the praises of his new home on

Aberdeen: "with a nice big back yard, nice porches, and four bedrooms. . . . I am sure you will like this place very much, and we would be glad to have you and Mr. Dakin come up and visit us, or come up and stay any time you see fit." It was signed, "Sincerely yours, C C Williams."[11]

That Cornelius chose to write to Grand may simply have been because of his recognition of her practicality. But it is likely that he was also demonstrating a growing animosity toward Mr. Dakin, compounded of jealousy that Tom had always acted toward the old gentleman more as a father than a grandfather, and, perhaps more significantly, of loathing for the qualities of gentleness that both the minister and Tom shared. He could understand a gentle lady like Grand, whom he always treated with utmost consideration and respect, but not a gentle man. Conversely, that "masculine" attitude in his father would alternately attract and repulse Tom and become the psychic makeup of many of Tennessee's male characters.

Tom's new room was in the attic, and he noted that his father "complains because he will have to heat it for me in the winter. But maybe—when winter comes—I will not be living there. Maybe I will be living a new, exciting life somewhere else." But now it was summer, and since it was impossible for him to write in the unventilated and sweltering heat of the attic, Tom sought refuge in the residence of Mr. and Mrs. McBurney, Clark Mills's parents. Tom wrote:

> That summer Clark and I started what we called a "literary factory." It was located in the basement of Clark's home at 7541 Westmoreland Av., in Clayton—in the basement because it was cooler down there and it offered a minimum of distraction. For instance that bane of all writers, the vacuum cleaner, sounded to us, in our subterranean retreat, as only the faintest rumor, mistakable for the murmur of distant waves or wind among branches. Over the windows we had dark blue drapes—Clark said it gave a sort of deep-sea effect—indirect lighting and a small victrola. However there was not a thing luxurious or "decadent" about the atmosphere. Furnishings were broken-down pieces that Mrs. McBurney had discarded. We worked at old kitchen-tables, seated in old kitchen chairs—no temptation to lean back and "relax." The walls were stacked with old magazines, manuscripts, books. On a shelf was a cocktail shaker and some glasses—occasionally one of us went into the garden to gather some mint. But this was only during rare periods of relaxation. Eight hours of each day, upon an average, we were typing the nails off our fingers—Clark upon a new group of poems, I upon a new play.[12]

Tom subsequently entitled the play *Fugitive Kind*, and Mills remembered him working on it in their literary factory. "He told me he had spent a couple of nights in or investigating a flophouse in St. Louis. That was the setting of the play. As Tom said later on, 'Ideas from my poems went into his plays, and ideas from his plays went into my verse.' Well, that's true. I wrote a poem called 'The White Winter,' which was all about a snowstorm in St. Louis. And in his play, there was a snowstorm falling outside the flophouse."

Mills said the literary factory came about because he and Tom both had the same problem: There was no place to write at home. He went on to describe it: "I lived in a sort of glass bungalow. My parents were fresh-air nuts. All the walls were glass, and all the doors between the rooms were glass, so that there was no privacy and no quiet. So, what happened was: I got some tongue-in-groove lumber, very plain boards, and we set up one corner of the cellar. We put up two walls, and *primitive* was the word, the most god-awful cellar you ever saw, with a coal furnace and a washing machine. But at least it was a bit cooler there and also, since it was one whole floor removed from the rest of the house, it was quiet—we could type. We had two typewriters, two kitchen tables, two hard chairs, a bookcase, and a very beat-up studio couch, just a mattress on box legs. And that was the whole of the literary factory. It was pretty pitiful, but that's where we wrote—just Tom and I. Occasionally, when he wasn't around, I'd invite a girl there—but that was not for literary purposes; it was because there was no place in my glass house where I could entertain *anyone*. My parents were all over the place, and there wasn't much seclusion even in the basement. As Tom wrote later, my mother visited us more often than the muse."

Undoubtedly, Tom felt closer, more drawn, to his friend than Clark realized at the time. He noted in his journal that he was lonely and feeling "shy and remote now that school is out and I'm so much by myself." Clark, by comparison, was as gregarious and busy socially as ever. He had been sexually active with a variety of St. Louis girls for years, the first when he was fourteen, and by 1937 he was recognized as having attained an impressive track record. What bound Clark and Tom was the camaraderie of a couple of frustrated writers. "We had a very happy sort of relationship, full of uproarious humor," Mills said. "Half the time we were making wisecracks and yelling with laughter—or rather, he screaming, with that laugh of his."[13]

What impressed Mills the most, though—as it did Willard Holland—was Tom's "fanatical and inexhaustible energy in his writing." Mills said, "His persistence was almost grotesque. It was Dionysian, demoniac. He wasn't aiming basically at material success. He wrote because it was a fatal need. Here was this lost member of his family trying to learn playwriting entirely in the dark."[14] Later, Mills observed, "The way Tom learned to write a successful play was by first attempting countless versions that he then discarded, finally arriving at one he felt might be accepted. *That* was his greatness, as I saw it—what set him apart."[15]

The literary factory remained open until the end of summer, when Clark was due to leave for the Sorbonne to write a study of Jules Romains, and Tom for Iowa, although he did not know it at the time. This would be the last of the "innocent summers." In his journal, Tom spoke of his uncertain future and of "warm, moony summer evenings, the cicadas in good voice—a faint cool breeze now and then," and of dreamy summer afternoons when "I would like to be lying in a pile of hay—mellow lotus!—way out in the country. I should have been a shepherd—I have such a taste for pastoral life. Alas, the day of shepherds is past—poets have got to live in cities and adjust themselves to a social system which was definitely not made for poets. But maybe I am not a poet but just a blooming idiot."

With Morning on Her Lips

Wed—or Thurs. A.M. . . . 11 till about 2 a.m. . . . drove Mother to sanitarium to visit R.—waited about an hour—M. came out crying—R. has taken a dreadful turn—become raving—won't eat—thinks she is being poisoned—can't sleep—disturbed the whole ward, so has been isolated—looks a wreck M. says. She could not tell me about it till after we reached home. This of course made me feel very wretched.

Then ride with D. [Dad] who was mean as the devil—cutting remarks—felt so inadequate and helpless and hated him so. He is sick himself, I suppose—and one cannot blame him for being disgusted with me—I *am* such a fool. . . . Maybe I will go to Clark's in morning and write—*something!* If only I could leave here—go to camp—is there any possible chance of it? The beastliness of life frightens me so—R.—when such things can happen to people, how to believe in any good power over us mortals? The fear—the helplessness—*what can we do?*

Then there was disastrous news. Tom confided, "Our worst fears about Rose were confirmed. Her trouble has been diagnosed as dementia praecox. The doctor at St. Vincent's said Insulin shock was about the only hope—it is not decided yet whether to give her that—a catastrophe worse than death. I slept fitfully last night—that thought woven through my dreams—a living nightmare. Grandfather says, 'She is God's child and He will do what is best for her.' Why must a child of God have dementia praecox? His ways are indeed mysterious. I am driven more and more to the conclusion that individual lives do not matter much in the cosmic scheme of things. If only I can keep my sanity I shall count myself a fortunate man."

Finally, he added a thought he would return to at a later, more crucial time: "Lay cowering on my bed for a while and then got up with the reflection that nobody ever died of being strong."

Dakin, who had graduated third in a large class and whose scholastic achievements were in glaring contrast to his brother's failures, was packed off to camp for a week at Mutton Hollow in Hollister, Missouri. Tom despaired, "My chance of getting away seems increasingly remote." By the end of July, Tom's feelings of confinement—the panic of being shut in and cut off from life—had become so intense that he was unable to get an uninterrupted night's sleep. At four in the morning, he would still be awake and writing: "Nervous frenzy—no sleep—can't even lie still—no sleeping pills left. Must keep hold of myself—don't want to go mad—or am I already?"

Later the same morning, he wrote, "Slept about three hours after daybreak. Wakened by the old man pounding on my door and yelling at me that 'I had to do something around here'—he raved at me for some time in this vein. That on top of everything else—I am just about driven to the last ditch." He commented that if only he was not "so completely disorganized" and not so "sick, body and soul," he might be able to make a complete break—"the curse of inaction!" What troubled him most was Rose—what was happening to her and the fear it could happen to him. The feelings he harbored were mixed and conflicting—of concern for his sister and egocentric self-concern, being drawn to her plight and at the same time being repelled by its threat to him. He was reminded, "Whom the Gods would destroy they first make mad."

Edwina was keenly aware of his state of mind, and it frightened her. But her anxiety was lost on Cornelius, who saw Tom's inaction as lazy self-indulgence. In turn, Dakin resented the burden it placed upon him to be the only one able to drive his mother to see Rose: "My sister was a raving maniac at the time and had no thought pattern at all. It was very unnerving to go there and hear your sister screaming incoherently like a wild animal."[16] At another time, he said, "Often I would hear her screaming long before the Catholic sisters would usher us into her presence at St. Vincent's. Our visits were almost always depressing disasters. Between screams and the most vile cursing, she would be chain-smoking and pacing up and down the corridor or visiting room. Finally the Mother Superior advised us there was no future for Rose at St. Vincent's, which was primarily equipped for 'custodial care.' "[17] Dakin felt that Tom was at fault: "Rose had always been extremely close and emotionally dependent upon him, and he certainly did let her down when she desperately needed him."[18]

Early in August, Edwina wrote to her parents, saying that she had held off writing the tragic and sudden turn of events in regard to Rose.

> She is now in the State Hospital in Farmington. Cornelius had her taken there on Saturday and Dakin and I will motor up this morning as I wish to talk to the Superintendent about her. She became violently insane just after you left and they placed her in a room off from the rest and told me they would advise insulin immediately as the only hope for her. They admitted this would be very expensive, so Cornelius got busy right away and had Dr. Satterfield and another [doctor] visit her and sign the necessary papers. They all agree that this is the only hope and that Farmington is the best place, so there was nothing for me to do but consent.

In signing the admission papers, Cornelius gave the power to the state hospital to make all determinations and decisions regarding Rose's therapeutic treatment. Edwina said that this sorry event, together with packing and moving five people and cleaning both houses, "taxed every ounce of strength that both Susie and I had. . . . Dakin had only a week in the Ozarks—not enough to do him much good but with all the expense the best we could do for him." It was the same for Tom, who had been ill ever since the Dakins had left. "So I sent him to the Ozarks day before yesterday. Rose's trouble has been a blow to his already nervous system."

Subsequently, Edwina wrote,

> Have just returned from Farmington Hospital where I interviewed Dr. Hocter [sic], the Superintendent. Couldn't see Rose but they say she stood the transfer nicely, seemed to enjoy the ride over. She was quiet and quite responsive, and he felt sure I had every reason to hope for a cure. He has recently sent home thirty girls treated with insulin for Rose's trouble—all well. He will commence the treatments as soon as he has completed his own laboratory tests of her and said he would let me know. He was perfectly lovely toward me and inspired me with confidence that he will do the right thing by her. He is of fine moral & Christian character also Roman Catholic.[19]

On July 31, Rose was admitted by Emmet Hoctor, M.D., to Farmington State Hospital as case number 9014, the hospital records describing her as suffering from "Dementia Praecox (Schizophrenia) Mixed Type, Paranoid Predominating." On her admission sheet, her "Environment and Economic Status" were designated as "urban" and "comfortable," and her mental condition was listed as "passive." The word *no* was written after "suicidal" and "homicidal."

There was no reference to specific hostility toward her father, nor were there any intimations that he had made improper advances toward her, but it was stated on the admissions report that Rose had "delusions of sexual immorality by members of the family." The report went on to say, "The patient has periods of great excitement and confusion. Delusions of a somatic nature (gastric distress etc. . . . Sent here for Insulin Shock treatment.) Came in as a City of St. L., patient but an effort will be made to have her changed to a [private] patient."[20]

A letter from Isabel to "Dearest Brother" said, "My heart and prayers have certainly been burdened with dear Rose as she is sent for this treatment which we trust will mean restored health to her. I think you did the only thing you could wisely do to take the course which alone held out hope for her recovery." This letter, dated August 7, 1937, has often been misconstrued to mean the treatment was a prefrontal lobotomy, when in fact Isabel Brownlow was referring to insulin shock therapy and was approving the move to Farmington

State Hospital for that purpose. Whether Edwina intended to mislead readers of her memoir in order to place the ultimate responsibility for the operation on her husband or whether she misinterpreted the content of Isabel's letter can only be left to conjecture. The lobotomy did not actually take place until six years later, under very different circumstances. Not only Edwina but also Tennessee, unwittingly or not, perpetuated the fiction that the operation was performed in August or September of 1937, when even medically this was an impossibility.

Isabel concluded her letter, expressing concern for Tom, whom she had not seen since he was a child: "I so long to see him. I have so much confidence in his success as a writer. I know he will one day really distinguish himself."[21]

Before Tom left for his week in summer camp, he penned a poem for Rose titled "Valediction":

> *She went with morning on her lips*
> *down an inscrutable dark way*
> *and we who witnessed her eclipse*
> *have found no word to say.*
>
> *I think our speechlessness is not*
> *a thing she would approve,*
> *she who was always light of wit*
> *and quick to speak and move—*
>
> *I think that she would say goodbye*
> *can be no less a lyric word*
> *than any song, than any cry*
> *of greeting we have heard!*[22]

Sunday—(Aug. 7 or 8)—Returned from camp after one short week— freedom! Escape! It was so comparatively sublime. Now I have come back and almost wish I had not gone—the time was so short and the return so desolate heartbreaking. . . . I have been harassed by the blue devils since leaving camp. . . . We all (Dakin, M. and I) went to Early Communion to pray for R. . . . I've got to pity M. and stop pitying myself.

The question of Tom's continued education, and especially the furtherance of his writing career, had been a matter of discussion for several weeks, both between Edwina and her parents and among Tom's friends. Although he had benefited from some of the courses he had taken at Washington University—a "lost year," as he would come to regard it—his only valid credits were those he had earned at the University of Missouri. Willard Holland, who had returned from his screen test on the West Coast, felt that Tom would benefit most from going to the University of Iowa, where he could finally earn his undergraduate degree and, more important, where there was a drama department that espoused his philosophy of a theatre in *action*. Clark Mills, who was preparing to leave for the Sorbonne, concurred. Once again, Edwina and the Dakins gave their support, Cornelius abstaining.

In his journal, Tom wrote that he was "holding my thumbs for Iowa," which he felt at that point was "still a fabrication of dream. Will it be reality? Oh, how I hope!" A week later, Tom reported, "Still looks as though I will go to Iowa but now I begin to have doubts about advisability of it. Of course I will go if I get the chance—but feel something will probably develop to impede." On Sunday, he said that he had visited Rose at Farmington, "where she is undergoing insulin treatment. Much better than I expected. A horrible business though. She is unconscious half of every day—swollen and exhausted physically but in remarkably good spirits—laughed and joked about other patients. Chief worry is her hair which she thinks is falling out."

> Thursday. Sept. 16. . . . Dakin is at S.A.E. House for his first rush date. I am waiting up—in my garret room—to let him in. This is a charming room. I almost hate to leave it. You see, I feel in my heart that I will never really return to this place. Whatever happens good or ill, this next year, I think it will surely divorce me at last from the paternal roof—wish-fulfillment! But of course my life has been a series of returns. I do not seem to have much capacity for exploring new fields although I have no lack of desire.
>
> My play [*Fugitive Kind*] is all but finished and I feel pretty well satisfied with it. Now I yearn for work on a new one—will not be content till I have made a good start on it. The next play is always the important play. The past, however satisfactory, is only a challenge to the future.
>
> I want to go on creating. I *will!!!*

About this time, there was turmoil in the Williams household. Dakin was threatening to go to a university other than Washington because the SAE brothers had decided against him. Edwina told her parents, "He feels badly about it, of course, but I think Cornelius feels worse. He said in amazement, 'Why I thought everyone would like Snookie'!!'"

A new doctor, C. C. Ault, had begun attending Rose at Farmington, and Edwina noted that she had called him and "he said she was still re-acting nicely to the insulin but had 'her ideas' just the same which doesn't sound encouraging. He said I could come to see her every two weeks giving him 'three days notice.' I feel sure she will be cured."[23] She also mentioned that she was putting the "finishing touches" to Tom's wardrobe, a preoccupation he was glad to leave to her. Packing for him meant his books and manuscripts and what was to become the ubiquitous volume of Hart Crane he had "borrowed" from the Washington University library.

Before boarding the train, he made a last entry in his journal: "No, I haven't forgotten poor Rose—I beg whatever power there is to save her and spare her from suffering."

On Wednesday night, September 22, Tom wrote, "The miracle has happened. I'm on the train for Iowa City. At least I will get there—*Deo volente* I will *remain*. Feel pretty good—less nervous than I expected and rather jubilant. At last I am really doing something. Making a definite move—that is a satisfying thing. It is interesting to speculate upon the possibilities of this coming year. So much may or may not happen! Of course I am a little frightened—*ça va sans dire*—but I think I will carry it off okay—"

In the pages of his journal, he also wrote a letter to Clark, but—like the many letters written during his lifetime that were never mailed—he just left this bound in the little account book, a copy of it finally delivered to Mills some forty-five years later.

> Dear Clark:
> I am seated in a coach bound for Iowa City—it is 11:45 P.M.—and I feel such a prodigious excitement—in spite of a double sedative—that I must communicate my feelings to someone or else *blow up*. . . . But of course the *important* thing is that I am actually going. I never really believed in its possibility until I got on the train.
> I spent this evening with Bill Smith and the Filsingers [who were sisters]. We drank great quantities of beer, criticized Bill's new verse—which is rather good, shows progress—and laughed almost continually. I felt quite hysterical with joy over my imminent departure. I want you to know that I have already purchased a pint of good whiskey to fortify myself against the rigors of a northern winter! . . . I will probably call up Schramm and Mabie soon as I get in town and invite them both out on "a colossal binge."
> Bill and I called up your mother tonight and she said she had recovered from her illness which I'm sure you are glad to know. I will at least add my address to this letter when I get to I.C. so you can drop me a line before sailing.
>
> > Sincerely your friend,
> > Tom

ABOVE: Tom as a freshman at the University of Missouri

RIGHT: Tom and Rose in front of their Enright home, the tenement model for *The Glass Menagerie*

29

ATO brother Jim Connor would give
his name to the gentleman caller in
The Glass Menagerie

30

Tom's roommate Mitch, whose name
would be immortalized in *A Streetcar
Named Desire*

31

Mrs. Cornelius Williams on ATO
Mother's Day, 1930

32

Rose at St. Vincent's Sanitarium

TOP: Washington University in St. Louis

LEFT: William J. Smith, friend and fellow poet

RIGHT: Clark Mills McBurney, Tom's first close friend at Washington University, his literary mentor and fellow poet

First Row—WILLIAMS, FERRING, THYSON, KEALHOFER, SCHWEIG, GUIDRY.
Second Row—CLARK, LORENZ, DUSARD, EXTEIN, PICKERING, HOTCHNER.

Staff of *The Eliot*. Tom is at the far left, front row.

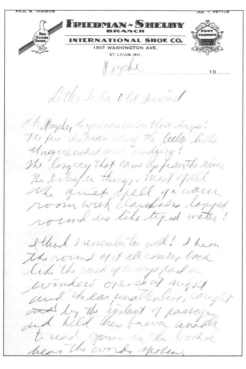

37

38

". . . I was fired for writing a poem on the lid of a shoe-box."
The Glass Menagerie

39

The celotex interior

Edwina and Cornelius—
together apart!

THE GARDEN PLAYERS

present

"CAIRO, SHANGHAI, BOMBAY"

by

BERNICE DOROTHY SHAPIRO & TOM WILLIAMS

Directed by: ARTHUR B. SCHARFF

Cast in order of first appearance:

GEORGE MADLINGER
LOLE ROSEBROUGH
MRS. HUBERT HASTINGS with
  BABY MARY LOU HURT
CATHERINE GIBSON
MARY BETH CLOWER . . . . as MILLIE
DOROTHY WILSON . . . . as AILEEN
ARTHUR B. SCHARFF . . . . as UNKNOWN AUTHOR
FRED FAEHRMAN . . . . as FAMOUS AUTHOR
HARRIETT LOOP
TOMMY SANDERS . . . . as CHUCK
CHESTER LOOP . . . . as HARRY
HARVEY PIERCE
RAYMOND HURT
HUBERT HASTINGS

TIME: TODAY
PLACE: A SEAPORT TOWN

SCENE I. A park facing harbour; early evening.

SCENE II. A cheap Oriental Garden; 2 hours later.

SCENE III. A backyard; few hours later.

SCENE IV. Another part of the park, as in Scene I;
one-half hour later.

The first playbill to
bear Tom's name

Tom's second place prize in a 1936 poetry contest was a silver service dish.
He would have preferred money.

44

43

ABOVE: A production still from *Fugitive Kind* with (left to right) Samuel Halley, Jr., Willard Holland, and Viola Perle

ABOVE LEFT: Willard Holland

FOR THE FOURTH PRODUCTION OF THEIR NINTH SEASON

MUMMERS
OF SAINT LOUIS
PRESENT
on
THURSDAY, MARCH 18
SATURDAY, MARCH 20
at
THE WEDNESDAY CLUB
AUDITORIUM

"CANDLES TO THE SUN"
By THOMAS LANIER WILLIAMS
Directed by Willard H. Holland

CAST

BRAM PILCHER	Wesley Gore
HESTER	Genevieve Albers
STAR	Jane Garrett
JOEL (as a boy)	Donald Smith
MARY WALLACE	Jean Fischer
TIM ADAMS	Al Hohengarten
FERN	Viola Perle
LUKE (as a boy)	Lewis Turner
MRS. ABBEY	Mae Novotny
ETHEL SUNTER	Mary Hohenberger
LUKE	Sam Halley, Jr.
BIRMINGHAM RED	Willard Holland
JOEL	Gene Durnin
WHITEY SUNTER	Fred Birkicht
SEAN O'CONNOR	Frank Novotny
1st MINER	Leland Brewer
2nd MINER	Ralph Johanning
3rd MINER	George Drosten
TERRORIST LEADER	Joseph Giarraffa
MINERS' WIVES	Lucile Williamson, Ann Bono,
	Irene Wisdom, Lillian Byrd

Other Miners, Women and a Gang of Terrorists.

SCENE: THE PLAY TAKES PLACE IN A MINING CAMP IN THE
RED HILL SECTION OF ALABAMA.
SCENE 1. BRAM PILCHER'S CABIN.
SCENE 2. THE SAME. THAT EVENING.
SCENE 3. THE SAME. FIVE YEARS LATER.
SCENE 4. STAR'S CABIN. FIVE YEARS LATER.
INTERMISSION
SCENE 5. BRAM'S CABIN. FEW MONTHS LATER.
SCENE 6. THE SAME. LATE AFTERNOON.
SCENE 7. THE SAME. EVENING.
SCENE 8. STAR'S CABIN. TWO DAYS LATER.
SCENE 9. THE SAME. IMMEDIATELY FOLLOWING.
SCENE 10. BRAM'S CABIN. SOME WEEKS LATER.

In "CANDLES TO THE SUN," the Mummers bring to their audience the third
new play by a St. Louis playwright to be produced within the last year. We feel that
the production of new plays is a necessary and important contribution to the growth
of the non-professional theatre. Other St. Louis playwrights are urged to submit their
scripts for reading.

4477 OLIVE   THE MUMMERS OF SAINT LOUIS   FRanklin 8416
BOARD OF DIRECTORS—Sam Halley, Jr., Genevieve Albers, Bernard Galvin, Leland
Brewer, Frank Novotny, Wesley Gore, Mae Novotny, Viola Perle, Ruth Moon.
TICKETS—Aeolian Ticket Office, 1004 Olive, CHestnut 8828.
ACTIVE MEMBERSHIP—Mrs. Frank Novotny, 4477 Olive, Franklin 8416.
GENERAL PROGRAM—Rehearsals, Classes, Business Activity at Mummer Studio.
4477 Olive, FRanklin 8416.
PRODUCTION STAFF—Leland Brewer, Robert Bennett, John Allen, Miriam Schwarz,
Ruth Moon, Gene Durnin.

COMING! — TWO SPRING COMEDIES

"THREE IN A ROW"	"GENTLEMEN WEAR GLOVES"
THE WILD PIECE OF NONSENSE ABOUT THE MURGATROYD TRIPLETS, SET AGAINST THE BACKGROUND OF THE ELEGANT 'EIGHTIES.	THE DROLL STORY OF A MAN WITH NEW IDEAS ABOUT STARTING A BANK PANIC.

45

FOR THE FIRST PRODUCTION OF THEIR TENTH SEASON

The MUMMERS
OF SAINT LOUIS
PRESENT
on
TUESDAY, NOV. 30
SATURDAY, DEC. 4
at
THE WEDNESDAY CLUB
AUDITORIUM

"FUGITIVE KIND"
By THOMAS LANIER WILLIAMS
Directed by Willard H. Holland

CAST

TEXAS	Frank Novotny	TERRY	Willard Holland
JAKE	Kenneth Sheehan	REPORTER	Ann Bono
OLSEN	Bernard Galvin	GWENDLEBAUM	Louis Prince
PETE	Victor Zuzemek	LEO	Samuel Halley, Jr.
ROCKY	Carl Koenig	TRANSIENT	Ralph Johanning
GABE	Carl Hohenberger	O'CONNOR	Albert Hohengarten
ABEL	Warren Metzinger	INTERNE	Kenneth Kimball
CHUCK	Leland Brewer	DRAKE	Robert Baum
GLORY	Viola Roth	BERTHA	Mary Hohenberger
MRS. FINCHWELL	Erna Roth	FEDERAL AGENT	Fred Birkicht
SYLVIA	Lucile Williamson		

Girls of the Junior Welfare League: Jane Garrett, Dorothy Timmerhoff,
Lucllea Mick, Jean Fischer.

Scene: The play takes place in a flop-house in a large middlewestern
city during the holiday season.

Scene 1.	Xmas Eve	Scene 5.	December 30
2.	Xmas Day	6.	New Year's Eve
3.	December 28	7.	One Hour Later
4.	December 29	8.	Five Hours Later

(12-Minute Intermission After Scene 4.)

In "Fugitive Kind" The Mummers of Saint Louis present the second play by their
own playwright, Thomas Lanier Williams. "Fugitive Kind" justifies The Mummers'
conviction that Mr. Williams has an important contribution to make to the American stage
in the field of realistic drama.

THE MUMMERS OF SAINT LOUIS
BOARD OF DIRECTORS

Wesley Gore, Genevieve Albers, Robert Bennett, Fred Birkicht, Leland Brewer,
Jean Fischer, Sam Halley, Jr., Albert Hohengarten, Amber Gleave, Ruth Moon, Miriam
Schwarz, Dorothy Timmerhoff, Walter Geary, Mary Hohenberger, Viola Perle.

TICKETS FOR INDIVIDUAL PRODUCTIONS—$1.00, 75c and 50c

SEASON DISCOUNT BOOK CONTAINING FOUR $1.00 TICKETS—$2.00

For information on ticket reservations, season membership, associate membership, active
membership, classes for non-members, write: The Mummers of Saint Louis, 4477 Olive St.

THE MUMMERS BRING TO ST. LOUIS
THE OUTSTANDING NEW YORK SUCCESS
MAXWELL ANDERSON'S
COMEDY

"HIGH TOR"
DRAMA CRITICS' 1937 PRIZE PLAY
WATCH FOR PRODUCTION IN JANUARY

46

47

48

TOP: Milton Lomask

TOP RIGHT: Professor E. C. Mabie,
University of Iowa

RIGHT: Truman Siltor

49

50

Tom on stage as one of Falstaff's soldiers in *Henry IV, Part I* at the
University of Iowa, in 1938

722 Toulouse, where
Tom waited on tables
in exchange for a bed

En route to Mexico
with Jim Parrott

D. H. and
Frieda Lawrence

PART III

Outer Space
1937–1939

---

*"They change their clime, not their
disposition, who run beyond the sea."*

12

Iowa

Fall 1937

When Tom arrived on the campus of the University of Iowa, he quickly learned that neither Wilbur Schramm, who was both a faculty member and the editor of *American Prefaces*, nor Edward Charles Mabie, head of the theatre department, was a likely candidate for "a colossal binge." Mabie's students and associates called him "the Boss." Within the university's theatre, he was seen as the counterpart of the old-time manager, the kind of all-powerful, omnipresent producer who is now all but extinct. He personified a *passionate* commitment to the American theatre. It was his belief that the only way a student could learn was to make that same commitment while working in all phases of a department that itself resembled the actual conditions found in the professional theatre. He eschewed separating the writing of plays from the active participation in their production.

Mabie became a faculty member in 1920, when he was twenty-seven years old, and in 1925 he was appointed head of the Department of Public Speaking. By 1937, Mabie's single-handed efforts had transformed a department of speech, noted for its debates, into a theatre department that had gained a national reputation. He also had a reputation for being a rigorous taskmaster, proper and disciplined in the same manner that he expected of his students.

The year before Tom arrived on campus, a true theatre plant had been opened, which had many unique facilities, including a revolving stage thirty-six feet in diameter. Even more extraordinary was Mabie's fierce dedication to the uncovering and nurturing of creative talent, especially that of the playwright. He was ultimately to win his fight for academic recognition by offering a degree in Experimental Dramatic Production. But his one driving interest was the discovery of new playwrights through active participation in the production of their and other original plays. Tom could not have hoped for anything more in keeping with his own ambitions. The problem was that the Boss was not only autocratic and prone to rages when encountering ineptness or radical departure; he was also an archconservative in his concept of theatre, if not in his politics.

When Tom entered the registrar's office, there was some question whether he would be admitted to the department. A student could elect, but Mabie was the one to select, and if there was a most unlikely recruit in Mabie's eyes, it was Thomas Lanier Williams. Alarmed and uncertain of what action to take, Tom wrote immediately to Willard Holland, telling him of his plight. A reassuring reply was dispatched in the mails on September 26:

> Dear Tom:
>   Just received your note. Will get manuscript off to-day. Will write Mabie later to-day special delivery and get [critic Colvin] McPherson to do the same. Hope everything gets there on time to do some good.
>   Willard[1]

In a subsequent letter to his mother, Tom airily dismissed the whole matter by saying that it was Holland who "apparently became very alarmed because he sent Prof. Mabie, head of the Dramatics Dept., a long telegram urging him to admit me and also got Colvin McPherson, dramatic crit. of the Post-Dispatch, to send a Special Delivery letter. All of which was quite unnecessary as the delay was purely routine and I was attending classes just the same. Holland even sent my new play up special delivery to show Mabie." He assured his mother that, although there had been a delay, his Missouri transcript had finally been sent to the registrar, and "I am fully registered."[2] What he neglected to tell her was that he had been admitted "on probation" because of his unsatisfactory scholarship at the University of Missouri. Apparently, he ignored this as a minor point, as he did his classification as a student but not a candidate for a degree at Washington University.

Tom's first lodgings were at 225 North Linn, and on his first day in Iowa City, he wrote home: "I am very well satisfied with this place. I get both board and room here." He said that the "excellent" meals cost twenty-one dollars a month and the room ten dollars in advance. He was also delighted with the city—"very much like Columbia," an opinion he would shortly reverse. The university campus he found "much larger and handsomer" than Ol' Mizzou. Finally, on a practical note, he added, "I find that on unpacking that I have left only two articles at home, my shaving brush and tooth brush."[3]

Leaving his home in St. Louis at this time in his life was not the rite of passage Tom had hoped for. In becoming Tennessee Williams, he would never become so much the free spirit he wanted to be, but, rather, always an exile in flight doomed to come full circle. His were more explorations into outer space, for there would be numerous occasions that lay ahead when he would be forced back into the dreaded confinement of his home, back into the family—no lasting escape, particularly from the hold his mother and his sister had upon him. The irony was that the very thing he abhorred most—the dread possessiveness of family and friends—*he* would arouse through his own need for them, creating conversely in himself a dependency that he hated. There was in his nature, in his manner and aspect, his slight build, a quality of vulnerability—a muted cry for help—that would both excite the maternal instinct and stir in others a natural desire to render assistance.

Not merely his dependency but *all else* that would be characteristic of him as man and artist was by now established. The contradictions and the paradoxical behavior that he saw in others he failed to see in himself, creating an ambivalence toward everyone: suspicions that gave rise to a sudden, antipodean swing between affection and disaffection. His reaction to any adversity, particularly criticism—or rather the failure on the part of others to affirm his work—became a paranoid resentment. His pains, both real and imagined, and his inability to understand the psychosomatic nature of his illnesses sent him in desperate search of addictive pharmaceutical remedies: pills and palliatives for a whole range of afflictions—most notably insomnia, irregular heartbeat, and a dread of suffocation—that incessantly tormented him.

For all that he suffered, there was solace in his obsessive need to set down his feelings and to transform experience and observation into story form—to communicate with the world outside. Exacerbated by his aloneness and his fear of enclosure, there sprang a desperate desire for an itinerant way of life, an escape from the specters of madness and death that haunted his thoughts and dreams. Fighting against what he called his "pathological shyness," he forced a boldness of behavior, an outward thrust that opened the way to making new friends and meeting those he thought might be influential in furthering his career. Almost all these conflicting feelings were hidden and kept private, and the fears they generated were released only in his writings:

Sat. Oct. 9—Been up here over two weeks—love the place but am disgustingly ill and nervous—have jolting sensations in heart and almost constant tension. I intend to avoid getting panicky about it.—I must keep my head on my shoulders—but it is not very pleasant. Do other people have lives like this? Yes—some do—and endure it. . . . I think of Rose [in] wonder and pity—but it is such a far away feeling—how bound up we are in ourselves—our own miseries. Why can't we forget and think of others? It is in the nature of the beast!

He mentioned having received an "encouraging and enthusiastic letter" from Willard Holland about *Fugitive Kind*. Writing to his mother, he said that Holland had "read it to the Mummers and received 'God! What a reaction!' It seems they are very enthusiastic about it and are going to give it all they've got—he is planning to run a feature article about me and the play pretty soon in one of the papers and wants me to have a picture taken."[4] At the same time, he got off a letter to Holland, giving a new address at 3255 South Dubuque, regarding it as a better location at the same price:

Dear Willard: Your letter with the encouraging news about the reading arrived at a perfect psychological moment as I was feeling quite low, due to the fact that it is raining here and rain is definitely unbecoming to Iowa City. I can't understand how any town could be so dry in one sense of the word and so interminably wet in the other. Last night myself and some confederates toured the town in search of a whiskey label (one of those treasure hunts) and found nothing more exciting than Goetz Country Club Beer. When you feel like drinking up here you are supposed to make "needle beer"—which is near-beer spiked with alcohol, the very description of which is enough to turn anyone's stomach. So I am learning how to spend sober week-ends if nothing else in this region of the blessed. . . .

In this boarding-house there is a young Jew who has spent several summers on the bum and he has given me a lot of information about the characteristics of transients. He has slept in flophouses, jails, jungles, been deported, Etc., and so provides excellent material of the sort I am interested in [for *Fugitive Kind*]. . . .

I am having a play presented in the "laboratory theater" next Thursday. . . . These dramatizations are written in competition by the playwriting class. The three best are selected each two weeks and produced in what is called "a living newspaper." . . . Assignments keep me so busy I hardly have time for independent work. However I am still planning to write the "Van Gogh" for which I have chosen the title "The Holy Family" suggested by an anecdote from his life. He took a prostitute to live with him who soon gave birth to an illeg. child by another man. V.G.'s friend, Gauguin, tried to persuade him to leave the woman but V.G. remained devoted to her. In disgust, as he left, the friend exclaimed, "Ah! The Holy Family—maniac, prostitute and bastard!" Does that sound too profane? I think the real story of the relationship is rather beautiful and would make good dramatic material. But at the same time I am going ahead with "April Is The Cruelest Month" [*Spring Storm*] which stage facilities here would make possible and am also planning—if others are discarded—the study of an ordinary middle-class family in a city apartment, supposed to show the tragedy of bourgeois stagnation. . . .

I have had a short-story ["The Red Part of a Flag," later renamed "Oriflamme"] tentatively (almost positively) accepted by AMERICAN PREFACES, published here, which O'Brien (short story anthologist) rates as one of the three best literary publications in the country. The editor happens to be my professor in an English course.

This is all very diffuse and windy but I hope it makes sense—a football game is being broadcast in the next room.

Good luck—

Tom[5]

As it turned out, the "living newspaper" dramatization would be enlarged the following year into a full-length play about a prison scandal—which Tom would call *Not About Nightingales*—while the tragedy of middle-class stagnation would remain in gestation until its emergence a few years later as *The Glass Menagerie*. It would appear that Tom also told his intention to others on campus, because, long after, there were those who were sure that Tennessee Williams had started writing *Menagerie* at Iowa. In truth, he was still living his way into it.

Those Flames, Tinder-Quick

Although Tom made friends at Iowa, the only close confederate he had was a thirty-four-year-old graduate assistant to Professor Mabie, Marian Gallaway, who in 1935 had been director of a community theatre in Cedar Rapids. Tennessee later remembered Marian as "one of those persons who lived and breathed theatre and somehow managed to infect her associates with her own religious excitement about it."[6] Gallaway, like her boss, had a conventional view of what constituted good playwriting, namely the well-made play, subscribing to the German school of Lessing; she always insisted that a play must reach a climax, even though she was chided by some who called it a Freudian viewpoint.

With the Mummers' production of *Fugitive Kind* finally set for later in the fall, Marian offered to work with Tom on sorely needed revisions. Although in her opinion the play was poorly plotted, she, like Holland, saw real strength in its dialogue and characterizations. She may not have been aware that Tom's was potentially a new voice in the theatre, but she did have faith in him. And, more than that, she genuinely liked him. As she recalled, "Tom was as self-conscious about his writing as a duck is swimming on water. He was neither apologetic nor aggressive about his talents. He wrote only what he wanted to write, whatever the assignment may have been. He did not worry at all, to my knowledge, about Mr. Mabie's impression of him, nor about anybody else's."[7]

It *can* be said that E. C. Mabie's impression of Thomas Lanier Williams was, in fact, less than favorable. A classmate and later a producer, Norman Felton, remembered that Tom was once assigned a "living newspaper" play on the topic of "socialized medicine." When Tom turned in his play, Felton said, "it was as if a volcano had erupted. You see, 'the Boss' had many friends among doctors of medicine at the University. The next day I heard that he had torn up Tom's script, and I asked a young lady in the office if that was true. Her answer was to close the door and whisper to me to shut up and not to ask again."[8] If Tom knew this, he made no reference to it.*

He did speak, though, of his friendship with Thomas Pawley, his one black classmate, in whose play *Ku Klux* Tom was enacting, because of his southern accent, the role of a Negro chairman of a church convention. He told Willard Holland that Pawley exhibited real talent. Pawley recalled Tom Williams as shy, reticent, taciturn, and unkempt; because he didn't attend classes frequently enough, he got poor grades. "Once I arrived in Iowa City," Pawley said, "I quickly discovered there was absolutely no social contact between blacks and whites. The town and the University were segregated: I could not eat in the restaurants or the Student Union, and I was told I could not stay in the dormitory." But Tom, he said, "was always cordial to me. I was genuinely surprised at his apparent sympathy for Negroes." Pawley, who went on to become a distinguished professor at Lincoln University, added however that, had he known Tom was a native Mississippian and not simply from St. Louis, he would not have been so friendly, as Mississippi had "an unsavory reputation."[9]

In the academic year of 1937–1938, nineteen plays were given completely mounted productions at Iowa, and in addition there were many others staged experimentally. If Tom thought he would be enjoying an artist-in-residence status, such as he had had with the Mummers, he was mistaken: That was not what E. C. Mabie considered proper training for an aspiring playwright. Tom soon found himself employed in every phase of production, and it was expected that he would be punctual and would carry out his assignments.

But he was beginning to repeat once again the same pattern of ignoring— as he had the previous year at Washington University—anything that might distract him from writing. One of his courses was in stagecraft, which meant building, painting, and hanging a show: the nitty-gritty of carpentry, paint buckets, and carrying lights up a mile-high A-ladder. His instructor, Arnold Gillette, a noted designer, assigned him to a crew that was building the sets designed by Gillette for the production of a Katharine Dayton–George S. Kaufman play, *First Lady*, to be directed by Mabie. Gillette's one and only memory of Tom was that "he was a God-awful student."[10] Marian Gallaway, who worked on costumes and makeup for the production, commented that, as a crew member, her friend "excelled in goofing-off."

This was the first time Tom was to witness Mabie directing one of the season's major plays, and apparently in the heat of production he picked up an

---

*On one occasion, Williams submitted a script to the "living newspaper" based on Robert Browning's "The Last Duchess," the source of which had hardly been wrested from the day's headlines. Although never published or produced, Williams named this intended play *Balcony at Ferrara* and as late as 1978 was still carting it around from one location to another in his script bag.

unfounded rumor and promptly reported it to his mother: "Prof. Mabie, head of the dramatics department, is a brilliant man but slightly unbalanced at times. He has been confined occasionally in the university's psychopathic ward—he has terrible tantrums. On one occasion, when he attended the final dress rehearsal of a play, it displeased him and he threw his glasses at one of the actors: kept them rehearsing from eight o'clock that night till noon the next day and made the author re-write the last act of the play."[11]

Another rumor had it that Mabie was suffering from an inoperable brain tumor. Mabie's daughter, P. A. M. Stewart, characterized this as "absolute, unmitigated nonsense!"[12] Mabie was a man of intense intellectual interests and emotional opinions; he had a keen feeling for the social issues of the times; and he was an eager participant in reforms, especially those affecting the theatre. Until 1935, he had been the Midwest regional director of the WPA-sponsored Federal Theatre Project and was in 1937 the first president of the American Educational Theatre Association. In his view, plays with political significance were what mattered; those that delved into human character to the depth that interested Tom were in Mabie's opinion more tracts for the medical than the theatrical profession. Also, there was the problem of Tom personally; he was living proof that one need not know a Fresnel from a Leko to write a great play; even after he became Tennessee Williams, Mabie stubbornly refused to produce any of his plays.

His prejudice was directed against both the plays and the playwright. Homosexuality was in his eyes a despicable perversion, and he referred to Tom Williams as "that pansy." Although at Iowa Tom still had not accepted the meaning of his feelings, there were among the theatre's older, more experienced and sophisticated members those who could recognize the telltale signs. Given the sexual mores of 1937 and his devoutly Christian background, Tom simply was unable to reconcile an inclination with what he knew to be wrong, a sin, and utterly unacceptable.

Mabie was well aware, painfully no doubt, that the theatre attracted "that kind," and for him, this only compounded the anathema. An incident that his daughter later recalled took place during the spring term in the greenroom of the university theatre. "Tom was on the couch lying on his stomach, avoiding contact between his sunburned back and the furniture. He was in a t-shirt and complained of the itch from the burn. I was sitting on the broad arm of the couch, so I idly started scratching him between the shoulders." Mabie suddenly came down the stairs from his office and roared at his daughter to leave the greenroom. "He couldn't have been more vocal about my avoiding contact with Tom Williams."[13]

After Edwina had insisted that Tom copyright *Candles to the Sun*, he placed it with an editor/agent, Olga Becker, in New York. She had been circulating the play among Broadway producers and wrote to him on September 22 what was a compendium of maddening generalities:

She said that she had submitted *Candles* to a producer who would be interested in the play provided that Tom revised it to speed up the first act, eliminate the propaganda, and contrive some better curtain lines, and also make it less like *Tobacco Road*. Miss Becker added that she didn't really concur with this latter point.

She had given the play to Edward Sargent Brown, who as a favor agreed to read it free of charge, although he usually received $50 to critique plays. She said, "He conducts a course in playwriting and I believe he is very good." However, she warned that he was rather less supportive than others had been thus far, but she did feel Tom could benefit from Brown's feedback that the play lacked a central character, the first act was flat and would not arouse audience interest, and the overall structure was weak.

Mr. Brown was of the opinion, though, that the play was "not beyond repair" and suggested that if it were rewritten it might be something for the WPA theatre. Becker said that, while she knew Tom was aware of these faults and she was returning his manuscript, she would be happy to show the producer she had mentioned, as well as others, the revised version and would enter it in the WPA contest. He would not give up the right to a professional Broadway production by applying to the WPA except that, should it be sold beforehand, the WPA would not then produce the play. She concluded by saying that the deadline for the contest was October 31 and that she hoped her letter wasn't too discouraging.[14]

As if this was not enough, Miss Becker also enclosed a critique that ran to seven legal-sized pages. Working under the WPA program was one of Tom's aims, and though by the time he received Becker's letter it was apparently too late to meet the October 31 deadline, he was aware that Mabie had been active in the Federal Theatre and doubtless had contacts.

Concurrent with Mabie's production of *First Lady*, Tom was also put to work on an experimental play called *Dude Ranch Mystery*. This time, he was not only a member of the building crew but was also designated assistant stage manager. This might have been enough to cause the stage manager to abandon his chosen profession, except that the production was slated to go up on November 27 and December 14, a time when Tom was also expected to be in St. Louis for the premiere of *Fugitive Kind*.

Of course, Edwina, preoccupied with settling into her new home on Aberdeen Place, was elated at the prospect of Tom's play being presented during the holidays, and as always she was making her regular reports to her parents: "Yesterday, Dakin drove me over to see Rose and she seemed about the same in mind. The insulin is making her so fat that I'm distressed to see her. The doctor says it gives them a tremendous appetite. He has now given her thirty of the forty treatments she is supposed to have. It will take two more months and then they will let her rest from them for a while. He didn't seem to think she was showing enough improvement though he said she was some better." Edwina added a note of optimism, however: "I'm glad that Rose is in good spirits, still, even though she has to wear 'night-gowns of unbleached domestic' they have given her, and she showed me the cotton stockings remarking, 'They don't look so bad!' She asked about you both." Concerning Dakin at school, she said that he was "much pleased with himself in his uniform as he joined the R.O.T.C. He does look good in it. Cornelius bought him a handsome tweed suit . . . as compensation for not getting in fraternity and has told him he can 'go away' to college next year."[15]

With both Rose and Tom out of the house and neither of them an expense, Cornelius now had his home, his younger son, and, to some extent, his wife the way he wanted them. Dakin had damaged Cornelius's car in an accident, but C.C. took it in stride and bought a new Buick. Describing his good mood, Edwina mentioned that he had been vacationing in Knoxville and had been "entertained every minute of his stay." All of this was duly reported to Tom, and, as usual, his replies, like her letters, were calculated to present the sunnier side of his life:

> Dear Mother: I only have time for a few lines before supper. I got your letter this morning and was pleased to hear the encouraging news about Rose. Does the Doctor also feel that she has improved? . . .
>
> I had a short play presented very successfully last week and another one will be put on next week, a satire on Hollywood producers. They are giving it the best director and a cast consisting of the university's best players and so I think it will turn out fine. It is about an ignorant Jewish movie producer revising a great classic for the movies. American Prefaces are still holding my short story. The editor says it is "going the rounds" which means I suppose that every one in the English faculty is passing judgement on it. They have also asked to see some of my short plays.[16]

By the end of the month, he was again writing his mother and telling her that, under pressure from his fraternity brothers, he had moved into the ATO house and was delighted with it: "Grand piano and radio-victrola, beautifully furnished. I have a study and a bed in the dormitory both very comfortable and the first decent meals since leaving home."[17]

At the same time, however, he was telling quite a different story in his journal. He confessed that he was

> Home-sick! Yes, I really am. Most of all I miss little "Jiggs." It is strange how deeply I love that little animal. Mother's last letter said Rose was "reasonable" on last visit. I have been neglecting my school work and done not a lick of good new writing—all because of this awful sick, neurotic condition. . . . I must admit that I have felt very beast-like lately, and if things turn out well for me it will be better than I deserve. My virtues—I am kind, friendly, modest, sympathetic, tolerant and sensitive. Faults—I am ego-centric, introspective, morbid, sensual, irreligious,

lazy, timid, cowardly. But if I were God I would feel a little bit sorry for Tom Williams once in a while—he doesn't have a very ~~gay~~ easy time of it and he does have guts of a sort even though he is a stinking sissy!

Sat. Notes from John Keats letters—"Is there another life? Shall I awake and find all this a dream? There must be, *we cannot be created for this sort of suffering!* . . . I wish for death every day and night to deliver me from these pains and then I wish death away, for death would destroy even those pains which are better than nothing."

Keats, did God pity and love you as much as I? You will be always remembered. I will be forgotten. If only we could stretch out our hands across these dark spaces of death and time—clasp hands and walk into the dark together. Why must our deaths be so separate—so lonely? I am not *one*—now I am you and all the others—I have broken the walls of self—I have become a part of you all—lost myself in you—no, I am not afraid now! . . . The dark has no peril that love and courage cannot face when friends walk together!

Despite his fears and self-doubt and the pain born of his tensions, Tom persisted in his writing. Plays, stories, and poems were written with amazing profusion, and there were those, such as Wilbur Schramm and others on campus, who were aware of his talent. Tom wrote that Schramm had "almost definitely accepted" his story "The Red Part of a Flag," which he felt was his "best piece of writing." He made the entreaty, "If only I could go on and write more things like that! I could if only I could go on!!"

He admitted that he was becoming morbid. "I've got to get up and laugh some more. Laughter is my only escape these days. I have never laughed or jested so much in my life—and never been more miserable!" Years later, he would say that his laughter was only a substitute for weeping. Ruth Holwill Morgan, a student who knew him at Iowa, said that what drew her attention to Tom Williams was his "obnoxious laugh"—more like a bray. But on reading one of his short stories, she remembered it to be sensitively written. Long after, when she had occasion to read the short stories of Tennessee Williams, it was their sensitivity that made her realize that Tom and Tennessee were one and the same person.

In St. Louis, Tom's poetry was being published regularly in *The Eliot*. The university magazine's managing editor, John Pickering, was one of those, like Clark Mills, who recognized early on Tom's poetic gift, and he was to observe years later that memory and loss and thwarted desire were the main themes of that early poetry, presaging their use in the great plays that were still to be written. Now, they spoke from the torment of a young, bridled talent.

Odyssey

It seemed infinity to him
With eagles crying in the dawn.
Importunately then he dreamed
Of lands forever leading on!

A boundless continent was this
The early morning of the mind—
But evening heard a serpent hiss
Or moth wings fluttering the blind.

And presently the pilgrim turned
Exhausted toward the nearest gate
And as a final lesson learned
That even Death could make him wait![18]

The poems themselves were conventional in form: sonnets, ballads, songs, odes—mostly iambic and rhymed. Although, at the time, Tom would have liked to have been considered a poet in the sense that his friend Clark Mills was—the solitary poet, that most heroic of literary figures—he was beset now with an equally strong, divisive pull toward becoming a playwright. Clark was his ideal, and it would have astonished Tom to know that Mills, too, was beset with doubts and apprehensions. During his recent trip to New York, Clark had suffered dire premonitions of some terrible disaster awaiting him, and when that failed to happen, he became certain that the freighter he was taking to France would sink mid-Atlantic.

In a letter written to Tom before he sailed, Clark said that he had been to Boston briefly, where he "had lunch with some of the less Olympian editors of *The Atlantic*, who seemed to me to be very ordinary people, such as yourself and myself. It is clear to me now how necessary it is to know the people of influence in the east to get anywhere writing these days." He also found New York City "more disturbing than I had expected it to be, and it is absolutely impossible for me to get any work done." But he confessed that he was "most delighted with the subways!" Along with his letter, Clark enclosed the program of a French film he had just seen, Jean Renoir's *The Lower Depths*, saying that he thought it paralleled Tom's *Fugitive Kind* "to an amazing degree. The locale is different, but as you can see from the resumé, the characters are rather similar, and the atmosphere and dialogue are almost identical. It seems that you and Gorki see things in much the same light!"[19]

Across the Space

Rehearsals were now under way in St. Louis for a November 30 opening of *Fugitive Kind*, and Tom told his mother that Willard Holland had sent him names of the cast among whom were his best players. He said that a friend of Holland's in Hollywood who worked for Paramount studios had read the play and wanted a copy. But he said he did not want anybody to have it till it had been copyrighted.

His journal, as usual, saw the gloomier side of his life: "Iowa City is really a very unattractive place—no charm of atmosphere like Columbia, Mo., or southern towns. I am dull and weary tonight . . . I am lonely and bored. Among interesting people and in a pleasanter atmosphere I would soon forget my sickness and get well. Why not be a man and throw it off anyway?" He punctuated this with an underscored *"En avant!!"*

From then on, *En avant!* ("Forward march!") became a signature that Tom would use repeatedly for most of his life as a challenge to himself. Apparently on this occasion, he did press forward, for with this entry in his journal he made no further record of his feelings for nearly six months. Later, in 1940, he made a marginal comment: "Sometime during this interval the course of my life subtly but definitely changed. I began to integrate more firmly—to grow more independent, detached, balanced, sophisticated. A deep physical love affair with a girl and freedom from home were important factors."

When finally, in the spring, he resumed writing in his journal, he reflected upon what apparently had been an ephemeral attachment. "I did have a passionate physical love affair for a few months (last winter)—it ended very badly. I was thrown over by the beloved bitch—but the experience was valuable." It would be his last such experience with the opposite sex, and although he wanted and tried to effect a reconciliation with the girl, she wasn't interested. Her name was Bette Reitz, and, according to her roommate, Jean Fitzpatrick, she aspired to a career in the theatre, mainly as an actress. At the time Tom met her, Bette was working on props for *Dude Ranch Mystery* and he, who was supposed to be an assistant stage manager, was preoccupied instead with both Bette and the revisions to *Fugitive Kind*, which Marian Gallaway still found "too talky."

He was doing poorly in school and knew it. Mindful of the sacrifice his grandparents had made, he painted as reassuring a picture for his grandfather as possible:

Last night I heard the famous English novelist, J. B. Priestly [*sic*] give a lecture. Two weeks ago we had Stephen Vincent Benet, a famous poet. The cultural opportunities here are remarkable for a mid-western school. They even have a fine free symphony orchestra. Also a radio broadcasting station—even television! Almost every evening there is an interesting public lecture, debate or round-table discussion in the Student Memorial

Union—which is a beautiful recreation hall containing a library, magazine room, cafeteria, dance hall, lounge and auditorium—furnished like an expensive hotel!

From my two windows I now have a beautiful view of snow-covered hills and woods and a frozen river and am receiving over my room-mate's radio a broadcast of classical music from the University studio. But unfortunately I have to put on my boots for another trip to the campus.[20]

At about the same time, Tom dispatched a letter to Willard Holland in which he said he was "highly satisfied with the cast" of *Fugitive Kind* and added, "I will probably get down for the Saturday performance. I don't envy you these early rehearsals—they must be ghastly things." "Ghastly" applied more to his own ineffectiveness as a member of a stage crew, and although his department head took a decidedly different view, Tom boasted that he was learning much about the theatre technically. "Believe it or not, I can actually build flats and put up sets. Next term I will learn all about lighting.

"But," he added, "the life here has many unpleasant aspects. For one thing my father is not contributing one cent to my support as he disapproves of all my activities—my grandparents send me thirty a month which is scarcely adequate for the barest living expenses. I get a bed in the frat. dormitory and breakfast and lunch in the fraternity house at reduced rates by coaching the Freshmen in their English and make a small commission selling tickets to the University theater—but have gone to bed numerous nights without supper." He said that such an austere existence was probably excellent for the soul, but should some New York producer offer him a fat check for *Fugitive Kind*, it would find him in a most receptive frame of mind. "Anyway you see I have some reason for disagreeing with Pangloss about this being 'the best of all possible worlds.' "

He also told Holland, "I'm having another short play, 'The Family Pew' produced this afternoon. The others were 'Quit Eating' on the prison hunger strike, 'The Big Scene' satire on Hollywood and a fourth one 'So Glad!' which will be produced later. Each two weeks three plays are chosen from the class for production. Despite the short-time for rehearsals, the performances are usually letter-perfect." His principal effort at the moment, however, was focused on writing one of three full-length plays to be completed by the end of the term, *The Holy Family*, his play about Vincent van Gogh. He told Holland that he had on his desk five volumes of van Gogh biographies and letters but that he had written very little dialogue thus far. "Perhaps that is better because usually I plunge into dialogue before I have even formulated a plot which leads to a great deal of re-writing and confusion." His main problem, though, was that there was just

too much dramatic material. It is hard to make a selection. Van Gogh was a great social thinker and artist—had a tremendous love for humanity and believed in the community of artists—he painted common people at work and tried to establish an art colony in southern France—but he was constantly misunderstood and persecuted—crowds gathered outside his window, shouting "Fouroux"—"The red-headed madman"—that suggests a main theme—a man with a great love for humanity whom humanity rejected—he formed many disappointing relationships—his brother Theo was his only supporter—his work did not have any success till after his suicide in a fit of insanity.

The Holy Family was intended to be the story of "an artist's relations to society—not one artist but all."[21] Tom never completed the play, but within it he discovered a theme that became an undercurrent in many of his finest writings.

Marian Gallaway offered to drive Tom to St. Louis in time to make the December 4 performance of *Fugitive Kind*. A news item heralded Tom's arrival:

MUMMERS TO GIVE PARTY FOR PLAYWRIGHT

Invitations have been issued by The Mummers of St. Louis for a reception late Saturday evening, Dec. 4, at The Mummers' Studio, to meet Thomas Lanier Williams, author of "Fugitive Kind," which will be presented that evening at the Wednesday Club.

"Fugitive Kind" is the second play of the St. Louisan to be given its premiere production by The Mummers. Mr. Williams, son of Mr. and Mrs. Cornelius Williams, is studying at Iowa State University but will come to St. Louis for the reception.

Willard Holland's belief, probably more of an instinctive faith, in his young playwright friend was set forth in the house program for the play: "In 'Fugitive Kind' The Mummers of Saint Louis present the second play by their own playwright, Thomas Lanier Williams. 'Fugitive Kind' justifies The Mummers' conviction that Mr. Williams has an important contribution to make to the American stage in the field of realistic drama."

Looking back on his production during an interview years later, Holland remarked:

To me "Fugitive Kind" was one of the best things ever written by Tom . . . [but] it was a flop in the sense that the plot structure was too phony and along too melodramatic lines. . . . All the revisions of "Fugitive" were carried on by mail because Tom was at Iowa. Tom to me was like a typewriter that never stopped writing. All I could see were pages and pages flying out of a typewriter, piling up on the floor and into cor-

ners. We literally pasted "Fugitive" together. We would read a page of
dialogue between two players and decide that two-thirds of it would play
better in an earlier scene, scissor the stuff we liked and then pasted it into
a scrapbook until we got the whole thing the way we wanted it.[22]

As the play finally evolved, some twenty-five characters were in eight
scenes set in the "lobby of a flophouse in a large middle-western city, the
action taking place between Christmas eve and New Years eve." There was
never any question that the city was St. Louis, its blemishes in full view: the
ugly sores of poverty and crime opened, to the chagrin of the city's more comfortable West-end citizens, like Cornelius C. Williams. Tom was adding his
protest to the clamor of many 1930s intellectuals, saying that society's evils,
carefully disguised behind the cosmetics of hypocrisy, were being maintained
by capitalist greed. This was the hue and cry of the Mummers, as it was the
manifesto of the Group Theatre in New York, and in Williams's second play
its central weakness. Clifford Odets was at that time the theatre's radical
voice, while in *Fugitive Kind*, Tom's voice was a distant echo.

Time and again during his life, Tennessee Williams was accused of being
insensitively apolitical, though repeatedly, in one form or another, he made it
very clear that he was acutely mindful of what was happening in the world
outside the theatre. But his was the poet's view of the hapless creatures of God
and country: To him, that was social comment enough.

The first review written December 1, which Tom saw before leaving Iowa
City, was by Colvin McPherson, drama critic of the *St. Louis Post-Dispatch*. In
September, he had written to E. C. Mabie in praise of the aspiring playwright.
But now it was November, time to review a new play, and McPherson wrote
that, although *Fugitive Kind* "describes vividly the life in a big city 'flop-
house,' " there is "no plot arising out of its situation and all considered, is a
weak play." McPherson concluded his short review by saying, "Even with the
best of acting, 'Fugitive Kind' would still be somewhat amateurish and the
performance is spotty. Some extraordinary credit should go to the Mummers,
however, for giving a local playwright his forum and for attempting to present
the life close at hand in the theater." Tom was stung, as he always would be,
by negative criticism. The implication that he was still an amateur at his craft
was enough to send him into a rage.

On December 1, Anne Jennings, a more perceptive critic, pointed out
that "Thomas Williams is not only a playwright, but a poet of exceptional
merit as well." On the same date, Reed Hynds, critic for the *Star-Times*,
was also more charitable in his assessment: "That Thomas Lanier Williams
is a playwright to watch was demonstrated again by the Mummers last
night when that dramatic group produced his new play, 'Fugitive Kind.'
While less intense than his 'Candles to the Sun,' [it is] a consistent, vital
and absorbing play to the audience . . . and one marking a step forward for

the young St. Louisan." Hynds compared Williams to dramatists Sidney Howard, Ben Hecht, and Maxwell Anderson but qualified his accolade by pointing out that "Williams shares some of the faults as well as some of the virtues of the lions of the day . . . he wants to say something forceful and true about the chaos of modern life. But, like them, he seems clearer about the way to say it than what to say. His play has theatrical substance, but its thought is confused."

Tom immediately drafted a letter to Hynds, but, apparently in his haste to leave for St. Louis, he failed to mail it.

> The reviews of my new play just arrived and your sympathetic criticism is all that prevents me from changing my mind and not driving down for the Saturday performance. Had I read only Mr. McPherson's [review], I would hardly venture within shooting distance of my home town. I don't need to say that I'm extremely grateful for your more generous estimate of the play. . . . I have read enough of your literary criticism to place a special value on your appraisals.[23]

Once Tom arrived in St. Louis—after what he remembered as a wild, non-stop, overnight ride with Marian Gallaway at the wheel—the December 4 performance confirmed his worst apprehensions. Tom's not being at rehearsals to work closely with the director, as he had on *Candles to the Sun*, placed the full burden on Holland. The play that emerged in performance proved in many ways to be more of a surprise to Tom than to anyone else. He was witnessing the alchemy of a group of artists and artisans transforming the written page into a form of life itself, much of it a marvel and much simply tangential and disorganized. Clearly this was not the play *he* had envisioned. As Williams was to learn, the transcription of written word from script to stage—the literal act of putting a play on its feet—demands the presence of the originator as much as it does the interpreter.

The holidays were dispiriting, in part because of Tom's reaction to *Fugitive Kind*, even more because this would be a Christmas spent with Rose miles away, shut within an institution that she would not be leaving for many years to come. The family made the trip to see her, and Edwina told her parents, "When we took Rose's Christmas box to her, we saw Dr. Hoctor and he seemed much more optimistic about her recovery. For the first time she told us she wanted to come home. She also asked to see Cornelius and made a big fuss over him which pleased him and made him think she was 'about well.' "[24] However, a summary made by Dr. C. C. Ault on December 16 told quite a different story: "There has been very little change in this patient. She received a course of insulin shock therapy and is now considered to have had a mere remission. She is not as bizarre and more cooperative, but still thinks she is filthy, remains to herself and frequently becomes overtalkative. Delusions are still very prominent."

Dr. Ault also reported that "considerable information has been gained from conversation with the mother and other relatives. It appears that [Rose's] father has been eccentric most of his life, but never to the point of mental derangement." Significantly, the report made no reference to a matter of speculation, whether Cornelius had ever made a sexual overture toward Rose, nor was there any record of her accusing him of such an act. He had always, in fact, been coldly distant and withheld the affection she craved. Any of the normal hugging or kissing between father and daughter would have embarrassed him, as it would have been discouraged by Edwina, who held such rigid attitudes toward sex. Moreover, she would have instantly separated from Cornelius had he ever approached her daughter.

The report continued: "Mother appeared of fairly good intellect and normal in talk and actions. Maternal grandmother has appeared overtalkative and somewhat eccentric." Ault went on to say that Rose's first manifestations of mental illness were her delusions of sexual immorality within the family, thoughts that she had on one occasion expressed before guests in her home. Since that time, for the past seven or eight years, the doctor reported, "Symptoms have been continuous with periods of exacerbations . . . great excitement and confusion, and somatic delusions consisting of gastric distress chiefly."

In the main, Dr. Ault was of the opinion that the information Rose gave was both meager and not very reliable. "She stated that her father was 50 years of age and her mother was also living, age not stated, but that both of her parents had lost their minds," and, in fact, that "all of the family were mentally deranged." More than that, he said, "She later insisted that her mother also had illegitimate children—thinks her stomach trouble is caused by her family's dissipation. She thinks a doctor has the family under his influence, that her family are impaired because they had children before they married. Thought her grandmother tried to poison her at one time, but only through a doctor's efforts." At present, Ault reported, "Rose is generally cooperative, complaining mainly about her stomach trouble and tending to be reclusive. She believes that her doctor is related to her and that everyone in her ward are her relatives." He concluded that her mental deterioration was of a functional type and that "the prognosis for a full remission is very poor."[25]

Clearly, Rose still had her "ideas," according to Edwina. She in fact suspected that Dr. Hoctor's optimism was more Christmas greeting than the truth about Rose's condition. But in her letter to her parents, she decided to impart nothing but family news: Dakin was ill, though recovering; Cornelius would be away during the New Year's week; she had an infected finger that had to be lanced and "left me awake two nights"; and Cornelius's best friend, Warren Hatcher, and his wife had invited the whole family to Christmas dinner. She also said that they had seen "little of Tom as he was in the attic at his type-writer all day and out every evening."[26]

Hazel and her husband, Terry, were in St. Louis for the holidays, and Tom must certainly have thought about her in relation to Bette Reitz, whom he believed was waiting for him in Iowa. His feelings concerning the failure of *Fugitive Kind* to meet his expectations were revealed in a letter that he started to Willard Holland, a fragment he was writing more to hear himself think. Acknowledging that the play was perhaps "too hastily written," he complained that "the whole burden was thrown on *me*—on the *lines*—in the latter half." He asserted that the atmospheric buildup he had specified was lacking and that "the lighting was all wrong—there was no large window to bring the city and snow onto stage. What became of the Cathedral-like effect we had agreed upon? The neon sign? and the lines—they were rushed and jazzed and moaned—"[27] He stopped there and doubtless on second thought decided not to lay this added stress on his friend. Holland didn't need to be reminded of what the antidote of money could have cured. Tom ended his complaint in midsentence, probably recognizing that the fault was as much his as Holland's.

The new year was at hand—Tom had another play, *Spring Storm*, he hoped the Mummers would undertake in their 1938 season—and, more than that, he was not about to say anything that would alter Holland's belief in him. His reaction would become typical of Tennessee Williams, who to the end would cry out at the injustice of his failures, then pick himself up, brush off his hurt and indignation, and start all over again.

I3

The Island of My Self

January–December 1938

Edwina headed a letter to her parents "Jan. 1st. 1938!" and then went on to say, "Tom is having friends in for Egg-nog this after-noon, so I haven't time to write more. He returns to Iowa tomorrow. . . . Hope we will all have a happier New Year!"[1] The next day Tom wrote to his grandparents from a hotel in La Salle, Illinois: "I drove up here with Hazel and Terry on their way back to Madison—it is just a short distance from Iowa City, so I am saving a good deal on train fare." He told them that he had had "a very happy and pleasant time" during the holidays. "We went out to see Rose and I thought her surprisingly well—her manner was more animated and friendly than any time before."[2]

During the return trip with Hazel and Terry, Tom could feel he was not any longer the third person, but had a girl of his own to look forward to. Bette would disappoint him, however. At first, she refused to see him, since she was dating someone else. Looking back on his and Bette's affair, Tennessee wrote in *Memoirs* that, while it may have been short-lived, the romance was "a very deep one we'd had and I think that she had loved me as long as I'd satisfied her but now she was with a real stud and she was letting me out."[3] He described her as having an Etruscan profile and as being sexually attractive, with beautiful breasts and a terrific build. In his disappointment, Tom tried to date other girls, but somehow he wasn't able to impress them enough. Later, when he resumed writing in his journal, he asked himself, "Why do women ignore me so consistently these days? Sometimes they look at me as though I weren't there. I believe it's because I am so damned short, and then I'm too lazy to be interesting when I'm out among people I don't know well. And when they ignore me it hurts my feelings—a vicious circle."

An even more vicious circle, as he would subsequently come to recognize, was his deeper preoccupation with self: self-fascination and self-torment, the self-imprisonment that his work demanded. In time, that circle turned into a vortex, drawing him into its center and, along with him, those closest to him, those whom he loved and who would love him. Many, though, like Bette Reitz, understood what the personal cost to them would be and shunned his importuning. They simply realized that he would never be free from the bondage of his work.

Bette was a girl somewhat ahead of her time. As her roommate, Jean Fitzpatrick, and others remembered her, she knew her way around. If she didn't recognize Tom as gay, she knew that he was sexually inadequate to meet her desires and that she had to lead him into the act itself. In *Memoirs*, he threw the weight of his inadequacy against what he saw then as her promiscuity, but which by present-day standards of free love would be largely overlooked. In the months to come at Iowa, Tom would continue to pursue Bette for the illusion she was.

He, of course, found her rejection painful. But the disapproval of his work was far more unbearable, particularly when issued by such a respected source as critic Colvin McPherson. A letter Tom drafted, but apparently never posted, to McPherson attempted to rationalize his feelings about what he saw as the failure of *Fugitive Kind*. In some respects, it was more self-consolation than a defense:

> While temporarily painful, criticism of this sort proves of particular benefit to a writer in the long run, especially when his aim is toward technical improvement that may eventually enable him to say things he thinks worth saying rather than toward the enjoyment of a present success. Of

course present success has its advantages: it removes some of the formidable odds that stand against an inexperienced writer. But if a writer goes on despite these odds and manages to survive without the luxury of a quick success—if he recognizes his failures and has an ideal of perfection—then the ultimate outcome in his case may be better for those initial discouragements. If he does not do so—then the loss is not significant to anyone concerned.

As for the play itself, he admitted—as he had to Holland—that it had been "hastily done." Looking forward to the next Mummers production and, he hoped, to a better review, he ended his letter, saying, "Your sympathy has been too evident in the past for me to doubt its continuance. In my new work I shall be trying particularly to meet your exact standards and I'm sure it will be better on that account."[4]

For the moment, though, Tom's concentration was not on his new play but on cramming for the end-of-term exams. When he received his first-semester grades, he wrote to both his mother and his grandparents letters that were more fiction than fact. To his mother, Tom said, "It is quite a relief to be through finals and starting a new term. I got an A, two B's and two C's." That was the fiction; the fact was that his highest grades were B's in Mabie's course and in a Shakespeare course taught by Baldwin Maxwell, and the lowest, an F in Arnold Gillette's Stage and Technical Practice. In fact, his grade point average for the first semester was an unremarkable 2.0. To his unsuspecting grandparents, he compounded the fiction by saying, "The A was in Experimental playwriting, for which I have Mr. Mabie, who is nationally famous, head of the dramatics department."[5] He also told his mother that his schedule for the new term was considerably heavier due to the addition of a science course, which he said was "the only requirement for graduation which I have not yet filled . . . a course in advanced zoology, uninspiring but instructive."[6] He did not continue stagecraft. One F was quite enough. So was rigging, constructing, and handling scenery. His professor complained, "Williams never came. I saw very little of him. He was not interested in the technical side of the theater."[7] The F in stagecraft, like the F in Greek at Washington, would have to be made up, and once again it meant that Tom would not be graduating in June.

As for his playwriting, he told his mother that he intended to continue Mabie's course, Experimental Dramatic Production, which would require writing two long plays, one biographical and the other an adaptation from a mystery novel. Also, "I am having a series of short plays broadcast over the local radio station on the 'Little Theater of the Air.' The first went over very well, although a revolver, used for sound effect, failed to go off."[8]

A classmate, Rod Erickson, who produced the broadcasts over radio station WSUI, recalled that Tom had "submitted a number of experimental writings which appeared to be incomplete extractions of longer works." That was before Professor Clay Harshbarger "censored him out of business," Erickson said.[9] "In retrospect, the material he censored was typical Williams' downbeat Southern, featuring, as I recall, a mother-son relationship and the usual anti-feminine characters. The incident became a joke between Clay and me for many years."[10] Although Erickson fought for the plays themselves, he said the picture of Tom at Iowa was that of "a student who was not likely to leave many vivid paths behind him."[11] Norman Felton agreed: "If anyone had bet on who would be a successful playwright, I would have bet on anyone but Tom. In fact, I would have bet all I owned, as little as it was, on his failure."[12]

The editor of *The Eliot*, John Pickering, who had a more optimistic belief in Tom Williams, sent him a St. Louis newspaper item citing him as the previous year's "star poet." Pickering wrote:

> Dear Tom: As the best poet we've had in Eliot and a topnotch poet any-where you are the logical choice for the doubtful honor of judging the 2nd annual poem of our Contest Issue. If you can spare the short time necessary, we'll send you the 12 or 15 poems, in readable form, have you pick 1st, 2nd, & 3rd & return all. If you get them Feb. 11, can you drop them in the mail again Feb. 18? If you can't, we'll extend the judging period.[13]

On stationery he had cribbed from the Cadet Officers Club, and after he had performed the role of critic and judge, Tom wrote Pickering:

> Dear Jack: I'm glad to hear that a winner came through and that it's a girl, as I believe in the encouragement of female poets. Everything possible should be done to discourage the male ones, for their own good, unless they are exceptional cases like Wm. Jay Smith on the Washington campus who has recently had some works accepted by the *American Mercury*. Do you know Bill? Most of his stuff is too much in the complicated modern style for a college magazine, but he might have some things you could use. My own work has been running mostly to dialogue but enclosed are a few you might use when you reach the dregs of what I submitted last year. Thanks again for the honor—it really was very gratifying to learn that somebody thought me qualified to act as a judge of poetry.[14]

After Tom's visit to see Rose at Christmas and the encouragement he felt, Edwina withheld from telling him what she now had to confide to her parents: that Rose would have to go on the insulin treatments again. "I phoned her doctor and he said she just 'moped and wouldn't keep her clothes on' and they were putting her back into the hospital. I didn't think when I talked to her at Christmastime . . . that Doctor Hoctor was justified in his optimism to Cornelius, and a letter I had from her confirmed my opinion."[15]

Rose's letter, sent from Farmington, was misdated and handwritten in pencil on lined paper:

My dearest Mother:
I do so want you to receive this. I am *terribly* anxious to come *home*.

I wore the dress which you gave me to the church services. I like it very much, but think I shall be better pleased when I have black silk hose and slippers. I shall get some black patttin [*sic*] leather ones to wear with it when this closes. I want a hair brush and box of *face powder*. I like to brush mine at night and will be tickled to death if you send me a stiff bristled one.

They have been making me *unconscious* almost every day & keeping me that way. I hate it you will neve [*sic*] never know how much. I have to go to the dentist, have lost several fillings.

We dance in the evening. Bud Campbell is staying here. I want him to give me swimming lessons next summer. He is an expert. Carl Block is too.* He is nicer than erer [*sic*] ever. The Bishop's wife is here with him. She is charming. I need a tooth & *paste*. I do hope you can see me in a few days & make arrangements for me to come home.

Dr. Simon's sister is stopping here. She is one of our relatives. I like her ever so much and am going to knit her a scarf, let her select a shade.

Please make it snappy about getting me out. Tell Tom to come over and get Ashton. She is from New Orleans. He will like her. She is nice looking very southern.

Don't forget that I havn't powder.

Love,
Rose Isabel.[16]

In a subsequent letter to her mother, Edwina wrote, "With the bad weather and illness in the family etc. I haven't been able to go to see Rose. When I phoned Dr. Ault he said she had been asking 'When was I coming.' I feel as if I were neglecting her but it is all I can do to look after the family here." She then chronicled the usual head colds and attacks of flu being passed around from one family member to another like dinner dishes.

Tom had written his mother to say that a play of his was being broadcast, but he complained, "The irritating thing about radio-writing is the ridiculous censorship. My latest show was cut all to pieces because of my realistic treatment of the dialogue. You aren't even allowed to say 'damn.' "[17] Tennessee Williams would always be attracted to the wide-ranging latitude of radio and television, and particularly that of films, but the more important freedom of expression that only the theatre offered in those times determined the course his career would take.

In February, Pi Tau, a fraternity of honorary writers, listed Thomas Wil-

---

*Rose's reference to Carl Block, whom she obviously thought was with her in Farmington, was to the Reverend Karl Morgan Block, the rector of the Saint Michael's and Saint George's Church, who had prevented her from continuing to teach Sunday school.

liams as a charter member and playwright. With the publication of poems in *The Eliot* and *L'Alouette*—the last ones for some time—playwriting became Tom's main bent; his aim now was toward Broadway. He had entered *Candles to the Sun* in a competition sponsored by the Dramatists' Guild in New York, but the only encouragement he received was the Guild's reader reporting that his individual style was "pronounced."

The play that engaged his attention now was his van Gogh opus, *The Holy Family*. A St. Louis paper announced it as his next effort for the Mummers, but Tom was still mired in the biographer's problems of how to translate his research into a dramatic narrative. In this, he was assisted by Professor Edwin Ford Piper, who had spent half his life at the university and was a leading force in making Iowa a mecca for creative writers. A poet and regionalist, Piper taught poetry and Imaginative Writing, a course that Tom readily chose.

Although he finally abandoned the van Gogh play, it was not before another professor, E. P. Conkle, also tried his hand. Ellsworth ("Worth") P. Conkle was a recognized playwright, in addition to being an assistant professor at Iowa from 1936 to 1939. Mabie was particularly proud of Conkle, who had had more than ten plays produced when he was a student at the university. After he had joined the faculty, his play *Two Hundred Were Chosen* was selected as the first production at the inauguration of the university theatre in November 1936. At the same time, the play was also being staged in New York by the Actors' Repertory Theatre.

Mabie encouraged his students to write original plays, and furthermore he gave established playwrights like Paul Green, Lynn Riggs, Dan Totheroh, and Owen Davis a stage for their new work. Aspiring playwrights Richard Maibaum and Marcus Bach were among Mabie's protégés, and Thomas Williams might have been, too, had his plays been more to the professor's taste. But Tom was an original, as E. P. Conkle recognized. Though Conkle's plays were more political, he and Williams shared a common interest in the travail and valor of people who struggle against impossible odds. Virginia Conkle wrote, "I know my husband held Tom in high regard. He was one of the few students I ever heard him mention."[18]

On March 17, 1938, Conkle's most recent play, *Prologue to Glory*, about Abraham Lincoln, was produced by the WPA Federal Theatre Project in New York at the Maxine Elliott Theatre. Tom wrote his mother that the play had received "four stars, the highest award, by Burns Mantle, leading critic. Fortunately we get along well so I'm hoping he may give me some assistance in marketing my plays."[19] Later, he told her, "Dr. Conkle is a changed man since 'Prologue to Glory' achieved such an unexpected success in New York. He has been ground under Mabie's thumb for years, and had lost all his personality—but since this success he has shown a miraculous transformation in character. His voice, appearance, everything, is completely altered, and he has turned into a first-rate teacher as well as dramatist."

Tom was impressed not only with Conkle's "transformation" but also with the play's "marvelous publicity . . . broadcast on Rudy Vallee's program and illustrated in LIFE. It was produced by the WPA which are now holding 'Candles to the Sun.' I will send them 'Fugitive Kind' soon as I finish rewriting it." He also mentioned, "My new play [probably *Spring Storm*] is completed and turned over to the playwriting class. I am very hopeful about this play, as it is well-constructed, no social propaganda, and is suitable for the commercial stage."[20] In his journal, however, he subsequently had an unhappier report to make: "Badly deflated by Conkle & class this week when they criticized my play. Hardly a favorable comment. Conkle hesitated when I asked if it was 'worth working on'—and said, 'Well, if you've got nothing else—' Yes, I was horribly shocked, felt like going off the deep-end. Feared that I might lose my mind."

Two days later, the criticism still troubled him: "I don't believe the play is really that bad—its virtues are not apparent in a first reading but I think it would blossom out on the stage—but I see plainly now that I'm a distinctly second or third rate writer—and I wonder how I ever got into it so deep—now what?" He didn't mean just his chosen career. He was "in deep" with his mother and grandparents, and he added, "No degree—flunked 2 hours last term—have not yet broken the news to Mother—dread doing that. She has been so marvelous, so lovely, so generous. I think of her and Grand and poor little Rose a great deal."

Rather than confess anything now, he chose instead to tell Edwina about the move he was making from ATO to a popular rooming house called Scott's, which offered lodgings to a mixed group of theatre students and graduates writing their theses. Among them was a Turkish graduate student, Joseph Sofra, who, like Tom, was rather short but, unlike Tom, was given to extravagant gesticulations and loud talk, so that he came naturally by the sobriquet of "Joe the Turk." It is not known who chose whom, but Joe became Tom's roommate—for a time.

> Dear Mother: Your letter and the checks arrived yesterday. Thanks. I am now trying out something new—housekeeping! A young man who is a graduate in the dramatics dept. and I have rented a small apartment, two rooms and a kitchenette, which is located quite near the campus. We feel very elated about it. The place is only $24 a month, twelve dollars for each of us, and doing our own cooking we will save money. He is an expert cook. This morning we got six eggs for a dime and last night had a swell steak and spaghetti dinner for a total expenditure of forty cents. It is much cheaper and we can eat according to our own convenience and taste. The A.T.O.'s seemed to regret my departure but took it gracefully. Having a room to myself I find it much easier to work—especially since my former room-mate was pretty obnoxious. The complete quiet which we have here in the evenings is a relief. . . . I will stop now to cook myself some lunch. This is excellent domestic training! And I find it quite sim-

ple. But I must confess the garbage has not yet been emptied and there is quite a stack of dishes in the sink. We are going to invite some girls over to wash them for us.[21]

In a matter of days, he was writing his mother again, reality having considerably dampened his enthusiasm for housekeeping.

Now that I have no one to clean up for me I appreciate the difficulties of housekeeping. Even in this relatively clean community dust and dirt seem to accumulate with miraculous ease. My fellow resident is a graduate student from Constantinople, very cosmopolitan and refined, but he has Oriental fatalism in regard to such things as dusting and washing dishes.[22]

Edwina's only comment to her mother was: "Can't say I'm very pleased with the idea of Tom 'keeping house.' Well, I can't worry over *that!*" Indeed, she had more than enough to worry over. "What you really want to know is about Rose. I've had no good news about her. I phoned Dr. Ault yesterday. They have completed another course of treatment with little result. Her physical condition [is] good but not her mental. . . . Dr. Block called me and said he had 'just heard about Rose's illness,' was so distressed, etc. etc. and could he come the following Saturday and talk to me about her?" Instead, Edwina said she met him in his office and told him *"plenty."* Dr. Block had assured her that he would call and go with her to Farmington. "He seemed to think he could do something for her—seemed genuinely distressed."[23]

But a few weeks later, she reported that Dr. Block had said nothing more about going to see Rose, and the following month, a newspaper clipping she sent to her parents announced that Dr. Block had accepted the post of bishop coadjutor of the Episcopal Diocese of California. Edwina commented, "Think he'll make a better bishop than pastor. He's said no more about going to see Rose!!"[24]

Dr. Block was not the only one avoiding Edwina. A Mrs. Bernard Wells, who was actively campaigning for state regent of the DAR, gave a party for sixty guests and neglected to invite Mrs. Williams. This snub and its repercussions among the ladies clearly hurt and embarrassed her. She told her parents that it was causing considerable comment, and Tom wrote, asking her not to take the offense too seriously: "What else could you expect from a woman of her character? She probably thinks you have not been active enough in that idiotic campaign of hers."[25] Cornelius added his assurance that if he were Edwina, *he'd* "put the hooks into her!"

But he was giving her problems, too. She complained to her mother, "Cornelius stayed out again all night Saturday, coming home just as I was leaving the house for Early Communion. I delivered an ultimatum, and he promised, 'It is the last time,' and gave me thirty-five dollars for a Spring dress and hat—I mean it too, I've grown so nervous that I can't stand staying awake all night on top of all the other worries I have. I've reached the end of my rope and have just been exhausted."[26]

Cornelius evidently made other amends as well, for the following week he drove Edwina to Farmington. She wrote, "It was a very sad trip for me as Rose refused to talk to me and was very much upset when she saw me, told me I had put her into a 'charity hospital to be tortured.' She can't be blamed for feeling that way. Neither the Insulin nor the Metrizol have done much good for her Dr. Ault told me, and she has been placed in one of the cottages under another Physician, a Dr. Groves [who] asked me 'please not to come to see her often'! As this was the first visit since Christmas, I thought it unnecessary for him to say that." She added, "I've been so depressed since I came home I could hardly carry on."[27]

How much of this that she reported to Tom was not reflected in his letters, although subsequently he noted in his journal that he had "written a rather nice short story—'The 4-leaf Clover'—about a girl going mad—memories of Rose. Oh, God, have pity on my poor little sister!—this I mean if nothing else—pity her and forgive us all."

She was seated on the lawn in a white dress. It was five o'clock and the sun was directly behind her so that it was barely possible to tell where the light ended and the translucent edges of her figure began. She had washed her hair that afternoon. It still had a prismatic dampness in the sun. Her bare throat and arms were like the inner surface of a shell. She was as lovely and insubstantial as something remembered, something not actually seen.

As he came toward the swing where he usually read for a while before dinner, she looked up at him and smiled. "Look! I've found a four-leaf clover!"

Her smile was like a delicate web upon his face and hands that he had to break away from.

He rose quickly and went toward the house.

The downstairs was empty. From above he heard the now-familiar sound of his mother's weeping. He had climbed halfway up the stairs before he noticed a strangeness about it. This time it was wild and hysterical to a degree that it had never been before and it frightened him so that he could climb no further but stood on the landing in helpless foreknowledge of some unbearable hurt.

. . . Cousin Amelia's voice, hoarse from tears, offering a comfort which she herself rejected, "They have such marvelous sanitariums, new treatments and—"

. . . Arthur went slowly downstairs. The hall was flooded with a misty brightness which had its center in the swinging pendulum of the grandfather's clock. All of the afternoon's fading brilliance was concentrated in that metal disk as it swung leisurely from side to side in the glass cabinet.

Arthur watched it in merciful suspension of thought till the hypnotic gold had drained out and left only the dull brass and the sound that came from its motion was the repetition of one meaningless phrase.

The room was tired and full of shadows.

He moved thirstily toward the window's diminishing brightness. He looked out across the wide lawn and saw that she was still there in the one remaining portion of sunlit earth. Her head was inclined slightly forward and the last and purest light of the afternoon made a luminous cloud of her hair. She was looking at something, something that she held in the cup of her palm, and even from this distance he could see that she was smiling.

He recalled the troubled look in her eyes as he had gone by without speaking and then her voice which now had in his memory the persistently haunting sweetness of a child's:

"Look! I've found a four-leaf clover!—It means good luck!"[28]

April, the Cruelest Month

One of E. C. Mabie's requirements was that all the students in his department act in his various productions. The professor leaned toward more epic plays, like Shakespeare's *Henry IV, Part I*, in which Tom Williams was cast as a member of Falstaff's "Charge of Foot," which prompted him to tell his mother, "I am enlisted as a soldier in King Henry IV's army—next major play—fortunately they did not know about my record in the R.O.T.C."[29] It had been a year since he made his acting debut as an old man in Molière's *Scapin*, stomping about in a yellow fright wig and ad-libbing in French. At the time, he found to his surprise that he actually enjoyed the experience. However, French with a southern accent was one thing, Shakespeare another. Mabie wisely saw to it that he had only one line to deliver.

Tennessee's recollection was that "throughout the scene in which I appeared I had to sit on the forestage, polishing a helmet, all the while my throat getting tighter and tighter with apprehension at delivering that one line. I simply had to say that somebody had arrived at the gates. But when my cue came, the sound that issued from my constricted throat was quite unintelligible and would always bring down the house—it was like a mouse's squeak. They said it was effective, however."[30]

Marian Gallaway, who designed the play's costumes, had a different memory: "Tom did one acting job in Iowa that I shall never forget. He didn't want to act, but Mabie insisted. Tom played one of Falstaff's ragged soldiers. There was absolutely never such a *flat*, FLAT ON THE GROUND, lazy soldier in the world! He was 'feeling the part.' "[31]

Bette Reitz was a member of the stage crew, and Tom confessed, "Wish I could get things started again. We are now friendly but *pas de plus.*" About this time, he started a poem: "(For B.R.) Remember me as one of your lovers, /

Not the greatest of these, not the least, / But in some small way distinguished from all the others . . ."[32] Tom obviously had not given up, although Tennessee's recollection was that about this time Bette began to fade out of his libido and others of his own gender began to fade in. Two in particular whom he found extraordinarily handsome were Walter Fleischmann, who played Hotspur, and Lemuel Ayers, who worked on lights.

Fleischmann could not have been more of a campus idol if he had been the university's star quarterback. Not just students but faculty as well were attracted to him. Mabie and his wife invited him to their home, and he became especially close to Mrs. Mabie, whom he called every year on her birthday, until her death. Also, there was Mabie's daughter, who confessed to having had "the world's worst crush on Walter." Worth Conkle and his wife invited Walter to their home, and further, they helped him to go to New York to try his luck as an actor. Later, he toured with the prominent actress Katharine Cornell, and afterward he assumed the name of Anthony Dexter to play, among other roles, the lead in a film biography of Rudolph Valentino. Fleischmann barely noticed Tom among his many idolaters.

Lemuel Ayers went from Princeton University to Iowa for postgraduate study in the theatre. In a short time, he was destined to become a leading designer and successful producer, a meteoric career that ended with his death from leukemia at age forty. In *Memoirs*, Tennessee recalled him "walking around the men's locker room quite naked before a performance. He was like a young saint out of an Italian renaissance painting—darkly gleaming curls, and a perfectly formed body." Williams also remembered one occasion "at dusk in a tiny zoo on a hill" when he encountered Ayers. He said that no one was around, and there was only the sound of guinea hens fluttering their wings. "We lingered a while, which I would have liked to prolong, but Lem, I suspect, was accustomed to more aggressive types, and he smiled and he drifted away."[33] Not many years later, they would meet after Ayers had created the sets for the highly successful musicals *Oklahoma!* and *Bloomer Girl*, and again when they were both employed in Hollywood at Metro-Goldwyn-Mayer. Ultimately, Lemuel Ayers would design Cheryl Crawford's stage production of Tennessee Williams's *Camino Real*.

By midterm, Tom still had not written anything to his mother about not being able to graduate in June. Edwina informed her parents, "If Tom's commencement doesn't interfere with Dakin's finals, he can drive us up to Iowa. Cornelius says *he* can't go."[34] Once Tom learned of these plans, he got busy drafting a letter about "the painful news from the Registrar's office which I am very reluctant to communicate." Finally, he managed to come up with a more positive slant, making a lemon into lemonade, as his mother would say. Relating news he allegedly received from the registrar, he wrote, "It seems at the end of this semestre I will still be four hours short of the required thirty and to get a degree would have to stay for the 8-weeks summer session. It seems very silly and unreasonable since I already have far more credits than are ordinarily required for graduation, but they say it is a national ruling you must take at least 30 at the college granting the degree."

Whether he had caught his mother in the tangled web of his letter or not, it read as though he had convinced himself, too. "I took fourteen hours the first term and was intending to take sixteen the second to make thirty. I got a special permission to enroll for that many but after a few weeks I found that it was too much—I didn't even have a free afternoon for my writing—so I had to drop my Stagecraft course in which I was doing badly. It was nearly all carpentry, building sets and shifting scenery—and took far more time than it was worth. Dr. Conkle advised me to drop it." He concluded his letter by saying, "This academic red-tape has just crossed me up. Aside from this complication, everything is fine." He assured her that there were some very definite benefits he would get from the summer session. "I could get my new play produced here. It is now finished except for a few revisions and was enthusiastically criticized by Dr. Conkle and the class."[35] If Edwina bought Tom's elaborate circumlocution, it didn't seem to matter, because she told her parents, "I'm writing him that I will see him through. He must get the degree, especially as he is so near it!!"

The tragic news she had to convey was that Cornelius had suddenly been called to Knoxville. His sister Isabel had been taken seriously ill and was not expected to live more than twenty-four hours. "They have had two nurses and five doctors," said Edwina. "Blood poisoning starting from an infected tooth which was pulled scattering the infection. Will [Brownlow, her husband] had written Cornelius a few days ago that she was ill and in a hospital but they didn't think her condition serious, said she had been in a run down condition from doing too much! Her Bible classes!" The following day, Cornelius wired that Isabel had died. "I think that he had more affection for Isabel than any other member of his family and he was much up-set before he left. This is a terrible blow to Ella."[36]

Ella wrote to Tom: "Your poor Aunt Belle was surrounded by a solid wall of prayer but Death got through." It had been more than twelve years since Tom had last seen his aunt Belle, but she remained in his thoughts, a presence whose facets of character he drew upon in fashioning his enduring portraits of southern women. Isabel was named and appeared in his short story "The Resemblance Between a Violin Case and a Coffin," and when it was published, he appended, *"Inscribed to the memory of Isabel Sevier Williams"*—the only instance in which he dedicated a work of his to a member of his family.

With the resumption of his journals, Tom described an incident that would have had little meaning except that it provided insight into a malaise of mind that would prey upon him all his life: the burden of unfounded guilt. "A silly business has alienated me from the theatre crowd," he wrote. "One of the girls had a pocket book stolen and I became quite embarrassed while they were talking about it. Was afraid they might think me guilty—*for absolutely no reason!!!*—*idiotic*—have felt uncomfortable with them and avoided them ever since. One of the silliest things I've ever experienced. But it isn't insanity since I realize how ridiculous it is—but perhaps my queer actions have actually made them suspect me. Sounds like dementia praecox, doesn't it? But it's just the old guilt complex—the feeling of social inadequacy in a new guise." Here he was on "the island of my self" again, using his writings as a medium of self-analysis, attempting to defuse a gnawing guilt that went deeper, much deeper, than this superficial incident. Then he asked, "What do I want? I want love and creative power!—Eh bien! Get it!"

Throughout the spring and early summer, Tom started taking long walks by himself, wandering aimlessly about the city streets at night. The endless search for a companion had begun. In *Memoirs*, Tennessee recalled, "I was lonely and frightened, I didn't know the next step. I was finally fully persuaded that I was 'queer,' but had no idea what to do about it. I didn't even know how to accept a boy on the rare occasions when one would offer himself to me."[37] If this awareness had actually reached levels of consciousness, there was nothing of the sort confided to his journal. On the contrary, he was still hoping to take up with Bette again, and in the main he kept the company of his Turkish roommate, who in turn kept the company of women. In his journal, Tom said only, "Drove out in country with Joe the Turk—me driving—and it gave me a thrill. I still respond quickly and sensitively to the beauty of things." His main problem, it would seem, was not so much with Joe Sofra as with another Turk, Sedat Sorah, who was tall and handsome and in determined pursuit of Bette Reitz.

Truman Slitor, who lived in the same rooming house as Tom, said, "One night, Sedat, Bette and Tom were visiting in the upper room above mine where Tom lived. I was reading when I noticed the noise level from Tom's room was increasing as the evening wore on. When I heard some very loud thumping sounds that shook my ceiling, I went upstairs to investigate. I found Tom and Sedat fighting over Bette. They were dragging the helpless girl about the floor like puppies playing with a rag doll. Tom held Bette by the arms while Sedat pulled from the ankles. I could not be certain if it was a real fight or simple rough-house play." The rumpus continued for a while after Truman returned to his room. "Finally the noise subsided. I opened the door of my room and looked out into the hallway. There was Sedat passing by my door with Bette slung over his shoulders, her head and arms hanging down, as he went on out to the sidewalk. I then went upstairs to check on Tom. I found him lying on the floor completely exhausted but unhurt. I had a feeling that the romance between Tom and Bette might have been terminated that evening."[38]

Slitor's memory of Bette Reitz was that she was not "a real beauty, but slightly unkempt and hyperkinetic. Tom and I would sometimes talk about girls. He would tell me how sultry Southern girls were. According to him they were *smoldering*. We would laugh and then agree that smoldering Southern girls could be very interesting. In the back of my mind I took his opinion of Southern girls as an exaggeration but never argued the point."

> May 30—Memorial day—Spent a delightful afternoon on the river— canoeing—with Truman Slitor—we went to Coralville and got some beer and drifted back down to town . . . [In 1940, he commented on this entry, "Remember that afternoon very clearly—sunny water—bare skin—free, lazy motion—youth."] then drove out again with Joe the Turk in his car and drank with a bunch of Journalism students. . . . At the end of the year I have found very few friends—loads of acquaintances— Slitor is the best of the bunch and even he couldn't lend me a buck when I'm down to my last dime. Ah, well.

Tom would often tag along with Truman and his fiancée, Gwen, and once again he found himself the lonely member of a threesome. As far as their socializing was concerned, Truman said:

> We would meet at Smith's Café in Iowa City, a popular hangout for students in the Speech Department. Within a group, Tom would keep a low profile in contrast to the noisy ones who were demonstrating their speech projection. You could only identify him above the sounds by his occasional burst of high-pitched laughter. He was more of an observer than a performer. He was different from the other students. In our conversations, he would employ much color in his descriptions of ordinary observations and experiences. His remarks were carefully composed in perfect prose. He did not use the "machine-gun diction" that often characterizes small talk between friends. He must have been a compulsive writer. I would often find him on a sofa in the lounge of the Memorial Union writing in a notebook. He would sometimes read to me what he had written, using a somewhat poetical and theatrical cadence, and then he would pause with a smile that seemed to indicate satisfaction with his words. I do recall Tom's liking the sound of "Allamakee," as in Allamakee County, Iowa, my home county. He would repeat the name several times with a smile. Also we would sometimes listen to late-night mystery shows on the radio—on the order of *Inner Sanctum* or *The Shadow*. Tom enjoyed these "spook" shows for their melodramatic effect.[39]

Their friendship was all too brief, and after Truman's departure, Tom wrote in his journal: "Truman's left town—one fellow I really liked." He and Joe the Turk, though, had parted company acrimoniously, and he added the lament, "Poor Tommy is more or less by himself these days and is not quite the brilliant companion he would like to be!" There were those who couldn't agree more. Robert Leo Quinn, who took the same modern drama course as

Tom, dated Bette Reitz's roommate, Jean Fitzpatrick. He said that he kept his relationship with both Tom and Bette "as minimal as I could make it. She was a bit too crude for my taste and he was a rather unpleasant little person who always managed to be elsewhere when the check for drinks, coffee, or whatever, arrived."[40]

It was a monotonous fact that Tom was perpetually broke, and certainly his penurious state among those who knew how to manage their money did not inspire friendship. At least they *had* money to manage. Because of the small amounts sent by his mother and grandmother, he was constantly borrowing, and his income was largely committed before he received it. Since childhood, because of his father's niggardliness, he had been living like a poor relative in a home of obvious middle-class affluence, and now at the age of twenty-seven he was still made to feel like an arrested adolescent—which in many ways he was. It meant a reliance upon his mother, who was forever cribbing money from her household allowance and surreptitiously finding other ways to give Tom support. Where once she was regularly confronting her husband with his dereliction, now she was using it to ensure her son's affection and dependence. As he grew more beholden to her, he often felt fury and resentment at his sense of obligation.

A postcard he sent to his mother announced the fact that he had moved again to a rooming house at 126 North Clinton Street and had started a board job: "I am a waiter in the state hospital doctors' cafeteria—feel very professional in a white uniform—I get meals for three hours service—hope I can keep it."[41]

But what he recorded in his journal was a different story: "Been working exactly a week State Hospital waiting tables in restaurants—horribly exhausting, nerve-wracking work and it has made me nervous and ill—palpitat jolting heart and tension and gas—quite uneasy today—but not the old frantic fear that I used to have. Is this courage—? Or what? Anyway it's a blessing. No doubt I could be scared out of my wits again but at least I am *now* able to put up a fight." He described his new quarters as "pleasant—alone now but will have a roommate soon. Enjoy this quiet and tranquility after the noisy, disgusting Turk that shared my apartment—one of the most revolting persons I've ever known."

Earlier he had told his mother that he had received letters from both Clark Mills and Willard Holland. "Holland is leaving for another vacation in California and wants me to let him take one of my plays out there. Clark is having a hard time in Paris, living on about fifty cents a day, and waiting for money to get home on. He said they feel war is inevitable over there and expect to be defeated. Are very incensed against England for being so irresolute."[42] In March, Hitler had swept over Austria without resistance, and Tom commented to his mother, "It seems the whole world is in a state of economic and political chaos for which there isn't any immediate solution. Very hard on these young people on campuses who are going to have to deal with it in the future." Clark Mills would be one among them. In an unmailed note to Mills, Tom wrote, "Everybody is talking about the literary 'renaissance' at Iowa— there are five or six prominent writers here, all of which are now working on novels—"[43] He was alluding to the origin of the University of Iowa's famed Writers' Workshop, although it would not be named as such until the following year.

Another unmailed letter, to Willard Holland, said that he had just been rereading *Spring Storm* and concluded: "It really is a mess. I hadn't realized it was so bad or I wouldn't have let you see it. . . . The idea of the play as I see it now is simply a study of Sex—a blind animal urge or force (like the regenerative force of April) gripping four lives and leading them into a tangle of cruel and ugly relations."[44]

This "tragedy of sex relations," as he called it, was eventually abandoned, along with a number of unproduced plays, but it was significant because it was the forerunner of plays that, with few exceptions, were notable as studies of the ways in which sexual passion often frustrates and even destroys the rational basis of human life.

By mid-June, Tom had registered for two classes in the summer session: Mabie's seminar on playwriting and Conkle's course on problems in dramatic art. At the same time, he wrote in his journal that fortunately he had been given an easier job at the hospital "due to my inefficiency in the first. I didn't break any dishes—not one!—but forgot orders and got terribly nervous and confused."

Now that the summer session had begun and the campus had a somewhat leaner look, Tom's hope was that Mabie might take more notice of him. He told his mother that Mabie was about to lose his best playwright, Marcus Bach, and that "he has begun to take a special interest in me, possibly in hopes that I will come back. Of course I probably would if he could get me one of the Rockefeller scholarships."[45] Marian Gallaway had secured one, through Mabie's efforts, to work on her thesis. Even though he looked upon Mabie as a tyrant, it amazed him what the Boss was willing to do for his graduate students.

Later, he reported, "Mabie won't get me a scholarship." Worse than that, Tom had once again read *Spring Storm* aloud, this time to Mabie and his seminar, and wrote that "it was quite finally rejected by the class." As Tennessee remembered years later, "When I had finished reading, the good professor's eyes had a glassy look as though he had drifted into a state of trance." The reason, in all likelihood, was because Tom had tacked on "an alternate ending" where at curtain the woman character strips naked onstage. Tennessee's memory was:

> There was a long and all but unendurable silence. Everyone seemed more or less embarrassed. At last the professor pushed back his chair, thus dismissing the seminar, and remarked casually and kindly, "Well, we all have to paint our nudes!"

And this is the only reference that I can remember anyone making to the play. That is, in the playwriting class, but I do remember that the late Lemuel Ayers . . . read it and gave me sufficient praise for its dialogue and atmosphere to reverse my decision to give up the theatre in favor of my other profession of waiting on tables, or more precisely, handing out trays in the cafeteria of the State Hospital.[46]

Tom took long walks at night not only out of restlessness but also to escape the heat in his attic room. He was not alone. Another writer, Milton Lomask, who in later years became a prominent biographer and historian, recalled, "It was very hot in Iowa City that summer." Lomask and a friend, Hazel Teabeau, would go out walking in the evenings. "It was the only route to comfort in those un–air-conditioned days."

Hazel was from St. Louis and later became a teacher of English at Lincoln University, at that time an all-black institution in Jefferson City, Missouri. "Hazel and I met in St. Louis," Lomask recalled, "and came up to Iowa City in the summer of 1938 for some graduate study, she in sociology, I in the Department of Speech and Drama." Tom was, in fact, very impressed with the sophistication of his new friends: To him at that time, Lomask, who was white, and Hazel, who was black, would have to be radicals. Even in a northern state like Iowa and in a "liberal" university, it was unusual for an interracial couple to appear together in public. Tom thought it was marvelous to have such liberal friends.

Lomask said, "I can't recall where I first encountered Williams, perhaps in one of my classes, perhaps at the theater. My early impressions, never much altered, were of a lonely and vulnerable person, a perennial onlooker and likely to be ever a stranger at the feast." He did remember one evening when he and Hazel were out walking:

I noticed Tom Williams coming toward us. He nodded. I nodded. He joined us. There were introductions. After that, for the rest of the summer session, Tom accompanied us on our nightly airings and the three of us became friends.

One day he told me he'd written some plays. Would I care to read a script? Inwardly I groaned, thinking, "I won't like it and he'll know I don't and that will be the end of a beautiful friendship." Sure enough, I didn't like it. I've no idea what tactfully bland remarks I made, but I remember saying to myself, "No doubt this young man will make some noise in the world, but he'll never be a playwright!"[47]

With graduation only a matter of a few days ahead, Tom confessed in his journal, "I haven't the slightest notion what comes after this summer. Holland is about my last resource. If he likes [Spring Storm] and will produce it that should at least give me a spar to hang onto for a few months. I would do better to come back here but how?" In a letter to his mother, he remarked, "Mr. Mabie is much less indulgent than Holland—since he knows a great deal more about [staging plays]—so I have to have the script in best possible condition before he will consider it for production." He informed her that he could not have the play ready in time but considered that just as well since "the summer productions are much inferior to the others, due to the shortage of acting talent and the crowded schedule."

Then he received discouraging news: ". . . a woeful letter from Willard Holland last week. It seems that while he was in Hollywood with very bright prospects of crashing the movies—having a personal agent and all that—his salary was suddenly discontinued by the Mummers and he was stranded without funds. He had to come home immediately and there learned that a new board of directors had been elected in his absence and he had been discharged as director. They are willing to re-engage him provided that he surrenders his dictatorial powers—he urged me not to send them my script and says he is planning to organize a new company if they don't come to terms with him." Willard confided in Tom that he was "nearly insane with the suddenness and injustice of it all."[48]

While Tom still hoped that the Mummers would present *Spring Storm* during the season ahead, he could only wonder how Holland would resolve his dispute with the board members. Also, as he told his mother, he, too, was uncertain about what lay ahead: "Mabie thinks I'm coming back for a Masters—as all his writers do—but of course I would not consider it unless he offers me a job or a scholarship."[49]

By the end of July, Tom was again writing to his mother, saying how glad he was that she and Dakin were intending to come to Iowa for his graduation. He also mentioned that after graduation, Marian Gallaway was planning to drive up to Chicago for a few days and to return home via St. Louis, and that Milton Lomask was also going to Chicago to look for work. "I might inquire around too. . . . Marcus Bach who is new director of the Chicago WPA theater has asked me to bring some scripts and I would like to talk to him about them and the possibility of work in his office. I would only stay a day or two if I go and it would only cost a few dollars." He also announced, "I have a small part in the final play of the season, only two lines—as a page in *Richard of Bordeaux*."[50] He hoped she and Dakin could see the play, which was performed August first through fourth. On the fifth, Tom's graduation took place.

As it turned out, Edwina was unable to attend either the play or the graduation ceremonies, to her great disappointment, because Dakin had departed for camp at Lake Taneycomo; Grand and Walter had gone to a Monteagle Assembly in Tennessee, and Cornelius sent Tom a twenty-five-dollar check. And so, after five years and two months, Thomas Lanier Williams received his bachelor of arts degree.

Saint Louis: Good-bye Again

When Tom and Marian Gallaway left Iowa City and drove on to Chicago, the one question that troubled him was where best to go to ensure that his work would be produced. His experience with Willard Holland and at Iowa had taught him that a playwright writes plays to be *played;* otherwise, it is an act of futility, there being nothing as forlorn as an unproduced script. From this time until the very last production, he made it his business not simply to write plays but to search out markets, as well. Holland, because of his dispute with the Mummers, seemed a doubtful prospect. First, Tom would try his luck with the Federal Theatre Project, and if that didn't work out, the logical move was back to Iowa in the fall—anything to avoid coming under the "paternal roof" again.

On August 8, he wrote to E. C. Mabie to make "a formal application" to the National Youth Administration, which offered jobs at fifty cents an hour. "I am tremendously anxious to write a creative thesis for my Master's at Iowa but it is necessary for me to have work as my savings are exhausted and I can't expect any further help from my father who wanted me to remain in the shoe business." Williams added that he had worked in that business for three years. He also mentioned "spending a good deal of time with a notebook on the public beaches and stopping at a cheap South-side hotel to get authentic material for my flophouse play [*Fugitive Kind*] in case I ever get time to revise it."[51]

In all likelihood, this was another unmailed letter, indicating not only Tom's wavering intentions but also the fact that he was loath to admit his father's lack of support. To acknowledge that it was his mother and his grandmother who had made it possible for him to get through Iowa would be embarrassing, would make him seem a mama's boy. This clearly troubled him, and the most Tennessee Williams would ever admit even to close friends was that his beloved grandparents, especially Grand, were the blessed providers. He acknowledged Edwina's help by giving her a half interest in *The Glass Menagerie.*

Tom immediately dispatched a letter to his mother. He told her that he and Marian had driven to Chicago and that he might return with her to St. Louis. He said nothing about the Federal Theatre Project but told her, "I talked to Mr. Mabie and he said he would try to get me a $40.00 a month NYA job next year."[52] He assured her he would be home soon and would probably return to Iowa in the fall.

Milton Lomask and Hazel Teabeau took the train to Chicago, planning to meet their young friend there. Lomask, who maintained that Tom was on board with them, recalled, "Williams and I put up at the downtown YMCA. During the Chicago stay, a theater near the Y was being renovated, and one morning we dropped by to explore it. I remember Tom's animation as we stepped in. He examined the place as though he were planning to make an architectural drawing of it. Up the flies he went, down every backstage corridor, into every dressing room."[53]

By August 15, Edwina was fretting because she'd heard nothing further from Tom and also because she was about to turn fifty-four years old and was feeling it. In a letter to Grand, she complained, "On top of visits to Cornelius in hospital (he's in a villainous mood so I think he must be practically alright) I broke off a lower tooth." The twenty-five dollars C.C. had given Tom as a graduation gift, she felt, could not last long in Chicago. "It was too bad I couldn't go to Iowa City and pack up his things. His trunk arrived full of manuscripts—very few clothes! . . . P.S. A special delivery from Tom! Thinks he can get place on radio script dep't of local Writer's Project with salary from 65 to 95 a month. Will know definitely Monday."[54]

However, Tom was turned down for the WPA project on the basis of his being from a prosperous middle-class family and not qualifying as destitute and in need of federal aid. The other, unstated reason was that his work was just not radical enough. Increasingly, the Federal Theatre Project had been coming under the domination of Communists—at least that loud accusation in Congress would soon doom the project—and in the eyes of the theatre's administrators, Tom Williams was bourgeois: a term of opprobrium that amounted to a kiss of death.

Several months later, Milton Lomask received "a long letter, two or three pages, densely typed and postmarked New Orleans," and he remembered, "At Iowa City Tom often talked to me of his father. It's the only subject I ever heard him talk about at length. I forget what he said about the older Williams but I remember the tone: bitter. Ninety per cent of the letter was about Papa, and that, too, was bitter."[55] Now, of course, Tom had to face the old man again.

Back in St. Louis, Tom had no idea what, if anything, had been resolved between the Mummers and their former director, Willard Holland. It was not solely Holland's autocratic approach to managing the company and casting his favorite actors that was at issue; there was also his attitude toward the rivalry between the Mummers and the St. Louis Little Theatre, the more socially powerful and publicized of the two groups. Sam Halley, Jr., who had played in both *Candles to the Sun* and *Fugitive Kind*, remembered that Holland would become "highly indignant when actors in his company would choose the Little Theatre in preference to the Mummers." That Holland was actively seeking work in Hollywood was further cause for grievance among the committee members. In hindsight, Halley admitted that Holland's loyalty to the Mummers was compromised by his interest in films. "He got his concepts more from the movies than from any attraction to the stage."[56]

Wesley Gore, another member of the company, was Holland's best friend. He felt that Holland chose only those who were best suited to play the roles, and he recalled how close Holland and Tom Williams were as director to playwright: "Willard did all the directing—he would change some scenes and speeches around and maybe add more in stage direction—a dramatic high-light or something—and those were the suggestions Tom appreciated at that time. Often they sat with their heads together during rehearsals."[57]

Once back in St. Louis, Tom immediately took up with his friend Clark Mills, who had just returned from Paris and had accepted a teaching post at Cornell University for the fall.* For a short while, "the literary factory" was reopened for business. This time, though, the two writers transferred their industry to the Williams house on Aberdeen Place, prompting Edwina to complain to her mother that Tom had stayed out "three nights in succession 'till a wee hour in the morning. He now has Clark in the house at eleven a.m.—one writing in Dakin's room, the other writing in the attic!" Then she added that "in desperation I have locked my-self in my bed-room!!!"[58]

In the late summer of 1938, the warm friendship between the two poets prompted Tom to pen a tribute to Clark entitled "Return to Dust":

On the wall of our literary factory, directly before us was tacked up a little verse of our own composition which was to serve as a grim reminder—as some writers keep skulls in their studies—

> *"For lack of food some writers died*
> *while some committed suicide,*
> *and all though great or small in fame*
> *returned to dust from whence they came!"*

Then Tom set forth a credo that ultimately would apply more to him than to Clark: "For every artist, experience is never complete until it has been re-produced in creative work. To the poet his travels, his adventures, his loves, his indignations are finally resolved in verse and this in the end becomes his permanent, indestructible life."

And he concluded, "Yesterday I visited our old 'literary factory' in the basement of the McBurney home. Our grim little verse about the fate of all writers was still tacked upon the wall. I tore it off—and grinned. It no longer seemed appropriate on Clark's wall. Maybe I'll type it over and stick it on my own!"[59]

---

*Clark Mills McBurney completed his studies at the Sorbonne and the Alliance Française and was awarded the Diplôme Supérieur d'Etudes Françaises Modernes and, from the Collège de France, the Certificat de Phonétique. He was also recipient of the Abbé Rousselat Médaille for experi-mental phonetics. As a result, he accepted the offer of a teaching post at Cornell University, which he held until he enlisted in the U.S. Army, serving from 1942 to 1950 in Germany in counterintelligence, ETO, and with the CIA until 1952, after which he resumed teaching English at Hunter College and Fairleigh Dickinson.

"Suspended in the Mist Over Berchtesgaden, Caught in the Folds of Chamberlain's Umbrella"

The sounds of approaching war were coming in over the airwaves louder than ever, and the fascist menace had suddenly become as much a threat from without as within. The previous March Hitler had annexed Austria, and in the United States there were those in government and industry covertly supporting Nazism. Roosevelt labeled the Nazi aggressions "an epidemic of world lawlessness" and was searching out bipartisan willingness to maintain "standards of conduct helpful to the ultimate goal of general peace." In other words, he was advocating international cooperation to combat this threat.

Radio was playing the dominant role in a new war of nerves: The tense, elliptical broadcasting of CBS commentator H. V. Kaltenborn, in particular, transfixed the listener; added to that was the startling immediacy of hearing the actual voice of Prime Minister Neville Chamberlain in London on his return from a meeting with Hitler in Munich, announcing to a cheering crowd, "I believe it is peace for our time."

While radio was still offering its customary comedy hours and Sunday-night sermons, it took the wild, innovative genius of a young New York actor-director-producer, Orson Welles, to scare the country very nearly out of its wits. Although on October 30 the CBS radio audience was being assured that what it was about to hear was only a dramatization, Welles and his Mercury Theatre players broadcast *The War of the Worlds*—which depicted a supposed invasion from the planet Mars—so convincingly that thousands of listeners ran from their homes, flooded the streets, and drove off aimlessly in their cars. The panic and pandemonium caused many Americans the next day to laugh at themselves but, at the same time, to feel the tension between a dramatized Martian invasion and the threat of the Nazi Wehrmacht menacing world peace.

While plays and movies were largely escapist, one film in 1939, *Confessions of a Nazi Spy*, would forthrightly attack the existence of seditious Nazi bunds springing up across the nation—especially in cities like St. Louis, where there was a large population of German-Americans, many of whom were openly sympathetic to the Hitler regime and just as blatantly anti-Semitic. Across the North American continent, fall was turning toward winter, the days growing shorter, and at twilight dark clouds gathered ominously on the horizon. Anyone willing to look could see them.

Willard Holland, in a temporary pact with the Mummers, opened their season with Bernard Shaw's *Arms and the Man* and scheduled Sinclair Lewis's *It Can't Happen Here* as the next attraction. Tom was asked to write a promotional piece for the production and felt that he had come through with "a pretty strong denunciation of Fascism." He wrote in his journal: "I am at last becoming sincerely aroused in my social consciousness. I begin to appreciate the very real danger of Fascism." His program note read:

It is significant that the great thinkers and artists of Fascist countries have become voluntary exiles because they cannot exist and create in states where the science of government has become confused with that of penology. Thomas Mann, Einstein, Freud, Max Reinhardt, leaders in every field of science and art, have fled from the black-shirted countries. Without such men there would be no progress in civilization. Culture would become merely a product of the munitions factories.

Most of these great exiles came to America because they thought that America was free from Fascism. Is it possible that they were mistaken in that belief? Can Fascism come to this country?

You will find the answer in Sinclair Lewis' dramatization of his famous novel "It Can't Happen Here" which the Mummers of St. Louis have wisely chosen as their next production. It is a thrilling and powerful play and nobody who values his liberties can afford to miss it.[60]

Edwina, in a letter to her parents, commented, "Things certainly do look bad for the world at present, don't they!" Tom, she said, was hoping to get work at a new radio station, while "in his usual blunt frankness Cornelius opines that 'Tom's next job will be in the army.' "[61] Tom, though, was preoccupied not only with homegrown fascism but with other forms of social injustice, as well. Previously, on September 1, the *St. Louis Star-Times* had run a piece concerning the brutal murder of prison inmates—four convicts had died when steam was turned up full blast in a radiator-lined cell block called the "Klondike"—and it inspired Tom to write a strong dramatic protest. In his journal, he said that he had "turned down a chance of getting NYA work at Iowa City—drank coffee almost daily to work on new play *Not About Nightingales*—a melodrama based on the prison atrocity in Philadelphia County."

Since there was no further reference made to *Spring Storm*, Tom's hope now was that Holland would decide to put on his prison play. He felt that he had never written anything to compare with this in terms of violence and horror. But after the Sinclair Lewis play, the Mummers presented Rachel Crothers's *Let Us Be Gay*, a silly bit of badinage more suitable for the Little Theatre. Willard Holland's final effort for the beleaguered company was Clarence Black's 1909 melodrama *Jesse James*. He staged it on the *Goldenrod* showboat, and it was a great success. Tom was disappointed, but more than ever he was aware that the real forum for his work was in New York, and more than ever he thought of going there.

While his playwriting took precedence over everything and everyone, Tom also understood its worst penalty: loneliness. In college, he had learned to value his companions and recognize his need of them. Somewhat wistfully, he asked himself, "I wonder about my old friends. Jim? Milton? Bette? Mitch? Truman? Clark?" Beyond their mention in his journal, these special comrades of his youth would be engraved in the memory of Tennessee Williams: Jim

Connor, the gentleman caller; "a boy named Milton Lomask"; Bette Reitz, a girl free of inhibition; Harold Mitchell, desire unfulfilled; Truman Slitor, "one fellow I really liked"; Clark Mills, his closest friend, the poet whose "talent burned very bright in those early years."[62]

In his journal, Tom said that he and Clark had had a good time together before Clark left for Cornell: "much social activity." In one of his fragmented letters, Tom wrote:

> I have just taken a sleeping pill to which I am likely to succumb at any moment so you will excuse the brevity and dullness of this letter. I'm glad to learn through your mother that you've found comfortable lodgings with a beautiful blond in such auspicious proximity.
>
> Since you left I have been writing furiously—day and night—and all but completed my new play—there is something in what you said about the value of social isolation—I have seen nobody and done a great deal more—but now I am paying the piper as the strenuous work has resulted in something like nervous collapse. My blood pressure—which has always been my nervous barometer—jumped up alarmingly and I've spent several days and nights feeling like a smoking volcano.

He told Clark that they were still stringing him along at KXOK but that he had lost interest in a radio job, being at this point "almost fully determined to go to New York."[63]

Now that the Mummers held no promise, Tom turned his attention to the St. Louis Poets' Workshop, which he had formed with William Jay Smith. As Smith recalled, they met regularly at the Williams home: "We were soon joined by Louise Krause, who had attended Mills College in California and had come back to St. Louis to take a master's degree in English." Another recruit was Elizabeth Fenwick Phillips, "who later married Clark Mills and as Elizabeth Fenwick wrote several fine mystery novels." They had some stationery printed and "sent poems to all the leading magazines with a covering letter signed by a fictitious secretary of the workshop. In a few carefully chosen words the letter described the great poetic flowering then taking place in St. Louis. The poems enclosed, the secretary stated, were representative samples of this remarkable Midwestern Renaissance. The editors addressed were less impressed by our flowering than we were: the poems all came back."[64]

In mid-November, Tom drove his mother, Grand, and Jiggs to see Rose at Farmington. He wrote, "She is like a person half-asleep now—quiet, gentle and thank God—not in any way revolting like so many of the others. She sat with us in a bright sunny room full of flowers—said 'yes' to all our questions—looked puzzled, searching for something—some times her eyes filled with tears—(so did mine). Only the little dog stirred her—she was delighted with him—held him and gave him water. She said once 'I can't believe he is!'—meaning 'alive' I suppose, as she always feared so much for his health. Strange, sad— It rains tonight, lightning, low thunder—"

The means needed for Rose to achieve a full recovery now seemed to be beyond medical capability. Edwina and Grand had not lost hope, Grandfather prayed, Cornelius remained stoically aloof, and Tom wondered if perhaps he might have "a touch of my sister's disease?!" Looking back over his journal, Tom commented, "I notice that in Sept. of last year—before leaving for Iowa—I remarked that I felt I was leaving the paternal roof for good— Well, here I am back under it. Yes, my life *is* a series of returns." Once again, he was enduring in his attic room a terror he had not known in the year he had been away: the terror of being trapped and imprisoned, with the accompanying painful swings from one emotional extreme to the other. "Swam 20 lengths—felt swell afterwards—then the renewed illness began— Oh, I hope I can throw it off *soon*—I want to live, live, *live!!*"

A while later, Tom alluded to a scene with his father at which apparently his mother and visiting grandmother were either present or within earshot.

> Dad started griping about my lack of job, Etc.—Surely I won't stay on here when I'm regarded as such a parasite. Now is the time to make a break—get away—away. I have pinned pictures of wild birds on my lavatory screen—Significant—I'm desperately anxious to escape. But where and how?—No money—Grand & Mother the only possible source. What a terrible trap to be caught in!—But there must be some way out and I shall find it.

> Nov. 16 or 17—(I'm a bit vague about the calendar these days) I wish to report one happy circumstance—am almost definitely decided [on] departure for New York. Seems almost too fabulous, doesn't it? But no serious obstacles apparent now. My miraculous grandmother is going to finance the trip. Will it *happen? Can* it happen? I hope so!

The one really gnawing question that he kept turning over and over was why his father held him in such open contempt. Why wasn't *he* the one to encourage him and support his aspirations? And why wouldn't he pay for his trip to New York, which he could well afford? Tom could reason that, after all, he had written an impressive body of work and two of his plays had been produced. But in the six years since he had been removed from the University of Missouri, all his father had done was to provide him with room and board. Inevitably, Edwina's reaction was that of the protective mother who chooses to move closer to her son, thus making him his father's competition.

Having long given up any hope of winning Edwina as an affectionate wife, C.C. had increasingly taken refuge in drink and in the company of his poker-playing buddies Pat Shackelford and "Hatch" Hatcher. More than that, he had forfeited any future at the shoe company: He could go neither back on the road nor forward in management. What Tom presently saw was a man defeated, retreating and imprisoned by his own hand. He realized that this, too, would be his own fate unless he could escape. He also knew the only way he could win his father's affection would be to succumb to the same imprisonment C.C. was suffering at the shoe company.

He now saw his father as a failure, and so, too, his father's father. Failure was begetting failure. And instinctively he knew it was only his ungovernable desire to write that could save him. Tom had the inherent strength of his forebears: the Williams clan, Tennessee pioneers. But *his* frontier was the theatre—that was what held out the promise of setting him free—and by now he was fast building up an arsenal of one-act and four full-length plays.

As a result, what had been developing in Tom all these years, above all other traits, was a *passion* to write. And that passion emanated from a curious source: a fierce reaction to the repressed love of his father, while in Rose this same love for her father was suppressed, ultimately crushing her sanity. Although Tom's mother and grandmother were giving him the concrete support he needed, paradoxically it was not so much their inspiration as his rage against his father that inflamed his burning desire to write. Tennessee Williams's career could be called an act of revenge, until at length he entered analysis, understood his sublimated love for his deceased father, and turned his anger on his mother, thus changing the character of his plays.

Tennessee was to say that his failure to stand up to his father and his overt fear of him were interpreted by the old man as weakness and cowardice and that he loathed his son for it. But now, in December of 1938, the tables were turning. During all the years of his youth, Tom had looked upon C.C. as an overpowering figure of strength. But once the son had become a young man, he began to perceive in his father the same weakness and cowardice that the old man had attributed to him. This knowledge was enough to give Tom the courage he needed to leave and to say, once again, good-bye to St. Louis.

After Grand had returned home, Edwina reported the news that Tom had changed his mind about going to New York because of the expense and risk involved and had decided to try his luck in New Orleans. "I will finance his trip and board, long enough to look for a job. He wants to leave on the bus next Monday, the day after Christmas. Could he spend the night with you? He will get a little money from his 'Candles to the Sun' which is to be produced in Kansas City." She also said, "He is sending three plays to 'Group Theatre' contest in New York."[65]

Actually, Tom planned once he got to Memphis to mail four one-acts, among which were *Moony's Kid Don't Cry* and *The Dark Room*, as well as the full-length plays *Spring Storm* and, via his agent, Olga Becker, in New York, *Candles to the Sun. Fugitive Kind* and *Not About Nightingales*, he decided to take with him. He had finished a third draft of *Nightingales*. "It may be very good or very bad—I don't know—haven't read it yet—just writing, writing—drinking coffee nearly every day—and feeling well in spite of it. But it is only the prospect of leaving St. Louis that keeps me up."

In her frantic fashion, Edwina made the preparations for Tom's departure and the imminent Christmas festivities a campaign of nonstop shopping. For Tom, that also meant a routine medical checkup. She informed her mother that "Dr. Alexander has finished the examination of Tom and found no physical troubles—at present. However, his left eye *has* been permanently injured."[66] Although this was a developing cataract and a serious condition, Tom took the more poetic view. "Had my eyes dilated at oculist—thought of beautiful theme for a painting. Four people—eyes closed—in ante-room of oculist office—forced to sit with eyes closed—awake—possibly for first times in their lives. Each thinking of what?—Trivial things? Yes, but—there is beauty and wonder in it if you look deep enough."

Often, too, there is beauty and wonder in fate, for on the night of December 22, in New York, a tiny actress, in physical appearance much like Edwina, was making a comeback in a play entitled *Outward Bound*. In 1912, Laurette Taylor had shone in *Peg O' My Heart*, but in recent years her career had been virtually destroyed by a descent into alcoholism. Now, against enormous odds, she was making a triumphant return. Seven years later, in the same theatre, she would appear to even greater acclaim in a play about a writer named Tom Wingfield, his mother, and his sister called *The Glass Menagerie*.

At the moment, however, Tom Williams was getting ready to leave his attic room, for good—he hoped. More than simply moving out from under his father's roof, Tom had to change *everything* in his life. And, again as fate would have it, a play contest provided the incentive. The Group Theatre in New York was offering a five-hundred-dollar prize to the winner, and although the age limit for entrants was twenty-five, Tom made up his mind to send his plays for consideration, giving his birth date as 1914 instead of 1911. His rationale was that he had every right to deduct the three lost years of enforced labor at the shoe company. Also, he decided that he would go first to New Orleans and en route stop off to see his grandparents, give their address in Memphis, Tennessee, as his, affix the name of *Tennessee* Williams to his plays, and mail them from there.

Of the many versions of how Tom became known as Tennessee, the most persistently apocryphal and romantic assertion, fostered by Williams himself, is that his classmates at Iowa gave him the nickname. But no one at any of the three universities he attended had any memory of his being called anything other than Tom, which explains why so many for so long failed to connect him to the famous playwright. Williams was also fond of ascribing the change to a southern weakness for "climbing the family tree" and to his heritage as a Tennessee pioneer. Actually, he mailed his plays from Memphis to the Group Theatre contest, affixing the name of Tennessee Williams, because he wanted simply to win the five hundred dollars—money that would enable him to buy the time to write. Tom had not the slightest notion of where that name would take him, the persona it would create, and the confusion that eliminating three years from his life would entail. Long after, Tennessee worried that, having faked his birth date, his deception would be made public; he even instructed his agent to warn reporters not to bring up his age at any interview he might be willing to give. As a result, many yearbooks and library card files, including that of the Library of Congress, recorded his birth date as 1914 instead of 1911, and some often even listed both in the same file drawer.

In the Winter of Cities

The day after Christmas, Tom started on a journey that would last the rest of his life. He would return home again, but briefly, then take off, only to alight somewhere else. He had become a wayfarer. In the last entry he made in his journal before leaving St. Louis, he said that the move to New Orleans seemed his last or only hope. "May be a new scene will revive me."

> Dec. 28—1938—Wed.—How strange! Immediately after the above entry I find my self reporting that *here* I actually am in a completely new scene—New Orleans—the Vieux Carré. Preposterous? Well, rather! Somehow or other things do manage to happen in my life. . . . I am delighted, in fact enchanted with this glamorous, fabulous old town. I've been here about 3 hours but have already wandered about the Vieux Carré and noted many exciting possibilities. Here surely is the place I was made for if any place on this funny old world.
>
> I am lying on the floor in front of a gas grate at about 2 A.M. to make this entry. I feel very quiet & comfortable—but full of anticipation! If only it can be done—financially—if only *only!* Much will happen I am sure in the days, weeks or months to come—
>
> Sufficient to say now that I am sleepy and happy or as nearly happy as old T.L.W. is able to be! The bed looks clean—I hope it is!—Tomorrow I will go out first thing to locate a cheap furnished room in the artists' section . . . En Avant!

Arriving late at night in New Orleans after a long bus trip from Memphis, Tom had checked into a small, sleazy hotel off the Robert E. Lee Circle. His luggage consisted of a suitcase, a portable typewriter, and a windup phonograph. Packed in his suitcase was his copy of Hart Crane, which he would carry for years to come. Another item was the bound ledger that had become his journal and that, despite his tendency to misplace everything else in his life, went everywhere with him. His hair was neatly cut and his shoes polished; he wore a dress shirt, tie, and a conservative suit. To New Orleanians, he looked what he was: a tourist.

The next day, Thursday, Tom went into the French Quarter and found a small hotel room that would cost him four dollars a week. He immediately dispatched a postcard depicting the Vieux Carré to his grandparents, and to his mother he wrote, "This is most fascinating place I've ever been. Arrived late last night & spent morning finding room—very scarce on account of Sugar Bowl game. I am situated for a week at 431 Royal Street. Letter soon."[67]

Grand wrote to her daughter: "Tom sent his plays from here to New York and gave this address. Yesterday we received notice they had received them and wanted him to write them where he was born and how old, how much University education he had had. I sent the card to Tom and I am sure he will give them the information they want. It seems strange that they should require that."[68]

> Fri. [30th] Judas Priest!—It's no use denying the fact that I am very blue & lonesome—enough so to be really worried about the prospects. . . . Being completely alone for 48 hours, even in the most enchanting of cities, has gotten on my nerves.
>
> Something will have to happen to relieve my depression tomorrow *or*—perhaps all will be lost. Nothing constructive done so far except a brief meeting with Ashton, Director of the WPA Theater, who told me to see a young lady about submitting my scripts—think I'll do that tomorrow. I *must* do something.
>
> Somebody has just moved in the room next door—even a stranger across a wall is comforting to me in this state.

Wayfarer though he might be, Tom was discovering the brutal truth that escape from his father's jailhouse did not in and of itself set him free from the self-imprisonment of his anxieties.

On New Year's Eve, Edwina sent off a short letter to her son, and as always it showed her concern over the practicalities of his existence, though a remarkable restraint for one who must have felt his absence keenly: "Your postal just received and I'm hastening to send you ten more until I hear how much more you need as rooms may be higher when so scarce. Also I'm sending your shoes which I had half-soled etc. I knew you'd find New Orleans interesting. Let me know where you are all the time. If, and as soon as you move, let me know immediately. Haven't time to write. Good luck—Happy New Year. Love, Mother."[69]

As she had when Tom was at Iowa, Edwina sent small amounts of money cribbed—doubtless without Cornelius's knowledge—from her household allowance. Grand was still giving music lessons and was able to send contributions, usually a ten-dollar bill, carefully stitched to her letters. Together, they would be the young playwright's principal backers for some time to come.

Once Tom was living in the French Quarter, it didn't take him long to cast off the garb and other telltale aspects of a tourist.

New Year's Day—1939—What a nite! I was introduced to the artistic and Bohemian life of the Quarter with a bang! All very interesting, some utterly appalling.

New Orleans and Tennessee Williams had found each other.

14

Vieux Carré

January–February 1939

TIME: The period between winter 1938 and spring 1939.

PLACE: A rooming house, No. 722 Toulouse Street, in the French Quarter of New Orleans.

THE SETTING OF THE PLAY: The stage seems bare. Various playing areas may be distinguished by sketchy partitions and doorframes. In the barrenness there should be a poetic evocation of all the cheap rooming houses of the world. This one is in the Vieux Carré of New Orleans, where it remains standing at 722 Toulouse Street, now converted to an art gallery. I will describe the building as it was when I rented an attic room in the late thirties, not as it will be designed or realized for the stage.

It is a three-story building. There are a pair of alcoves, facing Toulouse Street. These alcove cubicles are separated by plywood, which provides a minimal separation (spatially) between the writer (myself those many years ago) and an older painter, a terribly wasted man, dying of tuberculosis, but fiercely denying this circumstance to himself.

A curved staircase ascends from the rear of a dark narrow passageway from the street entrance to the kitchen area. From there it ascends to the third floor, or gabled attic with its mansard roof.[1]

In New Orleans, and most particularly in the Vieux Carré, the young Tennessee Williams first became aware of a dark side of life that seemed to drift timelessly, exhibiting a laissez-faire attitude that characterized the mores and amorality of the most colorful segment of humanity he had ever encountered. From the first, he became deeply attracted to the strangely sovereign life of the Old Quarter, existing apart from the rest of New Orleans: a cloistered heart of the city.

In the early 1920s, the French Quarter was rescued from decades of neglect by an influx of writers and artists who began restoring the old buildings and gradually transforming a slum area of New Orleans referred to disdainfully as "Frenchtown." In time, the Vieux Carré became identified with a burgeoning literary life, inaugurated by New Orleans chroniclers Roark Bradford and Lyle Saxon; soon such writers as William Faulkner, Ernest Hemingway, Edmund Wilson, and Sherwood Anderson were among the many who migrated there, who wrote and were published in a literary magazine called *The Double Dealer*. Artists of all kinds also came to the Old Quarter, lured by its promise, often its delusion, of freedom. Tennessee Williams recognized it as "a place in love with life."[2]

By the unseasonably warm month of January 1939, the Vieux Carré had become, as it remains, an asylum for every conceivable form of human, poor and rich, maverick and ne'er-do-well, the dispossessed and the misbegotten intermingling and cohabiting with casual industry and insouciant air, each with his own arcane system for survival. Below sea level, suffocatingly humid in summer and penetratingly cold in winter, the city has an atmosphere that is languid, and the sky seems so low that its drifting clouds often appear to be within reach. The effect is of life compressed and borne in on itself, a characteristic of so many who live in the Quarter and who would enter the plays and stories of Tennessee Williams.

Although on this first visit he stayed only a few weeks, Williams would return year after year to his "favorite city of America . . . of all the world, actually." He would always maintain, "My happiest years were there."[3] And though he was desperately poor and forced to hock everything he owned except his typewriter to get by—and that, too, on one occasion—his first experiences in New Orleans did not leave him, as in St. Louis, with bitter memories.

Whether the events he related much later in the play *Vieux Carré* and in the short story "Angel in the Alcove" actually occurred in the time and place he recounted is a matter for speculation. In both the play and the short story, Williams depicts Tom's seduction by a tubercular painter who is vainly denying the encroachment of death and is grasping at life, which is embodied in the ingenuous young writer. When the writer admits having had a previous one-night love affair with a paratrooper, the painter says, "Love can happen like that. For one night only."

Many years later, during a television interview, Williams remarked, "In New Orleans, I discovered a certain flexibility in my nature—it happened on New Year's Eve."[4] But which New Year's Eve? Given Tennessee's inclination to re-create his life in keeping with remembered emotions, it is more likely that his sexual encounter with the paratrooper was telescoped with experiences he had on his return to New Orleans in 1941, just prior to the attack on Pearl Harbor; by that time, the United States had been hastily mobilizing for war and the Quarter was overrun with servicemen. If such adventures did take place in the early winter of 1939, Tom made no mention of them in his journal. Possibly they did, and the "angel in the alcove" might have been the symbol of guilt for something at that brief period in his life he would not have admitted to God, to his journal, or to *anyone*. It is more likely, however, that the New Year's Eve festivities as he described them to his mother were a reasonably accurate account of what actually occurred, considering how prone he was when writing her to color his experiences in rosy pastels. Edwina was seldom fooled, though; with a husband like Cornelius, she had become quite adept at reading between the lines.

On January 2, Tom wrote to his mother on stationery cribbed from the St. Louis Poets' Workshop,* giving a new address, 431 Royal Street, in the French Quarter:

> The city has been wild with the football and sport carnival crowd—the big game was today so they will be gone tomorrow. I rented a room here in a cheap but clean hotel for four dollars a week. He would give me a month for twelve dollars—but I think I will find something better (for that price) soon as the crowd is gone.
>
> [The Knute Heldners] have been lovely to me. They invited me to a New Year's Eve party which lasted till day-break and traveled through about half-a-dozen different homes or studios and I met most of the important artists and writers. They are all very friendly and gracious. Roark Bradford, famous author of negro literature, and Lyle Saxon, who wrote Fabulous New Orleans,† both live in the Quarter and I am promised introductions to them. I met Mr. Ashton, director of the WPA theater. Their program will be open after the first of March and so could use some of my plays. I'm going to submit Fugitive Kind soon as I've made a few changes. They have a swell theater, large as the American in St. Louis, and their plays run for a week or more—but apparently they lack good material as the play I saw was quite feeble in plot.
>
> I'm crazy about the city. I walk continually, there is so much to see. The weather is balmy, today like early summer. I have no heat in my room—none is needed. The Quarter is really quainter than anything I've seen abroad—in many homes the original atmosphere is completely preserved. . . .

---

*Evidently, Tom Williams had packed some of the Poets' Workshop stationery, and the use he found for it was in writing various letters and in drafting pages of his plays. A blank piece of paper, especially stationery, had become by now, like Gulley Jimson's blank walls in Joyce Cary's *The Horse's Mouth*, irresistible. Many of the draft pages found in Tennessee Williams's archives were type- or handwritten on stationery with imprints ranging from the Plaza Hotel in New York to the Towers in Miami to the Caribe Hilton in San Juan, even to the House of Lords in London.

†Allean Hale writes in "Two on a Streetcar" (*Tennessee Williams Literary Journal*, Spring 1989, pp. 31–43) that "Lyle Saxon was the ambassador of the French Quarter, promoter of Mardi Gras, and genial host to all the famous who passed through. His *Fabulous New Orleans* had become such a best seller friends suggested it should be packaged with a praline as a tourist attraction."

The Quarter is alive with antique and curio shops where some really artistic stuff is on sale, relics of Creole homes that have gone to the block. I was invited to dinner by some people who own a large antique store. Their home is a regular treasure chest of precious objects.

Food is amazingly cheap. I get breakfast at the French market for a dime. Lunch and dinner amount to about fifty cents at a good cafeteria near Canal Street. And the cooking is the best I've encountered away from home. Raw oysters, twenty cents a dozen! Shrimp, crab, lobster and all kinds of fish—I have a passion for sea-food which makes their abundance a great joy.

The court-yards are full of palms, vines and flowering poinsettia, many with fountains and wells, and all with grill-work, balconies, and little winding stairs. It is heaven for painters and you see them working everywhere. Mr. & Mrs. Heldner (Alice Lippmann's friends) say that if I get desperate I can earn bread as a model—but I trust something better will turn up. The Heldners live in two rooms with a baby girl—he is brilliant and very good-hearted. Showed me his canvasses which have won fine critical comment but during his whole sixteen years in New Orleans he has only sold four. They are very modernistic so are not popular as decoration for homes. He has a red beard and often forgets where he is going when he leaves the house—but not as bad as Mrs. Lippmann! [Alice Lippmann was early champion of Williams.] There is a writer's project here and many of the writers I have met are on it—perhaps there is room for more. Lyle Saxon is at the head of it.

The fine weather and much walking have cured my cold and I am feeling splendidly. Will be here till Thursday and then will send my new address. . . . Mailed my plays from Memphis in plenty of time.[5]

Tourists, attending the Sugar Bowl game or Mardi Gras, flow into the Quarter as though on the crest of a high tide, flooding its streets and shops and bars, swiftly receding, often overnight, to leave the shop owners, street artists, and wily panhandlers a little richer for the wear. Everything and *everyone* immediately become available at much lower prices, and so Tom readily found a rooming house at 722 Rue Toulouse, with a dormer room on the third floor, for ten dollars a month.

Signing in as "Tennessee Williams, writer," he had moved from one attic to another. As Williams later described it, "in this old house it was either deathly quiet or else the high plaster walls were ringing like fire-bells with angry voices, with quarrels over the use of the lavatory or accusations of theft or threats of eviction. I had no door to my room . . . only a ragged curtain that couldn't exclude the barrage of human wretchedness often exploding. The walls of my room were pink and green stippled plaster and there was an alcove window."[6]

No longer attired in the raiment of a tourist and now looking like any other

Quarter resident, Tom had no problem in meeting people who composed a cross section of New Orleanians; as he told his grandparents, they were a mixture of writers and painters, radio announcers and "officials in an advertising company," and the heads of both the Federal Theatre Project and the Federal Writers' Project. Tom was still busy revising *Not About Nightingales* and had submitted *Fugitive Kind*, believing that these plays would provide good examples of his social consciousness.

However, it was a long way from Chicago to New Orleans, where social consciousness had an entirely different connotation. Tom wrote his mother: "The WPA theater has sent Fugitive Kind to their Regional Director in Florida for his judgement. They like the play better than any submitted so far but are afraid the social message might be too strong for a southern city."[7] Too truthful might be more like it. Of course there were always those in coffeehouses like the Café du Monde and in bistros like the Napoleon House who could deal with the truth and would be discussing the encroaching fall of Barcelona, which would mean the end of the Spanish Civil War, a victory for fascism, and a guarantee of world war.

But many New Orleanians had a cultivated faith in the homegrown fascism of Huey Long, and corruption in high and low office was de rigueur. In Walker Percy's view, "looting Louisiana with Protestant industry and Catholic gaiety" had resulted from the melding of the differences between the northerners who had emigrated from "up East" and the descendants of the Spanish and French Creole settlers. By the time Tom arrived in New Orleans, good politics consisted mainly in giving support to any politician who had the wit and guile to rival Louisiana's "Kingfish," as Huey Long was known. While not all could equal his guile, one governor, who had recently been driven from office in disgrace, did have the wit to announce, "When I took the oath of office, I did *not* take a vow of poverty."[8]

There was an additional reason for *Fugitive Kind* being rejected, of which Tom was not aware. By this time, Roosevelt's New Deal was a thing of the past, and the reputation of the WPA for harboring Communists prompted Congress to withhold any further funding and to investigate those suspected of being Party members. Hallie Flanagan, the national director since 1935 of the Federal Theatre Project, appeared before a congressional committee. When she spoke of "a certain Marlowesque madness" that permeated the Federal Theatre, she was asked by a congressman from Alabama in a low incriminating voice if Marlowe was a Communist.

Tom then turned to Lyle Saxon for assistance, but the Writers' Project, too, would not long survive the new emphasis in Roosevelt's administration on preparation for war. The Nazis were on the march again, breaking their promises at Munich, and in the Pacific, Japan was ruthlessly expanding its empire. In his journal, Tom noted that the "world [is] apparently on the point of explosion. War, war, war!—And I write fanciful introspective stories & precious verse!" He was not alone. Traditionally, the residents of the Quarter had always viewed the American annexation of Louisiana as a day for mourning. The lure that the Vieux Carré held out to the artist was *escape* from such mundane things as the internecine quarrels among nations.

Now Edwina had two correspondents: the Dakins and Tom. She told her parents that she had been "busy cleaning the attic and Rose's room which Tom left in a mess! I suppose he told you that Dr. Alexander said not to do anything about the eye unless it got worse. I have an idea the injury occurred when he had that high-blood pressure. I read the other day that it sometimes affects the eyes." At the same time, Tom learned that his brother was unhappy because a new ruling prevented him from getting his B.A. in two and a half years instead of the usual four and that he intended to take math in summer school "so he can be an officer in the R.O.T.C." and qualify for a law degree. His sister was under the care of a new doctor, who would only say, "She is just the same," prompting Edwina to complain, "They are always so uncommunicative!"[9]

Shortly after moving into his garret room overlooking Toulouse Street, Tom told his mother that his landlady, Mrs. Anderson, "is planning to open a boarding-house next week. She has promised to let me serve tables for my meals and says if the business is successful she may also give me my room and a few dollars a week. However her capital is very small and she plans to do the whole work herself—so I don't know how it will turn out. She's an extremely practical, energetic woman—a widow who lost her money in Chicago. With her enthusiasm and business-sense she may make a go of it. She's having some cards printed which I'm going to distribute for her."[10] To ensure that he would be suitably attired to wait on tables, he asked his mother to send his dark blue double-breasted coat and a black bow tie.

A week later, he wrote "Meals in the Quarter for a Quarter" across the top of still another letter to his mother. "I just have time for a few lines. Am enclosing one of our printed cards which I composed and have been distributing around town. The slogan is my own invention and seems to be effective. . . . I serve as waiter, cashier, publicity manager, host—in fact, every possible capacity, including dish-washer. When not busy in the dining-room I stand on the sidewalk and try to drag people upstairs!" Apparently, Mrs. Anderson was even more practical than Tom reported, for she hired a Mrs. Nesbit to do the cooking and put two other famished elderly women to work in exchange for their meals. He now described his landlady as a "perfect termagant" but said that "the cooking is the best I've ever tasted—the cook is an old lady who ran a restaurant in Florida till the depression. We all conspire to keep Mrs. Anderson out of the way as her sharp tongue kills the trade."[11]

The Window in the Alcove

By the end of January, Tom was out of work again. At midnight on the twenty-eighth, huddled in his candlelit cubicle, he wrote in his journal, "Well, the 'Quarter Eat Shop' had a very brief existence—exactly one week. It is now past history. Little Man What Now? I wish I knew. My life seems to be a pretty constant state of wishing I knew. Well, I've found out before—I shall again." To his mother he sounded a somewhat more promising note: "Today I got lined up for the Writers' Project through Mr. Lyle Saxon. It seems fairly sure that I will get on it pretty soon."[12]

This was not to be, but he did meet two other writers who became friends. One was Joe Turner, a merchant seaman who it was said later lost his life at sea, and the other Frank Bunce. His admiration was reserved in the case of Bunce, who, he told his mother, "writes for the *Saturday Evening Post* but doesn't like to write," although "he gets $500 per story and sells one or two every month. Since he has a car and many attractive girl friends, he has proved a very valuable friend to me." He added that they were planning to drive over to Gulfport "to visit some girls he knows there."[13] What Edwina's reaction to that plan was can be easily imagined. Tom did confess to his journal, though, that his and Frank's "viewpoints in art & life are so dramatically divergent that it is amazing that we should be friends. It struck me today as an idea for a novel or play—'Strange Companions'—in which a boy of my sort is contrasted to a fellow like Bunce, their reactions to each other, influence, Etc.—a psychological thing."

There were other acquaintances Tom mentioned. One was Dick Orme, who became a good friend in later years. Also, "a funny little fellow named Verbeck came running into the house in search of a lost black cat—turns out to be a poet who writes about 'dragons and chrysanthemums'—very *precieuse* [sic] but very nice." He added, "Life here has been rather even & pleasant since New Years Eve."

It was more like a hangover, however, because, as he recounted to his mother:

> . . . we've had a very hectic time at 722 Rue Toulouse. As I've probably mentioned, the land-lady has had a hard time adjusting herself to the Bohemian spirit of the Vieux Carre. Things came to a climax this past week when a Jewish society photographer in the first floor studio gave a party and Mrs. Anderson expressed her indignation at their revelry by pouring a bucket of [boiling] water through her kitchen floor which is directly over the studio and caused a near-riot among the guests. They called the patrol-wagon and Mrs. Anderson was driven to the Third Precinct on charges of Malicious Mischief and disturbing the peace. The following night we went to court—I was compelled to testify as one of the witnesses. Mrs. Anderson said she did not pour the water but I, being under

oath, could not perjure myself—the best I could do was say I thought it was highly improbable that any lady would do such a thing! The Judge fined her fifteen dollars. One of the other witnesses was the wife of Roark Bradford, who wrote [*Ol' Man Adam and His Chillun*, 1928, on which Marc Connelly based] Green Pastures, the famous negro play. Her dress was ruined at the party. I went to see her afterwards to assure her my part in the affair was altogether unwilling—she was very nice and cordial and assured me there were no hard feelings at least toward me. I also met Mr. Bradford and Sam Bird, a New York producer. As all my plays are in New York I had nothing to show him. I'm using my colorful experiences here as background for a new play which is well under way. . . . I'm completely out of funds now—so could use a few dollars if you're not in the same predicament.[14]

After a while, Tom became once again on more or less friendly terms with Mrs. Anderson, who began to feel motherly toward him and let him sample her gumbo or whatever else she had cooking on the stove. He desperately needed work for rent money and other basic needs and was faced with having to hock his riding boots and typewriter. He said regretfully that the Eat Shop had been perfect because it gave him something else to do, and it saved his eyes, his brain, and his money—"but like all lovely things it too proved fugitive."

News from home now only added to what already seemed a long night-mare: St. Louis had become a diminished reality, exchanged for a wholly new one in New Orleans. Tom also heard from Willard Holland, but that merely served to underscore how little progress he had been able to make, a failure that threatened him with a dreaded return to his father's dominion. Holland wrote, "I hope you keep your job until something more in your line develops. The Group Theatre simply *must* evince some interest." He added the wish that "the WPA will do one or more of your scripts and pay you for it. Have you tried the radio stations there?"

Lyle Saxon—"Mr. French Quarter," as he came to be known—tried to help Tom as best he could, referring him to editors of trade journals and man-agers of radio stations, but to no avail. The radio stations, Tom said, were too "impoverished" to pay anything. Holland did manage to lift his friend's spirits somewhat by telling him that Thomas L. Williams had made his "St. Louis radio de-butt. I condensed your Munitions King play [*Me, Vashya!*] to 7 min-utes. Called it 'Men Who March' and we stole the show. Every one com-mented on our thrilling material and your name was mentioned 3 times in the broadcast." Edwina heard the program and told her parents that it sounded fine. She thought that perhaps he might get there yet!

Holland also held out a tentative promise that the Mummers might pro-duce *Not About Nightingales* if the rights to another play they had in mind proved unavailable. Then he inquired, "Are you intrigued with N'Awleans? I always have thought of the word 'stagnant' as being particularly suited to the place."[15]

The pace of life in the Quarter—so laid-back that some said it was laid out—often involved a surrender to life for life's sake, and Tom found this unsettling. He had no wish or intention to take his place among the writers of unwritten works in progress. Equally threatening was a hedonism that both shocked and intrigued him, the classical Apollonian disciplines gone to Dionysian orgiastic rites. At once, an inner and lasting conflict was set up. In time, Tennessee Williams would come to call himself a "rebellious Puritan," and looking back upon the impact of New Orleans, he would say that there "I found the kind of freedom I had always needed. And the shock of it against the Puritanism of my nature has given me a theme, which I have never ceased exploiting."[16]

Many subsequent experiences and changes of scene would leave their imprint upon him, but none would make the deep, lasting incursions that those in New Orleans did on the young Tom Williams. A whole montage of disjointed memories would run over and over again through his mind and would infiltrate his writings: the voodoo cult in Congo Square; the shady ladies in Storyville; the Creoles of Color on Rampart; Basin Street and Dixieland jazz; the Musée Méchanique; the all-night chicory coffee and hot, freshly baked beignets at Café du Monde; "the peculiarly benign morning sunlight and those wheat cakes with corn syrup"; the sixty-cent lunch at Galatoire's: crawfish bisque, oysters Rockefeller; the seven-cent ride on streetcars named Desire and Cemeteries; the early-morning sound of a horse's hooves clip-clopping along streets like Chartres and Ursulines and along the oak-lined Esplanade; the raunchy Decatur Street bars; everywhere the redolent odors of gumbo, sweet olive trees, and musty courtyards; the mournful sounds of ships' horns at night and of a lone saxophonist leaning against the locked cathedral doors in Jackson Square; the calls of a coal peddler and the lyrical chant of a blackberry woman . . .

> *Black-berries—fresh and fine, I got black-berries, lady.*
> *Fresh from de vine, I got black-berries, lady,*
> *three glass fo' a dime,*
> *I got black-berries . . .*

. . . and always the ominous presence of the Mississippi, its brownish blend of marsh water and river mud snaking its way around the crescent curve of the city, pressing against the levees that keep the Old Quarter from turning into a vast swamp. Running parallel but ignoring each other were Royal and Bourbon streets: Royal, as the name implies, and Bourbon, vulgarity's epitome, the sacred province of the French Quarter pimps, prostitutes, and male hustlers. Then there were, as he titled his poem, the "Mornings on Bourbon Street":

He thought of the innocent mornings on Bourbon Street,
of the sunny courtyard and the iron
lion's head on the door.

He thought of the quality light could not be expected
to have again after rain,
the pigeons and drunkards coming together from
under the same stone arches; to move again in the sun's
faint mumble of benediction with faint surprise.

He thought of the tall iron horseman before the Cabildo,
tipping his hat so gallantly toward old wharves,
the mist of the river beginning to climb about him.

He thought of the rotten-sweet odor the Old Quarter had,
so much like a warning of what he would have to learn.

He thought of belief and the gradual loss of belief
and the piecing together of something like it again.
But, oh, how his blood had almost turned in color
when once, in response to a sudden call from a window,
he stopped on a curbstone and first thought

Love. Love. Love.

He knew he would say it. But could he believe it again?
He thought of Irene whose body was offered at night
behind the cathedral, whose outspoken pictures were hung
outdoors, in the public square,
as brutal as knuckles smashed into grinning faces.

He thought of the merchant sailor who wrote of the sea,
haltingly, with a huge power locked in a halting tongue—
lost in a tanker off the Florida coast,
the locked and virginal power burned in oil.

He thought of the opulent antique dealers on Royal
whose tables of rosewood gleamed as blood under lamps.

He thought of his friends.

He thought of his lost companions,
of all he had touched and all whose touch he had known.

He wept for remembrance.

But when he had finished weeping, he washed his face,
he smiled at his face in the mirror, preparing to say
to you, whom he was expecting,

Love. Love. Love.

But could he believe it again?[17]

Although Tom had also become acquainted with a few respectable New Orleanians, who lived "uptown" in beautiful old mansions in the Garden District, it was the subterranean world of the Old Quarter and its habitués—"Quarter rats," as they were called—that caught his imagination. In time, his reminiscences would become abstractions: elegiac evocations of places and events and gossamer apparitions of people, the pariahs—the lost and tormented, who would have long since disappeared down the corridors of memory were they not otherwise destined for an ongoing life in the plays and stories of Tennessee Williams.

By the end of January, and with the Quarter's feverish anticipation of Mardi Gras—as pagan a pageant as ever masqueraded as the religious advent of Lent—Tom began to feel apprehensions about staying on in New Orleans: "I swim every day at the 'Y'—eat at cafeterias, go to the movies—write rather badly—" At night, he was drawn more and more to wandering the streets of the Quarter, always the avidly curious observer, a part of and yet apart from the vagrant existence of those for whom a life clearly without purpose was not a means, but *the* end. Nowhere except in this most foreign of American cities could Tom have found a more darkly sensual environment where night shadows and sounds mingled as if they were issuing from a Dantesque vision of hell. And it frightened him: this pull within him, this desire—as he had declared so many times—just to "live, live, live!" It was a cry he could almost hear emanating from nearby St. Louis Cemetery, where the dead were placed in tombs and vaults above ground, because otherwise they would be buried in watery graves.

Though Tom was aware of death's haunting the Old Quarter like a specter on every corner, for him there was an even greater threat. He knew the worst possible eventuality would be the gradual erosion and ultimate abandonment of his writing. That *would* mean death—a prophetic conviction he held until at the last it became true. He had heard that many writers, like Faulkner before him, had fled the Vieux Carré for that very reason. "I write badly or not at all," he confessed to his journal. "Started a marvelously promising new play this week—but can't seem to get going on it. Dull, dull! I sit down to write and nothing happens. Washed up?—No!" He needed a new stimulus. And that stimulus was, as it would be all his life, to move on to a change of scene.

Later in the year, in looking back upon the relatively short time he had spent in New Orleans, Tom appended the thought to a journal entry that it was "a crucial time—might easily have ended in some form of disaster." He was alluding in particular to a question he had asked himself: "Am I all animal, all willful, blind, stupid *beast?* Is there another part that is *not* an accomplice in this mad pilgrimage of the flesh?" He had come as close as he could to expressing the accelerating attraction to members of his own sex. He had seen, if not yet experienced, uninhibited sex. The effect upon him was shock and revulsion and fear of what he might become if he remained much longer in the French Quarter.

Certainly there is no precise explanation of what determines sexual orientation or when it takes on a more definite direction. Whether the events of his few weeks in New Orleans—which proved to be portentous and decisive with respect to his career and to his itinerant lifestyle—might also have brought his homosexuality closer to the surface can only be conjectured. There can be no question, though, that the impact of New Orleans upon Tom's puritan nature was profound and lasting, nor can there be any doubt that these initial events affected the character and content of his writings. Although he was only a few months away from a decisive homosexual experience, the evidence is that Tom Williams was both captivated and frightened by the French Quarter's way of life. He knew only that he must leave, go elsewhere—anywhere but St. Louis.

By the middle of February, Tom was witnessing the mounting madness associated with the approach of Fat Tuesday, the day of rampant indulgence preceding the day of atonement. The parades and the balls and the hardly private parties celebrating Mardi Gras had begun, instilling in Tom a lifelong disdain for the event. Although in gay circles Tennessee Williams enjoyed the often hilarious ritual of antic camping—while seldom joining in himself—he was never able to reconcile himself to flagrant public displays, which he saw as a mockery not simply of women but of his own sense of manhood.*

With Mardi Gras only a few days away, providence took a hand. A young musician, a clarinetist named James Parrott, was staying in the Toulouse rooming house and was en route to Los Angeles. Jim was more the kind of

---

*In an October 1976 interview with George Whitmore at the Hotel Elysée in New York, Williams said, "I don't understand most transvestites. I think the great preponderance of them damages the gay liberation movement by travesty, by making a travesty of homosexuality, one that doesn't fit homosexuality at all and gives it a very bad public image. We are *not* trying to imitate women. We are trying simply to be comfortably assimilated by our society" (*Gay Sunshine Interviews*, vol. 1 [San Francisco: Gay Sunshine Press, 1978], p. 312).

young male Tom could relate to: He fit in with the heterosexual images of Clark Mills, Willard Holland, Stanley Kowalski, and Harold Mitchell, and so the two mavericks struck up an immediate friendship. Fond of jazz and the company of pretty girls, Jim also thought he might become an actor or a director. He had been an English teacher but had given that up as too dull. Now he planned to drive the southern route to the West Coast and excited Tom with the possibility of a career in Hollywood.

As a result, Jim and Tom agreed to pool their all-too-meager resources for the journey, optimistically expecting to find temporary employment in Los Angeles while living on a pigeon ranch owned by Jim's aunt and uncle. Armed with a clarinet and a typewriter, how could they lose? they asked each other. Their determination to get work in the film studios provided that added measure of youthful optimism to help fuel the trip.

Jim, who was athletic, of slender build, and about the same height as Tom, looked like he could be his younger brother. Although Tom was now in his twenty-eighth year, he told everyone he would be twenty-five in March, to be consistent with the age he had represented to the Group Theatre; in fact, he looked younger than twenty-five and often had the problem in bars of being regarded as underage. Had Tom stayed in New Orleans much longer in his present penniless condition, his mother would be sending him bus fare to come home, which was the last thing in the world he wanted. But Jim, with his buoyant good humor, enthusiasm, and confident view of life, offered Tom hope for the future.

On February 18, Tom mailed a postcard to Edwina with a message of inflated reassurance:

> A musician under contract in Hollywood has offered me free transportation to West Coast, no expense except meals on road, which seems too good to refuse, so I am leaving this A.M. We plan to take southern route along Mexican border, will stop several days at El Paso, Texas. You can write me there, General Delivery, enclose a small checque. Parrott, the musician, thinks he can get me work in studios. Will write letter first stop.[18]

On Monday the twentieth, the day before Mardi Gras, the two adventurers revved up Jim's Ford V-8 and departed New Orleans in high gear and high spirits. And so it was that Tennessee Williams, nomadic playwright, embarked upon one of countless journeys, which would continue unabated to the last restless days of his life.

15

West by Southwest

February–July 1939

En route to the West Coast, the two pilgrims met with the predictable adventures that come of no gas, no money, and no shelter at a time of year when the warm climate of Southern California must have beckoned them like a mirage. Knowing what an agitated state his mother must be in, Tom wrote an artful letter from San Antonio.

> No doubt you were surprised by my sudden decision to travel westward, I hope not too disagreeably. It seemed nothing was to be gained by remaining any longer in New Orleans—the cuts in the WPA made it uncertain when they could hire me and no other permanent work was available there. This fellow, Jim Parrott, was driving to the West Coast and invited me along free of charge. He's a swell young fellow—his family have a summer home in Lake George, New York, and winter home at Miami, Fla. He's a musician and has been promised work in Hollywood and thinks he could get me work there in the studios. We delayed our departure till Monday in order to see a little of the Mardi Gras—two days of it was quite enough.
>
> We are going over the "Old Spanish Trail" through southern Texas, along the Mexican border, New Mexico, Arizona and Southern California to Los Angeles. . . . The trip is a wonderful experience for me. I'm collecting lots of significant material on the way—it is all very stimulating. . . . I had not heard anything from my plays in New York when I left. I'm writing them tonight to hold the plays till I get settled somewhere. I will want to have them in Hollywood—I hope they have at least some encouragement for me (at the Group).
>
> We've been driving since sunrise so I'm dead tired. The air is delightful—dry and bracing—but makes me too sleepy to write. As I mentioned in the postcard I hope you can send me a small checque to El Paso, Texas, "Gen'l delivery"—to provide me with living expenses on the way. We have a pup tent and a couple of army cots—intend to sleep in tourist lots along the "Trail"—but tonight is too chilly for that. Ordinarily my expenses will not run over 50c a day as Jim is paying all the car expense himself. I think I was extremely lucky to get this chance—only hope you are not too disturbed about it.[1]

Stretching their funds to the limit, the two travelers often had to decide on a choice between fuel for their stomachs or for the gas tank. Hunger won out, and so the Ford was sometimes kept in motion by their siphoning gas from parked cars. In her memoir, Edwina Williams rather indignantly doubted this, saying her son would never be guilty of such a thing, much less could he "operate a siphon if his life depended on it. He has no mechanical skill."[2] Likely, though, the clarinet player did, while the writer kept careful watch.

Edwina's only comment to her parents regarding his letter sent from San Antonio was: "I suppose he has written you of his sudden decision to try his luck on the West Coast. I don't know how he expects to get back! I sent fifteen $'s to him at El Paso where he expected to be on the twenty-third or fourth—says he's enjoying trip immensely and does not remember ever feeling so well—so I suppose I must not worry *too* much about him!"[3]

By the time Tom and Jim arrived in El Paso, they were broke. Jim began looking for work in a band to help provide enough gas and food money to make it to Phoenix. And Tom decided to put his writing skills to work and composed a form letter meant to wring the hearts and pocketbooks of editors at large.

> Dear Editor: The author of these poems and his friend, Jimmy, a jobless musician, have run out of money and gas in El Paso, Texas. There is a terrific dust-storm raging and a sheriff named Fox who puts undesirable transients in the house of detention [for] thirty days. The author and the musician, a good tenor sax player, are not quite sure of their desirability and would like to continue westward to California where they understand that unemployed artists can make fifty cents an hour picking fruit. Their jalopy, running on kerosene or low-grade gas, could make Cal. on ten or fifteen dollars. If you like the poems an acceptance would aid materially in the author's survival. He knows that such appeals to an editor are unfair and in extremely bad taste and that a rejection slip would be a deserved rebuke.[4]

Which editor, if any, received Tom's appeal is not known. Apparently, the adventurers made it to Phoenix, not on the dubious charity of a would-be publisher but, rather, on the strength of Jim's musicianship. In a letter written to his father, Tom said, "Parrott, the fellow I'm traveling with, has run low on funds so we've had to make a pretty slow trip, stopping off to earn gas money at various points along the way. . . . His clarinet was stolen in Texas which accounts for the difficulties. He had to replace it with a large portion of the travelling fund."[5]

By now, Edwina must have engaged in some melodramatic hand-wringing, because Cornelius urged Tom to contact Sam Webb, one of his shoe salesmen in Culver City, as soon as he arrived on the West Coast. In his letter, Tom assured his father, "We will reach Los Angeles in about a week and I will certainly see Mr. Webb the first thing. It will be good to have a connection like that. Perhaps he can give me some leads on temporary employment till I find an opening in script writing."

He also told his father, "We're stopping at a tourist camp owned by an Indian squaw, Mrs. Cactus Flower, who collects her two bits at sun-up and says she's got a load of buckshot for anybody who tries to break camp without paying." Whether this incidental information was subsequently given a dramatist's elaboration to turn it into a colorful incident is not known, but Tennessee later said that Tom and Jim were stealthily driving away at 4:00 A.M. when the Ford backfired, and as they crouched low, muttering something on the order of a prayer, Mrs. Cactus Flower, true to her word, let go with a double-barreled salvo. Shaken but unscathed, they apparently went on their way.

Driving through the desert and the Gila Mountains impressed Tom as "thrilling . . . like being on another planet, so totally different from the East. We have been cooking our meals over open fires along the roadside." Some of the things he saw, though, were more appalling than thrilling. He told his mother:

> I'm amazed by the number of destitute transients on the highways. You see them everywhere. Fine, able-bodied young men, who are unable to make a living anywhere, simply wander from place to place, begging for any kind of work. A few days ago we picked up a family of 3 on the road, including a little 4 year old girl. They shared our cabin with us and the wife cooked our meals. Unable to make a living in their home town, they were headed for California—had to sell their car as they couldn't buy gas. It is pitiful to see even little children along the road, but a valuable experience as it gives you a very clear, unforgettable picture of the tragic dilemma in which many Americans are now finding themselves due to the economic mess we are in.[6]

The "paternal roof" had shielded Tom from the realities of the Depression, but now he was witnessing its effects firsthand. Nearly a decade after the stock market crash, 9.4 million Americans were still unemployed, and what Tom was observing, probably for the first time, were desperate members of the one-third of a nation who remained, in the President's words, ill-housed, ill-clad, ill-nourished. Indeed, the Great Depression was not over and would continue undiminished until the country became involved in World War II.

Before Tom dispatched his letter, the only word Edwina had received was a postcard mailed from El Paso, in which he said they had been twice across the Mexican border through Ciudad Acuña and Juárez. Edwina's reply, sent to Phoenix, general delivery, was rather curt, an attitude she often took to hide her hurt feelings. "I trust you received the two small checques I sent to you, at El Paso—by air mail. . . . Let me know where and when to send your next checque and how *much* you need." Not merely curt but also coy, she needled at Tom's sense of guilt: "Aren't you ashamed of cutting me out of a trip to New Orleans to see you?"[7] The amazing thing about the umbilical cord is how far it will stretch, and Tom could never bring himself to sever it. Destitute as he was, he nonetheless was "the fastidious hobohemian who sent his laundry home to mother"[8] and who, on those occasions when he was flat broke, could depend upon her or Grand to send "a small checque."

As Jim Parrott recalled, "The Border authorities in California held us out for a time, said we looked like 'Okies' to them!"[9] But late in the afternoon of Monday, March 6, Tom and Jim arrived in Los Angeles, "the apparent end of our journey," Tom wrote in his diary. "I went to the 'Y'—got a room—Jimmie had supper with me and then drove on out to his Uncle's." Suddenly out of the company of his newfound friend, he wrote, "Quite appalled at my isolation! I have never felt lonelier in my life—or less enterprising, so the fate which now faces me is inscrutable to say the least. Oh God, be a little sorry for Tom tonight and let him sleep and wake up stronger & able to go on."*

By Tuesday, Tom—not having heard anything from Jim—wandered about the streets of what must have seemed to him a dead city, as eerie a place as he had ever seen and, unlike the Old Quarter, utterly devoid of character. By 1939, the Depression years had corroded the boomtown look of the 1920s. Such prosperity as there was among the fortunate few moved westward to West Hollywood, Beverly Hills, Brentwood, Pacific Palisades, and Malibu, all within reach or in the vicinity of the movie studios. But downtown Los Angeles looked as though it had been hit by a blight. The once-elegant Biltmore Hotel faced Pershing Square, a small city park grown over with rat-infested palm trees and run over with human relics: the homeless, mute, wasted, and defeated, the many who had traveled thousands of miles across the country in search of work, some modicum of security, only to give up in despair.

Nearby, a two-story cafeteria, Clifton's, with the slogan over its portals PAY WHAT YOU WISH, VISITORS WELCOME, catered to the poor and near starving and had about it the aspect of an elaborate funeral parlor, with live organ music, meant to cheer its woebegone patrons. For thirty cents or less, a customer could buy a full meal, and those who arrived after dark saw a cascading waterfall glow with blue, yellow, pink, and green lights while neon flowers burst into bloom. Sitting in a terraced dining room under a thatched hut, Tom was appalled not only by the man-made waterfalls and rainstorms but also by the aquariums and aviaries, with the trilling song of innumerable birds accompanied by organ music. The cafeteria hosted some eight thousand customers each day and became a monument to the rampant kitsch for which the "city of

---

*A few months later, Williams appended a note to this entry, saying, "I felt like I was going to cry—could scarcely control my voice—Jim left me at the Y.M.C.A. and I was completely lost. I shall never forget that lonely night in the Y.M.C.A. room in the heart (?) of downtown Los Angeles."

angels" has since gained a certain fame. Tom could not have landed in a more nightmarish place.

> Awful! Awful! Such appalling loneliness. Jim didn't call—met no one and feel too miserable to live—but will have to just the same. Remember the little grey fox you saw chained to the wall in a little Texas town on the way here? He looked at you with frightened, miserable eyes—then shuddered and buried his little face in his fur—shutting out the sight of the world that made his little savage heart a captive. Tonight he is my brother, he is my *self*— The Little fox and I are together in our great loneliness, our lostness and desperation.

Unable to face a third day alone at the Y, Tom called Jim and headed out to the country. It was raining hard that night when he arrived "like a wet dog" at Adelaide and Fred Parrott's doorstep. He was warmly welcomed and fed a good supper. The next day, he got in contact with Sam Webb. Edwina commented to her parents, "At last, Cornelius feels that he should be-stir himself a little for Tom, so he wrote him a letter at Phoenix and a letter to his salesman, Sam Webb, in Los Angeles to look out for him."[10]

Finally, Tom sent his mother the reassuring news she had been waiting for:

> I am now staying (of all places!) on a "pigeon ranch" in Los Angeles County. It's owned by Jim Parrott's Uncle. I arrived here with a terrific cold and they insisted that I stay with them and have treated me like a member of the family. I'm paying them $3.00 a week for room and board. They are not very well off so I thought I had better pay them at least the cost of feeding me.
>
> Jim is staying at another relative's and both of us are looking for work. Sam Webb took me over to the Broadway Dept. Store where . . . I spent an afternoon pulling sticks out of shoes—for nothing!
>
> I haven't heard a word from New York concerning my plays. . . . I won't stay here long unless I find work as I think L.A. is a thoroughly unattractive place to live unless you own a car and can drive about the beaches and the hills.[11]

Tom confided to his journal that, although at first it was "a sublime relief to be out here in the country" with the Parrotts, ". . . I got lonesome again—isolated feeling returned—today I felt panicky—went out to see Jim. . . . Got him to drive me to a bar where I drank a hi-ball & two beers—a good substitute for suicide—but it didn't last long—depression returned & I left before supper feeling quite desperate. This really does seem rather like 'Custer's last stand'—but this journal is a succession of such apparent finales which turn out to be continued in the next issue."

What many found puzzling about Tennessee Williams was his propensity

for writing volumes of letters, so many of which were never mailed. They
were unmailed not only because he might lack postage or an envelope but
more often because of the driving need he felt to set down his thoughts, to
communicate more with himself than others, the need to *write* when others
silently talk to themselves.

Then there were those he forgot to mail that turned up later lost in the
pages of a manuscript, such as one addressed to his St. Louis friends Anne and
Blandford Jennings:

> . . . I was offered a free ride out here with a high school English teacher
> from New York State who was fed up with his profession and wanted to
> rough it a while. . . . I am boarding here on the pigeon ranch with his
> Uncle and he with his first cousin—I'm working for my board, killed and
> picked sixty squabs yesterday and drove them into the markets. We're
> about twenty miles out of L.A.—of course I had some interest in Holly-
> wood but that expired after one disgusted look at the place. . . . The
> owner gets dead drunk every night and one of my principal duties is
> to take him home and keep him out of communication with the local
> police. . . .
>
> I may start selling shoes Monday—one of Dad's salesmen is getting
> me a job I don't want in a retail shoe store—but I need the money to pay
> some debts—I skipped out of New Orleans owing everyone. I still love
> that old town and want to go back—but probably won't for sometime.
>
> All of my plays are still in New York—I haven't heard a thing about
> them. Perhaps they're all lost in the mail—which possibility does not dis-
> turb me too much as I suspect I'm better at picking squabs than writing
> plays. Oh, yes, I also shovel manure on the ranch—which should prove
> excellent preparation for Hollywood if I go back there. . . .
>
> So long—10.*[12]

At about the time he wrote to the Jenningses, Tom also got off a note to his
father, saying that Sam Webb had told him to come down to Culver City to
start work. Plainly bulling the old man, he said he would enjoy getting some
retail experience. Also, after Webb had visited him, Tom assured his father,
"Sam's impression of the pigeon ranch was not altogether correct. The pigeons attract a great many flies but the house itself is perfectly clean."[13]

In yet another unmailed, partially completed letter to an unknown correspondent—written on International Shoe Company stationery with Sam J.
Webb's Hayward address imprinted—Tom wrote that he had just received a
card from the Group Theatre informing him that one of his plays had not yet

---

*This is the first known instance in which Tom used the numeral 10, alternating with Tenn and
Tennessee; any one of the three he would append to his letters from then on—excepting, of
course, those to his family, to whom he was forever Tom.

been eliminated from the contest and that probably he would hear from them within the next few days. "I think it is beastly of them to tease me along that way!!! 'Incidentally,' said the Group 'your friend in New York did not give us *Candles.*' There were no tear stains on the paper—but it shows they are getting Williams conscious up there—I hope."[14]

The "friend in New York" was obviously Olga Becker, who, as it turned out, had misplaced her copy of *Candles to the Sun,* prompting Edwina to exclaim, "I'd write a letter to that Olga and burn her up for losing your play in N.Y." It is not known whether Tom complied, but he did agree with his mother: "I think it is outrageous that Olga Becker lost my copy of 'Candles.'" He asked Edwina to contact a theatre group in Kansas City to whom he had sent his "last remaining" copy.

In still another letter to his mother, Tom said that Sam Webb thought he could employ him "selling shoes during the Easter season, though he feels I'd do better writing for the movies. . . . It will take time to crash the studios so I'm awfully anxious to get any type of work now." He also mentioned that "Jim Parrott got a job in an airplane factory at $18.00 a week—his cousin is employed there. I also applied but they gave me a rigorous physical test and my vision proved too defective. If you don't think America is preparing for war you ought to see the boom in plane-building out here! They're hiring workers daily and turning out planes at top-speed."

He also mentioned "getting free art lessons" from Adelaide Parrott, who was an art instructor in a WPA program. "I've made 3 oil paintings of scenes out here which are really *good*—she says I have a remarkable talent so maybe I'll come back East in a beret." Doubtless, Edwina thought, That's all Cornelius would need! Finally, stretching the facts in his fashion, Tom announced that he had "some bad news!—I broke my glasses driving over the mts.," his only pair, which in truth he had left in New Orleans. A new pair, he said, would cost only "$8.00 with an exam. thrown in and two dollars cheaper if they have the present prescription. So you might phone Aloe's to send my right eye prescription out here—I don't need a left lens as I can't read with that eye anyway."[15]

Understandably, Edwina became alarmed, especially when the family oculist told her that it was very important that Tom keep after the problem and see him immediately upon returning. Seizing on this, she wrote, "Don't you think you'd better return now and get busy on it?" As an inducement, she said that she and Cornelius were about to buy a house. "It has a perfectly luxurious attic with *bath!* Wouldn't you love that?"[16] She enclosed a check and cautioned him not to use his eyes too much. Tom was hardly tempted to return to St. Louis, but the family's planned trip to the New York World's Fair made a return "very enticing." He told his mother that it was New Orleans, not St. Louis, that made him quite homesick, Los Angeles being "so barren-looking and the people generally so common. . . . From the morning papers (which I read with my new glasses) it looks very much like a *general* war. Hope Dakin has some disability like mine that will keep him out,"[17] referring to his impaired vision.

The Turning Point

On March 20, six days before his twenty-eighth birthday, Tom received the best possible greeting of all, a wire from New York:

> THE JUDGES OF THE GROUP THEATRE PLAY CONTEST ARE HAPPY TO MAKE A SPECIAL AWARD OF ONE HUNDRED DOLLARS TO YOU FOR YOUR FIRST THREE SKETCHES IN AMERICAN BLUES.
> HAROLD CLURMAN, IRWIN SHAW & MOLLY DAY THACHER

Tom immediately wrote to his mother:

> Some *good* news at last. Mr. "Tennessee" Williams got telegram last night from the "Group Theatre" saying they were happy to make a special award of $100.00 for my group of one-act plays American Blues! . . . This should give quite an impetus to my dramatic career. At least it should make the studios and producers pay some attention to me, as it is some degree of national recognition. . . . Do not spread this around till the *checque has arrived*, as some of my "friends" in St. Louis such as W. G. B. Carson might feel morally obliged to inform the Group that I am over 25—probably that wouldn't make any difference but I'd rather play it safe.

He was writing from Culver City and said that he had started work at Clark's retail shoe store, one-half block from the Metro-Goldwyn-Mayer studios. "My boss is a young fellow—I think we'll get along fine. Salary—about $12.50 a week—hours—9–6—Sat. later—which is pretty bad—but I can get more and better hours when I learn the trade. I may as well stick at this till something better." He mentioned having bought an old bicycle to ride to work on with ten dollars Grand had sent him. "There are no trolley connections between here and Hawthorne and the Parrotts are giving me such reasonable board I don't want to move."[18]

Sam Webb, who was taking more of a fatherly interest in Tom, got him his job at Clark's Bootery. On his secondhand bicycle, Tom pedaled back and forth between the ranch and the shoe store; as he shuttled past the massive MGM studio, guarded as if it were some military post, he could hardly have imagined that someday he would be working there. Right now, however, although he would readily have accepted a film deal, his focus was on a street in New York called Broadway.

Edwina wrote to him immediately, "Your letter containing the good news just received. I'm bursting with pride and can hardly wait to tell everyone I know."[19] At the same time, she sent a letter to her parents with the news, adding, "I had a telephone call from Cornelius' secretary, Miss Starr, this morning, who as Cornelius is on short business trip opened his mail finding a letter from Sam Webb. She knew I'd be interested in the news it contained." Webb had written that "any boy who would ride a bicycle twenty-four miles a day (12 each way) to work, is bound to succeed." Edwina exulted, "I wouldn't take any-thing for his writing that to Cornelius. You know how horrid Cornelius has talked to Tom, and about him. . . . I don't forget what he has been through."[20]

Having to face Edwina's proudly uplifted chin and being confronted with praise coming from one of his salesmen prompted Cornelius to dictate a letter to Miss Starr, who probably had to hide her own smile:

> Dear Tom,
> I got a pair of woven shoes for myself today, that were samples, and they had an extra pair, which I am sending to you today by parcel post. They are made in two widths, narrow and broad, and we only had the broad in samples, which is about like a D width, which is a little broader than you wear in a shoe, though I imagine they will fit you all right.
> I hope you are getting along nicely in your work, and we were all very proud you won the $100. prize.
> Hoping this finds you well, and with love from us all,
>
> Affectionately,
> C. C. Williams[21]

The moment Tom received his one-hundred-dollar check, Edwina told the news to everyone she knew, informing Tom that "Holland was much thrilled over your prize, and immediately notified the Star and McPherson. The Star had the inclosed notice in last night's paper." The *New York Times* carried a brief news item, headed "Naya Wins Play Prize," mentioning a Tennessee Williams as the recipient of a special award. The word went out, and the machinery that would propel his career toward the New York theatre was suddenly set in motion.

Molly Day Thacher had been appointed head of the play department at the Group Theatre by its managing director, Harold Clurman. She was the wife of a young Group actor and director, Elia Kazan. In a letter to Tennessee Williams, which followed the award announcement, she said that under the terms of the contest the judges had planned to award only one prize of five hundred dollars, which was won by Ramon Naya for his full-length play *Mexican Mural*. But it was the uniqueness of Williams's talent that caught her interest, and it was she who persuaded the Group's treasurer, Kermit Bloomgarden, to make a special award.

Thacher immediately contacted a friend of hers, prominent literary agent Audrey Wood, saying that he was her kind of writer. In her letter to Tennessee, she expressed the hope that "this award will be the beginning of a fruitful association with the Group Theatre, that you will keep us in touch with your work and that it will not be too long before you come to New York to get acquainted with our theatre."[22] Enclosed was a citation that read: "To Tennessee Williams, twenty-four years old, of New Orleans, for 'American Blues,' a group of three sketches which constitute a full-length play." Now there was Thomas Lanier Williams of St. Louis, born 1911, and Tennessee Williams of New Orleans, born 1914. And henceforth the man and the persona would ever be at odds.

Had Tom been in St. Louis and under the influence of Willard Holland, doubtless he soon would have found himself on a train en route to New York. Any beginning playwright would have found Thacher's invitation irresistible. Instead, Tom decided it was safer for the moment to remain on the West Coast, lest it be discovered who Tennessee Williams really was, where he actually lived, and how old he was. Although Tom knew who the principals at the Group Theatre were by reputation, he did not fully comprehend the importance of Molly Day Thacher's letter.

By 1939, the Group Theatre had attained a stature exceeded only by the formidable Theatre Guild, which was the first major American theatre company, the "home" of Eugene O'Neill, and the sponsor of a number of American and European playwrights. The Group, which owed its inspiration to Stanislavsky's Moscow Art Theatre, was initiated in 1931 as the result of a number of lectures on collective theatre endeavors given by Harold Clurman that grew in attendance and frequency until at length an actual company was formed.

A triumvirate headed the company at its inception: Clurman, an esteemed critic and director; Cheryl Crawford, who became an independent and highly successful producer; and Lee Strasberg, a gifted teacher and director and later head of the famed Actors Studio, itself a direct outgrowth of the Group.* The company was composed not only of an impressive list of actors—including John Garfield, Lee J. Cobb, Ruth Nelson, Karl Malden, Frances Farmer, and Franchot Tone—but also of playwrights—Clifford Odets, Paul Green, Irwin Shaw, Sidney Kingsley, and Robert Ardrey. Originally, the Group was founded more as an actor's theatre, its chief purpose being to broaden the range of actors' roles and break down the exploitative strictures of stars and typecasting. But the company achieved an even greater, unexpected distinc-

---

*When the Group was founded, Harold Clurman, Lee Strasberg, and Cheryl Crawford were employed at the Theatre Guild. Crawford, whom Clurman regarded as a more practical and tactful person than either he or Lee Strasberg, made a personal appeal to the Guild's board both for financial support and the release of one of its optioned plays. She received a thousand dollars, Paul Green's *The House of Connelly*, and also two actors under contract to the Guild: Franchot Tone and Morris Carnovsky. Strasberg directed, and the play and the Group Theatre were an instant success. In later years, both Crawford, as producer, and Clurman, as managing director, would play important roles in the career of Tennessee Williams.

tion as the original producer of a number of plays that have since become part of the classic American repertoire: Odets's *Awake and Sing!* and *Golden Boy*; Kingsley's Pulitzer Prize–winning *Men in White*; Shaw's *The Gentle People*; Green's *The House of Connelly*; and Ardrey's *Thunder Rock*.

Following the success of several plays by Clifford Odets, beginning with the phenomenal reception of his *Waiting for Lefty*—at which audiences led by actor Elia Kazan stood up and shouted, "Strike! Strike! Strike!"—the Group decided to set up a special department to encourage the work of new playwrights, headed by Molly Day Thacher. Being an aspiring writer herself, she worked diligently to uncover the talents of unknowns such as Tennessee Williams.

Southward on a Highway Called the Camino Real

Not long after Tom received the Group award, he wrote his grandmother: "Right now I am 'at liberty' again as the business in Culver City went flat due to suspended production at neighboring studio [MGM]. I have a great deal of correspondence on my hands with N.Y. agents who want to handle my plays so it is just as *well*."[23] Among these was a letter from a feisty lady named Frieda Fishbein, who said, "I thought if there was no agent representing you, I would be pleased to do so."[24] To another agent who said she was interested exclusively in "vehicles for stars" and asked if he had any, Tom was said to have replied that the only vehicle he had to offer was a secondhand bicycle. But the letter that most interested him came from Molly Thacher's friend Audrey Wood.

> Dear Mr. Williams:
> I have heard of your successfully winning one of the Group Theatre prizes recently distributed. It seems to me, from what I have heard about you, that you may be exactly the kind of author whom I might help. I have a reputation for showing interest in the talented unknown playwright, which was proven rather forcefully a few weeks ago when four of the six Rockefeller Fellowships awarded were given to clients of mine. I can refer you to the Dramatists' Guild for further information regarding my status as a playbroker.
>   I should like very much to be aware of your work if you are not at this time tied up with any other agent.[25]

Wood recalled that it was quite a while before Tom mailed a response. Finally, he wrote to say that he had received her letter along with several from other New York agents. According to Wood, "He was thinking the situation over and he would let me know what his decision was. At the time, I thought all this rather amusing. After all, we were an established agency—even in California people knew who Liebling-Wood, Inc. was—and here was a struggling author with no credits whatsoever."[26]

The letter Audrey Wood received from Tennessee Williams was in actuality a polite reply thanking her for her interest and saying that Molly Day Thacher had recommended her agency. He said he was considering another offer and could not make an immediate commitment but hoped she would read the plays he was sending; then, if she was still interested, he would decide. Among the manuscripts he mailed was a short story, "The Field of Blue Children," which particularly moved Wood and excited her interest.

On Easter Sunday, Tom went back to his journal in a very different mood, which he later described as "manic elation" brought on by the Group award, a new confidence in himself. "My next play will be simple, direct and terrible—a picture of my own heart. There will be no artifice in it. I will speak the truth as I see it—distort as I see distortion—be wild as I am wild—tender as I am tender—mad as I am mad—passionate as I am passionate. It will be myself without concealment or evasion and with a fearless unashamed frontal assault upon life that will leave no room for trepidation . . . a passionate denial of *sham* and a cry for beauty."

Tennessee Williams had written a manifesto for all the plays and stories to follow. He had also provided the impetus for his first major play, the tidal effort that would carry him into the New York theatre. It was the award that provided both the stimulus and the insight. In many ways, the artist's manifesto had about it the portent of a volcanic rumbling of anger and of welling emotions too long repressed. Throughout, there was the Lawrencian passion, for Tom was now more than ever involved in the writings and pervasive philosophy of D. H. Lawrence.

He was also dealing with the emerging persona of Tennessee Williams—a creation that was quickly coming to life. Tom Williams and much that he had written would soon be put away with the things of youth and become mainly a reference to receding times and events. Within that old frame, there would remain certain of his friends and, always, his family: his mother, his sister, his brother, his beloved grandparents, and the father he thought he hated.

More than an invention, Tennessee Williams, the persona, was becoming a refuge for the artist who until now had been imprisoned. Though both Molly Thacher and Audrey Wood found that his full-length plays lacked realization and the ability to sustain a dramatic idea, he knew that they reflected more than structural problems: The plays of Thomas Lanier Williams omitted *him*, and he was determined that the plays of Tennessee Williams would rise out of a seething inferno *within* him.

From time to time, because of the vicissitudes in his life during the climb to eventual success, Williams would of course waver in his determination and attempt to make his work accommodate what was expected, often demanded, of him. On such occasions, he would be overtaken by a recurrent plague of blue devils, anxieties arising from self-doubt and self-loathing, and a diffidence that caused him to take flight, frequently at the most inopportune times. This would become a lifelong idiosyncrasy: He would simply disappear from the most critical rehearsals and meetings.

Now he was about to do much the same thing. Instead of using the one hundred dollars to take off for New York, he and Jim decided to ride their bicycles down the Southern California coast to Mexico. Edwina first learned of their latest safari when she received a postcard mailed from Laguna Beach, while about the same time Cornelius received yet another letter from Sam Webb, saying, "Tom just left my sample room, he just ask[ed] me to cash his 100.00 prize check, which I did. Business was so slow in the Culver City store the owner of the store just could not stand the expense so had to let Tom go." Then Sam, without realizing what an assault he was making on his boss's fixed opinions, remarked, "Tom is quite a boy and I agree with you, about all he is interested in [is] his plays and story writing. I have often read that people with this inclination live in a world of their own and are happy doing what they like to do. Tom certainly fits in the books I have read and you will never change him."[27] Now Edwina had even *more* reason to gloat.

Sam Webb's letters had the effect at least of compelling Cornelius to take a second look at his errant son. In Hollywood, after all, Tom might amount to something: make some money, get married, and have a home of his own. C.C. offered some fatherly advice: "I just had a letter from Mr. Webb stating that he had expected to spend the weekend with you, but you had gone off down to San Diego on your bicycle for several days. He writes that when you find time, he has made arrangements to have you meet a friend of his who is connected with one of the motion picture companies, in the book review department, and he felt he would be able to do you some good. While you are out there you should certainly take advantage of every opportunity you have to get lined up with someone in the work you like to do."[28] But the only thing that Tom wanted to take advantage of was to live and write—and write about what he was living.

Crossing the Mexican border on their bicycles, Tom and Jim visited Tijuana and Agua Caliente. Since, as Tennessee recalled, these were quite primitive border towns, inevitably the adventurers met with a familiar misadventure. They departed considerably poorer and "considerably less enchanted with Mexican *cantinas* and their clientele," and "started back north on the camino very real. In fact, we no longer had the price of nightly lodging along the way, but there were comfortable fields to sleep in under big stars."[29]

Returning north through San Diego, Tom found a letter in general delivery from Audrey Wood, forwarded from Hawthorne: "I have been in touch with the Group Theatre and they are going to send me copies of the material they have on hand they think I should see. I'll let you know whether I think I can help you after I see your work." In his previous letter, he had mentioned being "high and dry on the beach," and Miss Wood suggested, "If you are financially embarrassed why don't you apply for a Rockefeller Fellowship which are being given through the Dramatists' Guild. These fellowships amount to $1000.00 each and are given solely on the basis of need and merit."[30] Tom replied, "I shall appreciate hearing from you as soon as possible as Miss Fishbein has definitely offered to act as agent and I am holding her off till I hear definitely from you. I may follow your suggestion about the Rockefeller Fellowships—though that would require a long time I imagine."[31]

When Tom and Jim reached Laguna Beach, "a lovely town in those days" about halfway back to Hawthorne, they rode a short distance up a canyon, where "we happened to pass a chicken ranch at the entrance of which was a sign that said 'Help Needed.' And since we needed help, too, we turned onto the dirt road and presented ourselves to the ranchers, an elderly couple who wanted to hire custodians of their poultry for a couple of months while they went on vacation somewhere . . . all they could offer us in the way of remuneration was the occupancy of a little cabin at the back of the chicken run. We assured them that our passion for poultry was quite enough to make the job attractive."[32]

By the time the "custodians" had returned to Hawthorne to make preparations for a summer in Laguna, there was still another letter from Audrey Wood. She told Tennessee that she had read *American Blues*, the short plays, and the full-length *Fugitive Kind*. About the one-acts, she said she was "deeply impressed with your simple yet very true kind of character writing. Your attempt here to dramatize these different milieus comes off, in my opinion, very successfully." Her only reservation was "how limited the market is in the commercial theatre for short material. It is a very special medium and one that is not too commonly used." However, she felt that the short stories were so well done that they "should be shown to the trade as an example of a very promising talent." She said she intended to send them to Whit Burnett, editor of *Story* magazine.

As for *Fugitive Kind*, she felt it should not be sent out in its present shape. "One of my virtues, unfortunately, is extreme honesty and I cannot at this point promise you any kind of a quick sale on anything. As a matter of fact, the theatre isn't an easy market and one has to, very often, play a waiting game before the breaks come. Also, on the basis of what I have read, you are not a finished dramatist although I do say I think you are highly promising."[33] She'd felt him so promising that years later she would confess, "I never in my life had such a hunch on anybody."[34] More than anything, it was her virtue of extreme honesty that convinced Tom he could depend upon an honest opinion from Audrey Wood, whether right or wrong and whether he liked it or not. A relationship had begun that would last for nearly thirty-two years.

Before he departed for Laguna Beach, Tom wrote to Audrey, "I have stalled Miss Fishbein off in the hope that you would come to a favorable conclusion about my work. Apparently you have and I am very glad of it." What followed was a somewhat romanticized account of his life and work, but he added with more honesty than modesty, "It surprises me a little when people take my work seriously at all—perhaps that is not a good thing, especially out here in the 'Capitol of Blah' as the Mummers director calls Hollywood—but at least it makes me properly grateful when somebody like you shows an interest in my work." As for future efforts, he said, "I have two long plays in progress and another probably the best, only in mind." He was not more specific but stressed how tied into financial underwriting any "sustained creative work" was: "For instance I have about thirty bucks and when that is gone I shall have to start writing desperate letters home, hocking my typewriter and my guitar." He felt that kind of living might be exciting but hardly conducive to emotion remembered in tranquillity, "from which the finest art is supposed to spring! I would like to settle for a year in a cabin that I discovered in a lonely arroyo [along the California coastline], live a completely primitive, regular life and devote myself to writing one long, careful play. That is really my only ambition right now."[35]

Audrey Wood spent a large part of the next thirty years just tracing the whereabouts of her famous "gypsy" client. The "flights," as he called them, were in the beginning more often survival strategies than mere efforts to escape—that is, he turned them to some purpose other than the pursuit of pleasure. Invariably and at the very least, no matter where in the world he might be and no matter the circumstances, he wrote unceasingly.

With what little remained of the one hundred dollars, Tom and Jim set out on yet another adventure. They packed their bicycles in an ailing Ford, along with Tom's portable typewriter, guitar, windup phonograph, and box of paints—as well as his script bag, his journal, and the volume of Hart Crane—and embarked upon a memorable summer, an enchanted few weeks Tennessee Williams would always remember as "the happiest and healthiest and most radiant" of his life.[36]

The Careless Days

Dear Mother: The days have gone by so furiously I can't believe it's been nearly a month and that I probably haven't written you in that time! I have never lived in such an ideal, enchanting place as Laguna Beach. It is one of the country's main artists' colonies for obvious reasons. Everyone here, almost, is engaged in some kind of creative work. It is located on a bay surrounded by beautiful wooded hills and is just opposite Catalina Island. The water is the amazingly clear color you must have noticed when you took your trip to the island. The surf-bathing and swimming here are excellent. I spend the mornings writing and afternoons on the beach. Jim Parrott and I got a cabin two miles from town, up a canyon road, for fifteen a month—only $7.50 each—and it is marvelously comfortable and attractive with gas-range, hot shower, complete housekeeping equipment, orange trees and vegetable garden at our disposal. We have a radio, two bicycles and Jim's car—there is a swell little theatre—delightful people—endless places to visit and things to see! These conditions seem to accelerate my pen—or typewriter—and I'm making good progress on a new play—so naturally am not in haste to leave. Jim plans to drive East about the first of August and could go by way of St. Louis so it seems quite practical for me to leave then—which would considerably reduce traveling expenses if not eliminate them altogether. Of course I'm running short on money right now. My agent, Audrey Wood, says Whit Burnett, editor of STORY, has promised to use some of my short material which I've sent her to market for me—but payment is not till publication. She also thinks it likely that I may get a Rockefeller fellowship. So if you want to advance me $7.50 for next month's rent, the chances are fairly good that you *could* get it back before the dollar becomes extinct as coin of the realm! I miss you and Grand a great deal and hate staying away from home so long—but home was never like *this!*—You know what I mean. . . .

I work some nights in a bowling alley (setting up pins) and Jim plays Saturday nights in Los Angeles bands so we do some toiling and spinning in return for our magnificent raiment![37]

Forwarding the letter to her parents, Edwina added a notation, "I sent Tom $15.00." To his grandmother, Tom elaborated, "There are two beautiful twin girls we met in Los Angeles who entertain us frequently at their beautiful house on the beach—so we are ideally located. I have a nice outdoor studio in which I do my writing and painting—Oh, yes, I'm quite an artist these days! . . . I'm feeling fine and beginning to look like 'Tarzan of the Apes.' Housekeeping is very simple—our landlord is away so we have all the eggs and milk we can eat in return for watching the place."[38]

He said nothing about his financial straits, though, and unaware that his mother forwarded his letters, he thought Grand's gifts were purely spontaneous. One of the things that Tennessee carefully omitted from the biographical sketch he gave Audrey Wood—and never mentioned to *anyone* in later years—was how Tom depended on checks from his mother. The difference between her help and Grand's, he felt, was between parental obligation and the gifts of an angel.

Through his mother, he sent word to "C. C. Williams" that Frieda Fishbein had referred him to "a film writer, very successful, who has promised to teach me movie technique and all 'the ropes' out in Hollywood."[39] C.C. found it difficult to understand why his son would not search for other work with Sam Webb's help, and worse, why he would spend the one hundred dollars on so foolish an escapade as a summer on the beach, miles away from Los Angeles.

In those halcyon days before the outbreak of war, the little community of Laguna, more artists' colony than city, was truly at peace with the world. Its steep hillsides and verdant sloping canyons comprised an area of no more than five square miles, with a mere three and half miles of oceanfront. For Tom, after the hell of St. Louis, it was as if he had arrived at a way station to heaven. "Those were care-less times," Tennessee said. "Care-less is the best time in a person's life, and once you lose that, you can never be as happy again"—no matter what bounty success brings.[40]

> May—26 (?) Thursday Evening . . . Life here at Laguna Beach is like that haunting picture of my favorite painter Gauguin—"Nave Nave Mahana"—The Careless Days. It is like a dream—life—nothing of importance occurs but it is all so quiet and sun-drenched and serene—with just a little shadow of sadness in the knowledge that it will have to pass away. It has been years since I have felt so calm and relaxed . . . under the benign influence of this glorious sunlight, starlight and ocean. Mornings writing or lying around—afternoons at the beach—I am brown and firm-muscled—feel like a perfect young animal—and love it.
>
> Only I wonder, with some uneasiness, if the old passion and unrest is gone and with it the rebellion that expressed itself in my lyrical writing. But that is foolish of me—this is just a little sunny interlude. The great storms will come back too soon and with them the old lightning that I put into my work.

On the other coast, meanwhile, Audrey Wood had started to move. Tom had written her from what she imagined to be a woefully impoverished state. He wrote to her, "I would jump into the arms of any agent who could assure me the quick sale of anything—even my soul to the devil."[41] Miss Wood found that selling his talent was more within her purview, however. Along with sending an application for the Rockefeller fellowship, she gave *Story* magazine Tom's one-acts and the short stories he had mailed to her. She also sent *American Blues* to the Actors' Repertory Theatre, the group that originally had produced *Bury the Dead* and E. P. Conkle's *Two Hundred Were Chosen*.

From the beginning, Tom wrote to Audrey Wood not only as an agent but as a personal friend, and though she was by reputation "all business," even before she met her new client she began to respond to his "lost and vulnerable quality." She would come more and more to look forward to his letters, which gave her both enjoyment and concern. With his previous "long descriptive letter," he had enclosed a snapshot of himself, and she replied, "Thank you so much for sending a picture of yourself. It is refreshing to find an author on a bicycle for a change." Audrey Wood had no children of her own, and now it was Edwina Williams, unaware, who had formidable competition. Audrey concluded her letter, asking, "Do write me in detail because I am very anxious to help you."[42]

In response, Tom described a play he had in mind about the poet Vachel Lindsay. "Nobody with a desire to create," he said, "has ever put up a braver, more pitiful struggle against the intellectual apathy and the economic tyranny of his times! He was, as you know, for many years a tramp selling his poems for two cents—from door to door." The play, as he was conceiving it, would illustrate "the whole problem of the poet or creative artist in America or any capitalistic state."

His intention was to set the play during the closing chapter of Lindsay's life in Springfield, Illinois.

> That old yellow frame house intrigues me as a background for a poet's tragedy! The high-ceilinged rooms, the awkward, ugly furniture it must have contained—what marvelous stage sets they'd make! Then I'd weave into the plot the personality of a younger writer—some unknown like myself—who had approached Lindsay, perhaps for confirmation and help. "To you from failing hands we throw the torch, ETC.—" . . . The play would terminate, of course, with Lindsay's suicide—that awful, grotesque crawling upstairs on hands and knees at midnight!—but would strike some positive, assertive note—I mean I would not want it to be just another futilitarian tragedy about a beaten-down artist.

Referring to the extraordinary propensity most writers have for talking about themselves, he said, "Since I am now living in a lonely canyon with a minimum of social intercourse I see no promise of checking that tendency in myself, as letters are just about my only means of advertising my ego at the present time." And with that, he launched into the kind of detail concerning his life in "Bootleg Canyon" which appealed to Wood's sense of humor. He told her that the owners had left temporarily, "allowing me tenancy of the shack in return for tending the poultry, cat, goldfish and garden. Written instructions say that I should 'give the little chicks enough growing mash so that they will not be without it' which sounds simple but is horribly complicated by the fact that the little chicks eat continuously."

He said that on the previous day, after a long siege at the typewriter, he had found

> three of them legs upward in a state of *rigor mortis*—and as the food trough was empty I could not decide whether the poor little bastards had starved or foundered themselves! Do literary agents dispense any advice about feeding small chickens? I hope so. We also have a little bantam rooster, full-grown but tiny, confined to a coop with eight enormous red hens—his activities are a continual source of amusement and amazement to me and make me doubt, almost, the superiority of the human race! I suppose I'll come out some morning and find him in the same condition as the three small chicks, but if I do, my coroner's report will be filled out with much less hesitation.[43]

During his first month in Laguna Beach, Jim quickly made some young friends, whom Tom described in his journal as "people of the sort who bore

me and I bore." Occasionally, Jim would take off with his friends and leave
Tom at the local bowling alley, where he had found work setting pins. It was a
job that suddenly ended, however, when he sustained an injury to his kneecap.
Afterward, he explained to Audrey that he had failed to get out of the way of a
strike quickly enough. Occasionally, too, Jim would go off to Los Angeles
without telling Tom why. "Today Jim mysteriously disappeared," he wrote in
his journal, "left a cryptic note saying not to worry till I saw him again. He is
just about as crazy as I am which makes us excellent companions. And has
problems so similar to mine that it is almost like having a younger, clearer
image of myself to study and work with. It is good for me to have somebody
around that I can feel an unselfish affection for. I usually forget my own problems sometimes considering his—and feel quite fatherly—though God knows
that Jim is probably better able to take care of himself than I am! . . . I feel a bit
lost by myself in a lonely cabin. I hope Jim comes back tomorrow."

Another Awakening

Then, in mid-June—for the first time—he wrote about a homosexual encounter. Jim was away again for the weekend, and Tom confessed that on
Saturday he had had a "rather horrible night" with a picked-up acquaintance,
a certain Doug, whose "amorous advance made me sick at my stomach. Oh,
God— It is dangerous to have ideals." A few days later, his mood had deep-
ened into depression. "The downward turn of the cycle continues—a week or
so ago I seemed to be living in a state of enchantment so marvelously calm and
serene. Then quite strangely everything went sour. I had the experience Sat.
night which confused and upset me and left me with a feeling of spiritual
nausea."

He quickly left for Hawthorne "to escape"—but, hitchhiking back to Laguna, he began feeling nervous again. Finding that Jim had returned to the
cabin, he felt some relief, but that was quickly dispelled when they rode their
bicycles into town to join some of Jim's beach friends. Later, Tom wrote, "I
don't fit in with the careless young extroverts of the world—people of my own
kind are so difficult to find and one is always being disillusioned & disappointed. Oh, hell! I must learn to be lonely and *like* it. At least there is something clean about being lonely—not cluttered up and smeared over with
cheap, filthy personalities who take everything out of you that is decent and
give you nothing but self-disgust."

> Sunday—June 25—I seem to be my *normal* self again—full of neurotic
> fears, a sense of doom, a dreadful lifeless weight on my heart and body.
> Oh, of course that isn't *quite* my normal condition. But without periodic
> spasms of it (from which I had been rather free the last few months) I
> would not be Mr. Thomas L. Williams. . . . Funny, isn't it, how time
> sours a thing? Jim and I are like strangers and I am now quite alone. . . .

He was not as alone as he thought, however. Word from Audrey Wood brought some good news: "I have just heard from Whit Burnett that Story Magazine has decided to accept your story entitled The Field of Blue Children. Story, as you know, pays very little money and I am only able to get you $25.00 which will be sent to you on publication." She said she was delighted about this because "I think it is a tremendous beginning for your literary work."[44] Which it was, because in those years, *Story* was widely read and respected, especially by both aspiring and established authors, by editors of all the publishing houses, and by the heads of film story departments: It was *the* prestige market. Also, this was the first published work of someone oddly named Tennessee Williams, who sounded more as though he was writing in a cabin in Tennessee's Great Smoky Mountains than in Laguna Beach.

Now, finally, the author Thomas Lanier Williams was a thing of the past—anyway, as he told his mother, his was a name that sounded like William Lyon Phelps or like a pretentious writer of bad poetry. What he had wanted was a name that marked him as an avant-garde writer, not a university pundit. "I had already tried being Valentine Xavier," he said, "but that seemed a bit pompous."[45] He used it instead as the name of the principal character in his next play. At that time, his choice of Tennessee was thought by many to be, if not affected, then vaguely ludicrous, prompting Dorothy Parker to exclaim, "*Tennessee* Williams! I might as well call myself Palestine Parker."[46] Shy he was, but paradoxically he also had a canny instinct for promoting himself, and he simply said, "I think it helped me. I think it caught people's eyes."[47]

It certainly did. However, when readers encountered "The Field of Blue Children," they found to their surprise that it was not a mountaineer melodrama but, rather, the sensitively realized story of a boy and a girl, students at a midwestern university similar to that of Missouri, who are drawn to each other by the emotional force of the boy's poetry, "poetry of a difficult sort . . . parts of it reminiscent of Hart Crane, others almost as naively lucid as Sara Teasdale's." The girl says, "There was something about a field of blue flowers. . . ."

"Oh yes," he whispered. "The blue children you mean. . . . I want to show you the field I describe in the poem."

It wasn't far. The walk soon ended and under their feet was the plushy coolness of earth. The moon flowed aqueously through the multitude of pointed oak leaves: the dirt road was also like moving water with its variations of light and shade. They came to a low wooden fence. The boy jumped over it. Then held out his arms. She stepped to the top rail and he lifted her down from it. On the other side his arms did not release her but held her closer.

"This is it," he told her, "the field of blue children."

She looked beyond his dark shoulder. And it was true. The whole field was covered with dancing blue flowers. There was a wind scudding through them and they broke before it in pale blue waves, sending up a soft whispering sound like the infinitely diminished crying of small children at play. . . . He led her out over the field where the flowers rose in pale blue waves to her knees and she lay down among them and stretched her arms through them and pressed her lips against them and felt them all about her, accepting her and embracing her, and a kind of drunkenness possessed her. The boy knelt beside her and touched her cheek with his fingers and then her lips and her hair. They were both kneeling in the blue flowers, facing each other. He was smiling. The wind blew her loose hair into his face. He raised both hands and brushed it back over her forehead and as he did so his hands slipped down behind the back of her head and fastened there and drew her head toward him until her mouth was pressed against his, tighter and tighter, until her teeth pressed painfully against her upper lip and she tasted the salt taste of blood. She gasped and let her mouth fall open and then she lay back among the whispering blue flowers.[48]

The boy and girl have only this one night together. She marries another student but long afterward returns for a last time to the field of blue flowers and falls sobbing among them. As in "The Accent of a Coming Foot," Tom is coming to terms with Hazel's rejection, the imagined effects upon *her*. Love, its ephemeral nature living only in memory, engaged Tom all his life, those remembered fragments, the dreamlike, composite makeup of characters, and glimpses of settings.

And blue, the color of distance and memory, with its many emotional shades—his and his mother's favorite color—pervades the writings of Tennessee Williams. So does the influence of D. H. Lawrence in this and others of his early works, an attraction that was intensifying during this summer in Laguna Beach. Like Lawrence, Williams had become deeply preoccupied with the dualism of the body and the spirit. The images of the fugitive fox and the helpless moth symbolize not only male and female but also the inner conflict between the sensual and spiritual, the lifelong, irreconcilable split within Williams's own personality.

Lorenzo, the Transmitter of Life

Writing to Audrey, Tom said that he was "almost deliriously happy with the news of Story's acceptance, since, as I've told you, I hitched my wagon to that star at the very inception of my writing career but had lately given up all hope of landing there. Well, I thank devoutly whatever accounts for my good luck in bringing us together as that accident seems to have had an effect on my fortunes directly opposite to that incurred by the wanton shooting of an albatross at sea!"

He added that he had filled out the application for the Rockefeller fellowship, mentioning the Vachel Lindsay play as his work in progress. Not understanding that *Story*'s payment upon publication meant waiting for several weeks, he announced, "The twenty-five dollars loom quite large in my own perspective—in fact on the strength of it I'm having my typewriter repaired and am planning a trip to Frisco to see Wm. Saroyan and the World's Fair!"[49]

San Francisco was holding an exposition on a landfill that became known as Treasure Island, located midway across the Bay Bridge that connected the city with Berkeley and Oakland. With his newfound confidence, if not with *Story*'s twenty-five dollars, Tom headed north on the Camino Real.

> Thursday—July 6—Went to Frisco on my thumb last week-end—on the whole a very profitable experience. Learned that I could survive on my own—take care of myself—and met a truly delightful personality who picked me up at Santa Monica and drove me all the way into Berkeley—one J. Brecheen, a salesman, with an extraordinarily sensitive and philosophical mind. We talked rather quite beautifully for hours and it left a very nice taste in my mouth after the many hurts and loneliness of the recent period. Strange experience to suddenly delve so deep into another lonely human heart just in the course of a few hours. I might have looked him up afterwards but somehow the experience was too perfect and complete, as it was, to risk a continuance that might have detracted from that perfection. Relationships shouldn't be carried beyond the point of complete revelation, perhaps—except in rare instances where a tranquil sharing of life is possible.

Again he was addressing the poignant impermanence of love, the transient love, as that in the field of blue flowers. In this instance, he could well have been struggling with mixed feelings for Jim Parrott, where a deeper difference between their natures made reciprocation inexpressible, impossible. After his cathartic experience with Doug, Tom was now facing the fact of his homoerotic, if not yet homosexual, feelings.

Though Tom did not meet William Saroyan during his trip to San Francisco, he did tell his mother that the fair was "indescribably beautiful. Stayed at A.T.O. house in Berkeley across the bay from Frisco and got free rides both ways."[50] On Telegraph Hill, he wrote a poem, "The Gravedigger's Speech," but what mainly engaged his thoughts now was a volume he had checked out of the Laguna Beach library.

> Today I read from D. H. Lawrence's letters and conceived a strong impulse to write a play about him—his life in America—feel so much understanding and sympathy for him—though his brilliance makes me feel very humble & inadequate. Still—perhaps I can do it—why not say I *shall!!*

In mid-July, he wrote to Audrey:

I have shelved the Lindsay idea for a much more compelling impulse to dramatize D. H. Lawrence's life in New Mexico. I feel a far greater affinity for Lawrence than Lindsay and the elements of his life here in America are so essentially dramatic that they require little more than a re-arrangement to be transferred directly to the stage. . . . I intend to run down to Taos, New Mexico on my thumb before long—I understand Frieda Lawrence still lives down there, also Mabel Dodge Luhan and possibly Dorothy Brett who were intimates of Lawrence during this period. I want to take some pictures and absorb the atmosphere of the place and then start right to work if circumstances permit.

He also told her he was considering the possibility of spending some time in New York in the fall, "as I've never been really exposed to the professional theatre. I think I'd learn some craftsmanship—(badly needed)—by attending a lot of Broadway plays." He hoped he might find some employment while there. "I probably would have gravitated that way sooner except that I don't like the crumby sort of Bohemian studio life that an impecunious writer is subjected to in a large city—I got too much of that in the 'Vieux Carré' and it's taken five months of California sunlight to fumigate my soul. Also it is impossible to starve in rural California, with so many orchards and truck farms—though you can get an awful nostalgia for proteins. In New York I don't know. Somehow I think it is more dignified to climb a fence and steal avocados than to stand outside a soup kitchen."[51]

On June 30, the WPA Federal Theatre Project in New York had ended, and for a moment Tom thought that a play about the plight of the fired writers might be a good idea. Audrey replied, saying, "The WPA situation right now is so involved as well as precarious that you might find your play out of date before you finish it."[52] She was also skeptical about his idea for a play about Lawrence, mainly because she had heard that his widow, Frieda, could be extremely difficult. Unless he had Frieda's consent in writing, she felt, it would involve too much of a risk.

Tom wrote in his journal: "Jim & I are getting along fine—now that my nerves are better. It is hard to remember—but necessary—that I discolor the whole world and everybody in it, at times, by my own restless, acid humors." He was alone in the cabin, trying to read with Jim's glasses, which, he said, "I'm afraid are not very good for my eyes—why do I risk blindness? Must take trip to Hawthorne & get my own glasses back. Dead broke & rent due in couple of days!—Jeepers!"

Money, or, more precisely, the lack of it, was the main source of trouble in their paradise. Jim would get an occasional gig, and on this, together with Tom's checks from home, they managed—barely. By the middle of July, Jim took off again and drove up into the hills—this time, as Tom wrote, "for an indefinite period. Paid all but $2.50 of our rent, which was my shamefully small contribution. I'm really in financial hot water—not a red cent and no credit, no groceries but dried peas and a few potatoes. But I will survive somehow."

In *Memoirs,* Tennessee remembered this as the longest time in his life he had ever gone hungry. A plague had also overtaken the chicken flock and suddenly a third of the feathered population were "lying on their backs and sides with legs extended . . . and the survivors of this flash epidemic were not in much better condition. They were wandering dizzily about their enclosure as if in shock or sorrow for their defunct companions and now and then one of them would squawk and fall over and not get up again." After three days of semistarvation, he said he stopped feeling hungry. "The stomach contracts, the gastric spasms subside, and God or somebody drops in on you invisibly and injects you with sedation, so that you find yourself drifting into a curiously, an absolutely inexplicably, peaceful condition, and this condition is ideal for meditation on things past and passing and to come, in just that sequence."[53]

Jim returned toward the end of the month with some cash and plans to move to Pasadena. Parrott remembered that "by that time these two young bachelors were beginning to grate on each other's nerves. I was too critical of his writing (I would say stuff like 'They'll never produce it, Tom; people can't *talk* like that on a stage!') . . . His major criticism of me was that as an actor and future director I had neither joined the Laguna Playhouse, nor had I tried to be interviewed by any of the Hollywood studios. 'You're not *dedicated* enough!' were his exact words. He was right, of course. But be it as it may, I couldn't wait for his departure."[54]

In one of Tom's letters, he asked Audrey if she wanted him to send her his poems, and she answered, "I'm sorry to say I don't handle poetry. As a matter of fact, I don't think most agents do and I think you will have to fight the good fight yourself."[55] But she was anxious to learn whether he had a novel in prospect, "since Story Magazine has, as perhaps you know, a publishing tie-up with Harper's and would be interested in seeing whatever long fiction work of yours is coming along at this time."[56] Now *he* was sorry to say, "I don't like novels—they seem purely esthetic, not *living* as plays are—(this in confidence!)—but I have several ideas for short novels and the temptation to wallow in words may some day impel me to write one."[57]

Tom also informed Audrey that he had been offered a ride to St. Louis by way of Taos, "where I can see Frieda and discover whether or not she is the ogre that you suspect her of being. I have always gotten along rather well with female ogres. I don't expect to write a Lawrence play *next* but am not willing to shelve the idea permanently just because his wife is still living."[58] On July 29, he wrote a somewhat inflated self-appraisal:

Dear Mrs. Lawrence:
Writing this letter is rather insane as I have no idea of your exact address, I am only vaguely persuaded that you are still living in New Mex-

ico, in the vicinity of Taos. Briefly, I am a young writer who has a profound admiration for your late husband['s] work and has conceived the idea, perhaps fantastic, of writing a play about him, dramatizing not so much his life as his ideas or philosophy which strike me as being the richest expressed in modern writing.

I am now associated as a playwright with the GROUP THEATRE in New York, having recently received their national award for young dramatists, and have had plays produced in several large Middlewestern cities, stories in STORY magazine, and a good deal of verse published. My New York agents are Liebling-Wood, Inc., 30 Rockefeller Plaza, in case you should wish to direct some enquiries about me. Frankly they have advised me against undertaking this play because of your possible opposition. However it doesn't seem likely to me that you would oppose it. I have read your deeply moving biography "Not I But The Wind" and am convinced that you would be entirely sympathetic toward any work undertaken to advance the world's knowledge and appreciation of your husband's genius. Provided, of course, that it accorded with your personal knowledge of the facts.

I am leaving California in a few days and will pass through Taos on my way East. I'm writing to know if a meeting could be arranged between us. Could you let me know by return mail? Excuse the abruptness of this. Geographically my life has been very much like your husband's—nomadic, restless, uncertain.

Even without this project in mind I should enjoy meeting you and talking with you tremendously.[59]

Although there appears to be no record of a reply to Tom's query, Frieda later acknowledged having received more than one of his letters. Inspired nonetheless, he noted in his journal: "The D. H. Lawrence project grows strong and clear—like the beginning of a great new day—sunrise. It is like being dedicated to something big at long last! Hope I can find strength for it. I *must*—I *shall*—somehow."

When Cornelius learned that his son might be coming home again, he stepped up his campaign to help find work for Tom in Hollywood. He knew that writers who worked in the film studios were well paid, and he saw this as Tom's only prospect and the only way to keep him away from home. An associate of his, W. Ed Campbell, knew Jimmie Fidler,* the radio columnist, and

---

*James Marion Fidler's broadcasts were heard over 480 radio stations and his gossip reported in 360 newspapers. He paid a network of spies to provide his columns with news, usually to the detriment of anyone who did not cooperate with him. He was in a league with Hedda Hopper and Louella O. Parsons as a power broker and long outlasted his two rivals, retiring from radio in 1983, when he was eighty-four.

asked if Fidler would be willing to meet with "Mr. Thomas L. Williams who writes under the name of TENNESSEE WILLIAMS."[60] Fidler's film gossip was broadcast nationally and was delivered in a breathless, rapid-fire style, with a whine only Louella O. Parsons could match.

Writing to his mother, Tom commented pointedly, "I was glad to get Mr. Campbell's letter, though I don't think much could be accomplished through a meeting with Jimmie Fidler." Although he said he might enjoy meeting the columnist, he added, "It looks like my Laguna period is drawing to a close quite rapidly as Jim has decided to go to Pasadena where he can work in the theater and it will be too expensive for me to remain here alone." He admitted that "I went to Frisco and back on my thumb—hitchhiking—but [I'm] rather uncertain about getting as far as St. Louis that way."[61] This was too much, not only for Edwina but for C.C., as well. When Edwina forwarded Tom's letter to her parents, she noted, "Cornelius is sending Sam Webb money for Tom to come home on the bus—stopping off at 'Taos.' That will probably make the trip easier."[62]

At the end of the month, Sam Webb motored to Laguna Beach, but he missed Tom. He told C.C. that he had waited about four hours and then left ten dollars with a note that Cornelius had sent a check for sixty dollars to finance Tom's trip home. "Also talked to the lady he rents the cabin from. She said his rent was up on the 13th of each month. I told [him] in the note to write me when he wanted to leave and I would drive down for him. My wife and the children want him to spend a few days with them. Tom plays the banjo, my little girl at the Piano and my boy the Accordion and they are not going to let him get away until he has given them a few lessons."[63] Tom was nowhere to be seen because he was hiding.

Shortly after, he wrote to his father, explaining that he had missed Sam Webb's visit because he had gone to Pasadena to attend a Maxwell Anderson Drama Festival and had been visiting some studios in Hollywood. He said he would write to Sam to apologize for the effort he had gone to but would ask that he mail the money, "as I can catch the bus directly from this point with only forty cents additional charge which will save taking all my stuff into L.A." And he added, "I greatly appreciate the money and the trouble you've taken."[64]

Edwina's only news about Rose told little other than the fact that she was "about the same." With a return home imminent, Tom's thoughts dwelled on his sister:

Rose, my dear little sister—I think of you, dear, and wish, oh so much that I could help!—Be brave, dear little girl. God *must* remember and have pity some day on one who loved as much as her little heart could hold—and *more!* Why should you be there, little Rose? And *me here?*—no reason—anywhere— Why?—why?

Also I think of Grand. And love her and miss her. And hate myself for staying away—selfishly—so long. But, oh, Grand, you know how hard it is at home—and here I am *free!* But I remember and love and am sad. God bless you tonight—my dear "Two Roses."

16

Orpheus Ascending

August–December 1939

By now, both Jim and Tom felt that they were becoming too close for comfort. The problem was not only cabin fever but also the tendency toward narrow-mindedness when two people, *any* two people, are imprisoned, even in paradise. They were good friends and they wanted to keep it that way. Tennessee's recollection was that "the careless days" lasted "till the month of August which is the month the sky goes crazy at night, full of shooting stars which undoubtedly have an effect on human fate, even when the sun's up. . . . This was the end of *Nave Nave Mahana.*"[1]

That was true of the world as well during the last summer and the last month of "peace for our time." Soon the headlines would announce: NAZIS AND SOVIETS SIGN 10-YEAR NON-AGGRESSION PACT, binding each other not to aid opponents in acts of war. The subhead read, too late, "Britain and France Mobilize." On September 1, Hitler's Wehrmacht would invade Poland, and on the third, a shaken British prime minister would announce that his country was at war with Germany. Millions of youths enjoying the summer sun would soon be in uniform and ultimately more millions would die.

Tom now thought he was living in a "strange trance-like existence—the dreadful slipping by of the days like oxen on a hot dusty road. Soon this little encampment will break up, is already fundamentally broken. We live a few sad, brief days on the verge of departure—a sort of *fin de siècle* is in the air about this place."

Jim has gone again into L.A. to see a semi-official at a studio.

We are not happy together as we were. He is very generous, even patient with me but I demand so much, I *give* so much in a relationship—so there is a desert between us. My loneliness makes me grow like a vine about people who are kind to me—then it is hard to loosen the vine when the time has come for separation. All my deep loves & friendships have hurt me finally—I mean have caused me *pain*, because I have felt so much more than the other person could feel.

Then I am so pursued by blue devils—no wonder I cling for salvation to whomsoever passes by!

Now I must make a positive religion of the simple act of *endurance*—I must endure & endure & *still endure*. For the break would mean, I'm afraid, to follow my sister—and one of us there is enough.

The heart forgets to feel even sorrow after a while—everything is trampled under the feet of these slow, terrible oxen.

A letter from Audrey Wood informed Tom that he was likely to hear from Edwin Knopf, a West Coast story editor for film producer Samuel Goldwyn, and she cautioned him *not* to discuss money but to refer Knopf to her. With the rent on the cabin paid up to the middle of August, Tom waited on the possibility of word from Knopf. By the tenth of the month, he wrote to his mother that he was "still waiting to hear from the fabulous Mr. Knopf." He had already purchased his bus ticket and felt that Mr. Knopf could reach him in Taos if he was that interested. "I may run out of money in Taos, due to this delay in leaving, so you might, if possible, send me a small checque there."[2]

At the same time, he wrote to Audrey, commenting, "My reactions to the possibility of studio employment are rather confused. Pleased and excited, yes, but also a little worried. Would getting this work preclude my chances of a Rockefeller scholarship? Naturally a year of independent writing would do me more good than hack writing for a film company." But he agreed to rely on her judgment, admitting, "I would love to see the inside of Hollywood, it would certainly open up a new social vista which might compensate even for temporary creative extinction. Not to mention the charms of a pay-check." He closed his letter with a bit of blarney she was not above enjoying: "I think it would surprise you a little to know the fabulous image that you have pro-jected on my little cave of consciousness out here."[3]

He told his mother that the September–October issue of *Story* was due out on the seventeenth and that he would get his twenty-five dollars then "minus Audrey's ten percent." He said, "She also gets a rake off on my salary if she gets me a job which explains her anxiety to do so. However she seems to have wonderful contacts and to be extremely efficient so I guess this is only fair. It is only a question of time, with her behind me, till I get some place out here or in the East."[4]

By August, it was barely eight months since Tom had left St. Louis—for the last time, he had hoped—but now he saw no alternative except to return home. He would be glad to see his friends, the former members of the short-lived Poets' Workshop. Louise Krause, for one, sent him a card saying, "I am holding an M.A. which does me no good since the Diploma is in Latin and I can't read it." She said Bill Smith was waiting on tables. Clark Mills had com-pleted his first year at Cornell as an instructor in French and was preparing for his marriage to Elizabeth Fenwick Phillips. But Tom was pulled eastward to the New York theatre—that, he knew, was where he belonged.

After paying some of his debts, he had enough money left for bus fare as far as Taos, where he expected that Audrey would have sent *Story*'s twenty-five dollars. Jim saw him off and said that, among his belongings, he was carrying the old guitar that someone at the Hawthorne squab ranch had given him. Parrott recalled that his guitar "took on an unexpected importance. He tied a rope around it and wore it all the way to Taos. He later explained to me that the guitar had opened up great avenues of conversations with strangers! . . . Remembering back to the sight of his walking down the aisle of that Greyhound bus as he departed for Taos, I think he might have been the first 'hippie'!"[5]

Cornelius had laid the groundwork for Tom to see one of the shoe company's regional salesmen in Taos, a Mr. Gusdorf. But first Tom had to change buses in Santa Fe, where he met with the poet Witter Bynner, who had originally welcomed D. H. Lawrence to New Mexico. To his mother, Tom said that D. H. Lawrence was "a perfect god to all his old friends, and so they are eager to give me every encouragement."

After Tom left Santa Fe, he traveled across the high desert through the Rio Grande canyon toward Taos, in the foothills of the Rockies. He wrote, "The country around here is wild and beautiful—scarcely inhabited. Real Indians in blankets and braided hair in adobe pueblos." Arriving in the village of Taos, he was somewhat dismayed, though, to find it had the appearance of an abandoned phoenix's nest. "I will probably get all I want from this place over the week-end & go on then to St. Louis." As a postscript, he assured his mother, "Will see Gusdorf the salesman soon as I rest & clean up a bit."[6]

It turned out that Alex Gusdorf was a prominent Ranchos de Taos merchant, who carried Red Goose shoes, and that his wife and daughter were in charge of the Harwood Foundation's museum and library. To his surprise, Tom found that they were very cultured people and that "the museum was Mrs. Gusdorf's old family home—she is a descendant of Spanish first settlers and very proud and aristocratic. In the library they have everything written by or about Lawrence!"[7] Writing to Audrey, he told how Witter Bynner had given him "letters of introduction to the Honorable Dorothy Brett, Mabel Dodge Luhan, Spud Johnson & of course Frieda. It seems she is not at all unapproachable, in fact she has gotten a new boy-friend, an Italian army officer, and is very much on the *qui vivre* [*sic*]." He reassured her that the Lawrence opus would not be his next play but that it made sense for him to gather background material for it while he was among Lawrence aficionados.

In fact, he had no intention of lingering. "I don't like it here. Frankly these people are like the country—which is like a dead planet, the moon! They have a brilliance but it is not living. Whatever was living in them must have died with Lawrence—anyway it is certainly dead. They are a bunch of tired esthetes. Hollywood would be better—at least there is a commotion in Hollywood, an atmosphere of life!"[8] But he had private, ambivalent feelings: "In Hollywood I am a worm. Prostrate. Crawling. Pathetic and evil. Maybe here is a place I could be alive. If I could stand the grandeur and loneliness of it. Metamorphosis, where are you?"

Spending the night in a tourist camp, he wrote in his journal, "I am *bored—lonely*—I wish I were back at Laguna—*dread* going *home.*" He also confessed, "I miss Jim but feel good about the way it closed—nothing but good feeling on both sides and I think a solid, enduring friendship."

Tom was soon captivated by the lingering legend in Taos of D. H. Lawrence, whose death Tennessee Williams would depict in a play called *I Rise in Flame, Cried the Phoenix.* Now he was to meet Frieda, the keeper of that flame, and Lawrence's other disciples.

First, Mrs. Gusdorf arranged an appointment with Dorothy Brett in her studio, a ramshackle affair located close to Los Piños. Brett was a painter, whom Tom described as the daughter of the English Viscount Esher and the sister of the Rani of Sarawak, wife of the only Anglo-Saxon raja. She continued to live on a parcel of land given to her by Frieda Lawrence until her death in 1977 at age ninety-three. Because she had always been partially deaf, she used an ear trumpet, which only accentuated her probing, insistent, and eccentric nature. She also kept a pair of field glasses at hand, and whenever she spotted anyone en route to Frieda's house, she would promptly abandon her paintbrushes and take off uninvited to join them. Brett had about her a gregarious affability that wore down the resistance of any and all within her reach. Tom told his mother that she greeted him wearing "a cowboy hat and blue denim trousers and is simple as an old shoe." Then she invited him to drive up to Frieda's Kiowa Ranch, located in the Lobos Mountains on 160 acres twenty miles north of Taos.

Tom now had a change of mind about the local "esthetes," reporting that "some people on the next ranch were giving a luncheon which I crashed. Everybody was very cordial and I had a marvelous time. Frieda Lawrence was there, we had a long talk, and afterwards she invited me up to her ranch where we went in swimming. They treated me as though I had known them all their lives, the social atmosphere around here is the nicest I've found anywhere and yet the people are by far the most important I've ever met. Frieda is accustomed to entertaining people like Marlene Dietrich and Lillian Gish and Aldous Huxley. Their names were in the guest-book a few lines above mine—she speaks familiarly of Bernard Shaw!"[9]

Regarding Frieda, he jotted down his observation of her on a scrap of paper: "You should see her. Still magnificent. A valkyrie. She runs and plunges about the ranch like a female bull—thick yellow hair flying—piercing blue eyes—huge. She dresses madly—a hat & coat of bob-cat fur—shouts—bangs—terrific! Not a member of the female sex—but woman."[10] He told his mother that she "spends her winters in Hollywood and is in the cream of society there, so knowing her would be very useful if I ever worked in Hollywood." That possibility, however, he shelved for the time being on receiving "a letter from the movie man, Knopf inviting me to see him—but it is too late now. . . . I told him to write Audrey if he had any position for me."[11]

Although Frieda and her friends had treated him cordially, Tom noted in his journal that he had written Audrey, asking her to send him his check as soon as possible, because he was unable to leave until it arrived. He also told her that in visiting an Indian pueblo, he was so absorbed that he left minus his wallet, "which possibly made some redskin five or six dollars richer, but myself infinitely poorer. I can understand now why my Tennessee progenitors had so little affection for the varmints."[12] His story had a familiar ring—reminiscent of the time when he had claimed to have lost one hundred dollars to some pickpocket artist under the Eiffel Tower.

Dorothy Brett must have felt a sense of kinship with this young fugitive writer, because she mounted an all-out effort to introduce him to other members of the Lawrence clan. They were certainly a motley bunch, and each made claim to a special relationship with Frieda's Lorenzo, as they called Lawrence. One such member, Mabel Dodge Luhan, Lorenzo's millionaire padrona, was nearing sixty at the time Tom met her. First a widow, then twice a divorcée, she went to New Mexico in 1917 after years abroad and married her fourth husband, Tony Luhan, a Tiwa Indian who already had an Indian wife. Mabel had found a cause in the plight of the American Indian, and after reading Lawrence's *Sea and Sardinia* invited him to Taos to write about the American Southwest and Indian culture. Tom made no further reference to her; she was probably in his view the ultimate American bitch goddess. Lawrence and Frieda arrived in the United States on September 11, 1922, Lawrence's thirty-seventh birthday. Two years later, after traveling to Mexico and other places in the Southwest, the Lawrences settled down at Mabel's Kiowa Ranch for what was a productive but often a stormy stay.

What really attracted Tom was Frieda's unbridled dynamism. He could imagine her as the aristocratic cousin of the German World War I air ace Baron Manfred von Richthofen; he could envision her deserting her English professor husband and three children; and he could understand her running off with an impoverished writer solely because she knew he needed her, as she declared, to set free his genius. And Tom could readily comprehend why Frieda's Lorenzo could not live without her, even as he struggled against her overprotective domination. Their battles were by this time legendary. But she would laugh and say simply that her Lorenzo saw through her like glass, through her hard, bright shell, and touched a strain of tenderness in her. Now, as Tom saw Frieda Lawrence, she remained an epic in herself.*

---

*In a review of Richard Aldington's *D. H. Lawrence: Portrait of a Genius But* . . . , critic Lewis Gannett wrote in the *New York Herald Tribune* of 19 May 1950 an apt description of Frieda Lawrence as "the only person besides [DHL's] mother who took the trouble to stand up to him, give

The Italian army officer to whom Tom had referred was her lover, Angelo Ravagli. He, like Tony Luhan, was also married and had a wife and three children in Italy. Frieda married him anyway, with the Luhans and Brett as witnesses. Although Lawrence had died at the age of forty-four in 1930 and was buried in southern France, Frieda sent Angelo to Europe in 1935 to have Lorenzo's body exhumed and cremated and his ashes brought back to Taos. Mabel, aided by Tony and Brett, then set out to steal the ashes and scatter them over his ranch land. But Frieda outwitted them; she had Lawrence's remains mixed in a ton of concrete and above her ranch house she erected a shrine on a hill facing the Sangre de Cristo Mountains, at the foot of which, in 1956, she would be buried.

The fox as fugitive moved Tom, as it fascinated Lawrence, and he wrote:

Cried the Fox
For D. H. L.

I run, cried the fox, in circles
narrower, narrower still,
across the desperate hollow,
skirting the frantic hill.

And shall till my brush hangs burning
flame at the hunter's door
continue this fatal returning
to places that failed me before!

Then, with his heart breaking nearly,
the lonely, passionate bark
of the fugitive fox rang out clearly
as bells in the frosty dark,

Across the desperate hollow,
skirting the frantic hill,
calling the pack to follow
a prey that escaped them still.
                                        Taos, 1939.[13]

Although Tom still did not have a specific story concept for his next play, it was, as he had said in his letter to Frieda, the "ideas or philosophy" of D. H. Lawrence that inspired him and in which he was now engrossed. In Taos, the

---

him back abuse for abuse, let him rage and boil and employ every device of dishonest casuistry in argument, and afterward would bear him no ill but on the contrary love him as much as ever."

pervasive spirit of his revered predecessor made a deep impression upon him. He spent long hours in the Harwood Foundation library, where he was able to search through the writer's papers and in doing so experience the ineffable thrill of handling documents and manuscripts in Lawrence's own handwriting. It was the letters, though, as Tennessee would say many years later, especially their candor and insight, that had the greatest impact.

What stirred Tom most forcefully were the striking parallels between his and Lawrence's early lives. As children, both were slight and frail because of a life-threatening illness. Both had unhappy, abusive fathers whom they hated and possessive mothers who fought endless battles with their husbands in an effort to protect their sons. And both had chaste childhood sweethearts. Edwina bore more than superficial resemblance to Lawrence's mother, Lydia, who was middle-class but ensured that her son would not become a mired proletariat like her spouse. Both women stood between their coarse and insensitive husbands and the sons who held out a promise to them of some kind of vicarious achievement.

But the ideas now forming in Tom's mind would emerge not long after in plays and stories by Tennessee Williams, particularly in his next play. The revelation he found in Lawrence was that the sensual and the spiritual in man should not be at odds. But since both writers suffered the deeply ingrained restraint of puritanism, what was a conscious awareness became nonetheless an interior conflict. This dichotomy in the two writers would manifest itself in their inner torment and would become a discernible theme throughout much of their early writings.

Lawrence held the conviction, as did Williams, that his own sexual character was dual, not entirely male, but male and female at variance, with the male always struggling for superiority and dominance. It was a conviction illuminated in both the male and female characters in Lawrence's and Williams's works. The ambiguity of the male fascinated them, and although Lawrence did not subscribe to the practice of sexual affection of one man for another, he did believe in "man-for-man love," the *Brüderschaft*, or the deep alliance of male friendships. He believed that a man's love for a woman was not by itself enough, and he once said that the nearest he had come to perfect love was the bond he had had with a young coal miner when he was sixteen. Tom could understand this and wish that he had such an attachment in his own life. But, as he complained, the intensity of his feelings for others was never reciprocated. A liaison with someone like Doug he had found repugnant, while, sadly, friendships with Harold Mitchell, Stanley Kowalski, and, lately, Jim Parrott stopped short of the classical Greek ideal of "passionate friendship"—the physical and spiritual devotion of sharing and, if necessary, sacrificing life itself one for the other.

What D. H. Lawrence and Tennessee Williams had most in common, what most profoundly affected their writings, was a failed relationship with their fathers. Tennessee began to exonerate his father early on in his plays and stories, whereas Tom in his personal life found this an impossibility. In actuality, the *impossible* existed in Tom's vain pursuit of open affection and respect from his father. But in *The Glass Menagerie*, Tom Wingfield's attitude toward his absent father, more one of envy of a heroic figure, is in sharp contrast to Amanda's bitter and rueful recollections. The characteristics that Tom Williams openly despised in C. C. Williams, his insensitive posture even toward his own deeply buried feelings, made of the father an enigma that Tennessee Williams secretly admired and, with respect to his drunkenness, poker playing, candor, and sensual desires, finally emulated.

Autobiography transmuted into fiction often becomes a form of therapy for the writer, and *The Glass Menagerie* is a prime example. Until Tom went to Taos, he felt locked in, very much alone in his emotional life—almost as though he were the only such creature on earth—but in Lawrence he found an intellectual bond. Tom also shared Lawrence's belief in "spontaneous mutability"—the freely creative as opposed to the preconceived—making the nomadic existence of each more quest than flight.

Tom may not have been fully aware of all this during the few days he spent in Taos, but these and other of Lawrence's ideas would be germinating in the weeks and months to come. The birth and rapid growth of Tennessee Williams had wrought great, irreversible change in Thomas Lanier Williams, and now a return to the life-denying existence of his home was something he knew he could not and would not long endure.

As much as Tom would have liked to stay on in Taos, to experience the milieu as he had in Laguna Beach, it was clear that there was no work he could do to sustain himself. More than that, he had committed himself on the strength of his father's sixty dollars to return to St. Louis. Now he had to admit that he had not bought the full bus fare home, and on a penny postal card, he informed his mother, "I seem to be *stuck* here. I wrote Audrey a week ago to send me the $25.00 for my story but she has *not* done it yet."[14] He said he could get home on five dollars if Edwina would send him that much. The bind he was in was more than financial; admitting that he had used part of the sixty dollars to pay off debts before he left Laguna would have constituted an unforgivable deception in the eyes of *both* his father and mother.

Not knowing what else to do, he sent Audrey a dramatized plea:

AMERICAN BLUES
(In Taos)

BRETT: And then Lorenzo said, "Mabel—"
TENNESSEE: (*rises abruptly*)
BRETT: (*focussing ear-trumpet*) What's the matter, where are you going?
TENNESSEE: (*frenziedly*) I've got a luncheon engagement!
BRETT: (*focussing ear-trumpet*) Who with?

TENNESSEE: Nobody! But I can't stand to sit here and listen to you when I'm half-dead of starvation!

BRETT: Starvation? Incredible!—What do you mean, young man?

TENNESSEE: My agent hasn't sent me my STORY checque yet and I'm living on my landlady's trust in human nature which was exhausted last night.

BRETT: Sit down. How do you like your eggs?

TENNESSEE: In large quantities. —Miss Brett, I'm not going to write a play about Lawrence, I'm going to write a play about YOU! D.H. will enter in the last act and ask where the bathroom is. . . .

CURTAIN

(This play has a social message)

OR MORE EXPLICITLY—if my receipts from STORY (I suppose it *was* published, I haven't found the magazine out here) are not yet mailed, please, oh please send by return Air-mail. This is an arid country and I haven't quite cultivated an appetite for cactus, though they do say it makes delicious candy! When I hear from you I'm going home and live on the folks for a while till I get a play finished. Please don't be annoyed by my importunities about that money but I am in a bit of a mess right now and even the smallest funds look very imposing.[15]

His next message to Audrey was a postcard mailed on the twenty-eighth: "I am leaving here at once for St. Louis. My address there will be 42 Aberdeen Pl., Clayton, Mo., but God knows when I'll get there as I only have a ride as far as Denver."[16] At the time Tom hit the road, the *Story* check was arriving in Taos. Edwina told her mother, "Every day I've been expecting him but I'm afraid he's had to wait at Taos to get his check. He seems to be enjoying it there, however. Tom's story in 'Story' magazine is *good*. I've only been able to get one copy. As soon as I can get more, will send you one." Grand was ill, and Edwina promised, "When Tom comes we will drive down some week-end and bring you home with us." There was nothing said about Rose except that a planned visit had been postponed because of rain and Dakin's illness.[17]

When finally Tom made it home by thumb to his attic studio, he wrote Audrey to tell her that after leaving Denver, he'd gotten as far as Dodge City, where he was stranded for several days. He said that he would unhesitatingly nominate it as the least-attractive town in the United States. He acknowledged that the *Story* check had been forwarded from Taos. Also, he said he had received a polite personal letter from Mr. Knopf of the Samuel Goldwyn office and that he had expressed interest in the Lawrence play and hoped that Tom would come by the next time he was in Hollywood. Now, Tom considered working his way back to the West Coast, feeling that without complementary work of some kind—a dependable income, perhaps at the Goldwyn studio—he could not get any appreciable writing done. He asked Audrey whether there was any reason to expect that he might get the Rockefeller fellowship. One thing was certain: He knew he could not remain very long in St. Louis.

The Mummers were defunct and Willard Holland had returned to Los Angeles. Clark Mills was at home but would soon resume his second year at Cornell. They had a rollicking reunion, and in a letter to Audrey, Tom said, "A Cornell professor has offered me a ride as far as Ithaca, New York. I think I may go on from there for a very brief visit to New York City in which case I will drop in your office and see what can be done about patching up some of my scripts."[18]

There was *some* comic relief during the doldrums of his homecoming: a letter from "Lubino Gooch, Cal." addressed to " 'Volunteer State' Williams" from J. Parrott. From his twenty-five dollars, Tom had sent him the vast sum of one dollar. "Tom, Old Man—Why you big-hearted bum. Geez that buck made me get very sentimental and incidentally came when I was absolutely flat & hungry. Since then however have received check from home—whew!" He ended with:

"Knopf, Knopf . . ."
"Who's knocking?"
"Success." (Laughter)[19]

On the eve of his departure for New York, Tom noted in his journal: "Saw Marian Gallaway & B[landford] J[ennings] tonight. Pleasant enough but I felt on the defensive."

Sunday—9/16[17]/39—End of the St. Louis period—leave tomorrow midnight for New York. Time here has passed in a flash. Nothing happened. *Nothing* at *all*. Written practically nothing & so I don't feel too good. Had hoped—*intended*—to go to N.Y. with new play script. But I go almost empty handed because I want to go somewhere—to get away—the old flight motive— May God be merciful to me and open some door, some avenue of escape.

"New York, New York, It's a Helluva Town!"

Tom did not hitchhike to New York, as mythology has it, but rode with Clark Mills in a car driven by Frances Van Metre, to whom Clark was "semi-engaged," according to Tom—another parcel of his dramatic imagination, as Frances was soon to return to St. Louis with the intention of marrying someone else. He wrote to his mother saying incidentally he had left his hat in Frances Van Metre's car but had found another one in a telephone booth. He added that she might phone Frances to return his hat.

As Tennessee recalled, he arrived in New York broke, unshaven, and looking "pretty disreputable" but went directly to the offices of Liebling-Wood,
which were located in Rockefeller Center. This imposing complex encom-
passed the only group of skyscrapers in New York to go up in the thirties, and
Tom would have been impressed by the sleek, cool design of the towering
buildings. The firm of Liebling-Wood, Inc., founded in 1937, was a husband-
and-wife team. *Liebling* was the diminutive Audrey Wood always used to refer
to her husband, William, because it meant "darling." He was a highly successful talent agent before they met—the "king of 45th Street," as he had
crowned himself. Short of stature and soft-spoken, a gentle man and generally
liked and respected in his profession, Bill Liebling, like his wife, was truly cast
against type. Nonetheless, they were a dynamic duo: he, managing performers, and she, playwrights.

At their first meeting, Audrey remembered, the person who called himself
Tennessee Williams appeared slight of build and looked like a teenaged country boy. Judging from the vigor of his letters and the rather athletic-appearing
photo he had sent her, she was expecting someone more in the southern mold
of a Thomas Wolfe. When Tom shyly entered the agency offices, Liebling
was interviewing a roomful of girls for the chorus of a musical. Liebling finally
noticed him sitting quietly on a bench to one side of the room and thought
Tom was an actor, and so remarked, "Sorry, nothing for you today."

Tom answered that he didn't want anything today except to meet Miss
Wood, who, on entering the room at that point, asked, "Did you want to see
me about something?" He nodded. "If your name is Audrey Wood, I do. My
name is Tennessee Williams." As Williams recalled, her reply was, " 'Well,
well, you've finally made it,' to which I replied, 'Not yet.' I meant this not as a
witticism but quite literally, and I was rather discountenanced by her frivolous
peal of laughter."[20]

Tennessee's memory of her was that of "a very small and dainty woman
with red hair, a porcelain complexion and a look of cool perspicacity in her
eyes."[21] She, on the other hand, was surprised and charmed by his unassum-
ing, almost inarticulate manner, and she was also struck by a quality of serious
resoluteness: He told her he quite understood that he "must get through a
certain period," against what he realized might prove formidable odds. And
indeed, the odds against success in the New York theatre of the thirties and
forties were as great as they have always been, particularly for the aspiring
playwright.

Fellowships and grants-in-aid were few and far between. There was no
Off- or Off-Off-Broadway theatre to provide the playwright with an experimental stage, nor were there regional theatres that presented new plays, with
their sights carefully set on a move to New York. In 1939, Broadway was *the*
theatre and for the playwright, it was a mecca. As a result, there could be no
success other than a commercial success. Achieving anything less than that
was to take up residence in oblivion. In those times, a playwright who did not

consider the commercial possibilities of whatever he wrote would be considered a ludicrous eccentric. Only Eugene O'Neill had consistently defied the system, but by the fall of 1939, he had not been heard from for nearly six years. Even the Group's shining light, Clifford Odets, had "gone Hollywood" and was trying to reestablish his reputation with a new play, *Night Music*, soon to go into rehearsal. Tom's schooling at Iowa and his alliance with Holland had taught him the need to write for the theatre that *exists*, and Tennessee was never anything less than a commercially oriented playwright, much as he deplored and increasingly resisted it.

Commercial often meant the fashioning of vehicles for name actors and actresses. Star power sold tickets, as every Broadway producer knew, and he also knew that any play that survived the critics by a few weeks was generally sold to the movies. Although Broadway was ostensibly disdainful toward Hollywood, behind the front it put up, the theatre employed much the same "closed shop" tactics that made the West Coast studios inaccessible. For Tennessee to have an agent like Audrey Wood, who was shrewd and business-minded while at the same time dedicated to her clients, was to be twice blessed. But Audrey would never have given the time to her young client had he not already demonstrated his willingness to consider the commercial appeal of his work. All the same, there was still no guarantee of success in Audrey Wood's being his "representative"; they both knew it would take a great deal more than even her steadfast industry to make of him a recognized playwright—more than anything, it would require *his* hard, painful, unshakable tenacity. Much as she was fond of him personally and dedicated to him professionally, the one thing that kept Audrey working for him and that convinced her he would make it was his incredible desperation to succeed, even if occasionally it meant compromise.

Tom's first letters home were optimistic and proved that his representative was taking more than an ordinary interest in him. Audrey and Liebling took him out to dinner on more than one occasion and were so "marvelous" to him that he said he felt ashamed he had earned them only a $2.50 commission thus far. "Audrey has taken me right under her wing and made a succession of dates. Today we went to the Group Theatre together and had a long conference. They are going to try to get me work that will support me here while I study the professional theatre firsthand which they think is all I need to make me a finished dramatist."[22]

He also reported having had appointments to meet the head of the Actors' Repertory Theatre and a Bertram Bloch in the eastern offices of the Goldwyn studio, "just to get acquainted." He told his grandparents, "In one day I had as many as six appointments and a dinner and a cocktail party. Audrey Wood and Molly Day Thacher of the Group Theatre both want me to stay here for the theatre season to attend plays and study the theatre and they are bending every effort to find me some kind of work."[23]

Although the war had begun in Europe and an era had ended, jobs in the United States, except those in defense factories, were still hard to find. For the next two years, the country would live in a never-never land of supposed neutrality, and Tom was to discover New York work opportunities frozen in suspended animation. Liebling tried through a friend to get him a job at Macy's and a girl Tom had met thought she had a connection at Lord & Taylor, but to no avail. To make matters worse, Molly Thacher would soon resign from the Group in protest against what she felt was Harold Clurman's autocratic rule, so there was nothing for Tom there. The Group, in fact, was foundering and would soon go under. Robert Ardrey's symbolic fantasy *Thunder Rock*, directed by Elia Kazan, although a success in London, would close after only twenty-three performances. This was the fatal blow, and the failure of Odets's *Night Music* in February would deliver the coup de grâce to a marvelous and in many ways revolutionary theatre.

Getting located in New York was Tom's first problem. Until he could find something, he suggested that his mother write him in care of Audrey but cautioned, "Do *not* use *fancy* stationery as my circumstances are supposed to be desperate." After a brief stay at the Sloane House YMCA, he rented a room in an apartment around the corner from Columbia University. The apartment was occupied by Mrs. Juliet Alves, whom he described as "an aristocratic Kentuckian" and whom he had met through Clark Mills.

Thanks to Audrey, he was regularly seeing plays, including Lillian Hellman's *The Little Foxes* with Tallulah Bankhead. That the play dealt with the conflict between the Old and the New South, and that it was written by a southern playwright and starred a member of a prominent southern family, impressed Tom deeply. Although most producers were busy with plays they were preparing for the new season, Audrey managed to get him introductions. Molly Day Thacher met with him on several occasions at the Group Theatre, and with her guidance he completed the first draft of a new play, which he would describe later to Audrey as "Opus V—Written on Subways."

He told his mother, "You really need to *push* your own work in N.Y. The agencies are perfect madhouses, swarming with desperate, unemployed actors. I am always ushered in ahead of everyone else—to the private office—taking precedence in Dakin's threadbare topcoat over beautiful ingenues in Mink coats, which demonstrates the value of playwrights. But naturally they even forget what scripts I have given them, they are so rushed all the time. I have gotten things moving a little but still not enough. Last year [Liebling-Wood] sold *Room Service* to the movies for $250,000.00—so you see there *is* money in show business."[24]

He mentioned that there were some friends in New York from the University of Iowa, including Lemuel Ayers, who had recently designed the sets for two important revivals at the majestic Empire Theatre, R. C. Sherriff's *Journey's End* and Sidney Howard's *They Knew What They Wanted*. Tom also reported that Willard Holland had written from Hollywood, saying "he has nothing to do out there and wants my prison play. I may suggest he come to N.Y. if our plans progress well."

> Tuesday—Oct. 2, 1939—New York City—Met lots of people here but nobody does me much good. They're all so involved in their own lives. I need somebody to envelop me, embrace me, pull me by sheer force out of this neurotic shell of fear I've built around myself lately. Defeatist attitude toward work is the main difficulty. Loneliness next. Between the two of them I feel all but annihilated. Yes, something *does* have to break and damn soon or I *will*. Think I may look up some people tonight. I *hate* New York—long for the Taos desert or the Pacific—or what? Anyhow I long for something I haven't got.

By mid-October, he had moved several times, the "aristocratic Kentuckian" having objected to his typing at night, and now he was staying at a men's residence club on West Fifty-sixth Street. There he would get his first glimpse of men in residence in a way he had never seen before. He was intrigued by what he saw, and if he was not as repulsed as he had been by his encounter with Doug, he had not yet accepted that he could be a part of such a scene. Once again, he was spurred to leave—that is, run away. And once again, Edwina sent him bus fare.

It was clear that he could not survive in New York without work, and, as he had written to Audrey from Laguna, he preferred stealing avocados to starving in a cold-water flat in Manhattan. There were two things motivating him at this juncture: developing a satisfactory treatment of the play "written on subways" and winning the Rockefeller fellowship. It made sense, much as he hated the prospect, to return to the St. Louis attic and dig in. At least it was a garret in which he would not have to worry about going hungry and being evicted into a snow-covered city.

On the stationery of the Hotel Rex, "2 blocks from Rockefeller Center," he penned a hasty note to Audrey. "I dropped in this A.M. to receive your final benediction but you and Liebling had flown the coop." After suggesting one of his short plays, *Death is the Drummer* [*Headlines*], as a curtain-raiser for the Actors' Repertory revival of *Bury the Dead*, he granted it was "theatrical hokum but sensational over the radio in St. L." He added, "I hope you haven't come to regard me as the Seven Plagues of Egypt! My *very best*, Tenn. Wms."[25] Perhaps to ensure that he returned alive, some last-minute rescue plans were made, if what Tom told his mother was true, and as she related it to Grand: "He made a quick trip home with some acquaintances of Liebling who were coming to St. Louis in a car. They rode all night. He turned in the return trip ticket on bus. Seems to feel the stay in New York helped him immensely with his play-writing."[26]

"Opus V"

In a letter to Molly Thacher, Tom said that he was "writing furiously with seven wild-cats under my skin, as I realize that completing this new play is my only apparent avenue of escape. My method of writing is terrifically wasteful. I have already written enough dialogue for two full-length plays, some of the best of which will have to be eliminated because it flies off on some inessential tangent. I wish to God I could write under some one's direction. That I could get back to New York." He admitted that his attack was "purely emotional" and that under good direction the play would work itself out in rehearsal. "Because of the almost insane violence of my present attitude (loathing of St. Louis and humiliating dependence) I have to write everything to tone it down, to eliminate the lunatic note." Eventually, though, "the final product should emerge as something worth while and the author will then depart for one of three places, New York, the bone-orchard or the state sanitarium."[27]

He also sent Audrey what he called "a very hasty, rough description" of his unnamed play, labeled "Opus V." He was halfway through a second draft but anticipated a tremendous amount of work because of "the violent, melo-dramatic nature of the material. . . . You won't like the pathological characters or violent theme but I'm hoping my final treatment of it will please you some-what better. After I've married the banker's daughter or received the dramatic fellowship I may be in a mood to write something sweet and simple. Jesus, I hope so!"[28]

Audrey wasted no time in replying. She had read his synopsis and declared, "Don't ever think I don't like violent themes. Also don't think I go for plays about hearts and flowers. If you can write a play with a violent theme well enough to make me think it is commercial, I will go screaming down the street like a mad woman and deliver you a sale as soon as I can get someone to go mad with me."[29] "Opus V" was provisionally titled *Shadow of My Passion*, and eventually it would become *Battle of Angels*.

It was at this time that Edwina's constant fussing over Tom began to ex-tend to censorship, as well. He had brought home several of D. H. Lawrence's books from the library, and leafing through them she—like Amanda in *The Glass Menagerie*—would have denounced "that insane Mr. Lawrence." Since the play Tom was writing contained plot and thematic elements strikingly similar to those of *Lady Chatterley's Lover*, this was probably the novel that Edwina would have regarded as "the output of a diseased mind." An exas-perated Tom complained to Audrey, "If Mother doesn't launch one of her literary purges during my infrequent absences from the attic I should be able to complete a presentable script in a few more weeks."

He then described "the maddening situation here. My life is hopelessly circumscribed by the wholesale shoe business on one side and the D.A.R. on the other although I must admit there is considerably less anxiety about the next meal than there was on the Coast." He reminded her that in his last conversation with Molly Thacher she had said she would see what could be done about the Rockefeller fellowship. He asked, "Does that mean she can exercise some kind of pressure? Please don't think I'm a whining spineless sissy. I'm really not—or *am* I? Noooo! I'm only thinking about my ART!! (I suppose you can hear that horrible deprecating laugh of mine.)"[30]

By mid-November, *Battle of Angels* was nearing completion. Tom told Audrey that he was relieved to know that she was not "too unfriendly" toward the work in progress. "I started out, frankly, to write a commercial play but I now hope that the final result will have some artistic merit as well. The two things are not completely incompatible, do you think?"[31] He later explained, "Writing for me is a continual see-saw between rapture and despair which leaves me so exhausted, nervously and physically, that I actually believe each play reduces my life expectancy by several years."[32] While admitting this last was something of an exaggeration, he maintained that—with or without the fellowship—he would have to run off someplace as soon as the play was completed.

To his journal, he confided that he looked upon the grant as a last chance.

> The waiting is almost unbearable and I dare not think what it will be if this last, wild hope is snatched away from me. I'm finishing up a play of highly uncertain quality. But I don't feel the strength in me to start something new without relief, the escape that the award could give me. I must, however, steel myself for the shock of rejection. I can't let it break me. I must remember that my method of survival has always been a very oblique method, a kind of success through failure program of dogged resistance to discouragement and constant bobbin-up again after apparently final slap-downs and knock-outs. I must keep moving onward and outward to ward off the threat of regression.

In setting forth this "method of survival" in his journal, Tom had defined a modus operandi for Tennessee Williams that would guide him the rest of his life. Presently, Tom wrote, "I am stronger than I used to be but my situation is alarmingly static. I keep making these humiliating, inglorious returns to a place I thought I was leaving forever . . . *En Avant!*"

In November, Willard Holland wrote to Tom from Hollywood, saying he had answered an inquiry from the fellowship committee and "told them plenty! Gosh, I hope it all works out."[33] Holland was not making any progress on the West Coast and had severed his connection with the Mummers, who hired a new director for the 1939–1940 season and then expired. Tom also heard from Jim Parrott, who had recently met a writer from Taos, a friend of Frieda Lawrence, by the name of Bright Canoe, "who when I tell him I know a writer just left Taos for New York—Williams—this guy setz there calm as a bump on a log and says, 'Yeah, fine chap I met him in Taos'!!! And him a perfect stranger whom I met purely through coincidence. He and his wife and

Frieda were quite impressed—even hinted they thought you might possess
that rare quality of genius. Seems Frieda is coming out here for the winter. . . . My best, Tom—Jeem."[34]

Finally, on the last day of the month, Tom sent a draft of *Battle of Angels* to
Audrey:

> Well, here is the play—and I feel like Singapore Lou, waiting to see what
> color her baby will be! This really wasn't intended for a final draft, as you
> can tell by the varieties of paper used, but the season is rolling along
> pretty fast and you say you are going out to the West Coast this winter, so
> I thought I'd better not delay shipment any longer even though the prod-
> uct is unrefined. . . . There is a kind of spiritual fungus or gangrene which
> sets in here after the second or third month's residence. At the end of
> four you are pronounced incurable and committed to the wholesale shoe
> business for the rest of your life.[35]

Audrey had left for Los Angeles, and a secretary acknowledged receipt of
the manuscript. This was all Tom would hear for some time. Audrey and
Liebling were exploring the possibility of setting up a West Coast office
and even a production company of their own, which meant that Tom had
to suffer the agony of wondering about both Audrey's reaction to the play
and the status of the fellowship. Meanwhile, he filled his time making a
fainthearted attempt to write a play for actor Francis Lederer, whom he
had just seen playing opposite Katharine Cornell in S. N. Behrman's *No
Time for Comedy*, which he found "exquisite" in the urbane Behrman style.
He was also swimming, seeing friends like Louise Krause and Bill Smith. In
his journal, he mentioned: "Jane [Garret] married—Frances Van Metre
getting married—lives are progressing all around me—mine stands still—
But maybe it is actually moving—imperceptibly—faster and more directly
than I dream. Oh, Molly—oh, Audrey—Oh, Dramatists' Guild—oh God—
Why don't you help me a little? I'm stuck. . . . The walls here are closing
in on me tighter and tighter. Humiliation, dependence, frustration—they're
bearing down heavier all the time—I've got to get *Out Out*. How can I? I
have 9¢—and no guts."

Then he confided, "I have an idea for a new long play—rather, a *character*
for a new long play—in New Orleans—Irene—" At this time, he also wrote to
Audrey, "The girl Irene in this from my projected novel 'Americans' will also
be, most likely, the subject of my next full-length play, making a southern
trilogy: Spring Storm, Battle of Angels and this last one which I plan to call
The Aristocrats."

It would be years before the last of these would take the ultimate shape of
A Streetcar Named Desire and Irene would become Blanche DuBois. Tom
would return to the idea again and again. "As you have observed by now," he
informed Audrey, "I have only one major theme for all my work which is the

destructive impact of society on the sensitive, non-conformist individual. In this case it will be an extraordinarily gifted young woman artist who is forced into prostitution and finally the end described in the story. In 'B. of A.' [*Battle of Angels*] it was a boy who hungered for something beyond reality and got death by torture at the hands of a mob—I hope that idea got across in the script." Not having heard from her, he added, "Your protracted silence has begun to disturb me, my dear! I am still here in St. Louis by virtue of necessity—the *smother* of invention! All optimism has departed—I suspect and expect the worst."[36]

In a letter to his grandparents, he said, "I am enclosing a letter which I want you to mail for me from Memphis to the Dramatic [Dramatists'] Guild. It is to enquire about the fellowship. I don't want to mail it from St. Louis as I wish to keep my address here unknown." *And* his actual name *and* age *and* his family's middle-class affluence, he failed to add. "When the answer comes, I wish you'd forward it to me."[37]

In mid-December, he received at least a note of encouragement, and he wrote in his journal: "I'm happy to report a real resurgence of hope through a letter received from Luise M. Sillcox, Exec. Secty. [of the Dramatists' Guild] of the Authors' League of America—I am among 22 survivors of eliminations and she will try to facilitate things by making extra copies of my stuff. Sounds very encouraging. Do I dare to *hope?* At least it gives me a new lease on life for the time being—relieves the depression and strain."

Edwina was feeling the strain as well, and she complained to her parents, "Tom is very restless. Do wish he were settled!"[38] He wrote every day, always *something*. In his journal, he described this as part of a routine that included riding his bicycle, going downtown for a swim, taking Jiggs for long walks, and after supper reading Lawrence or Joyce or Faulkner's *The Wild Palms*, which he characterized as:

> such a mad book—by distortion, by outrageous exaggeration he seems to get an effect closer to reality (or my idea of it) than strict realists get in their exact representation. You say while reading "This is delirium" but the after-effect is a close approximation of the actual.
>
> I feel strangely remote from everything—insulated—cut off from the main stream. Home—the attic—the literary life—the creative trance—it makes you feel like you have practically stopped living for a while. I want life and love again—and a swift flow of significant experiences.

Almost all of his friends were married by now, and visiting them only made him feel more isolated. Among them was his classmate at Missouri, the gentleman caller whom he at one time had brought home, at his mother's insistence, to meet Rose: "Went to Jim Connor's last night, drank too much beautiful whiskey. . . . Jim has a lovely wife and a very attractive apartment, a beautiful car. But he has gotten fat and I think is a little ashamed of his bourgeois position. Not unhappy—in fact I suppose much happier than in his wild, free days—but I felt sorry for him somehow although he certainly has an abundant supply of good whiskey and the little wife looked like good stuff, too. Alas, poor Yorick or something—I knew him well."

The life and love he sought now was outside the pale of marriage; it left him searching and lonely. "I'd like to see Jimmie tonite. I'd like to ride my old bicycle up Canyon Road an' look at the stars and hear the ranch dogs barking. I want to be free and I'm going to find a way to be soon as I can." There was someone else now, whom he never identified except by a genderless initialed code in his journal, a practice he would use while he was at home. "There is one titillating prospect—Friday evening at V's. We drank together Sat. nite and exchanged some interesting confidences. Ah, well—let us be prepared for any eventuality." Later he wrote, "V. is the only thing worth thinking about—here is a new possibility that will be very exciting to explore—a whole new landscape appearing—will it prove a mirage? If so it will probably be my fault—my lack of finesse." Finally, he reported, "No dice with Va."; then, "Can't feel any sincere sentiment for anyone tonight—I guess the experience with Va. knocked a lot out of me."

Everything in Tom's life now was thrown into doubt, and in his journal he made a statement exemplifying the division in his artistic personality that would become the hallmark of Tennessee Williams's writing. "Today I wrote one very good line—'The past keeps getting bigger and bigger at the future's expense.'—Too good to be good in a play. The tragedy of a poet writing drama is that when he writes well—from the dramaturgic, technical pt. of view he is often writing badly. One must learn—(that is the craft, I suppose)—to fuse lyricism and realism into a congruous unit. I guess my chief trouble is that I don't. I make the most frightful *faux pas*. I feared today that I may have taken a distinctly wrong turn in turning to drama. But, oh, I do *feel* drama so intensely sometimes!"

There was still no word from Audrey, nor anything further from Luise Sillcox at the Dramatists' Guild. Edwina was busy buying and wrapping Christmas gifts and pressed Tom to take her to Farmington to see Rose, a prospect he tried to avoid. Cornelius faced the holidays as though they were a conspiracy against him personally. Dakin, as usual, was down with a cold.

Beginning December 19, over the course of the next three days, Tom's life underwent a profound change:

> Tues. nite—Grouchy—tired—spiritless today. Did nothing but drive Mother down to office to mail Xmas boxes. Loathed going in the old shoe co.—makes me feel so humiliated somehow. . . . My eyes are a worry these days. Left gone out completely—right none too good. I'm a decimated individual but I still got hopes.

Wednesday—Visited Rose at sanitarium—horrible, horrible! Her talk was so obscene—she laughed and talked continual obscenities. Mother insisted I go in, though I dreaded it and wanted to go out, stay outside. We talked to the doctor afterwards—a cold, unsympathetic young man—he said her condition was hopeless, that we could only expect a progressive deterioration. It was a horrible ordeal. Especially since I fear that end for myself.*

Life—life—how uncomprehendably brutal you can be—why?—That question is much too old. It does no good to repeat these old questions— except in art when we can give them, possibly, some kind of poetic expression. But everything seems ugly and useless now—hideously smirched. After all, her naked subconscious is no uglier than the concealed thoughts of others.—And is sex ugly? Not essentially—not from a cosmic viewpoint. But when it is divorced from reason—it looks like slime—it seems horrible if you can't reason it away. Poor mad creature— if only it didn't make you so hideous you wouldn't dread it so much. . . . I am unnerved. The old man was nasty to me this evening about two trivial things. . . . How can I *stay* here? . . . Have dizzy attacks and feel an alarming dullness and lethargy—it scarcely seems worthwhile to move from one room to another. Catatonic? Jesus. No.

After seeing Rose under such nerve-racking circumstances, the very next morning he received the news that seemed, by contrast, to be a miracle:

Thursday—Wow! Received fellowship!—Was awakened this A.M. by arrival of congratulatory telegram from Audrey. Mother literally wept with joy. I felt numb—great merciful acts of this kind never give me a big immediate reaction—they sort of spread through me like a new, warm season. I have had to insulate my spirit against shocks in order to survive—result I'm dulled even to happiness.

Audrey's wire, dated December 22, read:

SO PROUD THAT YOU WON ROCKEFELLER FELLOWSHIP. LIEBLING AND I DELIGHTED. HAVE READ NEW PLAY AND LIKE A GREAT DEAL OF IT. WILL WRITE YOU.

---

*Rose's medical report, signed Kuhlman/Whitten and dated 14 August 1939, in Dakin Williams's collection, read: "Does no work. Manifests delusion of persecution. Smiles and laughs when telling of person plotting to kill her. Talk free and irrelevant. Admits auditory hallucinations. Quiet on the ward. Masturbates frequently. Also expresses various somatic delusions, all of which she explains on a sexual basis. Memory for remote past is nil. Appetite good. Well nourished."

Tom spent Thursday afternoon at the newspapers "giving them the tidings—then went swimming." That night he, Louise Krause, and her boyfriend visited Mrs. Alice Lippmann. "Read us some poems and fed us pie so terrible that Bob stuffed his in his overcoat pocket." He noted a possibility of seeing V. that evening, then made no further mention of it in his journal. As it was, he had more than enough social activity. Old friends and new converged upon him. In his journal, he noted that "poor Jim wrote me such enthusiastic congratulations from California. His play company folded up—poor dear—and I guess he's about ready to throw in the sponge. Wish there was something I could do." Marian Gallaway also wrote "a very sweet letter—things apparently not going so well for her either."

Among his new friends, one in particular, Anne Bretzfelder, was planning to leave soon for New York. She later said, "In St. Louis, Tom and I were sore thumbs—we just didn't fit in. We were artists. I had always wanted to be a sculptor as much as he wanted to be a writer."[39] She recalled an evening when he had arrived at her home conspicuously under the influence, much to everyone's discomfort, liquor and the fellowship lifting his spirits to a new high.

In his journal, he wrote, "Happy? Yes, yes, yes!!—It still seems like a dream—trite statement but, oh, how true. Freedom—the one desire—now possible—for 10 months! A miraculous amnesty for this weary battle-worn veteran of many wars. . . . It seems truly like an Act of God."

Of course he wrote to Audrey immediately: "Your telegram and the letter from Miss Sillcox arrived simultaneously." In fact, Luise Sillcox, the administrator at the Dramatists' Guild for the fellowship, had sent her congratulatory message to the Memphis address, where presumably Tennessee Williams lived. To make this geographic distance between St. Louis and Memphis more melodramatic, he said that the messages arrived "while I was somewhere along highway #67 with a truck-load of shoes. . . . I deeply appreciate your part in this good fortune—I am warm all through my very bones with gratitude for everyone involved."[40]

Tom was not certain of his immediate plans, although he expected to arrive in New York sometime after Christmas to "settle down to a studious, uninterrupted siege of the Broadway theatre." Edwina, of course, had all but run the news up a flagpole and naturally wanted Tom home for Christmas, if simply to make him the center of the festivities. Cornelius had not only to face the Christmas bills but now this. Although he could not articulate the pride he felt in his son, he knew that what Sam Webb had written him—that Tom would never change—was something he would have to live with to the end of his days, as would Tom himself.

The fear he had voiced in his journal that he might now be taking "a distinctly wrong turn in turning to drama" would drive him to reconcile the irreconcilable, antithetical pull of the poet, his truer self, against that of the dramatist. These opposing forces, set in motion by the two most profound influences in his young adult life, Clark Mills and Willard Holland, became the genesis of a unique American phenomenon: the poet-playwright Tennessee Williams.

On Thursday night, December 29, Tom wrote, "Leave for Memphis Saturday to see Grand and Grandfather and possibly a little of Mississippi—then N.Y.C.!" The first fellowship payment of one hundred dollars had been sent to Tennessee Williams of Memphis, Tennessee.

The one person he felt was lost to him forever was Rose, helplessly insane, an unbridgeable distance between them. He felt guilty, and he confessed in his journal that he didn't really deserve his good fortune. "If only I could share a little of this blessing with my little sister—beyond the reach of joy. Perhaps also beyond the reach of sorrow. Good night and God bless the tortured world."

PART IV

Wanderings
1940–1943

———

*"I didn't go to the moon,
I went much further—
for time is the longest distance
between two places."*

17

Broadway

January–June 1940

When Tom Williams said good-bye to his grandparents after celebrating the new year with them, it was to board a train, with his new identity going ahead of him: He was playwright Tennessee Williams, age twenty-five, from Memphis, Tennessee, his official place of residence. Except for Audrey Wood and Molly Day Thacher, that was as much as anyone else in New York would know about him for some time to come.

During the long train ride, now that the euphoria over the fellowship had passed, he began to feel more apprehension than elation: What if the Dramatists' Guild was to find out that he had misrepresented himself to win the Group Theatre award and the Rockefeller fellowship? This guilty secret would be a matter of concern to him for many years, his fictional birth date of 1914 appearing in everything from publicity accounts to library records. As late as 1988, a *Playbill* was headed: "Tennessee Williams—An American Master (1914–1983)."

His anxiety went deeper than that, however. The conflict between Tom and Tennessee would torment him for the rest of his life. With him, first the artist, then the rational man did not apply; it was, in fact, quite the reverse: In him, the artist was the rational force and the man the irrational dissembler. "Mad" Shelley had written, "The poet and the man are two different natures; though they exist together they may be unconscious of each other, and incapable of deciding upon each other's powers and effects by any reflex act." In Tennessee Williams, there was a psychic split between the gentle, poetic Dakin side of his nature and the hard, aggressive Williams side, an irreconcilable division that made him "half-mad," as he would say over and over again.

Sunday—Jan 6—on train about 1½ hours out of N.Y.
　　Sorry to report I feel rather dull due to the blue devils of defeatism

which nearly always rear their ugly little faces in reaction to some period of triumph or elation. Will have to beat them out once more. They're such a damned nuisance. Which is stronger, my will or these reasonless fears? I must ride them down like a nest of snakes, trample them under my heels! . . .

Dream—a woman who was a giant jack rabbit, rather attractive in an esoteric, repugnant way—sitting with me in a bar and saying, "I've never tasted alcohol before *except in sewers.*"—Where did my subconscious get that from? Page Mr. Freud!

Where will you be tonight, Tom? I'll tell you later. We are now in Schenectady. So long. Good luck, old soldier, and keep your chin up!!!

Leafing through his journal, he came across an entry made in 1937, when he was still living at home: "Lay cowering on my bed for a while and then got up with the reflection that nobody ever died of being strong." He appended, "Remember that *now*, Mr. Williams. 1/6/40."

On his arrival in New York City, Tom went directly to the West Side YMCA on Sixty-third Street and checked into a tenth-floor room with "a *view* of Rockefeller Plaza where [my] agent is. Will stay here permanently while in N.Y. I think, as rent is just $7.50 a week which includes use of the pool."[1] The next day he walked down to Rockefeller Center and afterward dispatched an airmail postcard to his mother: "I have just seen Audrey. She told me that I had come in *first* of all the Rockefeller applicants and introduced me in the office as 'our sweetheart.' One reader at the 'Group' is excited about my new play (they now have it at their office) and is trying to get the head director [Harold Clurman] to read it."[2]

Tom could not help but reflect now upon the comparison between his life in New York and that in New Orleans only a year before. Audrey saw to it that he was very busy for the next few days. She and Liebling made daytime appointments with a cross section of important theatre and literary people and at night took him out to dine and to openings of new plays. Luise Sillcox at the Dramatists' Guild also gave him passes, and there were second-balcony theatre tickets available for as little as forty cents at the cut-rate booths in the basement of Gray's Drug Store on Times Square. Molly Day Thacher arranged for him to sit in on rehearsals of Clifford Odets's new play, *Night Music*, and observe Harold Clurman direct Elia Kazan in the lead.

Kazan would soon be giving up his career as an actor in favor of being a director. Like his wife Molly Thacher, he, too, would be leaving the Group Theatre. Clurman said her letter of resignation was "a lengthy analysis of the causes that had transformed me from a true leader into a would-be dictator."[3] With the Hollywood studios regularly raiding its talent bank—for a time tempting Clurman himself—Clurman felt the company could survive only under the firm hand of a producer. Inevitably, there is an attrition that corrodes art by committee, ending up, as it too often does, in factionalism and

internecine disputes. He had only to point to the mighty Theatre Guild itself
as an example, for it also had much the same beginning: Originally directed by
a group composed for the most part of actors, it was known as the Washington Square Players, but finally it evolved into the Theatre Guild under the
direction of Lawrence Langner and Theresa Helburn. But even here, as Tom
was to learn, two heads proved one too many.

> Friday nite in N.Y.—(been here 5 days now)
> Been spending money like water for practically nothing—feeling
> pretty blue most of the time—the ole blue devils got my spirit still. Fall-
> ing off a little though. Think I'll throw 'em tomorrow 'fore they throw
> me. I'm writing like a nigguh cause ah jus' been to see "John Henry" with
> Paul Robeson singin' it, boy! Audrey & Liebling took me after dinner
> with them.

He was now, in fact, receiving the exposure to professional theatre that
Audrey and Molly Thacher felt was a prerequisite if he was ever to achieve
stature as a playwright. In letters to both his mother and grandparents, he said
that he was spending about four hours each day watching the *Night Music*
rehearsals. "This is the first time I've ever seen a professional play in rehearsal, of course, and since it is being directed by the finest director in the
country and with some of the finest actors, the experience is tremendous to
me. I met the author and also Irwin Shaw whom you may have heard of—
another distinguished young Group theatre playwright. In fact I had a date
with Odets sister, Florence. Unfortunately she is Jewish. But very nice."[4]
    "Jewish but very nice" was illustrative of southern anti-Semitism and typi-
cal of an attitude Tennessee Williams would hold privately but always without
malice, not very different from his view of Negroes. He was often, literally,
surrounded by Jewish theatre associates, many of whom would become close
and cherished friends. The America of 1940 was still distanced from the
Holocaust, the civil rights movement was yet to come, and such epithets as
"kikes" and "nigguhs" were commonplace. At the time, to refer to someone
as a black was taken more as an insult.
    To his mother, Tom confessed, "I'm afraid this city would not do for me to
write in—there are too many diverting things going on." In spite of the distractions, he said he was working on the last act of *Battle of Angels* and felt that
the Group would be pleased with it. "Clurman, their head director, introduced himself to me at the rehearsal yesterday and said he had my new play on
his desk and would read it as soon as he gets the present Odets play on the
stage." Then he added, "After seeing some of this season's productions I
don't see why my work should be neglected much longer by the commercial
theatre. There is a pitiful lot of plays going on right now."
    The one exception he cited was the Abbey Theatre's revival of Sean
O'Casey's *Juno and the Paycock*, which he said was magnificent. "I was stand-

ing out in front of that play when Audrey and Liebling came along—Liebling gave me a box-seat."[5] He said he was the only person sitting in a box and felt very elated—so much so that Audrey Wood's memory of the occasion was the sound emanating from that box: shrieks of laughter at the performances of Sara Allgood and Barry Fitzgerald. O'Casey's quick interchange of comedy and tragedy would markedly influence the conception of *The Glass Menagerie*, which was gradually taking shape in his mind.

With the new decade, Tom was an unaware witness to the end of an epoch in the American theatre: the conclusion of nearly twenty years during which the playwright was the thing and the drama flourished. Eugene O'Neill, Robert E. Sherwood, Elmer Rice, Clifford Odets, Philip Barry, Maxwell Anderson, Paul Osborn, S. N. Behrman, Lillian Hellman, George S. Kaufman, Moss Hart, Paul Green, George Kelly, and now William Saroyan were among an aristocracy of American dramatists whose names alone could attract New York audiences to their plays.

Control in the theatre, though, was in the firm hands of those who produced plays. If the playwrights were aristocracy, then the producers and actor-managers were royalty: Langner and Helburn at the Theatre Guild, Brock Pemberton, Gilbert Miller, Herman Shumlin, Vinton Freedley, John Golden, Eddie Dowling, and the partnership of Katharine Cornell and Guthrie McClintic—these were a few of those who established symbiotic bonds with the playwright, bonds that even the foremost stars of the day could not equal, unless, like actress Cornell, they were also managers. The stars—Tallulah Bankhead, Helen Hayes, Alfred Lunt and Lynn Fontanne, Ethel and John Barrymore, Ruth Gordon, Jane Cowl, Judith Anderson, Paul Muni—were nonetheless among a ruling class, and established playwrights were not above fashioning vehicles for them. The net effect was to make of the theatre a hard and brutal temple of commerce. Despite the fact that twenty-two productions were running on Broadway, there were still thousands of trained artisans out of work, and the young novices had no chance of employment. There were few alternative theatres Off-Broadway, and newcomers were up against a closed shop. Tom was only vaguely aware of how fortunate he was in being admitted to the inner circles—that is, for the moment.

Nor did he understand how inexorably, insidiously, a change was being forced upon the theatre, while simultaneously across the nation a greater change was reaching into everyone's lives. Although naïvely regarded at first by most Americans as Europe's "phony war," the conflagration was compelling change, as war always does, and by January 1940, with the fall of France imminent, England, as a last bastion of European civilization, was engaged in a life-and-death struggle. Most Americans wanted to believe, as they had in 1914, that the United States could and should stay out of the war. Powerful isolationist forces cried out *America First!* But the majority of theatre people were in favor of intervention—or at least aid to those beleaguered countries resisting the Nazi blitzkrieg. Like many of his contemporaries, Tom felt a sense of futility, if not indifference, toward the encroaching debacle and focused his energies on what most concerned him: his career. In his journal, he wrote, "Came home and heard the war news—Disasters abroad merely add an edge of excitement to our evenings in America. *C'est la vie, c'est la guerre, c'est l'amour!* Holocaust in Europe—it really does sicken me, I am glad to say. Of course my reactions are primarily selfish. I fear it may kill the theatre."

As Tom wandered about the Theatre District, the marquees were ablaze with stellar names and attractions. Broadway was at its zenith, and not in his most wishful imaginings could he have believed that so many of the great theatre artists and film luminaries would someday figure prominently in his life and career. There was Tallulah Bankhead, whose career was cresting in her long-running success, Lillian Hellman's *The Little Foxes*. Appearing at the Booth in Saroyan's *The Time of Your Life* were Eddie Dowling and Julie Haydon, who in a few years would be playing stage images of Tom and Rose in *The Glass Menagerie*. Laurette Taylor, who would be enacting Edwina's "alias," had recently concluded a highly successful run in *Outward Bound*. At the Shubert Theatre, Katharine Hepburn and Shirley Booth, both of whom would star in different television versions of *Menagerie*, were playing in Philip Barry's *The Philadelphia Story*. And at the Martin Beck, Helen Hayes, who also would act the role of Amanda Wingfield in revivals at home and abroad, was starring in Ben Hecht's and Charles MacArthur's *Ladies and Gentlemen*.

Cheryl Crawford, who would produce several of Tom's plays, was presenting Celeste Holm in *Another Sun*, and one other, who would also become his producer and friend, was a young lawyer from St. Louis, David Margulois. Recently, Margulois had walked unannounced into producer Herman Shumlin's office and offered to invest five thousand dollars, part of a twenty-thousand-dollar legal fee he had received, in a play that opened in January at the Cort, Elliott Nugent and James Thurber's *The Male Animal*. It was an instant success, whereupon Mr. Margulois gave up the law and changed his name to David Merrick.

Those who would soon figure prominently in Tom's *Battle of Angels* were Margaret Webster, set by the Theatre Guild to direct Helen Hayes later in the season in *Twelfth Night;* Miriam Hopkins, starring in the film *Virginia City* at the Strand; Doris Dudley, playing opposite an ailing John Barrymore in his last stage appearance, *My Dear Children;* and Wesley Addy, cast as Benvolio to Laurence Olivier's and Vivien Leigh's Romeo and Juliet.

When Tom wrote his mother that there was "a pitiful lot of plays going on right now," he was stating a fact. Despite all the great talent on the boards, there were no *new* playwrights offering plays of lasting distinction. Once the United States became involved in the war, the theatre would be put on hold, offering fare that was attractive but oddly passé, the mood being either resolutely light or blatantly patriotic.

Audrey and her husband, Liebling, were busy trying to keep their protégé properly and, they hoped, profitably employed. Liebling had asked Tom to read Frederic Prokosch's novel *Night of the Poor*, which Bertram Bloch of the Samuel Goldwyn New York office was considering for a film adaptation. Acknowledging that Prokosch had an excellent prose style, Tom wrote Liebling that "in this instance [he] is handling material which he doesn't know as well as I do . . . the lives of the 'fugitive kind.' "[6]

Bertram Bloch was also giving a seminar in film writing at the New School for Social Research, an institution noted both then and now for its challenge to academic orthodoxies. Located on Twelfth Street in Greenwich Village, the New School attracted many of the world's foremost scholars as instructors and speakers. On January 15, Erwin Piscator became the head of its Dramatic Workshop. Then a forty-seven-year-old German émigré, Piscator had been a director and scenic artist and one of the leaders of the left-wing theatre in pre-Hitler Germany. As director of the Volksbühne during the mid-1920s, his most celebrated production was *The Good Soldier Schweik*. The settings he devised were of a Constructivist type that often employed moving pictures to accelerate a play's action and give it dimension. He believed in the supremacy of the director and relegated playwrights to the status of any other theatre craftsperson. Although Tom would come to despise Piscator's methods, he was impressed with the use of cinematic techniques onstage.

There was, however, one among the school's instructors who regarded the dramatist as the theatre's primal being. Teacher, critic, theatre anthologist, and author John Gassner ardently espoused new and disturbing voices in the theatre. He was also a reader for the Theatre Guild, and, together with the Guild's Theresa Helburn, he was conducting a playwriting seminar at the New School. During the semester from January to June of 1940, a number of guest speakers were slated to appear there, among them Harold Clurman, Eddie Dowling, the Guild's Lawrence Langner, Iowa's E. C. Mabie, and Audrey Wood. Audrey had managed a scholarship for Tom, and he found in John Gassner a lifelong advocate. Years later, Tennessee Williams would say, "Gassner was one of the first to recognize my work. I liked him very much."[7]

Gassner's connection with the Theatre Guild proved the main inducement for Tom to go back to school. The possibility that the Guild might take an interest in *Battle of Angels* was too much to resist. Tom told Audrey that he had made some important changes in the script, but since Harold Clurman had the only existing copy, he had to work from memory. "Act three, Scene one, (between the two women) was formerly the weakest thing in the play, but I believe it is now the best scene with this re-writing which I have done. Audrey, I have a profound conviction that this play can be successfully produced—it's the first time I've felt that way about any long script, as I've probably told you . . . as it is not laden with social significance and would be equally suitable for any good producer who is not afraid of strong stuff."[8]

In another note to Audrey that mentioned Clurman might do his one-act plays if Odets's play was successful, Tom added, "Afraid the '*if*' clause is a big one." One of his short plays, *The Long Goodbye*, was scheduled for production in the New School's basement early in February. Although it was to be directed by John O'Shaughnessey of the Actors' Repertory company, Tom complained, "Saw a *stinking* rehearsal—student actors at the School for the Feeble-minded! . . . Hope no one I know is there unless it improves vastly. John *wrote* a soap-box oration himself and *inserted* it in script to give it a social message. Oh, well, I guess it isn't a crucial production, although my first in N.Y."[9] Giving the play topical significance, as the director saw it, was something that Piscator would certainly have found defensible, but Tom was determined to throw off the burden of sociopolemical writing, the distant sounds of the 1930s having suddenly become overwhelmed by the rumblings of war.

The Long Goodbye was a precursor to *The Glass Menagerie*, and in its narrative technique there is a similarity to the flashback method—through which the action is largely memory—that Williams would employ later. In both plays, a young writer is struggling to free himself from painful memories of his mother and sister and endeavoring by moving on to distant places to find escape and, through it, hope. A theme, an undercurrent in these memory plays, surfaces in the words of the writer in *The Long Goodbye* when he says to his friend, who objects to what he regards as aimless wandering, "You're saying goodbye all the time, every minute you live. Because that's what life is, just a long, long goodbye!"[10]

Newfound Friendships

Tennessee Williams once said that desire is rooted in a longing for companionship, a release from the loneliness that haunts every individual. While he was enjoying the new experience of attending plays and rehearsals and meeting important people in the profession, he felt a gnawing need for something else. It made him feverishly restless and involved him in furtive episodes with companions he would identify in his journal only as B. or P.N., initials devoid of proper nouns that would reveal them as male, casual encounters that were evidently homosexual.

> I live from day to day attending Group Theatre rehearsals, walking about town, eating, meeting people, falling into bed now and then with or without an accomplice. I ache with desires that never are quite satisfied. This promiscuity is appalling really. One-night stands. Nobody seems to care particularly for an encore. I'm too pure I suppose.

A new acquaintance he had made, Harold Vinal, was editor of the poetry magazine *Voices*, in which Tom had been previously published. Vinal had turned his ancestral home on the island of Vinalhaven in Maine into a summer retreat for writers, and during the winter he stayed at a Madison Avenue hotel. They had dinner together, and Tom wrote in his journal: "Vinal introduced me to a new crowd—starving artists from Georgia. Became pretty absorbed in their problems—various complications, Etc." The artists were Donald Windham and Fred Melton, recently arrived from Atlanta, who had taken a room on Fifty-second Street, then called "Swing Alley" because of its profusion of street-level nightclubs housed in three- and four-story buildings. The landlords of these former brownstone residences derived income from the nightclubs as well as rents from small furnished rooms inhabited mainly by working musicians. Donald and Fred were not exactly starving, nor was Tom absorbed in their problems as much as he was in their friendship. At first, he was attracted to Donald, whom he called "dreamy eyes," and immediately he made a futile pass at him. But what most intrigued him was their obvious devotion to each other.

> The big important love doesn't develop. . . . No great source of joy in my life—like a real love affair or big artistic triumph—but an interesting flow of daily events—& comfortable living *with* money!

The fellowship money—income that his new friends assumed was coming from his occupation as a writer—set him apart. Tennessee Williams was, after all, represented by a prominent agent and apparently on the brink of success. That is how he appeared to everyone. But to Donald Windham, he also had the valorous dimension of the artist: a courageous nonconformist who gave to his writing a veneration that surpassed even the ardor of a lover. Windham remembered the developing cataract in Williams's left eye, the fact that he smoked cigarettes placed in a long holder, and that his mode of dress had the sartorial flair of a collegian. He took notice of the clothes that Tom now at last could afford to buy and the variety of footwear, which Donald had no way of knowing consisted of the samples that his father had sent him. Windham remarked that there was always something askew in his dress: colors that clashed, mismatched socks, or some piece of apparel that was ill-fitting.

Tom might now be appropriately dressed for college, unlike the days at Iowa, when one of the girls described him as having the drab look and nervous disposition of a brown sparrow. But with or without the colorful plumage, he still had the same disheveled appearance about his person that he gave to his possessions. To the eye of the beholder, everything in his life was sheer chaos. Since there was no longer a mother or maid to pick up after him, leaves of manuscript were spread over his bed, piled on the dressertop, and stuffed in the drawers. Dirty clothes were heaped in a corner and the remnants of food, a half-eaten hamburger or a cup of cold coffee, were apt to commingle with his shaving gear and hair tonic. So it was and always would be in hotel rooms around the world, wherever Tennessee Williams took up transient residence.

What made his behavior even more puzzling to the managers of these hotels, his agent, and his apprehensive friends was his total lack of concern not simply for his clothes but for belongings he needed in his work and for survival. He would depart, usually on the spur of the moment, leaving behind an expensive jacket, pages of manuscript, or even his glasses, which, if the hotel help or his variety of friends were honest enough, would be forwarded to him. Anne Bretzfelder, Tom's friend from St. Louis who had recently arrived in New York, recalled an occasion when "he wanted me to take home some of his short stories to illustrate, and I promptly left them on a subway seat! They were in an envelope addressed to Whit Burnett at *Story* magazine."[11] Although this caused her considerable anguish, Anne remembered Tom's reaction as casual, almost indifferent. Years later, she encountered Burnett at a meeting, and he said he thought those must have been the stories someone had apparently found and mailed to him. Audrey and Liebling warned Tom to make copies of his work. Originals were out everywhere; he was forever being given the gift of carbon paper, which he would also misplace. With him, it was not so much an absence of mind but, rather, a matter of where it was focused at any given moment; his attention quickly shifted away from the minutiae that largely consume most lives, or, as in Edwina's case, become the whole of it.

Then there are those who wallow in the details of their existence, and such a person was Gilbert Maxwell, another indigent poet from Atlanta. Maxwell at least had the distinction of having been published, and he had come to New York in hot pursuit of a success that was always to elude him like some dogged quarry. He was talented and witty, but he was also unintentionally funny in his postures of self-importance. Maxwell resided at the George Washington Hotel, in rooms he referred to in all seriousness as "Poet's Corner," a small space he shared with a young Irishman whom he dared to call "the mick." Donald Windham and Fred Melton first took Tom to meet Gilbert, who gave parties to which he expected the guests to bring provender and spirits; he saw nothing unusual in this, as he was, after all, *giving* of himself, reading with ceremonial airs from his work in progress. Overcome by a sense of his own eminence, Gilbert was simply unaware of the kind of entertainment he provided for his friends.

The one thing that struck these new young friends of Tennessee was his commitment: Uppermost in his mind and foremost among his priorities was the *need* to write, by now an absolute compulsion. Anything or anyone who might get in the way was thrust aside. Gilbert Maxwell told of a festive occasion when Tom, being one among several guests, chose to sleep on the floor of Maxwell's apartment, rolled up in a blanket. He was up, bathed before anyone, asking to borrow Maxwell's typewriter, and "while the rest of us were showering, using electric razors, shouting back and forth from bedroom to bath above a raucous radio, he sat typing ninety words a minute, plainly deaf and blind to all the bedlam. After half an hour he whisked a last sheet from the typewriter, sat back and sighed."[12]

When asked, Tom explained he had just written a new scene for *Battle of Angels*. Donald Windham, in recalling those first months in New York, remarked that a good deal of the time his friend was literally punch-drunk from writing and that his dedication was exemplary. As Fred Melton aptly nicknamed him, he was "Tennacity" itself.

Tom's first moves into the gay world were tentative, arising more out of loneliness and in response to an adventurous curiosity than from sexual desire. He was like a latent alcoholic enjoying his first evenings of drink and convivial company, yet apprehensive of where they might be leading. Although in the eyes of his new friends he may have seemed exclusively homosexual, Tom made no such admission in his journal. He felt that most people were ambiguous sexually and that he was in no sense stereotypical. His reading of Philip Horton's biography of Hart Crane had left no doubt of Crane's sexuality, but the curious ambivalence in D. H. Lawrence's writings created a kind of reserve in Tom's attitudes, if not his actions. Like many young men "coming out," he was regularly going back into the closet, confused by a deep but inactive attraction to women and a drive toward the easier sexual outlet he had found in the company of gay men.

He sought out the company of Anne Bretzfelder, whom he had described in his journal as a "glamorous personality." She was staying in the West Seventies, not far from the West Side Y, and she and Tom met for occasional luncheons and dinners. Later, when Anne located a studio on Washington Square, she would often feed Tom and listen to him read a new short story or fragment of a play. She remembered his being perplexed by the stormy relationship with his father and by the fact that both he and Cornelius had obstructed vision in their left eyes and an occasional hysterical paralysis of their left arms.

At this time, Anne introduced Tom to a friend of hers, Sidney Edison, the son of one of the heads of the International Shoe Company; she described Edison as "an interesting, attractive, very amusing, imaginative, and spoiled young man from a very rich family." Tom noted in his journal, "I had lunch with interesting new personality, Sid. Edison. We got along swell together, his ideas falling in with mine quite remarkably. Then I spoiled things (I'm afraid) by upsetting a table and spilling whiskey and water all over the rug."

Although apparently Edison had no real interest in him, for a spell Tom thought he might be the close friend he hoped to find. "Been over to Sid. Edison's—met Gordon Sager there. We played records & drank apple jack brandy with beer chasers. Argued about Lawrence—Sager insisted (ridiculously) that he was anti-semitic." After that, his references to "S.E." expressed the hope something more permanent would come of their friendship, a hope that later, he said, came to a calamitous end.

Undeterred, he also tried to make such a friend of Harry Ellerbe, the fine actor he had seen several years previously in St. Louis playing opposite Nazimova in *Ghosts*. "Saw H. Ellerbe last night—had 3 scotches and a pretty good time though nothing significant occurred." During this period, he was also pursuing "D." (a friend of Gilbert Maxwell). He said that neither S.E. nor D. was a "bitch," but both were the masculine type he liked.

> Sunday night—Another *mad* weekend with G.M. & D.—who is sort of a current major theme. Went to D's last night—D. was lucky Pierrette which caused a very dramatic scene. Rather disappointing outcome as G. was never quite mad enough to leave. Rather touching—though farcical—display of jealous devotion. G. and I went to Harlem—visited Father Divine's [Gospel tabernacle] and were tossed out for invading the Sisters' quarters. Then went to Apollo & saw good negro stage show. . . . Frittering my time away—or am I? Maybe this period is really what I need to straighten me out.

After the opening of *Night Music*, Tom noted in his journal, "Odets'[13] play flopped as I expected. Met & talked to him in theatre lobby this P.M. when I took Anne to see play. He was nice & I liked him for the first time—sympathy for the defeated. He nervously fingered his watch and looked deeply hurt— almost completely deflated. Ought to do him good as an artist." If ever there were words that would come home to roost in Tennessee Williams's life, he had just set them down.

Soon after this encounter, Tom wrote in his journal: "Anne leaves tomorrow [for St. Louis]. We had a little love ~~sequence~~ episode in her apt. one night but didn't mean much. Still I like her remarkably—for me." Anne's own recollection of this and other such incidents was: "He kept making advances that displeased me mightily. I felt pressured to the extreme by him—so much so that finally I would flee from him and hide from him—which was not very courageous, I know. But it was just unfortunate for me that I happened to be in his life at that time. And I didn't realize then, not until I was older and knew more about such things, that he was probably profoundly being pulled in two directions."[14]

The truth, by his own admission, is that Tennessee Williams was never freely or wholly able to move in either direction. At the center of his existence, there was the pull of his family: his love for his mother, intertwined with the more intense, guilt-ridden attachment for his sister, further bound in by his love-hatred toward his father. Homosexuality, despite its being fraught with the dangers of police entrapment and public revelation, nevertheless offered Tom the deepening appeal of nonconformist exploration and the illusion of escape from the imprisonment of family.

For the moment, the only friendship that seemed to be taking root, free as it was of the tensions of sexual involvement, was Tom's with Donald Windham. To Tom, Windham and Fred Melton appeared to be role models, while to Donald, the independence of his new friend was nothing less than heroic.

On Valentine's Day, Donald and Fred went trudging through a snowstorm to the New School's basement theatre to see the opening of *The Long Goodbye*.

The *New York Times*, in its daily column devoted to drama news, mentioned that a new play by Tennessee Williams would have its premiere performance at the New School; at the same time, the chief organ of the Communist party, the *Daily Worker*, treated the event as a news item: "The young Southern winner of a $1000 Rockefeller Playwriting Award, Tennessee Williams, will have the first New York showing of his play, *The Long Goodbye*, in a student production this evening."

Evidently, the director had pulled the production together, because Tom in his journal now saw it in an entirely different light: "I was rather pleased with the play—stimulating to see how good my lines can sound when they're well-read." An adventuresome critic who braved the winter weather, Fleet Munson, was equally, if not more, impressed. He wrote to Audrey Wood:

> Last Saturday night I had the good fortune to watch a group of not too fumbling student actors perform a piece called The Long Goodbye. I cannot know how it was to be a member of the Provincetown audience in the early days of O'Neill but I do know that I have been profoundly moved by the playwriting talent of one whose ability is as clearly recognizable. I am told that The Long Goodbye is but one of Tennessee Williams' lesser works, not considered worthy of much attention by such prize awarding bodies as the Group Theatre. Well—I am glad you are handling him because I think you've got something there. . . .
>
> I'm sure you know how good Mr. Williams is but even so, I am impelled to add my small word. Gentle him, for pete's sake. Don't let the drones get him.[15]

Although Harold Clurman had shown no interest in an undertaking as large as a full production of *Battle of Angels*, Tom did mention in his journal, subsequent to the New School presentation: "Current possibility is news that Group is *thinking* of doing a one-act program. *Maybe* some of mine—*maybe*." By mid-March, with nothing conclusive happening, he was foundering: "D. doesn't call but is nice when we meet at D. & F.'s [Donald and Fred's]. Still it offends my pride and my heart a little. The big thing hasn't come yet. Will it ever?"

To offset his discontent and restlessness, he planned a trip to Mexico, sailing on a Cuban mail ship from New York on April 5. With the approaching end of the theatre season, he felt the only things of any consequence that had happened to him were the scholarship for the playwriting seminar at the New School and the production of *The Long Goodbye*. He mentioned in his journal that he had just written a one-act play, *Portrait of a Madonna*, which he thought might be "kinda good." It would prove to be one of his major creations.

L'Heure Bleue, Les Heures Perdues

"I feel old and unattractive lately," Tom wrote. "I don't seem to cut much ice these days with people I want to impress. I look kinda dreary. Sallow, heavy. Need a good, intense affair to bring me back to life and restore my spirits. Yeah. The big emotional business is on the other side of tomorrow." A few days after he had turned twenty-nine, he wrote in his journal: "Something has happened to the fellow that's been writing in here lately. He doesn't sound like the guy that I used to know in the days gone by. Sounds listless and coarse. Needs a good emotional shot in the arm. Something exhilarating. Some spiritual champagne. Maybe it's the end of youth, my dear . . . hope not—it *mustn't* be!"

Now he was determined to sail for Mexico. He told his mother that the New School was organizing an excursion to the drama festival in Mexico "by boat and rail, complete trip only $55 on a 1st class boat (Cuba Mail Line) and I am crazy to go."[16] He told her he planned to stay about a month, and in his journal he tried to reassure himself: "Maybe that will work the necessary charm although I'm not too expectant of that. Probably be lonely and unhappy down there, too. Anyhow I'm *going*—this dullness can't go on—even the fire is better than the cold grease in this frying pan. Bad image I know. John Gassner at the Theatre Guild has taken an interest in 'B. of A.,' but I'm not banking on that little development."

To him nothing seemed more beyond reach than the Theatre Guild's taking an interest in *Battle of Angels*. His focus was on the journey to Mexico and in announcing his travel plans to Audrey Wood. Tom said that he would be taking with him the draft of his new play, *Stairs to the Roof*, and that he was completing a one-act, *Portrait of a Madonna*, which he proposed be bound with two other new ones "possibly under the inclusive title of 'The Lonely Heart' as all 3 are about rather desolate people and nostalgic in atmosphere."[17]

In *Portrait of a Madonna*, the changing image of Irene underwent yet another transmutation, becoming Lucretia Collins, a deranged and "middle-aged spinster, very slight and hunched of figure with a desiccated face that is flushed with excitement. Her hair is arranged in curls that would become a young girl and she wears a frilly negligee which might have come from an old hope chest of a period considerably earlier."[18] The picture is a composite of Rose and Edwina, as "she" might have appeared in later years, alone and confined with her shattered pieces of memory, her nightmarish and imagined experiences at "the Church of St. Michael and St. George at Glorious Hill, Mississippi," where her father was rector.

As for *Battle of Angels*, the hope that Harold Clurman would direct it was abandoned finally with the failure of Odets's *Night Music*. For the Group Theatre, this was the mortal blow, and with the failure again of one more play directed by Clurman, the beleaguered company, after a decade of eminence, passed out of existence in the spring of 1941. Also, Tom had received the discouraging word from Audrey that producer-director Guthrie McClintic had turned down *Battle*, saying that he did not care for the style and that the play did not appeal to him at all. Tom protested to Audrey, suggesting that a copy be sent to the Theatre Guild. "I do think this play is *Commercial!*—Capital 'C' as in CASH! I have been thinking about John Garfield as the male lead—Stella Adler as Myra—Sara Allgood as Vee!—I suppose to be consistent, Shakespeare should have written the play!"[19]

He noted in his journal: "Tomorrow Gassner at New School—nervous. Rather momentous. Wish it were all over and done with and I were dying of a new kind of ennui in Mexico." Instead, he received the "emotional shot in the arm"—the "something exhilarating" he had hoped for—and he wrote immediately to his mother:

> My Mexican trip has been postponed, at least till the Fifth of April. The Theatre Guild has taken a sudden, unexpected interest in my new play. Audrey called up yesterday morning and said their play-reader, John Gassner, who is also my instructor at the New School, was "tremendously excited over it" and wanted Elmer Rice, the playwright, to look at it soon as he got back in New York, April 2nd. I saw Gassner this afternoon and he confirmed Audrey's report and said it was the best play he had read in a year and if the other two readers, who took it to Nassau with them, liked it as well as he, there would be a production next Fall!![20]

In a subsequent letter to his mother, he told her that he had met at the New School with Theresa Helburn of the Guild and that his play had been read to Gassner's class. Helburn had taken him home in a cab and said that they would pay him one hundred dollars as an option on the play, which he understood to be "the first step toward a complete sale."[21] When he told Helburn he was planning to leave for Mexico, she suggested that he wait until he had done some necessary rewriting. He was undeterred, though, the option money being all that he needed as the final inducement. By now, the ship had departed, and Tom's plan was to travel overland by train and meet it in New Orleans. Anne Bretzfelder had returned to New York, and although Tom wanted her to go with him, that was as far as she intended to travel.

Once on board the train, Tom wrote a letter to Bertha Case, one of Audrey's assistants, confessing, "I made tracks out of town as soon as that checque came through and if the deal is illegal, I'll probably be 'South of the Border' before anybody can stop me. No copy of contract was enclosed with the checque, just a note saying here is $100 'advance royalty' on your play. And by G. I see no earthly reason why I should refuse it—do you?" With Audrey away on the West Coast, there was one down-to-earth reason: The Guild was trying to "buy him cheap." He did at least raise the question, before making any further revisions: "Don't you think I ought to demand more payment though?"[22] Later, in his journal, he explained what had happened: "During this interval I left New York—with reading option checque for $100.00 from the Theatre Guild—went to St. L—Memphis—Clarksdale, Miss. & returned.

So beginneth the 3rd N.Y. period. I was called back for further consultation with the Guild. *So* Mexico is at least temporarily postponed. May *sell play.*"

When Audrey Wood learned that her client had departed with the loot, she sent an urgent letter to St. Louis, which Edwina forwarded to Memphis: "Upon request of the Dramatists' Guild, you are under no circumstances to accept the check you received from the Theatre Guild, which is, as was explained to you, a violation of the basic minimum agreement. I am sure that upon receipt of the check, the Dramatists' Guild will have no difficulty in making the Theatre Guild sign the regulation agreement which will satisfy everyone concerned."[23] Upon his return to the West Side Y, Tom wrote home, saying that he was

> in the middle of very dramatic negotiations with the Theatre Guild. The changes they wished were relatively slight to what I expected and I think have already been satisfactorily worked out. The Dramatists' Guild and my agent are now putting pressure on them to make a different type of contract with me as the one I signed does not give me as much money as I should get. There is quite a battle in progress between the Dramatist and Theatre Guilds over this point. Both Miss Helburn and Mr. Langner spent half an hour bawling at them over the telephone while I was there, and were practically besides themselves with fury when the D. Guild refused to yield a point.

He went on to say that the Guild's "new Saroyan play laid a terrific egg last night, the reviews were merciless—I attended the opening night and the play was as sorry and absurd a spectacle as I have ever seen in spite of a very fine production. So they are more up in the air than ever."[24]

That the Guild would be negotiating with a new and untried playwright at the same time their prodigal son, William Saroyan, had proved such a disappointment would seem a most unlikely turn of events. Flush with the success of *The Time of Your Life*, winner of both the Drama Critics Circle Award and the Pulitzer Prize—which he had declined with much fanfare—Saroyan had become the theatre's enfant terrible. But despite the magic of Walter Huston in the lead, the play *Love's Old Sweet Song* lasted only forty-four performances.*

---

*Actor Alan Hewitt maintained (in *On Broadway*, photographs by Fred Fehl and text by William Stott with Jane Stott [Austin: University of Texas Press, 1978], p. 8) that the play could have been a success if "Saroyan had left it alone. He insisted on being co-director with Eddie Dowling, and

In March, Tom had written Saroyan, and later he received a friendly reply, explaining that "when your letter reached me I was at work on the last play of mine to be produced. . . . My plays appear to be the kind I must stick with all the way through or else they will be somebody else's plays, or nobody's. I was delighted to hear from you, as I had been watching with interest the announcements of your arrival in the goofy world of letters and drama."[25] By this time, Tom had begun to look somewhat suspiciously upon Saroyan as a possible rival, a new presence, like his, in the theatre and someone to whom he might be compared.

Langner and Helburn had something else to consider: Their great resident playwright, Eugene O'Neill, had dropped out of view and out of mind, his only play of consequence in nearly a decade being the uncharacteristically gentle comedy *Ah, Wilderness!* Clearly it was time for the Guild to dismantle its reputation as a warehouse and move ahead with fresh and innovative talent, lest it meet the fate of the Group. The times were indeed changing. In addition, there was the persistence of the Guild's play reader, John Gassner, who convinced Langner and Helburn that Tennessee Williams had a new, distinctive, and potentially powerful voice to bring into the theatre.

Finally, on May 8, Tom sent a wire to his mother:

THEATRE GUILD SIGNS REGULAR CONTRACT TODAY. MUST STAY NEAR NEW YORK. FALL PRODUCTION LIKELY. INFORM GRAND AND GRANDFATHER. . . . LOVE—TOM.

That same evening, Anne Bretzfelder, Windham, and Melton joined him in celebrating the news at the Greenwich Village Barn.

Edwina wrote, "It's too bad you can't make the trip to Mexico, but you couldn't afford to displease the Theatre Guild!" She had good news of her own: "The next time you come home we'll be in 53 Arundel [Place]. Your father is still much enthused; bought some chairs for the rathskeller and a Saronk oriental rug for the living room. I'm having a hard time holding him down, he is in such a buying mood."[26] Mr. and Mrs. Cornelius C. Williams were now the proud owners of their own home, a two-story residence that included eight rooms and two baths and, for Tom, an attic studio with dormer windows, which held as much appeal for him as the return to a jail cell.

Instead, in early May he took the four-dollar train trip to Lake George, located in upstate New York, as the guest of Jim Parrott's parents, to "check the swimming." He found it too cold, and on returning to New York City, he decided to share an apartment at 151 East Thirty-seventh Street with Wind-

---

couldn't stop changing things around. He rewrote freely, redirected—he even brought in people off the street, people who had never seen a play before, and insisted that they be cast in the play." As a result, Hewitt added, the production came into New York "a mess, instead of being a fairly neat play."

Audrey Wood with husband
William Liebling (left)
and author Sinclair Lewis at
Lewis's California home,
c. 1940

Dear Mother — I have just seen Audrey. She told me that I had come in first of all the Rockefeller applicants and introduced me to people in the office as "our sweetheart". One reader at the "Group" is excited about my new play (they now have it at their office) and is trying to get the head director to read it. My address is at The 63rd street Y.M.C.A. Please forward this card to Grand + J. — I will be very busy the next few days. Tom.

A card to his mother carried good news.

Tom met dancer Kip Kiernan (right) at Captain Jack's Wharf (above) in Provincetown during the summer of 1940.

Bottom: In P-town (left to right): Joe Hazan, Tom, Ethel Elkovsky, Walter Hollander, and an unidentified friend

Celebrating the good news from the Theatre Guild in the Village Barn (left to right): Tom, Anne Bretzfelder, Fred "Butch" Melton, and Donald Windham

Tom's "kid brother" Dakin, drafted into the army as a noncommissioned officer, was to serve overseas in South Africa, India, and Burma.

MIRIAM HOPKINS

WILBUR THEATRE
TWO WEEKS ONLY
Beginning Monday Eve. Dec. 30
MATINEES THURSDAY & SATURDAY
Prices: Evenings $2.75, $2.20, $1.65, $1.10
Matinees $2.20, $1.65, $1.10

MIRIAM HOPKINS

BATTLE OF ANGELS

BATTLE OF ANGELS

THE THEATRE GUILD

presents

MIRIAM HOPKINS

in

BATTLE OF ANGELS

A New Play

By TENNESSEE WILLIAMS

with

DORIS DUDLEY *and* WESLEY ADDY

Directed by MARGARET WEBSTER

Scenery designed by CLEON THROCKMORTON

Music by COLIN McPHEE

Production under the supervision of
THERESA HELBURN & LAWRENCE LANGNER

Battle of Angels

by Tennessee Williams

Pharos: Numbers 1 & 2

Spring, 1945 - $1.50

63

64

Wesley Addy

65

Doris Dudley

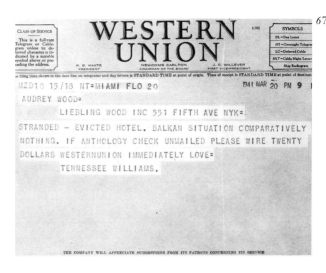

```
CLASS OF SERVICE          WESTERN    1201   SYMBOLS
This is a full-rate                          DL=Day Letter
Telegram or Cable-        UNION              NT=Overnight Telegram
gram unless its de-                          LC=Deferred Cable
ferred character is in-   R. B. WHITE   NEWCOMB CARLTON   J. C. WILLEVER   NLT=Cable Night Letter
dicated by a suitable     PRESIDENT    CHAIRMAN OF THE BOARD   FIRST VICE-PRESIDENT   Ship Radiogram
symbol above or pre-
ceding the address.
```

The filing time shown in the date line on telegrams and day letters is STANDARD TIME at point of origin. Time of receipt is STANDARD TIME at point of destination

MZD10 15/18 NT=MIAMI FLO 20   1941 MAR 20 PM 9

AUDREY WOOD=
    LIEBLING WOOD INC 551 FIFTH AVE NYK=
STRANDED - EVICTED HOTEL. BALKAN SITUATION COMPARATIVELY
NOTHING. IF ANTHOLOGY CHECK UNMAILED PLEASE WIRE TWENTY
DOLLARS WESTERNUNION IMMEDIATELY LOVE=
    TENNESSEE WILLIAMS.

THE COMPANY WILL APPRECIATE SUGGESTIONS FROM ITS PATRONS CONCERNING ITS SERVICE

A distressed and depressed Tom left for Miami following the failure of
Battle of Angels in Boston. He would end up at the Trade Winds in Key West
(below), and Marion Black Vaccaro (above, with her husband, Regis) would
become a close life-long friend.

Jordan "Big Daddy" Massee and son, Jordan, Jr.

70

71

LEFT: The "legendary" Paul Bigelow

RIGHT: Jordan Massee, Jr.

BOTTOM LEFT: James "Jay" Laughlin

BOTTOM RIGHT: Horton Foote

72

73

Charge to the account of_____ $_____

CLASS OF SERVICE DESIRED	
DOMESTIC	CABLE
TELEGRAM	ORDINARY
DAY LETTER	URGENT RATE
SERIAL	DEFERRED
OVERNIGHT TELEGRAM	NIGHT LETTER
SPECIAL SERVICE	SHIP RADIOGRAM

Patrons should check class of service desired; otherwise the message will be transmitted as a telegram or ordinary cablegram.

WESTERN UNION

1206

CHECK

ACCOUNTING INFORMATION

TIME FILED

A. N. WILLIAMS
PRESIDENT

NEWCOMB CARLTON
CHAIRMAN OF THE BOARD

J. C. WILLEVER
FIRST VICE-PRESIDENT

Send the following telegram, subject to the terms on back hereof, which are hereby agreed to

WANT A REPLY?
"Answer by WESTERN UNION" or similar phrases may be included without charge.

APRIL 30TH, 1943

MR. TENNESSEE WILLIAMS
53 ARUNDEL PLACE
CLAYTON, MISSOURI

COME AT ONCE TO NEW YORK. HAVE ARRANGED WRITING DEAL
PICTURES WHICH NECESSITATES YOUR LEAVING NEW YORK INX TIME
ARRIVE CALIFORNIA AROUND FIFTEENTH OF MAY. FARE TO CALIFORNIA
PAID BY PICTURE COMPANY. ADVISE WHEN ARRIVING NEW YORK.

AUDREY WOOD

DAY LETTER * Charge Liebling-Wood
551 Fifth Avenue

74

ham and Melton; they had both found work, Donald selling Coca-Cola at the World's Fair and Fred working as an apprentice in an architect's office. Shortly before moving in, Tom was engaged in making revisions suggested principally by Theresa Helburn, while the lawyers for all concerned were hourly adjusting semicolons in their fashion. The fine points were of no interest to Tom: If Audrey said sign, he signed. He seemed almost naïvely removed from the extraordinary events taking place in his life, as if they were everyday occurrences. His main concern seemed to be the hope that the right person would soon appear.

> May 25 or 6—Sunday midnight
> ... my emotional life has been a series of rather spectacular failures—so much so that I am becoming pretty thoroughly despondent about it. . . . I am losing my looks alarmingly. Haggard, tired, jittery, fretful, bored— that is what lack of a reciprocal love object does to a man. Let us hope it spurs his creative impulse—there should be *some* compensation for this hell of loneliness. Makes me act, think, *be* like an idiot—whining, trivial, tiresome.

> > You *coming toward me*—
> > please *make* haste!
> > J'ai soif! Je meurs de soif!
> > (*You—You—is* this *you?*
> > "*Coming toward me?*")

At the time Tom moved in with Donald and Fred, he received a letter from Bertha Case in Audrey's office, enclosing copies of the Guild's option agreement for his signature, and he quickly complied, saying, "Nice going! Does this mean I am getting another hundred out of our friends?—SWELL! Between you and the Dramatists' Guild I will eventually have to start worrying about an income tax." He also mentioned that "Langner and Helburn seemed to be very pleased with the changes I have made. They came right out and mentioned Madame X last time but stressed the necessity for absolute secrecy about it."

The X in question turned out to be Joan Crawford, who in those days was suffering a doubtful future, her tenure with Metro-Goldwyn-Mayer at an end. The quintessential movie queen was totally inexperienced as a stage actress; the idea that she would ever appear on Broadway looked more like copy from some studio publicist. But in fact, Crawford was reading play scripts and looking for something suitable. If she was to make a New York debut, she would settle for nothing less than a Theatre Guild production. Langner also knew that, like other film stars who had appeared on Broadway, she would likely bring money to invest.

Tom greeted the possibility of Joan Crawford starring in his play with a slight sneer: "I'm sure you can surmise what ardent hopes I am now entertaining—of a somewhat sinister nature. But that is strictly between us. I'm not supposed to mention Madame X to you even." Langner had also suggested Miriam Hopkins and Tallulah Bankhead, and Tom responded enthusiastically: "I think Hopkins would be magnificent, and, oh, Tallulah! Wouldn't that be something?"[27]

Now that he was being received at the Guild's headquarters, Tom formed what would become a long-lasting friendship with Jo Healy, a rather stout, red-haired switchboard operator. Since the switchboard was located in the building's vestibule, she also acted as receptionist. Irish, hearty, and outgoing, she greeted everyone with an infectious friendliness. Celeste Holm, who had acted in the Guild's production of *The Time of Your Life*, recalled, "They paid her about twenty dollars a week, and I found her jolly, jovial, and an astonishingly self-confident creature. I don't think most telephone switchboard operators would expect to have dinner with Katharine Hepburn, but Jo was kind of like that. She told me, 'I have a playwright friend—he's got a funny name, but he can write gorgeously. And I try to feed him. I can only afford spaghetti.' And when I asked his name, she said, 'Tennessee Williams.' I was terribly impressed that Jo saw his talent—she recognized it in his scripts and obviously had read *Battle of Angels*."[28]

Toward the end of June, Tom was the houseguest of the Lawrence Langners at their farm in Weston, Connecticut. Langner gave him a little summerhouse in which to continue work on the play. But after returning to the city, Tom felt restless and sought a place to go for the summer, an East Coast resort that would have about it much the same aura that Laguna Beach had had the previous year. Audrey Wood suggested Provincetown, on Cape Cod. Because of the number of summer theatres in the vicinity, she believed "P-town" was a good place for him to go. She was aware that he was distracted by city life and was tending to squander his energies, and although closemouthed as always, she also knew that her innocent was moving in gay company. While she understood that the artists' colony in Provincetown had a reputation for the wild and free, her hope was that Tennessee would at least be inspired to write, as he had been in Laguna.

Williams's own recollection was of friends seeing him off on the train to Boston. "In those days people were always putting me on trains or buses like I was a pawn in a chess game. Well, I must have wanted it that way. And that's the way I got it. How very kind they were to me, in those long ago days!" Once in Provincetown, "the first few days I stayed in a rooming-house, a charmingly casual old frame building with a swing on the verandah. The house was tenanted by equally charming and casual young people. There was a blond youth who succumbed to my precipitate courtship the first evening.

"Yes, you see, now I had finally come thoroughly out of the closet: I was not a young man who would turn many heads on the street. . . . The pupil of my left eye had turned gray with that remarkably early cataract. And I was still very shy except when drunk. Oh, I was quite the opposite when I had a couple of drinks under my belt."

Of that first month "at the frolicsome tip of the Cape," Tennessee wrote, "There is a magic about a frame rooming-house with a verandah and a porch swing, whether it be North or South. And it is *l'heure bleue*, so flattering to blonds." He said that despite the youth's protestations that he was "straight," it took no more than ten minutes to convince him that "his life would not be complete until he'd passed an evening in my embrace."[29]

Tennessee was again creating a dramatic identity—the bravado being something he later acquired among the privileges of fame—for Tom's journal told a somewhat different story. The "blond kid" was admittedly and openly gay, and, in all probability, the one who did the importuning. The evidence confirms the fact that at this stage Tom was both appalled and at the same time driven by the pursuit of sex. The final emptiness of most one-night stands seemed only to raise the hope that there might be a companion to share his bed and, more importantly, his life.

18

The Broken World

July–September 1940

To anyone struggling in the theatre of the 1930s and 1940s, the fact that this character who called himself Tennessee Williams could have a play optioned by the Theatre Guild was extraordinary, to say the least. Equally extraordinary was Tom's attitude. A legion of playwrights, not all beginners, was struggling for just such an opportunity and, instead of hying off to a summer retreat, would have haunted the Fifty-third Street offices of the Guild. But Tom gave the appearance of being almost indifferent, as though he was taking his good fortune for granted. As an artist, it was simply something he expected and always would.

Tennessee remembered his first meeting at the Guild with Lawrence Langner, who "had a desk the size of a President's and it had been covered that day with more playscripts than I had imagined to exist in the world. In one great gesture, he swept the desk clean of all scripts but mine and said, 'I have no interest in anything but *genius*, so please sit down.' "[1] This, too, Tom accepted, with the remark that such tributes only caused him to check to see whether his wallet was still in his pocket. To be considered a genius did not embarrass him; outwardly he took it as a matter of fact, although privately his journals reflected the torment of self-doubt.

What many saw as an insouciance or conceit in Tom was actually an unshakable confidence, more compulsive than presumptuous. This could also explain why he was innately shy but at the same time bold in making his contacts—in his desperate quest now for someone whom he could love and who would love him in turn. What he was seeking, as he had said, was not a deep but a "satisfactory relationship." He was about to receive, however, an answered prayer: a love that went deeper than any he had ever known or thought possible, possible for *him*, at least. He was to refer to this as "that pivotal summer when I took sort of a crash course in growing up."[2]

In the few months since his arrival in New York, Tom had entered a gay life beyond his imagining, as liberating as it was fatally fascinating: a heterodox underground activity that existed in a very large "closet," indeed. Those in the straight world rarely recognized homosexuals except for an effeminate minority within the minority. For young women, in particular, to suspect the nice young men they knew of doing such things would be quite literally unthinkable.

Since "good girls" in those days did not live with their suitors, let alone openly indulge in prenuptial affairs, *roommates* was a term generally applied to members of the same sex. As a result, two young men could live together for years without arousing suspicion, regarded simply as eligible bachelors saving money for their eventual marriages. Many wore engagement rings to stave off the attack of some curious would-be bride and mother-in-law.

Tom saw in these hidden friendships an ideal he would pursue all of his life, its genesis being in the *erastes-eromenos* relationships of ancient Greece: He would, more because of circumstance, always be the older to the younger man. However bizarre his sexual behavior would become, Tennessee Williams never covertly lived the lie. And in those days, that took courage, because exposure could and often did ruin the lives and careers of even the most powerful. He was not making convenient and often tragic marriages and hiding behind other such camouflage. Pretension of that kind he felt beneath him, and although he did not strut his homosexuality, he was living free of the closet, sometimes dangerously, long before the word took on its present meaning.

While the beachfront life of Provincetown in the summer of 1940 was no less sexually frenzied than that in New York, at least it was washed with sun and ocean breezes and blessed with the hungover quiet of mornings, in which Tom was able to write without distractions. But once darkness descended on the colony, he felt only the hollow loneliness of sex in the night, that passing glimpse of love that merely intensified his desire for some one friend in his life.

Provincetown, once a quaint fishing village at the tip of Cape Cod, Massachusetts, had, by 1940, long since become a place where one takes his pleasures as he finds them, where winter restraints and inhibitions melt under a summer sun and where the wily New Englanders, their puritanism set aside, cash in at their registers. Artists of every kind—painters, poets, and dramatists—make P-town their refuge.

Among the playwrights at the original Provincetown Playhouse on the wharf, Eugene O'Neill became the most famous. In 1924, the theatre was closed, but by the summer of 1940, a founder and actress-director-producer, Catharine Huntington, had rebuilt and reopened the theatre. Tom attended a performance of O'Neill's *Diff'rent*, and perhaps in the character of Emma Crosby he glimpsed an hysterical precursor of Alma Winemiller and Blanche DuBois in *Summer and Smoke* and *A Streetcar Named Desire*.

To Bertha Case in the Liebling-Wood office, he described his life now as idyllic: "It's great to be back on the beach again! The lovely sand-dunes and sea-gulls are a marvelous katharsis after Manhattan. They say I brought fair weather to the Cape. The sun is out pretty consistently and the water getting warmer."[3] He also told her, "I am working on a new long play *Stairs to the Roof.* If somebody else were writing it, it might turn out to be a 'great American drama,' as the theme is pretty big, more cosmic than sexual for a change."[4] The play, first named *Beauty and the Beast*, was developing into a "fantastical" view of his years at the International Shoe Company, but it would not receive its one and only production at the Pasadena Playhouse until 1947.

His next address was 30 Commercial Street, and in letters to Donald Windham and Fred Melton, he spoke of the beach crowd's behavior as shocking, even as broad-minded as he felt he was. In keeping with a custom of many gays who indulge in a mockery of themselves and the so-called straight world, he referred to himself as an old auntie who had left her glasses at the apartment. His was hollow and halfhearted ridicule, though, since at the same time he vowed in his journal to rid himself of his bitchery.

Kip

During the first days of July, Tom met Joseph Hazan and his friend Kip Kiernan. Joe and Kip shared a two-story shack on Captain Jack's Wharf, as well as an interest in dance. They had previously studied in New York at the Madame Duval Ballet School, but Joe's interest had turned to East Indian dance and philosophy and Kip's to modern dance. Both had decided to take different professional names, Joe's being Joss Hassan and Kip selecting the Kiernan from a telephone book; a Canadian of Russian Jewish descent, Kip's actual name was Bernard Dubowsky. Collaterally descended from the great Ukrainian opera singer Alexander Kipnis, "Kip" became his nickname. He had another reason for changing his name: He was an illegal alien at a time when Canada was at war.

Kip was uniquely handsome, with an impressive build and winning smile.

He was not a good dancer. "To confuse Kip's charm with his ability to dance was naive to say the least," Hazan said. But he easily found work modeling at the Provincetown extension of Hans Hofmann's famed art school. Although they were good friends, in later years Joe complained that Kip was always stealing his girls.[5]

Tennessee remembered, "Some casual acquaintance took me to the wharf one noonday, clear and blue. At the stove of a little two-story shack on this wharf built on stilts over the incoming, outgoing tides was the youth to whom I dedicated my first collection of stories. He had his back to me, as I entered, since he was facing the stove, up-stage, preparing clam chowder, New England style, the dish on which he and his young (platonic) friend Joe were subsisting that summer through economic need. He was wearing dungarees, skin-tight, and my good eye was hooked like a fish. He was too preoccupied by the chowder-cooking to more than glance over his shoulder and say 'hello.' " When he finally turned around, Tennessee was struck by his likeness to the young Nijinsky. "Later he was to tell me, with a charmingly Narcissan pride, that he had almost the same bodily dimensions of Nijinsky, as well as a phenomenal facial resemblance. He had slightly slanted lettuce-green eyes, high cheekbones and a lovely mouth."[6]

As much as Kip resisted any involvement in the colony's gay life, for a short while he shared an intense intimacy with Tom. Both Kip and Joe found Tom gentle and charming company and invited him to share their quarters. Tom slept downstairs on a cot in the same room with Joe. Kip had the upstairs bedroom to himself. He realized that his young writer friend was longing for him and was finally so moved by Tom's importunings that he gave in fully and passionately. Broke and lonely and in need of someone to befriend him, he gave an initial response to Tom's worshipful love that was reciprocal, albeit ephemeral.

Tom now had a certain professional reputation. This, together with his obvious commitment to his writing, impressed Kip, who hoped Tom might help him in his aspiration to become a dancer. Tom had recently been publicized in the Sunday *New York Herald Tribune*, and in mid-July he returned briefly to New York in order to find out what progress the Guild was making with his play. But his thoughts were centered on his affair with Kip, and he wrote in his journal:

It is a rather pale bright summer morning, weak lemony sunlight on the brownstone fronts. I am playing "La Golondrina" and feeling rather weary of it all. Yes—in spite of the fact that the great anticipated thing occurred—not once but apparently twice—or maybe this wasn't what I meant. Love to be love has got to be love. . . . Why am I always restless, searching, unsatisfied? My work lags, production plans uncertain. Writing this journal doesn't interest me much anymore. I will probably forget it entirely after a while. I have been taking too much nicotine, coffee, alcohol—try to cut it out reduce it. Have got to save myself for my work—such as it is. Unbearably stupid today—gbye."

He had phoned the Guild offices and talked with Langner and Helburn and was upset by their lack of commitment, or so it seemed to him. On his return to the Cape, he wrote to Langner, requesting more definite information about their production plans. He also sent a letter to Bertha Case during Audrey and Liebling's absence in Beverly Hills, where they had opened new offices.

> When I was in New York last week neither Langner nor Helburn had anything to say, I only talked to them over the phone for a minute. One highly significant fact came out however—which is that [Joan] Crawford regarded the part as "low and common"—and is apparently eliminated from the picture. I regard this as an act of God—but cannot exclude the suspicion that the Theatre Guild might have purchased the play mainly because they thought *she* would like it. If this were the case, they might now lose interest in it. I expressed this apprehension to Bennett Cerf [of Random House, whom he had met earlier] when I saw him—he assured me that they were primarily interested in the play itself and that Crawford was just a subsequent "brainstorm." However *I* don't *know!!*—nothing surprises me much anymore.[7]

In an effort to resolve the problem of a leading lady, Tom bicycled to Dennis Port, where Tallulah Bankhead was appearing at the Cape Playhouse. Since the Theatre Guild had publicized the fact that it would produce *Battle of Angels* only after it had secured a star, Tom overcame his shyness and visited Bankhead backstage to tell her he was convinced that she would be the perfect lead in his play. Flattered, "Tallu" was all southern charm and promised to read the script. When he returned to meet with her shortly after, she drawled in her famous baritone, "Oh, it's you. The play's impossible, darling, but sit down and have a drink with me."[8] It would be the first of many they would share in the years to come.

The Guild had also sent a copy of the script to Miriam Hopkins, who, like Bankhead, was touring in summer stock that year. Writing to his mother, Tom said, "She has my script and has promised to read it this week. They are all afraid of the other woman in the play who has a dangerously good part. I don't think the Guild will announce any production plans till after the actress problem is settled. I am not told anything at all. They had so much trouble with Saroyan interfering in his productions that I suppose they think it best to keep the playwright as ignorant as possible till everything is settled."[9] In his journal, he reported:

> Fri—July 27—Back at the Cape. Should be sublimely happy. Instead rather miserable due to one of my oldest neuroses coming back on me.

Plagues me viciously, makes it hard for me to bear the strain of people. I wear dark glasses almost continually—even this does not seem an adequate protection. It is worst in the early mornings such as now when I face another whole day of this tortured evasion. . . .

But love—which I have been needing—only somewhat thwarted by this damnable tension.

A day or two later, he wrote to Donald Windham about Kip and the second-story room they now shared:

The ceiling is very high like the loft of a barn and the tide is lapping under the wharf. The sky amazingly brilliant with stars. The wind blows the door wide open, the gulls are crying. Oh, Christ. I call him baby . . . though when I lie on top of him I feel like I am polishing the Statue of Liberty or something. He is so enormous. A great bronze statue of antique Greece come to life. But with a little boy's face. A funny turned-up nose, slanting eyes, and underlip that sticks out and hair that comes to a point in the middle of his forehead. I lean over him in the night and memorize the geography of his body with my hands—he arches his throat and makes a soft, purring sound. His skin is steaming hot like the hide of a horse that's been galloping. It has a warm, rich odor. The odor of life. He lies very still for a while, then his breath comes fast and his body begins to lunge. Great rhythmic plunging motion with panting breath and his hands working over my body. Then sudden release—and he moans like a little baby. I rest with my head on his stomach. Sometimes fall asleep that way.[10]

In *Memoirs*, Tennessee wrote, "I remember that the first day after the first night, when we were crossing the dunes to the ocean-side cabin of a dance critic, Kip and I lingered behind the others in the party and Kip said to me, 'Last night you made me know what is meant by beautiful pain.'" In the loft, Williams said, he wrote his only verse play, *The Purification*.* "I had set up a little writing-table, a wooden box with my portable on it, and in that play I

---

*If Williams's memory was correct, this may have been a first draft, although in his journal he attributes the origin of *The Purification* to a date in the spring of 1941. On the other hand, Williams may have been alluding to an early draft of a short play he subsequently titled *The Parade, or Approaching the End of a Summer*. This was written in anger, as he told his bibliographer, Andreas Brown, in a letter dated 19 February 1962, "The character Dick in PARADE is very, in fact completely different from Kip as he was." Williams thought perhaps this discrepancy was due to his having written the play after their emotional crisis, when he was angry with Kip and sorry for himself. "When someone hurts us deeply, we no longer see them at all clearly. Not until time has put them back in focus." In 1962, Williams gave the play a new title, *Something Cloudy, Something Clear*, and finally in 1981 it was produced under his supervision in an Off-Off-Broadway theatre.

found a release, in words, of the ecstasy of the affair. And also a premonition of its doom."[11]

> Sun. night—Went to chamber music recital—K. moody—rushed off by himself. Moves me to find someone afflicted as I am with mental conflicts. Think I understand a little— Still it troubles me—this is so much what I need, what I want, what I have been looking for the past few months so feverishly. Seems miraculous. It is too good to be true.
>
> I can't feel sure of it. Can't believe it will go on. So K's moods worry me—I fear his being lost to me already. If that happened I suppose I would go on outwardly very much as usual but, oh, what an ache of emptiness I would have to endure—for now, for the first time in my life, I feel I am near the great *real* thing that can make my life complete.
>
> Oh, K.—don't stay away very long. I am lonely tonight. It's after midnight—I am here alone.

Unaware at first of Kip's confusion and distress and unable to accept the youth's moods as attempts to escape him, Tom felt that his lover was perhaps bisexual. Soon after, his "premonition of doom" was personified in the form of a girlfriend of Kip's. She had warned him that continued association with Tom could result in his, too, becoming homosexual. In a letter to Fred Melton, Tom quipped that having a *woman* as a rival was competition in restraint of trade and that Fred was fortunate to have a lover who was *gay* and not bisexual like Kip.

Tom was, in fact, wildly, hopelessly in love with Kip, incontinent in his desire for him, and he believed Kip loved him in return. But the idyll was about to end. One day, when Tom was "on the dunes with a group that included the yet-unknown, or uncelebrated abstract painter, Jackson Pollock," Kip suddenly appeared on his bicycle looking very solemn. As they rode back to town, Tom on the handlebars of the bike, Kip said with great care and gentleness that their affair was over. It was his intention to marry someday, as eventually he did, and more than that he felt the gay world and homosexuality itself "violated his being in a way that was unacceptable to him. He told me that the girl who had intruded upon the scene had warned him that I was in the process of turning him homosexual and that he had seen enough of that world to know that he had to resist it."[12]

Later, Tennessee recalled, he was upstairs in Kip's room and hurled a boot down the steps at the girl, cursing her. In his journal, Tom said he had "made a horrible ass of myself this A.M.—insulting a stupid little girl because she had been instrumental in my unhappiness." After that, Kip withdrew, remote and silent, and Tom's despair was "consummate." Alone, isolated, and desolate, he could feel only a gnawing emptiness and a desperate desire to escape, in hopes of alleviating the pain—"to find in motion what was lost in space." Tom wrote:

Tuesday—C'est finis—
I can't save myself—
Somebody has got to save me,

I shall have to go through the
world giving myself to people
until somebody will take me.

We are moving into a new studio at the front of the wharf—I am a little drunk—the pain is dulled a little.

There is nothing. T.W.

Still, he felt that somehow he had to go on, and he planned to leave for New York at once. "It can't be much worse the next few weeks than I expect it to be, since I really expect it to be next to unbearable—and I am pretty badly frightened. Well—to *hell* with it. I am going to see it through. No bug-house for me, baby." As for Kip, he said, "I must not write about him now because I couldn't do it fairly. I feel that I have never given my love more uselessly in any whore house. No, that's not true. It's my hurt pride crying out again. This has got to stop—pass away—it can't continue. How will it be on the boat tomorrow? How will it be in New York? Oh, Christ, how will it be!"

He wrote, "Joe has been swell—a grand guy—kind, understanding—the kind of friend I would like to take through life with me, but know that I can't because I can never stand still. I'm always the fugitive—will be till I make my last escape—out of life altogether." Immediately on arriving in New York, he sent word to Hazan, "I had an awfully strange feeling as the Boston boat sailed slowly around the light-house point and then distantly—austerely—past the new beach and the glittering white sand-dunes. Saw P-town dwindling sort of dream-like behind me. Not real at all. The Pilgrim monument getting smaller and smaller till it was just a tooth-pick—'mad pilgrimage of the flesh' is what it seemed to stand for. This awful searching-business of our lives." He added, "Leaving always makes you conscious of that fatal, inevitable forward motion in life which at other times can seem so curiously stagnant. When you see a shore-line recede behind you, you realize very keenly and bitterly and excitedly what is happening to you all the time of your life—the Long Goodbye."[13]

Sunday in Manhattan—August 18. A grey sultry heavy-lidded day—felt quite weighted down with fatigue when I awoke to face it. Bad cold on chest uneasy feeling which probably means the blood pressure is up.

He mentioned that a blond friend of Windham's, a coworker at the World's Fair, had come by the previous night. "What once was so desirable—though I wanted it as an hour's diversion—seemed pretty empty and sordid.

Still it helped me over a bad night and cost nothing."

He had just read an article about travel in Mexico, and this renewed his desire to go there, but this time as an escape.

Perhaps this proposed trip will revive me. But, oh, K.—if only— only—*only*—

What is the use of such thoughts? I have loved once in my life—and now it is over.

Now is the time for waiting for the heart to close in on itself, for rest, for recuperation.

Somewhere there is another rare and beautiful stranger waiting for me. And this one, perhaps, is the one who will *take* what I give. And I will stop being *lonely*.

Monday . . . Took a long walk in the rain along Broadway and enjoyed it. Felt quiet and relaxed—only a little bit blue—for first time in days— and days—

Bought "Sonnets from Portuguese" for K. and "Rubayat" for Joe. Cheap gifts but my heart goes with them. I mark Sonnet XLIII for K's attention.

Silly of me! He'll probably think so, too. . . .

A drunk wobbled up to me and caught my arm and called me "darling."

Strangers still look at me with interest—sexual interest in spite of the fact that I begin to feel old and jaded.

I think almost continually of K. Memories—dreams—longings—little hopes and great desolations— Will he ever come back? Can there—will there—be someone else? Or will I always be walking around streets at night all alone? Standing wearily in front of bright windows? Wondering where to go, what to do, when only someone I loved could give me a real direction in which to move. K., if you ever come back, I'll never let you go. I'll bind you to me with every chain that the ingenuity of mortal love can devise! . . .

K.—dear K.—I love you with all my heart. Good-night.

Joe responded to his letter, and on Tuesday Tom wrote gratefully again to the one person he now regarded as "closer than a brother." "Joss" had apparently counseled him to seek in meditation what was rationally inaccessible, and Tom replied, "Oh, if I only had this ability to lose myself in 'beauty' which you speak of, but too often it only hurts me in that it makes me more conscious of my isolation, and I am afraid that I will always be casting myself against the stones of the world in an effort to be 'absorbed, included' to escape from aloneness. I pray for the strength to be separate, to be austere. That is the best future for me—ascetism [*sic*] and concentrated work. But remember what an animal I am! And don't expect too much of me."[14] In his journal, he wrote:

> Oh, God, how desolate and lost I feel—how utterly *alone*—alone.
>
> It no longer seems likely that we will ever really come together again. Of course the play production seems a tremendous amount. Audrey does not want me to count on it—and I don't. But what else can save me now? . . . Oh, K.—what have you done to me?

The Heart Forgets

Tom wrote to Audrey at her new offices in Beverly Hills, "I wish you all the luck in the world though of course it is a little painful to see you so firmly established at the other side of the continent." He said that neither Langner nor Helburn had divulged any actual production plans. "Hope things turn out well for both our sakes. If they go badly or not so well as expected, I may come out to your west coast and sell what is left of my soul to the cinema people."[15] Audrey replied, "Liebling writes me that he saw Theresa Helburn the other day and she said your re-write on the play was greatly improved. I am keeping my thumbs crossed for you and so is he. I am still hoping very big things for you, since I still believe in you tremendously."[16]

Clark Mills was in New York at that time, prior to the start of the school term at Cornell, and remembered going to the apartment where Tom was staying. Someone else had let him in, explaining that Tom was expected shortly. Clark said that there was a baby grand piano in the living room and on it a note that he thought was a message for him. It was an impassioned love letter signed "—10—." From what Mills read of the letter, there was no doubt that Tom was writing of his love for someone of his own sex. Clark said that discovering this made no difference in his regard for his friend, although he had never before suspected it: "Obviously Tom felt constrained, and it was just unfortunate that something that need not have come between us ultimately did."[17]

In the early hours before his departure for Mexico, Tom wrote to Hazan that Clark "came over last night and told me quite seriously that he had decided to kill himself within the next year. He is tied to an academic job at Cornell which smothers his creative life, and he sees no possible escape as his poetry, very fine but completely uncommercial, could never support him. I reasoned with him for a long time about the infinite value of life, the miracle of simply being alive, and through this I think I convinced myself of it."

He said he had a number of addresses given him by Bennett Cerf at Random House and by Langner at the Guild and expected to make friends in Mexico pretty rapidly, leading "a gay-mad sort of life the first week or two in reaction to what I've been through. Then settle down on the beach and try to catch up with myself." He expected to live in Mexico "till the play goes into production as I no longer have money to live well in New York, the Rockefeller funds being used up and just option money, which fortunately goes up to one hundred next month."

Finally, he thanked Joe for his emotional support during the previous month's crisis. "Funny—in my wanderings about I have met a great many people nearly all friendly, many of whom I was fairly intimate with in one way or another, but nobody has seemed as close in spirit as you are. That was why I thought only of you at those times when my life seemed in danger of falling to pieces. It was a cumulation of tension that I have gone through here in New York, constant suspense and nerve-wracking excitement, which I evaded with drink and with sex. It all came to a climax in this neurotic condition just gone through—but I think is now over."[18]

The means Tom chose for going to Mexico was through an agency called Share-A-Ride. People with cars who were looking to share expenses would notify the agency of an intended trip, and someone like Tom, who did not have much money, could arrange via the agency for low-cost transportation. The car Tom was to travel in, for a twenty-five-dollar fare, was owned by a young Mexican, a somewhat-impoverished member of an otherwise-wealthy family, and his bride, who were returning to Mexico City after a whirlwind visit to the New York World's Fair.

Before Tom left, he wrote one last plea:

Dear Kip:
Fuck the whys and wherefores. Just write me a letter because you're my friend and you know I want to hear from you. The rest has gone under the bridge and way, way, way out to sea! Five o'clock in the morning I leave for Mexico. Will you write me care of Wells-Fargo, Mexico City? Almost immediately after that I expect to go to Taxco and then on to Acapulco to resume my life on the beach with a slightly more tropical setting.... God knows, perhaps I'll be stranded on the beach at Acapulco without a fucking penny twixt me and the hairless chihuahuas. In which case, will you come down there and keep me? No?

I will be a nice, lazy beachcomber the rest of my life, dozing under a big wide sombrero and in my dreams I will see entrechats, pirouettes and marvelous arabesques....

I'm sorry I can't be as monkish as Joe would like me to be. After all, would that be *me?* I feel right now a definite reaction against all sobriety, my nigger laughing and dancing which Joe likes is part of this me and not the other me and this is the me people like. Except you. Or do you?

I hereby formally bequeath you to the female vagina, which vortex will inevitably receive you with or without my permission.

But I love you (with robust manly love, as Whitman would call it) as much as I love anybody, and want you to write!

—10.[19]

When Kip finally did write, his reply was distant, as though he was writing a casual friend. Tom had already heard through a friend about "K.'s indifference to any mention" of him. There was, in truth, nothing that Kip could say—*any* word would only add hurt and, worse, give hope where there could be none.

Leafing through his journal, Tom came across an entry he had written in August of the previous year, when he observed that all his deep loves and friendships had hurt him finally because he had felt so much more than the other person could feel. Now with the loss of Kip, he recognized that the "experience has repeated itself—only more bitterly."

What he had written was the painful solace that "the heart forgets to feel even sorrow after a while."

La Golondrina

Flight could be called Tennessee Williams's natural existence. Wherever he alighted in new or familiar environs, he would soon feel only discontent among the earthbound and would suddenly fly off. As he had told Joe Hazan, "I'm always the fugitive—will be till I make my last escape—out of life altogether." The images of birds stirred his imagination and became woven symbolically into his writings.

Travel, with its illusion of perpetual mobility, had by now grown into a driving necessity, a component of the very activity of writing, a way of life. There were those among Tennessee Williams's friends who viewed his birdlike migrations as more madness than method, more circle than direction. In the beginning, it is true, these peregrinations were just aimless wanderings, but finally, they became voyages. Certainly this curious impulse to move about—toward friends and then quickly away from them, to foreign places and then back to familiar ground—was a protective measure. He came to look upon himself as "a moving target," travel becoming his way to avoid a life of being possessed by possessions and to evade those who would possess him. To keep moving enabled him to free his mind from niggling hour-to-hour, day-to-day demands; to prevent events and family and friends from closing in and suffocating him; and, above all, to accommodate his overwhelming desire to write.

For Tom, writing was no longer simply putting words on paper but also using words to release a banked flood of reflections and impressions and cruel memories. More than any vainglory in success or beckoning lure of escape in travel, there was the terrible, primal passion to give vent to emotions he could no longer repress. And to write them down was the only means by which he could elucidate and communicate them. At length, writing had become an act of survival, a flight from madness.

The love that Tom had hoped to channel through Kip into his work, now thwarted and turned in on itself, left him stranded in an arctic aloneness. Although he would go on seeking sexual outlets in brief affairs and one-night stands, he knew this to be a drearily repetitive pattern, what he described to Joe Hazan as "this awful searching-business of our lives." He had equated his and Kip's relationship with Donald Windham and Fred Melton's as "beyond shame." And in doing so, he revealed a deep, enduring reservation and hope that beyond promiscuity there must be something or someone beyond shame whom he could love unreservedly. A conflict had been set up that would follow and torture him the rest of his life: a vacillation between the open, often "scandalous" pursuit of sex and the conscience-ridden desire to "return to my goodness."

Olé

On the drive to Mexico, there was not only Tom, the husband, and his bride in the car but also three other male Mexicans who took turns at the wheel. And since the group spoke little or no English and Tom scarcely any Spanish, the problem of road directions and other communications difficulties resulted in a chaotic trip with the car zigzagging from highway to side roads and back again, much to everyone's chagrin and confusion. Tennessee later described the journey as erratic as a blind bird's and taking twice as long as expected.

En route, the party stopped over at a hotel in Monterrey, where Tom wrote to Bennett Cerf, asking him to be sure that the formidable and acidulous critic George Jean Nathan received a copy of *Battle of Angels*. Knowing that Nathan had virtually ushered Eugene O'Neill into the American theatre, Tom wrote, "Nobody's criticism could be more important to me, so if he has time, will you suggest he let me know his reactions?" Cerf subsequently responded that Nathan did not give his unqualified approval of the play but said that Tennessee Williams as a playwright showed most unusual promise.

Tom also gave Cerf a graphic account of his trip thus far: "Drove down in a jalopy with some Mexicans and a gallon of dago red which now is exhausted and the bottle re-filled with tequila. They drink and fight among themselves—I sit back and sing 'God bless America' so loud I can't hear them and utter an occasional prayer to 'Our Mother of the Highways' when the road becomes very exciting. . . . Everything fell out of the car at Sabinas Hidalgo— it is being put together if possible. Then we shove on to Mex. City. Two more days of all this—and heaven, too!"[20]

While in Monterrey, the "bride" confessed to Tom, a somewhat abashed gringo, that she was not married, that she was in fact a prostitute by profession, and that she was quite understandably apprehensive at being introduced into her "husband's" wealthy family. Tennessee recalled, "She had perched herself in an attitude of more and more permanency on my bed and at last I thought it best to inform her that I was quite ineligible as a surrogate for her bridegroom. And I told her why. She nodded sadly and there was a little respite of silence. . . ." At length, she sighed and got up, remarking, " 'I guess you're lucky, honey. Female hygiene's a lot more complicated than men's.' "[21]

What had begun as a chest cold developed during the trip into a bad cough that caused Tom to expectorate blood. He was so miserable in his forlorn hope that there might be a reconciling letter from Kip waiting for him in Mexico City that he wished the cough would become a symptom of tuberculosis or that an accident on the road would relieve him of his misery.

Once in Mexico City, Tom found to his surprise that there was word from both Joe and Kip. Lonely and desolate, he wrote the first of several remarkable letters to Joe Hazan:

> I am leaving in a couple of hours for Taxco and Acapulco. Mexico City is too big to take in one gulp so I am going away to the beach till my throat stops aching and then come back and try to swallow some more. At first I thought there was nothing here: mistaken: there is a tremendous lot but I am not strong enough for it right now. I go up and down, up and down the seesaw of moods, because my nerves are exhausted. . . . Last night, for instance, I was entertained at the home of Juanita, who is the queen of the male whores in Mexico City. They accosted me on the street and took me there. Such strangeness, such poetic "license"! We sat in a room with pale pink walls and an enormously high ceiling, covered with pictures of nudes and pictures of Saints and madonnas. The bed was very wide to accommodate several simultaneous parties and was covered with a pale lettuce-green satin spread. Above it hung a handsome black and silver crucifix and Jesus with great sorrowful eyes looking over the pitiful acts of lust that went on there. No doubt thanking his lucky stars that he remained a celibate on earth, because if he had not—it is quite likely he would have been a fairy. Some of the whores were very, very lovely with eyes dark and lustrous as those of the Christ and smooth olive skins. But I stayed out of bed with them because I suspected they were all rotten with disease. I could speak no Spanish but "Mana [mañana] es otro dia," they could speak no English, so there was none of that tiresome necessity for conversation which I despise so much. We laughed and drank together and three who had exquisite high voices and a feminine quality that was graceful and charming . . . sang a beautiful song called "Amor Perdida"—very haunting. They were like sad, wonderful flowers—Fleurs de mal—their price was two pesos, the equivalent of forty cents. And one was so lovely that when he kissed and embraced me, I had an orgasm, but I showed more than my usual discipline and kept out of any real mischief. . . .

The following morning he woke up feeling "very low" and began packing, determined to leave for Acapulco. At the Theatre Guild, he had been given the address of a woman and told Joe that this was the kind of human contact he needed, saying that "all my neurotic symptoms disappeared after her gracious reception."

> She seemed to understand intuitively the state that I was in and her whole manner was brimming with kindness. My nerves straightened out and my head became cool and quiet. It was like having a raw wound wrapped in a long white bandage. I feel now that it will be a woman I will finally go to for tenderness in life. The sexual part—if there has to be any—would probably adjust itself in a while, since I am so easily directed in that way.
>
> The mood that you were in when you wrote [your] letter is so much like mine! We are both standing on the outside of reality, looking in, and it appears all fantastic and empty. We are clutching at hard, firm things that will hold us up, the few eternal values which we are able to grasp in this welter of broken pieces, wreckage, that floats on the surface of life. . . .

He felt that it was possible to build stone pillars that hold the roof off one's head but that it takes time, infinite patience, and endurance. He said that one had to make a religion of endurance, and he entreated Joe:

> Read the collected letters of D. H. Lawrence, the journal and letters of Katharine Mansfield, of Vincent Van Gogh. How bitterly and relentlessly they fought their way through! Sensitive beyond endurance and yet *enduring!* Of course Van Gogh went mad in the end and Mansfield and Lawrence both fought a losing battle with degenerative disease—T.B.— but their work is a pure shaft rising out of that physical defeat. A permanent, pure, incorruptible thing, far more real, more valid than their physical entities ever were. They cry aloud to you in their work—no, *more* vividly, intimately, personally than they could have cried out to you in their living tongues. They *live*, they aren't dead. That is the one ineluctable gift of the artist, to project himself beyond time and space through grasp and communion with eternal values. . . . And so we come back to the word "beauty"—which I thank God is significant to us both. Let us have the courage to believe in it—though people may call us "esthetes," "romantics," "escapists"—let's cling tenaciously to our conviction that this is the only reality worth our devotion, and let that belief sustain us through our black "tunnels." . . .
>
> Kip wrote me a nice letter. He is living behind a wall without even a grated window for you to look through, you have to peek through the cracks, through the broken mortar, but when you do, you count more flowers than weeds on the opposite side. . . . Give him my best. . . .
>
> Devotedly your friend,
>
> 10.[22]

Tennessee Williams seldom traveled anywhere without leaving a variety of problems in his wake for friends, associates, and strangers to handle as best they could. During these early improvident years, he also left behind a goodly number of unpaid bills. After he departed from the YMCA in Mexico City and arrived, broke, at the Hotel Costa Verde in Acapulco, he still owed three dollars' rental on his bicycle in Provincetown as well as rent on the Thirty-seventh Street apartment and its furnishings, such as the piano, and the type-writer he had with him. As far as his unpaid bills were concerned, well, in a letter to Fred Melton he likened artists to little gray foxes and the rest of the world as hounds, their natural enemies.

The Lemon Tree

En route from Mexico City to Acapulco, Tom first traveled by bus to Taxco and then hitched a ride the rest of the way. Tennessee recalled the event, saying he had "joined a group of American students who drove me to Acapulco. We arrived at dusk at a seaside resort called Todd's Place, charm-ingly primitive, and with a very rough surf. We went swimming that night with the surf roaring in. I contrived to be washed repeatedly against and over the most attractive one in the group. I think he got the general notion but could not be separated from his companions."[23] After they had arrived at Aca-pulco, Tom continued his quest; in his journal, he said that he "carried on with a blond boy here—on the beach and in bed—and shocked a bunch of nice young American college boys—[ATO] fraternity brothers, inciden-tally—with my drunken candor about homosexuality. One was very nice—Jerry. Tried to put me into bed. To save my honor! or the fraternity's. The affair was no fun but it relieved the monotony."

Sunday Sept 7 or 8, 1940
So I begin a new journal. Not a very auspicious day—not in a very auspi-cious time. This is the period after heartbreak and it is full of the dullness and tedium of mind that no longer cares for its existence. Yet is desperate to continue to survive, to fight the way through a mind that fears break-ing because of its constant neuroses. But must and will *not*.

I have come to Mexico running away. I have settled down (?) for a while at Acapulco. My brain is curiously dead. I find it difficult to carry on conversations—need companionship dreadfully but can't talk, can think of nothing to say. Well—nothing but stupidities. I have always dis-liked conversation but now it is all but impossible for me. . . .

Tried writing yesterday. Did some work on Stairs to the Roof. Not much energy but accomplished something. Even coffee doesn't wake up my torpid brain cells. Such heaviness, such dullness, appalling.

Well, it is bound to get better. It couldn't get worse. The cause—

heartbreak over K.—is all but forgotten. The effect will run its course also.

In Acapulco, Tom ran into the writer he had seen recently in New York, Gordon Sager, who was in the company of writer and composer Paul Bowles. Tom noted in his journal they "got very drunk—rum, beer, tequila." A subsequent meeting with Bowles and his wife, novelist Jane Bowles, was characteristic: He just appeared at their door. Although this meeting was as casual as it was brief, the three were destined to become lifelong friends. At the time, Bowles remembered being somewhat struck by the maverick personality of the young playwright:

> He came to the house. We lived on the Avenida Hidalgo there. And one morning we were just about to go out to the beach, and the servant came and said there was a gentleman at the door and I went, and he said, "I'm Tennessee Williams. I'm sent here by Lawrence Langner. He told me you were here. The Theatre Guild is going to do my play *Battle of Angels.*" I said, "Come in, but you must excuse us because we are about to go to the beach for the day and since we have been invited, we can't take you. But here is the house. Here is the patio. Here are hammocks. Here's a new bottle of rum and there's plenty of Coke. You just call the servants and they'll bring you whatever you need . . ." and when we came back at five o'clock in the afternoon, he was lying in the hammock, and he'd drunk a good deal of rum and lots of Coke, and was very happy and was reading books. And that's how we got to know him.[24]

In his autobiography, *Without Stopping,* Bowles described Tom as "a round-faced, sunburned young man in a big floppy sombrero and a striped sailor sweater."[25] Tennessee remembered that "Paul was, as ever, upset about the diet and his stomach. The one evening that we spent together that summer was given over almost entirely to the question of what he could eat in Acapulco that he could digest, and poor little Janie kept saying, 'Oh, Bubbles, if you'd just stick to cornflakes and fresh fruit!' and so on and so on. None of her suggestions relieved his dyspeptic humor."[26] The impression he had of Jane and Paul at that time as very odd and charming was reciprocal. Although Tennessee had only the vaguest memory of Jane Bowles on that occasion, he would come to revere her.

Another who would also earn his admiration and become a close personal friend was Carson McCullers. Tom, in fact, had just discovered McCullers, and in a letter to Bennett Cerf, he wrote, "I brought one novel down here with me called 'The Heart Is a Lonely Hunter' by a young girl named Carson McCullers. It is so extraordinary it makes me ashamed of anything I might do. Are you familiar with her work?—What a play she could write!—Let us hope that she doesn't—or that she *does*—however it might deprecate other works in that field." He also told Cerf, "I will either leave this place in a strait-jacket or a much better integrated person than when I arrived, depending on how I react to almost complete isolation. . . . [There is] only one person near who speaks English and he is usually too drunk to speak anything but the language of pigs."[27] He added that he had selected Acapulco as the place to finish his play *Stairs to the Roof* and perhaps start a novel about an actress, to be called *The Bitch*.

What he had actually begun to write, however, was a short story, "The Night of the Iguana," set in the same Hotel Costa Verde at which he was staying. He described it as having ten sleeping rooms, each with a hammock slung outside its screen door; and, directly below the cliff on which the hotel was located, there was a small private beach for the hotel guests. It was a still-water beach bordered by a tropical rain forest. To the west of the peninsula was the Pacific Ocean. Underneath the hotel, some Mexican youths had tied an iguana to be fattened and then eaten at a later time.

Irene, who would ultimately materialize as Blanche DuBois, had yet another incarnation as Miss Edith Jelkes, a lonely spinster and art instructor from an Episcopal girls school in Mississippi, who had "given up her teaching position for a life of refined vagrancy." With "a wistful blond prettiness and a somewhat archaic quality of refinement," she belonged to "an historical Southern family of great but now moribund vitality whose latter generations had tended to split into two antithetical types, one in which the libido was pathologically distended and another in which it would seem to be all dried up."[28] The story is essentially a character study of Miss Jelkes and her fascination with two male writers, an older man and his younger lover.

As he wrote to Joe Hazan, the older writer he apparently abstracted from the wealthy, spoiled son of the manager of the Pullman Company, who "has surfeited his senses so he can't find zest in anything. He raves continually about his sex experience which has been infinite and altogether with women, but horribly dull, and love is impossible for him. He despises women but wants to fuck all the time. He even says he finds their bodies disgusting when they take off their drawers. He is terribly lonely but too selfish to be absorbed in anyone but himself."[29] In a subsequent letter to Donald Windham, Tom said that he had had a long and dull affair with the older writer, who wanted him to share an apartment during the winter in New Orleans or Key West.

Although the creation of Edith Jelkes at this writing grew more out of the conflicting elements of the Dakin and Williams families and from the original model of Irene in New Orleans, the characters of the two writers were evidently based upon the hotel guest and Tom himself. As there are traces of his own personality in Miss Jelkes, as well as a projection of what might have become of Rose, there are also the glimmerings of a fanciful relationship with Kip in the depiction of the two writers. As always, it was the transmutation of actual persons into living characters and the employment of actual places and events that gave verisimilitude and distinguished his writing. Twenty years later, Edith would reemerge as Hannah Jelkes and the world-weary, burned-out writer as a defrocked priest in the play of the same title, *The Night of the Iguana*. At this point, though, Tom was simply absorbing the colorful detail that would become the play's setting.

"The people here," he wrote Joe, "are of two classes, those who are waiting for something to happen or those who believe that everything has happened already. That is, the Americans and other outsiders. Their life is lying about the beaches usually in a hypnosis induced by strong drink and hot sunlight and lack of any exertion." Nothing seemed to surprise or interest these expatriates "as they sit in a cantina on the square and squeeze a drop or two of lemon into their rum-cocos. And the dark, slow natives drift around them like figures in a dream. The juke-boxes play on every side of the plaza, furiously bright posters announce three bulls will be killed this week-end." All this inertia and indifference, he observed, while the world is "cracking up all around them."[30]

Tennessee recalled that Mexico during the 1940 summer was overrun with Nazi Germans and that a party of them had arrived at the Costa Verde hotel, apparently overjoyed at the news of the firebombing of London. To Joe, Tom wrote:

> I am in a bad humor tonight. There is a hard tropical downpour which has driven all the guests onto the back verandah and me into my room to escape them. They are predominantly pro-Nazi Germans, coarse, loud, overwhelmingly arrogant, descended on the hotel in a swarm the last few days. I tried to speak to one of the girls yesterday and she said, "Excuse me, I don't speak Yiddish." Apparently she thought I was Jewish or else regarded all Americans as Jews—anyway the remark struck me as incredibly revolting in its racial nastiness and smugness. . . . Hitler has ruined the Germans, he has so thoroughly sold them on his lowest of bourgeois ideology. If the whole world falls into this state—and some people say we must be Fascist to fight Fascism—it will be well nigh impossible to live in during the remainder of our generation. Gentle ideals were impotent enough before—what will become of them now? What will become of *us?* What will become of our passion for truth in this great Battle of Lies? Who can we speak to, who can we write for—what can we *say?*—Nothing but GOD BLESS AMERICA?—Oh, God, Joe— We have to get out and stay out of this damnable mess 'till it's over!

Joe and Tom had the idea they might share an apartment once they returned to New York. But now Tom was saying:

> If only I can get my play on this year and make money, money, money!— which is escape. A yacht! Yes, that is a beautiful idea.—Where we can go places like this but stay just outside the stink of the people on shore.

There are some British people doing just that. Mexico and Chile are the only countries that will admit them so they move between those two in their boat—which is a sailing vessel with an auxiliary motor. There are six of them, two of them writers—very charming young men—and all of them the wise, tolerant, gracious sort who are naturally exiles from this world.

Yes, if I get a good deal of money, that is what I will do, buy a boat and stay mostly off-shore till La Paloma flies back with the leaf of an olive! However the things that I have to sell in my work—what little I can give to the world in the way of poetic truth—is going rapidly down on the war-time market, and lies and manic laughter and nationalistic hoopla are soaring dizzily up!

One of the German girls has just been bit by a scorpion and is screaming. I hope she dies.

The rain makes a loud, continual noise and the lightning glares balefully through my screen door. I think I will take off my clothes and go for a walk among the elements. Maybe God will be in a conversational humor tonight—for a change—and explain some things to me which I find most confusing.[31]

With the older writer about to leave for Mexico City, Tom found a new lover. "Not knowing the language I have learned to be very direct," he told Joe. "I dispense with all the tedious subtleties and merely say, 'Usted amor muchachos or muchachas!'—Carlos said 'Non importe!'—so we go up on the 'playa,' under the moon and the whispering mango trees, and the restless beast in the jungle under the skin, comes out for a little air."[32]

What Tom was discovering for the first time was an openly primitive and uninhibited sexual experience with native youths, similar to that which his idol Hart Crane had also encountered in Mexico, as being in "the fullest masculine tradition." Except for a shrug or a knowing smile, little was made of males pairing off. Some good, vigorous sex, like some good, hard drink—it was all the same and very different from the New York gay life, with its in-house parties and the often furtive, anonymous, and dangerous search for sex in bars, rest rooms, and alleys. Tom was now enjoying a casual and ingenuous form of sexual gratification, devoid of any sentimental or protracted companionship. Certainly there was seldom the sort of deep, wild, emotional attachment that Tom felt for Kip. Though he assured Joe with transparent bravado that he had put Kip out of his blood, Tom conceded that he still had "a feeling of friendship" for him.

The posture he was striking, the feigned indifference, was hardly an uncommon reaction to unrequited affection. But breaking up with Kip was more disturbing than he was admitting even to himself: an affliction of the heart, the searing pain of rejection and loss, the constant intrusion into his thoughts of something finished but not past, the rage at his own helplessness, and finally, at the last, a dull, hollowed-out, hopeless acceptance. Tom would in time love another companion, but never again would he surrender his affections to anyone so completely, so passionately. To do so, he knew, would be to risk everything: his health, his sanity, and the one thing that would stir him more profoundly than any human being possibly could—his writing and the career that was now enveloping it. In later years, he would write, "All my life I have been haunted by the obsession that to desire a thing or to lose a thing intensely is to place yourself in a vulnerable position, to be a possible, if not a probable, loser of what you want most."[33] Later, he would tell Donald Windham that his relationship with Kip was something that never entered his mind. Looking back on their affair and the intensity he had felt at the time, now it all seemed unreal, more like fiction. But his love for Kip did not end as easily as that. In truth, it remained in the recesses of his "leftover heart" for the rest of his life.

During the few weeks he was in Acapulco, Tom wrote several poems. One in particular, "How Still the Lemon on the Branch," would eventually be adapted for *The Night of the Iguana*. On the original version, he made the notation "Written on the verandah of the hotel Costa Verde, over the Pacific Ocean, as I watched the daylight fading on a tree of big golden lemons."

How still the lemon on the branch
observes the sky begin to blanch

Without a cry, without a prayer,
with no expression of despair!

Sometime while night obscures the tree
the zenith of her life will be

Gone past forever, and from thence
a second history will commence,

A chronicle no longer gold,
a bargaining with mist and mold,

And finally the broken stem,
the plummeting to earth, and then

An intercourse not well-designed
for creatures of the golden kind

Whose native green mists arch above
the earth's obscene, corrupting love

And still the lemon on the branch
observes the sky begin to blanch

Without a cry, without a prayer
with no expression of despair.

O courage could you not as well
select a second place to dwell,

Not only in the lemon tree
but in the frightened heart of me?

When finally, toward the end of September, his royalty check arrived, Tom left Acapulco and headed home for St. Louis. If in running away to Mexico he had hoped not only to forget Kip but also to leave his creation "Tennessee Williams" behind in the care of others like Audrey, he was mistaken. He was chained to it. And more than that, through it the artist in him spoke. Try as he would over and over to elude this new identity, he would find there was no escape.

19

Battle of Angels

October 1940–April 1941

But they, being lost,
could not observe an omen—
They knew only
the hot, quick arrow of love
while metals clashed,
a battle of angels above them,
and thunder—and storm!
                    —NEW MEXICO, 1940

Returning to St. Louis, Tom took the same route he had the previous year from Los Angeles. By contacting Audrey's Beverly Hills office, he probably had learned that the Guild was still negotiating with Miriam Hopkins and that she should soon be making a decision.

As Tom traveled through the parched auburn landscape of New Mexico, the specter of Lawrence strengthened its grip on his imagination. Here were the natural environs of the two poets: a sidetrack from the invented reality called civilization into the reaches of "a divine unconscious"—still, at that time, uncorrupted by speculative money. In this painted desert with its mockery of time—man's pitiful measure by clock and calendar—what the young poet had learned from the older was clear as the constant blue sky.

Each in his way was an errant spirit. And in *Battle of Angels*,[1] the fugitive kind was personified in the character of Valentine Xavier, named after a Williams ancestor, Valentine Sevier, the pseudonym Tom had considered before he chose Tennessee Williams. The love that the name Valentine suggests, combined with the sanctity of Xavier, symbolizes the conflict between the sensual and the spiritual—a conflict now heightened by Tom's recent torment over Kip—which becomes the young drifter's ill-fated struggle in *Battle of Angels*.

Lawrence's theme of the tragic irreconcilables of body and mind had fastened itself on Tom's imagination, and as he passed through Taos and the many languid southern cities on his way home, he could picture Val Xavier arriving in the rural town of Two Rivers in the Mississippi Delta, hoping to escape from the dissolute lifestyle of New Orleans. Carrying a guitar and sporting a snakeskin jacket, an emblem of his feral nature, he is virile and handsome and seeks simply the itinerant existence. But being a loner, he is also a "fox in the chicken coop," attractive to women of the town and the hunter's quarry to its men. He represents something wild, free, and alien that both women and men resent and try in various ways to capture and imprison.

Val soon finds himself drawn to the center of a mortal confrontation between Myra Torrance and her dying husband, Jabe, owner of their dry-goods store. Myra is friendless, embittered at having been abandoned by a former lover, who deserted her in order to marry into wealth, and she is desperately striving to be free of Jabe's tyrannical hold on her. Afflicted with terminal cancer, Jabe is confined to his bed in the apartment over the store, and he telegraphs his constant demands by banging a stick on the floor.

After Val takes a temporary job in the store, selling shoes along with other merchandise, Myra gradually succumbs to his sexual magnetism, and there awakens in her a hope she might escape with him into a life together. But Val is unable to make a commitment that could lead to the restraint of marriage: "I made up my mind about something and I've stuck to it ever since. To live by myself." From the time he was fourteen, he tells Myra, he has lived like a fox in the bayous. He used to lie out naked in a flatboat with the sun on him. "I had a feeling that something *important* was going to come *in* to me."

When Myra asks, "In? Through your skin?" he replies, "Kind of. Most people don't expect nothing important to come *in* to them. They just expect to get up early—plow—rest—go turtle-eggin' an' then back to bed. They never look up at the sky, dark—or with stars—or blazing yellow with sunlight—and ask it, 'Why? why? why?'" Val's one desire now is to make the solitary effort of writing a book about "Life." Although he admits to being "tired of moving around and being lonesome and only meeting with strangers," he asks, "How do you get to know people? I used to think you did it by touching them with your hands. But later I found that only made you more of a stranger than ever. Now I know that *nobody* ever gets to *know* anybody. Don't you see how it is? We're all of us locked up tight inside our own bodies. Sentenced—you might say—to solitary confinement inside our own skins."

Along with Myra, two women in particular are captivated by Val's elusive stoicism: one a town outcast, Sandra (Cassandra), prophetess of his doom, who tries to seduce him and lure him back to a dissolute life in New Orleans, and the other, Vee Talbott, the sheriff's wife, a religious fanatic, who, to everyone's horror, paints portraits of young men as saintly figures whom she secretly desires. The picture of Val she paints is a representation of Christ among the twelve apostles under a lynching tree in a nearby cottonwood grove.

Later, after months during which Val and Myra have become sexually involved, still another woman arrives in town searching for Val, claiming he had raped and jilted her. Bent on vengeance, she enlists the help of the sheriff and his deputies in tracking Val down. Val tells Myra that she doesn't know what it is to be hounded by someone's hate, but she replies that it isn't hate, it's *worse*, "it's a terrible, twisted kind of love." Now both Myra and Sandra beg him to leave town, Sandra declaring that the atmosphere is so heavy with imminent disaster that she can even *hear* it: "A battle in heaven. A battle of *angels* above us! And *thunder!* And *storm!*"

Finally, Myra confesses that she is with child, theirs, imploring him to let her escape with him. But Val refuses, insisting he must go it alone, though he admits he is in love with her. As a last, irrational resort, trying to keep him from leaving without her, Myra phones the sheriff to say that Val is robbing her. Val protests he is only taking his pay, when Jabe, who suddenly appears on the stairway like an apparition of death, loads a revolver and calls them both buzzards. "You think you've got a corpse to feed on, but you ain't! I'm going to live, Myra!"

She taunts him for being "rotten with death," declaring that she's glad he's going to die. "Because I'm not barren. I've gotten death out of me ... I've got life in me." Leveling the gun at Myra, he shoots and kills her. As Val wrests the weapon away from him, Jabe shouts, *"You* shot her!" With the sheriff and his posse closing in, Val quickly retreats into an adjoining confectionery, which he and Myra had hoped to open two days later, on Easter Sunday, but which is now set on fire with a blowtorch.

In an epilogue, we learn that Val was captured when he tried to escape the burning building. "They torn off his clothes an' thrown him into a car. Drove him right down the road to the lynching tree." We are also told that Sandra drowned herself by driving her car into a flood-swollen river and that "the Jesus picture" was the last thing that Vee painted before she lost her mind. All that remains a year later is Val's snakeskin jacket.

As in O'Neill and in Shakespeare, the melodramatic plot is often an allegory. In Tennessee Williams's major writings, conflicts point by analogy to the artist's struggle against society. And while *Battle of Angels* is clearly freighted with symbolism, pagan (Cassandra, fire and water, a bird with no feet that must sleep on the wind) and religious (Val as a Christ figure, the snakeskin jacket as the Robe, the lynching tree as the Cross), far more pervasive is the influence of D. H. Lawrence in melding purity with passion. There are undeniable similarities to *Lady Chatterley's Lover* in the basic situation of Myra (Lady Chatterley), Val (Mellors, the gamekeeper), Jabe (Clifford, the invalid husband), but what sets *Battle of Angels* apart from *Lady Chatterley's Lover* is the violence of the conflict and its tragic denouement—in short, its intense dramatization.

Langner and Helburn and others at the Theatre Guild must have been struck by the comparison of their young prodigy to their titan O'Neill. In employing the Greek concept of fate and Greco-Christian symbolism, and in conveying the internal power of outward melodrama, Williams was giving actors not only an opportunity to strut their hour but poetic dialogue to read, as well. Dominant, though, was Tom's attraction, both as disciple and as a puritan in revolt, to Lawrence; but in addition, Williams's themes of guilt and the quest for God were unique personal expressions and rooted in his own identity, that of the alienated artist. More important than the influence of Lawrence was the repository of Tom's memories and his need "to release and purify the storms" of his youth.

Williams later wrote, "The stage or setting of this drama was the country of my childhood. Onto it I projected the violent symbols of my adolescence. It was a synthesis of the two parts of my life already passed through. And so the history of the play begins anterior to the impulse to write it. It begins as far back as I remember, in the mysterious landscape of the Delta country, the smoky quality of light in the late afternoons when I, as a child, accompanied my grandfather, an Episcopal clergyman, on seemingly endless rounds of rural parishioners." He remembered a lady named Laura Young, "a bright, misty lady" who was "the beginning of Myra Torrance—even that long ago!" He could see her still "dressed in checkered silk. She had a high, clear voice: a cataract of water. Something about her made me think of cherries and she was very beautiful. She was something cool and green in a sulphurous landscape. But there was a shadow upon her. There was something the matter with her."

Little Tom could not have known then that she was soon to die, nor that "it was for that reason we called upon her more frequently than anyone else. She loved me. I adored her. She lived in a white house near an orchard and in an arch between two rooms were hung some pendants of glass that were a thousand colors. 'That is a prism,' she said. She lifted me and told me to shake them. When I did they made a delicate music. This prism became a play," eventually subtitled *The Memory of an Orchard*.[2]

On Tom's arrival in St. Louis, it was mid-October—an autumnal calm before a storm of a kind he could not have imagined. In New York, there was a great deal of excitement over this "lyrical play about memories and the loneliness of them" and curiosity about its precocious young author. The wheels of production were slowly beginning to grind.

When Tom returned home, he entered his parents' new house at 53 Arundel Place in Clayton. It had taken her a little more than twenty years, but Edwina had at last attained her goal: a house of her own in a fashionable suburb of St. Louis. According to her, Cornelius had bought the house in a moment of rash generosity, a handsome two-story building with a large attic and lawns covered over in spring with her favorite jonquils. She felt they could live in such a house with a minimum of friction. In fact, they were getting along better than they ever had since they had been married. With Dakin distinguishing himself academically in his second year of law school at Washington University, with Rose sequestered in the state asylum, and with Tom away from home for nearly a year, Cornelius had at last become the center of Edwina's attention. Although they still slept in separate bedrooms, at least the house was free of the tension that he felt Rose and Tom had created. For a time, C.C. and Edwina were happily preoccupied with furnishing their new home and entertaining friends.

Cornelius's was an ephemeral peace, however, for Edwina's parents would soon be coming to live with them. There was ample room for the old minister and his wife, seriously ill with a suspected cancer; by now, they could not properly care either for themselves or for each other. Edwina had also fixed up a spacious attic bedroom-studio for Tom. This was her beckoning candle in the window, and much to Cornelius's chagrin, Tom would return over and over again to his mother's protective comfort before he could afford a place of his own.

But now he was anxious to get back to New York as soon as possible. To Joe Hazan, he admitted that the "lights, theatres, city glitter and excitement draw me back like a moth, I can't stay away very long. A month or two and I'll be surfeited with that once more." Then he planned to return to Mexico, although he confided in Donald Windham that he had some reservations about that. The food was hard to take, he complained, nothing but grease and beans, to the point Acapulco was renamed "frijole junction." He said that the sleeping porch sounded at night like a shooting gallery.

Writing to Bennett Cerf, he mentioned having been told "that Miriam Hopkins is definitely interested in 'Battle of Angels.' . . . But she is not quite sure yet whether she can make arrangements to get free from Hollywood." He added, "I don't know the extent of your influence, moral or otherwise, but

I feel that this is a consummation so devoutly to be wished that any degree of persuasion should not be left unsolicited—*soooo!*—is there anything you can do? That is, short of abduction from the studio lot— No, I won't even make that limitation." He also mentioned that he had finished another long play, *Stairs to the Roof,* "this one a serious comedy, wishfully written for Burgess Meredith."³ In November, Tom would accept a one-hundred-dollar advance from Cerf, giving Random House the option to publish his next play at their discretion—this without the knowledge of Audrey Wood.

Miriam Hopkins was delayed because of her contractual obligations at Warner Brothers, begun auspiciously enough playing opposite Bette Davis in *The Old Maid;* the two films that followed in 1940 left her career in limbo, if not in doubt. Thirty-eight years old, she felt it was time for her to make a career change, and she turned to the theatre, as she had years before—this time to the eminent Theatre Guild, to star in a promising play. She had faith enough in the venture to invest her own money, a not-altogether-altruistic gesture, since it gave her more control than she would normally have had in a theatrical production. A southerner, born in Georgia, Hopkins never quite lost her accent, and considering her disappointment at not being cast as Scarlett O'Hara in *Gone With the Wind,* it was understandable why the role of Myra Torrance appealed to her.

While Tom waited for a signal from Helburn that it was time to leave St. Louis, word arrived from Roberta Barrett in Audrey Wood's New York office. She said that although the Guild remained silently in possession of his play, "other managers ask, wistfully, whether it has been released." In the meantime, she inquired whether he would be interested in dramatizing some sketches at one hundred dollars each for a radio series about Abraham Lincoln originated by his Iowa professor E. P. Conkle. Also, William Kozlenko was editing an anthology of plays entitled *American Scenes* for John Day Company and wanted to include *American Blues* for "the usual anthology fee of $25."⁴ In a subsequent letter, Barrett wrote, "Glad that you approve of the anthology. Another anthology, *The Best One-Act Plays of 1940,* to be published by Dodd, Mead and edited by Margaret Mayorga, wants to include *Moony's Kid Don't Cry* for the princely sum of $20. She would like to omit that one line about 'kissing the Aunt Fanny—the play is just as good without it.' Will you let her do it?"⁵ She also commented that Burgess Meredith was on the coast making pictures and that Audrey, who was still in Beverly Hills, could talk to him there about *Stairs to the Roof.*

With all the excitement surrounding *Battle of Angels,* Cornelius's hostility toward Tom had leveled off into a kind of cold war. As always, the "old man" was unable to articulate his feelings save for some grudging compliment. Edwina, on the other hand, was gloating all over the place, happily making preparations for Tom to leave and deciding to accompany him to New York. For her, it was time to exchange old dreams for new dreams, hopefully to enjoy a vicarious success.

Life on the Wicked Stage

In New York, everything was about to go into high gear: Audrey sent the news that Miriam Hopkins had committed herself. At the Guild, design and other preproduction preparations were under way. Paul Bowles had heard the incidental music by Colin McPhee and thought it fine. *Battle of Angels* now had a projected out-of-town opening in New Haven, Connecticut, on December 27. Tom boarded the train, the Spirit of St. Louis, admitting to himself that things had a somewhat brighter appearance.

On their arrival, Edwina checked into the fashionable Barbizon-Plaza Hotel on Central Park South, while Tom returned to a room at the West Sixty-third Street YMCA. He immediately dropped Roberta Barrett a postcard: "This will indicate my return to Manhattan. Will drop in to see you all soon as I've shown mother Grant's Tomb, etc."[6] And for the next few days, Tom became the reluctant tour guide as Edwina marveled at everything: the interesting shops and double-decker buses on Fifth Avenue, the Automat, where you put nickels "in a slot for each item of food." Edwina wrote home, "I'm delighted with New York, so clean and bright . . . and the people friendly and courteous."[7]

She was not all that pleased with the October 30 issue of *Variety*, which headlined a story: HOPKINS MAY PLAY HILLBILLY'S 'ANGELS' IN N.Y. and went on to say, "It's a first play by Tennessee Williams who, like his name, is of hillbilly background." Tom could well imagine C.C.'s thunderous response. He could not have been too amused to read an Associated Press story written by Karl Barron headed COLLEGE TRAINED WAITER GETS ACROSS FIRST SHOW. However, the November 1 issue of the *New York Herald Tribune* reported that "Miriam Hopkins is in town ready to begin rehearsals in *Battle of Angels*, the Tennessee Williams play which the Theatre Guild will probably send into production next week."

Actress Doris Dudley, who most recently had played opposite John Barrymore in *My Dear Children*, was among the first to be cast, and Edwina, having been introduced to various people at the Guild, made Dudley her particular favorite—and her target. Exercising her southern charm in all its calculated grace, she enlisted the actress as a go-between in order to be sure that Tom was taking proper care of himself. Once she had her liaison, she was content to return home for the holidays and, on her arrival, hastened to spread the good news among Tom's friends and associates.

The St. Louis papers all covered the story, while Reed Hynds, who was both friend and critic at the *Star-Times*, wrote a full account. Then Mark Barron of the Associated Press filed an extensive profile headed "Newest Find on Broadway Is a Mississippi Playwright Named Tennessee Williams," accompanied by a captioned picture of a broadly smiling Tom Williams. Barron wrote that *Battle of Angels* was "swinging into rehearsals with as high powered a lineup of talent as even Bernard Shaw or Eugene O'Neill could command.

But Williams already is yearning to move on from the bright lights and has no intention of staying in their glow a minute after his play opens."[8]

Tom quickly found himself swept into preproduction meetings and consultations with the play's director, Margaret Webster, and he was clearly bewildered by the speed—"the machine-like haste"—of the professionals, not to mention the sight of his script marked in red throughout with coproducer Theresa Helburn's suggested revisions. Soon he would be contending with more and more such suggestions-cum-demands from Helburn, Miss Hopkins, and others creating the production. Although Tennessee Williams was often extremely malleable toward making changes, *Battle of Angels* suffered both from ill-conceived intrusions and from his inability to cope with the suddenness of it all. This being his first professionally produced play, he was vulnerable in many ways.

John Gassner, who never lost faith in the play, later said of Williams, "He was so poorly guided in the revisions he made for the Theatre Guild that the play as produced was inferior to the script that had been accepted, and he also appeared to have been fixed on D. H. Lawrence somewhat too strongly at this stage to be able to master the play's problems."[9] In the interview that Tom gave to Mark Barron, he said that he intended to write a play about Lawrence, acknowledging the novelist's influence over his writings and adding, "I've dedicated *Battle of Angels* to him."

Barron's story for AP also made much of the fact that "Hollywood's Miriam Hopkins" was to star in the play, omitting any reference to her considerable stage experience. No one at the Guild ever questioned that the incendiary actress was a perfect choice for the lead, but because of the snobbery of the times, she bore the stigma of being a *film* star. A high-spirited southerner and a performer with a remarkable range, she nearly drove her coworkers mad with her antic energy and magpie volubility. In films, the temperaments of superstars like Bette Davis and Edward G. Robinson were taxed to the extreme by the unpredictable pyrotechnics of Miss Hopkins, and consequently good roles were becoming more and more difficult for her to get. Ultimately, only director William Wyler continued to employ her in excellent, though supporting, roles in *The Heiress*, *Carrie*, and finally *The Children's Hour*, originally filmed in 1936 by Wyler as *These Three*, starring Hopkins. Recognizing the actress's enormous talent, Wyler withstood her incessant chatter simply by turning a literally deaf ear.

On one occasion, Lawrence Langner said that Hopkins "became so excited that she took careful aim at my head with the manuscript, which happily missed me by a couple of inches."[10] Tom's experiences with the actress, however, were rather different. Margaret Webster, who found the actress "lively, restless, stimulating," recalled the first encounter of the seasoned star with the uninitiated playwright. He arrived for their meeting at Hopkins's luxurious hotel suite nearly an hour late, "dressed in a shabby corduroy jacket and muddy riding boots," which he put up on a yellow satin chaise longue. Although Tom was amiable enough at first, "after we started to talk about the play, he didn't seem much interested; when Miriam became a little vehement, he prefaced his reply with 'As far as I can gather from all this hysteria . . .' "[11] Hopkins appeared suddenly speechless at the finality of his attitude. He had confronted her with the southern gentleman's classic put-down of a southern lady, and then and there they seemed to have reached a respectful understanding. Hers was a disposition that Tom could readily understand, and although she was never again to play one of his imposing heroines, they remained good friends until her death in 1972.[12]

Margaret Webster's principal problem centered on neither the star nor the playwright, but on the play itself. Staging material so distinctly and regionally American was a formidable assignment for an English lady whose reputation rested chiefly on her fine direction of Shakespeare. Moreover, when she read the play, she did not find it a very good one. Still, she conceded, "there was power in it and some splendid, multicolored words, and I believed the author would one day live up to his obvious potential talent and write a dazzler. . . . [Battle of Angels] provided an unexpected and extremely inauspicious start for a young playwright with the improbable name of Tennessee Williams."

Webster believed that everyone concerned with the production had been "deceived by the maturity of the play into misjudging the immaturity of the author. . . . Tennessee concealed it, for a time anyway, by getting increasingly vague, Southern and other-world; and when confronted with really desperate demands for rewrites, he would repeat his routine of lying down on the nearest suitable piece of furniture, putting his feet up on the cushions and closing his eyes."[13]

Williams later admitted to having fooled just about everyone: "Because certain qualities in my writing had startled them, they took it for granted that I was an accomplished playwright and that some afternoon when I was not busy with interviews, casting, rehearsals, I would quietly withdraw for an hour or two and work out the dramaturgic problems as deftly as such things were done by men like Barry and Kaufman and Behrman. They had no idea how dazed and stymied I was by the rush of events into which my dreamy self was precipitated."

As bewildered as Tom obviously was by the ways and means of the theatre, Peggy Webster was equally at a loss to understand the ways and customs of the Deep South. In an effort to learn about southern mores firsthand, she and Tom caught a plane to Clarksdale to explore the Mississippi Delta. "We spent two days down there," Tennessee recalled, "introducing Peggy to the South—visiting country stores and talking to Delta people. Peggy absorbed the South in twenty-four hours. It was a bit too much for her. She began to look a little punch-drunk, seeing just enough of this extraordinary country and its people to make them more mysterious than they were before." The net result of the trip for Webster, as she remembered it, was that she had grown very fond of this strange young playwright—and had acquired a slight southern accent!

After that, the nightmare began in earnest. It was mid-November, and as Tennessee described those last weeks before the opening:

> Toward the end of rehearsals, a series of frenzied conferences were held. Miss Hopkins, who played her part with heartbreaking beauty and something that only a woman of poetic understanding and deep experience could give—whenever the confusion lifted sufficiently to give her a chance to do so—was now becoming definitely frightened. She looked to me for salvation. After all, I—poor captive thing—was the author. How it wrung my heart that I could do nothing for her! She had staked so much on this play. It was to mark her triumphal return to the stage, where her talent as a dramatic actress could operate without the bonds that bad screen vehicles had recently put on her. One could easily see why she regarded the production almost as a matter of life and death.

At length, he said, "all the conferences only added to my feeling of impotence. Miss Hopkins' pleas and protestations—'For heaven's sake, do something, something!'—only made it more impossible for me to do anything at all."[14] Finally, he went to Webster, pleading that, if only there was more time, if only the imperturbable producers could be persuaded to delay the opening and he could have some concentrated time alone, then he could make the needed revisions. But that, after all, was the purpose of out-of-town tryouts, he was told.

During the final New York rehearsals, Miriam Hopkins became dissatisfied with the leading man, Robert Allen, and demanded a change. Initially, she had wanted Raymond Massey, but he had other commitments. Wesley Addy, the replacement, remembered that "Peggy Webster came over to the theatre and talked to Helen Hayes and got me out of *Twelfth Night*, which Peggy had directed for the Guild. While Tennessee would occasionally confer with Webster, I never spoke to him; he was always in the back of the auditorium during rehearsals." As far as Addy could recall, "He never gave anybody any input. What changes were made were evidently written before we went into rehearsal, or at least before I got into rehearsal, because we went with what was on the page."[15]

Still, although troubled over his shortcomings and uncomfortable among the experienced professionals, Tom was enjoying the excitement surrounding him. He and Joe Hazan had recently moved into shabbily elegant rooms in the residence of a lady identified only as a countess. Tom rented a piano and gave parties for his friends. What struck Clark Mills, who was invited to one of them, was Tom's strange, almost light-headed attitude toward the production of his play. Attending a rehearsal with Tom, Clark observed his friend acting more like an amused spectator than a serious young playwright watching over his creation. "Sometimes Tom had a naïve quality that shocked me. In New York, when they were in the midst of what looked like a dress rehearsal—at least they were using props—and Margaret Webster was directing—an actress was carrying around some paintings depicting churches with red steeples. That was all right, but it seemed unnecessary that Tom would be digging me with his elbow, saying, 'Get it? It's symbolism, Freudian symbolism.' This shocked me because it seemed a little naïve that he would have to explain the obvious. And then he would cackle, the way he did."

At that same rehearsal, Mills said that Webster was over on one side of the auditorium, "while Tom and I were sitting farther back on the other side. She was a very dynamic director, very vocal in a loud, elevated voice—she was directing, then halting, moving about, and then sending the play on. Suddenly, she sat down and jumped up with this wild roar, 'Jesus Christ! What *is* this? What in the name of God *is* this!' There was a deathly silence all over the theatre. Then, from somewhere in the dark, a nervous voice volunteered, 'Oh, that's Tennessee's custard cream pie.' He ran to the nearest exit."

Clark also recalled what he said was "one of the strangest things about Tom. We went to a movie on Times Square. There was a newsreel and it showed a British mine disaster—the wives were all at a mine entrance—and it was raining and a dismal scene—and the husbands were being brought up from the mine shaft either dead or dying—and the women were just wailing and screaming and screeching various exclamations in a cockney accent. Well, you would think this was a pretty heartrending scene, but Tom went into hysterical laughter. He couldn't stop. Everyone around us was outraged, and an usher came down. Here was this horrible scene on the screen, and Tom's cackle that could be heard in the third gallery. I don't remember if we were thrown out or asked to leave—but this was another Tom—some kind of a dark, sardonic quality making him capable of laughing at unlikely moments. I couldn't help thinking that perhaps he found such a thing so uproariously funny because he was evaluating what was supposed to be a dramatic dialogue and found it pretty ridiculous."[16]

Another who remembered Tom at that time was Elaine Anderson, who then was married to the actor Zachary Scott and was later to marry novelist John Steinbeck. Initially, Elaine worked at the Guild's summer Westport Country Playhouse and was brought into New York in the fall to be assistant to the production stage manager, John Haggott, on *Battle of Angels*. She recalled, "It was my first play for the Guild—and you must understand I was an absolute neophyte—but that's when I met Tennessee. I read the play and I was thrilled at the poetry—that was the word we all kept using to describe it. I remember there was great enthusiasm at the Guild—everyone kept remarking about the poetry in the writing."[17]

Unexpectedly, the December 27 New Haven opening was shifted instead to Boston on the thirtieth. This proved to be a disastrous decision, Boston being at the time a bastion of prudery and intellectual snobbism. Perhaps Langner thought the inevitable publicity would enable Tom's play to battle its way through to New York. To compound the obstacle of a hostile Boston reception, the new date also coincided with the out-of-town premiere of Gertrude Lawrence in Moss Hart's big musical *Lady in the Dark*.

On opening night, her dressing room filled with flowers and congratulatory wires, it was Miriam Hopkins who sent Tom a telegram:

DEAR TENN, SO DEEPLY HOPE FOR YOUR SAKE YOU WILL BE AS HAPPY AFTER THE PERFORMANCE AS THE DAY YOU SOLD THE SCRIPT. FONDLY, MIRIAM.

"And Thunder—and Storm!"

That the actors had to face a Boston audience was bad enough, but they became the center of an onstage fiasco, as well. Cleon Throckmorton, a prominent designer of O'Neill's plays both at Provincetown and on Broadway, had built a fine but complicated set, one that had to accommodate all sorts of mayhem. The cue sheet for Tennessee's battle called for "endless sound effects, drums, guns, lightning and thunder, offstage pinball machines, wind, rain, guitars, songs, 'hound-dawgs' and musical noises," in addition to a simulated offstage fire. At the dress rehearsal, the fire amounted to a little puff of smoke. Realizing that the apocalyptic blaze Tom had written into the stage directions really needed, as Webster saw it, "the resources of MGM, Wagner's fire music, and Bernhardt to play the second lead," she extracted solemn oaths from the technical staff that on opening night there would be a fire "even if it meant self-immolation."[18] It nearly came to that. The next night, Doris Dudley, the hapless second lead, was delivering a long speech while billows of black smoke were sent into the faces of a Boston audience already burning up over the play's inflammatory content.

Tennessee remembered it being like the torching of Rome, with great, sulfurous clouds of smoke that

> rolled chokingly onto the stage and coiled over the foot-lights. To an already antagonistic audience this was sufficient to excite something in the way of pandemonium. Outraged squawks, gabbling, spluttering spread through all the front rows of the theatre. Nothing that happened on the stage from then on was of any importance. Indeed the scene was nearly eclipsed by the fumes. Voices were lost in the banging up of seats as the front rows were evacuated.
>
> When the curtain at last came down, as curtains eventually must, I had come to the point where one must laugh or go crazy. I laughed. There was little joy in it, but knowing I had to laugh, I found that I could. Miriam Hopkins accepted the same necessity. I see her coming out to face

her audience. The stage is still full of smoke. Before her smiling face she is waving a small white hand, to clear the fumes away. She is coughing a little, apologetically touching her throat and chest. Their backs are turned to her, these elegant first-nighters, as they push up the aisles like heavy, heedless cattle. But she is still gallantly smiling and waving away the smoke with her delicate hand. The curtain bobs foolishly up and down to a patter of hands in the balcony that goes on after the lower floor is emptied.[19]

Elaine Anderson said, "Although the opening night was a mess, always on the road after the first performance, the Guild would have the company meet to get not only the director's notes but to have a general discussion of the play. On this occasion, the Langners, Theresa Helburn, Margaret Webster, and Tennessee, of course, were all there, including the principal actors. They all had their say, and it was considerable. It went on for a long time—Tennessee just listening, sometimes looking far away, not saying much.

"There was discussion of audience reaction, and among other things it became obvious that Tennessee didn't know how to listen to an audience and he really had not become expert in *visualizing* what he had written. Finally, we all turned to him, expecting him to say, 'All right, I'll start work on the changes right away,' but his *exact* words were, 'I put it down this-a way, and that's the only way I know to put it down.' And there was a deadly hush. Everyone was aghast and realized that he didn't know how and didn't have any intention of fixing his play. From then on, we all knew we had no show."[20]

Among those who were present at the opening was St. Louis poet William Jay Smith, who remembered Tom being "stunned and speechless" as he and Audrey Wood left the theatre. Audrey kept reassuring him that everything would be all right. "Tom asked me to stay on with him for a while, and indeed he appeared so depressed that I hesitated to leave him." After they had gone to his hotel room, Tom "went to his suitcase and took out an anthology of poetry and asked me to read aloud to him the poems of John Donne, which I did for the next few hours."[21]

Looking back at the calamity that befell her young client, Audrey Wood mused, "The Theatre Guild's plan to open such a play in Boston seems, in retrospect, to have been a manifestation of a deep collective death wish. Philadelphia, Washington, New Haven—perhaps such towns might have appreciated the onslaught of Tennessee's first drama. But Boston?" "Banned in Boston," she said, has since come to mean censorship. "In the case of *Battle of Angels*, that saying was quickly altered to bombed in Boston."[22]

Tom, the young Tennessee Williams, had endured his first theatrical failure and would have to wait a long four years before there would be another such opportunity. As he told his friend Joe Hazan, the answer was to make a religion of endurance.

So Many Dark Angels

With most of the blame being fixed on the inadequacies of his play, Tennessee, on reflection, puzzled that no one had expressed any apprehension over the choice of Boston as a testing ground. Immersed as the company was in production problems, apparently no one ever considered that the play might be attacked for its morals—least of all the playwright.

> If it was in the minds of others, certainly this suspicion was never communicated to me. Was I totally amoral? Was I too innocent or too evil—that I remained unprepared for what the audiences, censors and magistracy of Boston were going to find in my play? I knew, of course, that I had written a play that touched upon human longings, about the sometimes conflicting desires of the flesh and the spirit. This struggle was thematic; implicit in the title of the play. Why had I never dreamed that such struggles could strike many as filthy and seem to them unfit for articulation? The very experience of writing it was like taking a bath in snow. Its purity seemed beyond question.[23]

Tom had created the furor himself to some degree by telling a reporter prior to the opening that he had written "a sex play with cosmic overtones," using the same theme as that in Lawrence's story "The Fox"—that of a woman's spiritual awakening through sexual union with a young man of virile grace. The audience, composed largely of sedate Theatre Guild subscribers who already regarded D. H. Lawrence with disdain, had been told that they were about to see a play employing Lawrence's view of purification through sexual love. By this time, their jaws were set, but more than that, they were witness to the melodramatic violence, as one reviewer put it, of "seduction, adultery, nymphomania, shooting, lynching, flood and fire."[24]

Langner and Helburn, while trying to decide whether or not to close the play, considered the possibility of bringing in a "play doctor" to assist Tom with revisions. At the same time, they also had to examine the reviews. One tempered view was taken by critic Alexander Williams of the *Boston Herald*, who wrote, "Mr. Tennessee Williams has certainly written an astonishing play, one of the strangest mixtures of poetry, realism, melodrama, comedy, whimsy and eroticism that it has ever been our privilege to see upon the boards. In a sense there is something for every taste and equally something that will irritate any customer, who more or less knows his mind about theatrical matter."[25]

On the other side of the ledger, the *Boston Globe*'s critic felt that "the play gives the audience the sensation of having been dunked in mire," adding, "There never was a play crammed with more disagreeable characters."[26] *Variety*'s reviewer chided the Guild, saying that they "may have heard that somebody struck gold down the old tobacco road and decided to dig up a little dirt down along the Mississippi Delta to see how it would pan out."[27]

Actually, hostility toward the play came not so much from the press as from the Guild's powerful subscribers, whose protests echoed in the chambers of the Boston City Council. One council member, admitting he had not seen the play but had heard enough about it, damned it as "putrid." Then the police commissioner demanded changes in the dialogue, which he judged to be both "improper and indecent." The assistant city censor concurred, maintaining, "Too many of the lines have double meanings."[28]

For Miriam Hopkins, the event was as much of a crushing personal catastrophe as it was for the young playwright. To her credit, though, the lady spoke out, giving the press good copy, recommending, for example, that the members of the city council be dumped, as British tea once was, into Boston Harbor. As for the accusation that the play was "dirty," she called it "an insult to the fine young man who wrote the show, and you can tell them for me that I haven't gotten to the point where I have to appear in dirty plays."[29] Then, taking aim at the opening-night audience, she added that the dirt was in the mind of the beholders.

William Hughes, who was studying at Harvard and who was later to pursue a long career in theatre and films, attended one of the remaining performances, having prearranged an interview after the play with Hopkins. He sat among a small audience, and at the curtain, he remembered, "There was nothing but silence, the deadliest silence I have ever heard in the theatre. The curtain came down—there was a lull—and no applause. I felt kind of embarrassed for her and the whole company, knowing that when the houselights remained dark, they were lined up onstage behind the curtain, waiting to take their bows. But there was absolutely no applause, only this awful hush. The curtain stayed down."[30] Backstage, after a reasonable wait, Hughes was met by a polite but crestfallen star. She had little to say about her battle with the angels, choosing instead to talk about her next film project.

At first, Tom thought he would stay through to the last performance. He wrote to Joe Hazan of his plans, telling how "the bright angels" had been "pretty badly beaten" and saying that their landlady should be notified that "the large room with the grand piano" would be available after January 15. "I will take what money I get, possibly between 500 and 800 dollars and lam out for Florida, Mexico or the Gulf Coast to re-write this play and finish the new one." He was in trouble with the draft board, and he asked Joe to notify them that he would be back in New York in about two weeks. He concluded his letter by saying, "Joe, you're a good boy and I love you—(spiritually!) 10."[31]

Edwina, worried over Tom's reaction to the play's failure, had made several phone calls to Doris Dudley. Once, when he was in Dudley's dressing room as a call came in, he signaled the actress to say he was not there. Among a variety of other concerns, Edwina wanted to be sure he had changed his underwear! She meant that, because of the cold Boston weather, he should change to wearing a pair of long johns, but it made a better story the other way. The message traveled throughout the company and brought a much-needed note of comic relief.

Langner and Helburn were not finding much to laugh at, though; in fact, they were stunned by the subscribers' complaints and by the sight of them furiously stomping out of the theatre, one irate codger actually shaking his fist at the cast. A spokesman for the Guild said that changes would be made in the text, eliminating some of the offensive language, but "that, in any event, the play would close . . . unless a collaborator could be found to help the author to rewrite it."[32] In a letter to the Guild's subscribers, Langner and Helburn defended their decision to produce *Battle of Angels:* "We chose it because we felt the young author had genuine poetic gifts and an interesting insight into a particular American scene." They pointed out that only by presenting experimental plays "can we feed new authors into the American theatre." They cited Saroyan's *The Time of Your Life* as an experimental play that was "badly received in Boston but was later awarded the Pulitzer Prize as well as the Critics' Award, and was felt to have an important influence on the American theatre." The letter concluded, *"Battle of Angels* turned out badly but who knows whether the next one by the same author may not prove a success."[33] The next play, though, would not be produced by the Guild, to its everlasting regret.

All things considered, particularly Tennessee's lack of experience and inability to make a whole range of changes, Langner and Helburn decided to close the show and summoned Tennessee and Audrey to the swank Ritz-Carlton Hotel. Before the meeting, Wood sat with her client in a drugstore, both of them downcast as they drank their morning coffee and studied the play's reviews. When the hour was at hand, they crossed the Common, anticipating a reception as dour as their own mood. Just then, a small boy fired a cap pistol, and at the sudden pop they clutched each other, Tennessee crying out, "My God, it's the Guild, they're shooting at us!" Audrey recalled, "We both rocked with laughter because we knew in a few minutes it was all about to begin and there wasn't time for anything other than laughter."[34]

They were still laughing as they entered Langner's elegant suite, where they were met by the grim visages of Langner, Helburn, and Margaret Webster. Langner told Tom that his play would have to undergo extensive revisions before it could possibly open in New York and that it would close at the end of its Boston run. Anticipating this, Tom offered a changed ending that he begged them to accept. "On that occasion," he said, "I made an equally dramatic statement, on a note of anguish, 'You don't seem to see that I put my heart into this play!' It was Miss Webster who answered with a remark I have never forgotten and yet never heeded. She said, 'You must not wear your heart on your sleeve for daws to peck at!'" At this point, Theresa Helburn also made a remark that Tennessee never forgot or forgave: "Well, at least you're not out of pocket."

Langner quickly made it clear, however, that he had not given up, and he said that if Tennessee would go off somewhere and rewrite the play, it might be reconsidered for production next season. "Whereupon my agent, Audrey Wood, inquired cannily, 'What about money?' " There followed a calculated pause, during which "I continued to gaze, I hope not too piteously, at either Miss Helburn or Mr. Langner, and for the first time they gazed, or probably just glanced, at the unabashed face of my agent."[35] After another pause, Langner offered Williams an immediate hundred dollars, with the additional assurance that he would continue to receive further advance royalty payments during the spring, when he was to complete the revisions.

There would be many revisions. Tennessee Williams looked upon *Battle of Angels* as the emotional record of his youth, and even after the success of his next work, *The Glass Menagerie*, he would still refer to the earlier one as "a much better play."[36] In time, he would modify this opinion to accord with historical judgment, but the manuscript would remain on his workbench for more than thirty-five years, undergoing revisions and an unsuccessful reincarnation in 1957 as *Orpheus Descending*. In 1960, it was transferred to film as *The Fugitive Kind*, and finally, in 1974, *Battle of Angels* reappeared in a revised and critically successful New York production. A London revival in 1988 of *Orpheus Descending* met with extraordinary success and prompted the *New York Times* critic to write: "In death, Tennessee Williams is more often regarded by the American theater as a tragic icon than as a playwright worthy of further artistic investigation. The reverse is true in London, where the Williams canon, neglected by the major companies during the writer's lifetime, is suddenly being rediscovered."[37]

With this one drama, Williams projected multifaceted images of the alienated artist into many of his subsequent stories and plays, and on Margaret Webster's personal prompt copy of the original typescript he paid tribute to its inspiration, "For D. H. Lawrence—who was, while he lived, the brilliant adversary of so many dark angels and who never fell, except in the treacherous flesh, the rest being flame that fought and prevailed over darkness."[38]

On January 11, 1941, *Battle of Angels* closed, and the next day, Elliot Norton of the *Boston Post* wrote, "Mr. Tennessee Williams need not consider his lost battle as a decisive defeat. It is true that he was guilty of errors in craftsmanship and was also guilty of errors in taste." Referring to Miriam Hopkins's role as a backer of the play, Norton commented, "On the other hand, he was done in by actor politics, for one thing, and by direction which was altogether too arty and consequently confused. If he can learn more of the practical side of playwriting and keep his heart in the right place and his head clear of rubbish; if he can learn to walk with the theatre's craftsmen, he may find himself riding the clouds with the theatre's dramatists. His talent is most interesting." Much as he wanted to see *Battle of Angels* revived, Tom now needed to move on with his writing. Where he would go, he hadn't the slightest idea. Finding a place to write and a way to keep writing was all that mattered to him. His projected play about the Lawrences engaged his thoughts, as did further work on *Stairs to the Roof.* But Langner's expectation that he could begin revisions on *Battle of Angels* so soon after its calamitous closing only compounded Tom's feeling of exhaustion. To turn now to something new or turn back to an uncompleted manuscript was a necessity, a personal defense. He would gravitate toward his work only as impulse drove him to it, not on Langner's order.

While still in Boston, he wrote:

Speech from the Stairs

O lonely man,
the long, long rope of blood,
the belly's rope that swung you from your mother,
that dark trapeze your flesh descended from
unwillingly and with too much travail,
has now at last been broken lastingly—

You must turn for parentage toward the stars . . .

Tom might now turn to the stars, but he would still find himself pulled by "the belly's rope." On his arrival in New York, he wrote his mother from the West Side YMCA: "Doris Dudley called from Boston this morning and said you were worried about me. I'm o.k.—I was fully prepared for our difficulties in Boston—disappointed, of course, but feel that in the long run things will work out better." Then, picking up on what critic Elliot Norton had to say about "actor politics," he shifted blame and asserted what was more figment than fact: "The play is not ready for New York, due mostly to my ill-advised efforts to make it a starring vehicle satisfactory to Miss Hopkins rather than to my own best judgment. It is sadder for Hopkins as she is washed up in pictures and looked for this play to bring her back. But she messed things up herself by firing 3 [*sic*] leading men and finally opening with one who hadn't even had time to learn his lines."

It is not likely that Tom knew Hopkins had been a backer until he read Norton's review. In writing to his mother, he fixed the blame on the actress rather than on his own ineptitude, saying that the present ending of the play was "one the Guild insisted upon to satisfy Hopkins who wanted to remain on the stage all the time and consequently twisted the script around quite a bit." The paragraphs in Norton's piece that probably made him feel blameless for his play's failure read: "It began as a story of a man and three women and, in rehearsal, was altered and edited, and apparently wrenched, till it became pretty much a story of a man and one woman. The reason for this last change was undoubtedly Miss Hopkins, who, being star and angel of 'Angels,' naturally wanted to seem just that, in performance. She was that and her acting ability is not in question. She is a good actress. However, if she hadn't been an angel, perhaps 'Battle of Angels' might have been something closer to a winning battle."[39]

Tom told Edwina that "I will probably leave town in a few days."[40] And in another undated letter, he said that he was having his left eye examined by "a fine ophthalmologist . . . who says there is a cataract on the lens which should be removed. . . . the defect is disfiguring as the lens is opaque and a slight cast has developed." This was the first of what would prove four cataract operations. Subsequently, the operation at Saint Luke's Hospital was reported as successful by a nephew of the Reverend Dakin, who reassured the family that Tom was all right and had left the hospital on January 27.

(The Legendary) Paul Bigelow

Finally classified 4-F by his draft board because of poor eyesight, Tom moved into an apartment shared by Donald Windham and Fred Melton and their friends Paul Bigelow and Jordan Massee. Melton spoke of Paul and Jordan as inseparable companions: "You never thought of one without thinking of the other." Jordan had first met Paul in Atlanta, where Gilbert Maxwell had rented, as Jordan remembered it, "a funny little house in the backyard of somebody else's home."[41] Gilbert Maxwell described Bigelow as a small man, narrow-faced, with bright birdlike eyes and tight-curled black hair, and he said that he spoke with an accent that combined New England with Britain: "Paul could tell marvelous stories about the world of arts and letters in which he apparently knew almost everyone—but somehow there was about him . . . an air of reticence, even of mystery. . . . I knew that he had been educated in England, had lived in Greenwich Village in the twenties, in Hollywood (where he had been a newspaper reporter), as well as in Mexico in the thirties, that he had a sister and stepmother in California, that he'd been married."[42]

Paul had a deeply instilled sense of privacy, and only a very few like Tennessee shared his confidence. During the summer of 1904, his mother had died giving birth to him. His father, a prominent physician from Boston, grief-stricken and embittered, left the infant with his great-aunt, in effect disowning him. She not only raised Paul but wanted to give him her name. Educated at Cambridge, he became, in his words, "a professional catalyst," his work confined largely to the theatre. His marriage ended in divorce when his socially prominent wife objected to his association with theatre people. More than anything, it was his wit and sense of humor that bound him and Tennessee in a lifelong friendship.

New York was the beacon summoning this group of southerners to what they hoped would be their success, and even Paul, whose goals were less defined, also pursued the elusive bitch goddess. The apartment where Tom stayed with his friends following the eye operation was located on Seventy-third Street off York Avenue, near the East River. Until he recovered sufficiently to travel, he enjoyed Paul's invigorating companionship and the company of other friends. He would say that, more than anyone, Paul not only appealed to his sense of humor but gave him the kind of support and encouragement of an older and wiser man.

At about this time, Tom received a long and friendly letter from Margaret Webster saying she was sorry to learn that "the tale of our Boston immorality penetrated to Clarksdale. I must admit that for a week or two I scanned the papers, fearful of seeing a headline YOUNG AUTHOR LYNCHED IN HOMETOWN!" Referring to an editorial in the *Clarksdale Register* attacking the play as "dirty," she added, "I'm glad your grandfather remained sympathetic. He must be a very swell person." The letter concluded, "Let us know when you will be around again. Meanwhile write good, and all lovers of the English language will have cause to love you." Then she repeated Audrey Wood's constant plea, "Are you using carbons?" and his mother's clarion call, "Are you wearing your red flannel underwear?"[43]

Except for the vague hope that the Guild might yet produce *Battle of Angels* in New York, Tom realized that a playwright seldom survives an initial failure. Actors, designers, even directors often have several flops among their credits, but a producer will rarely take a second chance on a failed playwright. In those times, he might be conscripted into the lucrative anonymity of a Hollywood studio, at best, but it was more likely that he would quietly return from whence he came. Tennessee Williams, sponsored by the mighty Theatre Guild, had been briefly the new playwright most likely to succeed; now he was regarded as a might-have-been among those who thought of him at all. Even the film studios weren't interested, the rule being that a play must have at least a few weeks' run on Broadway before a movie company might acquire both the property and its writer. However, Tom had the benefit of a hard core of believers, such as John Gassner, Margaret Webster, and especially his torchbearer, Audrey Wood.

He once confided, "I always think that things will be better some place else." On departing for Miami, he sent a penciled note to Audrey saying that he had picked up his advance check and also fifty dollars at the Dramatists' Guild: "They say this is an outright loan and don't expect repayment till my next play—okay!" He asked if he might be eligible for the Sidney Howard Award of two thousand dollars and added, "I'm going to range around the 'Keys' or 'Fla' on a bike."[44] Arriving by train in Miami, Tom was met by his friend Jim Parrott, who was staying at his parents' winter home while taking a flying course. Since Tom took an instant dislike to Miami, Jim suggested that they drive down to Key West together. Writing to Jo Healy, his friend at the Guild's switchboard, Tom said, "Friday morning I was in Miami and Saturday night I was in Sloppy Joe's bar in Key West." He described the southernmost resort as "the most fantastic place that I have been yet in America. It is even more colorful than Frisco, New Orleans or Santa Fe. There are comparatively few tourists and the town is real stuff. It still belongs to the natives who are known as 'conks'. Sponge and deep sea fishing are the main occupations and the houses are mostly clapboard shanties which have weathered grey with nets drying on the front porches and great flaming bushes of poinsettia in the yards." He added somewhat wistfully, "I will appreciate a little news of Broadway now and then if you get sufficiently untangled from those telephone wires to drop me a line."[45]

Aware that his family would be apprehensive concerning his cataract operation, he wrote reassuringly that he could now distinguish light and dark in his left eye but that it would take several weeks to determine whether the vision would return enough to be useful. The removal of a cataract in those years was a primitive procedure and, as he said, "quite a bad ordeal. I suffered very severely for the first few days after the operation and they had to give me typhoid fever injections to combat the inflammation in the eye—it seems an artificial fever will accelerate absorption. The injections gave me high fever and chills that nearly shook me to pieces! I got wonderful attention at the hospital, though." He also commented that "several columnists carried reports of my operation so I received a great many sympathetic calls. Everybody in New York has been marvelous to me—considering what a hard-boiled town it is supposed to be."[46]

In Key West, Tom stayed in a tiny cabin in the rear of a 125-year-old mansion, the Trade Winds, a beautiful old antebellum structure built entirely of mahogany by an old sea captain whose intention was to lure his fiancée in New England to come live with him. Trade Winds was then owned by a retired Episcopal clergyman's widow, Mrs. Clara Atwood Black, and she let Tom have the entire slave quarters for eight dollars a week. Jim Parrott had returned to Miami, and despite the attraction of numbers of soldiers, and especially sailors in their tight-fitting uniforms, Tom was feeling very much alone. Key West was as far away from New York and the Broadway theatre as Tom could get traveling south. Eventually, he would make Key West his home, and what he entered in the Trade Winds guest register became a prophetic truth:

Name	*Residence*
Tennessee Williams	Where I hang my hat!

Marion Black Vaccaro, Clara Black's daughter, would in later years become one of Tennessee's closest friends. In *Memoirs*, he described her as well-educated and a very fine poet. "She was not a classic beauty but she had great charm and animation." He said that by the time they first met, her husband, Regis Vaccaro, had become the worst alcoholic he had ever known.

He was a likable guy, but he was giving Marion and Mrs. Black quite a good deal of trouble. When he wasn't on alcohol, he was on ether. He had to be on one or the other, either alcohol or ether, that was how bad he drank, and he took a liking to me and he was continually coming back into my cabin while I was trying to work. And I have a horror of the smell of ether. As a child, I had my adenoids and tonsils removed and was circumcised at the same time under ether, and I received anesthesia shock, which has lasted ever since.

This man would come in there exhaling these fumes of ether and glaring at me with his glass eye. I must have been much better natured in those days because I never threw him out. Of course, I probably couldn't have thrown him out because he was physically powerful. Well, he was part of the local color at the time, and he was giving Marion a really hard time which she bore with great fortitude.

Before she married Vaccaro, Marion Black earned her living as tutor and companion to Patricia Ziegfeld, the daughter of the musical showman Florenz Ziegfeld, Jr., and his wife, actress Billie Burke. As the young wife of an alcoholic, the irony was that she, too, in later years would come under the influence, with Tennessee as a "drinking buddy."

Williams remembered Key West in those remaining months before the United States entered the war as mainly "a wonderful colony of artists," including the venerable philosopher John Dewey. Although Ernest Hemingway had long since departed the island, everyone seemed to foregather at Papa's former hangout, Sloppy Joe's. His ex-wife Pauline Pfeiffer Hemingway was still a resident, "living in that lovely old Spanish colonial house on Whitehead Street. And they had a dance band at Sloppy Joe's, a really good black dance band that played wonderful dance music. Key West had in those days a very authentic frontier atmosphere which was delightful."[47]

Now it was Clara Black whom Edwina fastened on to, and eventually they became good friends. "Mrs. Black informed me, knowing I was worried about Tom, that, although depressed, he was trying to write." Once Mrs. Black's maid wanted to throw away crumpled paper scattered on the floor in Tom's cabin, but Mrs. Black refused, saying there might be something he wanted saved. She had discovered one page with the same seven words written over and over: "My head is a block of stone."[48]

In an unmailed letter to Lawrence Langner, Tom tried to describe his frame of mind, all the while realizing that it might cause Langner to forego any further subsidy for *Battle of Angels*. "I spend my time on the beach absorbing sunlight and sorting out past experiences and trying not to feel too much concern for the future. I had made up my mind not to write for a while but have broken that resolution." He said that his nerves were exhausted, that he felt like a broken string, and that, because of the Guild's latest failure, Philip Barry's *Liberty Jones*, he didn't know what to make of the theatre. "I am far, far more confused by it than when I first came to New York. I am sure I have learned some important lessons, but so much and so many that I am a little punch-drunk right now."

The crux of the situation, as he saw it, was that "the serious artist and the audience are pulling in opposite directions, the one toward truth and the other toward entertainment. Isn't that it? As for the critics, they try to ride both ways without being dismembered. This impossible trick is something that playwrights must learn. I think our best audiences are in the future when the permanent values that a serious artist deals with are not obscured by little details like the war. Our work can live in the future but unfortunately we must survive the present. I am learning how to fish. And how to be charming to widows. Practically the same thing."[49]

Tom was not making any progress revising *Angels;* instead, he wrote a one-act, *The Case of the Crushed Petunias,* "a lyrical fantasy—respectfully dedicated to the talent and charm of Miss Helen Hayes," one of several tributes to actors, such as Lillian and Dorothy Gish, Sydney Greenstreet, and Burgess Meredith, whom he envisioned in his plays and whose interest he sought to capture. He knew that playwrights should be charming to celebrities, too.

D. H. Lawrence and, in particular, his story "The Fox" were traceable influences in *Petunias,* as was the lingering rancor Tom was feeling toward Boston. Set in the town of Primanproper, Massachusetts, "within the cultural orbit of Boston, the action of the play takes place in the Simple Notion Shop owned and operated by Miss Dorothy Simple, a New England maiden of twenty-six, who is physically very attractive but has barricaded her house and her heart behind a double row of petunias."

A large, strong, and virile Young Man has deliberately stomped the petunias into the ground. The flowers, he explains, represent a self-planted ring around her heart. The complete restitution he offers are seeds of wild roses.

> DOROTHY: Wild? I couldn't use them!
> YOUNG MAN: Why not, Miss Simple?
> DOROTHY: Flowers are like human beings. They can't be allowed to grow wild.
> [Young Man goes on to ask her, "What do you make of it all?"]
> DOROTHY: I don't understand— All *what?*
> YOUNG MAN: The world? The Universe? And your position in it? This miraculous incident of being alive! *(Soft music background.)* Has it ever occurred to you how much the living are outnumbered by the dead? Their numerical superiority, Miss Simple, is so tremendous that you couldn't possibly find a ratio with figures vast enough *above* the line, and small enough *below* to represent it.
> [Finally, Young Man proposes that they meet that night and take a ride to the cemetery at Cypress Hill.]
> DOROTHY: Why there?
> YOUNG MAN: Because dead people give the best advice.
> DOROTHY: Advice on what?

YOUNG MAN: The problems of the living.
DOROTHY: What advice do they give?
YOUNG MAN: Just one word: *Live!*
DOROTHY: Live?
YOUNG MAN: Yes, live, live, live! It's all they know, it's the only word left in their vocabulary.[50]

The cemetery, Cypress Hill, on "a beautiful windy bluff just west of the Sunflower River," became a metaphor for life, while the remark that "dead people give the best advice. . . . Just one word: *Live!*" would be incorporated into the eventual revisions of *Battle of Angels*.

The One-Way Street

From the moment Tom arrived in Key West, Audrey Wood began writing to her client regularly. One letter enclosed a twenty-five-dollar check, which she referred to as an installment on the Guild's "loan," adding, "I hope you're well and happy."[51]

He was neither. As always in times of despair, he turned to his journal:

Sunday Feb. ? [16th] Been here about 8 days. By myself since Jimmie left. No friends except a young transient, "Chuck" who calls himself, "My Pardner" and has sort of moved in on me. Definitely a problem but better than being altogether alone—I am not in a sociable state and making friends would be difficult even if I tried. Oh yes, I have one other—an elegant old lady from England who allows me to sit on the porch of her cabana at "Rest Beach." . . .

This is the most crucial period in my life. God knows what will become of me if I don't meet the demands of the situation and I am tired, dangerously tired—and not well—an almost continual ear ache which plagues me—letting up a little. . . .

I sit by my little fire—electric heater—with my typewriter and my books—"Leaves of Grass"—"For Whom the Bell Tolls"—"Look Homeward, Angel." . . .

It is rather nice in here. Pale green wood with lemon yellow curtains at the windows—a wide comfortable bed with fairly fresh covers—a lamp beside it and a heater—my body naked and warm and still young—capable of passion and tenderness—my mind—vague, dreamy, but sincere and thoughtful and with a wealth of experience—my heart still with a purity after all this time—(Sentimentality about myself)—but there is only me right now. . . .

Tuesday . . . I am afraid this town is bad for me—water, water everywhere—and I am not a voyager any more. Bars alone—beaches alone—movies alone—I feel quite unable to speak to anybody—I wrote a 1-act and a few poems but do little on "BATTLE." . . .

> Sleepless—now six—raging ear-ache—plagued by the nightingale [his
> private code word for sexual liaison or desire], Etc. Don't see how I can
> stick it out here— Even dread the beach tomorrow.
> Roof drips slowly with moisture all night—crickets.

In a letter to Audrey, Tom admitted that his nerves were harassing him:
"So much has happened to discourage me about myself and my work." Still,
he said, "you cannot give way to such feelings. And I don't. This is a one-way
street that I have chosen and I have to follow it through with all the confidence or courage that necessity gives you." He also said that he was "working
hard on the 'Angels.' " The character of Val, he told her, was receiving daily
injections of iron and beef extracts and should soon have plentiful hair on his
chest. One of the criticisms he would be dealing with, not just in *Battle of
Angels* but in others of his plays as well, was the need to strengthen his male
characters, who often paled by comparison with the vitality of his leading ladies. He added the assurance, "For the first time in my life I am practicing
self-discipline and doing what I know I ought to do rather than what I feel like
doing."

Then in the same breath, he announced, "I am going to leave on a hitch-
hiking tour of the State to refresh myself for further operations of the play."
He asked her to mail his next check immediately and questioned how much
the Theatre Guild had so far advanced, so that he could plan on what to expect. He had begun his letter somewhat artfully: "When anyone's real nice in
Mississippi they are described as 'precious' and that is what you are. I hate for
you to bother sending me those goddam little checques—God bless them!—
with all the other nerve-wracking business you've got on hand."[52] By now,
Audrey had become well aware of how Tom managed money: He spent it as
fast as he got it, no matter the amount. At the moment, he was broke, and even
when he wasn't, he felt broke, anyway. Wisely enough, Audrey went on parceling out the money. Ultimately, he gave her power of attorney so that she
was able to manage it more providently. Parceling out the checks and prod-
ding him with cautious optimism became the perfect combination: A little of
each went a long way. Primarily, it was Audrey's constant practical encouragement, tempered with maternal concern, that kept the young Tennessee Williams going in the right direction.

Although the market for one-act plays in the theatre was virtually nonexistent, Audrey sent *The Case of the Crushed Petunias* to Cheryl Crawford, who
had expressed an interest in producing a program of one-acts. Hume Cronyn
was another who was giving serious consideration to the same idea. Meanwhile, Audrey continued pressuring for the revisions to *Battle of Angels*, and
she exhorted Tom to "keep giving Val those daily injections of iron. He'll be
a better man for having them."[53] And in a subsequent letter, she wrote, "Remember, the American theatre and Audrey Wood are depending on you to

hold both of them up this next season. Sit up straight, Mr. Atlas."[54]

"Audrey, dear," Tom answered, "it is nice to be called Mr. Atlas but I fear your eye like that of a horse has a magnifying lens inside it that imparts a fictitious grandeur to all that it gazes upon." She had prodded him enough, though, that he gave her a synopsis of the proposed changes. His mood clearly on the upswing, he reiterated his intention of taking a short trip around the Florida peninsula and asked her to send another check, since "I don't want to get broke on the road as they would pick me up for vagrancy and Langner would have to bail me out of the clinker. He once said to me in all seriousness, 'The *only* thing that I am concerned with is *genius!*' —If the old fool still thinks that I am a genius he certainly wouldn't allow me to perish on a Florida chain gang. —Or *would* he?"[55]

Before he left Key West for a short trip to Miami, Tom wrote a letter to his father, complaining that the people in Boston were "small-minded" and unable to see anything but sex in the play. He felt, too, that the Theatre Guild people had been intimidated by Boston's puritanical reaction and were perhaps becoming too old and conservative. And in a letter to his mother, he lamented the failure of the Guild's most recent plays. He said they were "mercilessly assaulted by the critics . . . serious, poetic plays which have not had a fighting chance this season. Drum-beating, flag-waving, and pure musical comedy entertainment are the chosen fare. The dice will be loaded against us till after the war—but of course popular stuff dies quickly and the future accepts more readily what the present rejects."[56]

On March 26, Tom turned thirty and Tennessee twenty-seven. His only comfort was that he looked even younger than twenty-seven. Turning thirty may not have been cause for celebration, but a wire from the Dramatists' Guild most certainly was:

FELLOWSHIP COMMITTEE HAS GRANTED YOU FIVE HUNDRED DOLLARS TO WRITE NEW PLAY. MONEY TO BE GIVEN ONE HUNDRED DOLLARS A MONTH TO BEGIN WHENEVER YOU CAN COMMENCE WORK. WRITING FURTHER PARTICULARS—

LUISE M. SILLCOX[57]

Audrey, while dispatching a twenty-five-dollar check as another payment from the Guild's advance, also enclosed an article from the *New York Times* announcing the additional Rockefeller fellowship. "Both Liebling and I are delighted about this, since we both know how much it means to you." Actually, the money was inadequate to meet his needs, his management of it chaotic; he left a trail of debts wherever he went, and as a result, he was forever trying to pay off old debts and living in arrears. The fellowship added five hundred dollars to the original one thousand, but this exacted a price: Tom was obligated to begin work on a new play while at the same time he was committed to finishing his revision of *Battle of Angels* for the Theatre Guild. He was accepting money for both promises but writing what he pleased.

On his return to Key West, Tom was invited by his landlady, Mrs. Black, to a dinner party. During the meal, Regis Vaccaro became incensed at criticism of his behavior, which included drunkenness and gambling, and threw his glass eye at his mother-in-law, and it landed in her soup plate. Removing it with a spoon, she passed it to Marion, saying with imperturbable dignity that she believed it was something that Regis had lost.

> Dear Audrey:
> Barely time for a note! Very, very happy and relieved about new funds.
> Back on keys but leaving in a few minutes for Brunswick, Ga. Land-lady's son-in-law, habitual drunkard, has run up gambling debts far in excess of his ability to pay—I have to smuggle him off the keys at once, his life being threatened—to Georgia where I have instructions to keep him sober till his wife gets there in about ten days. What a job! But they have been so wonderful to me I can't refuse. Driving his car up—leaving right away. This done, I will probably come back north. . . .
> PS.
> Only got to Miami with charge who is now in Sanitarium. Send me one more checque of Theatre Guild—to get home on. Will leave here soon as it comes and return East in a week or two after visiting folks. . . . Play rewrite about ready for typist.[58]

He was not writing, and he turned to his journal, saying:

> Wednesday April (?) Coral Gables
> Worn out completely.
> Situation improved.
> $500.00 from Rockefellers "to write new play"—I think I have the basic situation for it. A Woman's Love for a Drunkard.
> Regis and Marion.
> Strange, melodramatic little interlude that was! Too tired to write about it or anything.
> The nightingale sang sweetly once last week. . . .
> Must start long uphill climb to refresh myself and revitalize my system for work on a new play, only thing worth doing—I am selfish, small—impose on my friends and neglect them—my kindness and sympathy are much too passive—all is overshadowed by my own selfish needs, hungers, longings.

Germany is striking in Balkans—apparently with brilliant success.

Will there be any decency, any peace, and reason, any sanity in our time? In *mine?* I would forget all this to hear the nightingales—and not in Berkeley Square!

He regarded Coral Gables as "the worst place I've ever tried to live in— even worse I believe than Clayton, Mo." But he thought he might as well "fly away home"—for a while.

20

A Reckless Voyager

April–August 1941

Although Tennessee Williams would return to Key West again and again and would eventually think of it as the best place for him to write, he also likened himself to a footless bird that must die suspended in flight. The image was hardly inappropriate: He saw life and looked upon its hapless populace from aloft as always a tragic and ironically ridiculous spectacle, making him cry and laugh.

Now, in the spring of 1941, genocide was spreading like hellfire around the world. The tension from abroad could be seen reflected in every American's face, and the only question was, How and when would the inevitable be brought home? Thousands upon thousands of vibrantly alive young men lived on a precipice, doomed to be killed or maimed or traumatized. And—except for a simple childhood mishap—Tom could well have been among them.

As he was to say, "rare and peculiar things" happened to him all of his life, strokes of two-sided fortune. The ophthalmologist who had recently operated on his eye thought that Tom must have received an early injury, "and I had, indeed," he said, "in a childhood game of considerable violence. This was in Mississippi and we were playing Indians and early white settlers. The early white settlers were in a shack that was being besieged by the redskins. I was an aggressive kid and I led the charge out of the shack and was hit in the left eye by an 'Indian' with a stick and he fetched a considerable clout. I had a swollen eye for several days, but no sign of lasting eye damage till my late twenties."[1] This, and the crippling illnesses of his childhood, not only had created the ambiguity of a protective shield but had given a distinctive shape to his mind, as well. Set apart from the war as he now was, Tom's driving need to write only further divided him from friends and strangers on whose kindness he depended.

To many writers, the very *act* of writing, the painful exertion, seems virtually incompatible with *living:* For them, it is like working in a hostile state, as though the everyday flow of life itself amounts to a conspiracy to interrupt or frustrate the artistic process. For Tom, until the last months of his life, this was seldom the case. Nothing—sex, the telephone, hangovers, a lover's harangue, bodily ills—kept him from going the morning round from bed to typewriter, even if it meant going back to bed afterward. The difference now, though, was that a kind of paralysis had overtaken him, stemming from his recent inability to make script changes during rehearsals. He was beset by a drive to write what impulse dictated, as opposed to what commitment demanded, and he kept this conflict even from Audrey, leading her to anticipate a revised *Battle of Angels* suitable for production. She never at any time knew what to expect from Tennessee, and despite her strict business attitude toward her work, she was always deeply concerned about him.

The older he grew, the more helpless he got when it came to contending with the mass of details that governed other people: minutiae so habitual, so embedded, that these daily concerns become bands of petty thieves stealing away whole lifetimes. As a result, Tom's concentration on his work, if not total, came perilously close to it. Consequently, he was always in danger of one kind or another, and those close to him, like Audrey now, had reason for apprehension. What they saw as an absence of mind—in actuality, a concentrated *presence* of mind—made every street corner an abyss, although strangely every oncoming vehicle seemed to have a guardian angel at the wheel. Even his impaired vision *added* awareness, for it made him always the keen observer and absorbed listener: He was attentive and he listened closely to what others merely saw or heard. An infirmity had become a source of strength, the vision of "something cloudy, something clear" (the title he gave to a play), which he said symbolized the two sides of his nature: the aesthetic Dakin side and the aggressive Williams side.

In these early years, writing had become a release, a purging of deeply repressed feelings, an outcry that would leave Tom exhausted but cleansed. Although in later years, Tennessee would suffer attrition from the dredging of his emotions and from the expectations his place in the theatre imposed upon him, at this time he was drawing upon everything in his past and present, the names, personages, places, events, impressions—the stuff of his life—fast becoming the body of his work. Audrey and others were struck by this remarkable, compulsive outpouring of someone whose very appearance seemed to belie his authorship. Among them at this time, impressed by the uniqueness of his work, was the young actor-director Hume Cronyn, who was looking for material both to produce and direct and to whom Audrey had sent Tom's one-act plays.

About mid-April, Tom wrote to Audrey from Miami, saying, "I have decided to take the Georgia trip after all although the alcoholic case will remain here in sanitarium. His wife has given me permission to stay at their farm as long as I want and eat all the fresh vegetables and eggs on the place. It is in the heart of the interesting Gullah negro country on the Ga. coast-line so I feel I should 'take it in' for a while. Please mail Th. Guild checque #7 to General Delivery, DARIEN, GEORGIA. Put 'Please Hold till Arrival' on envelope as I am hitch-hiking up there and exact time of arrival is uncertain though it shouldn't take me more than two or three days. I won't use any of Rockefeller money till I return to N.Y."

He added that a girlfriend in St. Louis had promised to get his revised script typed for him. He also commented, "The world situation seems appalling right now," and then on a more cheerful note he added, "I am sending you and Liebling a FLOOGIEBOO, or LUCKY WORRY BIRD who is supposed to remove all anxieties from the [recipient]. I have been completely light-hearted since getting mine—hope it will have the same effect on you and Liebling. Very easy to take care of. Lives on radio news bulletins and interviews with actors and authors."[2]

Audrey replied, "Your 'luck bird' arrived this morning and while it looks very dismal and blue he may well be filled with the qualities you insist he has. He looks exactly like Lawrence Langner's brother to me. Can't you find a bird that looks like Miss Helburn, I would like to mate them. Please advise."[3] Enclosing another Theatre Guild check, she said she would not send any further money until he informed her of his next address—a sensible precaution, since his stay in Darien at the Vaccaros' home, Marsh Haven, numbered only a few days. It did at least inspire him to write a poem, "Dark Arm, Hanging Over the Edge of Infinity." "Suspense is ended—Heaven is full of the sound of shattering glass!" it said.

Although Tom planned to leave St. Louis soon after he got there, the pull now to go home proved irresistible—particularly the desire to see his beloved Grand, who was slowly dying of cancer. On his arrival, a letter awaited him from Fred Melton that had been trailing him from Darien, Meridian, Savannah, Atlanta—what Tom aptly described as his "erratic course." In response, Tom told Fred of his adventures on the road, having been picked up by everyone from millionaires to "lovely truck drivers." One misadventure involved a woman driver who had escaped from a hospital after suffering a brain concussion in an automobile accident. He said he couldn't get out of the car until she wrecked it. But he managed to make it home intact.

He was still living off the Theatre Guild and saving the fellowship money until he got back to New York. A New York news item concerning the Guild's summer playhouse in Westport announced: "Lawrence Langner, Armina Marshall and John C. Wilson will open June 30th with Tallulah Bankhead in 'Her Cardboard Lover.' Among the tryout productions will be the Tennessee

Williams play, 'Battle of Angels.' " Tom thought that the revisions on *Battle of Angels* were good enough to warrant the Guild's renewing their option, in which case he would have enough money to enjoy his carefree lifestyle. With world conditions what they were, he felt he should take his pleasures selfishly at any price—except at the expense of his work.

On arriving at his parents' new home, he was soon discontent and made no attempt to contact anyone outside his family. By now, most of Tom's St. Louis friends were either married or soon going to be. Both Clark Mills and Willard Holland were engaged, and the pressure on "eligible bachelors" from married friends and family was constant: "When are *you* going to get hitched?" For Tom, the gay life had become an attractive refuge and straight company deadly dull, as he saw it. Having come out at the advanced age of twenty-nine, the emotional contrast between before gay and after gay was like night to day. What is more, his bachelor life complemented his need to be free—to write.

Still, he was not reconciled toward being homosexual and never would be. He simply saw it as irreversible, as a natural inclination toward his own sex. Many among his gay friends cited his bold pursuit of sexual partners as evidence that he had chosen homosexuality as a way of life. But it never was a matter of choice—or so-called "preference"—he had only accepted the fact of it, as well as his own ambivalence toward it. He was still attracted to the ideal of a lasting partnership, and he always would be, but for the moment his experience with Kip seemed to preclude that.

What made a meeting now with Clark Mills "intolerably strange," as he anticipated it, was a painful self-consciousness and the fear that family and friends in St. Louis would learn the truth. The sad consequence was that both Clark and Willard would become among the deliberately estranged. Years later, Mills reflected, "I don't know if he was gay when I first knew him in St. Louis. To me, there were no visible signs. But later on, before *Battle of Angels* had gone into rehearsal, we met at a bar for drinks. It was a very peculiar thing—I had the uncanny feeling sitting there having drinks with the usual 'how've you been' and 'what's new' that a half-inch plate-glass window had suddenly come down between us. Something had closed off completely. He seemed like a different human being, not at all as he was in St. Louis." Clark said Tom's being gay didn't matter to him. "Tom was my friend. *That* was what mattered. I wrote to him after the war, but he never answered. It's too bad anything so unimportant could have come between us."[4]

Not only Clark but Rose, too, seemed now to be remotely a part of Tom's past. She was nowhere to be found in his letters and journal entries, and only abstractly in his writings. Edwina continued to send her packages of clothes and to visit her at Farmington whenever Dakin was able to drive her there. Rose's medical records showed that her condition had not changed and that she was not, for the time being, receiving therapy of any kind.

Once the family had moved into the Arundel Place home, Grand and the

Reverend Dakin rented their house in Memphis and went to live with Edwina and Cornelius. C.C. loathed the old minister and made no effort to disguise it; there was immediate and increasing strain between them. Although Tom was concerned for his grandmother's health, he seemed removed during his short stay at home from what was going on around him, if not oblivious.

> *Friday Night*—May [9th]—Clayton, MO.
> Leaving tomorrow for New York. Feel better—jittery—one of my anti-social neuroses—will make short shrift of it however—with luck.

On returning to New York, he first checked into the West Side YMCA, where Audrey had written to him to say that she was busy lining up several appointments, including one with Hume Cronyn, who had been impressed with the uniqueness of the short plays. At the same time, Tom had submitted his rewrite of *Battle of Angels* to Lawrence Langner. In *Memoirs*, Tennessee recalled that "after some weeks of reflection, Mr. Langner phoned me. (I mean *he* answered when I phoned *him*.) 'About this rewrite, Tennessee. You have gone like the Leaping Frog of Calaveras County, you know, that Mark Twain story, I mean you rewrote it too much like the frog jumped out of the county.' And that was that."[5] It was indeed, and there would be no summer tryout in Westport. The Theatre Guild and Tennessee Williams parted company then and there, although he continued to think fondly of Langner, if not Helburn.

Soon afterward, Tom moved to the Woodrow Hotel on West Sixty-fourth Street. He told his mother it was only a block from the Y, so he could still swim there every day. Paul Bigelow thought that the management at the Y had raised either Tom's rent or hell over his habits. One thing was clear: He was reacting to the enforced celibacy of life in St. Louis and, by his own admission, brazenly approaching practically anyone he found attractive. Fortune favors the bold, he had learned. Whatever the reason for the move, Paul remembered the Woodrow as a singularly bleak accommodation. "It was very bare—the *lobby* was very bare—nobody ever paused in the lobby—people rushed in the door and rushed into the elevator to get out of that awful lobby." Then there was the sun roof. "Everybody went up there for the sun, but, unlike a young man's hostel, it was run over with the most bedraggled old dames, heavily made up, and *tough*—all of them ancient and tough. Tenn would just look at these old alligators, blinking in the sun, with a sort of fear."[6]

It was not long before Tom began visiting Bigelow regularly and staying occasionally at his East Seventy-third Street apartment. On June 27, he turned back to a journal he had begun in Mexico the previous September:

> 9 mos. later I resume this journal. How full the past months have been! I did not even faintly surmise what a dramatic period in my history was just around the corner when I made the last entry!

It ended rather disastrously in failure—but it gave me a taste of glory—it brought me within sight of the "bitch goddess"—then whisked me rudely back to the near oblivion I came from.

I survived it all fairly well.

Now I am entering another phase—

Seems more dangerous perhaps than anything yet

Revised script rejected

$280.00 total funds

No new scripts

Two months to find some solution

Then destitution

Then what?

So endeth the lesson.

I am fatigued, I am dull, I am bitter at heart.

But I do not suffer much. I have diverted myself with the most extraordinary amount of sexual license I have ever indulged in.

New lovers every night, barely missing one, for a month or more.

I love no one.

I am loved by one whom I do not care for.

Paul B. and I are together every day.

He is a charming companion—one of the "truly civilized"—one of the "genuine sophisticates." *The* most stimulating, entertaining ever brilliant companion I have ever had.

Without him I must confess my life would be as empty as a broken egg shell.

Nothing romantic of course, just a love of the spirit.

Although Tom complained of feeling mentally torpid and attributed it perhaps to excessive sexual activity, Paul remembered his young friend going to his typewriter every morning as if to an altar. Nevertheless, he felt unable to create.

Perhaps I have really burned my daemon out.

I don't think so. I think he is still a phoenix and not a cooked goose.

But I must find purity again. A whole, undivided heart. Something simple and straight. A passionate calm. Where?

This conflict between what appeared to be an almost insouciant attitude toward sex—seemingly the more the better—would be followed by a cry he would utter privately again and again: the need to "return to my goodness." And this may well have been what prompted Tom's meeting with Kip early in June. Bigelow wrote to his friend Jordan Massee in Macon, "Do you remember Kip, the dancer with Hanya Holm,* who came to dinner with us once?"[7] Tom had brought him by the apartment, and although he would see Kip again on occasion, it was clear that their affair was over. Paul recalled, "He told me at the time that Kip was the greatest love of his life, but he never said that Kip did not return his love. I didn't ask him about it. But then, our friendship centered mainly on things that we *enjoyed* talking about endlessly. When it was a confidence, that was what it remained."[8]

Now Tom's longing for a place of "passionate calm" brought back memories of New Mexico, the desert landscape and the search for God. He was contemplating a full-length play about the years Lawrence spent in New Mexico with Frieda. Paul's recollection was that Tom's stay with him during the month of June became a warm and rewarding occasion for them both, the inception of a friendship that had that rare quality of never suffering a sea change—this despite vastly different temperaments and lifestyles.

Unlike other friends of Tennessee Williams, Paul had a way of controlling him with a reserve and detachment that demanded respect. Although Bigelow looked upon Tom's chaos as an "artist's order," at times it became too much. On one occasion, Paul had to make a wild dash to a laundry to recover two checks that Audrey had sent, which Tom had left in a shirt pocket. They were found after much frantic searching through bundles of laundry about to be dropped in steaming tubs. Finally, as Paul wrote to Jordan Massee, he decided to pack Tom off to Gloucester, where there was a theatre group with which he might become associated. "He had a horrid carbuncle on his shoulder blade which I tended as carefully as I might a rose garden . . . the combination of the carbuncle, the heat, and Tennessee was too much for me, and when he began to be restive in New York, I packed all his things firmly, picked out Gloucester as a respectable, cool place, and sent him to it."[9]

Paul remembered seeing Tom off on the train for Boston. "He was always without roots in New York, and he was always unhappy there. He would come back because of the theatre, but New York was never his town. He did not deal well with the pressures of life and, particularly, the pressures of city life."[10] They planned to meet again later in the summer at St. Simon Island, off the coast of Georgia, and the two friends parted on that prospect. Audrey, aware of Tom's promiscuous behavior, could only hope that the quiet of the ocean resort would divert his energies into writing.

Upon his arrival in Gloucester, Tom wrote immediately to Audrey: "I am situated at this anciently elegant place on a cliff over the sea," at a hotel called the Moorland at Bass Rocks. As for the local theatre group, he said that he

---

*In March, Kip had appeared with Hanya Holm and Dance Company at the Mansfield Theatre in "The Golden Fleece, an Alchemistic Fantasy," in which he danced Saturn to her Mercury, with music by Alex North, theme and costumes by Kurt Seligmann, and masks executed by Kip Kiernan. This premiere performance preceded a concert tour that lasted through 1941–1942.

"got theatrical rates through Mr. Levin who runs the Bass Rocks Theatre. They have been very cordial to me and I think I will like it here. It will seem very quiet after Broadway and I ought to get some work done." He concluded with "Spit in Langner's face for me—and 'in your orisons, be all my sins remembered!' God help us and the Russians, [signed] *Tovarich!*"[11]

The Sound of Shattering Glass

A few days before he left New York, the war news on everyone's lips was the wholly unexpected attack by the Nazi armies on the Soviets, and the hope and prayer now was that Hitler's legions, like Napoleon's, would be swallowed up in Russia's vastness, and further, that this would keep the United States out of the war. *Time* magazine's report read: "Like two vast prehistoric monsters lifting themselves out of the swamp, half-blind and savage, the two great totalitarian powers of the world now tore at each other's throats." Along with most Americans, Tom found the enormity of such an event all but incomprehensible. The news had the effect of making people silently hope that the two monsters would kill each other off, while at the same time all anyone could do was go about one's own business.

Audrey's next missive contained a letter from the actor-producer Martin Gabel about *Battle of Angels*. Gabel wrote, "It shows again that Tennessee is an extraordinary talent—potentially of the first rank. His work has tremendous emotional power, a terrific sense of the tragedy of the little people of America, and a gift for dialogue that is at the same time real and poetic."[12] However, he did have some reservations about Tennessee's ability to develop a strong story line.

Nonetheless, Audrey felt that Gabel was impressed enough to "make a deal" for Tom's next play, "whatever that's about—we, I don't know." She urged Tom to meet with the producer as soon as possible, and added, "I'm seeing Langner and Helburn (tra-la) today and I'm going to make another effort to vamp back your manuscripts."[13] The Guild held an option either to produce Williams's works or, if not interested, to release them. Now that *Battle of Angels* no longer interested producers, all that Audrey had left to promote were his short plays, and she set her sights on Hume Cronyn.

Tom intended his next full-length play to be either *Stairs to the Roof* or the opus on Lawrence and Frieda in New Mexico, which he thought might also include an epilogue on Lawrence's death in France. One play was in progress and the other in gestation, and so for the moment Audrey found herself unable to make a deal with Gabel or anyone else. In Gloucester, as in New York, he wrote mainly poems, two in particular, called "The Siege" and "Shadow Boxes."

In a letter to his mother, Tom described the "very elegant old hotel," the Moorland, as "extremely quiet, nearly all old ladies," lined up on the porch in their rocking chairs and looking down aghast at the theatrical crowd, who were "not permitted to go on the beach in shirtless trunks."[14] Possibly it was a restriction that proved too much, for Tom soon took off for Provincetown, where he could bathe in the nude among the dunes. He found Joe Hazan back on the Cape. Kip had remained in New York with the Hanya Holm dance troupe and with what Joe described as a "new crowd."

Hazan had rented a large house for the summer, the Cogan House, and was letting out rooms to a wide and wild variety of characters. This was clearly Tom's milieu, as the elegant Moorland certainly was not, and in a long letter to Paul, he wrote at the very top: "Please keep this description of life in 'Cogan House'—I want it in my memoirs." First, he said that he had two reasons for remaining in Provincetown, "or perhaps several, but the most active right now is lack of funds to return as my last five dollars was just commandeered for house-rent—I have written off for my second-to-last Rocky check."

Since then, he said, "a certain element of fascination has crept into my horrified observation of activities under this singular roof." He claimed that one of the crowd had been trying to "rape" one of the guests, "but it seems she is only physically attracted to homosexuals and all of her great, throbbing heart belongs exclusively to me! She will only sleep in my room and abases herself to wash my feet, light my cigarettes, butter my bread, and even button my pants, but this, my dear fellow, is not my other reason for remaining [in] Provincetown."

Rather, he was in pursuit of an "impervious blond—the vast impervious blond of my thwarted libido!—I have declared my love and embraced him madly and he has laughed and said, Tennessee, you amaze me!—and that is how things stand—and I don't mean *lay*. It is kuite, kuite mad in this place. Most of our table talk yesterday was about orgasms—" His lady friend, he said, would have nothing to do with the men "because it seems she had no orgasms the times they invaded her body and she has drawn great, metaphysical conclusions about the malevolent male universe from these misadventures in bed. She regards me with glittering, speculative eyes that make me shudder. Well, Friday nights we have great orgies with fifty cents admission to raise the rent-money. Of course I got kuite drunk and due to my frustration over the blond I carried on in a way that shocked everybody including myself."

He wrote that "four of us girls" had retired to an upstairs bedroom, "from which only occasional news-bulletins were issued to the party below till it ended." One of the four, it seemed, had escorted a girlfriend to the party, and she kept "bawling at the locked door and shrieking downstairs that she knew her dear Eric was being held incommunicado against his will. At one time she wailed, Why does it take those bitches so long to come? I could have come ten times already since they have been up there! All of this would have been very well (from all but the aesthetic pt. of view) had it not been for the fact that better than half of the persons attending the party were strictly jam and of a character corresponding closely to Theatre Guild subscription audiences in

Boston. Well, my dear, when I now appear in public the children are called indoors and the dogs pushed out!"

He also said that at night "an utter delirium settles upon the house. Like frenzied rats they go scuttling about in the dark on various errands, mostly profane or insane—there is great shuffling about of bed-partners, only the blond remaining aloof from it all and I, who am fully content with singular slumber. The household shifts in number from seven to twenty—we eat fish at every meal because we get it for nothing. My cumulated sexual potency is sufficient to blast the Atlantic fleet out of Brooklyn! Perhaps I shall when I get back to N.Y." He said that he had had three affairs and in all had been "trade"—that is, he had pretended to be only passively interested.

Langner, meanwhile, had written Tom "a honey-sweet letter—he says when he gets time he will sit down and make a great play out of 'Battle of Angels'—I think that is very nice of him. —No mention of payment in the meantime. —I write every day, have started what may be a novel about a male prostitute, written a good short story and a remarkable *kuantity* of verse."[15] He told Paul that he was thinking once again of leaving for Mexico.

In his sexual forays, Tom was wearing the urbane veneer of a sophisticate whose guard was up and who was no longer the naïve and vulnerable person he had been the previous summer. Seeing Kip again in Provincetown would have been like encountering a dream in the light of day. He would have felt nude and embarrassed except that by now he had taken on an air of cynicism, often adopted by those burned in love. His posture, the cigarette in its holder, and the dark glasses shielding his "White Eye" identified him as *perhaps* a person of importance. And in the gay world, he had become something of an anomaly—passive in manner but sexually the aggressor.

During these few weeks in Provincetown, Tom met a gifted painter from New Orleans, Fritz Bultman, then studying under Hans Hofmann, who had established art schools in New York and on the Cape. Bultman remembered Tennessee at the time as being "very hopeful and eager, but at the same time knowing and sophisticated about the theatre world and about people." Still, Bultman observed him as a bohemian in his lifestyle and said, "He was very amusing and witty, and he could be absolutely charming. But there was an undercurrent of self-absorption."[16] Another New Orleanian he met on the Cape was Oliver Evans, a young professor whose behavior out from under the groves was anything but academic—in fact, it was downright scandalous.

Tom told Audrey that he had not had much energy for sustained work and that his experiences with the Guild had caused a tired and listless feeling. In his journal, he wrote:

Provincetown—July 27
    Well—I sit in a lonely woods, besides a still lily pond—among the dunes of Cape Cod. I am too tired to write.
    I am too tired

I am too.

I am.

I.

When Tom returned to the Seventy-third Street apartment early in August, Paul was recovering from an injury to his leg but was preparing nevertheless to leave soon for Sea Island, Georgia, to join Jordan Massee and his family. After Tom met with Martin Gabel and told him the synopsis of a play he was planning to write, and after telling the same story to Luise Sillcox at the Dramatists' Guild, he gave Paul one of his best poems, "The Ice Blue Wind,"[17] and departed from New York, but without notifying Audrey.

Arriving in the town of Sea Island, located on St. Simons Island off the coast of Georgia, Tom stayed for a few days with Paul and Jordan. Jordan's parents had rented a large and handsome home for the summer. Jordan Massee, Sr., an imposing southern gentleman whose granddaughter had dubbed him "Big Daddy," was a true raconteur and used expressions such as "nervous as a cat on a hot tin roof."* He was also endowed with an inexhaustible supply of stories about plantation life "on the richest land this side of the Nile." Tom was clearly in awe of the huge elder Massee in his white linen suit. Jordan said that they got along famously: His father's infectious sense of humor had the one roaring with laughter and the other shrieking.

On Sea Island, Tom was exposed to still another southern way of life, the summer retreat to the Georgia coast. Everywhere he looked on what was once an Indian hunting ground, he saw tropical plants and close-cropped lawns spotted with red hibiscus and snapdragons and the yellows of alamandas and marigolds. On Friday nights, there were the plantation suppers with colored folk singing slave songs and spirituals. Beautiful, weathered houses were vine-covered, and those along the sandy beaches were of Spanish and Mediterranean style. This was a kind of southern grandeur that Tom had never seen before, and a mansion he would have noticed, the Casa Genotta (so named for Gene and Carlotta), had once been the home of the Eugene O'Neills on this, "the blessèd turned to damnèd isle."

Unfortunately, the few days he spent there ended with his leaving for a small town nearby, also named St. Simons Island, where Tom chose to stay at the Golden Isles Beach Hotel, at that time a decidedly humbler accommodation. Tom was never the ideal guest, and Paul had gently persuaded him to move back to New York. There was also a matter of money, or, as usual, the lack of it, and Jordan remembered that this was Tennessee's main concern. A wire had been sent to Audrey asking that Luise Sillcox forward his next check immediately and assuring her that he would be sending a new one-act and synopsis of a full-length play in return.

---

*Many southern expressions like "cat on a hot tin roof" had their origins in countries abroad (see: Henri Troyat's monumental biography of *Tolstoy* [New York: Doubleday, 1967, p. 549]).

Audrey's reply to her peripatetic client was immediate: "God knows where you will be on Monday, but if by some mad chance you're still in St. Simon's Island, Ga., I hope this will reach you. I am enclosing a check for $25, which is the first payment [from a two-hundred-dollar option on the short plays] of the Hume Cronyn money. I will draw up a contract between you and Crony some time next week. Please give me some definite idea where you will be all of next week so that a letter can reach you."[18] In response, Tom wrote:

Audrey—I thought I had better write Cronyn a thank-you note of some kind. If this will do, let him have it.

I thought to turn the new one-act over to you before now but it seems good enough to justify longer attention. It will be done this week-end, and I think may be a very moving little play. "The Front Porch Girl," or "If You Breathe It Breaks."

If money cannot be extracted from Mr. Gabel, perhaps I had better try the synopsis on [John] Gassner. He would like this material and might extort some further payment from the Guild.

Somebody has suggested I write a starring vehicle for Langner and Helburn in which he takes a bath in the last act in a tub of ass's milk, poured into the tub by Helburn wearing one of her most outrageous hats and nothing else. I think that would have all the elements of good theatre, including social significance, and sex.[19]

The return trip from St. Simons Island, Tom noted in his journal, was "a fiasco." It seemed that he had decided not to wait for the Dramatists' Guild check to arrive but had left instead for New York with a small amount of money, which he had stowed away in his suitcase for safekeeping. When his train made a long stop in Washington, D.C., Tom decided to do a little sight-seeing, and so, of course, the suitcase, his typewriter, and his manuscripts all journeyed to Manhattan without him. When later he discovered that the train had departed, he wired a friend in New York, Charles Criswell, for a loan. Criswell's answer being delayed, Tom then went to the nearest hotel that had a telegraph office and wired Jordan for help. In the meantime, Charles's money order arrived, and Tom left town intending that Jordan's money should be returned to him, except he couldn't remember the location or name of the hotel.

Tom later revealed to Paul Bigelow why he had forgotten the location of the hotel: He had met the handsome son of one of Washington's department store owners, and after the nightingales sang, he found his way back to Union Station. He told Paul that "the time spent seeing Washington the *hard* way did not leave me with a too favorable impression of our nation's capitol, long may she wave, Etc. Patriotism *died* forever when I walked across town for the fifth time to the main post office and still found no remittance from the

Damnest Guild and came back out and saw old glory still waving blithely on the capitol dome."

On his return to the Seventy-third Street apartment, he wrote to Paul, saying the place was a shambles ("There are scraps of paper and trash all over the floors and dust and complete disorder") and admitted to being drunk a good deal of the time. "I went out cruising last night and brought home something with a marvelous body—it was animated Greek marble and turned over even. It asked for money, and I said, Dear, would I be living in circumstances like this if I had any money? It sadly acknowledged that it guessed I wouldn't." Tom added that, after he had sent the "trade" on his way, he locked himself out on the street until three or four in the morning, leaning against lampposts and on car fenders, until the milkman came and let him in.

Finally, he confessed, "Sometimes I would just like to say about life—'The incident is closed!' Carry on—yeah. God only knows when I will be galloping off again. It's a disease . . . I think I am going to leave very soon for New Orleans. . . ."[20]

Along with his letter, he enclosed something he had written earlier for his friend:

Poem for Paul

> I think the strange, the crazed, the queer
> will have their holiday this year,
> I think for just a little while
> there will be pity for the wild.
>
> I think in places known as gay,
> in secret clubs and private bars,
> the damned will serenade the damned
> with frantic drums and wild guitars.
>
> I think, for some uncertain reason,
> mercy will be shown this season
> to the lonely and misfit,
> to the brilliant and deformed—
>
> I think they will be housed and warmed
> and fed and comforted for a while
> before, with such a tender smile,
> the earth destroys her crooked child.

Paul returned to his apartment in an effort to make it livable again. He found not only its rooms but also his young friend's mind in disarray. Tom was cornered and facing conflicting commitments: unfulfilled promises to Luise Sillcox at the Dramatists' Guild, to producer Martin Gabel, and, most troubling of all, to the patient Audrey Wood. He felt the need to escape and break the block between him and writing a full-length play, and he was undecided where to go: To Taos? Acapulco? New Orleans? Typically, he would make a last-minute decision.

On Sunday, September 7, Tom hastily wrote a note to Audrey: "I am leaving in an hour for New Orleans, address will be care of General Delivery till I get settled. And I do mean settled this time—if I have to chain myself to a bed-post." He had written a synopsis of a play, presumably of *Stairs to the Roof*, which Audrey liked "tremendously" and found better conceived than its initial draft. He also asked her to send another twenty-five dollars ahead to New Orleans "so I will have something there if I arrive without money." Once there, however, he warned her, "I may take little excursions around the South on a bicycle or my thumb, so do not be alarmed if I am temporarily out of touch at times. I will get as much work done as possible. . . ."[21]

This posted, he and Paul went to the same Share-A-Ride agency that had provided transportation the previous year to Mexico. On an early overcast morning, the itinerant Tom drove off with a young couple, heading once again for New Orleans.

21

New Orleans Revisited

September–December 1941

New Orleans—Sep. 11, 1941 (Friday) [Thursday]
The second New Orleans period here commences.

The much-bedeviled pilgrim—the fox who runs in circles—has returned to one of those places that failed him (?) before.

He still looks for sanctuary. Still hopes some new move will appease his interest.

But he has grown skeptical and sometimes thinks to *sleep* is the best thing, merely to sleep.

When Tom arrived in the Crescent City, a check for twenty-five dollars awaited him at general delivery, sent from the Liebling-Wood office as "a further advance on the Hume Cronyn money." He immediately wrote home,

"Had a beautiful trip down here, by car, through the mountains [of] Virginia. I have a room at 1124 St. Charles on Lee Circle, and find the city about right for me in my present circumstances. But too much *rain!*"[1]

Within the next few days, he had bought himself a bicycle for ten dollars and paid up a week's rent of $3.50. On Saturday, he reported, "Tonight I have heartburn. I am going to dress up and cruise about the old French Quarter. Maybe something will happen." It did, either by coincidence or prearrangement: He met the professor whom he had recently encountered in Provincetown and who was in a distinctly different mood regarding his life, which usually was about as gay as gay could safely be in those times.

> Oliver Evans—a sad but poignant episode. Macks [bar] and the St. James bar. "We ought to be exterminated" said Oliver, "for the good of society." I argued that if we were, society would lose some of its most sensitive, humanitarian members. "A healthy society does not need artists," said Oliver. [I replied,] "What is healthy about a society with no spiritual values?" "Then you think spiritual values are identical with *us?*" said Oliver. "No," I admitted sadly, "but we have made some unique contributions because of our unique position and I do not believe that we are detrimental to anyone but ourselves." "We are the rotten apples in the barrel," said Oliver. "We ought to be exterminated at the age of 25." "But Shakespeare had written no great plays at that age." "He had written *Romeo and Juliet,*" said Oliver. —"Yes, but he had not written *Hamlet.*" And so on— "If you think we are dangerous, why do you act as you do? Why do you not isolate yourself?" "Because I am rotten." —How many of us feel that way, I wonder? Bear this intolerable burden of guilt? To feel some humiliation and a great deal of sorrow at times is inevitable. But feeling guilty is foolish. I am a deeper and warmer and kinder man for my deviation. More conscious of need in others, and what power I have to express the human heart must be in large part due to this circumstance. Someday society will take perhaps the suitable action—but I do not believe that it will or should be extermination. —Oh, well.

In time, the shadow of guilt would cast its dark cloud over Tennessee Williams, and he and Oliver Evans would become deeply ensnared in self-destructive behavior. Evans, born in New Orleans in 1915, always thought he was a year younger than his friend, when in fact he was four years his junior. At the time they met, Evans had just received his master's degree at the University of Tennessee; eventually, he became known among his gay friends as "the professor." A respected scholar, author, and poet, he went on to teach creative writing and "business English" at various American universities. He never settled in any one place for very long, largely because of his promiscuous homosexual conduct, which brought him into conflict with authorities on and off campus.

A day after their meeting, Tom wrote in his journal, "I go now for a long ride on my bicycle, probably out to Lake Pontchartrain for a swim and something more clarifying than last night."

> *Later*—My bicycle trip was cancelled by rain and I was stranded for over an hour in the door of a warehouse in the colored section across from the "Star Club" where I watched the careless, infantile play of negroes . . . an ant with partly crushed body struggling to crawl across a concrete space with no companions and no apparent objective. I thought about the "hostilities of chance" that can foil an innocent outing. Not very novel reflections. Finally I braved the rain and came home. Now the rain still continues and I lie on my bed, smoke, and enter these banalities. I have such an ordinary type of mind, only a little more sensitive than most others, only my longings and my critical faculty, my sense of my own unfitness, has any dignity. I feel stunted. I should have grown bigger than this. Certainly as an artist. I should have grown much bigger and stronger and more durable. I am like, in my work, that half crushed ant dragging itself wretchedly and almost pointlessly forward. . . .
>
> *Later* Went to Gluck's [cafeteria] and had a 30 cent turkey dinner—good. Then along Canal Street and dropped in to see a sentimental slush film about an orphanage—pretty bad. . . .
>
> Tonight in the show I thought of a possible new play. Hawk's Daughter. A man like my father. Sensitive, terrified children. Same two as in Portrait of a Girl in Glass. Begins [with] drunken father's entrance early morning. The girl in the bedroom and all the little colored glass.

Tom soon moved into the French Quarter, staying at a rooming house at 708 Toulouse, near the corner of Bourbon Street. For him, the Quarter epitomized New Orleans. Existing apart from the city, the Vieux Carré offered its inhabitants a degree of personal freedom found nowhere else. In the fall of 1941, however, mainly because of the presence of hordes of servicemen, ubiquitous MPs and the shore patrol regularly policed the Quarter's nightspots. Gay bars in particular were frequently raided, and often Tom barely escaped from places he had begun to haunt, bars like Mack's and the St. James and the Wonder Bar out by Lake Pontchartrain. But more than the furtive gay life, the diversity and abandon that *everyone* enjoyed in the Quarter attracted him and appealed to his desire for freedom.

This second New Orleans period, of several months' duration, made a deeper, more indelible impression than the first. Tom had since "come out," and in accepting his sexual identity, he had confronted, if not shed, many of his painful inhibitions. Restlessly moving about and always observing and listening, he felt an affinity with the Quarter's pariahs and outcasts that drew him into their lives and bound them into his writings.

* * *

Toward the end of September, Audrey sent a fourth check from "the Hume Cronyn money" and enclosed a letter from John Tebbel, the managing editor of the *American Mercury*, "which I think you should have framed and look at every night before you go to bed." Tebbel had written, "Williams is sort of D. H. Lawrence and Hemingway and Thomas Wolfe rolled into one and leavened by a style which is not at all eclectic. I have a feeling that he'd be a better novelist than a short story writer. He has something to say and knows how to say it, which is more than can be said for nine-tenths of the American writers currently practicing."[2]

About this time, Tom also received a letter from John Gassner, who was still championing *Battle of Angels*. He, like the Boston critic Elliot Norton, felt strongly that Tom had been a victim of production politics and, in particular, the revisions that Theresa Helburn insisted upon. He wrote, "I hope everything turns out well for you, and that you can reward those who have had faith in you. Meanwhile, you can tell them—if my name and opinion mean anything to them that regardless of the outcome I think you have written one of the most promising scripts I have read in years."[3]

For Tom, Tebbel's and Gassner's praise had a more heartening effect than Audrey could have imagined. He wrote to her, "I don't believe anyone ever suspects how completely unsure I am of my work and myself and what tortures of self-doubting the doubt of others has always given me. Well, as long as some people think well of my stuff I don't care terribly whether it's printed or not as that makes me feel that it may eventually have some lasting place and not be wasted." Then he added, "Oh, Christ, how I want to do something really worth while—Before some truck runs me down on my new bicycle. If that should happen, by the way, you must tell my parents that I instructed copies to be made of everything at their expense (They will pay for it) and please be sure that no single copies of anything falls in their hands as my Mother wrote me the other day that the plays in 'American Scenes' were 'ugly details about indecent people' and a disgrace to the kinfolk mentioned in the preface."

Edwina's distress probably stemmed not so much from "the ugly details" in the plays as from Tom's description of family members: "I am also related to the late Senator John Sharp Williams who was a famous silver-tongued orator of Mississippi and also one of the State's best drinkers, who said when he retired that 'he would rather be a houn-dawg an' bay th' moon from his Mississippi plantation than a member of the United States Senate.' " In asking Audrey to look after his manuscripts, he said of his mother, "I am afraid she would burn them in order to save my reputation. The poetry and other scripts I carry around with me should likewise be kept from them and sorted out by you and Clark Mills and Paul Bigelow. I bring this up because my defective vision and absent mind make an accident far from improbable."[4] In time, Edwina's built-in mechanism for failing to recognize what she refused to see would apply not only to the "ugly details" in his work but to his homosexuality, as well.

Tuesday Night I am waiting for a friend who has just stepped down the Gallery for a minute which seems like an eternity to me. I will tell you later how it was.

Still waiting. Footsteps!

I had another friend last night.

Later The cold and beautiful bodies of the young! They spread themselves out like a banquet table, you dine voraciously and afterwards it is like you had eaten nothing but air.

Wednesday Started to work but found no energy in me in spite of the week's rest. I suppose the reason that I am living is because I have spiritually surrendered life.

Sometimes living matter assumes such charming forms and then such hideous forms without apparent choice. . . . But you have become, through practice, so horribly expert in the administration of palliative drugs—amusements, indulgences, little temporary evasions and escapes—you use them instead of warfare with the final, inner antagonist—maybe because you are not quite sure *what* he is.

I play my portable victrola and think of Strindberg and great artists who had an unfailing fire in them to strike out profiles of life. I—with my little embers, my tiny broken forge! . . .

Late Night . . . Bought the pocket book of verse and [went] home to read it.

Cardiac neurosis.

Verse soothed me as it always does.

Crane is so much bigger than them all, as Chekhov is alone above all prose writers.

Hart Crane and Anton Chekhov—breathe into me a little of thy life!

This life is all disintegration here in N.O.

All the old habits and more.

Liberty, Poverty, and Fertility

By week's end, however, Tom had fought off his blue devils. Abandoning himself to the sensual life of the Quarter, he began writing numerous short pieces—stories, plays, and poems—some that would achieve an existence of their own, others that would become the fragments of the larger works that he now resisted. Despite the New York pressures and expectations under which he labored, he still was not ready to write another full-length play, but most of what he turned out would become short stories and one-acts of lasting distinction.*

---

*According to Allean Hale, "Williams had the idea for *Vieux Carré*, a book of nine short stories of rather esoteric subject matter: 'One Arm,' 'Desire and the Black Masseur,' 'Blue Roses and the

Once again, he had moved, and as he told Paul Bigelow, " 'Cher,' I have a room on Royal right opposite *the* gay bar—The St. James, so I can hover *like* a bright angel over the troubled waters of homosociety and I have a balcony and everything but a mantilla to throw across it. But I *do* wish you would mail me my laundry. You don't want people to whisper—'The poor girl's putting up a very bold front, but actually doesn't have a *shirt* to her *back!'*—Dish, dish!—No kidding—please *do* mail it to me—538 Royal Street." Years later, mention of the missing laundry would still prompt Bigelow to emit an audible sigh: The "damned laundry" had been duly wrapped and mailed to Tom's various changes of address and just as regularly returned to the Seventy-third Street apartment.

In his letter to Paul, written on the impressive stationery of the New Orleans Athletic Club, Tom confessed:

> I got reckless and invested half of my current checque in a membership at this rather exclusive Club, but it is worth it as there is a marvelous salt water pool, Turkish bath, Etc., and the prettiest Creole belles in town. I am already well-established in their circles and my particular intimate is a Bordelon, one of the oldest families in the city. Such delicate belles you have never seen, utterly different from the northern species. Everybody is *"Cher!"*—I actually pass for "butch" in comparison and am regarded as an innovation—"The Out-door Type"!—and am consequently enjoying a considerable *succès*.

Feuding between Creole families, whose French and Spanish forebears had settled the city in the Vieux Carré, and the despised northerners, who lived across the great divide of Canal Street in the Garden District, was no longer as open as it had been after the Civil War. But the antagonism remained, and Tom found himself caught in the middle. Eloi Bordelon, who exhibited the airs of disenfranchised nobility, and Fritz Bultman, the painter Tom had met earlier in the summer in Provincetown, were at the opposite ends of the New Orleans social scale. The Bultman family were prominent, but, as Tom told Paul, "they are *not* accepted. It seems the grandfather used to ride a hearse," and as wealthy morticians, he said, "They only go out among the *nouveau riche*, and when I stopped to speak to his sister at 'Le Petit Theatre' the Creole belles I was with dispersed in a panic until she had disappeared. Such nonsense!—although I must admit she is not my dish."[5]

In another letter, Tom told Paul, "Well, darling, I met the Bultmans, they are sort of a multiple Bumbleshoot [Fritz], especially the sister who even jigs

---

Polar Star,' 'The Man on a Wall' ('The Malediction'), 'The Rich and Eventful Death of Isabel Holly,' 'A Letter from the See,' and 'Miss Jelkes' Recital.' All were set before that milestone date December 7, 1941" ("Two on a Streetcar," *The Tennessee Williams Literary Journal*, Spring 1989, pp. 31–43).

her Adams apple like his. She is what is known as an *ex*-cellent conver*s*ational-
ist—in other words talks your head off with absolute banalities. Classifies everybody according to ability as talker." She complained that a friend " 'never
opened her mouth except to say hello,'—Well, I only opened mine to *yawn*
which I did constantly all evening."[6] In time, Muriel Bultman Francis would
become a warm personal friend of Tennessee Williams and ultimately a leading figure in New Orleans society. His reference to Fritz as "Bumbleshoot"
stemmed from an occasion when Paul observed their short, plump friend
walking along a Village street carrying a large umbrella tied in the middle like
a nineteenth-century bumbershoot. At one point, Tom was invited to "spend
about 48 hours in their mortuary [and] burnt a cigarette hole in one of their
finest old antique tables."[7] He was obviously more at home in the Quarter and
in the company of Eloi Bordelon and a new acquaintance.

> . . . Bill Richards who is 27 and never had a real consummated affair—he
> says. Loves with his spirit—yet lusts with the flesh—he says. ???—!!! I
> told him pleasure was too important to be left out. But he believes in
> Plato. We read—*I* read aloud—Milton, Keats, Crane, Chinese verse—
> Nice. Swam at Athletic Club—then dinner & movies— Home and to bed
> sans cruising.

Tom wrote his mother, "I know you will be interested in hearing that the
son of Dr. Richards of Columbus is living a few doors from me. He is an
awfully nice boy—a painter—I cannot say whether his work is good or not as
it is very modern and hard to judge. He said his parents remember you and
Grand and Grandfather very well and spoke very highly of you. They are now
living on the Gulf Coast at Ocean Springs, Miss., and the doctor has been
retired for quite a while it seems and is considered very dreamy and impractical. The mother would like to get back to Columbus but he refuses to go."
Tom also told his mother that he expected to be in New Orleans "quite a
while yet" but said he planned to go to St. Petersburg, where Edwina was
visiting her childhood friend Claire Singleton and vacationing in the sun with
her parents. "I am so anxious to see you both, but I think it is much better
away from home. I just cannot live in the house with Dad, and you understand
why. You will not show him this, of course. I have nothing bitter against him
but don't feel up to contending with the strain of his presence."[8]
Early in October, Tom received a letter from his grandfather:

> . . . I was so pleased with the compliment paid you by "American Mer-
> cury"—that means a lot.
> If you stay long enough in N.O. I may have you get me a room; for
> after January I am going somewhere.
> I give your mother 40.00 a month for my board—Grand 10.00 which

leaves me out of my Pension $33.00—of *this* I am putting aside for my trip about $20.00 a month.

I had a fine time in Florida. . . . If I hadn't got a vacation from your father's presence when I did, I believe I would have "exploded."

He don't even say "good morning" to me now: I only see him at dinner, as I go immediately to my room after dinner. I don't enjoy my "eats" at all.

If Grand were only well I wouldn't stay any longer: however, I shall go to Florida *or somewhere* in January. . . .

We are hoping Grand will have a thorough examination at Barnes Clinic—her cough continues bad and she is weak.[9]

In his journal, Tom said that he had been "writing like mad." He had completed another short story and "a 1-act about D. H. Lawrence which is probably mostly shit." This he would entitle *I Rise in Flame, Cried the Phoenix*.[10] He had not given up his intention to write the full-length opus, and in an unmailed letter to Lawrence Langner, he wrote, "Most of my time is taken up now with a long play about D. H. Lawrence and Frieda called 'The Long Affair' which I want you to see as soon as it's near enough finished. It might interest the Lunts." The reason he decided not to mail his letter appears to be contained in the next paragraph: "I enclose another ending for 'Battle of Angels' which seems the best so far devised—I have substituted dogs for fire and fox-skin for snakeskin and worked out a clean-cut end which does not require either conflagration or regurgitation."[11] This, too, in all probability was an intention.

Paul had sent Tom his typewriter—whereupon he confessed to his journal: "Pawned my typewriter today—broke!" Soon after, he borrowed another typewriter and pawned that, too. Then he wired Audrey: PLEASE MAIL NEXT CHECK RIGHT AWAY. HARD AT WORK. GOING NICELY. Her reply cautioned him that she was sending the twenty-five dollars even though she had not yet received the month's installment from Hume Cronyn; he had been appearing in a play that, despite its being produced and directed by George S. Kaufman, closed after seven performances.

Tom answered, "Thanks for your prompt and trustful remittance. I did not know of Cronyn's misfortune nor that he had made such a small initial payment or I would not have lived so recklessly here. I lost one typewriter (mine), borrowed one from a friend and then hocked it for a meal-ticket at Harry's! It will be retrieved this afternoon.

"I seem to do *more* writing with a *pencil*. Completed first drafts (practically) of *two* new plays—one, mentioned previously is now called 'A Daughter of the American Revolution,' is predominantly humorous now, a sort of 'life with *Mother*.' The other a play about D. H. Lawrence which absorbs me more at the moment because of my long and deep interest in his work and ideas.

Maybe *Cronyn* would like to play Lawrence. Lawrence was a funny little man, a sort of furious bantam surrounded by large and impressionable hens—excluding Frieda who is truly magnificent. . . . As you suggest, the theatre contains a great many surprises, delightful and *otherwise*, and a minimum of expectation is the best defense. I have lived behind the mobile fortress of a deep and tranquil pessimism for so long that I feel *almost* impregnable.

"I think I will give up this room and sort of live on my bicycle along the Gulf Coast till we have more knowledge of Cronyn's reactions—leave my stuff with a friend—just take a notebook, tooth brush & extra shirt."[12]

Both Bill Richards and his friend Eloi Bordelon had taken rooms at 722 Toulouse Street, where Tom had stayed when he first went to New Orleans. But now, there was a new landlady, Mrs. Louise Wire, who would make a fictional appearance in a story, "The Angel in the Alcove," and a play that Tennessee would later write, *Vieux Carré*. He described her as "the archetype of the suspicious land-lady" and "a woman of paranoidal suspicion."

Saturday Night [October 4th] I cruised with 3 flaming belles for a while on Canal Street and around the Quarter. They bored and disgusted me so I quit and left Saturday Night to its own vulgar, noisy devices and went upstairs to my big wide comfortable bed and my book of Lawrence's letters—always so rich and friendly.

Bill, the decent one of the crowd, left for Ocean Springs, I think I may follow on my bicycle soon as this condition permits.

Got disgusted with the Lawrence play—it suddenly seemed to be shit. But this A.M. I wrote a new scene for it that revived my hope. I am a rather bad artist most of the time—alas!

Such drunken confusion on the street—the night in full flower, bottles breaking, soldiers bawling, singing, traffic—

The sea would be pleasant. Also good, solid work.—I am disappointed in Bigelow. He has not sent my laundry—or mentioned it. Afraid he is not such a true friend after all. I rather idealized him in New York. Right now I am not terribly concerned about anybody—vaguely friendly toward all—of good will. It is so long since I have seen or heard from Clark [Mills]—There is a personality with some solid foundations.

Sunday stares me in the face not too pleasantly—well, let's sleep. *Bon soir.*

Tuesday—Oct 7—
I'm going to give up this room, leave all my junk with the Bordelon, and hit the road on my bike. Audrey sent a check with the barely stated suggestion it might be the *last*. In that contingency—little man, what *then?* I can think of *no answer.*

En Avant!   *En Avant!*
What is it Lear shouted into the storm?

What tortured fearless cry?

Well, that's what I've got in my heart.

No, the Lawrence doesn't seem very possible—But getting moving again.

Must cash my check, get the borrowed typewriter out of hock—and *away!*

The next day, Tom set off to join Bill Richards and his family. On his return to New Orleans, he wrote to Paul Bigelow, detailing his adventures on the road: "I have just returned from a bike trip along the Gulf Coast which terminated at Bay St. Louis a short distance outside of which I collided in the darkling hours before moonrise with a nervous cow who kicked the rear wheel out of line. I had to leave the wheel to be repaired & procede [*sic*] on my thumb; as I wore boots & khaki cap and appeared rather military I got along famously. I spent a night and day with the object of this pilgrimage, a youth named Bill who is the son of the Doctor who brought me into this world and apparently is trying to compensate for this injustice by providing me with such a congenial fellow-sufferer. . . . Cronyn's play closed on Broadway and I do not know how this will affect our artistic liaison. Sort of holding my breath till I hear from Audrey." He added that he was not doing much cruising: "This is a rather peaceful period for me, for the first time in yrs. I find it not only possible but pleasant to sit at home & read & talk or meditate in the evenings."[13] But on the same day, he wrote in his journal:

> *Saturday Oct 11*—One of those queer, lost mornings. Love-life resumed with a vengeance last night—2 in the night, 1 in the morning. Enjoyed it, the first couple. Then a bit sordid. Ah well, I guess it comes under the heading of fair entertainment. The blue devils have sort of squatted dumbly at the foot of the stairs as it were. . . .
>
> Love is what makes it still seem nice after the orgasm. Then is when sex becomes art—after the orgasm. One must be an artist to keep it from falling to pieces uglily. Up to then it is simply craftsmanship and of a pretty crude and simple kind. It is also art, of course, when you first meet the person—selecting the attitude and sticking to it.

Having gone from check to check, Tom was now going from hand to mouth. There would be many months of a marginal life ahead, scraping together the means for basic survival:

> *Friday midnight*
>
> Difficulties—financial. Blue devils dispersed. I am flat broke—stony—literally—not one cent. Bummed a couple of cigarettes off a queen at Jean's. Guess I'll have to sell a suit tomorrow. Hate to. But I do love to eat and one must have beer money on Sat. Night in the Quarter. —Rent

overdue 3 or 4 days. The Lawrence play goes nicely. I think, well—let's hope a gift arrives in the mail. En Avant!—10.

Sat. A.M. I wake up with no money for breakfast and the land-lady right outside my door.
Midnight—Bill loaned me 5.00—God bless him!—I still have my good suit.

Had a pretty satisfactory "roll in the hay" this evening—then a long, dull round of the gay places to kill time. I have nothing to say to these people after I've been to bed with one of them—then it all seems utterly vacuous. I prefer to just sit and look at Bill and say nothing.

Come Sunday morning, he discovered, "I have 'crabs' again and can't even afford to buy 'The Personal Insecticide.' Literally a lousy writer, that's me. A lousy guy. Want excitement! —Move? Florida?—No. Taos? Wish I could. —New York? Maybe soon, but I am probably better off here—relatively speaking. I am satisfied and the life is (relatively) pleasant. And there is Bill— maybe the nicest guy I've ever known. —Moscow is being sieged—a footnote to all this trivial chatter. Typical bitch Tennessee. —Almost. —10."

Monday—Very, very blue!
A charming little incident climaxed an already miserable evening. The lover of Saturday night stopped me and said, "Say, do you know you have crabs? You gave them to me."

Enough of that! Tomorrow I sell every suit I own, if necessary, to buy an insecticide and be purified at last of my parasite companions. A nasty, humiliating business. . . . In the A.M. wrote a new scene in play and a short story. . . . But no typewriter of my own. The one I borrowed from Chris in hock. I must be *mad.* Still it doesn't seem that I can help myself. What else could I do but go home—my father's house? *Impossible!—What else?* I must work out something.
Later—Drank a pitcher of water to relieve my hunger. Found a few grapes left in bottom of sack—*two* were eatable.

When hunger drives a man to a crime it should not be considered a crime—except against the man who committed it.
Later—Can't sleep. Empty stomach and "crabs."

Remember the New York days—the plus days when I had a room at the Woodrow, that pleasant little penthouse room that overlooked Central Park. The portable victrola by my bed and always money enough to eat or smoke or fuck or almost anything I desired to do. . . . The little deaf and dumb belle picked up on 57th Street and Bigelow coming over for lunch and the sun roof. And cruising the park at night. And eating, eating, eating! I wasn't so happy. But I was well off, huh? O, I want to have *money* again. I love the pleasures, the sensual pleasures so much. And how I loathe the squalor, the awkwardness, the indignity of being broke. I suppose I am too much body, not enough soul. But how can one maintain a soul with so little to feed on? Meditation? Is that what the soul feeds on? I meditate and arrive at *nothing—nothing.* My thoughts, such as they are—and they are pretty impulsive—go into my work. . . .

Tuesday Midnight—Good humor returned with the sale of a suit, good food, the writing and dispatching of a 1-act about the Spiritualist, and a kind letter from Audrey—mailed before she got my request for a check for it contained none.

The mulatto-looking youth in the next room is beautiful. We merely exchange shy greetings.

He has a lover— And I have crabs.

(Roaches in my big valise—I am a victim of the insect kingdom.)

He also noted that he had sent Bill Richards a letter to apologize for his various impositions. "Read Hart Crane. Now feel hungry. May go out again to spend part of my last 50 cents. Two dollars to Landlady—spent 1.50 today—how? Don't know. Well, let's see—Cigs .17, Breakfast (2—owed for one) .45, envelope and stamps .13, Supper at Glucks .30, Coke .05, sandwich .10 —Got in show for nothing, usher not looking –0. .05 to porter NOAC [athletic club] .20, 2 orange juices .05, penny taxes and various other things probably leave about 3 cents.—ought to have 53 cents—first time I ever figured money out like this—getting bourgeois—stuffy—no kidding? I could live OK on a dollar ten cents a day. I'm getting too Rotarian lately. Yep—goin' out now an' *eat. Love to.*"

New Orleans, it is said, is a city that one never leaves no matter where one is, its register on the heart ineradicable. Tennessee would come to speak of it as his "favorite city of America . . . of all the world, actually."[14] Tom's confession, however, was more cautious: "I guess I like N.O.—it will always seem kind of home-like to me after this."

"Home-like" was as much home as Tom could take at times like this, when all he was seeking was a refuge. As for a return to St. Louis, he noted: "No word from home lately but I am too hard to worry. Love Grand but don't think of her except casually—say, for a moment or two a day. I'm sorry I'm so selfish." When Edwina wrote, however, saying that Grand was almost down to eighty pounds, Tom answered, "Just received your letter. I am dreadfully worried about Grand. Please let me know how she is getting along. Of course I will come to St. Louis if needed." He added, "You had better write me c/o Bill Richards, 722 Toulouse Street after tomorrow as I am going to get a less expensive room and he will take my mail for me or any messages till I am re-settled. Give Grand my dear love."[15]

Monday Midnight
   I have moved out of that pleasant, comforting room to a horrible windowless brown cubicle with a lumpy bed and a musty odor and big roaches crawling about the walls. Sad to return to at night. . . . Still, I wrote a new 1-act today—"The Lady of Larkspur Lotion"—and feel not too badly.

Tom and Audrey, meanwhile, had exchanged letters that crossed in the mails. Her news was that Hume Cronyn was "thinking very seriously about your one acts." Cronyn had sent her a fifty-dollar check, and she said, "Let me know when you need that next $25."[16] His news told of progress on the Lawrence play, that it was proceeding more rapidly than he had expected, but he said he was afraid she might be disgusted with him for writing something so noncommercial. He said that he had named it *The Long Affair*—opening with Lawrence's first meeting with Frieda and concluding with his death. He thought that the total effect would be more tender than tragic and that he would invest it with a good deal of humor.

On October 21, he wrote to Audrey, "I do hope you have already gotten my last appeal for money, mailed, I think, last week and that the check will arrive before this—I have had to borrow on my nice tan gabardine suit. When I leave New Orleans I shall write a song called 'The Rampart Street Blues.' Some day I expect to pass along there and see myself hanging in one of the windows—'Greatly Reduced.' The Lawrence play is about ready to be rewritten. It seems to go very well because of my great interest in him. Walter Huston might like it or even the Lunts. —Might. —Shall I try to interest that *Life With Father* man [producer Oscar Serlin] in a description of it? I think he manifested some interest in Lawrence on one occasion."[17]

And to Paul, he wrote, "I am terribly distressed over my Grandmother who is in a St. Louis hospital, apparently fading gradually away, dear gentle yellow rose that she is—only eighty-eight pounds and would not give in till she collapsed. The only member of my family I cared for very deeply so you can understand how I feel. I dare not go and dare not stay." Because he had anticipated the problems of making theatre out of D. H. Lawrence's life while also making the play of interest to "people who think Lawrence fought Arabs," he told Paul he had written it as "primarily the story of a woman's devotion to a man of genius and a man's, a sort of modern satyr's, pilgrimage through times inimical to natural beings—a would-be satyr never quite released from the umbilicus."

He added that he was moving once again. "A misunderstanding about some sailors who come in occasionally to discuss literature with me provoked a tedious little quarrel with the landlady—I told her I could not live in such an atmosphere of unwarranted suspicion. There were 550 Argentine sailors here on a good-will visit last week and I must say that no particular malice was displayed. Pan-American relations are much improved. The lack of a common language had to be compensated by a good deal of prestidigitation. I rose admirably to that contingency assisted by the fact that they have only three top buttons and two on either side."[18]

For the moment, Tom's disposition was up, his mood swings relating directly to how well or badly his writing was going. Overall, though, he had the added burden of credibility, of making his creation—Tennessee Williams—a reality, not only professionally but to himself, as well. The rejection of *Battle of Angels*, now released by the Guild, was the hardest blow he had yet endured. But losing only energized him, and so poems, short stories, one-act plays were sent out like shots in the dark, and no one was more amazed at this outpouring than Audrey Wood.

"A play is a Phoenix," he wrote in his journal, "it dies a thousand deaths. Usually at night. In the morning it springs up again from its ashes and crows like a happy rooster. It is never as bad as you think. It is somewhere in between and success versus failure depends on which end of your emotional gamut concerning its value it actually approaches more closely. But it is much more likely to be good if you *think* it is *wonderful* while you are writing the first draft." Still, he would always be hounded by the compelling syndrome of success versus failure. And there would always be vacillation between his artistic integrity and the Broadway sellout. "An artist must believe in himself—possibly not so passionately as Lawrence—but passionately. Your belief is contagious."

Tom felt that this New Orleans period was drawing to an end. He found some satisfaction in the amount of writing he had done but said, "None of my essential personality problems are solved. I have not found the sustained desirable lover." Instead, in his uninhibited sexual escapades, he had for the first time been struck in the face by some "dirt." Also, he had had a run-in with Eloi Bordelon, Bill Richards's friend, and "raged at him like a fishwife." He averred that he hadn't done anything like that since his breakup with Kip in Provincetown. At length, because of Grand's illness, he sent a wire home for bus fare, but he debated about whether he would use the money for that or go elsewhere. "I can suspect myself of almost anything these days. Yes—I suddenly remember myself a kid of 9 drawing pictures in Red Goose sample books, waiting in Dad's office—Why?—Stupid!"

Edwina had wired him twenty-five dollars, and Tom headed home. Having paid some of his debts and left most of his belongings in New Orleans, he hitchhiked as far as Jackson, Mississippi, where on November 2 he wrote to Paul Bigelow that he intended to return to the Quarter briefly following his visit home, after which he would "settle somewhere else, probably, for the remainder of my southern period." The frenetic, hysterically gay side of "homosociety," as he called it, was something toward which he had sharp, conflicting feelings. "I am quite fed up with piss-elegant bitches (don't you love that phrase?) of the New Orleans variety."

Of his brief time in Jackson, he told Paul, "I love to be alone in a strange town at night—there is something cool and purifying about it. Does it give

you that feeling? Isn't it pleasant to be lonesome sometimes? Being with people is such a strain and there is so much unreality in it, unless you happen to
like them very much."[19] But in truth it was *being* alone, not living alone, that
created the hollowed-out void in Tom's feelings and that caused him to go on
endlessly searching for love until the last days of his life. It was a void that no
one could fill for long, because, ironically, he would not permit it.

His homecoming was not as bleak as Tom might have expected. Grand and
Grandfather and his mother were delighted to see him and showered him
with attention—but then, there was Dad, who was not so delighted. One
bright spot was a letter from Audrey, telling Tom that he should soon be
receiving a check from Hume Cronyn. She said, "I'm glad you're going to be
home for a while because Grandmothers can be a great consolation in a world
like this," and she added that she was especially excited about his short play
The Lady of Larkspur Lotion. "I really think this is a well written one act with a
good basic idea as well as a remarkably unusual curtain." She had given it to
editor Margaret Mayorga along with *Lord Byron's Love Letter*, but since only
one play could be selected, *The Lady of Larkspur Lotion* was chosen. This, she
said, "made me very happy and I know will please you."[20]

Referring to *Lord Byron's Love Letter*, Tom pointed out, "Byron died in
1824 and I have him making love in 1827, which is a wee bit ghoulish. Better
make that little change in the script. Thanks for the clipping about Eudora
Welty. She and Carson McCullers and Wm. Faulkner and Katherine Anne
Porter have practically got a deep southern corner on the best imaginative
writing in America."

He had just read William Saroyan's new play, *Jim Dandy*, in script form
that had been sent to the Little Theatre of St. Louis, and writing to Audrey,
Tom grudgingly admitted it was

> the maddest thing he has yet written. Still it has unearthly charm. People
> go round and round for no reason in [a] revolving door, walk with one
> foot in miniature coffins, sit in chair on table, dance, sing, change shoes,
> play cornet and pianola, recline on a Mae West bed, make rhapsodic
> speeches about the snow and the rain—all in a room of the San Francisco
> public library. In the end all kinds of bells start ringing—signifying death,
> I believe—and the characters wander off the stage continuing all their
> curious little practices as they go. —Undoubtedly a parable on the sub-
> ject of LIFE—I cannot understand the symbolism, more than barely. But
> I read it twice and I must admit I was fascinated and moved by the
> strangeness of it and occasional speeches ring the bell of pure poetry.[21]

In a letter written to Saroyan he said that he had "just finished reading your
play *Jim Dandy* which rings in my head and heart like the multitude of soft
and musical bells that bring down the curtain. It is a beautiful little mystery of

a play. . . ." On reading it a second time, he said, "it began to glow and vibrate, coming out like a star in 'first dark.' "[22] *Jim Dandy* was the kind of play that Tom wanted to write and that in later years Tennessee would, entitling it *Camino Real*.

He did not mention, though, that he had received a letter from William Saroyan forwarded from New Orleans. After saying how glad he was when he first heard that the Guild was producing *Battle of Angels* and how "burned up" he was the way things had turned out, Saroyan wrote, "If you want the truth, as I see it, there is no one in the American theatre who knows how to do anything other than the ordinary, banal, commercial and shabby—which makes writing plays a hopeless activity, unless one is one's self ready to put them on. Now, I know the little theatres of the [regional] Conference cannot stage Jim Dandy the way it needs to be staged, but I offered the outfit the play just the same—simply because I am fed-up with the fat-headedness of Broadway."[23]

> *Thanksgiving Day—1941* . . . Been here 2 weeks and crazy to leave. Waiting for checque from Audrey. Hatred of my father & *fear*—yes, fear—make it about as impossible as usual to live at home.
>
> Also poor Mother's gross lack of sensitivity. Grand has been ill and I returned partly to see her, partly because my finances got horribly muddled. Well, we leave in a couple of days *irregardless*. . . . Not well physically. Heart neurosis bad today. No sex here. None ever. And sex, alas, is necessary. Writing a bad play, a good 1-act, two poems. Shame. As an artist I seem weak & muddled today. Sorry.

Audrey wrote, "You will be amused to know I have the [New School] Dramatic Workshop interested in producing 'The Battle of Angels.' [Erwin] Piscator is going to have a talk with me and when he does I'll let you know more about this."[24] On the morning of his departure for New Orleans, Tom answered Audrey, telling her of his intention of going on from there to Florida. He also mentioned that he had just met with Gilmor Brown, the founder and director of the Pasadena Playhouse, who, he said, had heard "some favorable (!) reports on 'Battle of Angels' and wished to read it. I am sending him my revised script from New Orleans with these latest changes which I am also mailing you for Piscator."[25] Although Tom may never have known it, Gilmor Brown heard those "favorable (!) reports" from Willard Holland, who was spending the winter months working at the Pasadena Playhouse.

The World Is Lit by Lightning

Everyone knew that American involvement in the war was inevitable. The only question that remained was when and how. And when it happened, strangely enough, it was almost a relief. On December 7, "a date which will live in infamy," Tom was en route to New Orleans. When he arrived, he had the feeling he had entered a different city. What had once been a casual and carefree atmosphere had suddenly become one of either gloom or desperate gaiety. Those men already in uniform who flooded the Quarter would be the first to go overseas and, ill-prepared, be among the first sacrificed.

Tom's mood, too, had changed. Instead of returning to his former lifestyle, he chose to concentrate almost exclusively on his writing. He had abandoned the full-length Lawrence play and had turned back to work on *Stairs to the Roof*, which he hoped to finish before Christmas. In a letter to his mother, he said he had been writing all day to keep up with a self-imposed schedule and expected to leave soon in order to return home for the holidays. "The city is very dead because of the war—practically no tourists—business bad. The Russian successes very encouraging—would indicate that it may not last much longer. I don't think any of the Axis will stand up under defeat, and if the Germans crack up, the whole business will be practically over—I do hope, before Dakin is called. He should try to get in the intelligence service or something like that."[26]

During his few remaining days in New Orleans, Tom found temporary work at Gluck's Cafeteria on Royal Street, and since it was as a cashier, it turned out to be very temporary. He completed a draft of *Stairs to the Roof*, which he subtitled *A Prayer for the Wild of Heart That Are Kept in Cages*. A note on the original manuscript stated that he had written the play as catharsis for the years he spent as a clerk in the International Shoe Company. After the melodramatic power of *Battle of Angels*, an allegorical play would be met with disappointment, no matter what its social implications.

On Christmas Eve, Audrey received a handwritten letter from Tom on New Orleans Athletic Club stationery:

> Monday (blue)
> Audrey, Audrey!!
> Did you get my wire with new address and a request for check?!
>
> If Mr. Cronyn has discontinued his remittances please inform me quickly as possible so I can borrow money here and go home, Clayton, while considering the next expedient.
>
> I have completed the long play "Stairs to the Roof" and will mail it soon as I can afford to. I am pleased with the way it has turned out, though it may be more a play for tomorrow than today.
>
> Today is pretty dreadful, isn't it?[27]

A note from Audrey mailed the day before, the twenty-third, said only, "I am enclosing a photostat copy of your [draft 4-F] classification card. I'm keeping the original because I'm sure if I sent it to you, you might lose it. Be sure to keep it on you at all times. A blessed Christmas to you and a very Happy New Year."[28]

Tom Williams spent Christmas in New Orleans—in all probability at Gluck's for a thirty-cent turkey dinner—and New Year's in St. Louis with his family. Neither was a happy occasion.

22

At Liberty

January–August 1942

In the year since Boston and his failed promise, Tom had written a number of short plays and stories of lasting distinction. In addition to the Mayorga anthology, two one-act plays were published by editor William Kozlenko in *American Scenes*. A third, which Kozlenko had passed over, was alternately titled *Port Mad* or *The Leafless Block*. It portrayed an aging southern woman, disoriented and about to be removed to an insane asylum, who is lost in memories of a lover she thinks is still alive. Later retitled *Portrait of a Madonna*, it became a source for *A Streetcar Named Desire*.

The two plays that Kozlenko chose were combined under the title *Landscape with Figures (Two Mississippi Plays)*; both were two-character dramas, with the action taking place in the Deep South. One, *This Property Is Condemned*, is set on "a railroad embankment on the outskirts of a small Mississippi town" and concerns Willie, a lonely girl of thirteen, who dresses up in her deceased sister's worn party clothes and still carries her "extraordinarily dilapidated doll." She is caught up in self-delusion as she tells Tom, an older boy who has chanced upon her, about her beautiful sister, Alva, who "looked like a movie star" and, like Garbo's Camille, died of "a lung infection."

The other, *At Liberty*, set in Blue Mountain, Mississippi, is a duologue, a quarrel between a mother and her daughter, Gloria, formerly an actress, who has returned to her home consumptive and wasted. Clinging to illusions of youth and beauty long gone and to the fantasy that she will resume her career, she becomes a forerunner of Tennessee Williams's galaxy of doomed southern heroines. The play contains a line of dialogue that Tom had set down in his journal in 1939, citing it as the dilemma of a poet trying to write drama: "Today I wrote one very good line, too good to be good in a play, 'The past keeps getting bigger and bigger at the future's expense.' " It had only to be spoken by a Delta lady with a diminished future.

By now, in the cold January of 1942, Tom was like the former actress and so many others in the theatre, at liberty. Considering his impecunious condition and also his indecision where next to migrate, the name Tennessee became a fitting sobriquet for an itinerant—particularly since it was common among hoboes and bums in the Depression years to call one another by the name of the state from which they hailed. "Bum" was certainly the way C.C.

looked upon his thirty-year-old unemployed son. He was made to feel pretentious and vaguely ridiculous as "Tennessee" Williams. Worse, he was that
most unforgivable of all American species: a failure.

The conflict between father and son, however, took on a deeper significance, that of the struggle of the artist in society against the forces that define
success solely in terms of monetary gain. Even Tom's closest ally, Audrey,
being a realist in the New York theatre, saw it that way. Money ruled, period.
While, as Tom the poet, he pulled away from this reality, as Tennessee the
playwright, he was made to face it. His resentment, though, was always there.
More and more, his characters came to symbolize this clash with society, and
each finally was at liberty in another sense—that is, available to whoever
might desire them or pay for them, if not their talent. Tom had isolated a
theme that would engage him for the rest of his career: the artist as pariah,
cornered and exploited, driven and confined within his illusory self. Even
after his phenomenal success, he not only sought out the company of "the
strange, the crazed, the queer" but felt he was one of them. It had been two
years since Tom had left home on the strength of a thousand-dollar grant.
Except for the persistent faith Audrey Wood had in him and the belief of a few
close friends, Tennessee Williams in January 1942 was either forgotten or
remembered as a failed curiosity.

In a letter to Paul Bigelow, Tom remarked that he had just sent Audrey his
completed draft of *Stairs to the Roof*, "and every day I mail little changes to her
which must be driving her to distraction, especially if she doesn't happen to
like the play. I haven't heard from her yet. I think my next project will be a
group of about seven more or less associated stories of Bohemian life in the
Vieux Carré ending on December 7, 1941. Our *fin du monde*, as everyone feels
too distinctly."[1]

> Monday—Jan. 5, 1942
> So I begin a new journal—appropriately in the house of my parents,
> always a place to start from and commence a new phase.
> I am not well. A bad chest cold. A few days ago I surprised myself by
> spitting out a good quantity of blood.
> Weakness. Occasional vertigo. Sometimes an overactive heart. My
> complaints. I do not pay any more attention than is necessary. I write
> nearly every day. I have completed "Stairs to the Roof"—I now wish to
> do a complete set of new stories and new poems.

> Tuesday—
> I am frightened thinking of the changes or rather the increased vicissi-
> tudes the war may create in my life. . . . Well, I must get moving. Where?
> Undecided as never before. A letter from Audrey will probably precipi-
> tate a decision. Macon? New York? Back to New Orleans? Or even

Florida—Mexico? Mexico City would be lovely. Wish it were possible. No, I feel no desire to participate in war work. . . .

Proust writes, "For a long time I used to go to bed early."

Dear selfish, shameless, heroic, honest sissy—Proust. We would have understood each other, my dear. How we might have "dished" the world in that cork-lined room of yours.

Sending Audrey what he referred to as "another reinforcement for those rickety stairs," he also said that he had "just come from the eye-surgeon who thinks my second 'needle' operation ought to be done right away—I don't [know] whether to have it done here or by my original doctor in New York." Then he asked, "How is the war likely to effect Tennessee? Perhaps he is one of those unlisted casualties at Pearl Harbor." In a somewhat optimistic vein, he added, "I have two more one-acts whenever you want them and a new story."[2] Audrey replied, saying that editor Betty Smith was putting together a collection titled *25 Non-Royalty Plays for All-Girl Casts*. "She tells me that she had heard Tennessee Williams has a one-acter for an all-female cast. I may be dense, but I don't remember one, so I write to ask you."[3] *At Liberty* would be published once again, but never in any anthology or collection of his plays.

Although Grand's persistent illness had been diagnosed as cancer, she maintained her German stoicism in the face of family adversity, and her own. To Tom, as ever, she gave her love and encouragement. Edwina in her memoir said that "he wanted desperately to be a success while she was alive."[4] The truth is, she never saw him as anything else—as much as his father looked upon him as a failure.

Monday—Jan. 12
Again—Providence!

A telegram from Erwin Piscator—summons to N.Y.—the day before I was to have my second eye operation. O let us be hopeful! What is it? A play production? Too lovely to believe—almost. After this hiatus. . . .

Yes. Happiness. Hope. Good night. Love? The night after tomorrow night. I'm betting on it, baby!

Now it seemed as though Tom's creation of Tennessee Williams might have some meaning again. Piscator at the New School, assisted by Herbert Berghof and director James Light, had created the only experimental theatre in New York. As egocentric as Piscator undoubtedly was, he did sponsor new plays and at this time had in rehearsal one that eventually moved from his basement theatre to Broadway's Belasco Theatre. In addition to Berghof in its cast, it also had settings by Cleon Throckmorton, who had designed *Battle of Angels*. Tom had real cause for optimism.

Considerable optimism also existed within the family matrix as he prepared to leave—excepting C.C., who was more concerned about *his* boy, Dakin. Keeping him out of the draft had become Cornelius's chief worry, a matter for stratagems. In his final term before graduation from Washington University, Dakin had distinguished himself scholastically and would soon receive a degree in law.

On January 25, the *New York Herald Tribune* ran an item:

> Tennessee Williams, author of *Battle of Angels*, has arrived from St. Louis to work on script revisions with Erwin Piscator. Mr. Piscator is considering a Studio Theatre production of the revised version, with Francine Larrimore in the leading role.

In the dead of winter, the only way artists, then as now, could keep from freezing to death was to seek the shelter of more fortunate fellow artists. And so, Tom took to "crashing the pads" of his friends and even of strangers, among other enforced economy measures. Fritz Bultman, his painter friend from New Orleans, who eventually became recognized as an Abstract Expressionist, had an apartment in Greenwich Village at 319 West Eleventh Street, located near the Hudson River waterfront. But Fritz and Tom were as unlikely a pair of roommates as could be imagined. Sooner or later, they were destined to meet head-on. Fred Melton observed that "Tennessee was already considered an undesirable houseguest. He was socially crass and slovenly, and friends would say, 'Don't ever bring that man here again.' He could care less about proprieties."[5]

MacDougal Street was the center of gay life in the Village; in the bars catering to homosexuals, there was always among the flamboyant "queens" a sizable gathering of nondescript gays like Tom, men seeking partners who generally turned out to be one-night stands. Disappointed in not having found the unnamed "love" mentioned in his journal, he once again resorted to indiscriminate sex, as much and as often as possible.

His greatest disappointment, however, came with his meeting Erwin Piscator. He had run up hard against the German director's monumental ego. Piscator's method was not unlike that of the famed producer-director David Belasco, in that the hapless playwright's scenes were cut up and transposed and tacked up on a wall to effect a different sequence. Tom complained to his mother that Piscator was "a terribly dictatorial German, completely impractical," who was "trying to force me to turn the play into a dry, didactic sermon on social injustice, representing the South as a fascist state. To comply with his demands will destroy the poetic quality of the play. Right now we are deadlocked." He added, "Either he will give in or the production will have to be called off. I am going out to his country place tonight for another 'battle.' You can imagine how tiresome and discouraging this is!"[6]

Sometime later, Tom wrote to Audrey and asked:

Did I ever tell you about my first interview with him, or rather—the second? I arrived at this palatial estate on the Hudson, admitted by a Prussian butler. After waiting half an hour I was conducted to his bedroom. He was slightly indisposed with a cold. He was lying up in bed with his dinner tray. Over the bed was a fur robe—I believe it was mink—and he was wearing peach-colored silk pyjamas. He looked at me mournfully and said, "Mr. Williams, you have written a Fascist play—all of your characters are selfishly pursuing their little personal ends and aims in life with a ruthless disregard for the wrongs and sufferings of the world about them." A man that lacking in humor is not for me to deal with![7]

Clearly at an impasse, Tom informed his mother that the director had "not yielded an inch on his demands. I am re-writing the play, but not according to his wishes. Maybe he will compromise and maybe he won't."[8]

Finally, in desperation, he wrote a plea to the director himself:

Things have come to the "dead end" here in New York. I can no longer impose upon the hospitality of my friend and my meager resources are all used up. . . . I wanted to see you to find out if I could read plays for you as Mr. Berghof suggested I might. I have had no luck at obtaining other employment. And it appears that a production of my play is remote at best. Please let me know as soon as you can.[9]

Tom complained to his mother that there had been so much disagreement and delay over the play production that he had decided to have the eye operation because it would give him time to rest and think things over. Afterward, he assured her that his eye was reacting "exactly right" in Dr. Frey's opinion. In another letter, he reassured her that there had been "marked improvement" to his sight and that parts of the cataract had dissolved and that he had lighting effects like the aurora borealis. He added optimistically that one more "needling" might be necessary but that the prognosis was very favorable for normal vision.

Subsequently, he wrote to his family that he had found employment, of sorts, difficult as it must have been for his mother to imagine. "I have been working nights in a night-club run by a German refugee, Valeska Gert, my procedes [sic] being only tips which range from a dime to five dollars a night and average about eight a week but her nature is so erratic and her temper so violent that I don't know how long it will last."[10] Of course, Edwina didn't know the half of it: Her precious son was indeed working for tips in a Village bistro appropriately named the Beggar's Bar, a noisy, cramped cellar filled with intermingling odors of dense cigarette smoke, spilled beer, and a peasant soup of sauerkraut and sausage. In her wildest imaginings, she could never have conceived of Tom wearing a black eyepatch, on which Fritz had painted a glaring white orb, while he not only waited on tables but recited verse slanted to the inelegant tastes of the Beggar's Bar patrons. Unlicensed liquor was served in coffee cups or by other means, and as Tom found out, when the spirits were high, so were the tips.

The bar's basement brick walls were painted black; a battered old upright piano stood beside a small riser; tables were covered with oilcloth of different colors; and no two chairs or tables were alike. A weird lighting effect was created by pairs of blue and red lights fixed to the wall. At a moment when the spirit moved her, Valeska would signal for the lights to dim, and within a quivering spot, she would appear wearing some bizarre costume reminiscent of the apparel worn in the Berlin cabarets of the 1920s. A caricaturist, her forte was political satire.

More than anything, Tom was fascinated by Valeska's portrayals of society's castoffs. The poet Harold Norse remembered that in a heavy German accent she would deliver "an original political satire that was both funny and poignant. She always got enormous applause." Her style was known as *Sprechstimme*, which "was characterized by musical speech, rather like the tone of wonder one uses to tell fairy tales to children, but heightened and intensified by sudden dramatic variations in pitch, duration and volume, punctuated by eerie cries. It had a spooky appeal that audiences loved."[11]

Tom's association with Valeska was abruptly terminated, however, when "one night the Madam called the waiters together and announced a change of policy. She said that the waiters (there were three of us) had to pool their tips and then split them with the management, meaning herself. I told the lady that I had absolutely no intention whatsoever of pooling my tips with the other waiters and having it split with the management." At that point, the terrible-tempered Fritzi, who had been waiting for Tom at the bar, joined in the noisy confrontation. "Near the kitchen entrance there was a crate of quart soda bottles and as soon as he entered he began to hurl these bottles at the celebrated dance-mime. At least a dozen bottles were hurled at the lady before one of them struck her. The paddy wagon and an ambulance were summoned, the lady received several stitches in her scalp, and, needless to say, I was out of a job at that particular night spot."[12]

> Feb. 15 or ? (1942)
> . . . So now we live for a while on our last remittance which will melt like snow in the coming spring.
> Then?—ah, *then*—
> I try to write today but I am suddenly quite dead and disgusted.
> So I go back to bed.
> Singapore has fallen.
> Everyone in our little group is cynical and hopeless and without an ounce of patriotic feeling.
> We expect an air raid soon. We expect social disaster.

We go on with our little lives. We are kind to each other mostly. Sometimes we are hurt and cruel.

I do not write home—weariness, negligence.

Only once in a while I feel very desperate but even then I know how to soothe myself. . . .

My will is to live, to survive. To go on gathering the nights and the days.

But I have the will to continue creation; the need to say more and clearer and more intensely.

If only they would let me do it my way. Nobody loves another one's power of creation [enough] to leave it alone. . . .

Fritzi is tortured waiting for a lover. I am not waiting for anyone and that may be better. Or worse.

In New York, Tom was encountering once again a different kind of homosexual activity, more concealed and furtive than the comparatively open and ingenuous life in the French Quarter. He hated being alone at night; his was a craving for companionship, something more than just sex. Sometimes, too, his need was plain animal hunger, and like unemployed actors, he was not above dropping by at mealtimes, the fare of slightly more prosperous friends being a filling casserole dubbed "fairy pudding," composed of canned tuna fish, cheese, and (mainly) rice.

Greenwich Village in wartime was greatly changed from the more romantic Village of the 1920s and early 1930s. It was no longer a place where bohemians gathered together and read the poetry of Edna St. Vincent Millay by candlelight and where it was in style for anyone of intellect, either posed or real, rich or poor, to be considered a political radical. The streets of the Village were overrun with men in uniform and at night became a place where pleasure, *any* pleasure, was better than none at all, "for tomorrow we die." Young people of both sexes drank heavily and smoked cigarettes constantly; "sticks of tea"—marijuana reefers—imported from Harlem at anywhere from twenty-five cents to a dollar apiece were passed around at "tea parties." Also bennies were in if you were hep; one could buy a regular Benzedrine inhaler at any drugstore and, by removing the wick, soaking it in water, and drinking the solution, get a high. Tom was not at that time into the drug scene. He drank when he could afford to, mostly in the bars where the price of a short beer would bring him in out of the cold and hopefully into the embrace of another lonely wanderer. The Village was the one place in Manhattan that had much in common with the French Quarter in its isolation from the more staid neighborhoods of the city; it was the one place where Tom felt at ease.

"Weave Back My Sister's Image"

Feb. 25—
I have just finished writing "The Spinning Song," a play suggested by my sister's tragedy.
The end is good. It is something to work on. Hard.
Now I relax and smoke and listen to the radio.
War bulletins and Cuban rhumbas.
Later—go swimming—rest and purify the body and soothe the nerves.
Then cruising? —Nearly always seems the only thing to do.
. . . Evening is the normal adults' time for home—the family.
For us it is the time to search for something to satisfy that empty space that home fills in the normal adults' life.
It isn't so bad really.
Usually we go home with nothing.
Now and then we succeed.
Night before last a love affirmation in the shower—quick rubbing over—off—goodbye.
. . . I am spending my last ten dollars.
What then?
Money from home?
Orders to return home?
No—won't do it.
. . . I begin to see a little out of my left eye. Amusing. The world reappearing slowly before a blind eye.
What a world!
Why see it, darling?
Yeah, but I *want* to, though.
I must be able to be a post-war artist.
Keep awake—alive—New.
Perform the paradox of being hard and yet soft.
Survive with calcification of the tender membranes.
Be a poet. Be alive.
So long. —10.

March 2—
. . . Was flat busted when a little money from Mother arrived today.
I wrote an appeal to Dramatists Guild for a loan.
Letter to Eddie Dowling pleading for a one-act prod.
Saw Piscator.
. . . "Spinning Song" about ready to start 2nd draft.

In early March, Tom wrote reassuringly to his family, saying, "So many people here are interested in my work that I do not need to worry too much about the exigencies of living: I am sharing a friend's apartment and another friend has provided me with this excellent typewriter as long as I need it. The war seems to draw men of good will closer together and makes the need for mutual kindness and humanity more apparent. If one can just survive this frightful cataclysm, the times after may be the better for it."[13] He expressed his concern about Dakin staying out of the fighting end of the war. Cornelius was in complete agreement, and as Dakin said, "Dad went into his wallet to see that I went off to Harvard after I got my law degree from Washington University." Dakin was to graduate in April instead of June and would receive further study in business administration at Harvard as part of a program for officer training. Ultimately, he was drafted into the army as a noncommissioned officer, and he remembered his father driving him to St. Louis's Jefferson Barracks while warning him to "beware of camp followers."[14]

While he was living with Fritz Bultman, Tom would occasionally drop by Anne Bretzfelder's studio in the Village. She was shocked at his "ill-kempt and worn appearance"; he seemed so "vulnerable and inadequate" compared with when she had met him in St. Louis and last seen him in the spring of 1940. And, although she was willing to share her table with him, Anne felt that he had become so "self-absorbed and dependent upon his friends, it was difficult even to converse with him." His, she said, was "a sensitivity that was inordinate—but not toward other people."[15] Though he admired her work as a sculptor and would always hold her in esteem, he seemed to be unmindful of the simplest considerations or of any inconvenience he might be causing. Finally, she discouraged his friendship for another reason: She had fallen in love with a young doctor, Joseph Post, and was about to be married.

That spring, Donald Windham became convinced that D. H. Lawrence's short-short story "You Touched Me" would make a beautiful play, and he showed it to Tennessee, who recalled, "I was very tired when he gave me the book. I went to bed with it. But in spite of exhaustion I didn't sleep that night. Something kept saying 'you touched me, you touched me' like those skinny wood pyramids that music teachers have. All of a sudden, about 2 or 3 A.M., I sat upright and turned on the light. The play was born. I woke up Windham and said, 'It's all of life this story. You and me and the Touch. It's all of life.' "

At first, the narrative seemed to him to be "a fairly simple delicate love story of two lonely young people whose longing broke through to each other in spite of many little obstructions such as pride and gentility and the interference of others. But as I thought about the story the essential myth began to grow and unfold in my mind like one of those Chinese poems that are written in almost invisible script on an infinitesimal slip of paper. Dropped in a cup of hot tea the paper expands and unfolds and finally floating on the top of the cup is a poem."[16]

Tom and Donald began working together on the play, first at Donald's Leroy Street apartment, then at the West Sixty-third Street YMCA after

Windham moved there. Apart from his coauthorship with Dorothy Shapiro of *Cairo! Shanghai! Bombay!* in 1935, this would be Tennessee Williams's only collaboration. According to Fred Melton, initially Tennessee offered to help Donald, but then he gradually took over.

Tom could see all too clearly what was happening in the theatre uptown. Both from financial necessity and lack of interest, he kept away from it. He could not be other than painfully conscious of the contrast in his threadbare appearance with his prosperous look when he was last in New York. The Village offered a certain insularity within the city while it safely divided him from mingling in the theatre crowd. He had not even been to see Audrey and Liebling or any of "the office gang." Still, he considered himself a playwright, and it was expected, especially by Audrey, that he would write plays. Why else endure New York? His problem was that the Broadway theatre, always a mirror of the changing times, was presently preoccupied with a mixed bag of escapist fare tempered by one or two propaganda plays. At the Theatre Guild, Langner and Helburn were staging comedies, revivals, and imported vehicles, preferring these to the work of new playwrights like Saroyan and Williams. Everything was a commercial endeavor, and except for Piscator's polemical workshop, there was no other theatre that a poet-playwright could work toward.

It was clear, as Tom had said, he would have to wait to become "a post-war artist," and in his notebook he wrote:

> The experimental dramatist must find a method of presenting his passion and the world's in an articulate manner. Apocalypse without delirium.
>
> In considering this problem while at work on new scripts, I have evolved a new method which in my own particular case may turn out to be a solution. I call it the "sculptural drama." Because my form is poetic.
>
> The usual mistake that is made in the presentation of intensified reality on the stage is that of realistic action. If the scenes are not underwritten, the acting must compensate by an unusual restraint. We will find it increasingly necessary to write our emotions out. Correspondingly restraint in acting and directing must increase. A new form, non-realistic, must be chosen. This necessity suggests what I have labelled as "the sculptural drama." Obviously it is not for the conventional three-act play which is probably on its way out anyhow. This form, this method, is for the play of short cumulative scenes which I think is on its way in. I visualize it as a reduced mobility on the stage, the forming of statuesque attitudes or tableaux, something resembling a restrained type of dance, with motions honed down to only the essential or significant.

The theatre—"the sculptural drama"—that Tennessee Williams envisioned would be put on hold for the duration of the war. Eugene O'Neill, racked with a gradually disabling illness, was silent but laboring to complete a cycle of plays that could raise him to a place of unequaled prominence. His friend and catalyst, the drama critic Brooks Atkinson of the *New York Times*, would soon, at age forty-eight, be reviewing the war overseas as a foreign correspondent. And a legion of the theatre's most talented artists and artisans would also be drawn into the carnage—many never to return.

> Connie Boswell singing about the blue birds over the White Cliffs of Dover. I with a capital of six pennies have just taken a hot shower to quiet my nerves, agitated by coffee and an empty stomach. . . .
>   I have written a verse play *Dos Ranchos*.

Published two years later as *Dos Ranchos, or the Purification*, it was thereafter called solely *The Purification*.* In *Memoirs*, however, Tennessee Williams said that the play was written during the summer of 1940 in the Provincetown shack that he and Kip shared. Indeed, it would seem that *The Purification*, set as it is in New Mexico, more logically might first have been conceived in Provincetown rather than in New York, since Williams's visit with Frieda Lawrence had taken place the previous summer. Still, it was seldom that anything he wrote grew directly out of an experience, and very likely he completed the play in the spring of 1942. The *impressions* of things past, more than his re-creation of events, were what prompted him to write. *The Purification* is remarkable not only as his only play written in verse but as a relentless *tragedy*, as well, concerned as it is with the incestuous relationship of a brother and sister.

Elena, the sister, has been slain with an ax by her husband when he has discovered her lying with her brother, Rosalio. The play opens in a courtroom located in the ranch lands around Taos in the mid-1800s, and the husband, a rancher, has been brought to trial. As the story unfolds, his Indian servant cries out that Rosalio is "shameless," and the brother replies:

> *Yes, I am shameless—shameless.*
> *The kitchen-woman has spoken her kitchen truth.*
> *The loft of the barn was occupied by lovers*
> *not once, not twice, but time and time again,*
> *whenever our blood's rebellion broke down bars.*

---

*Critic Brooks Atkinson, writing in the *New York Times* of 6 June 1954, reviewed a performance of *The Purification* that he had seen in Dallas: "From the technical point of view, [it] is a compact, tense and vivid drama. From the artistic point of view, it is reverent and lovely." He felt that Williams used time efficiently and space organically, but he stressed that "the poetic approach to life is the rarest gift a playwright can have." To Williams, "playwriting [is] not a mechanical arrangement of material, but the expression of a point of view toward life in which feeling is more illuminating than logic or reason." And in this, Atkinson compared Williams not to Lawrence or Lorca, but to Chekhov.

Restless it was,
this coming of birds together
in heaven's center . . .
Plumage—song—the dizzy spirals of flight
all suddenly forced together
in one brief, burning conjunction!
Oh—oh—
a passionate little spasm of wings and throats
that clutched—and uttered—darkness . . .
Down
       down
              down
Afterwards, shattered,
we found our bodies in grass.[17]

The Purification was as close as Tennessee Williams ever came to dealing directly with incest, albeit in parable form. During the past year, he had hardly made any reference to Rose, although his mother no doubt gave him regular reports that would have informed him that since his last visit to Farmington in the fall of 1939 her condition had remained unchanged and her treatments had been halted. To Tom, this meant she was irretrievably lost, except as a memory, alternately recalled in pain and then shut out in self-defense. In a way, though, he was beginning now to deal with her reality as it affected his—that is, in his writings. "Weave back my sister's image," he cried out in *The Purification*, and in another play he was writing, *The Spinning Song*, "a play suggested by my sister's tragedy," there were also the first glimmerings of a drama that would evolve slowly over the next two years, haunting his thoughts until very gradually there would emerge from his and Rose's agony something imperishable he could give to the world.

To write such a play would take a strength he was surely developing but did not yet have, either in technique and style, or in his personal character, which was foundering in ungoverned self-indulgence, like a starving person brought to a feast. The changes that were surfacing in Tom may not have been outwardly attractive, but they were cabalistic systems of survival he had to learn in order to live in the jungle of the New York theatre and in the hard city itself. More than that, he had to endure—not only physically but emotionally—to fight off the always encroaching madness, the blue devils that had felled Rose. "For nothing contains you now, no, nothing contains you, lost little girl, my sister."

A Macon Summer

Outwardly, Tom's life was now drifting to no purpose. He was still scrounging meals and giving and taking favors wherever and whenever necessary. Always an asset, there was his obvious helplessness. This, together with the effects of wartime on his friends, aroused in them, as he had observed to his mother, more charitable attitudes. Any young man in—or out of—uniform in March 1942 might soon be fighting for his life on sea or in a foreign land. A new spirit of open friendliness among Americans, who felt their country and possibly they, too, were imperiled, made it easier than ever for Tom to move with the times—and from place to place. His friend Paul Bigelow had invited him to spend some time in Macon, Georgia, and Tom thought he might do that.

He would soon be moving from Fritz Bultman's apartment, having evidently brought a full dimension of chaos into Fritz's comparatively ordered existence. Preoccupied with his writing, Tom burned a number of coffeepots, among other absentminded fiascoes, which were climaxed by his bringing a contingent of merchant marines home on a Saturday night:

> Sunday—March 29—An inner equanimity of spirit sees me through and the neurosis thins out, dissipates itself.
>
> Today—I am dull but relatively at ease. Could not do any good writing. Last night the apt. was filled with merchant marines—this A.M. F's electric razor was missing.
>
> Which is *not* a *non sequitur*.

> Monday March 30—F. asked me to get out of the apt. last night, on account of "constantly disregarding his wishes"—precipitated, no doubt, by the loss of the razor. Holds me responsible for it.
>
> Don't know where I shall go. Very tired. I have $2.00.

But, as Tom said, there were always "surprising turns of fortune at the last ditch." Not long after leaving Fritz's apartment, he found himself living in the penthouse of songwriter Carley Mills. He had gone to dinner there and was invited to stay. Now his address was a swank 43 East Fiftieth Street, and his mode of dress went from bohemian to presentable. No one could have been more surprised than Tom, as he came to "the end of another journal: Yes—*En Avant*, and always *En Avant!* . . . I work on the comedy with Don and I eat well and regularly, I swim and live selfishly and cynically as a wise old alley cat. Integrity—I wonder. I keep a sort of it still: my own brand. I am not a snob and I can feel things deeply."

Tom not only felt things deeply; undercurrent hurts and long-ago resentments would surface suddenly, manifesting themselves in paranoid rages. In his book *Lost Friendships*, Donald Windham cited as odd, if not deranged, be-

havior the fact that Tennessee had greeted with wild laughter a newspaper
account of an old man who had burned himself to death when he fell asleep
with a lighted cigar in his mouth. The old man was Emil Kramer, who had
died of his burns in March 1942 (at the time Tom and Donald began their
collaboration) and who was the grandfather of Hazel Kramer, the love of
young Tom's life. Kramer and C. C. Williams had conspired to separate the
two at the time, in 1929, when it was their desire to attend the University of
Missouri together. Later, when Tom finally learned of Kramer's role in coming between him and Hazel, he openly hated and ridiculed the old man.

The move to East Fiftieth Street brought a change not only in Tom's attire, but in his attitude, as well. He had just turned thirty-one and was living
with a man of forty-five who was both kind and influential. Carley Mills was
also well known, having composed more than thirty published songs and having been an arranger for the popular radio program "Hit Parade" and for
orchestra leader Guy Lombardo. Tom's friends could say that he had never
had it so good, and he knew it.

Meanwhile, Audrey had written to him at Fritz's address, asking, "What's
happened on the new play and also what's happened to you? Why don't you
drop by once in a while and let me know what goes on in your life?"[18] In
response, Tom thanked her for forwarding a letter regarding wartime work.
"Sooner or later I will render some kind of patriotic service but not on paper.
I have not been in because I know you have troubles enough of your own
without being told about mine."[19] He had not been in because until now he
looked like the life he had been leading. He said he was a bad penny circulating among his various friends and hoped to go back south to work on *You
Touched Me!*—which he described as a comedy-romance.

On April 25, the actor-director Robert ("Bobby") Lewis initiated a project
that captured Tom's interest: an experimental production of *Mexican Mural*.
Lewis remembered that it was "a script I had read when it was submitted to a
Group Theatre contest for playwrights under twenty-five years of age. Tennessee Williams had won one hundred dollars for three one-act plays, but the
top prize of five hundred dollars went to Ramon Naya for *Mexican Mural*."[20]
Tom journeyed to one of the top floors of the Chanin Building on Forty-
second Street to see the quite literal Off-Broadway production and was
greatly impressed by Lewis's direction.

Among the cast members who were to become involved in the life and
career of Tennessee Williams were Libby Holman, the blues and torch
singer, and the young Montgomery Clift. Holman had decided she wanted to
become a dramatic actress and, in backing the play, called upon Lewis, her
former drama coach, to direct her. Monty was twenty-one and would in three
years' time be playing the lead in *You Touched Me!* John Anderson, critic for
the *New York Journal-American*, singled out Montgomery Clift in *Mexican
Mural*, saying that he had acted "with fine perception and great effectiveness.
If his vocal inflection and gesture remind us too often of Lunt, so, too, does

the greater quality of concentration in a young actor of unusual promise."[21] In 1940, Clift had played a strong supporting role with Alfred Lunt and his wife, Lynn Fontanne, in *There Shall Be No Night*, and it followed that Clift would be influenced, if not outright mesmerized, by the enormous talent of one of America's truly great actors. The play was not well received, though, and lasted only four performances.*

By mid-May, the wanderlust was stirring in Tom again. His hope of getting out of New York and basking in the sun was a spur, but, more than that, the situation with Carley Mills had become unbearable—a nightmare of drunken nights with the songwriter and his alcoholic friends, or so Tom said. But as Donald Windham pointed out, Tom was also adept at fabricating something for his own purpose, and the implication that he was being kept by an older man—an "auntie," as he described Mills—embarrassed him among his younger friends. There was no question that Carley Mills felt attached to him, nor that his young guest was biting the hand that fed him.

Characteristically, Tom wanted to leave the city at a time when it would have made more sense for him to stay. He and Windham were readying a rough draft of *You Touched Me!* for Audrey's perusal, and even then she would certainly need revisions before submitting it to producers. Instead, Tom used a blend of fact and fiction as an excuse to leave town. He wrote to Paul Bigelow, who had been in Macon for the past six months:

> Fritz and I have separated (and thereby hangs a tale or several tails) and life is relatively simple. Peut-etre trop simple—ah, well. At any rate, I am restless—planning, hoping, praying soon to leave New York. There are too many restrictions in my present situation and I was never one to brook very many restrictions. . . . I dream of collapsing a month or so on a beach in Florida, in which case I shall pass through Macon and see you. . . .

Tom had recently attended Fred Melton's surprise marriage to Sarah Marshall, a pretty young girl from Macon, and he told Paul, "Donnie is living at the West Side 'Y' and Fred is living with Sarah and her dog. I believe the dog is happy."[22]

By the end of the month, he wrote to Audrey that he had "cut away most of the adipose tissue" on *You Touched Me!* and said that he was "perfectly willing to acknowledge it now as a legitimate offspring." He added that David Merrick, then an associate of producer Herman Shumlin, had asked to see him. "He says their office has a strong social spirit—I think we might show him this script if he'll be careful of it."[23]

---

*In his excellent autobiography, *Slings and Arrows*, Robert Lewis wrote that long after his production, the *New York Times Magazine* "published a feature that posed the following question to a number of celebrities: 'What production that you have seen would you like to have revived?' " Tennessee Williams voted for *Mexican Mural*.

Tom planned to stay on in New York until the end of May, when, as he wrote home, Erwin Piscator was to present by invitation his one-act *This Property Is Condemned* at the New School. To Audrey, however, he complained that he had only heard about the program accidentally and too late to prevent it. "I attended one rehearsal, last night, and I hope that nobody will see it as it is done with complete lack of feeling, against a projection of 'War and Peace.' " He said he was "fed up with all of these little so-called art producers—they don't seem to have any better taste or feeling than the commercial ones." Then he crossed that out, appending "Bad temper." Donald Windham, though, claimed that Tom didn't hesitate to send out printed invitations to just about everyone he knew. His personal list, Windham said, included David Merrick, Libby Holman, Bobby Lewis, and Monty Clift.

Making no further comment about Piscator's production, Tom focused instead on his trip to Macon and the work he hoped to accomplish there. He asked Audrey, "Can you raise the transportation for me? The minimum is $12.50 but a few extra dollars would be useful—I think it is strategic to buy your first meal in a new town." The bait he offered her was hard to resist. "First I want to round-out the Lawrence play, then 'The Spinning Song's' second draft. Then I want to prepare a group of short stories to submit to book-publishers." He added that he had "a project with Mary Hunter which she will probably tell you about when it gets going."[24]

Hunter, a talented director-producer and radio actress, took an early interest in Tennessee Williams and particularly in his and Windham's *You Touched Me!* She and a young actor-playwright, Horton Foote, had formed the American Actors Company. Like Bobby Lewis and the Elia Kazans, who had been trying to found the Dollar Top Theatre, Hunter was endeavoring to establish an Off-Broadway theatre at popular prices.

Another lady producer whom Audrey targeted was Carly Wharton, one of the fortunate investors in *Life with Father*. With her coproducer, Martin Gabel, she had recently produced H. S. Kraft's *Café Crown*, which ran for 141 performances. Gabel had previously made known his belief in Tennessee Williams, and he and Wharton took an interest in being among the first to read *You Touched Me!*

The Broadway season that began in peacetime and ended with the nation at war was now a curious mélange of light-headed and serious fare. Among the moderately successful plays was John Steinbeck's *The Moon Is Down*, the one truly serious study of the Nazi tyranny in occupied Norway. But audiences generally were not in the mood to be serious, not in the theatre in any event, as evidenced by the predominance of such productions as Cole Porter's *Let's Face It*, Noël Coward's *Blithe Spirit*, and the slapstick *Sons O' Fun*.

On May 31, Tom left a note for Donald Windham at the Y, enclosing an invitation to *This Property Is Condemned* at the New School and mentioning that he had just written a new story, "One Arm," about a one-armed blond hustler in New Orleans. "One Arm" has since become a classic among Tennessee Williams's short stories and created a furor when it was first published, because of its ruthlessly honest treatment of male prostitution and capital punishment.

Writing to Paul, Tom asked, "Is there any swimming in Macon—a bicycle available? I have already been born, christened, married and divorced informally too many times so prefer not to be caught up in that cycle of events which occupy the Macon calendar, as you say—but only want peace and quiet and a single bed for a while. (I said for a *while*.)"[25]

The summer in Macon turned out to be providential. Had Tom had the money to take off for New Mexico, that's where he probably would have gone. Since he was at work on two plays, one about Lawrence and the other based on a story by him, it made sense for Tom to visit with Frieda Lawrence. But instead, he traveled south to Macon and once again found himself in the company of Paul Bigelow. The influence on Tom of a deeply disciplined older friend who was erudite, an avid reader, and a gifted raconteur was as profound as it was long lasting.

On his arrival in Macon, Tom was interviewed by a young sportswriter for the *Macon Telegraph*. Paul had called the paper, saying "a distinguished young man of letters, collaterally descended from the Macon poet Sidney Lanier, was his guest," and Tom told Windham that the article sounded rather like a sporting event but resulted in numerous invitations.

Writing to Jordan Massee, who was spending the summer on Sea Island, Paul commented that Tom had "hardly gone out of the house" since his arrival.

> He does go to swim every afternoon at the YMCA, but he has behaved with the greatest circumspection ever since he has been in Macon. I told him when he came, without mincing words, that it would not be possible for him to stay here unless he resigned himself to living exactly as he does when he is at home with his family in Clayton. . . . I spoke so sharply to him the first day he was here—because I felt I couldn't impress my circumstances and position on him any other way—that I wonder he stayed at all. . . . I felt that I could not face a struggle against Tenn's disorder and unawareness and I told him so in exactly those words. . . . I have never in my life spoken so unpleasantly to anybody whom I like, but . . . having decided years ago that no person has a right to confuse and obfuscate the purposes and roots of another's life, I had no alternative.[26]

Paul and Tom shared quarters on the top floor of a large Victorian house on a quiet street opposite a park. There were two bedrooms on either side of a wide hallway, which became more of a central living room. The owner, George Rosser, was a retired professor who lived alone and had been head of the department of ancient languages at Wesleyan College. Once, when Paul and Tom were on their way out to have their morning coffee, Dr. Rosser emerged from his bedroom and announced, "Gentlemen! I can recommend as the best stimulant to the appetite in the morning: the translation of at least one stanza from the Sanskrit!" Paul said, "Tennessee felt the good doctor to be very much like his grandfather—and the doctor was pleased with Tennessee. I had previously explained that Williams was not only a distinguished name but there were others, like the Dakins, in the family who were prominent. Dr. Rosser, who was a totally unreconstructed southerner, would have brief conversations, recalling to Tennessee names and exploits of ancestors from whom he could not quite believe he was descended."[27]

Tennessee would always look back nostalgically upon this time in Macon, and a year later he wrote:

> I am sure I felt a poetry in Macon that was only there for a stranger tired of New York and perfectly willing to be annihilated and absorbed by the elements. Still I will never forget those terribly hot sticky nights with the sound of Paul's electric fan droning across the hall and little flickers of heat lightning through those tiny transom windows as I sprawled on my enormous bed or the leather couch in the hall reading K.A.P. [Katherine Anne Porter] or Crane, the summer storm gradually approaching till all of a sudden it broke in a big windy clatter and splash and a lovely wet coolness rushed through all the windows and my eyes got heavy and I went to sleep.[28]

A Lost Friendship, A Friendship Gained

On Sunday, June 14, Tom began a new journal, entitled "The Macon Period":

> Been here a week and one day.
> I guess it's what I wanted.
> Quiet. Easy.
> A new problem came up where I should have found pleasure. . . . the pleasure problem is A. L. [Andrew Lyndon] . . . but it is all shadowed now by the new neurosis, the old conflict, desire vs. fear.

From their first meeting, Tom was attracted to Andrew Lyndon, whom Paul described as looking very young, much like a teenager, although he would soon be in navy officer training. In his journal, Tom asked, "Can it be that I *love* A?—and that's what does it?—Creates the block of fear?—And is it hopeless?"

> Monday—I demand of life some violence even when I run to peace. Is it the need of violence that I am the fugitive of? Then there is the block: the invented phantom adversary always where desire is. . . .

I receive a letter from Carley [Mills] with a check for ten dollars. Kindness. . . . Paul is sharp and irritable, probably because, out of ennui, I went [out] last night. The sexual neurosis continues to occupy the center of my emotional stage and I wonder if this recent invention will not be a fairly perennial one. —It blocks the one violence open. —No, I must meet it and be the master, it challenges the manhood in me.

An empty day—I go to the library and then swim. I come home to find Andrew—cool and remote and gossipy. Paul still cross. I write in this journal and wait for supper.

Next door to Dr. Rosser lived a Mrs. Griffin, who cooked meals in her home. Paul explained, "Not in her house, but her *home*, you understand. If you were known or recommended to her, you could go there and eat, and that's what we did occasionally."[29] In a letter to Windham, Tom dramatized his situation, saying that he was broke, that he owed Mrs. Griffin two weeks on his board and sat at her table warily, while Paul was heartily oblivious to the whole matter.

Paul's reaction to this was to laugh and remark, "Oh, no—those meals were all prearranged, since I was only too well aware of his financial condition. This is just Tennessee outlining a one-act play. I remember that summer so well, in almost every detail. Often it was hilarious, the times we had together. And I was never cross with him—only silent when he was contemplative or downcast."[30]

Tom usually turned to his journal when feeling downcast. "Tonight I may call H. Called everybody I knew—out. Walked a good ways with Paul—feel fairly quiet—a storm is coming up to cool things off. Tomorrow I swim at the lake with A. [Andrew]—Mailed letter to Carley—To bed—will try sleeping in the hall." Later, he wrote, "Just now woke up with nightmares—the vampire dream, this time about Paul—a frightful thing—also sex and Lyle Talbot [a film actor], of all things—the scene was the exact hall in which I was sleeping."

The lake where Tom swam was located on an estate about five miles out of town. Paul remembered it as "rather small, more like a pond, and seemed to me rather brackish. It belonged to a woman who was quite mad and who suddenly decided that it was not decent for men to go in swimming without trunks that didn't come to their knees and without tops. Since her sole income came from selling tickets and since the townspeople stopped coming when she imposed this restriction, she then announced that she had received further divine guidance and that everybody could go in the nude if they chose! Tennessee just adored that story."[31]

At the end of the month, Tom reported in his journal that he was feeling "Okay again. Writing really good scenes. Sex o.k." He had received "nice letters from Robert Lewis and David Merrick" and said, "Libby Holman likes plays and good prospect [for] production. I wrote a sketch for her. Pretty good." The letter from Merrick was forwarded by Audrey. She had sent *Stairs to the Roof* to him, and he told Tom that he had found it "interesting and beautifully written. However, I think it is unlikely that you can get a Broadway production. I don't think a producer would be likely to risk a more than average amount of production money on a fantasy or semi-fantasy at this time. Not unless it had a chorus of pretty girls, and [referring to *Lady in the Dark*] a part for Gertrude Lawrence." Merrick reminded him, "You told me that you were aware of the fact that your work was uncommercial, so I don't suppose this opinion will come as a disappointment. I don't think I should advise you to write about more commercial subjects because I feel that you write so well and with so much genuine feeling in your present form. Let's just hope that soon they'll get around to wanting something better."[32] Years later, David Merrick, at that time the most successful producer on Broadway, presented the later, more difficult, and certainly noncommercial plays of Tennessee Williams.

In her letter, Audrey mentioned that Alan Collins at Curtis Brown had finally heard from Frieda Lawrence concerning the rights to the story "You Touched Me." She had given her permission to proceed on the basis of 60 percent for the collaborators and 40 percent for the D. H. Lawrence estate. Audrey asked Tom to let her know how he felt about this. She said, "I still think maybe you should have a better deal and that you should get ideally 70%." She concluded with, "Let me know how things go in Macon and give my best to Mr. Bigelow whom I remember most vividly!"[33]

In his journal, he pondered:

> I lie on a couch in the hall and the great trees throw the wind through the windows like rushes of cool water. I read about Jack London. A hot and violent man, beautiful in his youth and his power, who wrote the brawling objective life of a young America. Not my kind but I like him. Paul says there are still those who knew him, in the Biblical sense, living on the West Coast—that he was "trade" for "everybody." I've read very little of his—*Burning Daylight* while [at Iowa]. I will probably get a good deal of work done this summer before the culminating disaster or the regeneration takes place—which will it be I wonder?

It was a near disaster. Early in July, on a dark night, Tom and Paul went strolling to escape the heat in their apartment. Tom had had his hair cut in the style of a Prussian crew cut; also, he was brandishing his long black cigarette holder and wearing his little dark-colored glasses. With the war on everyone's mind, any stranger in a place like Macon was looked upon with suspicion. Even in New York, Asians riding in the subways wore signs saying I AM CHINESE, and here was Tom looking like a road-company German spy. The result was predictable: "Picked up by police last night and questioned at Station because Paul and I were reported as 'suspicious characters' and I did not have my draft card. Surrounded by crowd on street. Shows the change of our world—personal freedom is gone, even the illusion of it."

Paul reminded him, "There *is* a war on, you know!" With the country being threatened with invasion on both coasts, the good people of Macon could readily imagine Hitler, like Sherman, marching through Georgia. Paul wrote to Jordan to express his distress that the Massees might be embarrassed: "Of course this has been profoundly disturbing to me. . . . Just as we were about to get on a bus what seemed like all the officers in Macon converged on us and demanded identification." He said, "It is true that Ten had on dark glasses which he must wear because of his bad eye, and that he has a haircut that makes him look outlandish and that we were both very dressed up . . . and of course I do not sound in the least like a Southerner." But the real problem was the fact that Tom did not have a draft card with him, and Paul, who did, had to explain why to "the captain of detectives."[34]

Simply remembering to carry a draft card would not seem to be much added responsibility, but this was Tom Williams. Once again, Audrey came to the rescue, responding to a wire from Paul: "I am enclosing herewith the very precious draft card of Tennessee Williams. I gave Tennessee a photostat copy of this which I suppose he's already lost. *Please both of you* be very careful of this since there are *no other copies* in my files."[35]

Thurs. [July 9]
My last day of work for a while—feel too shaky to add more. How will I fill the days?

Later—Read "Time"—News appalling—
What a world, what times confront us! Russia, Egypt crumbling—I cannot see ahead nor can anyone. But I suspect it will be especially hard for us who are not made to be warriors. Our little works may be lost.
Here in Macon the crickets make the only noise at this time of night. . . .

Saturday Midnight—I only laid off work 1 day—Today wrote "Dragon Country" [play]—I wistfully hope that tomorrow unless I feel better I'll lay off again. Tonight I am aching all over—half my bones cracking—felt about to collapse after supper. But days without work here are utterly void. . . .
It is curious how I have so little urge for the bed—of roses. Flying creatures—bugs—in the room—hate them. Just made a savage and successful attack on one. The sum of living organisms in the universe reduced by one. —I will go to bed now, drinking a glass of milk and maintaining some equanimity for the morrow. So long—10.

Sunday night, he wrote, "Well, I never did like Sunday. So I shouldn't complain now. I'd like to live a simple life with epic fornications."

A jumble of thoughts and emotions entangled his mind: He decided he would stop writing poetry, then composed a long poem called "The Angels of Fructification." He felt his poetry was "mostly crap" and declared, "Maybe my plays are a little bit better—I hope." Also, he was experiencing that "migratory feeling," as he informed Audrey, "and will probably forsake this town for one of the Florida beaches after a while."[36]

He had written both Audrey and Donald about Piscator having offered him a position in September as a publicity agent. He believed that not only would he receive money enough to live in New York but that the job could lead to an experimental production at the New School of *You Touched Me!*—which he felt would be better than endless revisions.

He urged Donald to call on William Saroyan at his suite in the Hampshire House, noting that, according to *The New Yorker*, Saroyan had "swindled" sixty thousand dollars from Louis B. Mayer, head of Metro-Goldwyn-Mayer. He wanted to know how Saroyan had managed it.

He also mentioned that Carley Mills had sent him a ten-dollar check, that Mills had written boastfully about his latest song being introduced by the Ink Spots, Guy Lombardo, and Danny Kaye, and that he would probably be insufferable after this. The song, "If I Cared," written to Tom, ran, "If I cared a little bit less and you cared a little bit more," lyrics that Tom might have written to Kip.

Tom had been discussing "mental double exposure—the intrusion of self-consciousness into experience" with a friend. "Apparently he has suffered a good deal though perhaps he is still an amateur beside me."

> Today the writing slowed a bit. I begin to feel qualms about "Dragon Country." It is too heavy and lacks grace and charm. Too macabre. A sombre play has to be very spare and angular. When you fill it out, it seems blotchy, pestilential.
> You must keep the lines sharp and clean—tragedy is austere.
> You get the effect with fewer lines than you are inclined to use.

He had just read O'Neill's *Desire Under the Elms* and felt the writing to be "incredibly bad." He also mentioned receiving "a sad letter from Mother—The old man is being devilish."

By mid-July, Tom had departed for Atlanta for a weekend, which "contained an evening with Eros but otherwise was sorrowful—Dull and dull. . . . The cold has gone on my chest and this morning I observe traces of blood in my sputum." He said that he had come home to work on *You Touched Me!* but that "the story is wooden, the writing is awkward, only the idea is good, the result is shit. . . . I think of Saroyan and how beautifully and effortlessly he puts words together—I feel hopeless."

Paul made a brief visit to Sea Island at the end of July and afterward wrote to Jordan, "I returned to find that Ten has revised the third act of his play once more and so I must rush to retype it. Audrey will have fits! The play is now two weeks over-due in her office. . . . I shall have to check it all over again, and get it ready to mail, for I could not trust him to put the pages together in numerical order."[37]

Tom wrote: "We read over the play to check the final draft . . . and while it is rather shabbily contrived—or maybe *very* shabbily contrived—still I feel it may very well have the elements of a successful play. In other words, I have hope it will sell."

About style, he said, "I think I should work for the simplest. . . . In other words, fewer and better subjects. One big project—a play or a truly challenging story." He had written Audrey to say that he had completed two one-act plays and was in the middle of a third short play "about the deep South, under the composite title of 'Dragon Country.' The third may expand into a fairly long script."[38]

Tom also wrote to producer Mary Hunter, hoping to rouse her interest in his and Donald's play. He said that he was laboring by day at his writing in an attic and by night as a busboy at the Pig n'Whistle ("Another one-act olio," according to Bigelow). "As for work," he said, "I have finally finished and just now sent off to Audrey the Dh. [*sic*] Lawrence short story play. The second draft of it took much longer than I had expected. I want Audrey to show you a copy when she is ready to send them about. But I have also had time to write a group of short plays about the deep South under the composite title of 'Dragon Country.' "[39]

Tom added that he had had encouraging letters from Bobby Lewis, who had said he would like to direct his one-acts in the fall with Libby Holman but was now employed at Twentieth Century–Fox as dialogue director. Tom inquired after Horton Foote, who recalled that Tom's unproduced one-act plays "were read avidly by all who could get copies, and many writers at the time were heartened and inspired by them. Tennessee's work has been known to us for so long now, it is almost impossible to describe what it meant to read these then unknown plays for the first time."[40]

Audrey was not long in acknowledging receipt of *You Touched Me!* "I have just begun reading it and will write you more fully when I finish it. I am very happy that the play really is a full-length script (for a change)." She wanted to know the specifics of his agreement with Donald and what split of percentages had been agreed upon. "May I suggest to you that if you've done all the writing, which I suspect, that you should get the greater percentage."[41]

Paul wrote to Jordan, discussing Tom and Donald Windham's collaboration:

Audrey is already mad as hops because of Donnie's intrusion into the scene as collaborator and has written (this is *very* confidential) that she does not think the contract between Tenn and Donnie should be on a fifty-fifty basis since she is absolutely certain that Tenn did all the work— she added—"probably with Mr. Bigelow's advice and assistance." . . . I told Tenn this morning that I would never reveal that I had anything whatsoever to do with the play, except to type it, and that I will certainly tell Audrey whenever we meet again that the play is entirely Tenn's work and that I did nothing with it. Tenn is devoted to Donnie and he is afraid that his feelings will be hurt if the truth is even suspected—but Audrey is too alert and too astute a judge of dramatic writing not to know exactly what happened, although I suppose for the sake of peace she is going to pretend she accepts Tenn's version of his collaboration.[42]

What Audrey suspected is what Tom wanted her to believe and what Paul also believed, having seen him at work on the script these past weeks and having typed what he thought was the completed play. In an earlier letter written to Jordan when Tom first arrived in Macon, Paul said that "he tells me, reluctantly I think, that Donnie did not turn out to be a good collaborator and that he must re-write the entire play he did with him before Audrey will submit it to anybody."[43] In actuality, Donald had contributed much to the draft that Tom took to Macon and would also make further revisions during the months before the play's New York production in 1945. Tennessee Williams's pride of authorship, his inability to accept a collaboration, and the fact that he never did anything to correct a false impression—in fact, he perpetuated the myth that he alone had authored *You Touched Me!*—became some of the erosive factors in what with time Donald Windham would label a lost friendship.

Although Tom often struggled against his emotional insecurity and pervasive fears, he would always look back nostalgically upon his summer in Macon and the bond he formed with Paul Bigelow. Other than Andrew Lyndon, he had made no lasting friends but made instead careful note of Macon society, in particular one Margaret Lewis Powell, a lively young woman known to her friends as "Maggie the Cat." Paul confided in Jordan: "It has not been completely easy for me to have him here, as you know, for it is like having a destructive, unretentive child to supervise day and night—I feel at times like a lost-property bureau in a large railway station—but considering that his work is far more tranquil and rhythmic than before . . . really exquisite and poetic writing, I think he has justified himself in terms of friendship for the wearing attributes which he cannot help. More and more I understand that a great part of his personality is shaped by his actual physical inability to meet the world . . . and his decreasing ability to see. . . . Also, for the first time, he has talked to me about his sister, who is confined in an asylum and will never be released, and there is apparently a gnawing fear that . . . the same mental disarrangement may develop in him. That is the major reason why he writes so constantly and so frantically. . . . I think he feels that Hart Crane, whom he admires more than any other modern poet, grew gradually demented and that he thinks there is a parallel there and that he must write more than Crane did, understanding what is happening to him, as Crane did not."[44]

23

One Hand in Space

August–December 1942

By mid-August, Paul had returned to Sea Island, while Tom traveled down the Florida coast to St. Augustine. He wrote to Andrew Lyndon that he was sunburned and in torment but that he had received a wire from Bigelow with the welcome news that one of his "remittance letters is being forwarded." It was a damn good thing, he said, as he was down to "smoking my last cigarette on the veranda of this old ante-ante-bellum house in the old, cheap, and unfashionable part of town, which is the part I always like best, luckily."[1]

> Dear Saint Paul—
> Dr. Rosser is right about you!—you are *spirituelle*. I shall have you canonized, only one degree lower than my Grandmother, when you "pass over." (Alas, I'm afraid I shall precede you!) I ate 1 hamburger, 1 doughnut, 1 cup of coffee yesterday and smoked 2 cigarettes. The letter got here at *noon* today. My dear, I was getting ready to eat a jar of vaseline and a tube of nauseous pink toothpaste! Well, the letter contained $10.00 cash—isn't that lucky? And I am to write when I need more.
> My maternal progenitors have the patience of Job.
> Paul, you would *adore* this place—but I will say no more.
> I must go out *quickly* and *eat*—I haven't in nearly *16* hours. Can you believe it?
> What a *fate* for the termite *queen!!!*
>
> Love—
> 10./[2]

It was Edwina, not her "progenitors," who came through with a ten-dollar bill and assured him that if he wanted to return home, she would also send the fare. Her letter again stressed Grand's failing health: "Down to eighty-three pounds, only, and can't seem to gain. I really dread next winter for her."[3] Ominously, there was no word about Rose.

Tom was relieved to hear from Windham that he liked what he hoped would be the final draft of their play. He told Donald that it had become impossible for him to make an objective judgment and knew only that he was desperate for it to succeed. Another letter went off to Paul, mentioning that he was staying with "a *horrid* little person—*venomous. My God!* I talked to her for quite a while before I introduced myself and she thought it ridiculous that a person with literary taste should like Thomas Wolfe."[4] Tom had been reading *You Can't Go Home Again* and said in his journal, "Scene after scene has the stamp of genius. The picture of Webber's homecoming—particularly Randy and his boss—are as fine as anything of the kind that I have seen—*finer*—men like Wolfe—and the mess of this world—how do you reconcile it? You don't—can't. The world is ruled by Randy's bosses. The Tom Wolfes are observers—but their work makes them a threat to evil masters. They lift the scales from the slaves' eyes—if the slaves dare to let them."

On his first day in St. Augustine, he wrote that he had gone immediately to the beach. He exclaimed, "Oh, how good it was to meet the ocean again! I swam and gargled the cold salt water and plunged and capered."

> Alone. Boys on the beach but I talked to no one. A rain came up. I put my clothes under a boat and swam. Rain flattened water—silver sheet to plunge around in. Walked home across causeway.
>
> Disagreeable aspect here is suspicion of strangers because of saboteur scare. I was stopped on bridge for identification and I feel self-conscious walking about town. My capital is about 1.70 to last till hypothetical letters arrive. . . . The spectre of destitution is, of course, not far distant.

He said he would try to meet someone—"solitude is the bogey man, nothing is fun when you are lonely." But he met no one and on the way home was stopped again on the bridge and questioned.

> *Monday*—Another lonely day. I get up early, read at library. . . . I do some good writings on the play which I am making from The Malediction [short story]. It has a promising look, so I write [Herbert] Berghof that I have a play for him to act in. Then the beach and I am spurned by the kid I tried to talk to—he is painting his boat and is not inclined to be friendly. I can feel only a little pleasure in the beach alone. Alone, I return home, and walk the whole long way. Alone to eat and alone I wander a long ways, through an ancient cemetery, around the old fortress. I go and sit in a bar—alone. Return home alone. I write down a new poem in my collection, I smoke a cig., I brood—gloomily.
>
> Now I prepare to sleep. Alone.

The next day, he noted in his journal that he had read the New York reviews of William Saroyan's twin bill of *Across the Board on Tomorrow Morning* and *Talking to You.* Staged by Saroyan, the program lasted only eight performances. "I was pleased to find the critics took him to task. The son-of-a-bitch had it coming. Writing is not that easy even for a genius with $60,000—yes, I am envious and malicious."

> *Sunday*—Yesterday I rode my bike 30 miles up to Jacksonville Beach and even further back, by moonlight—a physical ordeal but it was good for me. Saw a white horse standing motionless in a clearing, the moon just brightening and a little stream bubbling in the ditch. The horse was large and stood there like a marble statue looking at me, around it great trees, moss-draped, and dusk falling. . . . I have written home for bus-fare to St. Louis. It appears the die is cast and I go back *again!* Can't I ever get away?—and under the worst circumstances. How can I face them, answer all their questions? My father—how to meet him again? Will I be able to do it?—or will I run away again?—New York?—and cheat my poor mother who goes without a servant to keep me going?
>
> Oh, but this business of dragging myself back before them, again unsuccessful, again dependent, it is very, very hard for me to accept. Can I? Will I?—Je ne sais pas.

The trip to St. Augustine, he felt, had been a sorry idea, leaving him "wretched with loneliness and ennui. It begins to have a very stale, fetid atmosphere, this continual wretchedness, self-pity, and weariness of mine." Later, he tried to explain, "What taunts me worst is my inability to make contact with the people, the world. I remain one and separate among them. My tongue is locked. I float among them in a private dream and shyness forbids speech and union. This is not always so. A sudden touch will release me. Once out, I am free and approachable. I need the solvent which hasn't come to me here, this time."

> *Mon. Night*—This evening a stranger picked me up. A common and seedy-looking young Jew with a thick accent. I was absurdly happy. For the first time since my arrival I had a companion. I took him all over town, bought him a beer, found him a place for the night. He was a hitchhiker with a bag of cheese and rolls for food. It was like cool water after hot thirst, just being *with* somebody. Left me quiet and relaxed.
>
> I went home and read Robinson Jeffers' extraordinarily good and bad verse.

While waiting for his fare home, and on going to the library, he was struck with the idea of writing a play about Don Quixote. "The tragedy of the ideal—the truth of the matter is that all human ideals have been hats too big for the human head. Chivalry—democracy—Christianity—the Hellenic ideal of intellectual purity (the one I find most appealing) are too big a hat! Undoubtedly the Fascist 'ideal' of force which we are *supposed* to be fighting—is a closed fist. But will not the immemorial Don Quixote of the race—rebel at wearing a hat that fits with such humiliating precision? No, the hopeful thing is still that we wish we had bigger skulls, not smaller hats to wear." About a decade later, the play would emerge as *Camino Real*.

By the end of August, Tom had received the money to return to St. Louis. Stopping in Jacksonville en route, he wrote Paul Bigelow that to avoid going home he had applied for night work as a typist at the U.S. Engineer Office. Then he fired off postcards to both Paul and Donald announcing the same news: He had gotten a job operating a teletype, with hours 11:00 P.M. to 7:00 A.M., for a salary of $120 a month. He told Audrey that he had been given "a medical examination, been fingerprinted, sworn in twice, made out my will and infinite endless papers all day. Oh, God, how I loathe this sort of thing, this reduction of man to . . ."[5] He didn't need to finish it.

Erwin Piscator had written to say that, since he had not heard from Tom, he was "forced to make other arrangements" regarding his job proposal. "Piscator and I have been exchanging sharp letters," Tom told Paul. "I sent him an envelope full of sand from the beach at St. Augustine and suggested that he blow on it and tell my fortune. I received in return an irate letter saying the sand had spilt in his brief-case and he was unpleasantly reminded of me everytime he opened it. I replied that it was a privilege to be remembered at all. That I deeply appreciated his feeling that I should be 'free to write' and so I had gotten a job copying telegrams for the government."[6] He said he expected to hear from Piscator again, since he was not one to relinquish the last word.

Audrey wrote to Paul Bigelow, "I have just had a long letter from Tennessee Williams who is, as you know, now helping the United States Government to function. It might be just as well if Tennessee controlled the whole thing. It would at least have beauty of sound and might signify as much and more than it does sometimes while it is being run by gentlemen who are considered business men."[7]

England, His England

It was one thing for Tom to write a play about D. H. Lawrence, quite another for him to adapt Lawrence's short story "You Touched Me." Lawrence, setting his fragile story in post–World War I England and in the Pottery House of Ted Rockley, etched the picture of a shy, sexually repressed young Englishwoman, Matilda Rockley, who is dominated by her elder old-maid sister, Emmie. Rockley's adopted "charity-boy," Hadrian, had at age fifteen gone abroad and enlisted in the Canadian army, but he returns, to be confronted by Emmie's hostility, born of her fear that her ailing father will leave his fortune to his son. Rockley is, in fact, trying to arrange a marriage that he hopes will take place between Matilda and Hadrian—an unromantic marriage of convenience, as it turns out, but one that releases the physically imprisoned Matilda.

On top of these frail underpinnings, Tom and Donald sought to build a three-act structure in *You Touched Me!* Audrey was encouraged that at last Tom was grappling with a full-length play, but what neither she nor Donald nor Paul could suspect was a different alchemy at work. In the relationship of Matilda and her adopted brother, Hadrian, with Emmie, there were emerging the character traits of Laura and Tom Wingfield and their mother, Amanda, in *The Glass Menagerie*. The ghost of one play was hovering over the life of the other.

Tom had received a lengthy criticism by Alan Collins of Curtis Brown Ltd., D. H. Lawrence's agents, who said that *You Touched Me!* was "damned good" but took exception to the character of Matilda, saying that she would not be believable "even in hooped skirts"—that her "fear of the world" was neither explained nor understandable. Tom wrote Paul that he didn't see anything incomprehensible in Matilda. "These successful Broadway people cannot conceive of anybody being afraid of anything but the Axis or a decline in the market."[8] In Matilda, Tom discerned a pathetic figure locked not so much in the tyranny of her jealous sister as in a puritanical fear of sex—that is, until Hadrian, the figurative fox in a chicken coop, sets her free in a marriage of love, not convenience. Although a highly romanticized comedy, *You Touched Me!* was at least consistent with the Lawrencian point of view in the triumph of the spiritual over the sensually inhibited.

Audrey had forwarded Collins's letter, and in giving it more serious consideration, Tom sent her a remarkable analysis both of his personal self and of him as an artist.

Anent Matilda—
Her danger *is* psychological. Without intervention, she would drift into that complete split with reality which is schizophrenic. The fear of the world, the fight to face it and not run away, is the realest in all experience to *me*, and when I use it in my work, I am always surprised that it does not communicate clearly to others. Perhaps that is the trouble with writing one's *self* too much. The great psychological trauma of my life was my sister's tragedy, who had the same precarious balance of nerves that I have to live with, and who found it too much and escaped as Matilda is in danger of escaping. I want this danger to be clearly stated, but I do not want her character to have an unhealthy *clinical* aspect as Val's did in "Battle." . . . But there is no reason why a thing so tragically common in human experience as simple fear of reality cannot be feelingly communicated in drama and used as the all-powerful motivation that it *is* in all too many lives. . . . It is hard for a person with so many problems regarded as "special" (they are not *really* so) to address audiences which

are necessarily composed largely of extravert personalities—to talk to them about what is vitally *important* and *clear* to himself *without* bewildering and offending them with a sense of exaggeration. This, I suppose, is my great creative problem, if I may be permitted to assume one; if I take the easy way out and simply not deal with things I know *best*, I am being cowardly about it and really precluding what might be an individual, special contribution. But this problem is ubiquitous in my work. And the more I write from my inside, the more it will emerge. It is the purification, I guess.[9]

Although *You Touched Me!* was obscured by the overwhelming success of *The Glass Menagerie*, it was important not only in its own right but also in the metamorphosis of Tom into Tennessee Williams, of person into artist. Much of this change had been taking place in his short stories and one-act plays, but now there was another full-length play, which John Gassner felt was well structured and a major step forward from *Battle of Angels*. It was a debt Tom owed to Donald Windham, and he knew it. But at the same time, he had laid the groundwork for a lasting misunderstanding. Paul, who had returned to New York, wrote Jordan: "Audrey won't consult Donnie at all, and her air with me is that of a conspirator—she knows perfectly well that I helped Tenn with that play last summer and when I say Tenn decided to do this or that, she smiles very knowingly. . . . I didn't want her to regard me as a collaborator at all, or know that I did work on it."[10]

Tom had informed Audrey, "The 50/50 basis is okay with me, and all in all since Donnie discovered the story which intrigued me so much (I don't think it is *slight*, for it has all the suggestion of a lot more) he does have an equal proprietorship. I want money, yes—but mostly I want an *audience*. If I get *that*, I am satisfied, for then I can throw in their faces the things they won't take till they know me, all the little, helpless, unspoken-for crowd of sheep-like creatures I seem to find in the world and wish Quixotically to be the equally little and helpless voice of."[11]

As much as the playwright Tennessee Williams was emerging in these letters to Audrey, as in time he would emerge in the theatre, to the War Department he was no one other than Thomas Lanier Williams, No. 1340, Jacksonville District. He was satisfied with his new job as long as he could work the night shift and had enough money to buy cigarettes and meals. He wasn't able to save any money and discovered it was a newfound luxury just to order a good meal and cuba libres instead of beer. He had rented a bicycle and discovered a fantastic dive on Ocean Street overrun with servicemen.

But he was still being plagued by his blue devils, reporting that they "have barely left me for a day since St. Augustine. I have not tried to bridge them." His anxiety was in all likelihood precipitated by news from his mother. As he related to Paul, "I received a most horribly distressing letter from home about my father's ill treatment of my grandparents and I have written him in a coldly passionate fury exactly what I feel about his rudeness to these helpless old people . . . the man is evidently altogether out of his mind. He has been for most of his life, but has managed to conceal it from the world outside our own house." Tom urged his mother to leave, for the three of them simply to walk out for good. "It is just as well I didn't go home for I am sure that I would have attempted to murder him—successfully I hope."[12]

At the same time, he complained about receiving an "appalling" letter from Audrey. "She apparently wants me to come to New York and re-write 'You Touched Me' as a modern play against the background of the present war, upon the bare possibility—or meagre likelihood—that it would then be suitable to show to Langner and Helburn of the Theatre Guild. This being the opinion of John Gassner. . . . I am really painfully surprised at Audrey's writing me such a letter, and that she should suggest I give up my job to come to N.Y. for such a slight prospect . . . I would have to find some means to maintain myself—Mother would be disgusted at me for giving up work here."[13]

> Sunday—Oct. 11, 1942
> Been here nearly a month and a half. Two things have happened:
> (1) The hope of immediate salvation from play dispelled by news I have to re-write—from Audrey. Wants me to return to New York.
> (2) Sex—a rather tender but not quite adequate relation with a simple adolescent. Puppy love sort of thing, which I only press as far as the limit of prudence. Still, an attachment exists, and this is an act of God, as it provides my sole comfort. That is, aside from having money for an abundance of food. . . .
> Done—attempted—no work. Well, it will soon end, this period.
> I will accept Paul's and Audrey's suggestion and quit job and go back to New York probably the sixteenth [of November].

He had written Paul about an affair he was having with a blond teenager who worked as a movie usher and spent hours in front of a mirror fixing a wave in his hair. He admitted, "I am pretty tired of it here. The affair last mentioned has become more of a trial than a joy. That is the trouble with beautiful adolescents, at first they make you feel like June in January but soon it becomes more like January in June. The gulf of experience is too vast to bridge with understanding or any hope of it even. And simplicity is a clean piece of paper on which ugly words can be written as well as good ones."[14] It had been only two years since the summer in Provincetown when Tom cried out his love for "dear Kip." Now *he* was separating from someone who may well have uttered the same cry, suffered the same hurt, and lived to visit it on some innocent.

* * *

Audrey agreed with John Gassner that the chief problem with *You Touched Me!* was that "it is not identified with any particular period or locale." Gassner, she said, believed "if you were at all sympathetic with bringing the play up to date and making the action take place in an English village now, that the values of the play might be enhanced greatly. How much you know about contemporary life in England is something I don't know. However, that remarkable friend of yours, Paul Bigelow, assures me that he can get sufficient data for you from one or two friends who have recently returned from England."

She cautioned him, though, not to arrive in New York expecting anything definite to happen. "If you can afford to come and stay here a while and do some work I think it will all be on the right side for you and the play."[15] She also mentioned that Paul felt he had a friend who would put Tom up. For once, Tom was hesitant. He was not in agreement with Audrey and John Gassner about changing the period of the play to the present time and he thought that

> it really ought to be laid at the turn of the century. The quaintness and earnestness of the characters, even the poetic quality of the writing are distorted by the unnatural effort to fit them into an immediate present. . . . Without it we would have a clear and beautiful play with all its meaning and message intact and the quaintness—with a period background—would only make it more charming.

He told Audrey that Donald was in agreement with him and felt that "Mr. Gassner's advice, on which the present changes were made, was probably very casually given and without much genuine feeling for the play or the authors."[16]

Paul, who had returned to New York for painful treatments on his jaw, wrote a long critique suggesting script changes, and they gave Tom pause: "I found them extremely helpful and the term 'officious' is quite the contrary of anything applicable to your kindness in making them out, and I am hoping to get all the assistance from you you're willing to give in preparing the final draft in New York." He was also reminded that it was John Gassner who guided *Battle of Angels* to a Theatre Guild production. The important thing now was to get *You Touched Me!* produced, no matter what. If the consensus was to give the play a contemporary milieu, then he was willing to make the necessary revisions.

Tom expressed amazement to Paul over the apparent success of yet another Saroyan one-act play, *Hello, Out There*. On a double bill with G. K. Chesterton's *Magic*, Eddie Dowling not only produced and directed both plays but also starred opposite the lovely Julie Haydon. Dowling and Haydon had appeared with great success in Saroyan's *The Time of Your Life* and would act together again in Tennessee Williams's *The Glass Menagerie*. "When I read Atkinson's review," Tom commented, "I said to myself, 'Saroyan has gone in the army.' Three days later the confirmation of this appeared in the paper. I think it should be bruited about—before I return to New York—that I am in a branch of the military service. I think any success in the theatre is dependent upon such things at this time. It is a pity that Donnie was rejected."

He said that he was spiritually prepared for a return to New York, but "nervously and physically not." He had just written a "very difficult letter of resignation to be effective, provided I can possibly be replaced, on the first of November. I think if we are immured more or less in the artist's studio for about a week after my arrival, with our respective manuscripts for a sort of literary factory as Clark Mills and I once had, we will get everything thrashed out and ready to meet the world with."[17]

Before he left for New York, Tom wrote a chillingly ominous poem:

Lament for the Moths

A plague has stricken the moths, the moths are dying,
their bodies are flakes of bronze on the carpets lying.
Enemies of the delicate everywhere
have breathed a pestilent mist into the air.

////////
Manhattan Period VIII
The little slants at the top of the page are my computation of the times I've been in N.Y. with periods abroad being the separations. This is the eighth period, now under way for a week.

I am well, I am somewhat more than reasonably in good spirits. The 2 mos. employment in Jacksonville, a regular life with plenty of food and the fairly pleasant circumstances, gave me a new lease on life, badly needed after the hellishly close call in St. Augustine and the dragging summer in Macon, in that stifling attic. . . . Lincoln Kirstein [founder of the magazine *The Dance Index* and the School of American Ballet], through Donnie, has taken a sudden interest in my verse, though not, perhaps, a very judicial one. He may be helpful.

The play re-write, third and final, is complete. . . . For sex—two affairs, a beautiful cold prostitute from Texas, and all that implies—and a solid mature, rather Rubenesque person met in the steam room of this establishment whom I fucked twice both ways but probably won't look up again.

The sweet thrill of merely caressing my little one in Jacksonville was better than any of these.

The return to New York held all of the horrors Tom most feared. But, as a form of compensation he was unable to perceive then, the city offered him on this occasion an unusual opportunity to meet a variety of people—friends and acquaintances—who would eventually become influential in advancing his career. Such money as he had managed to save during the last two weeks on the job was meager and did not last very long.

By mid-November, he was living in a furnished room uptown, having hastily departed after one night's tenancy from the apartment-studio of painter Karl Free, whose eccentricities were apparently too much even for Tom. The world of painters and sculptors was populated then as now by as mad a collection of eccentrics as Tom would ever encounter, including those in the theatre. Among them was a painter, Olive Leonard, whom Williams first met in New Orleans, when she was known as Olive Leonhart and when her huge canvases were covered over solely with splashes of black and white oils. As Paul recalled, she would haughtily explain, "You see, I have *never* considered the practicalities of the use of color," a proclamation that greatly amused Tom and lingered in his memory. Years later, Olive would reappear as Moise in his novel *Moise and the World of Reason.*

Tom had met another struggling artist, Tony Smith, through Fritz Bultman. Tony became acquainted with Fritz when they studied in Chicago's New Bauhaus, modeled on the famed German school, which was destroyed by Hitler in 1933. Tom was struck by Tony's vivid red beard and vigorous demeanor and by his emerging talents and fame as a sculptor, painter, writer, and teacher among the modernists of art, architecture, and industrial design. They were to become lifelong friends.

During these last weeks of 1942, Tom reached, as Donald said, the absolute nadir in terms of his appearance. Although Edwina would occasionally send him shoe samples and other clothes, these were usually misplaced or simply left behind in a dirty heap as he moved from one place to another. He still had not rid himself of a persistent chest cold and, lacking clean handkerchiefs, was constantly coughing up sputum in wads of tissue that he then stuffed into his pockets.

Fred Melton and his wife, Sarah, planned a Thanksgiving vacation in Macon, and they agreed that Tom could stay in their Leroy Street apartment until they returned—*provided* that Windham stay there, too, to protect the place. Donald helped Tom to move and recalled that his room was a total disaster, his dirty clothes, shoes, and manuscripts either scattered around the room or piled up in corners. Windham was not being so much critical as concerned about his friend's habit of disappearing for days and the effect his erratic behavior had on his health.

By Thanksgiving, Melton had returned to his apartment, Sarah remaining in Macon for another week, and the three boarded a Fifth Avenue bus uptown to Lincoln Kirstein's apartment for a sumptuous Thanksgiving dinner. The following day, Tom moved back into the West Sixty-third Street YMCA for a while, until his money ran out. Paul, meanwhile, was assisting him in editing yet another revision of *You Touched Me!*—which had been requested by producer Carly Wharton. Tom told Windham that Bigelow had a real talent for editing, something he felt they both lacked. The revisions had mainly to do with making a change of setting and event to present-day wartime England. An epigraph reads "Revised version 'B' Nov 1942—'One must speak for life and growth amid all this mass of destruction and disintegration—D. H. Lawrence.' "[18]

With Lawrence's story originally set in the aftermath of World War I, to wrest it from that context was, as both Windham and Williams must have known, both a commercial expedient and a violation of the story's simple intent. Although one could understand John Gassner's reasoning as to why he felt the play should be placed in the present time and related in some way to the world conflict—it being a year since the attack on Pearl Harbor—there were impressive arguments against such a decision. The fact that a number of plays about the war, albeit more directly related, were on Broadway gave producer Carly Wharton pause. Commercially, the most successful was Maxwell Anderson's *The Eve of St. Mark*, which had opened in October and ran for 291 performances. Others with war themes or those crudely patriotic were: Emlyn Williams's *The Morning Star*; Clifford Odets's adaptation of Konstantin Simonov's *The Russian People*; D. L. James's *Winter Soldiers*, presented by Erwin Piscator; and Irving Berlin's drumbeating *This Is the Army*. Tom and Donald's play *You Touched Me!*—conceived and written as a sensitive romantic comedy—was never intended to suffer such inappropriate comparison, and, ironically, when finally produced in the fall of 1945, the war had ended and so had the play's contrived relevancy.

By December, everything Tom owned was either in hock or sold, including his typewriter. Donald was working in the office of *The Dance Index* magazine, and he remembered Tom coming in almost daily to type copies of his poems for Windham to give to Lincoln Kirstein, who said that he would submit them to his friend James Laughlin, the publisher of New Directions. It was during this time that Laughlin first met Tennessee Williams; he recalled, "I was at a cocktail party in New York . . . being given by Lincoln Kirstein, one of my idols. It was a pretty big apartment, and I could see this little fellow with baggy pants and a torn sweater sitting all by himself and looking very nervous. And I was a little nervous too, so I went over to talk to him. We started talking and we found out that we both loved Hart Crane, and we became almost instant friends."*[19]

---

*Shortly afterward, Tom wrote to Laughlin, saying, "I hope you remember our talk about my poems at Lincoln's Sunday night recently." He wondered if, instead of sending his poems, "it would not be better for us to get together and sort of go over and discuss them informally." He assured him that he would not be "the sensitive poet in the grand manner"; that their meeting would be "extremely simple and we would part on good terms even if you advised me to devote

Dec. 12—about 1:00 A.M.

Been here over a month now. Nothing really has happened to alter the situation. The play has been the rounds for about 2 weeks. One producer has shown interest. The others not heard from. I worked 2 days and quit—too dreary—teletype operator at British Purchasing Commission. Could not sit still. Now I have borrowed 50c (borrowed from Donnie) and nothing definite to depend on. I see Donnie every day, nearly—I feel a deep fondness for him and the resentment about sharing the play seems trifling now.

I have been happy, I suppose. Health good enough, no neuroses. An animal pleasure in things.

But there must be more important things to come.

I wait for them. I am waiting. In the meantime I must be patient and wise—and *good*. I must be a good boy. Goodbye.

The question of his being "a good boy"—let alone wise—could be raised, considering the description that Windham gave of their behavior in and out of the YMCA. Being a pair of civilians in wartime, and therefore considered suspect of most anything, left them more the prey than the servicemen they were pursuing in places like the Crossroads Bar at the Times Square stop of the Seventh Avenue subway. Windham said that Tom from the time they first met was equally shy as he was bold, and his sexual desire drove him to proposition or make a pass at anyone he found attractive.

Dec. 14—

Time roars quietly along. I have about $2.00 left and no job and the room rent overdue. . . .

As usual life in N.Y. seems diverting and formless. And not very much life-like. . . .

[Carly] Wharton seems on verge of buying play. Bigelow and I had lunch with her today.

I then went to Employment Agency. May go out of town for hotel work. Tomorrow. Unless Wharton buys play immediately—

80c left, room rent 4 days overdue.

Supper at Lincoln Kirstein's with Donnie. Fun. I am closer to D. than anyone else. Paul and I seem to be drifting apart. A mutual distrust seems to come between us. I hate distrust. I want so badly to believe in people. Their affection and honesty and good faith. I must try to be the things I want in others. Well, I am honest. Much as I like Paul, I don't believe he is. I hope this feeling is an illusion and will pass away. It frightens me. We were so close last summer and he's been so good to me.

myself exclusively to the theatre for the rest of my life." (TW to James Laughlin, letter, 15 December 1942, Laughlin collection.)

A miserable night in the Y. When D. leaves I am suddenly forlorn. The sordid itch of desire returns and the old shameful seeking.

The only purity, and rarely even then, is in work.

Crane. Dear Hart—

I embrace you.

Goodnight.

Having returned to his journal, Tom was experiencing the usual good days and bad days syndrome, and running through his friendships was what Tennessee Williams himself would acknowledge as his "galloping paranoia." It was like an infectious disease, these hidden suspicions or reckless accusations, afflicting his friends, often pitting them against one another, and creating lifelong enmities. No one, not Donald or Paul, was above suspicion. In time, Tom would generally forget, or, more precisely, fail to remember, his behavior. Paul usually shrugged it off as material for another of his "one-act melodramas," but Donald tended to take this more seriously, being left either hurt or angered. To be a friend of Tennessee Williams was to be a candidate for this sort of treatment, which often left him more distressed than his target. Oddly, though, there were comparatively few who ended up disaffected or disenchanted. On the contrary, many remained loyal to him despite everything. One such was the twenty-nine-year-old "Texas tornado," Margo Jones.

Tom and Margo met at the Liebling-Wood offices during the final weeks of November 1942. She had gone there to present an award to Audrey, whose reputation for promoting the work of new playwrights had spread into the hinterlands. Since 1936, Margo Jones had served as assistant director of the Federal Theatre in Houston, traveled to Soviet Russia for a festival at the Moscow Art Theatre, and founded and directed the Houston Community Theatre. She had recently joined the faculty of the University of Texas's drama department in Austin.

Helen Sheehy in her excellent biography of Margo Jones writes that Audrey Wood had given Margo a copy of *Battle of Angels* during a previous visit to New York. Subsequently, she wrote Audrey, "I don't believe I'd be stretching it much to say I'd read it a dozen times." She felt that the play had more beauty, theatre, and guts than any she had read, and she asked Audrey to send her any other scripts she might recommend. Audrey was quick to oblige with the early one-act plays in *American Blues* and gave her a copy of *Stairs to the Roof* and the latest draft of *You Touched Me!*

Sheehy notes that "Margo felt an immediate empathy for this writer whom she had grown to love through his work. Although they were about the same height, Margo's energy and booming self-confidence made her appear quite imposing. . . . Tennessee, overwhelmed and somewhat intimidated by his first meeting with the exuberant Margo, quickly took her to his friend Paul Bigelow's nearby apartment, in a brownstone just off Fifth Avenue." Nervously saying he had an errand to run and would return, Tennessee disappeared. "Margo stayed, and she and Bigelow got on famously as the day wore on and Tennessee did not return. Bigelow mixed Black Velvets, a voguish combination of champagne and stout then considered the very symbol of sophistication."[20]

Margo impressed Bigelow as "a perfect Amazon of a woman—and very handsome. She was like Texas itself, very much larger than any life she could aspire to. She scared the bejesus out of Tennessee! She dressed in a very dashing style—flowing capes and voluminous skirts, and, long before women started wearing them, high boots—all accompanied by a firm, loud voice. It was clear from the beginning that she was totally dedicated to Tenn and determined to produce his plays."[21]

Tom wrote home to report, "The director of the Texas University drama Dept. was in the city this past week, and she has plans to put on 'Battle of Angels'—to shock the South! That is, if the school authorities will let her."[22]

> Friday—Wharton still cagey—no money. Another dinner date with her Sunday.
>
> Margo Jones writes long, enthusiastic letter from Texas. Hopes to produce "Stairs to the Roof." I wake up this A.M. sick with cold and penniless. . . .
>
> The phone calls cheer me and I go out to Bigelow's and the Authors League where Audrey has arranged a $10 loan to tide me over the next few days. I think perhaps I will try to go home for Xmas. It is a year since I have seen the home folks and a year is such a perilously long time as the old folks get older. It would hurt, it would be very sorrowful but I want it—to see them again. I should. After all, it is the only bond in my life. Otherwise I am just a loose plank in the flood. If Wharton kicks in with any cash I'll do the rewrite down there.
>
> Bigelow was very nice today. He feels the separation and I think there is an affection in him, at least considerably genuine.
>
> From five o'clock on I am alone. I swim, exercise, and go out alone to the movie. I return and the floor is quiet. . . .
>
> I don't think much about losing my youth. It happens and is accepted gradually. I feel very young. In a way. And in a way very old. I do not feel the time sense of much longer living.
>
> No, it seems as though it would not be long to the finish. But I started feeling that a number of years ago.

At the end of the year, he wrote a long poem that concluded:

This point, this moment, this passage
a nameless place,
but holding forever curved
one hand in space!

I want to go back to *creation*.
Strongly, brightly, with a fresh and free spirit and a driving power.
To do the monument.

He would build the monument; he needed only one more crucial event in his life during the coming year in order to begin work and make of it an enduring creation.

24

"If You Breathe, It Breaks"

January–April 1943

As much as Tom wanted to be with his grandparents and his mother again, the prospect of seeing his father was too much to bear, even at Christmastime. Carly Wharton—whom he hoped would produce *You Touched Me!*—gave him what amounted to a reprieve. He wrote home, "I have been engaged in hot disputes and negotiations with a producer who has finally come across with two hundred dollars to support me for the next two months while I make some further changes in the new comedy."[1] And in his journal, he observed, "What is to come is still unclear but it looks like the play will go on. I have received an advance of $200, half of which is already spent—but the final and fourth revision is complete—I have worked on the play 11 months now." He failed to mention, though, that he and Donald were *both* at work on the script and that his collaborator, because he was employed, had generously let him keep the entire advance out of consideration for his dire circumstances. Tom owed money everywhere, his typewriter was still in hock, and he was in need of the simplest amenities, so much so that the one hundred dollars was quickly spent.

But money also meant the chance to move around, if not travel, and much to his friends' chagrin, he would just disappear. He could be gone for days before it would occur to him that he should let others know where he was. New York's network of subways was always a source of misadventure for Tom. Whenever he descended into one, he could seldom be certain where he would come up. Usually, it was Brooklyn. Sometimes he would stay on or take the ride out to Coney Island, a playland that he especially enjoyed in its winter desolation. Other times, he would wander along the promenade in Brooklyn Heights, overlooking the East River, and stare at the magnificent model for Hart Crane's *The Bridge*.

He wrote to his new friend and hoped-for publisher, James Laughlin, "Lately my enthusiasm has divided between Crane and Rimbaud." He wondered if he should write a play about Rimbaud. "A motion picture would be the ideal medium starting with 'Morte a Dieu' and ending with the pitiful conversion in the hospital at Marseilles. Not with pious implications, however."[2] But here in the Brooklyn environs, his thoughts were riveted on the tragedy of Hart Crane.

Now Tom could look back to the spring of 1937, during his last full year at home in St. Louis, and remember reading about Crane's "search of sailors and the blind escape he achieved through sexual gratification." Crane had had an affair with a seagoing friend. After that, "almost as though in revenge for having been thwarted of the fulfillment of love, he became more brutal and insatiable in his lusts [and] he was not above paying for his pleasures in the dark pungent streets and seamen's dives along the Brooklyn and Hoboken waterfronts."[3] The comparison with Tom's own experience with Kip and its often sordid aftermath was clear, as was Crane's path of self-destruction plain for Tom to see. It did not seem to matter what happened to him personally as long as he could channel his experiences into his writings. By the early winter of 1943, he was embarked on a suicidal course that could be stemmed only by some extraordinary change in fortune.

He noted in his journal, "The life here in Brooklyn at the St. George Hotel is comparable for sexual incontinence only to the early summer period at the Hotel Woodrow, Manhattan, summer of 1941." The fact that the St. George also had a huge and well-populated swimming pool undoubtedly influenced Tom to stay on for a while. If anything, though, cruising was considerably more dangerous in staid Brooklyn Heights than in Times Square, which was perilous enough.

Tuesday, Jan. 5, 1943.
    This is the first time that anybody ever knocked me down and so I suppose it ought to be recorded. Unhappily I can't go into details. It was a case of guilt and shame in which I was relatively the innocent party, since I merely offered entertainment which was accepted with apparent gratitude until the untimely entrance of other parties. Feel a little sorrowful about [it]. So unnecessary. The sort of behavior pattern imposed by the conventional falsehoods.

Donnie comforted me when he arrived on the scene. Now he is upstairs with another party procured in the bar. Why do they strike us? What is our offense? We offer them a truth which they cannot bear to confess except in privacy and the dark—a truth which is inherently as bright as the morning sun. He struck me because he did what I did and his friends discovered it. Yes, it hurt—inside. I do not know if I will be able to sleep. But tomorrow I suppose the swollen face will be normal again and I will pick up the usual thread of life.

The next day he commented, "There was something incredibly tender and sad in the experience. So much of life at its most haunting and inexpressible. Not that I like being struck, I hated it, but the keenness of the emotional situation, the material for art—these gave a tone of richness to it which makes the affair unforgettable among many that melt out of sight." His plea was, *"Give me time for tenderness."*

Wed. Night (4:20 A.M. Thurs.)
Can't sleep. Slept till 5 P.M. today. Did nothing but visit Bigelow who was too ill for typing script. We have grown closer again. I am on excellent terms with both he and Donnie despite their enmity for each other. I play a somewhat deceptive role, since I must amuse each at the expense of the other, though I remain fundamentally faithful to both.

By the middle of the month, he was reproving himself for not having sent home his Christmas presents: "Self, self, self—how wearisome and ugly. I think it poisons my work. I must purify it somehow before the end." He was aware that cruising, as a compulsive, rudderless drive, was beginning to distract and corrode his energies. "I don't think it's sex I want," he wrote. "It is the dread of coming up alone to this little room at night. And going to bed and turning my face to the wall."

Saturday night I had the most beautiful (looking) lay of my entire experience. Really flawless. Strange how little excitement I felt, however. Wanted money, paid $2. Then turned it over to Donnie who was waiting his turn downstairs.
I had better get away from all this, unless the play goes into production. . . . I remember when I first came to N.Y. . . . 3 seasons ago—I kept looking for "the big, important thing" to happen. Well, that summer I had K. [Kip]. It nearly killed me. . . . I couldn't stand an isolated life without a lover. But a life in a small place, with simple, honest relationships (friends), *and* some sexual partner or outlet accessible is what I should seek out for myself.

It would be several years away—he *would* have his life in a small place with a loyal lover at his side—but nothing would ever assuage his loneliness, nor would anyone reach into his feelings as deeply as had Kip Kiernan.

Tom felt that a long poem he was writing, "The Dangerous Painters," could be fine after more work, and this prompted him to send a batch of his poetry to James Laughlin at New Directions. In little more than a week, he had a reply and a lifelong publisher.

> Dear Tennessee—
> I am very excited with the poems you sent. It seems to me you ARE a poet. Some of the stuff is rough, to be sure, but it's studded with nuggets. You have some of the wonderful quality of Eluard—strange insights that reduce to highly poetic images.
> I'm keen on the stuff and want to do something about it. We must get together and plan it out. I'll call Lincoln's office when I get to town and leave word where I am staying.
>
> > Best wishes,
> > JL[4]

In 1934, when James Laughlin IV was nineteen, he was influenced decisively by the poet Ezra Pound. Laughlin had thought he might become a poet, like his idol, but Pound in his blunt way discouraged one aspiration while opening the way to another: publishing. It was good casting. Laughlin made a strong impression even at that early age; standing six and a half feet tall, he was handsome and an heir to a Pittsburgh steel fortune. Although he had an acute business sense, his greatest asset was a passionate commitment to the makers of literature. While still an undergraduate at Harvard, Laughlin had founded in 1936 the aptly named New Directions, which went on to publish, often for the first time, such authors as William Carlos Williams, Vladimir Nabokov, Dylan Thomas, Federico García Lorca, Yukio Mishima, Djuna Barnes, Rainer Maria Rilke, Lawrence Ferlinghetti, Henry Miller, and Ezra Pound. By 1943, Laughlin had published a number of young poets, including Clark Mills, and now his interest was in Tennessee Williams. Jay, as he was known to most of his writers, was seeking out the nonconformist and the unorthodox, those fearless in their artistry. And in Tennessee, both as poet and playwright, he recognized a new voice, one to elevate into the best company.

About the middle of January, Tom was still "cruising like mad" when once again he ran afoul of what gays call "rough trade":

> Late Thurs. Night—
> Probably the most shocking experience I've ever had with another

human being [was] last night when my trade turned "dirt." No physical violence resulted, I was insulted, threatened, bullied and robbed—of about $1.50 and a cigarette lighter. All my papers were rooted through and the pitiless, horrifying intimidation was carried on for about an hour. I was powerless. I could not ask for help. There was only me and him, a big guy. Well, I kept my head and I did not get panicky at any point though I expected certainly to be beaten. I didn't even tremble. I talked gently and reasonably in answer to all the horrible abuse. Somehow the very helplessness and apparent hopelessness of the situation prevented much fright. I stayed in the room while he was threatening and searching, because my Mss. were there and I feared he might try to confiscate or destroy them. In that event, I would have fought, called for help, anything! He finally despaired of finding any portable property of value and left, with the threat that any time he saw me he would kill me. I felt sick and disgusted. I think that is the end of my traffic with such characters. Oh, I want to get away from here and lead a clean, simple, antiseptic life—Taos—the desert and the Mts.

The next day, he wrote, "I spent a quiet, sweet evening with Donnie and Fidelma Kirstein. Nice dinner there, good companionship and reading Blake, Beaudelaire [sic], and Cocteau's *Livre Blanc* aloud. Fidelma is lovely. It was good after the horror of last night."

Saturday night, he told of "an experience just consummated twice—very lovely—makes up for the last unhappy episode. This was blissful." But bliss carries its price, too, for by "Monday night (about 3 A.M.)," he noted another development: "What Bigelow calls my 'occupational disease'—crab lice—is back on me. Only one discovered but I shall have to procure a bottle of 'The Personal Insecticide' tomorrow. Who shall I blame? Who is the father of these bastards I am reluctantly bearing? *Qui sait?*" He added, "Tomorrow I see Carly Wharton and a verdict will presumably be handed down on 'You Touched Me'—an occasion important enough to alter the whole future course of my strange term on earth."

Carly Wharton, a pert and pretty red-haired woman, had formed a partnership in 1939 to produce plays with actor Martin Gabel, whom she had met when he was appearing in Orson Welles's modern-dress *Julius Caesar*. Previously, in 1935, she had been engaged to assist the director of a play by Lawrence Langner and his wife, Armina Marshall, *On To Fortune*, at their Westport Playhouse. Her subsequent marriage to John F. Wharton, a prominent and respected theatrical attorney, resulted in a friendship with one of his clients, John ("Jock") Hay Whitney.*

---

*During a short stint in Hollywood, Carly Wharton had become convinced that three-strip Technicolor would become a standard in films and, as associate producer, she persuaded Whitney to invest in what turned out to be a highly successful short musical called *La Cucaracha*. As a

Whitney and his sister Joan underwrote the firm of Wharton & Gabel in the amount of $100,000, enabling the pair to set up impressive offices at 11 West Forty-second Street and to invest in two solid Broadway hits, *Life With Father* and José Ferrer as *Charley's Aunt*. Following this, in January 1942, the team successfully produced *Café Crown*, directed by Elia Kazan. And now in 1943, they were looking for another commercial enterprise. Carly Wharton's suggested revisions of *You Touched Me!* were more in the nature of trying to refashion a hat to fit the wrong head, however. Tom knew this, of course, but in the theatre nothing springs more eternal than hope.

On the morning of January 20, Tom journeyed to Wharton & Gabel's offices on the twenty-ninth floor and stared at the Statue of Liberty as Carly delivered the bad news. She felt the rewrite unsatisfactory, dropping the play and dealing a blow that he took stoically in his fashion as a "veteran of discouragement." He said they parted on good terms and added as consolation that he had had a "pleasant encouraging evening at Audrey's. Bigelow at his conversational best, very brilliant. I manage to stay on here—Audrey prefers it and home would be a retreat at this moment, not very strategic."

A Girl in Glass

Although once again without funds, Tom did stay on and was startled by a letter dated January 20 from home—from Edwina. "Now that it's over," she wrote, "I can tell you about Rose who has successfully come through a head operation. A letter from Dr. Hoctor and the surgeon said yesterday that she shows 'marked improvement and has co-operated through it all.' I shall be permitted to visit her Sunday."[5] Tom immediately inquired, "I did not at all understand the news about Rose. What kind of operation was it and what was it for?" Finally, he asked, "Please let me know exactly what was done with Rose."[6]

On January 13, 1943, a bilateral prefrontal lobotomy had been performed by Dr. Paul Schrader, with Edwina's trusted Dr. Hoctor in attendance. Before entering military service, Dr. Schrader operated on more than one hundred patients at the state hospital in Farmington, and Rose Isabel Williams was one among them. Edwina was to say subsequently, often in tears, that she had been strongly advised to accede to the operation and that she gave her consent only when, after nearly six years in Farmington, Rose had shown no improvement. Edwina trusted Dr. Hoctor implicitly—he was, in fact, regarded as a

---

result, Whitney financed a color-film company that underwrote Kenneth MacGowan and Rouben Mamoulian's production of *Becky Sharp*, the first full-length three-color Technicolor motion picture, starring Miriam Hopkins. And that, in turn, led to Whitney's participation in the phenomenal success of David O. Selznick's *Gone With the Wind*. In the labyrinthine ways in which connections in the theatre and film world intertwine, it would be Irene Selznick who would produce Tennessee Williams's *A Streetcar Named Desire*, with Jock Whitney one of its major investors.

friend of the family—and, as superintendent at the state hospital, he gave her every reason to trust his judgment. In later years, Edwina would maintain that Tom had never forgiven her for having given her approval without first consulting him.

But with both her sons away—Dakin in the service and Tom an unstable itinerant—responsibility for the decision to proceed with the operation fell mainly on the older members of the family. Edwina had only to recall Tom's violent reaction when he saw Rose confined to a mental ward and her own fear that she might have the two of them there. In the final account, the burden was on her, as it had been for the past six years, since Cornelius—always the realist—had given up on Rose. Although Dr. Hoctor had the final authority, Rose being a ward of the state, he left the decision to Edwina. Tom remembered her hysterical reaction to Rose's being committed to Farmington and knew that she might again faint or retire to her bedroom for a spell but that sooner or later she would summon the courage to make a decision. And that she did.

During the war, little was known about prefrontal lobotomy beyond what was being publicized at the time. Psychosurgery was a relatively new and decidedly controversial field, an outgrowth from the conflict between the practitioners of psychoanalysis, on the one hand, and clinical psychiatry, on the other. Rose had been diagnosed as schizophrenic, a disorder that yielded little to analysis or to the medical treatments of either insulin shock or Metrazol therapy but that devastated one's ability in the areas of thinking, concentration, memory, and perception. Countless thousands like Rose were confined to mental institutions throughout the world, morbidly unresponsive; as a result, anything that offered new hope was quickly—if too hastily—embraced.

In time, the lobotomy was largely discredited as a mutilating brain operation, but once it was devised in Portugal by Dr. Egas Moniz, later winning him a Nobel Prize in 1949, the word spread rapidly throughout the world medical community. Then, in Washington, two doctors, Walter Freeman and the neurosurgeon James Watts, formed a team and labeled their procedure a lobotomy. Dr. Schrader, who operated on Rose, was a proponent of the so-called Freeman-Watts standard lobotomy, a "precision operation" in which "the brain was approached from the lateral surface of the skull rather than from the top." Then "burr" holes were "drilled on both sides of the cranium," after which a "6-inch cannula, the tubing from a heavy-gauge hypodermic needle, was inserted through one hole and aimed toward the hole on the opposite side of the head." When the cannula was withdrawn, "a blunt spatula—much like a calibrated butter knife—was inserted about 2 inches into the track left by the cannula."[7] At length, four quadrants were cut, two on each side of the brain, and the results varied, generally producing a pacifying effect.

Although there were strong reservations within the medical profession, the news quickly spread that the wizardry of brain surgery was curing the hopelessly insane. Among many, Joseph Kennedy, the father of the future President, subjected one of his daughters to a lobotomy, from which she emerged worse than before. By 1943, numerous articles had appeared in the press and in leading magazines. The *Reader's Digest* and *The Saturday Evening Post* brought the "great discovery" to America's bastion, the middle-class reader. And *Time*, with its last-word air of authority, came out in late November 1942 with a positive view of psychosurgery, lending credibility to a medical breakthrough for treatment of those doomed as incurably insane. One can safely assume that Dr. Hoctor and other close friends of the family would have called these articles to Edwina's attention.

Tom's only reference to the news about his sister was set down in another journal, a spiral notebook:

> *Grand, God be with you.*
> *A cord breaking.*
> *1000 miles away.*
> *Rose. Her head cut open.*
> *A knife thrust in her brain.*
> *Me. Here. Smoking.*
> *My father, mean as a*
> *devil, snoring—1000 miles*
> *away.*

His mother would probably have sent reassuring letters, but, at any rate, he was in no mood to go home. With the war effort accelerating, jobs were beginning to open up, and by the end of the month he thought he would "try [a] job at the book store"—in this case Frances Steloff's famed Gotham Book Mart, where he was put to work as a wrapping clerk. "After Steloff whipped together a package with blinding speed, she held it up to the astonished Williams and said, 'That's a messy job. You can do better.' "[8] He then proceeded to show her what "messy" truly was, and so ended his one day's employment without pay.

During the final weeks spent in Brooklyn at the St. George, Tom saw his future as "a blank space" but said, "If you don't drive, you get punched in anyway." He described his mood as "reasonably blue." He felt that Paul had become "fed up" with him and was anxious to see him out of town, which was another way of expressing his own ambivalent feelings about returning home. Paul commented, "Tenn asked me if I knew anything about the lobotomy and its prognosis, and since I didn't and he had confided in me about his sister, I suggested that perhaps he should return home to find out."[9]

Tom's thoughts were increasingly of St. Louis and his memories of the years spent there:

One lives a vast number of days but life seems short because the days repeat themselves so. Take that period from my 21st to 24th years when I was in the shoe business. A clerk-typist in St. Louis at 65.00 a month. It seems like one day in my life. It was all one day over and over. Ben in "Stairs to the Roof."

Monday . . . Horton Foote, the playwright, told me about an elevator's union which he thinks will get me a job. I will see in the A.M. Also will move from the St. George back to "Y."

Eventful day. Met William Saroyan and went to Cornell production of "Three Sisters."[10] Both disappointing. Saroyan is likeable enough with his somewhat calculated but fresh candor and probably has for many a charm. I felt too much space between us. . . .

So we light the last cigarette before sleep.

The air is pregnant with change.

The few remaining weeks in New York were spent visiting friends and moving from one job to another. His first job as an elevator operator provided hotel guests with the adventurous alternative of either climbing up or stepping down to get out at their floor. After the hotel manager told him he was overqualified for the work, he wrote to Andrew Lyndon:

Right now I have another job which I like somewhat better than the elevator job. I am an usher at the Strand Theatre on Broadway, one of the swanky movie palaces. I have a morning uniform, rather like an Eton scholar's, and an evening uniform, midnight blue with satin lapels, and we are drilled like a regiment. I rather enjoy it. It is only eight hours, sometimes day, sometimes night; strenuous because one is constantly on the hoof, and has to deal with stampedes of old women crazy to see Humphrey Bogart [in *Casablanca*] and Bronx kids crazy to hear Sammy Kaye [the bandleader who was the stage attraction]. There is always a gang of standees that have to be held back in pens of velvet rope. An old woman slapped me yesterday. Another one broke through the rope and stampeded up the aisle. When I remonstrated with her, very delicately, she screamed, "Don't you dare be impertinent to me! Why aren't you in the army?" To love the masses you must observe them only in the abstract, in solitude; right now I believe in autocracy; almost.

I must say that Paul and Jordan have been extremely nice to me lately. I had to collect a number of articles used in the new job, such as shirt studs, cuff-links, flashlight. They were extremely accommodating, Jordan even did some sewing for me, and very well done, too. I never mention them to Donnie any more or Donnie to them, so I think the friction will dissipate itself. . . .

Jordan took me to hear Jascha Heifetz play for a radio broadcast a few nights ago and it was almost unendurably beautiful, he played something

by Saint-Saens, I think it was Rondo Capriccioso, and for I think the first
time, music had the value of experience for me. . . .

Lincoln [Kirstein] goes in the army this month and leaves Donnie in
complete charge of the office and magazine. . . . I must go to bed. —I am
on the night shift. The ushers at the Strand ought to have football uniforms with catchers masks.[11]

Tennessee would always look back upon this brief employment with a nostalgic fondness that exceeded, as such memories often do, the actual experience. "I loved it. It covered my room at the 'Y' and left me seven dollars for
meals. I've made a lot more money than that in my life, but it never made me
feel as rich."[12]

However, as it turned out, the money was not enough, and Gilbert Maxwell lured Tom back into the hotel business. A letter to his family, written on
Hotel San Jacinto stationery, said, "Now I am working at this fashionable
East Side hotel which is much the most satisfactory job of the three, and pays
adequately." He remarked on how easy it had suddenly become to get work
with employers "literally begging people to work for them. But salaries are
still not keeping up with the cost of living. When I was working at the Broadway theatre, strangers came up to me and inquired [about] my salary and offered me higher pay to work for them. What a difference from the depression
days! It is a pity it takes a war to create work for everybody."[13]

In *Memoirs*, Williams described the San Jacinto as "a sort of retirement
home for dowagers of high degree but diminished fortune who would spend
their last dime on a good address." To his family, he explained, "Some of the
rich old ladies here are regular dragons. They fight among themselves with
incredible ferocity and it requires very tactful treatment and restraint to get
along with them. But they are so amusing as characters I can forgive their
ferocity. A good many of them are in the social register but that does not
prevent them from acting like Irish scrubwomen."[14]

He remembered one, in particular, who "bore the stately name of Auchincloss and went into a manic seizure whenever she inadvertently found herself
in the elevator with another old girl who bore an equally prestigious sur-
name." Maxwell, who was on the desk, had warned Tom never to permit
these two dreadnoughts to occupy the elevator at the same time, under any
circumstances. "Well, it happened: they did. And the scene in that elevator
was like the climax of a cockfight. And (wouldn't you know) the elevator stuck
between floors! I tried to get it back up to the Auchincloss floor, and the other
dowager shrieked, 'Not back up, down, down!' I swung the crank and the
elevator stalled between floors nine and ten and the disturbance must have
wakened everyone in the building that midnight."[15]

Maxwell's employment, like Tom's, ended dramatically when one resident,
actress Cora Witherspoon, "landed spread-eagled, out on the sidewalk because of our having failed to switch on the portico lights." Miss Witherspoon

registered no complaint, but other guests did, particularly after it was discovered that Tom had left the doors to the elevator shaft on the fifteenth floor wide open. At that point, the management terminated their services. "It remained, however, for Cora Witherspoon to provide the climactic line to our little drama. 'Oh . . . we all miss Mr. Williams and Mr. Maxwell terribly—but somehow the hotel seems a so much safer place to be in, now that they've gone.' "[16]

Tom's next hotel experience proved to be even more disastrous. He and Donald had taken two sailors to the Claridge Hotel, off Broadway, and were duly beaten up. Windham thought that Tom would be better off even in St. Louis, and Tom was inclined to agree. Shortly before he left, though, he met Sandy Campbell, a new friend of Donald's. Campbell was destined to become Windham's lifelong companion and recalled this first meeting in the spring of 1943, when he was embarking on a career as an actor. He said that Donald had taken him to the West Side Y to meet Tom. "When he came down from his room to the lobby, he was smoking a cigarette in a long holder. It was the first time I had seen anyone use a cigarette holder except in the movies, but it did not seem affected. We walked to Child's on Columbus Circle for dinner. During the meal, Tennessee sucked his teeth noisily. Later Don told me that he had cavities he couldn't afford to have filled."[17]

Soon Tom would be dining at home again, his mother admonishing him to eat his food leisurely and chew, *chew*—or else repair to the trough on the back porch. Now he was thirty-two and had every reason to despair. To give in to his father's pressure to find a permanent job, he felt, would be a fatal mistake. At the end of his journal and "the eighth period" in New York, he asked, "When will I strike again the full white flame from the forge?" He was about to answer his own question.

"When you look at a piece of delicately spun glass, you think of two things: how beautiful it is and how easily it can be broken."

On his arrival at his home on Arundel Place—where he read in the attic and wrote in the basement—Tom sent a poignant letter to Donald Windham concerning the conditions he found at home: They were even worse than he had anticipated. Because of the presence of the grandparents and the strain between the miserably unhappy Walter Dakin and his belligerent son-in-law, Tom said that the family was not able to sit at the same table together and that his father ate separately. C.C. made it clear he did not want Tom to come home, and he immediately put him to work on menial chores like moving woodpiles and washing garage windows.

Although it was Cornelius who had at first invited the Dakins to move to St. Louis, Edwina was left to cope with her mother's illness and her father's discontent. The restless old gentleman wished to go off on various pilgrimages but felt compelled to stay close to his ailing wife. At the same time,

Grand was constantly trying to help around the house, despite Edwina's pleas that she stay in bed and conserve her energy.

Tom told Windham that his grandmother was deathly ill the previous week when the "old devil" decided to hold a party in the rathskeller. There was so much noise that Edwina had to ask C.C.'s friends to leave. He said that just for his benefit, Grand had gotten up out of bed, pretending to be well, and "goes tottering around the house, holding onto things for support, like a tipsy old crane in her pale blue kimono and pink cap and giggling apologetically when she nearly falls." Tom said that he was so moved that he could hardly speak.

Then Tom told of taking a long walk downtown along the old riverfront, which reminded him of Hart Crane. On his return, he went upstairs and sat with his grandmother and marveled at her extraordinary beauty. "Her face is very gaunt and beautifully chiselled and ivory colored. Her hair pure white and silky and her eyes a deep brown, still sparkling." He compared the vision of Hart Crane with the gentleness of his grandmother. He saw them both in a heroic light.[18]

Edwina had shown Tom a letter from Rose that the family found encouraging but in which she repeated her delusional conviction that Tom was lucky to be in a penitentiary as "hordes of hungry people are clamoring at the gates of the city." In an unmailed letter to Paul Bigelow, Tom, too, expressed cause for optimism:

> We drove out to see my sister yesterday and found the operation on the brain had accomplished something quite amazing. The madness is still present—that is, certain of the delusions—but they have now become entirely consistent and coherent. She is full of vitality! and her perceptions and responses seemed almost more than normally acute. All of her old wit and mischief was in evidence and she was having great fun at the expense of the nurses and inmates. She told me they were "mentally lazy, interested only in menial accomplishments." She herself is reading nineteenth century history and is particularly fascinated by Victor Hugo. Before the operation, she was unable to read at all and was interested in nothing. She showed me about her building and I noticed the other girls regarded her very nervously. She said she had "publicly denounced them" that morning.

This was the first time Tom had seen Rose in years, and he found it

> curious to see [her] delusions persisting along with such a brightness and vivacity. To me mental therapy is the most intriguing work there is, and if I could make a fresh start, I'd take it up instead of writing. Unbalanced minds are so much more interesting than our dreary sanity is, there is so

much honesty and poetry among them. But then, you wonder if there is such a thing as sanity, actually. Our own behavior, and especially our friends', does not provide a very good model, does it?[19]

It remains a mystery why Tom buried this in his memory and why Tennessee shifted the lobotomy to 1937, describing it as a cruel, desperate attempt on his mother's part to silence her daughter's obscenities: *"Doctor, cut those hideous stories out of her brain!"* The irony of it is that the last time Tom had seen Rose, in December 1939, it was he who had written, "horrible, horrible! Her talk was so obscene—she laughed and talked continual obscenities." If now, in the spring of 1943, he expected to find only the shell of his sister, he was amazed that she appeared outwardly much the same gentle, sensitive, and beautiful creature of their childhood, though inwardly she remained inaccessible. She wore that faint mocking smile that told others she knew what they could not possibly know. Like her brother, she was possessed of an unbridled imagination, and from then on it would bind them. Once again, they could enjoy the exquisite secrecy of being children together. And he knew that Rose's reality was never that far removed from his own.

Tennessee Williams's fascination with mental derangement—the perilous borderline between sanity and insanity, and the journeys back and forth over that line that his characters constantly traveled—was by now the hallmark of almost all his writings, and it would distinguish the greatest of them. On a fragment found among his papers, he had written, "Interested in all lunatics, especially myself—*chacun a son gout!*—what a marvelous gift to understand them."

Rose was not Edwina's only concern at this time. With war casualties mounting daily, with friends who had lost sons and husbands, she had Dakin to worry about, as well. Home on leave, in a few weeks he would be completing his training to go overseas: If it hadn't been for the fact that Cornelius had suddenly, inexplicably refused to pay his board at Harvard, he would have become a commissioned officer.

Tom told Paul:

I took Mother to see the road company of [Maxwell Anderson's] "Eve of St. Mark" this week. She started crying two seconds after the curtain went up and never stopped, as my brother completes his training period in a few weeks, now, and will probably go abroad. Have you seen the play? It is an interesting thing. The final scene in which the two remaining sons "join up," hard upon the news of the first one's glorious end, is comparable to nothing but the vomit of a hyena. The reviews in St. Louis were not good. I find that generally speaking reviews on the road seem much more intelligent to me. Our two reviewers in St. Louis both described the play as "amateurish" and ineffective even as propaganda. Well, this is the twilight of an era in the theatre. God knows what's coming next.[20]

Tom admitted to Paul that in the two weeks he had been home, he had begun to enjoy himself. Grand's condition had improved, and he said that she was perking up considerably. He was having a quiet time of it and was trying to decide his next move. "A little contemplation does the soul no harm, though it isn't so good for the figure. I have gained ten pounds since I got here due to no exercise and three enormous meals and a few snacks between."[21]

Not knowing that next month he would be meeting Christopher Isherwood, he wrote in the spiral notebook, "Reading Isherwood's Goodbye to Berlin. He interests me profoundly. . . . seems strangely like me—his mind—his attitude. Only clearer, quieter, firmer. A better integrated man." Although he had no real desire or, as he saw it, reason to return to New York, Tom was writing numerous letters in that direction. He had learned that James Laughlin planned to publish a volume later in the summer called *Five Young American Poets*, in which his poetry would take up forty pages; he had also learned that Laughlin intended to publish *The Purification* in the 1943 *New Directions* yearbook. Tom told Jay that at the moment, "I am poised in the mid-continent, trying to decide which way to jump. The west is the strongest attraction, but New York still has some strings on me."[22]

In addition, he wanted Laughlin to see a short play of his, *The Last of My Solid Gold Watches*, concerning a Mississippi shoe salesman named Charlie Colton—C.C.—an affectionate, slightly mordant portrait of a man whose time has passed and who pathetically echoes himself. The play is remarkable as one instance, among several, in which Tennessee Williams drew on those facets of his father's character he most admired; it was the artist's evocation of a sublimated, slowly emerging love, harbored in Tom Williams's consciousness as "hate."

At the moment, however, he reported to Windham that C.C. had just left on a trip to the West Coast after loudly accusing Edwina of hiding his poker chips. He hoped the old man would never come back, a wish he would fulfill in the play he was writing about his haunted home life.

Tom wrote Audrey that, although things were wretched at home, the good news was, "I have been able to do some sustained writing for the first time since last summer. The Gentleman Caller is developing into a full-length play and should be ready for you to look at when I return."[23] He told Donald that he might also call the new play *Not So Beautiful People* or *The Human Tragedy*, being a gibe at his favorite target, Saroyan, after *The Beautiful People* and *The Human Comedy*. Tom said that he had been working several days on the play and that it was taking on the atmosphere of his life at home, although its setting was drawn from his memory of the dismal, overcrowded apartment on Enright in University City.

Actually, the play was slowly evolving from sketches, story fragments, and one-acts, some written as early as 1938.* One he titled *If You Breathe, It Breaks*, which is about a lovely, shy girl with two brothers, one outgoing and the other, like her, sensitive and withdrawn. Their mother, Mrs. Wingfield, has tried to attract a gentleman caller to meet and perhaps marry her, but the daughter says she would rather be "a front porch girl" and watch the boys go by than have one persuaded to visit her. She has a collection of glass animals and when she adds a tiny glass unicorn to the menagerie, she declares it to be so fragile that "if you breathe, it breaks." Subtitled *Portrait of a Girl in Glass*, it was intended to be one of the "Mississippi Sketches," with the further identification of "Landscape with Figures."

After his arrival home, Tom became mindful once again of the dominant role his mother had always played in his and Rose's life: her southern illusions of grandeur, her ceaseless much ado about everything, her preoccupations with the Episcopal church and the DAR, and her forbearance in the face of adversity. And so he rewrote another sketch, which he had begun in New Orleans in the fall of 1941, called "Daughter of Revolution," and subtitled it "A Dramatic Portrait of an American Mother." On the cover page, he wrote, "This play is inscribed to Miss Lillian and Miss Dorothy Gish for either of whom the part of Amanda Wingfield was hopefully intended by the author." Then he renamed it "A Daughter of the American Revolution (A Comedy)," with Mrs. Wingfield at the phone; in total there are more pages of notes about the production of the play than there are pages of dialogue.

Amanda is described as

> a stringy little woman, about 48 years of age, in a boudoir cap and a dingy wrapper. Her personality jelled in its present form as a Southern belle in Blue Mountain, Mississippi, twenty some years ago. The voice, the mannerisms remain exactly as they were when she received her gentlemen callers on her father's front porch, the rectory in which her girlhood was spent. Her present life is far removed from there, geographically, and in the circumstances she now contends with. But she is struggling in Apt. F, 3rd Flo. So. (on Maple Street in St. Louis) with a world which she comprehends no more realistically than she did the outside world when she was an Episcopal minister's sweet and pretty young daughter. We dis-

---

*After visiting his sister at the state institution, Williams returned home with the intention of completing *The Gentleman Caller* as a full-length play. In this period, he began to weave together the threads of various writings about his family, the earliest being "Apt. F, 3rd Flo. So." (c. 1938, signed Thomas Lanier Williams); it concerns a brother and sister, Arthur and Valerie, and the setting, like Rose Williams's bedroom, is Valerie's room with its white furniture and curtains. Arthur had been working in a factory but is now out of work. It is only a sketch, but on the title page of a copy of "Portrait of a Girl in Glass," which he was writing in the spring and summer of 1943, he noted, "This is a short-story treatment of the material used in a play I am now working on, called 'The Gentleman Caller.' "

cover her in the act of soliciting a subscription to a magazine known as the "Housekeeper's Companion." Only her figure and the wall phone are spotted.

As Edwina busied herself about the house, tidying and phoning her friends, she was Tom's living model, while his recent reunion with Rose had brought back a flood of memories. In April, he wrote another "fragment of a one-act play," entitled *Carolers! Our Candle!* In this, his sister became embodied in a character he named Laura Wingfield and her brother was identified as Tom. A poignant vignette, it depicts the tenuous relationship binding them to each other, and Laura voices her fear that he will soon go away and leave her with their mother. He reassures her he won't leave without taking her with him. In his conception of *The Gentleman Caller*, Tom was fusing the various sketches of his sister and his mother into one full-length portrait.

His production notes give one of the best illustrations of what it meant for Tennessee Williams and other serious playwrights to write during the war years. In these notes, Williams set forth his vision of what would evolve into *The Glass Menagerie*. "In some respects," he wrote, "this play is a companion piece to an earlier full-length play of mine called 'Stairs to the Roof.' The former was a fantasy. This is a realistic piece. But both are social comedies with more serious implications than have been involved in heavier efforts of mine more gravely written." Even before it was produced, Tom was stating a truth about *The Glass Menagerie* seldom understood by its interpreters: that too often it is played as a light work, without any understanding of the depth of violence underlying its characters' motivations and the grinding impact of poverty on their lives.

He was also decrying "the type of criticism that has grown out of a nation at war: the prevalent attitude of Broadway that social criticism in drama, in fact any serious treatment of our social life that occurs during the present emergency of war, is out-of-place, irrelevant, untimely, unless it represents a war-time society; unless it happens to involve the war." War, he said, was "a phenomenon which has its origin in things preceding its outbreak, things deeply rooted in the societies among which it chances to erupt. . . . The privilege of writing about this war is an almost sacred one which belongs, I think, to the still anonymous young men (and women) who now happen to be too busily engaged in prosecuting it to set their feelings and ideas about it down in scribbled journals, let alone in the full-length manuscripts of plays." He added, "If you impose the necessity of dealing with martial themes upon your theatre during the time of war—this can only mean one thing—that for the duration, you have committed your theatre to the creation of only sham and claptrap." He asserted that his was not a personal plea, but "a general plea for a theatre based on *truth*."[24] As for what he referred to as his "little play," that would have to wait its time. He told Donald that he had been working on it with tigerish fury every day.

While Tom was lamenting the dispiriting prospect he saw in a return to New York, he received a cryptic wire from Audrey strongly suggesting that he remain in St. Louis for another ten days. She also mentioned that she was in touch with Guthrie McClintic and José Ferrer regarding *You Touched Me!* But she added, "No definite word yet."

Then, three days later, on April 30, another door opened "at the last ditch."

> COME AT ONCE TO NEW YORK. HAVE ARRANGED WRITING DEAL PICTURES WHICH NECESSITATES YOUR LEAVING NEW YORK IN TIME ARRIVE CALIFORNIA AROUND FIFTEENTH OF MAY. FARE TO CALIFORNIA PAID BY PICTURE COMPANY. ADVISE WHEN ARRIVING NEW YORK.
>
> AUDREY WOOD

In the spiral notebook, he wrote simply that he had received a telegram saying he had been "sold to Hollywood."

PART V

New Harbors
1943–1945

————

"where marble clouds support the sea"

25

"Metro Goldmine Mayer"

May–July 1943

The "picture company" mentioned in Audrey's wire turned out to be the mammoth Metro-Goldwyn-Mayer studio, which boasted "more stars than there are in the heavens." Tom could scarcely believe his sudden change in fortune. Edwina and the Dakins at last had reason to rejoice. And the news at least gave Cornelius pause, for he knew that writers made real money out there. As Tom soon discovered, the money was indeed real. As Audrey Wood related in her memoir, she told him he would be getting "two hundred fifty." "A month?" he exclaimed. "No," she replied, "a week." His response was, "That's dishonest!"

By the summer of 1943, MGM, under the command of Louis B. Mayer, had some 150 performers under contract and a whole stable of writers, as they were contemptuously referred to. The studio was prospering during these war years as never before and was soon to net a record $14.5 million. Because of the war, many of the world's greatest writers, actors, directors, musicians, designers, and artisans at home and abroad were readily put under contract. And while it took some hard selling on Audrey's part to promote a young poet-playwright with only one produced play to his credit—and a failure at that—she was able to include Tennessee Williams in a package deal. Designer Lemuel Ayers, Tom's classmate at Iowa, who had just conceived the settings for the musical hit *Oklahoma!*, was part of Audrey's package. The fact that many of the studio's regular contractees were going into the service also helped her make the deal.

On May 4, Tom arrived at the Liebling-Wood New York offices and signed a standard seven-year commitment, containing a six-month option devised to safeguard the studio in either event: success or failure. If the writer performed to the studio heads' satisfaction, the option would be automatically renewed every six months, with the weekly salary fixed regardless of what the writer, in effect, earned for them. If his work proved unsatisfactory, the studio had only to exercise its option and drop him. Eventually, this binding one-sided contract was successfully challenged in the courts.

Almost all the major studios employed leading novelists and playwrights. Among them were John Steinbeck, Thornton Wilder, Aldous Huxley, Christopher Isherwood, Lillian Hellman, Clifford Odets, Dorothy Parker, Robert E. Sherwood, Edwin Justus Mayer, Dudley Nichols, Katherine Anne Porter, Ben Hecht, and John O'Hara. Samuel Goldwyn, however, was the one independent producer who understood the symbiotic relationship that existed in the theatre during those times between playwright and producer. As a result, many of his films were characterized by a strong literary quality and are now regarded as classics.*

At the big studios, writers who worked within "the system"—even punching a time clock at Warner Brothers, as William Faulkner did—labored in an atmosphere of mutual disdain: Producers and particularly directors considered screenwriters on a par with union craftsmen. Often they were quartered in second-story, adjacent offices, prompting Dorothy Parker on one occasion to shout through Spanish-grilled windows to a startled guided tour group passing below, "Let me out of here! I'm as sane as you are!"

The one holdout among playwrights was Eugene O'Neill, who steadfastly refused numerous offers to write for the screen. In answer to an MGM producer's entreaty proposing that he name his price for writing a scenario for Jean Harlow and asking that he send a collect reply limited to twenty words, O'Neill's wire consisted of the one word, *no*, repeated twenty times. But O'Neill was then a wealthy and successful playwright, quite able to resist a Harlow or a Garbo—while the unsuccessful and unknown Tennessee Williams could not be quite so cavalier about his assignment.

On May 7, Tom boarded the Twentieth Century Limited to Chicago, where he would transfer to the Super Chief bound for Hollywood. In all, the trip would take three nights and two days. Donald Windham saw him off, a copy under his arm of *The Sun Is My Undoing*, a novel by Marguerite Steen of some 1,170 pages. Asked by a studio representative, who met him on the train, if he would undertake a screen adaptation of the massive work, he is said to have replied: "Yes, if I don't have to read it."

To a family eager for news, he wrote:

---

*While Jack Warner at Warner Brothers was referring to writers as "schmucks with Underwoods," Goldwyn took the position, "Writers should write and directors should direct!" When he first started making talking pictures, he announced, "The day of the director is over and that of the author and playwright has arrived." A. Scott Berg in his fine biography *Goldwyn* (New York: Knopf, 1989, pp. 192, 283) wrote, "With scripts detailing every camera angle and vocal inflection, and Goldwyn overseeing every piece of costume, construction and casting, directors on his sets were reduced to technicians. Invariably, they became his whipping boys."

I am ensconced in a compartment on the crack transcontinental train and traveling like rich folks for the first time. It is fun. When I think how often I've traveled on my thumb this elaborate transportation seems a little fantastic.

I will get in Hollywood Monday morning. . . . It seems they want me first to dramatize a long novel . . . and I will work with Pandro Berman at Metro Goldwyn Mayer. I get $250 a week, the first term expires in 6 months and may be renewed at a higher salary.

Audrey has appointed herself my "power of attorney" and all funds go through her. She will give me $100 a week and put the rest in an account she opened in my name at the Chase National Bank. She said she was afraid I would spend or give it away if it went directly into my hands. She is thoroughly trustworthy so I guess it's a good arrangement.

I got no sleep last night because of farewell entertainments lasting all night and can hardly hold my eyes open.[1]

After arriving in Los Angeles's ornate Union Station, Tom lost no time in making his way out to the massive, walled-in Metro-Goldwyn-Mayer studios in Culver City. He could not have failed to think how different everything in his life was now from what it had been the time, only four years before, when he had bicycled past the studio gates en route to his salesman's job at Clark's Bootery.

Soon after, he had located a small two-room apartment in Santa Monica at 1647 Ocean Avenue. It was what he would regard as funky, to his taste; it had a small stove and refrigerator, and it was located adjacent to the Pacific Palisades, a long, winding promenade that overlooked the ocean and the palatial beach homes of stars like Cary Grant, Norma Shearer, and Marion Davies, whose "castle by the brine" had been built for her by William Randolph Hearst. With the wartime blackout, the Palisades offered an unparalleled opportunity for anonymous sex, and once he had made this discovery, Tom would rack up an impressive number of indiscriminate one-night stands.

The Palisades proved to be more than an escapist refuge, however. The entire coastline was on alert for attack by air or submarine and was mobilized with turrets, training camps, and ports of embarkation. Try as he might to avoid the omnipresent reminders of war, Tom was made fully aware of them. The Palisades' long, curving walkway high over the ocean, with its shroud of arbors and gardens, royal palms and belvederes, offered one a mind's-eye confrontation with the realities of a war being waged remorselessly somewhere in the vast expanse of the Pacific. In a poem entitled "The Summer Belvedere," Tom wrote, "We live on cliffs above such moaning waters!"[2]

At home in St. Louis, war's immediacy was manifested by the sight of men leaving for the service or returning maimed or in coffins. Dakin would soon be departing for duty in the Pacific, and Edwina was trying to hide her dread. Her worries about Tom were confined to the usual gamut. Fussing over his health, she advised: "not so much smoking, no snacks before bed, only milk—earlier to bed and look after your *teeth*." She also cautioned him, "Take care of your money. It isn't what you make but what you save that takes care of you. . . . If you need more money than they advance, let me know. I'm enclosing a check for ten."

She also had the surprising news that, on Cornelius's return from his trip west, "Dad has been quite lamb-like. It always does him good to go away. He brought me a nice box of candy on 'Mother's Day' and took Grand and me for a ride on Sunday!"[3] The fact that the Reverend Dakin was excluded from the ride and that C.C.'s thirty-two-year-old son was away and off the family dole would have had more than a little to do with Dad's good humor.

Edwina had an unexpected visitor at about this time. When Tom was working as an usher in New York, he had met writer David Greggory, and they became good friends. "I invited Tennessee up to my room, and on my desk I had photographs of Chekhov and Hart Crane—and so we were off to a hundred percent start!" Subsequently, Greggory drove across the country to the Los Angeles offices of the advertising agency where he had been transferred, and en route he stopped off in St. Louis, at Tom's suggestion. "He gave me a note to give Miss Edwina, and I gave her the full southern treatment with the bow from the waist and the whole bit. Once she knew I was a southerner, Mrs. Williams was very courtly and I was very courtly, and later on she told Tennessee, 'I am very pleased to see you have one friend who is a gentleman.'" One trait Greggory observed in Edwina was "an ability that Tennessee also had: to rearrange the facts of life when they became too oppressive. I saw him do it too many times. Of course he wasn't always able to make it stick, but she was: If you don't like the flowers in a given situation, then you rearrange them, and, as time goes on, the picture you have devised is what remains—that's what you see. Most of the time he wasn't able to keep it up, but she was."

Having failed to give his friend a forwarding address, Tom wrote in the spiral notebook that he had run into David quite fortuitously. He said that they enjoyed the weekend together, saw Bobby Lewis's production of "Eve of St. Mark" at the Lockheed airplant, and noted, "I spent the night with David and he says I muttered aloud, calling my sister's name. . . ." David decided to take up residence in the same Santa Monica apartment building as Tom, and he described it as "an L-shaped building with obvious possibilities—one could look out the back at what someone was doing in the front—but the landlady was ideally designed for Tennessee, a very easy go, and herself busy with gentlemen callers." She was indifferent to Tom's idea of housekeeping: "She would go in with ammonia and a mop and tell him to get his ass out of there, and she would give the place a once-over. But he was capable of living in a shambles without seeing it—I mean, he *was* aware of it, but he wasn't about to do anything about it—because he had the same kind of upbringing I did: These trivial things were all taken care of for us; things were clean and orderly and you didn't know why or how, much less care, but they always were."[4]

The Walls Within Walls

As soon as he reported for work, Tom was assigned an office of his own and told that Steen's novel had been shelved until Clark Gable's return from service. Instead, producer Pandro Berman handed him a vehicle to rewrite for Lana Turner, who was pregnant and between films. Berman said it was best for him to break in on something simple, and it certainly was *simple*. Tom wrote Audrey to say that he had been assigned the task of fashioning "a celluloid brassiere" for Miss Turner. The improbability of Tom's assignment brought forth an immediate response from Audrey: "The letter announcing that you were suddenly submitting material for Lana Turner met with ribald laughter at this end. It all sounds too much like Hollywood to be true." Then she added a word from the wise, "I think what you should do is discreetly begin to know Mr. Pandro Berman and to have Mr. Berman get to know your work."[5]

Formerly, Pandro S. Berman had been head of production at the RKO studios, producing most of the Astaire-Rogers and Katharine Hepburn films. By 1941, he had moved to MGM and produced *Ziegfeld Girl*, in which Lana Turner, then a starlet, gave a surprisingly affecting performance; after that, Louis Mayer assigned him as her producer. Berman was virtually born into the picture business; he had inherited an astute, cost-conscious approach to making movies from his father, an industry mogul. He also had a respect for good writers and considered it "the hardest part of making pictures, finding stories and people who could write."[6]

At first, Tom was struck with the absurdity of his situation. He told Audrey, "I think it is one of the funniest but most embarrassing things that ever happened to me, that I should be expected to produce a suitable vehicle for this actress. . . . I feel like an obstetrician required to successfully deliver a mastodon from a beaver. A bad comparison, as the beaver is a practical little animal who would never get herself into such a situation. I no longer feel any compunction whatsoever about the huge salary I am getting, as I shall certainly earn it."[7] Entitled *Marriage Is a Private Affair*, the film was being produced by Berman because he and Turner had recently made a successful film, *Slightly Dangerous*. Lana Turner, like so many of the screen's goddesses, was a product of the studio system. She was groomed to her very eyelashes to make money for the studio. Despite much of the turgid material she was given, such as the impossible script handed Tom, she would prove herself to be a quite capable film actress in such movies as *The Postman Always Rings Twice* and *The Bad and the Beautiful* and, ironically, conclude her long career at Metro playing Diane de Poitier in a literate script by Christopher Isherwood.

Ensconced in his new office, Tom began writing letters to one and all on his ostentatious MGM stationery, including Paul Bigelow:

> I truly meant to write this sooner. The period of adjustment is not over yet and it has been pretty tough. . . .
>
> As for the studio itself, I have nothing but nice things to say. Everyone is lovely to me, almost embarrassingly because I keep thinking how they are cheating themselves. I am not their dish anymore than they are mine. But at least one of them, Pandro Berman's assistant Jane Loring, is really delightful. Looks like a weary lion with a flaming bush of red hair and always lounging around in Oriental-looking trouser outfits. We understand each other, thank God, and I can be honest with her about my feelings. . . .
>
> I have a really lovely little private office. An easy chair and a lamp table besides the business appurtenances—good big typewriter, cream-colored walls and Venetian blinds that can let in any degree of the usually terrific California sun. Right now I have a sort of Chekhovian twilight effect, which may account for the gently melancholy tone of this letter—well, I am still a bit lonesome too. The visit home was such a nice change, but the very niceness of it—was sad. It seemed so final—my grandparents you know, are both so old, and Grand so lovely and delicate, a leaf on a window-sill. . . .
>
> Living space here is virtually impossible to obtain and it was a choice between this sort of place and one of those ghastly pseudo-elegant pseudo-modern Shangri La sort of apartments which Santa Monica is peppered with. I chose the cheaper and less offensive sort. . . . But it is in view of the ocean—well, with a little craning of the neck. And the landlady has already provided material for an amusing one-act. She belongs to "the movement" but confuses it with sex. We get along fine—her first name is Zola and on her table she has Zola's book "The Human Beast." When she entertains soldiers she tells them it is her biography and the fools believe her. Well, she *is* rather beastly-looking, you know. Drinks a quart of beer for breakfast—usually in my kitchen.
>
> I am being very good, and you know what I mean.[8]

With Lincoln Kirstein in the army, Donald had the full responsibility of publishing *The Dance Index*. Windham said that he did the complete job of editing and getting out a monthly magazine—writing and commissioning articles and illustrations, proofreading and laying out the pages. Before Tom left, Windham had sent a letter of introduction to Christopher Isherwood, who by 1943 had achieved a degree of fame with his *Goodbye to Berlin*.* Two

---

*Later to be retitled *Berlin Stories* and adapted then to stage and film as *I Am a Camera* and once again as the musical *Cabaret*.

years before, he had contributed to the shaping of a screenplay for Joan Craw-ford at MGM, *A Woman's Face*, and could speak from experience to his new friend, whom he considered "a true exotic, with his southern drawl and wild talk." Isherwood, although somewhat wary at first, savored Tom's "scurrilous stories, and adopted the stance of a concerned older brother."[9]

Tom invited Isherwood to lunch at the fashionable Brown Derby and told Donald Windham that he recognized Isherwood at once because he looked rather as Tom imagined himself to look. He felt self-conscious and was, he thought, too effusive about Isherwood's writing, which he ranked with Che-khov's. He expressed a concern about being drawn into filmdom's glittering lifestyle to Audrey when he said, "Christopher Isherwood warns me that I must not take to drink, as most Hollywood writers do. —I am not going to."[10]

After some soul-searching, Isherwood had become a convert to the Indian philosophy of Vedanta, and, along with other writers such as Gerald Heard and Aldous Huxley, he joined in the meditations of the Hindu monk Swami Prabhavananda, even to the extent of living as a probationer in his guru's Hol-lywood ashram. Only recently, in an effort to restrain his strong sexual incli-nations, Isherwood had become a "monk," sleeping in a dark little anteroom of the ashram. He was making an effort to discover an alternative to his Chris-tian indoctrination—the precepts of sin, punishment, Hell, and mortifica-tion—and in Tennessee Williams he met another repressed Anglican puritan.

Not understanding Isherwood's silence following their first meeting, Tom took it upon himself to appear unannounced at the Vedanta Center's Branhamanda Cottage, located on a promontory in the Hollywood Hills. He found the absolute, meditative silence oppressive. When bored, Tom's yawn was accompanied, as Paul Bigelow described it, by a grimace and the sound of a wailing banshee, and he created further havoc when finally, to make conversation, he referred to Krishnamurti, who was the protégé of the eccentric Annie Besant. His faux pas was explained to him somewhat tartly when Isherwood suggested they take a walk. After that, Tom sent a placating but tactless letter to Isherwood, mentioning that James Laughlin had suggested he write an article about Christopher Isherwood and "the Movement, whatever it is" and requesting "another audience . . . either in the sacred precincts or something more profane like the Brown Derby."[11] Isherwood replied in a long letter in which he made an effort to relate the meaning of Vedanta, and Tom was quick to respond that "if I went into this Vedanta thing it would be with a serious effort to understand it and your relationship to it." He added that "I am a little distracted from ham-mering at a short story. It is one of those days when the power won't find the groove, and you know how awful that is. Time's Winged Chariot, oc-cupied by Lana Turner and Pandro S. Berman, is galloping madly up and down the corridor beyond my locked office door while I work on some-thing called 'Portrait of A Girl in Glass' about my sister."[12]

Mainly what Tom and Isherwood shared during this time was an acute

self-consciousness, a penetrating self-examination that far exceeded ego-
tism—an "instrument of sensibility"[13] through which to observe their fellow
beings, as Stephen Spender described it. Over the years, Christopher Isherwood wrote and spoke with increasing honesty about his homosexuality: It
became central to his life, like his Hinduism, ultimately paving the way toward
a lasting friendship with a gifted artist, Don Bachardy, thirty years younger
than he. Swami Prabhavananda relieved Isherwood's Christian sense of sin by
commenting on his sexual liaison with a male friend: "You must try to see him
as the young Lord Krishna." That he and Tennessee enjoyed each other sexually was acknowledged years later by Isherwood: "It was not a big deal, we just
found each other very sympathetic, and we went to bed together two or three
times, I imagine."[14]

With Isherwood, as with any of his sexual contacts, Tom was seeking a
release from six to eight hours of solitary work by day and from the loneliness
that came on at night. He simply felt he needed the sexual outlet as an accom-
paniment to the outpourings of creative endeavor; it was an avenue to and
from an often intimate human experience, and thus the stuff of his writings.
But unrelieved loneliness was often the end price he had to pay, and the one
thing he dreaded was being alone at night. Late in life, he was asked to define
love, and his reply was, "Not being alone."

Designer Lemuel Ayers on his arrival told Tom that Margo Jones was
coming out to the West Coast to direct at the Pasadena Playhouse. Subsequently, she wrote Tom that Audrey Wood had let her read *You Touched Me!*
and that she was very excited about it. She was certain that Gilmor Brown, the
director of the Pasadena Playhouse, would approve, and she was also confident that Lem Ayers could be persuaded to do the sets. Finally, she believed
that MGM or one of the other studios would be interested in backing the play
once they had seen it at the Playhouse, mentioning that *Angel Street* [then
being filmed at Metro as *Gaslight*] had had its inception there.

Tom was somewhat wary of Margo's unbridled fervor and cautioned Donald to exercise restraint until they had seen it was not one of those Texas dust
storms. But he was impressed that both Margo and Mary Hunter were genuinely enthusiastic about the play, and this left him convinced that it had a
future. It was the *future* of Tennessee Williams that primarily concerned
"Texas Margo"; it interested her even more than *You Touched Me!* Without
his mother to hover over him, Tom now had Margo as protector. David
Greggory said that she "tended to mother him a lot and was always seeing to it
that he was correctly dressed for whatever was going to happen. The fact is, he
liked being looked after—within reason. I'd heard it said and even read that
she entertained thoughts of eventually becoming Mrs. Tennessee Williams—
but *that* stupid she was not! It was probably more a fear or figment of his
imagination."

The true surrogate, however, was Audrey—his mother by remote control.

Greggory observed that "there were many paradoxes in his makeup. He, of course, liked being helped, being fussed over, being told what to do, while resenting it in the same moment. It was a no-win situation. Audrey was the one who could do the most, so ultimately she was the one he came to resent most—and I don't think she really quite understood that."[15]

During his time in Santa Monica, though, Tom was totally dependent upon Audrey's guidance. In his eyes, she was the source of all good things. He felt free to call on her for the most trivial of his needs, and she would always respond. Even when he didn't ask, she volunteered. One example was the saga of Tom's motor scooter, which he had bought shortly after his arrival. Audrey wrote, "The motor scooter scares the hell out of me. I remember the traffic vividly out your way and I'm including you every night in my prayers. Please be careful because you and I have to live a long time and do a great many things together. Stay off the scooter and all will be well."[16] Since Paul Bigelow knew that Tom hadn't been able to navigate a bicycle without running into a cow, both he and Audrey had "visions of his getting [not] a half mile down the road before driving smack into a stone wall."[17]

That wasn't what happened, although there were several versions of a "rather bad accident." Tom told Donald that a rear tire blew out as he was traveling along Wilshire Boulevard and that he was knocked unconscious; two days later, the front tire burst, and he returned the vehicle to the dealer. David Greggory remembered him saying that after the second tire blew, "he just left the scooter in the middle of the street and walked away from it—that was his solution."[18] One way or another, it evidently was returned to the dealer, and when Tom discontinued his payments, the owner started pressing his claim.

However, neither his unpaid bills nor his obligation to his employer to write the vehicle for Lana Turner engaged his thoughts. Instead, Tom was preoccupied with "a hastily prepared synopsis or film story treatment of 'The Gentleman Caller.'" He told Audrey, "I have worked this out in spare time since I've been here, but as you know the stage version, in a rough draft, [was] already written before I signed here. I feel that this could be made into a very moving and beautiful screen play—much better than the stage version could be—only it would have to run unusually long, about as long I should think as Gone With the Wind. I think the theme and treatment is sufficiently big in scope to justify such a length and long films are better anyhow."[19] He asked Audrey to advise him about showing it to Pandro Berman or other producers, and when answering him, she asked him to send her a complete list of anything written prior to his employment at the studio, cautioning him, "If and when Metro becomes interested in your finished material, said properties are not to be put in their laps, but sold to them separately."[20] She was particularly anxious that *The Gentleman Caller* be included on the list.

"Isn't Money Beautiful?"

For the first time in his thirty-two years, Tom was receiving what could rightly be called a decent income, diggings from what was then prevalently called "Metro Goldmine Mayer." And although Tennessee Williams's attitude toward money would always be erratic, during these six months at MGM he displayed a surprisingly provident disposition toward his good fortune. With a salary of a thousand dollars a month, going literally from rags to riches, he could well have "gone Hollywood," and no one would have been all that surprised. Instead, he not only accepted Audrey's proposal to withhold all but seventy-five dollars but he opened a savings account in Culver City and also sent his mother a weekly stipend. Edwina wrote, "Your letter containing check for our savings account was received and I think it is a fine thing. You'll be surprised at how small amounts grow and then, too, I know you'll like to feel I can do something for Grand with it, if necessary."

She added the proviso, "I want you to take care of your own needs first always, however. It's such a big relief to know that you can do so. You don't know how I have worried over you." Tom was concerned about her, too, and when at home recently he had commented about a blemish on her nose caused when Cornelius had slammed a door in her face years before. She was proud of her appearance, and she assured Tom, "I'm going to have it attended to soon and your father will pay for it. I'm simply going to have the bill sent to him after it's done. Now that you boys are independent, I shan't fear his explosions as I did when I had three children to provide for and he threatened to throw us all out whenever a bill was presented!"[21]

Grand was also in Tom's thoughts, as well as in his mother's: It was painfully obvious that the elderly lady had to be in the last months of her life, and he was quick to respond when Edwina first suggested, "It would be nice to feel I had a little fund I could use in an emergency like I had last winter when Grand was so ill and I couldn't afford a practical nurse to make her more comfortable."[22]

A letter from his grandfather confirmed that Grand was too weak to make a proposed trip to Tennessee, but he said that Pat Shackelford and his wife "took your mother, Grand and myself to see Rose yesterday and the trip tired Grand greatly; we found Rose about as *you* saw her, only a little heavier—too bad, she is too fat. I quite envy you being on the ocean: perhaps if Fate is kind, your Grand may get strong enough for us to join you, some day of days." He added, "I neglected to say Rose inquired about you yesterday."[23]

The plight of his sister, together with the apparent final illness of his beloved grandmother, placed the family foremost in Tom's mind. He wrote to Audrey that "my first obligations are to my mother and grand-parents and any extra money I have goes to relieving their insecurity and dependence. Then, also, I have to look beyond my term here. The situation at home is that my father has always used his money-control as a humiliating despotism over all in the house." In a postscript, he asked, "Isn't money beautiful?"[24]

Money may indeed have been "beautiful" after his long years without it, but, as he was made aware, it also brought with it new responsibilities and added personal expenses. Keeping what might euphemistically be called a "low profile" was for him, as it always would be, more a chosen lifestyle than an artful dodge. No matter how much money he would eventually make—and from this time forward he would become increasingly independent—he could never be accused of ostentation. He could not have known that his money worries were at an end, and to safeguard his immediate future, he opened three bank accounts, one in New York under Audrey's watchful eye, a joint one with his mother in St. Louis, and his own personal checking account in Culver City.

In mid-June, Margo Jones arrived on the scene, and Tom told Audrey that he had taken her to the Brown Derby and had spent the entire evening with her. He said that it had cost him ten dollars but was "worth it." After dinner, they called on Lemuel Ayers and his wife in their ornate home. The dancer-choreographer Eugene Loring, another member of Audrey's package, was staying with the Ayerses, and Tom was led to believe that Lem, Loring, and Aaron Copland would be working together on a movie short of *Billy the Kid*, that Miles White would design costumes, and that he would write the ballad for it.*

He conveyed all this to Audrey while confessing that he felt "a little guilty about the time I *don't* spend on the Turner script and there are days when just looking at it brings on amnesia, anemia and the St. Vitus dance!"[25] In a subsequent letter, he said he felt that he was "working out a satisfactory adjustment to life here. One thing I have to learn is to keep my gorge down when writing stuff that doesn't have the inner compulsion. Why I should find that so hard I don't know. Probably because I've just never done it before. But they are very patient with me here, extremely kind and friendly."[26]

Nonetheless, Audrey urged him to spend more time on his assignment; she knew MGM might have reason to drop him. David Greggory recalled, "He couldn't write on order, just *make* himself do it. I mean, I think he was in a state of shock."[27] By the end of June, Tom sent the news to Audrey: "I am removed, or shall I say liberated, from the Lana Turner script. I have never received any reverse of fortune with greater complacency, though I commiserate with whatever degree of heart-break it *may* occasion at Liebling-Wood!"[28]

---

*Miles White—who had designed the costumes at the same time Ayers designed the sets for *Oklahoma!*—remembered Margo Jones approaching him about a Tennessee Williams play and thought probably it was *You Touched Me!* White was not at MGM, however, at the time but, rather, working for the Samuel Goldwyn studio, which he described as "a class act" where Goldwyn did only one picture at a time and "nothing was spared to make it the best." The thought that White would be designing costumes for the *Billy the Kid* project was apparently wishful thinking on Tennessee's part.

Now he could turn his attention to *The Gentleman Caller* and give in to the urgent, inmost pressure to write what he must. To Audrey, he had written portentously, "As you can see, a lot of work and time would have to go into this script, but it would be a labor of love."[29] But neither he nor Audrey saw that he was laboring to deliver one of the most important plays of the twentieth century and the one that would establish his greatness.

The Lion Roars

During his first two months at MGM, Tom had made an effort to go with the system, but he quickly lapsed into feeling a cynicism prevalent among writers who considered they were demeaned by the material they were asked to adapt; the studio system had been set long before there were *talking* pictures. From the beginning, the director and producer established absolute control and had little need or use for a written screenplay or shooting script; a synopsis or story outline was considered enough. By 1943, many writers simply went along with the demand made upon them for a basic script, grateful for the money; others, who were veterans, surmounted it. There were, in fact, gifted screenwriters attracted and committed to films, such as Dudley Nichols,* who went all out to foster "screen literature" as an art form and to promote "the filmwright" as the counterpart of the playwright. But there was no way to dislodge either the supremacy of the director and the concept of film as a director's art or the commercial-mindedness of the producer and his notion of the story as a "property."

Originating work for the screen was generally discouraged because studio heads felt that stories should be based upon successfully published or produced sources—in other words, a more reliable evaluation than their own. Tom Williams could have *created* film plays had he acquired the skills and been able to work with such sensitive directors at MGM as George Cukor and Clarence Brown who gave first priority to a well-written film script. Considering the great variety of talent surrounding him at this, the most powerful of studios, Tennessee Williams might well have written the enduring classics for films that eventually he did for the theatre, but the system was clearly opposed to such a possibility.

The roaring lion as the MGM emblem and *Ars Gratia Artis* as the motto—flanked on one side by the word *Trade* and on the other by *Mark*—must have struck Tom as ironic as he went through the studio gates and saw the spectacle of a colossal factory, where anyone espousing the notion of "art for art's sake" would have been fired on the spot. Still, there were many true artists

---

*Dudley Nichols, with John Gassner, edited two volumes of *Best Film Plays* published in 1944 and 1945. Shorn of camera directions, with only a suggestion of scene and character angles, the plays become eminently readable, clear evidence of how much of the screenwriter's art is inherently a part of films as various as *Casablanca* and *The Ox-Bow Incident*.

employed at the studio, and in spite of New York corporate control, films were being made that would become acknowledged classics, if not immediate moneymakers. In fact, the popular B movies rolled up the profits that financed the prestigious A films, some of which starred players who would eventually appear in the plays and film adaptations of Tennessee Williams. Jessica Tandy and Hume Cronyn—Tom's benefactor—were both featured in *The Seventh Cross* (1944), Hurd Hatfield starred in *The Picture of Dorian Gray* (1945), Katharine Hepburn was in *Dragon Seed* (1944), and Elizabeth Taylor was playing her first leading role, in *National Velvet* (1944). At Warner Brothers, Miriam Hopkins was starring opposite Bette Davis in *Old Acquaintance*. Tom had only to walk across the studio lot or eat at the commissary to see luminaries to the left and right of him, but he was totally oblivious to the "glitz and glamour" of it all and always would be.

The problem of what to do with the young southerner named Tennessee Williams was passed on to an executive at Metro, Lillie Messinger, who had negotiated Tom's contract with Audrey. She and Pandro Berman had made the decision to take Tom off the Lana Turner film, and she introduced him to another prominent producer on the lot, Arthur Freed. Tom told Audrey that he and Lem Ayers would try to sell Freed on their *Billy the Kid* project, as well as on "an idea for a negro opera based on material of mine."[30]

Freed, whose career at MGM began as a lyricist on the "All-Talking! All Singing! All Dancing!" *Broadway Melody* of 1929, ultimately became an extraordinarily successful producer of Metro musicals, including *On the Town*, *An American in Paris*, *Singin' in the Rain*, and *Gigi*. He was searching for a vehicle for a precocious child actress named Margaret O'Brien, who was Louis B. Mayer's answer to Shirley Temple. In 1942, O'Brien had appeared in a surprise hit, *Journey for Margaret*, which was followed by still another big-money success, *Lost Angel*. During 1943, she was cast in three films, all of them successful, including her role opposite Judy Garland in the 1944 film *Meet Me in St. Louis*. Mayer's word went out fast: Stories and story ideas for the diminutive star were a top priority. Tom was one of the studio writers who received a note inquiring if he had a story idea for the child actress. He told Donald Windham that he did, but that it was nothing that could be put in print.

During this period, when he was awaiting a new assignment, Tom was at his happiest: For the first time in his life, he was being paid to write what he wanted. David Greggory recalled that "Tenn asked me, 'Do you think if I didn't go into the studio, they'd send me my check?' I said, 'It's worth a try.' So, for about three weeks, he just didn't appear, except rarely. He locked his door at the studio and left his desk in a condition that indicated he would be back soon, and they did indeed mail him his checks. But I think by that time he knew he was on the way out."[31]

His mistake, encouraged by the unfounded assurances of Lem Ayers, was the assumption that Arthur Freed had virtually assigned him to *Billy the Kid*, which was intended to be a short Technicolor film in the mode of the very successful *La Cucaracha*. As it turned out, Ayers was not any more successful in Hollywood than was Tennessee Williams, for much the same reason. He would soon return to his career in the theatre, designing many plays, including Williams's *Camino Real*, and finally coproducing as well as designing the outstanding Cole Porter musical *Kiss Me Kate*. Audrey inquired, "I keep getting excited correspondence from Lem Ayers regarding 'Billy the Kid.' . . . Lem wrote me you were seeing Freed on this. What was his decision? I'm curious for many reasons—primarily because my father produced 'Billy the Kid' as a melodrama when I was a child and the play, under his management, toured for about eleven years, so anything that has to do with 'Billy' seems a family matter."

In the same letter, Audrey commented on what was actually occupying Tom's time and attention: "I read your story last night called 'Portrait of a Girl in Glass.' I liked it very much. It's particularly interesting since I have been reading so recently the synopsis and the corrections you sent on 'Gentleman Caller' for pictures."[32] At this time there was not only the recent memory of Rose in the sanitarium to haunt him, but a letter as well, written as best her perceptions would permit.

> Dearest Brother:
> The Dr. wrote me a nice letter from you. I was pleased to receive it. You made a bad appearance the last time you called on me. You looked murderous. I'm trying not to die, making every effort possible not to do so. I feel as well as I ever did at my sickest, when I am about to fall unconscious. The memory of your gentle, sleepy sick body and face are such a comfort to me. I feel sure you would love me if I murdered some one. You would know that I didn't mean to, Dakin might.
> You are like Dr. Beckmann's pills 9681(4) "blessed" will love me no matter how bad I be.
> Every acquaintance we have they tell is dying.
> If we have to die I want to be cremated my ashes put in with yours.
> Go to Church for the sacriment [*sic*] & pray for your sister's body that it will become thin & strong & given a husband as good as I am.
> If I die you will know that I miss you 24 hours a day.
> "Sweet Heart If you Should Stay a Million Miles Away I'll Always Be in Love With You!"
> I want some black coffee ice-cream on a chocolate bar, a good picture of you.
>
> > Your devoted sister
> > XXX Rose.
>
> P.S.
> Send me 1 dollar for ice cream.[33]

"Portrait of a Girl in Glass," of course, was about Rose, of whom Tom wrote, "I don't believe that my sister was actually foolish. I think the petals of her mind had simply closed through fear. I see the faint and sorrowful radiance of the glass, hundreds of little transparent pieces of it in very delicate colors. I hold my breath, for if my sister's face appears among them—the night is hers!"[34] Tom wrote home, "It is obvious that she still has her delusions, and I don't see how she could live outside an institution of some kind. . . . I will try to find a suitable present for her and send it out there."[35]

Tom's concentration now was almost entirely centered on *The Gentleman Caller*, in both screen and stage versions. The "Provisional Film Story Treatment" that he sent to Audrey summoned not only his own memories of the Old South but primarily those of Edwina:

> . . . the wide flat fields, the dark cypress brakes, the Mississippi Delta, the river and the bluffs along it, the Negro sharecroppers' cabins and immense Greek revival mansions, the high windy bluff above the Sunflower River which let into the Mississippi. . . . Under willow trees the Rectory with its cover of morning glories and the garden with its profusion of jonquils, mother's favorite of all flowers. . . . the gentlemen callers on Sunday afternoons: rich planters' sons, sportsmen, a doctor, a lawyer and the one who works for the new telephone company, the one who married [Tom's] mother and became his father and went away, never to return. . . . the refreshments served of lemonade and cakes—the church picnic at Moon Lake on Blue Mountain.[36]

Conceding that "the material has color and mood and is certainly worth working on," Audrey felt that "its chief flaw rests in the fact that [it] isn't sufficiently focused on a character. I strongly suspect you mean this to be Amanda's story."[37] His was a prompt response: "Yes, the central and most interesting character is certainly Amanda and in the writing the focus would be on her mainly." He described her as "a conventional woman, a little foolish and pathetic, but with an heroic fighting spirit concentrated blindly on trying to create a conventionally successful adjustment for two children who are totally unfitted for it. The stage play ends in defeat—which she rejects at the very end and prepares to continue beyond. The film story would have a softer ending, I think."[38] Years later, Tennessee Williams commented, "Amanda represents the natural elegance in the old South. My main theme is a defense of the romantic attitude toward life, a violent protest against the things that destroy it. Amanda represents that."[39]

Audrey also felt that if Laura were to be played by Lana Turner, the part would have to be expanded and clarified. Tom reacted somewhat heatedly, "I must warn you that Lana Turner is no where figured in my calculations. The part of Laura is the most difficult to write and the hardest to portray and would take somebody more like Teresa Wright or possibly some very sensitive young actress discovered through a stage production of it."⁴⁰

Hesitating between film and stage, Tom at length did submit a screen synopsis to William Fadiman, Metro's story head. If Fadiman had accepted it, a play version probably would not have been written or produced. In those times, a story idea was purchased outright and then developed into a screenplay, with the carpentry frequently left to a group or succession of writers with credits. One can easily imagine that Louis B. Mayer, who believed with all his heavy heart in American motherhood, could have seen the film idea as a perfect vehicle for Margaret O'Brien as a younger Laura and Greer Garson as a younger Amanda. Naturally, he would have felt that the title would have to go, with the gentleman caller undergoing a sex change in order to become the character Tom's love interest, so that he could go on to great success while raising a family of his own. Add to this Technicolor and the Hall Johnson Choir and there would be de rigueur a happy-that-rhymes-with-sappy ending. As a matter of fact, Tom's own "softer ending" was not that far removed. During wartime, many films were aimed at box-office success by catering to a public that was willing to weep copiously but demanded an "all's well that ends well" conclusion.

Fortunately, Tom's main focus was still on the theatre and Margo Jones was there to ensure it. She had managed to get a commitment from Gilmor Brown to produce *You Touched Me!*—although she would have to direct it on the smaller of two Pasadena stages, the Playbox, without Lem Ayers's design—due, as Tom told Donald, to Brown's determination to produce a drama festival of Booth Tarkington plays. While Tom acknowledged Margo's incredible industry, he told Audrey that producer-director Mary Hunter, "with her relative detachment and her more objective approach, is more likely than Margo to do something really important with the play. I know that she wants to do it, and I really don't think there is a director in New York who would do it so lovingly or intelligently as she would, and it needs a woman's warmth. I know that, for curiously it is the women who like the play, or at least those with some womanly virtues. It ought to do very well at matinees if it gets on Broadway."⁴¹

Hunter had founded the American Actors Company at the Provincetown Playhouse in Greenwich Village and would have a distinguished career as one of the theatre's few women directors. Now there was a clear division in Tom's feelings toward the two women. He saw Margo as "a rare character, an Alice in Wonderland no matter where she goes. When I think she has spent a year in India and turned out a book on Hindu philosophy, gone around the world, and directed plays for seven years in Houston—and hasn't lost one bubble of her original effervescence, I feel that I should go out and build a shrine in the hills for her spirit. —She is a little worried about my air of detachment, she expected me to be a much more vital person, I believe."⁴²

If he seemed to lack vitality, it was probably more because of the way he would become quiet when his suspicions were aroused, for now his feelings were further divided by the arrival of Horton Foote, whom he saw as a rival for Margo's attention and as Mary Hunter's preference. He wrote to Audrey that Foote was in Hollywood "to work with his producer, the French actor Jacques Thiery (I think that's the name) on a new version of 'Only the Heart' which this producer will put on Broadway with the Actors Company, early next season. I do hope they make a success of it, so they could do work of mine."[43] His jealousy with regard to Foote was made even more apparent to Audrey in what he had to say about him: "It was not very smart of me to introduce him to Margo, for he is just as ingenuous as she is and I think he is much closer to her idea of a playwright. I regard Mr. Foote with a somewhat uncharitable reserve. Rivalry has something to do with it, I'm sure, but I find his great warmth and ingenuousness seeming a little spurious beside Margo's. —She doesn't. —The three of us get on well together, but I'm afraid I act like a Boston audience much of the time."[44]

Horton Foote recalled, "I was so in awe of Tennessee, anything I did was to impress him. I was an actor; I didn't think of myself as a playwright, even though I had written a play, *Only the Heart.* I wanted his friendship, and I had no idea he was resentful."[45] Audrey quickly saw through Tom's paranoid feelings toward Foote; she would be dealing with his darker suspicions for many years to come. As for Margo, Audrey reassured him that "if anybody could get that play on, Margo Jones will. You will be pleased to know that while she admires Horton Foote's work she still feels that yours is definitely the greater talent. So Williams still has first place in her affections."[46]

Tom complained to Donald about the amount of money that he was spending on entertaining his friends; he compared himself to a character he was writing about in a story called "The Rich and Eventful Death of Isabel Holly." Eventually retitled "The Coming of Something to the Widow Holly," the widow is depicted as the owner of a rooming house on New Orleans's Bourbon Street. Her home had formerly been open to paying guests, but they gradually became less and less paying and were now just residing there. At this time, Tom was suddenly going back into his store of memories of the French Quarter and was also writing his elegiac poem "Mornings on Bourbon Street."

Despite her son's increased spending, Edwina was able to report, "You already have a nice little nest-egg in the bank of seventy dollars which shows how small amounts saved regularly add up." As always, her letters kept him apprised of what was happening in the family: "We haven't had such a bad summer as to weather, and that has literally been a life-saver with Grand so ill and no servant. Even faithful Susie has only been out twice to 'clean up' for me." The good news was, "Your grand-father is in excellent health and able to go to the park and down to the library twice a week, also to the Early Communion at Church every Sunday without fail, which I think remarkable for his eighty-six years. The yard-men all have defence jobs so he also has kept the grass cut. [He] is pathetically eager to hear from you and haunts the mail-box."[47]

Although Tom was going to the studio only occasionally, he told Audrey that he, Lem Ayers, Eugene Loring, and designer Miles White were still hatching the *Billy the Kid* idea: "Mr. Freed is supposed to call me in for a conference on it. I see it as a sort of folk-opera with a fresh approach to the western material, songs and ballads and dances, predominantly with Loring as Billy." (In 1938, Loring had choreographed and performed the ballet to Aaron Copland's score.) "In the meantime, I am grateful for being left alone in my lovely white office."[48]

As for *You Touched Me!*—Audrey had forwarded a letter from Frederick McConnell, the director of the Cleveland Playhouse, asking permission to do the play in September or October. Tom was concerned lest Margo and Mary Hunter come into conflict with each other, since Horton Foote had told him that Hunter definitely wanted to produce the play, possibly opening the season with it, under her own direction. Hunter was the better choice, Tom thought, but he worried over Margo's reaction, because she was convinced that her Pasadena production would end up intact on Broadway. Tom stressed his faith in Mary Hunter to Audrey, too, but there seemed to be evidence in her silence that she had reservations. At any rate, he said, "I think it would be well to give McConnell okay on Cleveland production as one can never tell how amateur productions will turn out. The one here might not be as good a showing as he could arrange."[49]

"I Can Only Write for *Love*"

For all his seeming impracticality, Tom was demonstrating what made the historic partnership of Tennessee Williams with Audrey Wood distinctive. Their rapport was open and aboveboard and withstood the periodic disruptions of his suspicious nature. They were not always in agreement, and despite his often wildly vacillating opinions and contradictory actions, Audrey deeply respected him. Above all, she understood what rent him in being oppositely poet and playwright: the poet apart *from* and the playwright a part *of* the theatre. More subtle perhaps in this otherwise no-nonsense businesswoman was her maternal response to Tom's needs—*her* need to protect him and her enjoyment in his often antic behavior. What bound them, more than anything else, was their sense of humor: Throughout all the madness of their professional lives, they could always make each other laugh. By 1971, when that ran out, their association was at an end.

Probably a sense of humor was the trait above all others that characterized Tennessee Williams's enduring friendships. As he told Audrey, Paul Bigelow was writing him letters that made him howl with laughter. And Audrey, who was well aware of their special "in" brand of humor, said only that she was glad that Bigelow wrote letters that made him laugh. "I'm laughing already," she said. Now that *You Touched Me!* finally seemed to be under way, Tom wrote to Paul with the hope that his friend would get to see the play, his "having been such a devoted obstetrician at the long delivery." He added, "One of these days I am going to settle down, maybe a ranch in New Mexico, maybe a place in old Mexico. . . . Then you must come and spend your declining years with me. We will paint tea-cups and have an Indian to carry our market basket, maybe two of them with two baskets!"[50]

New Mexico (Frieda and Lorenzo) and Mexico (Katherine Anne Porter and Hart Crane) were on his mind. His thought was to carry a copy of *You Touched Me!* to Frieda and perhaps just stay on there. Donald had recently sent him a photograph of Katherine Anne Porter taken by Paul Cadmus, and he, in turn, sent Donald a note to be forwarded to Porter:

> Through the agency of Donald Windham and the photographer I have come into possession of a photograph of my favorite living American author, one Katherine Anne Porter, and I want to thank you for being the subject of it. You are sitting, or perhaps I should say curled up, in what appears to be an enormous chair of straw that is practically a cabana and you appear to be looking out at the world from the shadowy recess of the big chair with a smiling warmth and knowingness that is very endearing.
>
> Well, I am putting the picture up with the other two on the walls of my study. You will be [among] a triumvirate that includes Hart Crane and Anton Chekhov . . . I hope you approve of your company, as much as I do![51]

Porter surprised Tom by answering that she had some informal photos of Hart Crane in a happy mood, and he quickly responded, "I am wondering if you have any copies to spare. Not only would I love to have one, but feel sure they would be of great interest to all the few who love his poetry." Although he said he had read "the fine biography" by Philip Horton, he urged her to write about Crane "as you knew him in Mexico. . . . That is, when you have finished the novel."[52] Not until 1962, when *Ship of Fools* appeared after twenty years in the writing, did Porter have her first popular and financial success. A strikingly handsome woman and fiercely independent, Porter lived until an embattled ninety years of age. She left in her trail three failed marriages, four lovers, and more than fifty changes of address, sometimes two or three in a year. For the vocation of writer, she declared, "I was and am willing to die, and I consider very few other things of the slightest importance."[53] She had spoken Tennessee Williams's credo, as well.

As usual, Tom's moods were vacillating between euphoria and despair. In one letter to Donald, he said that he had been very happy of late and was luxuriating in the simple comforts and the freedom that money can buy. A week later, he said that his nerves were tied in knots, and in another impassioned letter, he confided to Windham the agony of the interior storms, which he had revealed only in his journals. It was the first time he had written to anyone about his blue devils. He spoke of them as a family trait, making a raging drunkard of his father, destroying his sister's mind, and creating an unbridgeable gulf between him and the outside world. He wrote bitterly about the lustful indulgence of parents who have children with a wanton disregard of their own inadequacies.

It was about this time that Tom met the actress Ruth Ford and her husband, Peter Van Eyck, at a cocktail party. A composer and actor, Van Eyck had recently played the role of a hysterical Nazi lieutenant in the film version of John Steinbeck's play *The Moon Is Down*. He had known Christopher Isherwood in Berlin ten years before and was the model for Sally's young lover in Isherwood's story "Sally Bowles," later dramatized in the play and film *I Am a Camera* and in the musical *Cabaret*.

Like Tom, Ruth was born in Mississippi and had even lived briefly in Columbus, where her father ran the Gilmer Hotel. Also, like Rose Williams, she had attended All Saints' College in Vicksburg and from there entered the University of Mississippi at Oxford, where she met and became a friend of William Faulkner. A stunning-looking young woman, she traveled to New York, became a popular model appearing on the covers of *Vogue* and *Harper's Bazaar*, and in 1938 joined Orson Welles's Mercury Theatre. In 1941, she migrated to Hollywood, where she and William Faulkner were employed at Warner Brothers.

Ford wanted to read *You Touched Me!* and Tom and Margo brought her a script, feeling that she could be excellent in the role of Matilda. Writing to Audrey, Tom told her that "Margo and I showed the script to Ruth Ford, and she has actually duplicated Margo's enthusiasm for it." He added that Carl Benton Reid had read the play and "says the Captain's part is highly suitable to him." Other candidates were possibly Agnes Moorehead as Emmie and probably Henry (later Harry) Morgan as Hadrian. Morgan had impressed Tom as Henry Fonda's partner in *The Ox-Bow Incident*, a movie he regarded at the time as the best American film ever made.

In a letter to Sandy Campbell, he described what would always be an agony for him. His method of writing, as friends like Clark Mills and Paul Bigelow observed it, was like an unleashed fury: paper going in and out of his typewriter with incredible speed and tossed all over the room. At the end of each day, he would gather up the usually unnumbered pages. Moaning and cursing and sitting on the floor, with sheets of paper all around him, he would try to assemble them in some order. Comparing it to childbirth, he told Sandy that reading what he had gathered together was an even worse experience, encountering such odd incongruities and contradictions that occured in his scripts.

But to Audrey, he declared, "Let's face it! I can only write for *love*. Even then, not yet well enough to set the world on fire. But all this effort, all this longing to create something of value—it will be thrown away, gone up the spout, nothing finally gained—if I don't adhere very strictly to the most honest writing, that I am capable of. . . . By the time my six months are up here, I hope that I will have been gripped by some really *big* theme for a long play, one deserving entire devotion. In which case, I would retire to Mexico and live on those savings until it is finished."[54]

Without realizing it, he was at that very moment grappling with one of the archetypal themes as big and universal as any in human experience—the family. He did not yet know of the existence of Eugene O'Neill's *Long Day's Journey into Night* or that another young aspiring playwright, Arthur Miller, would within a few years write *Death of a Salesman;* nor could he know that his play, which he tended to dismiss, would become *The Glass Menagerie* and rank with the others as an enduring theatre masterpiece.

26

Hollywood Lost

August–December 1943

Aug 11 or 12
Thursday
6 weeks lay-off from Studio. Started Monday. . . .
On way home walked into a plate glass door and shattered my false front tooth. Idiotic accident! Replaced this A.M. for $5.00.

Audrey, who regarded Tom's employment at MGM as merely a means for buying the time he needed to write what he wanted, informed him that he now had in his New York account some $650. This was fortunate, for soon afterward Tom wrote to her, with a mixture of anxiety and relief, to say that MGM's lion was "showing his claws! . . . I have just received a note informing me that I am to be laid off for six weeks without pay because there is no present assignment for me. This came up without any warning." He had been told that "the tentative Billy the Kid idea does not constitute an actual assignment. And just now a very curt young man has entered my office, without knocking, to inform me that I should move my stuff out as I could not hold this office during the lay-off—which is extremely inconvenient because of the large store of Mss., books, Etc. that I have here. . . . I will try to be properly penitent for my natural waywardness and act more like a Hollywood writer the rest of the time here. This puts quite a dent in our savings plan, doesn't it? As well as our *Amour Propre!*"[1]

With Audrey away on vacation, Liebling was quick to write to Tom, assuring him that the layoff was a provision of his contract and that the studio was still obligated to resume his weekly payments for an aggregate twenty weeks, on or off the lot. He offered the possibility that Metro might still pick up their option after the first six-month term and continue to employ him: "I'd like you to stay another few months. By that time you may get an excellent credit which will do you good in the future and also you may save by that time enough money to keep you going for a couple of years."[2]

In answer to a concerned letter from his mother, Tom was reassuring: "Don't worry about me not liking commercial writing. I feel about it the same way that you would about being paid to give up Christianity and go to the synagogue instead of St. Michael's. . . . During my lay-off I've been busier even more than usual, as the Goldwyn studios phoned me they needed a vehicle for Teresa Wright and wanted me to submit any suitable material. I thought of *Spring Storm*, and so I wired for it, and prepared a film story treatment which has kept me busy. If sold outright it would mean a good deal of money, anywhere from five to twenty-five thousand."[3] Subsequently, he gave a copy of *Spring Storm* to Bertha Case, who now had a West Coast office of her own and a "home-and-home" business relationship with Liebling-Wood. She soon returned it, saying that someone named Duggan [Pat Duggan, a story editor at the Goldwyn studio] liked it but that the producer had turned it down.

In late August, Tom encountered his old friend from St. Louis Willard Holland, as the former director was leaving his office at the *Hollywood Citizen-News*. His wife, Harriett, recalled, "Willard had been trying to reach Tom at the studio. Then we ran into him on Hollywood Boulevard and he almost cut Willard dead. He was with two or three other fellows—and the impression I got was he didn't want to see Willard at that time. This really hurt my husband, and he never tried to reach Tom again."[4] Nor did Tennessee Williams try to reach him, but, in the introduction to his 1945 collection of one-act plays, *27 Wagons Full of Cotton*, he paid eloquent tribute to the friend who was the first to recognize his talent and produce his plays. Holland died of congestive heart failure in 1963 at age fifty-five, without ever understanding what had happened to their friendship. What happened to Holland was what ended Tom's friendship with Clark Mills: a fearful, unfounded concern that they would spread the word around St. Louis that he was gay and it would then get back to his family.

On August 30, Audrey sent Tom some words of caution:

> Please do not sign any kind of contract that may be submitted to you by the National Theatre Conference, the Pasadena Playhouse, the Cleve-

Hollywood destroyed many writers but not the young Tennessee Williams. He was oblivious to "all the stars in heaven" and enjoyed the Chekhovian twilight of his studio office where he worked on *The Gentleman Caller*—to be renamed *The Glass Menagerie*.

76

His first assignment was to fashion what he called a "celluloid brassiere" for Lana Turner in *Marriage Is a Private Affair*. Removed from the film, then suspended and finally dismissed, he used his savings to complete *The Glass Menagerie*.

Tom described child-star Margaret O'Brien to Donald Windham as "a smaller more loathsome edition of Shirley Temple . . ."

LEFT: Christopher Isherwood

ABOVE: Tom with friend David Greggory during his suspension from MGM

"Two Moscow mules and a Singapore Sling"—Sculptor Tony Smith, his bride, actress/singer Jane Lawrence, best man Tennessee Williams

On the beach in Santa Monica, he wrote to his agent Audrey Wood,
exclaiming, "Isn't money beautiful!"

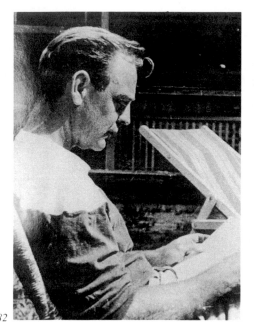

82

William Inge

83

Margo Jones, "the Texas Tornado"

84

85

"All that is not the worst of me surely
comes from Grand."

86

87

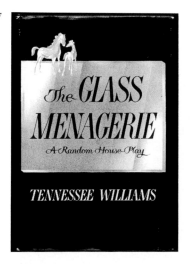

The play that transformed
the American theatre

88

THE GLASS MENAGERIE *was first produced by Eddie Dowling and Louis J. Singer at the Playhouse Theatre, New York City, on March 31, 1945, with the following cast:*

THE MOTHER	Laurette Taylor
HER SON	Eddie Dowling
HER DAUGHTER	Julie Haydon
THE GENTLEMAN CALLER	Anthony Ross

SETTING DESIGNED AND LIGHTED by Jo Mielziner
ORIGINAL MUSIC COMPOSED by Paul Bowles
STAGED by Eddie Dowling and Margo Jones

89

"The arrangement of Laura's hair is changed; it is softer and more becoming. A fragile unearthly prettiness has come out in Laura: she is like a piece of translucent glass touched by light, given a momentary radiance, not actual, not lasting."

90

"Laura? Laura Wingfield! You're keeping us waiting, honey!
We can't say grace until you come to the table!"

"A little silver slipper of a moon.
Look over your shoulder, Laura,
and make a wish."

Laurette Taylor with "Mr. Smith" in
her New York dressing room during
the run of *The Glass Menagerie*

93
94

The Chicago critics who saved *The Glass Menagerie:*
Ashton Stevens and Claudia Cassidy

95

Tom accepts the Drama Critics Circle Award from Howard Barnes
for the best play of 1945.

land Playhouse, or Margo Jones, personally. Tell them that all agreements must be read and approved by me before you can move on them. For instance, Frederic McConnell has already said that he would like a share of your royalties on "YOU TOUCHED ME," which he very obviously cannot have since you already have only a small share of royalties, what with Windham and D. H. Lawrence. Please be sure to tell Margo Jones that all publicity, unfortunately, must mention Donald Windham's name as co-author, which you agreed to when the contracts were signed. The story broke in the Times a week ago from California, not mentioning Windham's name and he is already disturbed.[5]

Tom was becoming troubled over his role as collaborator with Windham. He had already made one enigmatic remark about his hope that Donald had not grown to dislike him. Now he was anticipating problems over billing and publicity. Reacting to Audrey's letter, Tom quickly assured Windham that they would share cobilling in all publicity releases. He did feel, however, that the omission was due to the publicity value of his name and that they had better arm themselves against petty resentments and jealousies that could result from the fact that legally *You Touched Me!* was a joint property.

He also cited his contribution as being much the larger, saying that the credit and percentage are usually adjusted proportionately. For this reason, he claimed that he would normally receive a larger percentage in proportion to his contribution to the play; but he placed himself in the position of acceding to Windham's desire for a fifty-fifty division of royalties, when in fact Donald's only concern was that he have equal billing. In attributing to Windham what he himself had initiated with Audrey, he was in effect conceding to a demand that Donald never made. Actually, Tom was addressing something over which Tennessee Williams would forever stand guard: "the island of my self." He was attempting to say that because of their friendship, it was Donald and only Donald with whom he was willing to share such treasured territory. He said he was trying to avoid any resentment that might arise over their share in the accolades the play might receive, not in financial rewards.

This was the first injury of record that his and Donald's long and often troubled friendship would suffer. Still, Tom had not singled out his friend: *Anyone* caught in his orbit might circle, but never enter its center. In this way, he created his uniqueness and, conversely, perpetuated what he dreaded most, his isolation and loneliness. As for his professional reputation and the publicity value of his name, the young eagle was somewhat prematurely flapping his wings, although urged on to take flight by both Audrey and Margo.

Toward the end of August, Margo left for Texas, intending to go on to the Cleveland Playhouse in September to direct *You Touched Me!* She had received a letter from Hallie Flanagan, head of the National Theatre Conference, requesting a copy of the play. Margo replied, "I deeply feel Tennessee is the most talented young playwright that it has been my good fortune to know.

It would be difficult for me to express how deeply I feel that it is *my* job to see
that the world knows about Tennessee's plays."[6]

Writing to Donald, Tom told how Margo had managed to get funds from
the NTC to pay her round-trip transportation between Cleveland and
Pasadena while at the same time receiving a very good salary. He was clearly
in awe of her, the fact that she never seemed to tire or waver in her en-
thusiasms.

Although Tom was putting up a good front to all concerned, especially
Audrey, he was troubled by what his problems with the studio might do to his
relationship with her.

> 3 September 1943
>
>   The time is come to commence another journal. I hope it won't be
> as blue as the cover. It does not start off auspiciously, but let us leave that
> till later.
>
>   Today I picked up my check at Metro and went into LA. Very nervous
> and etc. but I went to a bar on Main Street and heard some ravaged old
> bags sing sentimental ballads. Then to *Watch on the Rhine* [film of Lillian
> Hellman's play] which was dull and false, one continuous fart from be-
> ginning to end.
>
>   How right I am to leave Hollywood! . . .
>
>   M-G-M called to inform me "things had not turned out as expected"
> and they were not renewing my option. . . .
>
>   Now the play will probably washout anyway, and me and the 8-ball
> will resume our rarely interrupted liaison. . . .
>
>   A siren races weirdly along the streets, receding. Fire or crime some-
> where. Everywhere, a dull sort of sick feeling in me, cough and cold.
>
>   Work pretty well, though, on The Spinning Song, which flowers into
> a newer, freer conception that might work out but would never solve an
> economic problem of the author. Never mind that, the author can bloody
> well take it.

"Cold, cold, cold / was the merciless blood of thy father"

This Tom wrote as the opening line in a poem he called "Cortege."[7] Written earlier in the summer, the poem expressed an unabated rage against his
father. But in *The Spinning Song* Tom was seeking a different dimension. The
play, as far as is known, was never completed. He signed the first long scene
with the name Thomas Lanier Williams; that identified it as having been
written before 1939. In 1942, he attempted to rework it with Rose in mind,
and now he was writing a fragmentary scene, which, although unsigned and
undated, appears in his journal to have originated in Santa Monica. A dramatic examination of the relationship between his mother and father, it pre-
cedes and lays the groundwork for the events depicted in *The Glass Menagerie*

and, beyond that, in *A Streetcar Named Desire*. A character named Blanche lives on a plantation called "Belle-reve." She is the mother of two children, a boy and a girl named John and Ariadne. The husband and father, Richard, is paying a periodical visit from New Orleans.*

Blanche tells him, "When you come back to Belle-reve plantation, you bring your turbulence with you. And when you leave, the columns are stained as if by muddy water."

RICHARD: You want me to stay away from here entirely?
BLANCHE: Yes, that's what I want.
RICHARD: And never see you?
BLANCHE: Not here where the children are. . . .
(He tells her he has to have "continual excitement.")
BLANCHE: Then, have it! But keep it from us!
RICHARD: Your blood is quiet and cool, but mine is always boiling.
BLANCHE: That's the trouble. Our marriage was a mistake.
(The light is dimmed, and there is "a confused murmur of voices and faint music of The Spinning Song.")
NARRATOR: Always before I sleep I hear that piece my mother used to play—"The Spinning Song." (music up a little) "The Spinning Song!" It takes me further than I could go on my thumb. North—through Baton Rouge—Natchez—Vicksburg—thirty miles north of that—Belle-reve Plantation! The earliest thing that I remember clearly—one Christmas morning—the set of Christmas blocks—the tree—my father's anger . . . (Scene: A small boy is crying at the foot of a Christmas tree—his blocks scattered on the floor beside him and the father glowering over him.)
FATHER: You've got to put them back the way you found them. You've got to be taught the necessity of doing things correctly. Slipshod ways will not be tolerated. I'm going to stand right here and watch you until you've put every one of those Christmas blocks back in the box exactly the way that you found them. Not jumbled up, but each one set in its proper place. Do you hear me? (The child stares at him with helpless fear.) Stop

---

The Spinning Song is excerpted here from a scene and fragment in the archives at the Humanities Research Center at the University of Texas, Austin.

Allean Hale points out that the young Tom Williams knew a woman in Clarksdale whose home was called Belle-Reve, a name he employed in *A Streetcar Named Desire*. Ariadne was named after one of Rose's friends at Hosmer Hall. Laura was taken from Laura Young, a parishioner of his grandfather's who had hung pendants of glass between two rooms in her home. These chimed when stirred and reflected myriad colors. "The Spinning Song" itself, a simple piece by Albert Ellmenrich, undoubtedly was used by Williams's grandmother in teaching him the piano.

As background for *The Glass Menagerie*, *The Spinning Song* is notable both for Williams's depiction of a scene cut out of his childhood and for the characterization of Richard as an absent and sympathetic father figure—the rationale behind the subsequent omission of Cornelius Williams from *Menagerie*.

crying like a baby and follow those instructions on the lid! Your mother's made you a sissy! (The Mother enters and moves to the piano. She plays The Spinning Song. The child runs to his mother for protection; she turns on the father.)

MOTHER: You've frightened him! . . .

FATHER: That's right! Turn the children against me.

MOTHER: They don't know you. You're a stranger almost. And it would be better for you to stay one than come home on holidays to shock them. (Ariadne enters clutching a doll. Stands frightened, staring. The Mother holds John against her.)

FATHER: They're my children.

MOTHER: You disowned them already.

FATHER: I've been cut off.

MOTHER: Yes, but you did the cutting!

FATHER: Laura, let's don't quarrel, not today!

MOTHER: (crying out) Look at poor Ariadne! Ariadne, come here! You've terrified her with your drunken shouting! (The little girl runs to her.) . . . See what you've done? You've spoiled their Christmas for them. They're not like other children. They're more easily bruised, they have to be sheltered more. . . . You bring a present and make it an instrument of torture! Ozzie! (The Negro nurse enters.) Take the children upstairs and give them their supper! (She kisses them.)

ARIADNE: (Gravely) Goodnight, Father. (John runs to the nurse, who lifts him and carries him out.) . . .

FATHER: I love the children.

MOTHER: You show it very strangely.

FATHER: I love *you*, Laura.

MOTHER: You show that strangely, too. . . . (He grasps her rigid figure in an embrace.)

FATHER: Find some way to quiet me, keep me still!

MOTHER: It's too late! . . . (The nurse is heard calling John. She appears.)

MOTHER: Hasn't he gone to bed?

OZZIE: No, Ma'am, he slipped away. (She sees him behind the column.) Oh, there he is, out on the po'ch ba'footed!

MOTHER: John, come back in here!
    (The child steps from behind the column.)
Kiss your father goodbye. He's leaving tonight.

JOHN: —No. —I don't like him.

FATHER: Goodbye, Laura. (He goes off.) . . .

MOTHER: John—sit on my lap.
Which is my little boy, which is he,
Jean qui pleur ou Jean qui rit?

As Tom personally struggled either to avoid his father or to banish him from his thoughts, the artist sought more and more to understand him. In *The Spinning Song*, he was seeking a resolution: how to explain the source within him of stifled rage and thwarted love. Finally, in *The Glass Menagerie*, Tennessee Williams's answer was to cast himself in the image of his father, in the more sympathetic mold of someone desperate for escape. "Tom who cried or Tom who laughed" had found a refuge for his father that Cornelius Coffin Williams was never to find in life.

Early in September, Tom reflected on the passing of summer. He acknowledged that it had been a full season in which he had had a surfeit of everything. Also, he had been virtually surrounded by "visiting firemen," past and present. Not only had he run into Willard Holland but Joe Hazan, Kip's friend, had also crossed his path. And Lem Ayers, Horton Foote, and David Greggory were regularly in touch. "Dear David," he wrote in his journal, "always with him I am especially shy and his understanding and caring seems only to make it more embarrassing." Jay Laughlin was planning to attend the play's opening in Pasadena in November, and even Cornelius was due in Los Angeles on business in October. And now his red-bearded friend, sculptor and painter Tony Smith, had suddenly appeared on the scene.

Janie and Tone

Tony brought the news that he was to be married as soon as his fiancée, Jane Lawrence, arrived from New York. Jane was a prominent member of the cast of *Oklahoma!* and had signed a six-month contract with Columbia Pictures at the urging of the composer Arthur Schwartz; he had become greatly impressed with her singing and acting talent and recommended her for the role of George Sand in *Song to Remember*, a film based on the life of Frédéric Chopin. Tom told Audrey that a distant relative of his, Jane (Lanier Brotherton) Lawrence, had arrived on the scene and that she was a wonderful girl.

"When I got out to the coast," Jane recalled, "we stayed briefly at that wild gypsy woman's rooming house where Tennessee was living, before we moved to a storefront apartment in Hollywood near the Columbia studios. I remember that at first Tenn and I were a little suspect of each other. He thought that Tony had made—as he told him—a *great* mistake. Then, a little later, he confided to me, 'Janie, I think you've made a *great* mistake!' "

"Tone and Janie," as Tom referred to them, were to become one of the prized and lasting friendships in Tennessee Williams's life. Although, as a young man, Tony Smith had painted extensively, he was a struggling architectural designer when he and Jane met. "He had been a 'clerk of the works' for the master architect Frank Lloyd Wright—he worked with Wright because at that time there was no school for creative architects." Ultimately, Tony would become a foremost educator and a renowned American sculptor. What interested Tom most about him was Tony's interest both in the theatre and, almost obsessively, in books and writers, in particular James Joyce. In addition, Jane said, "Tony was very theatre-conscious. Appia was his favorite designer."[8]

What struck Tony about Tom at that time was how removed he was, how he tended to keep life and love at arm's length. In his journal, Tom noted: "Tony says, 'Your hat is not in the ring! You're too young to be so outside of things.' " It had been only three years since his affair with Kip, when he said "good-bye to all that. What an eternity! But now everything seems running sand through tired fingers. I am unloved even by me. I love nobody." He was harboring feelings that would overtake him time and again all his life: a disconnection with the present and the need to move on and find the present somewhere else, a way to propel his writing: "With virtually no will and little enough consciousness I drift from one day to another, with energy that ebbs and flows within a shallow estuary. For quite a while I have had the same thought or feeling every night, that the shroud is already cut, that this period is sort of a final temporizing."

Toward the end of September, Jane and Tony married, with Tom acting as witness, the only person at the wedding. After a celebration with warm champagne and devil's food cake, they went to a nearby bar, where Jane said, "I sang until the wee hours—we got free drinks, not because of my singing, but because Tony had that red beard! It seems the owner was highly impressed with that—not many young men wore beards in those days. But Tennessee was my greatest fan, I think—whenever we were in a restaurant or a bar, he would always demand that I sing."

Jane said that after he had become famous, "Tennessee always walked *tall*—very tall—I think it was an image of himself—maybe how he would have liked to look—a tall, elegant man—and gentlemanly, cavalier, making you feel in his company very much a woman of whom he was proud. He always had an air—about who he was—a persona that was very special." But in September 1943, he presented a very different image. "I remember his attire—he sported a yachting cap, a long cigarette holder, and riding boots!" In fact, he never lost his fascination with hats, and one number he wore that summer was a narrow-brim Tyrolean hat adorned with a tiny feather. "He had a sense of the ridiculous though—the preposterous in life—and he could laugh as loudly at himself as he could at anyone or anything."[9]

> Tuesday Night
> Clean linen on the bed and a good book. Today no writee
> too sickee
> went into Hollywood dragged around my tired ass & came home
> about sundown.

No cruisee
no parkee
too tiredee
went to bedee
clean linen on bedee
kind of good bookee
shitee

Last night character from Ocean Park—writer and drunkard. Sweet. We talked about Tahiti where we both think of going après la guerre. Tried novel position in bed. OK till I came, then awfully tiresome. . . . Dull boy tonight. Excuse please. Very weak all day.

Wed. Nite

Pretty good work on verse play. Got check. Swam at "Y." Big swell dinner with cousin Jane (Lanier) Lawrence and Tony. Tony read Thoreau's Walden which impresses me enormously, not cold, not Puritan. An Elizabethan richness of language and deep lonely perception. I can use it in play. . . .

Tight-assed—Tony's expression for anything good. He calls Thoreau a "tight-assed old girl." So wonderful, I will probably use it. My contribution to our vernacular is bloomer girl. All the piddling literati I call bloomer girls, wonder if I am one?

No-o-o-o! Not me!

I am tight-assed (with bloomers). We were saying tonight writing will finally be more and more a projection of personality, direct, organic, less just writing.

Tony says I may finally stop being writer just be a person. Funny. Could be. writing disappear into life. the right direction.

On October 13, *You Touched Me!* opened in Cleveland, and because Margo wrote to him despairingly that under McConnell's direction "they mauled it," Tom chose not to go. Both Audrey and Windham attended the opening, and though Donald expressed dissatisfaction, her report was as favorable as the reviews. "It really all turned out much better than I think Margo Jones thought it would because, as you know, she was horribly depressed and disappointed and talked to me very sadly a long time before the play opened." Audrey felt, however, that despite Margo's disavowing any responsibility for the production, "I can tell you quite honestly that I'm more encouraged by the play now than I have ever been before."[10] Once Margo had returned to the West Coast, she and Tom continued to work toward a November 29 opening of the play at the Playbox.

It had taken Tom nearly a month to inform Audrey that he would not be given a new assignment and that his option would not be renewed. Paul saw his large, unearned compensation as "a triumph of art over commerce," but on receiving the news, Tom told Audrey, "I felt no kind of emotion, I merely thought, I wonder how dear little Audrey will feel about this? If you feel all right about it, then I do!" His reaction, he said, was to go on with "my own creations, which are two plays that I ricochet between and a group of stories I'm preparing for Laughlin maybe to publish." He thought that "something very, very good may come of it, as Laughlin regards me as you and Margo [do] with an affectionate blindness."[11]

In his journal, he noted that he had received a "brochure and nice letter from Laughlin. I am crazy about Jay. He has become my little shiny God. Why does he bother with me? It is so easy to ignore a squirt like me. My name in brochure and forthcoming works but Jay says they will be out late." His verse play, *The Purification*, was to be published in the anthology *New Directions 1944*. In addition, he told Audrey, "Laughlin is also bringing out 40 pages of my verse in his Young American Poets [1944], for which he has recently sent me a twenty-five dollar advance. Your two-fifty may be deducted from my next check to you. Laughlin is a rara avis, a very rich boy with a good heart and ready sympathy. . . . We need somebody like him in case we turn out something now and then worth printing."[12] Two stories that Laughlin would find worth printing in subsequent anthologies were "The Angel in the Alcove" and "The Mattress by the Tomato Patch."

The angel of the title is an apparition of a young writer's grandmother and it appears at intervals in the alcove of a garret the writer occupies in a New Orleans rooming house. He tells of being seduced by a tubercular artist who occupies the room next to his and who has awakened him and forcibly pressed his desires upon him. After the visitor's departure, the writer sees the angel in the alcove: "Yes, she was there. I wondered if she had witnessed the strange goings on and what her attitude was toward perversions of longing. But nothing gave any sign. The two weightless hands so loosely clasping each other among the colorless draperies of the lap, the cool and believing grey eyes in the faint pearly face, were immobile as statuary. I felt that she had permitted the act to occur and had neither blamed nor approved, and so I went off to sleep."[13]

During the time Tom was writing about his angel, Grand was still alive, although barely, and in his journal he expressed his guilt at not having written to her: "Disgraceful. I will, I will!" The specter of death was haunting him; in another entry, he said, "I only recently learned of the death of Miss Florence. So Mother wrote today. All those Saturday afternoons, Hazel and Miss Florence and I. It was really Miss Florence who was most tender toward me. She always spoke of 'your talent' when nobody else did. And in those times, dark, desperate days of adolescence, that meant something. Those afternoons were the bright spots of my life. Well, now she's dead. It brings death home."

There could be no better example of the extreme polarity of his moods than the fact that at the same time he was writing darkly of his angel, he was swinging into a light humor recounting his adventures in the Santa Monica rooming house, in a story entitled "The Mattress by the Tomato Patch." For anyone who visited Tom in his apartment (the combination dining room–kitchen that adjoined his "sanctified bedroom"), the experience was unforgettable. The immediate impression was that it had been ransacked by foreign agents. In the first draft of his story, he described how his typewriter reposed on "the green linoleum-covered table in the kitchen where the sun comes in like the gelatin flood of a burlesque show" and how Zola, his landlady, after sharing strong black coffee and confidences about *la vie horizontale*, would go out and sit on the front steps of the rooming house facing the ocean. "From there her indolent look can include everything from Marion Davies' beach home to the equally idiotic design of the roller-coasters at Venice."

The apartment building itself stood "directly above a municipal playground known as 'muscle-beach.' It is here that acrobats and the tumblers work out in the afternoons, great powerful Narcissans who handle their weightless girls and daintier male partners with a sort of tender unconsciousness beneath the blare and activity of our war-time heavens." And so it was that "the great white and blue afternoons of California go rocking over our heads, over the galleries, over the acrobats and Venice pier and the roller-coasters and hot-dog stands and the vast beach-homes of the most successful kept women, goes rocking and rocking, the giant white rocking-horse weather of southern California whose plumes are smoky blue ones the sky can't hold and so lets grandly go of!"[14]

No sex since last Thurs. probably my longest period of continence since early summer. Partly weakness—I am really near to collapse. Then luck when I go out is bad. I am not the radiant star of everybody's libido nowadays. My hair has gotten sort of ratty looking, my face dull and sallow, and my front teeth have two visible cavities that I am too lifeless to have fixed. It surprises me that even by moonlight I still sometimes attract a good party. These years, how does one go through them? Yet the loss of youth is never more than a peripheral concern of mine. My sorrows are all more phantasmic than that. I do not put much down even here, and so these notebooks despite their attempt at merciless candor about my life fall short, give very little, perhaps distort unfavorably for I seem inclined to note only the seedier things.

He had made no specific plans to follow the Pasadena opening of *You Touched Me!* He assured Audrey, "I find that I have accumulated a nice little savings account [here]. About three hundred. And with that and the N.Y. account I can live for about six months in some frugal manner in some remote place like New Mexico or Old, finish up one of the two plays and only emerge when the trumpet is blown somewhere."

As for his MGM misadventure, he allowed that his vine might have sour grapes, but he spoke a known truth that drove William Faulkner back to Mississippi and F. Scott Fitzgerald to drink: "There is a curious sort of spiritual death-ray that is projected about the halls of Hollywood. I sensed it first in the writers I met out here. All spiritual Zombies it seemed to me." He added, "I was frightened by the emotional deadness of these people, all superior craftsmen and many with really fine talents, but seeming all withered inside—the kiss of Lana Turner?"[15]

Go East Young Man

Toward the end of October, he noted in his journal, "Tomorrow I have to see my father in his hotel in L.A. Thank God Margo will go with me." His first fearful reaction was the imagined picture of Cornelius arriving at his apartment unannounced. He thought that he would give the apartment the look of vacancy with curtains drawn, doors locked, and a refusal to answer his phone. However, he was able to report that he had had "two more or less arduous meetings" with C.C. in his hotel room, where his salesmen were being given one of his sales talks and a plentiful supply of liquor. Tom wrote, "He appears very chastened and today we made talk alone for the first time in probably ten or fifteen years. A pathetic old man but capable of being a devil."

Bored and unabashed, Margo had more than a surfeit of drink and for the amusement of the salesmen did a wild dance. Cornelius, "dreadfully shocked," afterward sent Tom a wire asking to see him before he left the city. This time, David Greggory went with him, and he recalled, "Tennessee didn't especially want anyone to meet his father—and I was already disposed to hate him. I found it easy not to like him. I don't think he was very sober. He came off as hypocritical—Tennessee was on approval at all times, which is not a very comfortable feeling."[16]

Cornelius's purpose for the subsequent meeting was to urge him not to marry Margo. While C.C. admitted to having been "a slave to drink," and was in fact drunk when he said it, he also acknowledged that it was a family trait. He said that the Williams women had remained determinedly sober, and he hoped that Tom would never marry a drunken woman. Tom felt that their meeting might have been more endurable if his father had been his old self. As he looked upon him now, he could feel only pity for what had become of the Mississippi drummer, the opportunity he had lost and sacrificed to the practicalities of life, to marriage and the support of his children. But, as much as he loathed the old man, he knew that he was desperately lonely and starved for affection.

During November, Tom was mainly preoccupied with rewriting *The Spinning Song* in verse, and he provisionally renamed it *Presentational*. An entry made in his journal the day he met with his father mentioned, "Just read over the one fairly long thing I've done out here, the one-act version of The Gentleman Caller. It is appalling." But not long after, he noted, "I have returned to the original version of it. It won't be a total loss after all. But is very, very sentimental. Ah, well, I'm not Dostoyevsky nor even Strindberg. I must work within my limits. . . . So now I play my Hawaiian records and smoke my second pack of cigarettes for the day. This is hardly the behavior for a cardiac case but maybe my instinct tells me a long life would be evil and so puts the coffin nails in my hand and points to the hammer."

Tom now was, as he wrote in his journal, in a "happy state of mind and fairly creative too." He was tinkering with his story "One Arm" and felt that it had grown and had power.

> Sat. Night.
> Went to Olvera Street and Chinatown with Jane and Tony. Tired me dreadfully with all their shopping but we jested and camped merrily along. Tony in a beret and blue turtleneck sweater with his red beard Sensational. . . . They are good companions and real friends. I bought a lovely Chinese poster to hang in my room. . . . Feel phenomenally well. Why? Irresponsibility! Tony says I am a Chinaman. Last night the sweet writer who pushes wheelbarrows at nursery. I have always loved wheelbarrows. Jane and Tony say they do too.
> We all rode in them as kids. Writer pushing wheelbarrow made me happy somehow. We lay on sofa and heard symphony, quiet and warm. Room lighted only by gas range.

> Saturday—Nov. 6th
> GOD! I SEE! THE APE'S FACE! I'VE STOPPED WRITING.
> If I am careful this moment and from now on, I can maybe save myself from madness. It is worth doing anything to avoid that.
> So I will if there is any chance.
> Wanting the limitless, I am ruined by limits. My work breaks down into the slurrings of a crushed worm.
> If anything can break me, this thing will. If it doesn't I can die of attrition or turn into a watch tower.

> Sunday Nov 14
> Last Sat. I seem to have been a little upset. Was working on One Arm—read it over and decided that I had destroyed it.
> *Tant pire* [*sic*] but *no* call for hysterics. It is quite true that 97 percent of my work lately is abortive. Why? I can't say. It may be temporary—functional. It may be organic—incurable. All we can do is maintain our endurance—wait and see.

He went on to say, "I dreamt last night about J. Laughlin, that he had snubbed me when I called on him and the books left me out. Such appalling misery I felt, such desolation. A symbol of my worry about my weak writing."

The dream turned into a waking nightmare when Laughlin visited his apartment, which Tom described to Audrey as having "reached that state of disorder where just to look at it brings on a fit of the most colossal inertia, the way God must feel looking down at the human race in its present chaos! I have had no laundry done in weeks, I am wearing sweaters instead of shirts, unwashed dishes and pans have become a garden of fungi and a paradise of microscopic organisms who probably hold a better option on me than anyone else at this point. The California red ants are gradually removing everything that interests them." On viewing the spectacle, Laughlin left a note to call him, and Tom said that meeting him was worse than the prospect he suffered at confronting his father again.

Informing Audrey that Margo planned to leave for Texas the day after the opening, Tom said, "I will leave almost that soon for somewhere. God only knows how I will pack, how I will ever get moving! If I ever extricate myself from all this, I will let you know."[17] An act of circumstance gave him the decisive shove. The specter of the ill-fated scooter had raised its head. As David Greggory recalled, "He was owing several months' payments on it. And when he was pressed by the owner, he called me to say they were going to send a marshal, and he asked, 'What's a marshal?' I said, 'If the marshal comes to your door, you'll quickly know what it is.' So he took off for Hollywood to stay with Jane and Tony."[18]

As for the opening of *You Touched Me!* at the Playbox, he told Donald that it had been well received. He said that Laughlin attended the play and liked it, though Tom felt he was somewhat reserved.

Before departing for St. Louis, Tom spent his final week with Jane and Tony and met, among others, Man Ray and Henry Miller at Laughlin's suite. His report to Audrey was extremely enthusiastic: Although Ruth Ford had been compelled to drop out of the cast, Housely Stevens had replaced Carl Benton Reid, who had played the captain in Cleveland. But Tom felt the players, who were otherwise unknowns, were wholly adequate and told Audrey that the play was not only well received but, for him,

> a complete vindication of all the elements that McConnell distrusted and cut out in Cleveland. In fact that eliminated portion of the play was what seemed to entertain the audience most thoroughly last evening. The production had great warmth and charm and held the audience all the way through, the comedy and love scenes being greatly appreciated, the whole thing having a warmth, a lightness and a heart-touching reality which I had never guessed it could have.... This is the first time anything of mine has been done to my own satisfaction, so you know how happy I feel about it.[19]

Tom said that Margo had done a beautiful job of directing. He had stayed up all night to see her off on the train. There were smiles and a few tears as she waved out the window. David Greggory accompanied Tom and remembered him saying that he felt as though a tornado had passed through his life, a Texas tornado!

A letter from Dakin, home on a furlough, more or less determined Tom's decision to return to St. Louis. The principal motivation was Grand's illness. But for once he was not broke and could confront a "chastened" old man. Dakin asked, "Did Mother tell you we had a letter from Rose recently? It seems as though she must be much improved. I do hope that she is better. We are going to drive out to see her as soon as we can save a few gas ration coupons." He also said that he had been reading a copy of *You Touched Me!* "You must have left it the last time you were here for Mother found it and let me read it." He claimed he could hardly put it down. "We are all very proud of you, and I know that you are going to be very successful. Don't let anything discourage you."[20]

In mid-December Tom stopped off en route in Taos, and there he wrote to Tony Smith:

> I am spending a few days here on the snow-covered desert. Good news— Frieda Lawrence has received me very cordially indeed and has offered me a piece of her land, her ranch in the Lobos, to build on. For me it would be an ideal site. There is a spring which she has used to make a swimming pool. My heart skips around but I think that would be transitory. The snow is covered with tracks of wild animals, deer, fox, wolves, Etc. Frieda herself is a great animal—wears a coat and cap of bob-cat fur—shouts and plunges around—is wild-eyed. Could fuck you under the bed! Frieda gave me an unpublished play script of Lawrence's and a magazine published by Henry Miller in Paris called "The Phoenix." It is derived in philosophy from Lawrence but insincerely.
>
> There is a ghastly attack on *Joyce* in Miller's own article. How will you reconcile that with your admiration of Miller? It also contains a gratuitous attack upon *queens* in treating of Charles and Proust—"all beneath the banner of homosexuality."
>
> Calls Joyce a "Blind Milton" whose "vision has atrophied" and "who merely surrenders to darkness." In view of Joyce's actual struggle with blindness and the general triviality of the critique—however pretentious—I find the attack disgusting. The whole magazine an insult to Lawrence, really.[21]

Tom's anger at Henry Miller's denigration of Joyce may have been well founded, but for Lawrence, Miller had in truth "a passionate appreciation," the subtitle he gave to an unabashed paean. Lorenzo was still in Tom's view "a pure light in modern letters," and in Taos he visited again the small white chapel with the phoenix symbol atop—the final resting place of Lawrence's ashes.

Now, though, Tom was ready to return to St. Louis and from there to New York. It was Hollywood lost, permanently. He had arrived a playwright and, with the production of *You Touched Me!*, departed more a playwright than ever. While the experience left him with a distaste for art as a studio product, especially in its demeaning of the screenwriter, he was in fact deeply impressed with the wide-ranging, often poetic freedom of film itself, and this would influence his writing of *The Glass Menagerie* as well as other of his major plays.

27

"The Leaf on a Windowsill"

January–August 1944

I came home. It was a week before Christmas and there was a holly wreath on the door and somebody's next-door radio was singing *White Christmas* as I lugged my two suitcases up the front walk. I stopped half-way to the door. Through the frothy white curtains at the parlor windows I saw my grandmother moving alone through the lighted parlor like a stalking crane, so straight and tall for an old lady and so unbelievably thin!

It was a while before I could raise the brass knocker from which the Christmas wreath was suspended. I waited and prayed that some other member of the family, even my father, would become visible through those white gauze curtains, but no other figure but the slowly stalking figure of my grandmother who seemed to be moving about quite aimlessly to a soundless and terribly slow march tune, a brass band that was playing a "death march"—came into view!

No one else was at home, except Tom's grandfather, who had gone to bed. "Grand," he said, "was waiting up alone to receive me at whatever hour. I had not wired precisely when I might appear at the family door for this last homecoming of mine that she would take part in." At length, Tom knocked on the door. "I remember how she laughed like a shy girl, a girl caught sentimentalizing over something like a sweetheart's photograph, and cried out in her young voice, 'Oh, Tom, oh, Tom!' And as I embraced her, I felt with terror almost nothing but the material of her dress and her own arms burning with fever through that cloth."[1]

Tom had expected to find his grandmother bedridden. Instead, as he wrote Mary Hunter, she was "radiantly beautiful, all warm and white and shining" and spending the holidays fussing over her grandsons and assisting as best she could with household chores. Also, his grandfather's sight and hearing were improved, and as for his mother and father, he said they were "bravely continuing the quarrel that must have started the first time they found themselves in a dark room together."[2]

Years later, Tennessee recalled the night of his homecoming and told how he had heard his father stirring in the sunroom, where he slept. C.C. had arrived home drunk, and in his sleep was sighing and groaning and making "inebriate exclamations such as, 'Oh God, oh God!' He is unaware of my sleepless presence in the room adjoining. From time to time, at half-hour intervals, he lurches and stumbles out of bed to fetch a bottle of whiskey from some place of naive concealment, remarking to himself, 'How terrible!' At last I take a sleeping pill so that my exhaustion can prevail over my tension and my curiously mixed feelings of disgust and pity for my father, Cornelius Coffin Williams, the Mississippi drummer who was removed from the wild and free road and put behind a desk like a jungle animal put in a cage in a zoo."

The whiskey was all that transported C.C. from the reality of his day-to-day existence at the shoe company. As a rule, like clockwork, he came home evenings sober, ate alone, and took refuge in the one piece of furniture distinctly and obstinately his: an overstuffed chair next to "another veteran piece of furniture, a floor lamp that must have come with it . . . one of the most ludicrous things a man has ever sat under, a sort of Chinesey-looking silk lamp shade with a fringe about it, so that it suggests a weeping willow."[3]

Throughout Christmas and New Year's, Grand's remarkable display of stamina deceived everyone except Edwina, who kept saying to Tom, "She just won't give up!" Although her health had been slowly deteriorating during the past ten years, she had continued to make the long trips from Memphis to St. Louis until finally her strength gave out. She was down to eighty-six pounds and racked by a persistent cough, finally diagnosed as a spreading lung cancer.

In addition to her illness, what Grand feared most had also happened: She and Walter were now dependent upon their daughter and son-in-law. Although Cornelius was always respectful toward Grand, his open contempt for "the Parson" was one of the factors that kept her going. What would happen when she could no longer keep the peace between them? Her husband, now in his eighty-seventh year, hard of hearing, and with cataracts on both his eyes, might soon become helpless and be put away if Cornelius had anything to say about it. Without his wife to earn the extra income from sewing and music lessons, all the Reverend Dakin would have left was a small pension of eighty-five dollars a month and the little that remained from the sale of their home in Memphis.

But Walter Edwin Dakin had much in common with his grandson. Like Tom, he felt a restless urge to move about at the slightest excuse. A church conference or the marriage or burial of some distant parishioner was all he needed to go off on a bus or train. Often he would visit wealthier Episcopalians, who were always glad to receive him as their guest. Tennessee later characterized his grandfather as "an unconsciously and childishly selfish man . . . humble and affectionate but incurably set upon satisfying his own impulses whatever they may be." It was only at the last, when the old couple was compelled to go to St. Louis to live, that Grand began to rebel against his fitfulness, and that was only "for a reason that she couldn't tell him, the reason of death being in her, no longer possible to fly in front of but making it necessary, at last, to insist on staying when he wanted to leave."

The entire family had become so accustomed to Grand's gentle presence that even now it did not seem possible that death would soon overcome her courageous spirit. During her many years of personal sacrifice, her husband, the popular and charming clergyman, "would conduct parties of Episcopal ladies through Europe, deck himself out in the finest clerical vestments from New York and London, go summers to Chautauqua and take courses at Sewanee, while [Grand] would lose teeth to save dental expense, choose her eyeglasses from a counter at Woolworth's, wear at the age of sixty dresses which were made over relics of her bridal trousseau, disguise illness to avoid the expense of doctors."

On her visits to St. Louis, "She always came with a remarkable sum of money sewed up in her corset," the money she earned, which could be as much as several hundred dollars. It meant help for Edwina in augmenting Cornelius's stingy allowance and in meeting payments for the small grand piano in the Williamses' living room. For the children, it also meant "nickels for ice cream, quarters for movies, picnics in Forest Park, it meant soft and gay laughter like the laughter of girls between our mother and her mother, voices that ran up and down like finger exercises on the piano, it meant the propitiation of my desperate father's wrath at life and the world which he, unhappy man, could never help taking out upon his children except when the presence, like music, of my grandmother in the furiously close little city apartment cast a curious worldly spell of peace over all there confined. And so it was through the years, almost without any change at all, as we grew older. 'Grand' was all that we knew of God in our lives! Providence was money sewed in her corset!"[4]

On Epiphany, January 6, 1944, Grand died "after a spurious, totally self-willed period of seeming recuperation."

> I left the house right after dinner that evening. She had washed the dishes, refusing my mother's assistance or my grandfather's or mine, and was at the piano playing Chopin when I went out the door.

When I returned only two or three hours later, the whole two-story house which we now occupied was filled with the sound of her last struggle for breath.

I went upstairs. At the top of the steps, where my grand-mother's hemorrhage had begun was a pool of still fresh blood. There was a trail of dark wet blood into the bathroom and the toilet still unflushed was deep crimson and there were clotted bits of voided lung tissue in the toilet bowl and on the tiles of the bathroom floor. If an ox had been slaughtered in the bathroom there could not have been more blood, and later I learned that this incontinent giving up of her lifeblood had occurred almost immediately after I had left the house, three hours ago, and still in her bedroom my grandmother was continuing, fiercely, wildly, unyieldingly, her battle with death which had already won that battle halfway up the stairs. . . .

I didn't dare enter the room where the terrible struggle was going on. I stood across the hall in the dark room which had been my brother's before he entered the Army, I stood in the dark room, possibly praying, possibly only sobbing, possibly only listening, I don't know which, and across the hall I heard my mother's voice saying over and over again, Mother, what is it, Mother what is it, what are you trying to tell me?

I only dared to look in. My mother was crouched over the figure of my grandmother on the bed, obscuring her mercifully from me. My grandfather was knelt in prayer beside his armchair, the doctor was hovering helplessly over all three with a hypodermic needle and a bowl of steaming water and this or that bit of useless paraphernalia.

Then all at once the terrible noise was still. I went into my room.

My mother was gently closing my grandmother's jaws and eyes. . . .

Then a year or so ago my mother happened to tell me that she had finally found out what my grandmother was trying to tell her as she died, but hadn't the strength to. "Your grandmother kept pointing to the bureau, and later I found out that she had her corset in there with several hundred dollars sewed up in it!"

After Grand's body had been removed to a mortuary, Cornelius came home and received the news from Edwina, who said simply, "Cornelius, I have lost my mother." But a great deal more than that had been lost. The realization that the ballast during the many years of the family's life was gone so struck him that he dropped into his overstuffed chair and, "like a man who has suddenly discovered the reality in a nightmare," kept saying over and over again to himself, "How awful, oh, God, oh, God, how awful!"[5]

A gallant lady, Rose Otte Dakin typified a way of life of gentle strength and decency that at the very moment of her death was being irretrievably destroyed in a worldwide holocaust. Years afterward, her grandson wrote his reminiscence Grand, "in partial recompense for that immeasurable gift of the spirit that she had so persistently and unsparingly . . . pressed into my hands when I came to her in need."[6]

Tom did not attend Grand's funeral, giving as his excuse a disdain for such "bourgeois rituals." The truth was that he could not bear to see her in death. Instead, he chose that time to have another eye operation. It was "quite successful," he reported to Audrey. "Now with a thick lens I have 20/30 vision in the bad eye, which is certainly a great improvement over total blindness."[7] Tom had left Los Angeles with eight hundred dollars in savings and in addition had his St. Louis and New York accounts, but, regardless, his father saw fit to give him a hundred dollars to pay for the operation.

Despite his increasingly heavy drinking and the fact that he was ill a great deal of the time, Cornelius would live for another twelve years. Had it not been for the regard of his boss, Paul Jamison, for Edwina, C.C. would probably by this time have been retired or fired. A desperately lonely, unloving, and unloved man, he had every reason to die except for his fear of death. In contrast, the Reverend Dakin embraced life. With the arrival of spring, he would accompany his wife's body to Waynesville, Ohio, to the cemetery across the river in Corwin, where ultimately they would lie together. He was fond of saying that Rose Otte Dakin was born on All Soul's Day and died on the feast of Epiphany. He would die on St. Valentine's Day at age ninety-seven.

Tennessee in Flight

Tom remained in St. Louis until mid-March. He continued to work on *You Touched Me!*—incorporating changes suggested by Frieda Lawrence and writing "Homage to Ophelia," which he labeled "A Pretentious Foreword to the Play." In his letter to Mary Hunter, he told her that he had been looking mainly to her as both producer and director. He reassured her that he was not intending to make any commitments until he had heard from her. It irked him to read that producer Carly Wharton was backing the production of director Margaret Webster's version of Chekhov's *The Cherry Orchard*.

> Those two fine ladies! This is not sarcasm but tinged with sorrow. In the first place I think Carly might very well back *your* production of *The Cherry Orchard*—or even better, *The Sea Gull*—and in the second place I don't see Nazimova mentioned. In the third place—Mr. Chekhov is dead and I am the living author of one reasonably good play which I think might make her a lot more money. Does this sound childish? Yes—I do know better. My faith in Carly is not really affected but the Webster is still a red flag. She always makes me think of what Peg of Old Drury yelled to the mob that stopped her coach mistaking her for the king's mistress—"*I* am the *Protestant* whore!"

The quotation he cited was more the reflection in a handheld mirror. Of course, he did "know better." As the director of *Battle of Angels*, Margaret

Webster had accomplished as much for him as anyone could have under the circumstances, and she had been personally solicitous of him in his hour of defeat. But this was the emerging Tennessee Williams taking flight, and from this point on he would not just write his plays but would circle over them protectively, his eye fiercely fixed on their life in the theatre.

During his few remaining weeks in St. Louis, Tom concentrated his time and energy on writing, to the exclusion of almost everything else. Searching through his University of Iowa papers, he made a single-page outline of "A Balcony in Ferrara," then rewrote a short story, "The Red Part of a Flag." Renamed "Oriflamme," it portrays a young, fatally ill woman, who on the last day of her life is hysterically driven to purchase a bright red dress, "all wine and roses flung onto her body," and who in her attempt to evade death confronts "a gigantic equestrian statue . . . this menacing giant" with the inscription "Saint Louis," symbolizing the city that is her prison. She collapses onto a nearby bench to catch her breath, and all at once "the foam of a scarlet ocean crossed her lips." The image of his grandmother's death was still fresh in Tom's mind.[8]

Donald had sent him a copy of Chekhov's *My Life*, and, inspired by what he described as "the most curiously living thing" of all that he had read of Chekhov, he wrote one of his finest short stories, "The Vine." Here, Tennessee Williams was dealing with something he would never be able to reconcile in himself, the conflict between the dread of loneliness and the fear of a binding love. During his summer in Laguna, he had written in his journal, "My loneliness makes me grow like a vine about people who are kind to me—then it is hard to loosen the vine when the time has come for separation."

At once terrifying and poignant, "The Vine" is a study of two hopelessly dependent people, an unemployed middle-aged actor and his wife, entwined and doomed in their love for each other. The actor, apprehensive that his wife has left him, ponders, "When you came home alone after being alone on the street, how was it bearable not having someone to tell all the little things you had on your mind? When you really thought about it, when you got down to it, what was there to live for outside of all-encompassing and protecting intimacy of marriage?" What was the alternative? "Going to bed alone, the wall on one side of you, empty space on the other, no warmth but your own, no flesh in contact with yours! Such loneliness was indecent! No wonder people who lived those obscenely solitary lives did things while sober that *you* only did when drunk. . . ."[9] The emerging influence of Chekhov in this story without violence or melodramatic climax would ultimately pervade "the little play" that he was still calling *The Gentleman Caller*, which he had shunted aside for the time being.

Preoccupied with his writing and trying to decide what move to make next, Tom had not seen any of his old St. Louis friends during his stay at home. Hazel, inconsolable in her grief over the recent loss of Miss Florence, had returned to Madison with her husband. In the end, the greater dependency of

Hazel upon her mother, even in death, would destroy the lesser bond of her marriage. Tom could only ask himself whether it would have been any different if he and Hazel had married, or whether his would have become the same twisted, embittered married life of Edwina and Cornelius Williams.

Rose, who had been in a North Carolina convalescent home, was now back in the Farmington asylum and refusing to eat. In "Homage to Ophelia," Tom wrote, "When Wordsworth speaks of daffodils or Shelley of the skylark or Hart Crane of the delicate and aspiring structure of Brooklyn Bridge, the screen of imagism is not so opaque that you cannot surmise at some distance behind it the ghostly but ineluctable form of Ophelia." The homage he was paying was as much to Rose as to Ophelia, and there were elements in it of an evolving character he would name Laura.

He said that all the Ophelias of literature and life had about them an "inconstancy of heart and frailty of mind and body . . . a tendency toward schizophrenia and consumption." Still, for all her delicacy and tenuousness, Ophelia represented for him "the most precious archetype that our literature possesses."[10] Surely, Ophelia became *his* most precious archetype, as characters such as Blanche DuBois, Alma Winemiller, Catherine Holly, and Hannah Jelkes demonstrate, following after Matilda Rockley and Laura Wingfield.

In the aftermath of Grand's death, a pall had settled over the house. Edwina became unnerved and began nagging at Tom to stop writing and get his rest, "hollering down the laundry chute to go to bed." He wrote to Donald, complaining of a "*crise de nerfs*," of becoming so dizzy at times he couldn't stand up, of the reasonless feelings of panic, palpitations, nausea, chill, and finally he announced that he had contracted the seven-year itch. The seven years lasted only three weeks, during which he had to spend several days without bathing, wearing long underwear covered with grease, his outraged family saying that gentlemen just don't have such things. The more troubling itch, however, was, as always, the need to move on, although he still had no idea in which direction. Possibly he might return to New York, or maybe go to New Orleans or Mexico. But there would soon be a compelling reason to return to New York. Unbeknownst to Tom, James Laughlin had recommended him for a thousand-dollar grant from the American Academy and Institute of Arts and Letters, citing him as "the most talented and promising young writer whom we publish."[11] Writing to Jay Laughlin, Tom said, "the old fish-peddler [flesh peddler] Liebling woke me up early this morning on the phone saying he had a letter to read me. I was very indifferent as I supposed it was from those scooter people in California or something equally fatuous but disagreeable. Consequently I was a little thunder-struck when it turned out to be from Walter Damrosch . . . informing me that [the institute] was going to present me on May 19th with a thousand dollars. . . ." He went on to say that it was difficult to express his gratitude for Laughlin's "part in their dispensation."[12] On the promise of being handed this award, he left immediately for

New York. Now he would have the money he needed to go off to Mexico and write that "big" play.

> **"K.—dear K.—**
>
> **I love you with all my heart.**
>
> **Good-night."**

Shortly after his return to New York in mid-March, Tom was again confronted with the death of someone he loved deeply—the one person about whom he had once cared as passionately as he did about his work. Parting from Kip Kiernan in the summer of 1940, he had written in his journal, "The heart forgets to feel even sorrow after a while." But now he was to discover that as love resides in the heart, so, too, does sorrow.

Kip had married and had become a member of the Hanya Holm dance company. But a brain tumor that at first was thought to be benign had progressed to the point where it was now inoperable. At twenty-six, Kip was doomed. Tom was in Audrey's office when he received a call saying that his young friend was in Polyclinic Hospital, had only a short time to live, and was calling for "Tenny." Tennessee later recalled his feelings: "You know how love bursts back into your heart when you hear of the loved one's dying."

He asked Donald Windham to accompany him to the hospital: "I was afraid to go alone. As I entered Kip's room he was being spoon-fed by a nurse: a dessert of sugary apricots. He had never looked more beautiful, although the sugar syrup dripped from his mouth. His wife was there, too. They were calmly discussing taking a trip to the West Coast," and Kip wanted to know what it was like out there. Although it seemed that his mind was as "clear as his Slavic blue eyes," Kip's vision was severely limited, and he asked, "Tenn, sit there in the corner so I can see you." Believing that the surgeons had failed to remove sutures when they had operated upon him the year before, Kip also thought he would soon recover once they were removed. "But his eyes kept saying things to me," Tennessee wrote, "that controverted the undignified prattle. I longed to leap up from my corner and embrace him, but I observed the ritual of sprightly dissimulation." He wrote that finally, "I rose and reached for his hand and he couldn't find mine, I had to find his.

"When Donnie and I left, we went straight to the nearest bar. After several drinks, I went to a Japanese shop and bought Kip a lovely cream-colored Shantung robe and the next day I brought it to him. 'No visitors,' it said on his door. Inside, it was deathly still." It was not long after that Kip died. Although in time Tennessee would find a companion to give him the devotion he had wanted from Kip, he was never again to release, or openly display, the burst of feeling that he had had for this stricken youth. It was the full-grown artist now who would stand guard between him and a heart gone wild, for this bordered too much on an abandonment to madness.

A few years after Kip's death, James Laughlin published Tennessee Williams's first collection of short stories, *One Arm and Other Stories*. The dedication read "To the memory of Kip." For decades afterward, Tennessee carried in his wallet a photograph of the handsome youth, and he was to say, "Well, Kip, you live in my left-over heart."[13] But in the spring of 1944, the revenant presence of the youth who resembled the young Nijinsky hovered over him, and he wrote "Death is High"—"my longing was great to be comforted and warmed once more by your sleeping form, to be, for a while, no higher than where you are, little room, warm love, humble star!"[14]

Shortly after Kip's death, he had received direct word from Walter Damrosch, president of the American Academy and Institute of Arts and Letters, informing him that he had won the grant of one thousand dollars "in recognition of your creative work in literature and to further your efforts in that direction."[15] Tom immediately sent an effusive handwritten and somewhat fictional reply from his favorite West Side pension, the Sixty-third Street YMCA:

> This grant is really an act of God! I have just finished the first draft of a play in verse but doubted I would have the leisure to push it through. My Hollywood savings had dwindled to a point where the need was imminent of getting another job. Jobs mean the virtual secession of creative designs. Hence the almost supernatural atmosphere of this good fortune![16]

As for the dwindling of his Hollywood savings, there was still his New York account, which made it possible for him to rent a cottage on Ocean Beach at Fire Island for the month of May and to live in the same style as he had when he first came to New York on the strength of the Rockefeller fellowship. But he confessed to Jay Laughlin, "I am beginning to hate N.Y. again already—I spent the night before last in the Federal Pen. I was picked up crossing the park after midnight and didn't have my registration [draft] card on me. In fact I didn't possess one. Was turned over to the FBI and incarcerated for the night. I am now out with a subpoena while my cards are being sent from Clayton. The night in the Pen was fearful! But I have made some good friends at the FBI—they are really very gentlemanly."[17]

On May 9, he accepted the award given in the Academy's auditorium. Donald went with him; both found the ceremony comic and got the giggles, but they enjoyed meeting Eudora Welty. The award's citation read: "To Tennessee Williams, born in Mississippi, in recognition of his dramatic works which reveal a poetic imagination and a gift for characterization that is rare in the contemporary theatre." With the *New York Times* carrying the story, he was under pressure to write a play for Broadway.

It disappointed him to learn that Mary Hunter had elected to produce and direct Horton Foote's *Only the Heart*, which lasted forty-seven performances and delayed any possibility of her presenting *You Touched Me!* for the time being. Carly Wharton went ahead with a successful production of Chekhov's *The Cherry Orchard*, directed by Margaret Webster. Putting aside *The Spinning Song*, Tom decided instead to complete *The Gentleman Caller*, on the chance that it might appeal to a prestige producer. Then once again, he set off for another summer in Provincetown.

There was at this time an apparent strain between Audrey and Tom, which very likely had to do with Mary Hunter, about whom Audrey had her doubts. She had not written to him for a while, and he had asked, "Are we having a silent argument over something? If so, what?"[18] In negotiating directly with Hunter and mailing her the revisions to *You Touched Me!* without first sending them to Audrey, Tom was acting unilaterally, making in effect a commitment without the consideration of his agent. This was something Tennessee Williams would do over and over again, only to resort to profuse apologies and the making of amends—when amends were possible. Often he would turn angrily on the hapless person with whom he had made an agreement, never understanding that in the theatre a verbal deal was as good as a signed contract. And so Audrey was forever undoing his doings.

There was also the matter of money. Without any income, he was rapidly depleting his savings. His New York account, down to about five hundred dollars when he left for Provincetown, was what he hoped would carry him through the summer while he completed *The Gentleman Caller*. Once the script was in Audrey's hands, he intended to return to St. Louis briefly, where he had placed the money from the thousand-dollar grant in a savings account. Then, with his mother parceling out his month-to-month needs, he would be free to go off to Mexico City, which, he was convinced, would become the postwar Paris of the 1940s.

Although Audrey was not entitled to nor would she want a percentage of his grant money, here again Tom was bypassing her. Donald Windham recalled that Tom was often suspicious of her, displaying a paranoia that would periodically afflict their relationship. All that was needed to set off a seizure of dark doubts and misgivings was the mere suggestion that his trust was being abused in some way. Undoubtedly, Audrey's feelings were hurt, and in her fashion she chose the rebuke of silence.

On Tom's arrival in Provincetown, war news was on everyone's lips: D day had come at last, the Allied forces had established a beachhead in Normandy, and Paris would soon be liberated. Those at home could only imagine what it was like abroad. Dakin's troopship had made it to South Africa and from there would sail for India and Burma, although a companion ship had been torpedoed and all five thousand on board lost. But news of far grimmer statistics, of an unparalleled genocide, were beginning to emerge with the first reports of a Nazi "murder camp" near Lublin, on the eastern border of Poland.

American shores remained untouched. The summer ocean was as warm, sparkling, and inviting as ever, and only the Atlantic's horizon conjured up the unimaginable horror of the carnage abroad. Otherwise, as people often remarked uneasily, "You'd hardly know there was a war on." Tom quite naturally thought of his "kid brother" overseas and of friends like Clark Mills, who was now in the midst of the European conflict. But, although he experienced mixed feelings of guilt and concern over whether they were all right, the war's only reality for him was contained within the covers of *Time* magazine.

He told Donald that he was back on Captain Jack's Wharf. He had taken a one-room studio apartment close to the one where he had stayed with Kip, and he mentioned that Kip's friend Joe Hazan was there, too, and that it all seemed rather haunted, though pleasant. As for the colony itself, Tom observed that it resembled bedlam with a mixed bag of Manhattan migrants: Valeska Gert, Robert Duncan, Jackson Pollock, Lee Krasner (who married Pollock the following year), Fritz Bultman and his wife, Jeanne, and the music and dance critic Edwin Denby, who was hiding out in a rustic shack among the windswept dunes. Hans Hofmann and his wife, Miz, were taking in students at their summer art school.

Valeska Gert was apparently now on speaking terms with her former waiter. She told him that she had employed a seventy-year-old female midget called Mme. Pumpernickel, who went into jealous rages whenever Valeska was onstage. Fräulein Gert had been hauled into a Provincetown court for failing to pay her dancing partner and for throwing garbage out her window. Tom was asked if he would be a character witness, being no doubt considered an authority on how to dispense with an accumulation of garbage. His friends were surprised that he would testify for someone who had fired him, but he said simply that he liked her. Why had she fired him? Because, she said, he was so sloppy.

As Tom soon found out, there was little peace to be found in Provincetown in the summer of 1944. Not since the Roaring Twenties had there been such rampant hedonism. The mood was one of mounting optimism that the war would soon be over, and there was a pervading hope that those young men about to go into uniform or still waiting stateside might be able to avoid the bloodshed. Tom had heard from Dakin in Burma. A python had been killed outside his tent, and he had had to walk a mile to take a bath. Why bathing was a problem during the monsoon season, Tom couldn't understand.

After making possible the American Academy grant, James Laughlin was now undertaking the publication of *Battle of Angels* in *Pharos*, a new magazine he would be introducing. Tom was delighted at the news and also because Laughlin sent him one hundred dollars as half of an advance payment.

By mid-June, he had wired Audrey: PLEASE SEND ONE HUNDRED DOLLAR CHECK GENERAL DELIVERY PROVINCETOWN RIGHT AWAY. And then he inquired rather wistfully, LOVE? TENNESSEE.[19] Early in July, he wrote again to the silent Audrey: "I am moving into a little shanty in the dunes where I can avoid the summer crowd. I find this a good place to work and think I will get a play off to you next week, 'The Fiddle in the Wings' which used to be 'The Gentleman Caller' all done but the *first* scene which is a very tricky one, as it must establish all the non-realistic conventions used in the play." On July 5, he received a stiff little note from Audrey's secretary, saying, "Miss Wood has asked me to send you the enclosed check for $100 and to tell you that your bank balance, deducting this $100, is now down to $229.84 so go easy on it."[20]

Meanwhile, the indefatigable Margo Jones had returned to the Pasadena Playhouse for the summer and was readying a production of *The Purification*, due to premiere on July 27. She had hoped that Tom would want to be on hand, but there was not only the matter of money but also the problem of the damned scooter and a zealous process server. Apparently with the object of inducing Tom to make the trip, Tony Smith began a letter in which he told of attending Margo Jones's production: "I want you to know that seeing *The Purification* presented on the stage had the emotional impact of making me feel at home in America for the first time. It was a point of reference. It was something happening on a plane on which nothing of that sort had happened before. It was outside. It was real. There was nothing esoteric. Nothing ineffable. There was no cult. It was a solid, measurable piece of work."[21] Margo presented her production of *The Purification (or Song for the Guitar)* for three performances and directed it again in 1954 at her theatre in Dallas. When James Laughlin published *The Purification* in 1945 in *27 Wagons Full of Cotton and Other One-Act Plays*, Tennessee Williams dedicated it "For Margo Jones."

At the time *The Purification* premiered, Tom was still working on the play he now referred to simply as *The Caller*. He didn't feel it was very exciting, but it was a way of keeping busy until he could direct his energies into the big play he hoped to write in Mexico. His energies, to judge from the letters he wrote Donald Windham, were mainly devoted to life in and around P-town, to pursuit and being pursued—and in one instance, to avoid a determined second-night stand, he rode his bicycle two miles out to Joe Hazan's shack on the dunes. Since everyone was earning more and spending more than he or she had had since the twenties, Tom was finding it difficult to hold on to his self-imposed allowance. He sent another wire to the still-silent Audrey: PLEASE AIR MAIL OR WIRE ONE HUNDRED DOLLARS. PLAY NEARLY COMPLETED. LEAVING SOON.[22]

Though he may have had it in mind to return to New York, a plan was nothing in Tom's life if it could not be changed at the last minute. Suddenly, he decided to go to Cambridge in pursuit of a twenty-two-year-old law student, an acquaintance of the poet W. H. Auden. The student's name was Bill Cannastra, and one who knew him, Dorothy Farnan, described him as "having a coterie of admirers . . . he was frankly heterosexual and looked like Botticelli's Saint Sebastian."[23] Tennessee in *Memoirs* remembered him as "one of the aboriginal 'beats'—I mean he was beat before there were 'beats'; he was a beautiful gangling kid with dark hair and light eyes and a stammer." He said he was also a voyeur.

Having complained about Provincetown, Tom found the ivy-covered dormitories of Harvard hardly the ascetic refuge he had envisioned. "I was not yet quite through with my last draft of *Menagerie*, and I was not yet quite ready to return to Manhattan with it. This boy, Bill, had a group of friends at Harvard and they were all sort of freaked out, in varying degrees. One had attempted to slash his wrists a few days before—I remember how this attempt on his life had made him a celebrity in the group and the shy pride he took in exhibiting the scars when the wrists were unbandaged."[24] After partying among the "very mad crowd of young professors and students," Tom departed as precipitately as he had arrived—and as characteristically—judging from a letter from Bill that followed him back to Provincetown. "By now you probably know that you left unteen [*sic*] things here in Cambridge including your brief. I rather expected frantic appeals as to the latter but since you haven't written about it I've put it with your other things. If, however, you do want it sent on, I'll mail it or bring it to Provincetown on the 19th. You also left tooth brush, shaving equipment—I guess that's all."[25] The briefcase contained the draft of his nearly completed little play, which, if need be, he either would rewrite or would simply go on to something else.

In later years, Tennessee continued on occasion to see Bill Cannastra, who made an effort to bring him and Auden together. In one instance, he took Tennessee to Auden's apartment, and its disarray Williams ironically described as the worst he had ever seen. The poet was polite but conspicuously cool. Again in the early fifties in Italy, Tennessee and Truman Capote called on Auden, who refused to see them. "According to Wystan himself," Farnan wrote, "he behaved in the same way a year or so later when Somerset Maugham asked to visit him. When asked why, Wystan answered with that half-smile: 'He simply won't do, you know. He really won't do.' "[26] In time, Auden became bored with Bill Cannastra, as well.*

On Tom's return to Provincetown and with the return of his briefcase, toothbrush, and assorted accessories, he set to work again to complete *The Caller* and to move ahead with his plan to go to Mexico. He was regularly bicycling out on the dunes to see Joe Hazan, who was intending to drive to Mexico City in January with his mistress. Tom tentatively decided to go with them, hoping they would all live in a big house in the city.

---

*Cannastra was killed on 12 October 1950, at the age of twenty-eight, in a subway accident in New York—at the Spring Street station on the Seventh Avenue line. He was leaning out a subway window, waving to friends on the platform, when the train suddenly accelerated, and he was nearly decapitated by a column. When told of his death, Auden remarked that the most tragic thing about it was that it had caused a three-hour delay in the New York subways.

"La Fin d'Eté . . ."

He said it was the saddest thing of all, this end of summer. Provincetown in the early fall takes on a different, more casual pace: The vast beaches and dunes are virtually deserted, the windows of many houses are boarded up, the remaining stock in the merchants' shops is sharply reduced in price, the marigolds and zinnias replace morning glories and snapdragons, and the pubs are populated by familiar faces. Suddenly, there is relief from the frenetic social scene, which has moved back to New York; the "belles," as Tom commented, after their two weeks' vacation had gone back to Macy's counters and all things gaily au courant.

In September, New Directions published twenty-seven of Tennessee Williams's poems under the heading "The Summer Belvedere"; this was included in the *Five Young American Poets'* third series. In a preface, Tom wrote a warm and glowing tribute to his St. Louis friend Clark Mills, who was at this time a member of the army's counterintelligence, European theatre of operations, and would soon be fighting in the historic Battle of the Bulge.

A young gifted poet, a Mississippian from Columbus like Tom, Blanchard Kennedy, had spent a few afternoons with Tom and evidently received a lecture and an analysis from the older poet. Another visitor at this time was Harold Norse, also a poet, who shared with Tom a small log cabin belonging to the painter Karl Knaths. Norse recalled Tom as writing all morning, drinking endless cups of coffee, and spreading his work everywhere he could find space. He spoke, too, about his "woebegone, tragic, hapless personality" and about how this made one feel "protective, sorry for him." Norse saw him as a loner, terrified of poverty and failure: "It practically emanated from him like a physical substance." But, he said, "I learned very soon that beneath the guileless exterior there beat a heart of solid gold bullion. Tennessee was as shrewd and practical as I was rash and impractical. He never said anything openly critical or hostile to anyone, although he was waspish enough, at times, when they were out of earshot. He knew where he wanted to go and not for one moment wavered from that goal. And it was that very fall of 1944 that he reached it." When Norse inquired about the play he had written, Tom dismissed it as "a potboiler."

Norse recalled that at night they occupied a bunk bed, Tom in the upper bunk and he in the lower. "One night, before we went to sleep, we were discussing the difficulties of being homosexual. 'It's probably the worst kind of existence in the world,' I said. 'Having to hide such a great need for love and sex has got to be the most painful kind of life.' 'All homosexuals,' said Tennessee, in a choked voice, 'have to live with a deep wound that never heals.' "[27]

With his summer money about gone, Tom's departure for New York was imminent, and for the little time that he intended to spend there, he hoped it would be restful. Before leaving the Cape, he mailed his only copy of *The Caller* to Audrey. She was horrified that he would entrust it to the mails. No matter how much carbon paper was regularly sent to him by anxious friends and associates, Tennessee Williams was never much concerned: If it was lost, he would just do it over. Besides, he felt sure this little play would be relegated to what he had suggested to Audrey should be their "reservoir of noble efforts." And he vowed that it would be the very last one he would write for "the *now* existing theatre."

28

Chicago, Chicago

September–December 1944

The "now existing theatre" was in fact beginning to change, to become more open to innovation. A new mood pervaded both theatre and film as the country approached the postwar epoch. Plays sounding a clarion call to war were soon to be rejected in favor of those reverberating with the sound of taps. In the interim, however, audiences wanted to laugh, and Mae West was appearing onstage in *Catherine Was Great*, surrounded by a full gymnasium of the muscle-bound. The "magnificent bitch," as Tom referred to Miriam Hopkins, was starring in Samson Raphaelson's *The Perfect Marriage*. A six-foot-one-and-a-half-inch invisible rabbit named Harvey was the delight of the season. Two incomparable comedians, Beatrice Lillie and Bert Lahr, were convulsing spectators on- and backstage in *Seven Lively Arts*. Choreographer Jerome Robbins and composer Leonard Bernstein were collaborating on a musical about three sailors, *On the Town*. A comedy of Boston manners, *The Late George Apley*, was being directed by George S. Kaufman. And a twenty-nine-year-old playwright named Arthur Miller was making his Broadway debut with a play ironically titled *The Man Who Had All the Luck*, which ran for only four performances. But Miller, like the young Tennessee Williams, would have his second chance, too.

Life magazine was enthusiastically reporting that the "theater is enjoying its biggest boom," citing the musical *Bloomer Girl*, starring Celeste Holm, as "the first formal opening since Pearl Harbor." Forty-second Street was described as a conglomerate of amusement centers featuring "2 for $1" photos, pinball machines, weight-lifting tests of strength, and animated fortune-tellers. Movie houses like the Amsterdam, once the great Ziegfeld's famed legitimate theatre, and the Apollo, formerly Minsky's burlesque house, showed ten-cent double-feature films. And on the corner of Broadway and

Forty-second Street, one could buy five-cent hot dogs and orangeade at Nedicks.

The movies, too, were enjoying an unprecedented popularity. They ranged from Judy Garland in *Meet Me in St. Louis* to Cary Grant playing opposite Ethel Barrymore in *None but the Lonely Heart*. Elia Kazan, traveling between Broadway and Hollywood, had recently directed two theatre successes, Kurt Weill's *One Touch of Venus* and the Theatre Guild's presentation of S. N. Behrman's *Jacobowsky and the Colonel*, and had just completed work on the film *A Tree Grows in Brooklyn*. Darryl Zanuck was premiering his mammoth production on the rise and fall of a great American President, *Wilson;* at the same time, an even greater President, Franklin D. Roosevelt, was being elected to an unprecedented fourth term.

This was the New York that Tom had hoped would be "restful." It descended upon him more like a thunderclap. There would be more drama—offstage and on—surrounding his little play, once again named *The Gentleman Caller*, than anyone could have predicted or imagined. Audrey promptly had his single copy retyped, and although she shared his reservations about its salability, she set her sights on precisely the right person: Eddie Dowling.

By 1944, Dowling had become something of a legend in the theatre. He was a youthful forty-nine and Irish as all get-out, and he still had some of the bounce of the song-and-dance man he had once been. But he was also a shrewd and seasoned man of the theatre. Dowling first appeared in the *Ziegfeld Follies* of 1919, and by 1922 he was a star, coauthor, and coproducer in a long-running musical, *Sally, Irene and Mary*, in which he introduced Kate Smith, a singer who had been making her living as a barbershop manicurist. He told columnist Ward Morehouse, " 'Sally' was one of the biggest shows the musical stage ever saw . . . only cost buttons to do, the Shuberts pulled the costumes out of the warehouse and there were five companies."[1] He was making at times an aggregate ten thousand dollars a week.

In the mid-1930s, Dowling turned away from the musical stage and undertook several highly praised but commercially risky ventures. With Maurice Evans starring and Margaret Webster directing, he presented a very successful staging of Shakespeare's *Richard II*. Next he produced and played the lead in Philip Barry's mystical *Here Come the Clowns*. He introduced two plays by Paul Vincent Carroll, *Shadow and Substance*, followed by *The White Steed*, both well received. Finally, he coproduced with the Theatre Guild and played the lead opposite Julie Haydon in William Saroyan's *The Time of Your Life*, which won both a Pulitzer Prize and a New York Drama Critics Circle Award.

Dowling's wife, known professionally as comedienne Ray Dooley, first received and read *The Gentleman Caller*. Audrey had shrewdly told her that Dowling should look it over, not so much for a production but for an opinion of the playwright's unusual talent. Mrs. Dowling handed her husband the script, warning him that if he didn't read it then and there, she was sure that someone else would option it. At the moment, though, Dowling was working on another play with a coproducer named Louis J. Singer, a backer with little experience in the theatre. Singer was thought to be an investment broker, a hotel owner, and a member of the mob. No one at the time seemed to know exactly how he made his money. He was, in fact, a wealthy investment banker, and he had scant understanding of the theatre, despite the fact that he was obsessed with it. Singer and his associate, Joel Schenker, who was abroad, had planned to produce with Eddie Dowling a play called *The Compassionate Congressman*.

When Dowling told Singer that *The Gentleman Caller* was too important to resist, he is said to have replied, "Eddie, you've got a partner!" But Dowling needed an opinion on which he could rely, and he knew that his friend, the sixty-three-year-old critic George Jean Nathan, would level with him. Nathan had reservations about the play in its present state but saw it as a vehicle for his friend Julie Haydon, whom he would eventually marry, and he gave Dowling the nod.

Critics such as Alexander Woollcott and Louis Kronenberger were noted for their vitriolic comment, but in his time the acerbic Nathan was without peer. The theatre's sacred had much to fear from him, but not Eddie Dowling, of whom Nathan wrote, "I sometimes hear it said that I am prejudiced in Dowling's favor. What I hear said, believe me, is damned true. I am prejudiced in Dowling's favor as I would be in the case of any man who, like him, places the pride of the theatre above a potential fat purse, who is not afraid of risky but meritorious plays, and who is willing for weeks and even months to subsist on doughnuts and tea if it will allow him eventually to realize some little dream he may have."[2]

Not everyone in the theatre regarded Dowling so highly. To many, he was known as a "street producer," which meant a bit on the shady side. In that respect, he and that other Irishman, George M. Cohan, had much in common. But Dowling was unique; he had the poet's soul, the lilt was in his voice, and the glint in his eye. Nathan was right: One cannot be brave without being reckless at the same time, and it took courage not only to hazard the work of an unknown playwright but also to gamble on the quicksilver talent of a once-great actress, Laurette Taylor, who was Nathan's choice for Amanda Wingfield.

Taylor was as much esteemed by other actors as she was by critics. During her long career, she was considered peerless. While touring the United States in 1924 with his Moscow Art Theatre, the great Russian director Konstantin Stanislavsky hailed her as America's greatest actress and asked her to join his company. She and her husband lived in high style in their Riverside Drive and Long Island homes, where they were surrounded by visiting celebrities, including Noël Coward, who satirized their antics in his play *Hay Fever*. With the death of her husband in 1928, she took refuge in drink and for ten years afterward, because of unwise investments and indulgences, her fortune dwindled.

Laurette described her drinking as "the longest wake in history." She had been happily married, or so she romantically believed. In truth, she had been deeply dependent upon her playwright husband and manager, J. Hartley Manners, who had written and produced almost all of her vehicles. Chief among them was *Peg O' My Heart*, which premiered in 1912 and was revived over and over again. The play had also been made into a silent film, which was all that Tom remembered of her. He thought she must be dead or was ancient, while in fact she was only sixty years old. He had hoped Lillian Gish would play Amanda. Despite physical infirmities brought on by her struggle against alcoholism, Laurette talked and moved with a disarming, combative energy. Like Eddie Dowling, she was Irish and proud of it, and like her father, she had developed a love of a good fight and a thirst for good whiskey.

In 1938, after years of enforced retirement brought on by an Actors Equity suspension for drunkenly disrupting and closing a play, she made a comeback appearance on Broadway in a play called *Outward Bound*. Hers was a small role—she was one among a cast of prominent players—and yet her portrayal of a cockney charwoman was so moving that it overshadowed everyone onstage. She received twenty-two curtain calls. No one had questioned her artistry, however, as much as they had questioned whether she would even appear. Regarded as a hopeless alcoholic, her return was a cause for both amazement and celebration. For a brief time during the run of the play, she was once again a star. But nothing in the live theatre fades as fast as applause, and by the fall of 1944, Laurette Taylor was all but forgotten.

She was not forgotten *within* the theatre, though. It took only a notice in the columns that she might return in a given play for the rumor mill to put it out that she was too old, or that she was back on the bottle again, or—to her, the worst insult of all—that she could no longer remember her lines. She was drinking, it was true, but she was also reading play after play and turning down roles that she complained were hideous old silver-cord creatures or sappy *Little Women* mothers.

By 1944, Manners had been dead for sixteen years, and Laurette Taylor was living on the top floor of a modest apartment hotel at 14 East Sixtieth Street. She no longer could afford a maid and a chauffeur, but instead she enjoyed the companionship of a bright young actress named Eloise Sheldon. When Eddie Dowling went by her apartment carrying Tom's script, Laurette wearily took it in hand as probably just one more vehicle of the type that producer Guthrie McClintic had offered her, saying that she would *make* the play. She replied that she was tired of making the play, that she wanted a play to make her! Laurette stayed up most of the night reading the script, by someone with the odd name of Tennessee Williams, and the following morning she was on the phone: "I've found it, Eloise!" she cried jubilantly. "I've found the play I've been waiting for!"[3]

Her daughter, Marguerite Courtney, said that Laurette went down to Dowling's office that same morning. Later on, Taylor confided to a newspaper interviewer, "I wasn't too coy about business arrangements. When you haven't played for a while and the absolutely right part comes along, that's all that matters."[4] She wanted the role of Amanda so much that she even set aside the resentment she harbored toward George Jean Nathan because of his open contempt for her husband. "Nathan's criticism that Mr. Manners had never written a play which could 'possibly interest anybody over eleven' burned in Laurette's memory. Nathan, on his part, had never had much use for Laurette because he felt she had largely wasted her talent in her husband's plays."[5]

Nathan's real interest in *The Gentleman Caller* was the part of Laura, the shy, crippled daughter. He saw it as a perfect role for Julie Haydon. The fact that she was thirty-four years old meant that she would not appear too young to have Dowling as her brother. Actually, there could not have been a more appropriate choice than Haydon as Laura, "a role suited to her wan, ema-ciated beauty."[6] Often dismissed as more a personality than an actress, she had much the same angular beauty as Katharine Hepburn and an unusual alto-sounding voice. Tom had seen her extraordinarily moving performance op-posite Noël Coward in the film *The Scoundrel* and knew of her work costarring with Eddie Dowling in Saroyan's *The Time of Your Life*. He considered Hay-don as Laura ideal casting.

Julie Haydon's own personality was emotionally rooted in a pietistic atti-tude that existed beyond the reach of life's everyday realities, particularly the harsh life of the theatre. Tennessee Williams was to refer to her as never being in a mental or spiritual state short of ecstasy, but he saw her as a uniquely beautiful human being. Although Laura's is ostensibly a physical in-firmity, Haydon brought the added dimension of a frailty of mind that by the end of the play suggested oncoming madness.

While Eddie Dowling had begun to move with lightning swiftness, ensur-ing his financial backing and lining up his talent, Audrey Wood knew only that he was interested, and Tom knew nothing at all of what was going on. His plan was to get back to St. Louis, and from there, on the strength of the thou-sand-dollar grant money, move on to Mexico to write that big play. At this point, with one of the copies of *The Gentleman Caller* in hand, he stopped off at the Neighborhood Playhouse, where Horton Foote had taken over the di-rection of the Playhouse from Sanford Meisner during his absence. Foote re-called, "Tennessee left the play for me to read, and shortly after, I told him, 'Tennessee, I just love this play,' and he said, 'Nobody wants it.' So I proposed putting it on—but I couldn't cast Amanda—and all I did was the gentleman caller candlelight scene. Then afterward, a friend of mine ran into Tennessee and told him he had just seen a performance and how pleased he was. He said Tennessee turned white and exclaimed, 'Oh, my God, Audrey's just sold the play to Eddie Dowling!' "[7]

After Audrey drew up a Dramatists' Guild contract and Tom had signed it on October 21, he then met with Dowling, and a backstage drama was set. Now in the red glare of temperaments aglow—the internecine cross fire of professionals at odds—a production was beginning to take shape. Dowling signed Julie Haydon, having already advanced her career by casting her in several plays. She would always be grateful to him, but much to his annoyance, she gave her open admiration to Laurette. She was simply in awe of the great actress. With Eloise Sheldon out of town, Julie quickly assumed the offstage role of lady-in-waiting. And since Laurette, almost from the outset, made no secret of her feeling that it was ridiculous for Eddie Dowling at age forty-nine to be playing her son, their "Irish was up," in true O'Casey style. In time, he who had, after all, made the production possible, found himself pathetically isolated from his own company.

On October 30, Tom decided to return to St. Louis, anyway; he felt there was plenty of time. Shortly before leaving, he wrote to Margo Jones. It had been his intention to see her en route to Mexico, thinking that perhaps she would like to direct *The Gentleman Caller* as her initial production at the Dallas workshop. On the strength of a fellowship she had recently been granted from the Rockefeller Foundation, she was already at work on her dream of establishing in Dallas a working model for a national network of repertory theatres. Now he wasn't sure in what capacity, but it was his hope that somehow he could involve her in Dowling's production.

Margo dear:
I hope that my good news will not seem bad news to you. I am sure it won't, really, if it strikes you as being good for *me*. Any good thing for one of us is good for both!

This news just broke yesterday. I had no previous intimation of it, in fact never dreamed that any commercial manager, even one with Dowling's superior sensibilities, would think of doing the Caller on Broadway. I guess it's a sign that the theatre *is* changing. Before Dowling decided, he sent the script to Nathan and Nathan *liked* it. I guess that's why Dowling is getting Haydon. Everybody has liked the script so far, the first time this has happened with any of my plays, and it surprises me completely. Of course I liked the material because it was so close to me, but for that very reason I doubted that it would come across to others. It was such *hell* writing it! Dowling plans to play the narrator himself. He explained to me that he will look much younger on stage. Even so I think that will mean setting the play further back in time. I had thought of someone no older than myself playing the narrator. But of course Dowling is a grand actor and can get away with anything! As for Haydon, she is so physically and temperamentally right—has such a lovely quality—that her limitations as an actress don't seem important in this instance. Eddie will play her like a fiddle! He told me he didn't think the play would go on before late winter—he has another play to do first [a revival of *Little Women*], one he doesn't like much. In the meantime I think I will get out of town. I don't feel like being involved with a Broadway crowd, and you always are when a play is coming up. Then if I am not in telephone reach, they won't plague me so much about little changes that occur to them. If you were here now I would probably stick around, as your presence would give me a certain moral support in dealing with them, but as it is I feel safer at a distance. Not that I anticipate much trouble, but having been through the mill with Langner and Helburn I am twice shy! I hope you will be around when the production gets started. I could certainly use you. Perhaps by November fifteenth I will be ready to come back here. If you pass through Saint Louis we might leave together. You know how frightened I am of everybody! Especially people in the theatre. So—I need you![8]

Tom then wrote to Jay Laughlin that "everyone who has seen [read] the new play 'The Glass Menagerie' likes it, though I doubt it is for the commercial theatre. Haven't gotten Margo's report on it yet. As the title suggests—it is about the delicate feelings in life—that get broken."[9] Margo's reaction was what Tom could have expected. "It seemed to be the wisest procedure," she wrote, "to discontinue the fellowship and go to New York, for it meant an opportunity to practice what I had been preaching—the gaining of experience in all fields of the theatre. And I realized that I needed the added training of the Broadway stage. Another strong consideration was the fact that I believed in Williams and loved the play."[10] With the Rockefeller Foundation's approval, Margo set out on a tour of several regional and university theatres and en route stopped off in St. Louis to meet with Tom and discuss his play. He wired Eddie Dowling, suggesting that Margo Jones would be an ideal assistant director. Everyone believed that Margo was older, therefore more mature, than Tom, when in truth they were both born in 1911.

Tom had arrived home, to find his family in an uproar—not rejoicing over his good fortune but bemoaning the news, contained in a fifteen-page letter from Dakin, that he had converted to Roman Catholicism. Edwina was praying for him, and Cornelius thought the jungle had affected his mind. Tom told Donald that the letter, all about transubstantiation and the infallibility of the Pope, disgusted him. And the Reverend Dakin, who had baptized his grandson in the Episcopal faith, received the news as a personal affront, promptly departing St. Louis to take up residence at the Friends Boarding House in Waynesville, Ohio, the town where he had been born and near where Grand had recently been buried.

Tom wrote to his grandfather in Waynesville, telling him how "unexpectedly quick" the sale of his play was and how it had been bought "just one week after it left the typist. I had to stay over for conferences in connection with that. I am afraid my visit here may be cut short at any time by a wire to return, for Mr. Dowling, the producer, thought he might get started on it within the next few weeks. He plans to open it in Chicago around Christmas time . . .

before we brave the New York critics. I think you would like this play and wish you might get a chance to see it."[11]

On learning Tom's good news, his old friend and champion Alice Lippmann contacted the drama critic of the *St. Louis Star-Times*, suggesting he interview Tom. The newspaperman was William Inge, destined to become in his own right a highly successful playwright. "It was in October 1944 when I first met Tennessee," Inge recalled. "I did feature stories on public personalities, artists who came to town, and I had had a note from a nice old lady who was a friend of Tennessee's that he would be in town, that he was going to have a play in production soon called *The Glass Menagerie*." Inge phoned Tom at home and made an appointment. "I did the article and we became good friends."[12]

In fact, they had two weeks of intense, close friendship, frequenting bars and attending those music and theatre events to which Inge was assigned. Inge also gave a small party for his new acquaintance, and Tennessee was to say that he had never had as good a time in his hometown as he did during those two weeks. For his part, Inge listened with great interest to Tom's recounting of his early life in St. Louis—the background for his play—but in no way, he said, could he have suspected his friend's genius. He did plan, however, to travel to Chicago during December to cover the play for his paper.

One of Tom's reasons for returning home was to have another cataract operation, but in mid-November he received a wire to return to New York for rehearsals. Margo was in New York to attend the National Theatre Conference and "received a formal offer from Eddie Dowling to work [as his assistant]. Audrey Wood, who along with Williams had recommended her to Dowling, signed on as Margo's agent."[13] Margo's first challenge was to find an actor to play Jim O'Connor, the gentleman caller. Anthony Ross, like Laurette Taylor a troubled actor with a drinking problem, brought just the right balance between extroverted geniality and shaken confidence to the role. He was thirty-eight years old, and this pleased Dowling, who was becoming self-conscious of his age because of Laurette's mumbled asides about his being too old to play her son.

Rehearsals were scheduled to take place variously in Eddie Dowling's office, Laurette Taylor's rooms at Hotel Fourteen, and Donald Windham's Madison Avenue apartment. Julie Haydon and Tony Ross rehearsed at Donald's flat under Margo's direction, while Dowling began what was to become a struggle with Laurette. Although she listened attentively to his direction, her response was oddly vague. What he might have thought was an alcoholic stupor was actually an immersion in thought: She had virtually disappeared into the character of Amanda.

When Tom arrived at Laurette's apartment, he was astonished to find a little, vivacious woman, not unlike Edwina in many of her ways: She was opinionated, talkative, and imbued with a fighting spirit. He wrote his mother,

saying, "I met her for the first time yesterday. She is very cute and looks remarkably young. They say she has been 'on the wagon' lately and we are
counting on her genuine love of the play to keep her on it. We are having the
first complete reading of the play this evening at Miss Taylor's apartment."
The top-floor apartment struck Tom more like a stage setting, with its Italian
furniture, rich brocades, and the Steinway piano she had carted from one
place to another.

In his letter to Edwina, he only hinted at what was now the first real test to
which he, as a playwright, was being put. "Mr. Dowling occasionally suggests
changes in the script but so far Margo and I have managed to keep him in line.
I am lucky to have her, as I am less effective in arguments than she is."[14] Dowling felt there was too much in the play that was innovative and that would be
too costly to stage. He had to spend time "explaining" the script to Singer,
who found it beyond his comprehension, and he had the formidable Mr. Nathan's opinion to consider, too. The crux of the matter was a drunk scene that
Dowling felt should be added to show him off to better advantage.

In the middle of these discussions, on December 12, *Little Women* opened
at the City Center. Julie Haydon attended, escorted by George Jean Nathan,
who asked to meet with Tom after the performance. This was fine with Tom,
who had thought of approaching Nathan anyway, believing that so astute a
critic would advise Dowling to drop the idea of a drunk scene. Donald went
on to Margo's hotel, where she was giving a party, but it was some time before
Tom turned up. Separated from Margo, he had been led into the kind of classic trap that every new playwright can expect: the old wielding their superior
knowledge over the young. Both Nathan and Dowling were waiting for him,
with Haydon and Singer on the sidelines. It soon became clear that the drunk
scene was Nathan's idea. He discounted the play as being not very good, but
he said if Tom would entrust it to him and Dowling, they could make it into
something worthwhile. He added that Tom was not really a playwright, but a
short-story writer who had no real knowledge of the theatre. They then
handed Tom the scene as they had written it, the condition being that if he
would give them their way, he could rely on Nathan's support.

In *Memoirs*, Tennessee remembered Nathan as the instigator, writing that
"he got together with Eddie and between the two of them they composed a
drunk scene for Eddie which they thought the only possible salvation for the
play. This scene involved such things as a red, white, and blue flask, a song for
Eddie—'My Melancholy Baby'—and other unmentionables. This 'drunk
scene,' obviously composed in a state that corresponded, was given me as a *fait
accompli.*" He went on to say it was agreed that Margo would confront Singer
and "poor Eddie with a protest of the kind that had earned her the sobriquet
of 'Texas Tornado.' As usual, in such cases, a compromise was reached. I said
they would have their drunk scene but that I would accept no collaboration on
it. I wrote it and it is still in the script and I honestly think that it does the play
little harm."[15] On the contrary, Nathan's and Dowling's instincts, if not their

methods, were right: It is the one scene in which Tom and Laura appear close enough to be brother and sister. It needed only a director to point it out and a playwright to write it.

Margo did indeed meet with Dowling at his offices in the St. James Theatre building, and she argued that the integrity of the play would be at stake if Tom permitted the incursion of someone else's writing. Margo was Dowling's codirector, after all, and in the sober light of the morning after, he had much to consider. He knew she was right, and he also knew that both Audrey Wood and the powerful Dramatists' Guild would stand behind the playwright.

Like the best producers in those times, Dowling was inclined to give artists whatever they felt they needed to do their jobs, regardless of the added cost; the only safeguard was to hire a good general manager to sit on the checkbook. Alex Yokel, formerly the producer of Irwin Shaw's *Bury the Dead*, became company business manager, adding "last money" and bringing the capitalization to a total of $75,000, which was largely Louis Singer's money. In order to put up various bonds and other guarantees as typical preproduction costs, Eddie, with a very nervous and inexperienced Singer at his side, had already committed thousands of dollars. Neither he nor Singer was about to abandon the production and suffer the loss over the authorship of a single scene—not even to save Nathan's pride or to avoid his retaliation.

The original manuscript of the play contained many innovative stage directions, such as the use of slides and other cinematic techniques that related to Tom's interest in a kind of kinetic staging and a concept he called "plastic theatre." His most recent influences were Piscator's German expressionist school and the direct experience of working within a film studio. More generic to his use of a narrator, though, was the chorus of ancient Greek drama and the soliloquies of Shakespeare. He was seeking not simply to open up the otherwise rigid structure of a well-made play but, through the device of a play within a play, to give it an interior life, a new freedom and poetic voice, and Margo well understood this.

Normally, someone as perceptive as George Jean Nathan, who had championed the theatre's great innovator, Eugene O'Neill, would understand this, as well. He could recognize that even in its early draft, Tennessee's was a play conspicuously superior to what was currently being offered. So why his attempt to cheapen it? And why his ill-disguised contempt for Williams himself? There had to be something at work, consciously or unconsciously, in Nathan's effort to insert a single simpleminded scene and to destroy the fabric of a play whose potential he could readily perceive.

Nathan was Eugene O'Neill's most devoted critical guardian, a worshiper before the master's throne. The great dramatist's glowering visage had something of the aura of a god: His was a commanding presence, and simply to know him personally, as Nathan did, was to be in awe of him. Now, suddenly, here was this seemingly precocious and therefore, in Nathan's eyes, pretentious young playwright—this impostor challenging the existing modes and conventions of a theatre that had atrophied in the time that O'Neill had become silent. *Someone* had to take his place, and Nathan was certainly wise enough to comprehend this, resist it though he might.

Nathan was also wise enough in his ways, especially in the ways of the theatre, to have pegged Tennessee as homosexual, and he was outspoken in his loathing of sexual deviation. He was first among a few critics to let their homophobic feelings prejudice them against not only the playwright but his plays, as well. Nathan would ultimately give *The Glass Menagerie*—as a play apart from Dowling's production—a sneering review and finally, despite the great success of *A Streetcar Named Desire*, dismiss the playwright as "a Southern genital-man."

In balance, Nathan did make a number of suggestions concerning the first drafts of *The Gentleman Caller*. Now renamed *The Glass Menagerie*, the script called for a variety of visual effects and also an unusual number of auditory and music cues. Although Williams was aware that the German school had used the concept of leitmotif earlier, the increasing importance of sound effects and background music in films was the direct influence upon his integration of music within the play's action. The one person Williams knew who composed music for the theatre that had the quality of poetry was Paul Bowles.

Bowles, who had not seen Tennessee since his impromptu visit in Mexico during the summer of 1940, said that the playwright suddenly appeared at his New York flat in the company of Margo Jones and Donald Windham. "He had with him the script of a new play which he left with me. I read it and liked it. For a play aiming at a Broadway production at that time it was somewhat experimental, envisaging as it did the use of projected slides to serve as comments on, or asides to, the dialogue and action. The next time I saw Tennessee, the production was set, and what with the drawing up of contracts and my habitual refusal to write anything until I had stuffed an advance into the bank, I found myself with three days in which to compose and orchestrate the score."[16]

The New Frontier

With fewer than fifteen days to assemble and go up on the play in Chicago, once again Tom was caught in the whirlwind speed of a professional production. On a cold Saturday, December 16, the company gathered at Pennsylvania Station. Tom and Donald came together. Jane Smith, who shortly before had returned to New York, picked up Margo at her hotel. Eddie Dowling was already at the station with Louis Singer. Other company members on hand were Randy Echols, the production stage manager; his assistant, Willis Gould; Mary Jean Copeland, company secretary and understudy to Julie Haydon; and Joanna Albus, a longtime close friend of Margo who was an expert organizer and who from experience could work around Margo. Laurette Taylor arrived on the arm of Julie, temporarily pinch-hitting for her young friend Eloise Sheldon, who had been cast in the season's biggest hit, *Harvey*.

As the company boarded the train, Jane Smith remembered, "Donnie and I were left staring at each other. We went for a drink and after we got acquainted, I told him I was unhappy where I was staying—Tony was still out on the coast but on his way—and with Sandy [Campbell] touring in a road company of *Life With Father*, Donnie invited me to stay with him at his place on Madison Avenue."[17] Donald recalled that Jane stayed alone at Sandy's and his apartment when he went to the Chicago opening of *Menagerie*. Tony arrived shortly after, supposedly for a few days, but they all stayed into February.

On the following bitterly cold morning, the troupe "disgorged from the train into Chicago's barnlike Union Station. The impression was hardly that of a winning team. With scarcely a nod at one another they scattered in all directions." Laurette's daughter described the occasion, saying Dowling and Singer went off arm in arm, ignoring their tiny star, who stood hesitant and alone on the platform. "Julie, hatless and pinched-looking, flitted by as insubstantial as a puff of steam from one of the locomotives. Tony Ross, a six-foot-three protest against the cold and early hour, passed somnambulistically. The anxious author, who had forgotten something, dove back into the car and emerged again to feel the bleakness of the station like an unfriendly slap—a dismal portent of his play's reception. Desperately he longed for the sight of a familiar figure and at last saw one."[18] Tennessee recalled the event: " 'Laurette!' I called her name and she turned and cried out mine. Then and there we joined forces." Together they went in search of a taxi. "It was Laurette who hailed it with an imperious wave of her ungloved hand, hesitation all gone as she sprang like a tiger out of her cloud of softness: such a light spring, but such an amazingly far one."[19]

Tom may have become aware of the hidden tiger in Laurette, but, like everyone else in the company, he was puzzled by her odd behavior at rehearsals. Using a large magnifying glass, she hovered over her script, peering at it and mumbling her lines—this, while the other actors had memorized their dialogue and were following Dowling's direction. At one point, Eddie was heard to mutter, "That woman is crucifying me," and the nervous Mr. Singer, looking in on one of the rehearsals, cried out, "Eddie! Eddie! You're ruining me." Laurette's daughter wrote that her mother was simply "up to her old trick of watching the others, seemingly much more interested in them than her own part, neither learning her lines nor her business."[20]

Tennessee remembered that Laurette appeared to know only a fraction of her lines, and these she was delivering in "a Southern accent which she had acquired from some long-ago black domestic." He was even more disconcerted when she said she was modeling her accent after *his!* Tom wrote to Donald Windham, complaining that Laurette was ad-libbing many of her speeches and that the play was beginning to sound more like the Aunt Jemima

Pancake hour. To him, Laurette's "bright-eyed attentiveness to the other performances seemed a symptom of lunacy, and so did the rapturous manner of dear Julie."[21] He was witnessing a characteristic of many of the theatre's great actors who were quick studies but painfully deliberate in their approach to a role. As Laurette's daughter explained, "She seemed blandly unconscious of the discomfort of the others. . . . Amanda fascinated her. She could see whole facets of the woman's life before the action of the play and after it was over." This is what her husband had taught her was the test of a good part. "The outer aspect of this inner search concerned her not at all."[22]

Tom told Donald that he finally lost his temper when Laurette made some trifling changes. He said he screamed, " 'My God, what corn!" She railed that he was a fool, that she had been a star for forty years and had made a living as a writer which in her opinion was more than he had done. After they had returned from lunch, she "suddenly began giving a real acting performance—so good that Julie and I, the sentimental element in the company, wept."[23]

The company, including Tom, was housed in the Hotel Sherman, and they would meet after rehearsals for an extended nightcap. Other than Julie and Dowling, all concerned, including Laurette, enjoyed these late happy hours, with Margo leading the pack. The first performance was due to go up in another week, on Christmas night, and Laurette was being watched, however guardedly, with a natural apprehension on everyone's part. She was drinking, but so far there was no evidence of drunkenness.

Tom told Donald he was living luxuriously on his ten dollars a day and likened himself to the condemned man who ate a hearty breakfast. He still had his savings in his St. Louis bank account and, if worse came to worst, knew he could make it to Mexico and write with renewed confidence. Even if this venture closed out of town, like *Battle of Angels*, he now understood what it took to work with a group of professionals—fellow artists who knew how to breathe life into his play and construct a production to conform with his vision, the most important among them being the scene and lighting designer, Jo Mielziner.

Considered one of the theatre's great scenic artists, Mielziner would design nine of the major plays by Tennessee Williams. At the time he had been engaged to conceive the setting and lighting for *The Glass Menagerie*, he had behind him twenty years' experience designing Broadway productions. A protégé of the great designer Robert Edmond Jones, he began his career with the Theatre Guild, and in 1924 he designed Ferenc Molnár's *The Guardsman*. Four years later, Jones turned over an assignment to Mielziner—to design Eugene O'Neill's monumental *Strange Interlude*. Born in Paris in 1901, Mielziner began his career as a painter, and more than anything, this influenced his approach to set construction, in which light design—painting with light—was of equal importance to him. In the fall of 1944, the forty-three-year-old designer had been discharged as a major from the U.S. Army's Office of Strategic Services, and he was looking to break new ground in the postwar theatre. The demands of *The Glass Menagerie* offered him just the challenge he needed. "Williams," he said, "was writing not only a memory play but a play of influences that were not confined within the walls of a room."

Mielziner recognized that Tom, even though a largely inexperienced playwright, revealed a strong instinct for the visual qualities of the theatre. His desire to "depict the inner man as well as the external one" called upon Mielziner to employ extraordinary lighting effects and translucent scenery. Because Williams in his instructions said that his was a memory play, Mielziner felt it could be presented with unusual freedom from convention. "Expressionism," he wrote, "and all other unconventional techniques in drama have only one valid aim, and that is a closer approach to truth. When a play employs unconventional techniques, it is not, or certainly shouldn't be, trying to escape its responsibility of dealing with reality, or interpreting experience, but is actually or should be attempting to find a closer approach, a more penetrating and vivid expression of things as they are."[24]

With Dowling preoccupied with his performance and those of the other players and with Alex Yokel involved in front-office business matters, Louis Singer was moving back and forth and driving everyone to distraction with his nagging concern over negligible economies. He could not conceive how the chaos of the moment could turn into money at the box office. To guard his sizable investment, Singer called together Eddie Dowling, Tennessee, and Margo and told them that the play should have a happy ending, that Laura should marry Jim. Margo waited for the men to talk. Dowling didn't say a word. She waited for Tennessee to answer. Tennessee didn't speak. "Tennessee," Margo began quietly, "don't you change that ending. It's perfect." Then she looked up at Louis Singer, her cat's eyes narrowing. Making her hand into a fist, she said in a menacing tone, "Mr. Singer, if you make Tennessee change the play the way you want it, so help me I'll go around to every critic in town and tell them about the kind of wire-pulling that's going on here."

That ended that. Although Margo was actually the same height as Tom, she stood tall and firm. Singer may have lost that round, but it didn't stop his meddling and penny-pinching. Next, he was "supervising" Jo Mielziner's work. He decided that it would be better and cheaper to use canvas to back the set, but Mielziner in his calm though insistent manner wanted the more expensive lightproof black velour and got it. Then Singer refused to pay for costumes. Margo complained to Audrey Wood that it was absurd: "Laurette and Julie have had to buy their own clothes and sew them—Joanna [Albus], my friend, has had to help them and so have I." She said that Jo Mielziner had suddenly decided that Julie's dress should not be white and that, when Tom went out and bought it, "Singer wouldn't pay for it. It turned out that Eddie finally paid $20.00 of it and Tennessee paid $10.00."

Margo was now billed not just as assistant to Eddie Dowling but as assistant director and eventually as codirector. For her weekly $150 salary, she was also functioning as production manager. During the technical rehearsals, she sat in the orchestra, "taking notes, checking the blocking as the actors got used to the set, timing the music and sound cues, ironing out problems with light cues, prop and costume changes, and checking acting interpretations, especially Eddie Dowling's tendency to hoke up his performance."[25]

Tom, Margo, and stage manager Randy Echols scoured the city's secondhand stores for props, such as furniture pieces, an old typewriter, and an upright telephone that Tom especially wanted. He was also concerned that Mielziner highlight the little glass menagerie and the oversize picture of the grinning father in his World War I uniform.

Alex Yokel, the company manager, wrote to Ashton Stevens, his former boss and the drama critic of Chicago's *Herald-American*, telling him how "22 guys called stagehands are struggling with 'The Glass Menagerie' scenery, electrical equipment, props, furniture, and you name the rest." He said that Jo Mielziner was doing "the lighting job of his luminous life. Jo doped out an electrical scheme that is tremendous because I can't think of a bigger word. Where an ordinary show has one switchboard, Jo has seven. He has 57 sets of lines hanging from the fly gallery, 150 feet up, and is using every line to hang the electrical equipment." But, Yokel asserted, "Jo will get through that in about 24 hours, with coffee and sandwiches while he works, and then the real fun starts. We plunge right into our first dress rehearsal, and just before the curtain lifts on this formal preliminary, I'm going on stage to talk to the four actors of the cast and say that, God help them and me! they are now on their own."[26] As it turned out, Mielziner and his crew completed their work a mere three hours before the Christmas preview performance.

Integrating the scenery changes with Mielziner's light and Paul Bowles's music cues was difficult enough, but, as Bowles recalled, the dress rehearsal was a nightmare. "I flew out to Chicago [and] arrived in a terrible blizzard, I remember. It was horrible. A traumatic experience. And the auditorium was cold. Laurette Taylor was on the bottle, unfortunately. Back on it, really. She had got off it with the first part of the rehearsals but suddenly the dress rehearsal coming up was too much." Laurette was nowhere to be found. Finally she was discovered by the janitor, "unconscious, down behind the furnace in the basement. And there was gloom, I can tell you, all over the theatre because no one thought she would be able to go on the next night."[27]

Edwina had traveled from St. Louis alone. On Christmas day, she wrote to her father in Waynesville, "Last night I had dinner with some of the cast, and they are so enthusiastic about the play and love it—I think it's bound to be successful. I'm going to a preview this afternoon."[28] Because of Laurette, the opening had been postponed until the twenty-sixth. At the specially scheduled matinee, Edwina sat in an audience composed largely of four hundred uniformed members of the touring company of *Winged Victory*, Moss Hart's rousing tribute to the U.S. Army Air Force. Tony Ross had recently been a member of the company, and he said, "To make those guys rave it had to be good. The phony was something they couldn't use."[29] And rave they did. Now it was the critics' turn.

On opening night, December 26, Laurette had disappeared again. They were forty minutes from curtain. While Dowling checked with her hotel and restrained Singer from calling the police, Jo Mielziner decided to try the basement, as Paul Bowles had. He recalled:

> Far down a passage I saw a light and heard the sound of running water. There, in a sort of janitor's storage and washroom, was Laurette Taylor, dressed in a rather soiled old dressing-gown with the sleeves rolled up, bending over a washtub, wringing out the dress that she was to wear in the second act. Her hands and arms were dripping with lavender dye. I said, "Laurette, can't somebody do this for you? You should be resting in your room or getting made up." Her great, tragic, beautiful eyes smiled at me and she said, "No, it's all done."
>
> The dress was an important costume, a much-talked-about party frock. Early in the production I had assumed that the management would have something specially designed; but pennies were being pinched to such an extent that the dress had been "bought off the pile." At the dress parade the day before, Tennessee Williams had commented that it was far from right, and so Laurette Taylor, on her own, had bought some dye and was trying to remedy matters.

She thrust the soggy clump of costume into Randy Echols's hands with the command, "Here, dry this." He met the challenge. "The sweating Echols constructed a dryer of bits and pieces backstage, played lights on it, fanned it, blew on it, went quietly mad."[30]

Before the curtain's rise, a small storm-buffeted audience had made it to the theatre, including Chicago's two most formidable critics, Claudia Cassidy and Ashton Stevens. In her memoir, Edwina recalled that "everything seemed against the play, even the weather. The streets were so ice-laden we could not find a taxi to take us to the Civic Theatre and had to walk. The gale blowing off Lake Michigan literally hurled us through the theatre door."[31] Too nervous to sit and wait for the curtain, Tom went backstage, only to find the cast and crew even more gripped with fear than he was. Donald Windham arrived and sat next to Edwina. He recalled her remarking that the program notes were mistaken—Why, Tom was born in 1911, not 1914! she declared—and that was the way Donald learned that Tennessee was thirty-three, not thirty, as everyone had been led to believe.

Donald not only recognized Taylor's southern accent as Tennessee's but he also felt that she had co-opted a good deal more and had modeled her performance on her careful observation of Tom. "Her sideways, suspicious glances at her children when she was displeased; her silences that spoke more than words; her bright obliviousness to the reality before her eyes when she was determined to show that she, at least, was agreeable; and her childish pleasure in the chance to charm and show off her best features. . . ."³²

What Edwina was witnessing was in no real sense an autobiographical account of Tom's family life in St. Louis. It was a transmutation created by the artist who had taken refuge in the identity of Tennessee Williams—for it is true, as critic Frank Rich has said, that "anyone can write an autobiography, but only an artist knows how to remake his past so completely, by refracting it through a different aesthetic lens."³³ For Edwina, the play was more dream than memory—a flux of disordered images of "loss, loss, loss." There could be no avoiding the similarities between Amanda Wingfield's travail and her own: her faded southern gentility and its hold on her "writin' son," Tom; the gentlemen callers; her real love, John Singleton, who didn't propose; the jonquils. In the same way a dream verges on nightmare, there was Edwina's dread fear summoned up once more: Cornelius's unrelenting threat of deserting her to a life of poverty was made fact in the play. And there was the pain she had to feel in response to the reminders of Rose on that Christmas night, imprisoned in an asylum, with Laura's malformation acting as a metaphor for her daughter's enveloping madness. Then there was Tom's hope of escape—Tennessee's lifelong illusion—in pursuit of a father in love with long distances.

On one occasion, Tennessee said he could not remember his mother's reaction to the play; then on another he said that, as she sat listening to Laurette Taylor reciting her own utterances and aphorisms, "Mother began to sit up stiffer and stiffer. She looked like a horse eating briars. She was touching her throat and clasping her hands and quite unable to look at me." He thought that "what made it particularly hard for Mother to bear is that she is a tiny, delicate woman with great dignity and always managing to be extremely chic in dress, while Laurette Taylor invested the part with that blowzy, powerful quality of hers—and thank God she did, for it made the play."³⁴

When the curtain descended slowly, Edwina said, "At first it was so quiet I thought the audience didn't like the play. Then, all of a sudden, a tumultuous clapping of hands broke out." Backstage, Edwina told Laurette she was "magnificent." Laurette asked her, "Well, Mrs. Williams, how did you like yourself?" "Myself?" Edwina replied innocently. According to Tennessee, his mother did not pick up on this because she was bedazzled by Laurette's "somewhat supernatural quality on a stage."³⁵ Audrey Wood remembered inviting Laurette and Edwina to lunch at Sardi's a few months later. "Those were the days when we ladies wore tiny hats and gloves, and were, oh, so feminine." During lunch, "Laurette, with her wonderful fey Irish sense of humor, said to Miss Edwina, 'You see these bangs I wear? I have to wear them playing this part, for I actually have a high, intellectual forehead.' 'Is that so?' replied Miss Edwina, sweetly. She removed her tiny hat, and then she said, 'I wish you would look at my forehead, Miss Taylor. I hope you will notice I have an intellectual brow, too.' "³⁶ Although Edwina often declared, "I am *not*

Amanda!" she would on the appropriate occasion coyly refer to Mrs. Wingfield as her alias.

After congratulating Laurette and the other cast members backstage, Edwina recalled, "we returned to the hotel for a late dinner and wait for the reviews. Tom wanted to take me to a midnight service at the Episcopal Church but the weather was so ferocious we still could not find a taxi." Julie ate dinner with them, but Margo, who was supposed to join them, never showed up. "The excitement was subdued but intense," Edwina said, as they endured that special torture reserved for theatre folk: waiting for the notices. Then, "one by one the reviews came in, each more superlative than the last."[37]

The *Tribune*'s Claudia Cassidy said that the play "holds in its shadowed fragility the stamina of success," and she added, "If it is your play, as it is mine, it reaches out tentacles, first tentative, then gripping, and you are caught in its spell." Ashton Stevens of the *Herald-American* called *Menagerie* "a lovely thing and an original thing. It has the courage of true poetry couched in colloquial prose. It is eerie and earthy in the same breath." He added that fifty years of first-nighting had provided him with few jolts so "miraculously electrical" as Laurette's portrayal and that he had not been so moved "since Eleanora Duse gave her last performance on this planet."

Almost all the reviews were extravagant in their praise. Everyone had reason to rejoice—except the box-office treasurer. The second day's business amounted to a miserable four hundred dollars. Worse, despite the reviews, there was no advance ticket sale, a production's true barometer. Audrey wired Tom:

VERY VERY JOYOUS ABOUT BEAUTIFUL NOTICES. DOES CHICAGO APPRECIATE WHAT IT HAS? IN OTHER WORDS, ARE THEY BUYING TICKETS? UNTIL I KNOW I WON'T SLEEP SO PLEASE WIRE. HAVE THEY DECIDED HOW LONG PLAY WILL RUN CHICAGO? LOVE AND ADMIRATION TO YOU.[38]

Audrey must indeed have had several sleepless nights, as those in the front office did. The houses continued to be abysmally small. Louis Singer and Alex Yokel and even the press representative, Harry Davies, felt that there was no alternative except to close the show and stop losing money. Eddie Dowling was of a different mind, however: He felt they should keep on going. It was an opinion shared by Claudia Cassidy, who returned for three successive performances, admitting that that much exposure was "a risky business in the realm of make-believe." Ashton Stevens virtually moved into the theatre. Everyone was faced with one of the most heartrending experiences in the theatre: helplessly watching a beautiful, highly praised production slowly expire because of the lack of public response.

* * *

Edwina returned to St. Louis during the first weekend's performances, at about the same time William Inge arrived. Seeing that business was bad, he recalled, "I sat in a half-filled theatre but I watched the most thrilling performance of the most beautiful American play I felt I had ever seen. I had the feeling at the time that what I was seeing would become an American classic." But what disturbed Inge, watching the play with Tennessee and Donald in the audience, was Tom's Mozartian giggle regularly piercing moments of rapt silence. "I couldn't stand this because I was being overwhelmed by the experience," Inge said. "I was expecting a good play, yes, but I didn't know that I was going to encounter a work of genius. . . . The play itself was written so beautifully, like carved crystal and so it was a stunning experience for me and it shocked me a little, too, to suddenly see this great work emerge from a person that I had come to know so casually." From then on, he held Tennessee in a reverence "that made the casual quality of our friendship almost impossible . . . I think from that time on we were always a little self-conscious with each other."[39]

Laurette Taylor never lost an opportunity to divert the praise that was being heaped upon her to that "nice little guy," Tennessee Williams. She was always quick to remind her admirers that it was he, not she, who had written the lines that gave *The Glass Menagerie* its special power and beauty. And she told Tennessee, "It's a beautiful—a wonderful—a great play!"[40]

For his part, Tennessee Williams always said that, as much as he regarded Laurette Taylor a personal friend, he never ceased to be in awe of her. "She had such a creative mind," he once remarked. "Something magical happened with Laurette. I used to stand backstage: There was a little peephole in the scenery, and I could be just about three feet from her, and when the lights hit her face, suddenly twenty years would drop off. An incandescent thing would happen in her face; it was really supernatural."[41]

What was perhaps most extraordinary about *The Glass Menagerie* as a theatrical event was the meeting of these two great artists, one ending her career and the other beginning his. On that cold night of December 26, 1944, the convergence of two enormous theatre talents made theatre history: The performance itself became legendary, and the play became a classic in the literature of the American theatre.

29

The Glass Menagerie

January–March 1945

With the end of the first week's ticket sales adding up to a mere $3,670, it was only good business judgment to write off the venture as a costly artistic failure. Eddie Dowling could personally afford to jettison *The Glass Menagerie*, since he had already safeguarded himself, if not Louis Singer's investment; on the closing of the play, he intended to inaugurate a repertory season in Chicago at this same rarely used Civic Theatre, an ambitious undertaking to include Barry Fitzgerald and Jessica Tandy in *The White Steed*, Cedric Hardwicke and Sara Allgood in *Shadow and Substance*, Laurette Taylor in *Outward Bound*, and Julie Haydon and himself in *The Time of Your Life*. Chicago's mayor had already given his official support and offered a 50 percent ticket subsidy to keep *The Glass Menagerie* going.

The second week's business, though improved, was still cause for despair, with receipts amounting to only $7,860 and no advance sale. Good reviews or not, in the final analysis the public buys the ticket or it doesn't. In the theatre, the favorable word must spread like sheet lightning or the theatregoer is never given an opportunity to buy, much less become aware that there is something worth buying. Traditionally, plays are short-term ventures dependent upon instant success.

The demands made by Williams's original script and Mielziner's attempt to meet them made it obvious that the $75,000 capitalization, unusually high for those times, would soon be exhausted. Dowling, urged on by his business partners, seemed to have no choice except to post a closing notice. At this point, the set and multiple lighting effects were still evolving, with many of the cinematic devices being eliminated, until ultimately the play emerged in two versions: the so-called acting and reading editions. Among the few members who saw these first performances, the experience became literally unforgettable; these audiences were what led to the production's being acclaimed as mythical.

No one among critics or audiences could understand why this ostensibly slight play affected them so deeply. What they witnessed was the tragic failure of three family members to understand one another in their intertwined love, and the frustration they endure trying to escape from their isolation. Tom Wingfield appears both outside the play as narrator and within it as a character. While his plight as a would-be writer, held down by a menial job, is central to the plot, his mother, Amanda, is the pivotal figure. It is she who struggles valiantly against the threat of abject poverty. What binds her and Tom is the tragedy of his sister, Laura, crippled and withdrawn, an image he carries with him after finally he has left home.

In any but the hands of Tennessee Williams, such a simple plot might well have lent itself to outright bathos. But here was the poet in control of the playwright and, further than that, of the audience. "I give you truth in the pleasant guise of illusion." Family—his family and everyone's family—created the bond; in myriad ways, this theme was striking a universal chord. Almost all audience members could recognize facets of their own lives and families, and few left the theatre without being profoundly moved in some unfathomable way. In all lives, the separation between illusion and reality is often critically frustrating and often tragic in its consequences.

John Gassner characterized Tennessee Williams as "a dramatist of frustration," and therein lies the cauldron of the play, the helplessness of the characters to convey their emotions to one another. Amanda tells Tom, "There's so many things in my heart that I cannot describe to you!" Tom replies, "That's true of me, too." This painful distance between them, the inability to express their feelings, and their confinement, the need to depart not just from the home but from each other, creates a situation seething with frustration. The terrible realization for Tom is that it is his *love* for his mother and, above all, for Laura that imprisons him for the rest of his life.

The Glass Menagerie is a what-if depiction: what might have happened if, in true Williams historical tradition, his father had actually been the hero Tom wanted him to be. And Amanda is what Edwina might have been had Tom become the unwilling head of the family. Although the surface details of Laura resemble those of Rose, the character traits of Laura are also those of Tom Williams: his shyness, his reticence, his fears. As Tom Wingfield seeks refuge in his writing, his sister collects little glass animals, with the unicorn, a symbol of purity, her favorite. For a brief time, a gentleman caller, an "emissary from a world of reality," but in fact a prisoner within his own illusions of a successful future, awakens her love, accidentally breaks the horn off the unicorn, and then dashes her hopes by confessing he is engaged to be married.

If Tennessee Williams had hoped unconsciously that his little play as a confessional would become a catharsis, it failed him in that purpose. Subject as the play has been to innumerable interpretations, it can be looked upon as a study in the duality of male and female in his nature, symbolized by brother and sister, a theme that twenty years later he would explore in the most introspective of his plays, *Out Cry*, or *The Two-Character Play*. It can also be looked upon as the artist's expression of a deeply frustrated love for his father—a play inhabited by the memory of a freewheeling Mississippi drummer. Amanda, who has kept his picture prominently on the wall, confesses to Tom, "I've never told you but I—loved your father. . . . All he had to do was grin and the world was bewitched." At the end of the play, Tom Wingfield, as the surrogate of Tom Williams, makes the symbolic exit to become Tennessee Williams, never to escape the inescapable: the binding, incestuous undercurrent of attachment to his sister. "Oh, Laura, Laura, I tried to leave you behind me, but I am more faithful than I intended to be."

As undeniably fine as Laurette Taylor's performance was, buoyed by the excellent ensemble work of the other players, audiences were stirred by the words of this new playwright, as were three of Chicago's leading drama critics, Claudia Cassidy, Ashton Stevens, and the *Sun*'s Henry T. Murdock. They began exhorting their readers to support something extraordinary while they had the chance, reminding them that they were always complaining about bad second-string road shows. Joining these critics were the city's powerful columnists Dale Harrison, Irving Kupicinet, and Nate Gross. In addition, there were rallying editorials in the *News* and the *Sun*, and after that, the Drama League and local colleges began spreading the good word. Although there were critics like Lloyd Lewis who thought the play more artiness than art, most were plainly enthusiastic, and they all "chimed like one uncracked bell for the acting of Laurette Taylor."[1] The impact was decisive.

As a result, there was a dramatic increase in ticket sales of three thousand dollars at the end of the third week and an additional two thousand dollars' income accruing after the following nine performances. Calls were beginning to come in from individual and group ticket buyers and from ticket agents. Singer and Yokel were suddenly smiling, Dowling was exulting, and now the front-office arguments concerned whether the Chicago engagement should continue beyond mid-February and whether there should be negotiations for a New York theatre. For Tom, the rise from ten dollars a day in royalties to one thousand a week was equally dramatic. He told Donald that Audrey had come and gone, happy as a lark, giving him ten dollars and taking his 5 percent of the gross with her. He soon wrote his mother that with audiences close to capacity, the play was grossing fifteen thousand dollars a week. "I hope it keeps up!" he exclaimed. "Of course taxes will take an awful lot of it. Audrey sends me weekly statements and deposits my royalties in N.Y. account which she has opened for me. She was quite honest about the Hollywood savings so I feel safe with her doing this. However I will probably transfer most of the money to St. Louis when I get to N.Y."[2]

Tom wrote home the good news: that weekends were almost at capacity business and the other nights building. Everyone, especially Laurette, was anxious to move on to New York, except Dowling. He knew that Broadway critics often looked upon out-of-town reviews as a challenge to their superior judgment, but he made February 10 the cutoff date for advance ticket sales. Even if the play flopped in New York, Tom knew he could spend years in Mexico.

Although by now the production was just about set, Tom mentioned that his own drunk scene had replaced Dowling's ad-lib and that a second narration had been removed. The real difficulty was a growing animosity between Taylor and Dowling. Not only was she harping on the absurdity of a man Eddie's age playing her son but she also presented a gamut of other grievances: contract provisions, proper billing, and, primarily, press releases that suggested *The Glass Menagerie* was in fact the initial production of Dowling's repertory season and was not really Broadway-bound. She was going about lavishly praising Eddie as a director while in the same breath denouncing him as "a lousy actor." Finally, Ashton Stevens phoned her and warned that this was all the Broadway columnists needed in order to spread the word that a troubled and divided company was making its way to New York. In Stevens's view, "she was most traditionally Irish. She loved hard and hated even harder. God loved her loves, and the Devil had conditioned her as one of the world's most amusing haters. She was so witty about it that I sometimes envied her enemies."[3]

Promising to be nice to Eddie, she went right on telling him he was not only too old for the part but too mannered. Her daughter said, "She had, as was her way, picked to bits the parts of his performance she thought were not true or wrong for the play." Tom had her as an ally concerning the disputed drunk scene. When Taylor felt Eddie had elaborated it to the point of farce,

> her protest was vigorous and direct. She didn't call that feuding. She called it honesty and an honest concern for the play. When Dowling was noncommittal in response, it only confused her. Then she would hear from others that he was hurt by her criticism, deeply wounded because she talked behind his back. In she would stamp to his dressing room. "How dare you say I talk behind your back! I've never said anything I haven't said to your face. I've told you about that monkey hat you wear on the back of your head, that makes you look like a monkey. I've said that to you since the first day you put it on. I've told you and *told* you about those ridiculous pauses—'She touches my—' and you pause and wonder why you get a titter! For God's sake say *shoulder* and *then* pause."

Exasperated, she would say that it was like "wading through molasses to try to talk to him!"[4] From Dowling's point of view, he may have been her costar, but *she* was the one receiving inordinate praise. And, more than that, a backstage clique had formed around her, all but isolating him in his dressing room. His share was only in the profits. The company had pleaded with Laurette and Dowling not to bring their feuding backstage, so instead they carried it onstage, bringing a startling intensity to their fight scenes and revealing what depths of violence exist in a play that has too often been thought of as gentle.

The Telephone Man Who Fell in Love with Long Distance

Late in January, impressed with Tom's financial reports, Cornelius traveled alone to Chicago to see his son's play. Edwina said that the performance he attended had been sold out but that they put a chair in the aisle for him because he was the playwright's father. Tom told Donald that Cornelius stayed only one night and that he left him with Laurette, who was furious at being trapped with that "dull old man!" In reporting this to Windham, he also enclosed a subsequent letter from his father, who chastised him for his free-spending habits. C.C. complained that when he tried to reach Tom at the hotel, they were told that he and Margo were at the bar. He said that he had stopped at the Sherman Hotel, and knew what they charged for drinks there. With Margo's capacity, he said, it wouldn't take long to break him. He said she should buy her own drinks.

When Cornelius arrived home, Edwina said his only comment about the play was that he did not believe she was Amanda. He also took exception to the idea that he had ever left home. With his exclusion from the play, C.C.'s isolation now from the family was complete. He said that he didn't think the family portrayed on the stage resembled theirs. Many years later, Edwina agreed, telling a St. Louis interviewer emphatically, "Oh, no, the play isn't family in any respect!" But musing over a newspaper article that referred to her as a still-recognizable Amanda, she paused and said softly, "Perhaps I am."[5]

Dakin said that the characterization was so accurate, Edwina could have sued Tom. "Her fainting act and her 'suffering Jesus' facial expressions were the most lethal (and unendurable) bits of her repertoire." He said that the opening scene of *Menagerie* was also an accurate portrayal: "Don't eat too fast, Dakin. Animals have salivary glands, but we humans must masticate our food. Don't push with your fingers, Dakin!" As for the line in the play, "My devotion to my children has made me a witch," Dakin said that Tom's reply, "you are not a witch, Mother," was intended to dry her tears. "I'm sure that Tom would have agreed with me that Mother could, and often did, act like one! It contributed a great deal to the tragedy of her life, and ours, particularly Rose's. Dad's bad behavior only made matters worse."[6]

As Tennessee Williams would soon discover, success spawns a multitude of problems unknown to failure. In failure, he at least had had anonymity to protect him. But now he was trying to fend off social invitations and media hype, both of which he found a distraction. Laurette, on the other hand, gloried in them. When she was not being feted by Chicago's haut monde in their Lake Shore Drive mansions or in the fashionable Pump Room of the Ambassador East Hotel, she and Tom would take off for Riccardo's, an Italian restaurant in the Loop, under the El. It was their favorite after-theatre haunt, and in a guest book they added their names to an astonishing range of celebrities as various as John Barrymore, Sally Rand, Ramon Novarro, Judith Anderson, Harry Blackstone, Gypsy Rose Lee, and Tallulah Bankhead. Besides inscriptions to the owner, Richard Riccardo, there were pencil sketches and lyrical quotations, as well as Tom's not so lyrical doggerel:

Home Remedy

One time Mama took mighty sick
felt like she'd swallowed a dynamite stick.
Mustard plaster didn't relieve her,
quinine seemed to raise her fever—
Jumped right up to 104
death stood right outside the door—
Mama said, Papa don't you cry
Just knock off a piece and let me die.
I climbed on the bed like a 3-legged stool
I was hotter than Mama & she wasn't cool.
When I got through she hopped outa bed
pulled up her skirt & stood on her head.
Now every time Mama takes sick
the same ole treatment works mighty quick.
So now I'm passin' this on to you,
a remedy that's tried *an'* true!

10. Wms.—Jan. 1945

As the author of a hit play, Tom had found a remedy for ready sex that also worked "mighty quick." Suddenly, he was being approached by opportunists whose interest in sex often included a desire for other favors that only influence and a surfeit of cash could provide. Tom enjoyed casual, often anonymous sex, and if money was a condition, that was fine with him—particularly if the other party needed to be paid as an excuse for doing what comes unnaturally to the hustler. While he didn't object to paying for a one-night stand, from this point on Tom would be darkly suspicious in trying to distinguish between an extended hand of friendship and a sweaty palm.

Many in the *Winged Victory* company were gay actors, and many students on the University of Chicago campus were aspiring actors, but most all of them were just looking for a good time. Tom's sudden celebrity status, along with his accommodations at the Hotel Sherman, offered him the comforts of both laissez-faire and excellent room service. Incredibly, though, when scandal could easily have destroyed a budding career and brought Tom disgrace among his family and friends,* he was busier than ever in the pursuit of sex,

---

*The question whether his family and St. Louis friends knew Williams was gay was always more a question in his own mind. He made every effort to keep the knowledge from his mother in particular. If she was aware, nothing could have brought her to discuss it; a southern lady, as she

cruising the bars and other spots known to be frequented by gay men. He knew the danger but simply didn't seem to care. Although officials in the major cities kept a fairly open policy toward gay life, particularly in wartime, the military was vicious in its treatment of both a gay man in uniform and his civilian companion.

Tom's companion in these adventures was often the gentle and affable "gentleman caller," Tony Ross. Tennessee wrote, "Laurette was very fond of us both, she used to call us the Big Bum and the Little Bum. He and I went out together every night almost, after the curtain came down. We went out cruising together. I had more luck than Tony for the reason that Tony would get drunk, and drunks are not likely to cruise well in Chicago or anywhere. He was an amiable drunk, but something in Tony was broken and the fine performances that he gave every night were an extraordinary accomplishment for a man who had so much torment in him."[7]

More alcoholic than homosexual, Ross was tormented by feelings of insecurity and by deteriorating health. Randy Echols, who was both stage manager and Tony's understudy, was forced to go on when the actor was finally hospitalized. At the point when a replacement was being considered, Ross came to terms with himself in that standoff that alcoholics must confront if they are not to commit outright suicide. The company secretary, Mary Jean Copeland, was in love with him, married him a year later, and bore him a son. Afterward, his career flourished for a time, but in 1955, at age forty-nine, he died when, ironically, he was playing an alcoholic professor in William Inge's *Bus Stop*.

As anxious as she was to go on to meet the challenge of New York, Laurette was thoroughly enjoying her triumph in Chicago. She was the toast of the town, and her daughter quoted critic Ashton Stevens as declaring, "By virtue of the fact of *The Glass Menagerie* and Miss Taylor's presence in it, Chicago is for the moment the center of the theatrical world." He pointed out that "the town's most distinguished writers, players and social big shots nightly crowd her spacious dressing room."[8] The adulation Julie Haydon gave to her, however, proved to be too much. Despite Laurette's visible displeasure, Julie persisted during curtain calls in taking her hand and kissing it. On one occasion, the audience heard Taylor loudly warn her to "cut that out!" and on another, when Haydon stooped to kiss the hem of her skirt instead, Laurette pushed her into an awkward sitting position.

Eddie Dowling too was being eulogized at various testimonial affairs and

---

fancied herself, would simply shut such things from her mind. Tom was "different," that much she acknowledged, and C.C. could certainly agree with that. During his last years, the Reverend Dakin, when visiting his famous grandson in New York and Key West, enjoyed the gay life peripherally and was especially fond and approving of Williams's companion, Frank Merlo. In the private matters of one's sexual behavior, "mum was the word" in both the Dakin and Williams families.

given a reasonable share of media attention. Chicago's citizens and critics wanted him to remain in their city, and he was torn between an extension of the Chicago engagement and a commitment to a New York premiere. He and his partners could logically reason that to push back the Broadway opening, without losing the theatre for which they were negotiating, could mean not only amortizing their investment but sharing in some net profits during the Chicago run.

In other words, they could go into New York home free, regardless of what the critics thought. After all, they were businessmen, and where previously they had losses to dispute, now they had the prospect of profits to fight over. To anyone just dropping in, the front office had something of the atmosphere of a bookie's back room. Infighting was the order of the day. Yokel was threatening to sue Singer in a quarrel over billing. And Dowling was trying to shush Singer, who had announced to a reporter that the Shuberts could go to hell. Dowling tried to explain, "You have to go to the Shuberts to get a house for an opening. They own it all. I took 'The Glass Menagerie' to them. They told me to give it a tryout in New Haven, Baltimore or Philadelphia and they would come and give it a look." Determined to take his full share of the deep bows, Dowling told the newsmen that he had gambled with a play that even the author's agent had said would be a financial flop. Audrey Wood, he said, had sent it along to him as an example of Williams's style, in the hope that he would encourage Tennessee to write something more commercial. Dowling added that Wood had actually suggested he produce another play by another playwright. Whether this was true or not, it mirrored his intense dislike of Audrey Wood, whom Dowling eventually called "the damndest phony I know."

Dowling's bitterness extended to Tennessee Williams, as well—"the most ungrateful man (?) I have ever met."[9] This bitterness was shared by George Jean Nathan, who was receiving regular bulletins concerning the performances of Julie Haydon. It annoyed Dowling and Nathan that Laurette was the indisputable star of *The Glass Menagerie*. And they resented both Tennessee's resistance to their dialogue additions and Laurette's vocal support. Dowling would carry these feelings to New York and for the remainder of his long life. He was to write of Tennessee Williams that "it will one day, before long, be known to all who know anything about good plays [that] he has one good one that I made good, as George Jean Nathan told him to his ingrate face."[10]

Julie Haydon in no way shared these seething opinions. She was then and for the time she remained in the theatre grateful for both what she learned from the great actress and for the opportunity to originate the role of Laura. In her own gentle way, she was completely removed from the theatre's intramural sniping. As for the two scrapping Irish folk, Dowling and Taylor continued their pitched battle from Chicago through the New York engagement, until finally she became too sick to continue. She was already stricken with an undiagnosed cancer.

Louis J. Singer may have been given the title coproducer, but in actuality he was an associate producer, which in the theatre generally means a limited partner who contributes or raises the first money and keeps his mouth shut. That didn't stop Singer. He was like a religious initiate in his enthusiasm for having found a new religion. Everyone in the company was trying to avoid his blessings, and especially his opinions. In addition to taking potshots at the Shuberts, he was informing the press how he had given Jo Mielziner invaluable advice on ways to design the production. Tom forthwith dispatched a letter to Mielziner.

> Many thanks for your note—I guess you know by now that your lighting job is the first thing on everyone's tongue in connection with this show.
>
> It is nothing less than sensational—and now that the crew is working smoothly, it is far more effective than when you saw it. Now it goes like clockwork and is inestimably and very integrally a part of the play. I want to thank you for your patience—endurance is a better word—Margo is sending you a clipping about Mr. Singer's assistance to you that I think will give you the final sense of fulfillment!
>
> Well, business has picked up considerably—I am still going through hell with various dissenting opinions about the end of the play—but most of Eddie's mugging and ad-lib has been cut out—and of course you know that Taylor *did* know her lines—and gave a performance so astonishing that none of us still quite believe it!
>
> Hope I see you in New York soon, Jo—and that you'll stick with us—with or without Mr. Singer's expert assistance.[11]

James Laughlin arrived in Chicago early in February, saw the play, and told Tom that he wanted to publish *The Glass Menagerie*. His magazine, *Pharos*, was about to be released and it contained the first publication of *Battle of Angels*. Tom wrote to Audrey, "In view of Jay's kindness to me and the fact that he has already published my work and will continue to publish it I am firmly persuaded that he should do the book."[12] Audrey reminded him, though, that unknown to her at the time he had signed a contract with Bennett Cerf of Random House in November 1940 after he had returned from Mexico and that Cerf had paid an advance of one hundred dollars. The agreement specified that in the event the author did not wish to return the advance, he was permitted to keep it with the understanding that the one hundred dollars would be applied on the next work that might then be accepted for publication.

Tom replied, "In the years since Cerf made that payment he has not shown one spark of interest in my work or existence and while I don't feel any resentment of this—he had no reason to—I don't think I should now favor his firm instead of Laughlin's, especially since to be published by New Directions is far more of an honor to my way of thinking." He added, "I believe in dealing with people who have shown sympathy and faith in you—which isn't merely sentiment but also sound business practice."[13] He asked her to see what could be done to "extricate me gracefully—without unnecessary offense—from the Random House commitment."

At first, Audrey's business sense favored Random House "since they publish plays as well and better than any other publisher in New York at this time. They also publicize plays much more than any other publisher is interested in doing." But Audrey could take a certain assurance from Tom's loyalty to Laughlin; she knew very well that if he were now to become a successful playwright, other more powerful agents would try to lure him away with bigger money deals.

In her letter, Audrey mentioned that she had seen Margo, who was in town making arrangements for the incoming company, and that Singer had phoned to say the Broadway opening date was now set for March 6. Tom replied, "I am glad we are going into New York next month. Worried about Laurette. She got terribly drunk at a party night before last. Literally passed out cold and fell on the sidewalk—first time this has happened and she was okay for the next performance. But I know she is terribly lonely here and the sooner she gets back to N.Y. the better. Know you won't talk about this—I wasn't at the party but heard about it. I believe she restrains herself a little when I am around and that is one reason I'm staying."[14]

As much as she was being lionized in Chicago and was enjoying it, Laurette knew the fawning for what it was: skittering leaves in the Windy City. Offstage now, she was becoming bored and edgy and more and more in need of a drink. Tom felt that what she actually needed was the seclusion of her own apartment and the protection of her young actress friend, Eloise. One who could understand Laurette's quicksilver disposition was Helen Hayes, then in Chicago playing in *Harriet*. She remembered Laurette saying over and over like an incantation, " 'I'm going to break this witch's curse.' "[15]

Hayes said that Laurette was one of her idols and that they had been friends for a long time. "*Harriet* was closed on Sunday nights, and that was when I saw *The Glass Menagerie*. The play and Laurette were simply superb. Most nights after work, I would join her and Tennessee (they were very close) and Tony Ross, too, and we would go to their favorite bar. Laurette would order a double scotch, and when she saw my eyes widen, she reassured me that if she ordered a second drink, her deceased husband, Hartley, would come down and gently tap her on the shoulder. Being Irish, she believed that to be perfectly true."[16]

Hayes remembered that Laurette's career had nose-dived and that hers was "a daring attempt at a comeback at age sixty. . . . One night the phone was ringing when I returned to my suite at the Ambassador. It was Laurette. 'I can't go on tomorrow,' she said in despair. 'My throat hurts, and I'm losing my voice. If I don't go on, everyone will think I'm drunk. If they say I'm drunk, I will get drunk and stay drunk till I die.' Her cry for help galvanized me." Hayes said that she always carried an electric steam kettle when she went on tour, to which she could add medicine. "It had been helpful when I came down with bronchitis or laryngitis. I told Laurette I would come right away with the kettle . . . I taxied downtown to the Sherman House. I stayed with her through most of the night, making sure she was breathing properly . . . the next evening she gave a magnificent performance."[17]

The word had spread to Broadway and Hollywood, and the wagers were on: Would she or would she not make it back? Everyone in the Chicago company was now, by mid-February, plainly nervous. The more Laurette was surrounded by flattery and the excitement of prominent visitors, the greater was the strain on her to keep from joining in the carouse around her. The marvelously witty and stylish actress Ina Claire was in the audience every night, and Tom wrote Audrey, "Everybody stops off here between Hollywood and New York, so our social life is terrific. We've had Helen Hayes, Ruth Gordon, Katharine Hepburn, Terry Helburn, Maxwell Anderson, Mary Chase, Guthrie McClintic, Lindsay and Crouse, Raymond Massey, Gregory Peck, Luther Adler and God knows what all! Everybody has been favorable except Maxwell Anderson. He didn't like it."[18]

Neither did Theresa Helburn. Dowling had been hoping she and Lawrence Langner would accept the play for the Theatre Guild subscription season, but Helburn decided that it was just too fragile and Taylor too unpredictable for the Guild to risk. Moreover, the Guild was deep into plans for Eugene O'Neill's return the following year with *The Iceman Cometh*. Katharine Hepburn's enthusiasm for *The Glass Menagerie*, on the other hand, was such that she went straightway to Metro-Goldwyn-Mayer's Louis B. Mayer, saying that the studio should buy the play, assign George Cukor to direct, cast her as Laura and Spencer Tracy as the gentleman caller, and, above all, capture on film Laurette's incomparable performance. She was to say later that Amanda Wingfield was Tennessee's "most tenderly observed, the most accessible woman he ever created."[19]

Hepburn was in top form during her prosperous years at MGM and, in her inimitable fashion, undoubtedly gave Mayer a memorable sales pitch. She had done it before and sold him on two highly profitable film ventures, *The Philadelphia Story* and *Woman of the Year*. But she was not likely to know that Mayer and his legal advisers were already of the opinion that they owned the property, since Tennessee Williams had been writing it as *The Gentleman Caller* while employed at the studio—a contention disproved by Audrey Wood.

In her memoir, Audrey related how "L. B. Mayer, the titan, himself got into the controversy,"[20] claiming that the studio had rights to *The Glass Menagerie*. There followed the usual legal saber rattling, but as Audrey had sent

Metro a list of Tom's properties, including *The Gentleman Caller*, the studio had little claim. MGM executive Lillie Messinger wrote to Audrey, accusing Tom of biting the hand that fed him. Audrey wrote back, "This is America, this is Williams' play, and M-G-M has no claim whatsoever to it."[21] She might also have pointed out that he had offered a screen adaptation to story editor William Fadiman, who had flatly turned it down, forfeiting what might have been the studio's vested interest in the play. Instead, Metro-Goldwyn-Mayer suffered the further indignity of losing out to Warner Brothers, who ultimately bought the screen rights to the play.

In later years, MGM would produce the film version of *Cat on a Hot Tin Roof* and earn for itself huge profits and for its author some $500,000. There would also be the screen adaptations of *Period of Adjustment*, *The Night of the Iguana*, and, notably, *Sweet Bird of Youth*, the latter produced by Tom's former boss, Pandro S. Berman. As a further irony, Louis B. Mayer would live to see his daughter, Irene Mayer Selznick, produce Tennessee Williams's masterwork, *A Streetcar Named Desire*, then sell the movie rights to Warner Brothers.

Finally, along with the celebrities who had come to Chicago to see the play, a group of Tom's former classmates from Iowa arrived, among them his former mentor Marian Gallaway, who greeted him with, "Tom—Tom—when are you *ever* going to write a *play?*"[22] By then, Gallaway had become director of the theatre department at the University of Alabama, and the well-made play was as much her text as it was his aversion.

One who was not then a celebrity but destined to become a foremost interpreter of both Williams and O'Neill was José Quintero. In 1944, he was attending the Goodman Theatre School, and he said that seeing *The Glass Menagerie* reinforced his decision to go into the theatre. He recalled that after leaving the performance, "I walked all night long. I knew then something had made me feel whole. Here was someone who could feel my pain, my loneliness, and put it into such beautiful words."[23] He remembered this as the first time in his life that he stopped feeling alone.

"Y.T.M."

Tom had no reason to believe that if *The Glass Menagerie* was a success in New York, it would last any longer than Laurette Taylor was able to star in it. And while both Dowling and Audrey were of the opinion *Menagerie* should precede *You Touched Me!* into New York, it could be one or the other as far as Tom was concerned.

He was still holding out for Mary Hunter as producer and director of his and Donald's play. She had written him to say that she was now in a position to acquire the rights. Audrey had sent him a wire, cautioning him not to agree to an opening date or to make any other deals. Tom wrote her, "Mary Hunter called to say she has a man definitely interested in putting up all the money for

'Y.T.M.'—I agree it shouldn't be done before 'G.M.' has opened in N.Y. and would not permit it to. But I would still rather work with Mary on it than anyone else." He added, "She has the right idea about concentrating on the bright and lively values in the script and I think it would hardly be fair to snatch it from her hands when she has done so much work on it already."[24]

Now Dowling was under pressure to agree to a firm opening date in New York for *Menagerie*, not simply because Audrey was urging it upon him but because he had been made aware of the interest in *You Touched Me!* By mid-February, Audrey was writing Tom, "I Airmailed you a script of You Touched Me yesterday since you asked for a copy. I'm waiting for Mary Hunter to sign the contracts on the said play and will advise you when I get her signature."[25] Then at month's end, she wired him: ALEX YOKEL ADVISES YOU WANT HIM TO HAVE YOU TOUCHED ME. ALREADY SUBMITTED CONTRACTS HUNTER. WON'T TALK TO YOKEL TILL I HEAR FROM YOU.[26] The fact that Yokel had been the original producer of Irwin Shaw's *Bury the Dead* impressed Tom. Not only that, Yokel had held out the promise of a razzle-dazzle Broadway production, with a cast of stars and Jo Mielziner as designer, and "all the money in the world."

Because he was not getting billing in New York, Yokel threatened to sue Singer, while at the same time Audrey informed Tom that Singer told her he had been approached by another agent as to the status of the motion picture rights of *The Glass Menagerie*. "Do not discuss this matter with any second or third party and be sure that you tell anybody contacting you to get in touch with me. If you do this everything will work out beautifully. If you don't do this we'll be in a hell of a lot of trouble."[27]

Finally, Audrey wired: HAVE NOT YET BEEN ABLE TO DISENTANGLE HUNTER. ALSO QUITE HONESTLY DONT THINK YOKEL DEAL MUCH BETTER. IN RETALIATION HAVE SUBMITTED PLAY TODAY GUTHRIE MCCLINTIC AND IF HE WILL DO IT IS PERFECT WAY OUT. PLEASE KEEP THIS QUIET AND PLEASE REFER ALL INTERESTED PARTIES TO ME WITHOUT MAKING ANY PROMISE WHATSOEVER SO HELP YOU GOD.[28]

On March 2, Tom told Donald that he was in the doghouse with his producers on the one hand and with Laurette and Tony on the other. He had written a column for Ashton Stevens about "business men and gamblers" in the theatre, thus enraging Singer and Dowling.* As a reprisal, Dowling instructed the New York press agent to exclude Tennessee Williams's name from all publicity and even substitute Singer's profile in the first *Playbill* pro-

---

*Williams, writing in critic Ashton Stevens's column, "Excursions in Stageland" ("Pictorial Review" section of the *Chicago Herald-American*, 25 February 1945, p. 19), struck out, with the one hand, deploring the incursion of business opportunists taking over the theatre and, with the other, challenging those "select few of American drama critics who insist that the theater have another purpose than entertainment and profit." He insisted, "I am not speaking bitterly of businessmen and gamblers. Gamblers are exciting personalities and businessmen are not only respectable but often desirable members of any society. I am only speaking bitterly of them as custodians of an art which to me is religion."

grams. At the same time, Tony complained to Laurette that Tom was preventing him from going on the wagon, convincing her that he was a bad influence.

At this point, Tom decided to go home to St. Louis for a week or two, further spurred by the ghost of the ill-fated scooter and the price of success. He wrote Audrey, "Thanks for your note about the credit company. Those S.O.B.'s should be prosecuted but if there is no other way, pay them!"[29] He also wrote to his mother to say that he would probably be home before she received his letter but that he hoped she and Cornelius would consider going to the New York opening. "It is March 31st and New York ought to be getting very nice—or beginning to—at that time. If you can go, Mother, I would like to give you the trip as a much-delayed present."[30]

On his return to St. Louis, Tom contacted William Inge, and they went out almost every night. Inge, as a result of seeing *The Glass Menagerie*, was still in awe of his friend and confided in him "that being a successful playwright was what he most wanted in the world." But at a time now when personally Tom felt he should be most elated, he spoke instead of an ominous letdown of spirit that followed him like a shadow wherever he went. "I think Bill Inge had already made up his mind to invoke this same shadow and to suffuse it with light."*[31]

In addition, Tom's university friends gave him a homecoming party. For the moment, it was all play, but everything was beginning to change, particularly in Tom's attitude toward his friends and in theirs toward him. Now, more and more, there were concerns and decisions that Tom had to grapple with in the public person of Tennessee Williams. Although he would go on for the remainder of his life seeking escape from these onerous responsibilities, inevitably he would be drawn back to their genesis, the theatre. There he would find the ever-vigilant Audrey Wood watching over his career like a mother hawk. Although she would influence his decisions, as she very often did, he *made* them—not without vacillation, not without contradiction, and not without regret. Frequently they were hard, cruelly self-directed decisions, detrimental to anyone who might be in the way. In a secret hiding place where there was room for only one, there, deep within the recesses of the person, *Tom*, existed the fiercely protective artist, camouflaged in the world outside by the persona, *Tennessee*.

Before Tom returned to Chicago, Audrey sent him the news that Guthrie McClintic had come up with a $750 advance and had set an October 1 pro-

---

*As fate would have it, that ominous shadow did indeed hover over both playwrights. Inge's last successful play, *The Dark at the Top of the Stairs*—the title itself a tragic symbol—climaxed a series of successes, including *Come Back, Little Sheba*, *Picnic*, and *Bus Stop*. His career then went into a sharp decline, his last years, like Tennessee's, marred by one defeat after another, and ending with Inge in despair, committing suicide.

duction date for *You Touched Me!* She said, "I have not yet been in touch with Mary Hunter who also has not been in touch with me. I'm going to send her a letter saying that we have had to go ahead with another management and I shall send a copy of the said letter to the Dramatists' Guild." She added that although she had sent a wire to Donald asking him to call her, he had not as yet replied. She asked, "Did you ever make any agreement with Windham in writing as to what percentage he was to get on this play? I still think it's wrong to give him a half of your share which will mean that you will get only thirty percent whereas Frieda Lawrence will be getting forty percent. Won't you think about this and let me try to make a better deal with Windham?"[32]

One of the traits for which Tennessee Williams became only too well known was his skill at avoiding painful problems by delegating them to a third person. When it came to dealing with Mary Hunter, he could reason that this was business, after all, and within Audrey's province. But Donald was a close friend and confidant, and the eventual resolution of their stakes in *You Touched Me!* inflicted an injury, like something broken, that would never again be set right.

Shortly before leaving St. Louis, Tom wrote to Audrey:

> I fully participate in your happiness over the McClintic deal though I feel somewhat guilty and embarrassed over its effect on Mary.
>
> She woke me up at ten o'clock this morning with a long-distance call which went on for at least five minutes. She had received your letter which she said took her completely by astonishment and wanted me to explain as you were not in town. Having just awakened I was in no condition to cope with her verbally, that is, with any finesse, so I simply told her the facts as I understood them—that you and Mr. Collins [attorney for D. H. Lawrence estate] had not obtained her agreement to the contract or were not in accord on terms, and so you had to go ahead with another management. . . . I tried to be gentle and reassuring without actually misrepresenting anything to her—but of course I felt like a heel! Though actually I don't suppose any playwright would act differently under these circumstances. Do you suppose McClintic would give her some part in the production, co-director, assistant, or anything like that? That would certainly avoid a lot of unhappiness and disappointment for Mary and embarrassment to all of us—for I am sure Mary and Mary's friends will never regard Tennessee as anything but a snake if she is left out cold! I am putting all this in your hands! Can you hold it?
>
> Regarding Windham's percentage, I thought a contract had been drawn up a long time ago making that definite. There was some correspondence concerning it the summer I was in Macon and at that time I wrote you that if Windham wanted a fifty-fifty arrangement I did not want to antagonize him by holding out for more, though certainly I should have it. Since that time, however—as you know—I have re-

written the play repeatedly, worked on it always entirely without his assistance—since the first two months when collaborative effort on it was getting us nowhere. Actually at this time the whole play is my creation, dialogue and all inventions not drawn from the Lawrence story—which Windham had wanted to follow exactly to its death-bed conclusion. He never really liked what I was doing to the play and after I started making it a comedy, he seemed to lose interest in everything except its possible sale.

Windham's attitude is understandable, however. He discovered the short-story and it was his idea to make it a play—I volunteered to assist him—it just happened we couldn't work together and the final result was totally my own product.

Obviously the percentages are unfair, but I would prefer for any adjustment—*if* any is still possible—to be by friendly agreement rather than any pressure put on him. A fair arrangement would be for Frieda Lawrence and I to have equal shares and Don the remaining twenty, which is about as large a price as anyone has received for his amount of effort or contribution. If the matter were coming up for the first time, I would insist upon this division—because of all I've done on the script, and the fact that "Menagerie's" success is the only reason this one is sold. If he won't agree to change percentages, perhaps he would consent to smaller credit on the program—one or the other—I think it would be all right to talk this over with him and see if he is inclined to be unselfish. Let me know your opinion.

I have some revisions on the last scene of "YTM" which I will mail you before I leave Saint Louis—want to go over them once more.

I'm intending to leave this week-end, back to Chicago. Perhaps I will need an armed body-guard when I get there, with Yokel and Hunter both feeling betrayed. Love, /10.[33]

Donald's own contention was that in the spring of 1942, when they began their collaboration, the proportionate contribution was *much* greater on his side, changing only with Tennessee's commercially oriented additions and his unsuitably crude humor added during the summer in Macon, nearly all of which were eventually removed. But Audrey could only proceed on the strength of what Tennessee had set forth in his letter as the truth, and she drew up a document for Donald to sign, changing the distribution of royalties to 40 percent for Tennessee and 20 percent for Donald. Windham, unprepared for this turn of events, told Audrey that he would prefer to talk to Tennessee before he signed, and when he confronted his friend, Tennessee claimed to know nothing about it. Donald said that no one ever mentioned the matter to him again. Audrey would go on believing, as had Paul Bigelow during the summer in 1942, that *You Touched Me!* was the sole creation of Tennessee Williams.

Collaboration was something that Tennessee Williams simply could not abide. In almost all his communications, he treated *You Touched Me!* as *his* play, with his feelings for his friend clearly ambivalent. Without mentioning Donald, he wrote Guthrie McClintic that he had a good many ideas he wanted to discuss when he got to New York: "I think the plastic—visual, Etc.—elements in the play are unusually important . . . the play should have great lightness and charm and pictorial beauty. The atmosphere of Elizabethan comedy in a modern play is what I wanted to get."[34]

When Tom arrived back in Chicago, the situation was, as he had anticipated, in turmoil. Both Hunter and Yokel were complaining about his signing with McClintic, Mary imploring him to wait until he got to New York and Yokel reminding him that an option is not necessarily a commitment to produce. Because Mary Hunter had not yet produced on Broadway, Yokel could argue that, in addition to having produced *Bury the Dead*, he had had one of the longest-running hits, some 385 performances, in *Three Men on a Horse.**

As for Guthrie McClintic, what he thought about "plastic" theatre and "the atmosphere of Elizabethan comedy in a modern play" can only be conjectured. McClintic and his wife, the formidable Katharine Cornell, had for some twenty years an impressive track record of commercial successes that at least had the *look* of art. They were a producing team, he directing her in many of her appearances, such as *The Barretts of Wimpole Street*, *Candida*, *The Three Sisters*, and *No Time for Comedy*. No expense was spared to make these singularly beautiful productions. And Cornell, who may not have been the theatre's first lady, most certainly had the stage presence to be its foremost grande dame.

McClintic, apart from his wife's productions, directed many notable plays: *Winterset*, John Gielgud's *Hamlet*, *Yellow Jack*, *Key Largo*. His was a heavy hand—he had a definite feel for what was then known as "high drama"—but in a high comedy like S. N. Behrman's *No Time for Comedy*, it was the urbane flair of Laurence Olivier that gave the production its distinction, try as Cornell did as his costar to add a light touch.

Given his reputation for high-strung, volcanic rages, it was questionable whether McClintic was the right director for *You Touched Me!* After making the trip to Chicago to see *Menagerie*, he realized that something enormously powerful was approaching New York. And Cornell was hoping to work in new plays by a postwar playwright like Tennessee Williams. She was not right for *You Touched Me!* either, but shortly after she saw *The Glass Menagerie*, she

---

*In addition to their other concerns, Yokel and Singer were locked in various disputes. Yokel had finally gotten his title changed to general manager, but now his fight with Singer concerned his 5 percent interest in each partner's share, which he was to receive as a finder's fee for having brought Dowling and Singer together and, in effect, raised the capitalization. Later, in a court action, Singer "refused to turn over to Yokel the agreed-upon share of the show, although Dowling had readily done so. After months of controversy, the matter was settled, Yokel accepting $25,000" (*Variety*, 3 December 1947).

wired Tennessee to write her a part as fine as Laurette's; the telegram was signed Kit, the sobriquet used only by close friends and columnists.

A Chair in the Moon

Clearly, Tom was having difficulties adjusting to the new world of Tennessee Williams. When Tony Ross was hospitalized, Randy Echols substituted for him. Singer, of course, recognized the economy in having Echols carry out his duties as stage manager and also act the gentleman caller's one scene and thus eliminate one salary. Laurette warned that Echols could ruin the show. Tom agreed but was in a quandary as to what to do. Liebling wired him: YOU MUST PERSONALLY WRITE PRODUCERS IMMEDIATELY PUTTING THEM ON NOTICE THAT ECHOLS CANNOT OPEN IN NEW YORK. . . . YOU ARE THE COMPLETE AND SOLE AUTHORITY ON ANY MATERIAL OR ACTOR THAT IS TO BE IN THE PLAY. PUT IT IN WRITING AND BE TOUGH ABOUT IT.[35] He put it in writing, and Ross resumed his role.

Donald, too, was occupying Tom's thoughts. He began and abandoned a letter to him.

> Dear Donnie:
> With money rolling in at the rate of a thousand a week, all impulse toward action has been short-circuited in me. I have no reason to stay here and I can't think of any reason to go. I am neither elated nor depressed, just feel sort of dissociated from everything past or future. I mosey around town, usually with Tony and Laurette or the university kids, till five or six in the morning—go to bed and sleep till about four in the afternoon. Have breakfast sent up. Work desultorily. Smoke, swim, then to a movie, then call for Tony and Laurette at the theatre. What a useless existence! But this overwhelming security has made all plans or effort suddenly pointless and given life an air of extreme unreality. . . . I don't [know] whether it's a fool's paradise or purgatory! But I shall have to decide on something extraordinary soon or I will turn into a jelly-fish.[36]

The "extraordinary" he had decided upon was a play that at first he thought might be suitable for Katharine Cornell. A few days before the company was to leave for New York, Tom sent Audrey a letter in which he set forth a remarkably precise synopsis of a play that he would not complete for another two years. It would become the "big" play that he had planned to write in Mexico, what is largely thought to be Tennessee Williams's masterpiece, *A Streetcar Named Desire.*

> I have been buried in work the last week or so and am about 55 or 60 pages into the first draft of a play which I am trying to design for Cornell.

At the moment it has four different titles, The Moth, The Poker Night, The Primary Colors, or Blanche's Chair in The Moon. It is about two sisters, the remains of a fallen southern family. The younger, Stella, has accepted the situation, married beneath her socially and moved to a southern city with her coarsely attractive, plebeian mate. But Blanche (the Cornell part) has remained at Belle-reve, the home place in ruins, and struggles for five years to maintain the old order. Though essentially decent and very delicate by nature, she has gone for protection to various men till her name is tarnished. She teaches English in a small-town high-school but loses the job when her name is involved with a married man's. The place is finally lost, Belle-reve, and Blanche, destitute, gives up the struggle and takes refuge with Stella in the southern city.[37]

Having given the background of the play, he then went on for several pages to outline the action virtually scene by scene as he would ultimately write it.

On Sunday afternoon, March 25, Tom left for New York with the company. Checking into the Hotel Brevoort on his arrival, no one, including Donald and Audrey, had any idea where he was. In the few remaining days before the opening, he was attempting to settle his problem with Random House. He wrote Bennett Cerf a letter that is notable for its reflection of Tennessee Williams on the brink of fame, acting in his own business interests but also as a loyal friend of James Laughlin.

Dear Mr. Cerf—

I have reported our phone conversation to Laughlin and he feels that anxious as he is to publish The Glass Menagerie he could not very well repay the kindnesses you have done him by taking the book if you want it terribly badly.

Therefore I shall be willing to sign with you for it on your usual terms, provided they are satisfactory to my agent, Audrey Wood; and that you exercise your option by Wednesday, April 4th. The play opens tomorrow night and that should give you ample time to study the reviews and decide whether you can afford to risk your reputation on so dubious a venture.

One further provision would be that the contract contain no option on future plays or books. I have definitely decided that I wish to have my books published by New Directions because of my sympathy for the writers in that group and what they stand for.[38]

Laughlin had sent Audrey a check for $100 in the vain hope of paying off the advance made to Tom by Random House, but Cerf exercised his option in a graciously worded reply, "We will be very happy to publish The Glass Menagerie," and he added, "I understand that all future works of yours will be published by New Directions, and I appreciate Mr. Laughlin's attitude in this entire matter."[39]

Curtain!

Eddie Dowling had returned to his Forty-fourth Street offices, in close quarters with his warring partners. In addition to his problems of an orderly take-in of setting, lights, and props at the Playhouse, he had also to worry whether "that damned old woman" would fail to turn up on opening night or would go onstage drunk, as she had in *Alice-Sit-by-the-Fire*, closing the play. But, on the other hand, if she pulled out all the stops, how far upstage would that leave him? After an agreement on coequal status, the billing was now Laurette Taylor *and* Eddie Dowling over the title, with their separate pictures to the left and right on the house program. To that extent, there was a truce.

Laurette was well aware that both her disgrace in *Alice* and her come-back in *Outward Bound* had taken place on this same Playhouse stage. Across the street was the Cort Theatre, where her career had begun in the title role of *Peg O' My Heart*. She had much to look back upon, but the present confronting her was virtually unendurable. Back in her apartment, she found that her impulse was not to leave it and to seek escape in alcohol, but she also recognized this as an enemy that could bring upon her a terrible, final disgrace. In the hours before the curtain was to rise, she was under the watchful care of Eloise Sheldon, who had taken time off from her role in *Harvey* to be close to her.

The Glass Menagerie was scheduled to open on Saturday, March 31, Easter eve—a week after Tom's thirty-fourth birthday (his thirty-first, as far as his friends and the press knew) and the day before Laurette's sixty-first. Born a few weeks before Easter and reared in the symbolism of the Christian church, Tom saw this season as a special one, and he used the passage from crucifixion to resurrection as a constant theme in his work.

He had moved into the Shelton Hotel, and he and Donald spent the afternoon going in and out of Second and Third Avenue junk shops in search of a lampshade that might have been suitable in Amanda's eyes for the second-act dinner party for the gentleman caller. Donald said that Tennessee had only two tickets for that evening and that he took him along. Horton Foote said he had been promised a ticket, and Tennessee took him backstage to Eddie Dowling, who relieved Foote's embarrassment by giving him a house seat. Mary Hunter was in the lobby, and she and Tennessee embraced. Jane and Tony Smith were in the audience, and Margo Jones, accompanied by her beau, Sonny Koch, had flown in from Dallas. Paul Bigelow and Jordan Massee sent wires from Macon. And Audrey Wood was there with Liebling for an event that was to be in many ways her personal achievement, as well.

That afternoon, there had been a technical run-through and the usual chaotic dress rehearsal. Audrey wrote:

> I don't remember where the author was that last afternoon but I shan't
> ever forget sitting in an unairconditioned Playhouse Theatre. There was
> a frenetic veiling over everything—and everybody. The actors paced nervously before the run-through began. The light technicians tinkered
> with never-ending light cues and most of them came out just a little bit
> wrong. Having played their roles for months in Chicago meant absolutely nothing. This was the day of the New York opening. This was it. I
> kept remembering Liebling's remark, "You're only as good as the night
> they catch you."

Audrey recalled that when Laurette began her opening scene, she seemed
under control but "after a few words in recognizable anguish she said, 'I'm
sorry, I have to leave the stage. I'm going to be sick.' And sick she was offstage
and then returned to try once more, a little whiter." The illness continued all
afternoon.

Paul Bowles's sensitive incidental score roared out when it should have
sounded

> like circus music, away off in the distance of memory. Julie Haydon was
> trying to keep a stiff upper lip, but her concern for Miss Taylor was considerable. The two men, Eddie Dowling and Tony Ross, may also have
> been scared to death, but they made a brave attempt at pretending they
> didn't care a damn what day it was.
>
> The coproducer, Louis Singer, felt his way over to my side of the otherwise dark, empty auditorium where I was crouched down in my seat.
> Peering at me through the darkness, he said, "Tell me—you are supposed to know a great deal about the theatre—is this or is it not the worst
> dress rehearsal you've ever seen in your life?" I nodded "Yes." I was too
> frightened to try and open my mouth.[40]

During the rehearsal, Randy Echols had placed a bucket in the wings and,
except for the two hours that Amanda was onstage, Laurette was leaning over
it. Tony Ross later said, "It seemed incredible to us that by curtain time Laurette would have the strength left to give a performance. We went home for a
few hours for supper, but Eloise told me Laurette could eat nothing."[41]

In her dressing room, Laurette had placed in front of her a large framed
photograph of her husband, Hartley Manners. Among the many telegrams
and gifts of flowers filling the room, there was a present from George Jean
Nathan—a bottle of scotch. If he thought it might throw her performance off
balance in favor of Julie Haydon's, let alone destroy it, he was mistaken.

Subsequently, she sent him a wire: THANKS FOR THE VOTE OF CONFIDENCE.

Eloise had her dressed by the time of Randy's summons, "Curtain, Miss Taylor!" Tony Ross said that Mary Jean Copeland and Julie had to help her to her place onstage. "As the lights dimmed on Dowling at the end of his opening narration and began going up on the dining-room table we could hear Laurette's voice, 'Honey, don't push with your fingers. . . . And chew—chew!' It seemed thin and uncertain. Slowly the lights came up full, and as she continued to speak, her voice gained strength. The audience didn't recognize her at first, and by the time they did she was well into her speech, and kept on going right through the applause. They soon quieted down." The bucket stayed in the wings, and "the few minutes she had between scenes, she was leaning over it retching horribly. There was nothing left inside her, poor thing, but onstage—good God!—what a performance she gave!"

In the final tableau of the play, with Tom departed, Amanda hovers protectively over a broken, deeply dispirited Laura, symbolizing what Tennessee Williams saw in his own mother: "Now that we cannot hear the mother's speech, her silliness is gone and she has dignity and tragic beauty."

At the end, the audience roared its approval. There were twenty-four curtain calls. As Laurette took her bows, tears streaked down her cheeks and she smiled somewhat tentatively while she held out the pleated frills of her worn blue party dress and curtsied. Her daughter said that she had the look of "a great ruin of a child gazing timorously upon a world she found to be infinitely pleasing."[42]

At length, there were shouts of "Author! Author!" Eddie Dowling came down to the edge of the stage and beckoned Tom to come forward and take his place with the company. The young man who rose from the fourth row, his hair in a crew cut, his suit button missing, looked more like a junior in college than an eminent playwright. Standing in the aisle, he turned toward the stage and made a deep bow to the actors, his posterior in full view of the audience.

From this moment on, there was no turning back for Tom Williams. His prayers and those of his mother had been answered. Now he could give Edwina financial independence and freedom from the bondage of her unhappy marriage. To his father's dismay, the little boy who could not put his blocks back in the box exactly as he had found them had become the artist who would rearrange them in a lasting architecture. And now there was no escape save into himself, and no place in the world he could go where he would not be known.

He had become Tennessee Williams.

30

"En Avant!"

"the long-delayed but always-expected something that we live for"

After Tennessee Williams left the theatre, he and Donald walked about the city for hours. Finally, it dawned on him that he was expected to appear at a party being held in Audrey's suite at the Royalton to honor her now-famous client. Windham said that, in contrast with the exuberant way he felt, Tennessee was quiet and reflective.

Years later, Tennessee recalled that, after the opening, "I don't remember feeling a great sense of triumph. In fact, I don't remember it very well at all. It should have been one of the happiest nights of my life. . . . I'd spent so much of my energy on the climb to success that when I'd made it and my play was the hottest ticket in town, I felt almost no satisfaction."[1]

Except for his "nemesis," as he referred to George Jean Nathan, the reviewers generally conveyed some of the excitement of opening night, when the elite had joined the gallery on their feet, "clapping, shouting, whistling, shrieking approval." Within a few days, there were lines of theatregoers standing outside the Playhouse, buying tickets for weeks in advance of a run that would last for 563 performances. After Laurette Taylor's final illness forced her to leave the company, and before her death in December 1946, two road companies were formed, and they toured throughout the United States; in 1948, a production premiered in London with Helen Hayes as Amanda. By then, *The Glass Menagerie* was on its own. But Tennessee Williams had still to prove that this was not a writer's single autobiographical success.

On the day after Easter Sunday, the critical reaction, like that in Chicago, was uniform praise for Laurette Taylor. Along with all the critics, *P.M.*'s Louis Kronenberger praised Laurette, giving the best description of her "great performance, which out of many small bits contrives a wonderful stage portrait. She nags, she coaxes, she pouts, she fails to understand, she understands all too well—all this revealed in vague little movements and half-mumbled words, small changes of pace, faint shifts of emphasis, little rushes of energy and masterfulness, little droopings of spirit."

Laurette had good reason to wallow in the honors and praise being heaped upon her. She wrote to her son, Dwight Taylor, saying, "People are turning up that I haven't seen in years and years—Hoytie Wiborg and all the bejewelled social set Hartley and I used to mix with." She said she didn't harbor any bitterness, since so many of her peers in the theatre and those in films she most admired were sending her congratulations and offers. David O. Selznick offered her a deal to do pictures when she was free of the play. There were other offers, such as those from Adolph Zukor of Paramount Pictures, Walter Wanger at Universal, and her old friend at MGM, George Cukor, who expressed the hope he might direct her in *Menagerie*. But to her son, she said, "What I hope for, Dwight, (and this is between us) is that [James] Cagney, who is bidding for it, gets the screen rights. He would be wonderful as the son, a part which Dowling plays inadequately." She added, "Of all the extravagant praise I got, there is one sentence that pleases me most, but annoys everyone else: 'The old glamour-puss is back on Broadway and the toast of the town.' "[2]

Reviews of the play were generally favorable, tempered by various reservations. As was expected, George Jean Nathan, while calling the event "far and away the theatre's loveliest evening," dismissed Williams's work as "a freakish experiment . . . deficient in any touches of humor," except for what Eddie Dowling contributed.[3] In the same vein, the Associated Press's Jack O'Brien thought that either William Saroyan or Maxwell Anderson should have authored it, and *P.M.*'s Kronenberger thought Chekhov could have done better than either of them.

He did, however, grudgingly commend the play: "There is enough that is human, touching, desolate and bitterly comic about this family picture to keep one steadily interested. Moreover, Mr. Williams has told much of his story in little scenes that can be far more effective than conventional big ones. 'The Glass Menagerie' is unhackneyed, unhokumed theater."[4] While writing for *P.M.*, Kronenberger was concurrently drama critic on *Time* magazine and thereafter would consistently disparage Williams's work, often attacking him personally. Finally, in 1962, Ted Kalem succeeded Kronenberger and, in a cover story, called Williams, with the exception of Sean O'Casey, the world's "greatest living playwright."

Otis L. Guernsey, Jr., of the *Herald Tribune* found "the Williams script so full of gentle hints at atmosphere and character that it cannot be fully described in any space shorter than the play itself. The framework defies the conventions of playwrighting; the author has simplified his drama to a searching, but almost always loving examination of four ordinary people in hard times, giving it body by packing it with both visual and spoken commentary on this complicated business of living. . . . 'The Glass Menagerie' is a newcomer to be hailed with joy and admiration from end to end of Broadway."[5] But Lewis Nichols of the *New York Times* found Laurette's performance "memorable [while] Mr. Williams' play is not all of the same caliber."[6]

Within two weeks of its opening, *The Glass Menagerie* was voted on the first ballot the year's best play by the New York Drama Critics Circle. Of the fourteen votes cast by local newspaper and magazine reviewers, *Menagerie* won nine, with Kronenberger abstaining. The citation read: "To Tennessee Williams for his play 'The Glass Menagerie' and its sensitive understanding of four troubled human beings." Soon thereafter, he won both the Donaldson

Award, given by *Billboard*, and the fifteen-hundred-dollar Sidney Howard Memorial Award, sponsored by the Playwrights Company, extolling him as having "the sense of poetry and of character of which great drama is made."

During the week that followed the opening, Tennessee found himself swamped with phone calls and invitations. Journalists from *Life* and *Time* magazines, along with those from a variety of city and out-of-town newspapers, crowded into what one reporter described as "a tiny, unpretentious room at the Hotel Shelton. . . . Two photographers were 'shooting' him from all angles, maneuvering him into the most artistic and studious poses. Dressed in a gray flannel suit with a missing coat button, a conservative pale tie on a water-green shirt, and with his hair cut short, Mr. Williams appeared more like a farm boy in his Sunday best than the author of a Broadway success."[7]

Although pleased with the critical response, Tennessee questioned in a *Time* interview whether "the critics will like my future plays as much as this one. In this play I said all the nice things I have to say about people. The future things will be harsher."[8] A year later, he would assert that *"The Glass Menagerie* has for me the peculiar importance of being the first play that I have managed to write without succumbing to the undeniable fascination of violence. It is my first quiet play, and perhaps my last."[9]

For the moment, though, his principal complaint concerned taxes, which he called unfair. He pointed out that his income wasn't all that much after deductions and after taking into consideration his mother's half interest. Suddenly, too, there was the increased cost of a lifestyle that accompanies success, including a new suit costing $125. Of course it was expected that he would pick up the tabs not only of his indigent friends but also of those new "friends" emerging from the woodwork. Nothing was as he had imagined it would be. "I lived on room service. But in this, too, there was disenchantment. Some time between the moment when I ordered dinner over the phone and when it was rolled into my living room like a corpse on a rubber-wheeled table, I lost all interest in it. Once I ordered a sirloin steak and a chocolate sundae, but everything was so cunningly disguised on the table that I mistook the chocolate sauce for gravy and poured it over the sirloin steak."[10]

Throughout the month of April, Tennessee, both fascinated and repelled by his sudden celebrity status, found himself in the midst of a constant barrage of phone calls, scheduled meetings, and requests for promotional interviews, demands that were screened as much as possible by Audrey Wood. Donald Windham, who pointed out that Tennessee saw as many of his old friends as he could, kept a record of their times together. On April 4, the *New York Herald-Tribune* ran an article headed *"Menagerie*'s Author Calls Taxes Unfair," and in the evening he went to the theatre with Donald, Margo Jones, and Joanna Albus to see Tallulah Bankhead in Philip Barry's *Foolish Notion*. On the eighth Donald noted that Tennessee was working on a new play about two sisters in the South. The next day he went with Tennessee and Mary

Hunter to the Village to see a play and later waited while Tennessee talked to Laurette about Nathan's review.

On the ninth, Donald's friend Sandy Campbell was in San Francisco touring in *Life With Father*. At Mrs. O'Neill's invitation, he met with Eugene O'Neill, who inquired about Tennessee Williams. Later in the month, Donald went with Tennessee to the Office of War Information for an interview by Eugene O'Neill, Jr.

On the twelfth, the entire nation went into mourning with the news that Franklin Delano Roosevelt had died. Donald and Tennessee spent the evening together, walking until nearly midnight.

On the twentieth, Tennessee and Windham had dinner with Williams's mother and grandfather at Mary Hunter's. Two days later, Edwina dispatched an enthusiastic letter to Cornelius, telling him how Tom had met them at the station and how they had gone to see Katharine Cornell in *The Barretts of Wimpole Street*. She mentioned having had lunch with Audrey Wood: "I like her very much and she seems to have Tom's best interests at heart and is anxious for him to save his money. They are turning over one-half of 'Glass Menagerie' to me, and contract made. . . . Tom is giving a 'Tea & Cocktail' Party at Sherrys in honor of me and Laurette." She ended her letter with the hope that he was keeping well and signed it "Affectionately, Edwina."[11]

On April 22, Donald went with Tennessee to Guthrie McClintic's office to discuss the September opening of *You Touched Me!* On the twenty-fourth Donald took manuscripts of *The Glass Menagerie* given him by Tennessee to put in a safety-deposit box, and Tennessee signed an affidavit giving Audrey and Liebling power of attorney. The following week Donald accompanied Tennessee to the hospital for his eye operation, waiting until he was out of the operating room and conscious.

Both his eyes were kept bandaged during the next four days, and Donald stayed on hand to read to him. In this time, Tennessee was able to reflect upon his sudden success. He felt "a well of cynicism" rising in him: "Sincerity and kindliness seemed to have gone out of my friends' voices."[12] He had shocked and dismayed many of them by a remark given to the *New York Times:* "There is a kind of problem in personal integrity. The real fact is that no one means a great deal to me, anyway. I'm gregarious and like to be around people, but almost anybody will do. I'm rather selfish in picking my friends, anyway; that is, I prefer people who can help me in some way or another, and most of my friendships are accidental."[13]

On May 19, Donald and Tennessee had supper with Katharine Cornell at her and McClintic's home. The next day Tennessee and Margo left for Texas. Margo was undecided which play she would choose as the inaugural production for her Dallas repertory theatre. At first, she thought it would be *Battle of Angels*. Later in October, George Freedley, curator for the New York Public

Library's theatre collection (now housed at Lincoln Center), interviewed Tennessee on radio station WNYC. He referred to Williams as a member of Margo's board of directors and inquired what selection was being considered. Tennessee replied, "I read one particularly fine [play] that was written by the drama editor for the *St. Louis Star-Times*, William Inge, and we've taken an option on that already." The play Inge entrusted to Williams was clearly inspired by his seeing *Menagerie* and would be his most autobiographical; entitled *Farther Off from Heaven* and produced by Margo's Theatre 47 as her first offering, it reemerged in 1957 as Inge's last Broadway success, *The Dark at the Top of the Stairs*.

On his arrival in Dallas, Tennessee was caught up in Texas society, which proved as exhausting as New York's, and he quickly flew off to Mexico City. Checking into the Hotel Geneve, he started sending letters to Guthrie McClintic and Katharine Cornell that had more an antic tone than that of an important new playwright and that must have amused, if not puzzled, them. He told them he hadn't counted on the vitality of Dallas females, their poor husbands looking as though "they had donated too much blood and to the wrong cause [while] the women rock and roar in one continual effusion. . . . When they get a few drinks under their girdles, their talk becomes downright lascivious."[14]

Trying to decide whom to cast as Hadrian in *You Touched Me!*—Montgomery Clift or Phil Brown—McClintic put the question to Tennessee. In a wire, he replied, PRACTICALLY A TOSS UP. CLIFT HAS MORE EXPERIENCE AND CHARM. BROWN HAS MORE FOXY UPSTART QUALITY. I HAVE DYSENTERY. YOU DECIDE.[15] Shortly after, he wrote McClintic a letter describing his bout with "dysenteric colitis" and the treatment administered by a little Mexican doctor, who gave him shots "strong enough to kill a horse."

His main preoccupation, though, was with Mexico City's social life; he met there, among others, Leonard Bernstein, George Balanchine, and actress Dolores Del Rio, who entranced him with her beauty. Tennessee told McClintic he had seen his first Wagner opera, *Tristan and Isolde* with Helen Traubel:

> Some of the duets were magnifico but . . . the singers are so enormously fat. In the last act when the dying Tristan is lying under a tree, having delirious visions, it was uncontrollably funny. He was so fat and he kept billowing up and roaring "Das Schiff! Das Schiff!" and every time he did so a skinny little monkey of a Mexican singer would pat him sweetly on the stomach and tuck him in again, with despairing but tender glances at the audience. And in the Mexican Operas as well as the theatre it is not considered important to learn a part, as they have a prompter's box in the middle of the stage and lines are fed to them so continually you can hear them in the back rows.[16]

He informed Donald that he had attended the bullfights, which sickened him, and had heard Shostakovich's Fifth Symphony conducted by Carlos Chávez, which thrilled him. He told Audrey that among the letters he had received was one from "Lawrence Stanislavsky Langner, the one who operates that famous Art Theatre on E. 56th Street—saying that he still has the scenery for 'Battle' stored at Westport and has a new director in mind for it!" He added, "One cannot help loving people who make you laugh! This last communication has completed the cycle, often observed in life, from deepest tragedy to lightest farce!"[17] At the same time, a circumspect Tennessee Williams replied to Lawrence Langner tactfully, careful to keep the door to the Theatre Guild open, or at least slightly ajar. The Mexican sojourn over, he reluctantly returned to Broadway, to what O'Neill called "the most tawdry street in the world," the magnet to which Tennessee was irresistibly drawn for the rest of his life.

More than success in the theatre, though, more than a lover by his side, more than friends, what mattered most in life to the private person known as Tom Williams was his love for his sister, Rose, and what he had earned: the true artist's freedom to live excessively and write exclusively what he wanted, when he wanted, where he wanted. That the commercial theatre would exact an exorbitant price, however, was reflected in Williams's many public images, a deliberate artifice like the magician's sleight of hand. Not only did he appropriate the makeup of his characters from living models, but he also assumed many of these traits in composing his own chameleon personalities. And at the epicenter of these transformations, there were always his blue devils and their threat of madness.

On V-J day, August 14, the war ended, and the world shot forward into a new, atomic epoch. *You Touched Me!* was scheduled to open on September 26, and already there were critics who had come to believe that Tennessee Williams was in the vanguard with a new and exciting form of theatre. Instead, what they saw was a conventional three-act romantic comedy that bore only a slight resemblance to the D. H. Lawrence short story. What Donald Windham had first set out to do—to make a serious adaptation of the original—in the end was not only defeated by its transformation into a seriocomedy but was also suffocated by the production's lack of the very expressionistic virtues that characterized *The Glass Menagerie*, locked as it was into a box set and other such familiar trappings.

One has merely to assess the surprised reaction to *Menagerie* to see how rigid the critical precepts were at that time regarding what constituted the well-made play. Viewed as a romantic comedy, *You Touched Me!* was far superior to much that was as a rule popular with audiences. But it was a victim of bad timing, suffering an invidious comparison, and it closed after one hundred performances, prompting one critic to call it Tennessee Williams's "fall from grace." Placed in proper perspective, though, *You Touched Me!* was a major link in the evolution of *The Glass Menagerie*, and had it received a Broadway staging more imaginative than McClintic's and better timed, there is every chance that it would have been well received. The ultimate irony was that *You Touched Me!* was a box-office failure, and the play least likely to make it, *The Glass Menagerie*, was a huge commercial success.

"All poets look for God, all good poets do . . ."

While Tennessee was immersed in a play tentatively titled *The Poker Game*, *The Glass Menagerie* was establishing his, and separately its own, ongoing reputation. Curiously, Williams seemed never to have understood the inner strength of *Menagerie*. Like the play's critics, he was inclined to ascribe the power of the play to the voltage achieved by Laurette Taylor. As the *New York Times*'s drama columnist Benedict Nightingale pointed out in 1983, "Williams the man once scrawled 'a rather dull little play' on the typescript of 'The Glass Menagerie,' and from the first regarded it as too soft, too 'nice,' to be characteristic of the drama he felt he could and should write. He could not have been unequivocally delighted when Brooks Atkinson went so far as to proclaim it his most perceptive creation."[18] Tennessee's own ambivalence toward it was perhaps revealed when late in his life he said, "It is the saddest play I have ever written. It is full of pain. It's painful for me to see it."[19]

In his autobiography, Arthur Miller wrote, "The revolutionary newness of *The Glass Menagerie* . . . was in its poetic lift, but an underlying hard dramatic structure was what earned the play its right to sing poetically. Poetry in the theatre is not, or at least ought not to be, a cause but a consequence, and that structure of storytelling and character made this very private play available to anyone capable of feeling at all."[20]

From its inception, *The Glass Menagerie* has been the subject of countless examinations and interpretations, and many of the original criticisms have since been cited as attributes.[21] The use of symbols, which are embedded in almost all of Williams's plays, has been repeatedly called out as intrusive, if not excessive. *The Glass Menagerie* is notable for many, from the very title of the play, with its use of the mythical symbolism of the unicorn, to the father's picture on the wall (usually an enlarged, exact image of the son), meant to be an *ideal* representation of the telephone man who had the courage to escape the snare of the family.

A religious undercurrent, a struggle for faith, can be found throughout Tennessee Williams's major works. His self-proclaimed role as that of a rebellious puritan grew out of a little boy's search for God by "diggin' to de debbil" and the grown man's fervid prayers to an indifferent deity. The result was an alternation between puritan scruples and an attraction toward violence and a desire to shock. Withal, he remained to the last "de preachuh's boy."

As for literary progenitors, D. H. Lawrence professed one of Williams's basic tenets, that the sensual and the spiritual are inextricably intertwined, which in turn provided Williams with the rationale for his own homosexual freedom. Chekhov's writing was a *beau idéal*, reflected more in *The Glass Menagerie* than in any of Williams's other plays. One can find the trace elements of a number of writers, including Strindberg, Lorca, O'Neill, Ibsen, Melville, Pirandello, and even the more modern Harold Pinter, whom Williams both admired and envied. But in the end, however, the most pervasive influence in his life and career was that of the poet Hart Crane, to the same degree that Shelley influenced Crane. Crane was the true touchstone, Tennessee carrying the poet's book of poems with him everywhere, in the way his grandfather carried the Book of Common Prayer.

With the advent of *The Glass Menagerie*, and through the fusion of the opposite sides of his artistic nature, Tennessee Williams emerged as a poet-playwright and a unique new force in theatre throughout the world. By the end of 1945, he was absorbed in writing a play he would title *A Streetcar Named Desire*. Awaiting him was what he called "the catastrophe of success."

"En Avant!"

Tennessee Williams
Selected Writings

———

Plays

Candles to the Sun
Fugitive Kind
Battle of Angels
Stairs to the Roof
The Glass Menagerie
You Touched Me! (with Donald
    Windham)
A Streetcar Named Desire
Summer and Smoke
The Eccentricities of a Nightingale
The Rose Tattoo
Camino Real
Cat on a Hot Tin Roof
Orpheus Descending
Garden District: Something Unspoken
    and Suddenly Last Summer
Sweet Bird of Youth
Period of Adjustment
The Night of the Iguana

The Milk Train Doesn't Stop Here
    Anymore
Slapstick Tragedy: The Mutilated and
    The Gnädiges Fräulein
Kingdom of Earth (The Seven Descents
    of Myrtle)
The Two-Character Play
In the Bar of a Tokyo Hotel
Small Craft Warnings
Out Cry
The Red Devil Battery Sign
THIS IS (An Entertainment)
Vieux Carré
Tiger Tail
A Lovely Sunday for Creve Coeur
Will Mr. Merriwether Return from
    Memphis?
Clothes for a Summer Hotel
Something Cloudy, Something Clear
A House Not Meant to Stand

Short Plays

Moony's Kid Don't Cry
At Liberty
The Long Goodbye
The Purification
The Dark Room
The Case of the Crushed Petunias
The Long Stay Cut Short,
   or The Unsatisfactory Supper
Ten Blocks on the Camino Real
27 Wagons Full of Cotton
The Strangest Kind of Romance
Auto-Da-Fé
Portrait of a Madonna
I Rise in Flame, Cried the Phoenix
Hello from Bertha
The Lady of Larkspur Lotion
This Property Is Condemned

The Frosted Glass Coffin
The Last of My Solid Gold Watches
Lord Byron's Love Letter
A Perfect Analysis Given by a Parrot
Talk to Me Like the Rain and Let Me
   Listen
Three Players of a Summer Game
I Can't Imagine Tomorrow
Confessional
Demolition Downtown
Kirche, Kutchen und Kinder
Some Problems for the Moose Lodge
Steps Must Be Gentle
Lifeboat Drill
Now the Cat with Jewelled Claws
This is the Peaceable Kingdom,
   or Good Luck God

Short Story Collections

27 Wagons Full of Cotton
One Arm and Other Stories
Hard Candy and Other Stories

The Knightly Quest and Other Stories
Eight Mortal Ladies Possessed
Collected Stories

Original Screenplays

Baby Doll
Boom!
All Gaul Is Divided

Stopped Rocking
One Arm
The Loss of a Teardrop Diamond

Poetry

In the Winter of Cities

Androgyne, Mon Amour

Novels

The Roman Spring of Mrs. Stone

Moise and the World of Reason

Essays

Where I Live

Autobiography

Tennessee Williams: Memoirs

Letters

Tennessee Williams' Letters to Donald Windham 1940–1965

Five O'Clock Angel: Letters of Tennessee Williams to Maria St. Just

Music

"Blue Mountain Ballads." Lyrics by Tennessee Williams, music by Paul Bowles.

Lord Byron's Love Letter. Opera in One Act by Raffaello de Banfield, libretto by Tennessee Williams.

"Not a Soul; Blanket Roll Blues." From the film *The Fugitive Kind.* Lyrics by Tennessee Williams, music by Kenyon Hopkins.

"Shadow Wood, Five Poems of Tennessee Williams for Soprano and Large Wind Ensemble." Music by Warren Benson.

"Selected Songs." Lyrics by Tennessee Williams, music by Jeffrey Miller.

Notes and Sources

In quoting from correspondence and journals, I have made little attempt at corrections, except those of fact. It is hoped that the reader will realize that misspellings, mistakes of grammar, and other such idiosyncrasies are the province of the originators and not mine to alter, although obvious errors have been corrected. I have used the designation [*sic*] when it seemed propitious to signal the reader's attention to misspellings. Quotation marks indicate *actual* and never fictitious quotations. Williams's journal entries when dated are transcribed as such or they are placed in as close proximity as possible to the time and the events they describe, and for that reason they are not referred to individually in these notes. Another reason is that he kept concurrent spiral notebooks—now in university and private hands—often making similar entries when he misplaced his notebooks. Dates and page numbers of newspaper articles have been provided wherever possible. In the case of older, defunct publications that have been placed in vertical files or clipped, dates and page numbers could not always be ascertained.

Tennessee Williams was in the habit of omitting the date and origin of his letters and very often failed to mail them. I have tried to the best of my ability to identify his and other correspondence in these notes and sources. Since the endnotes are as fully annotated as possible, I have found it unnecessary to compile a more formal bibliography in this first volume. Because Williams wrote and rewrote, particularly his plays, there exist not just in his archives but in various publications markedly different versions. For this reason, I have not always cited a so-called standard edition but rather whichever version seemed appropriate within the context of what I was writing.

Abbreviations Used in the Endnotes

TW: Tennessee (Tom) Williams
RIW: Rose Isabel Williams
WDW: (Walter) Dakin Williams
EDW: Edwina Dakin Williams
CCW: Cornelius Coffin Williams
WED: Walter Edwin Dakin
ROD: Rose Otte Dakin

EW: Ella Williams
IWB: Isabel Williams Brownlow
AW: Audrey Wood
PB: Paul Bigelow
DW: Donald Windham
CMMc: Clark Mills McBurney
LL: Lyle Leverich

The Man and the Artist versus His Image

1. Subsequently, there were conflicting and unresolved opinions concerning the cause of death. Michael M. Baden, M.D., former chief medical examiner, city of New York, maintained in *Unnatural Death* (New York: Random House, 1989, pp. 69, 70) that the autopsy was inconclusive and wrote that the then chief ME, Dr. Elliot M. Gross, "found a long, thin rubber medicine bottle stopper" in Williams's mouth and had attributed his death to it. Dr. Baden was not present

at the autopsy but did attend a press conference where Dr. Gross exhibited a medicinal bottle cap similar to the one that he said he had found "displacing the epiglottis anteriorly." However, in his opinion, Dr. Baden felt that it was not wide enough to block Williams's air passage. In an interview (Baden to LL, 6-3-94, NY), he concluded that Williams had been drinking and had overdosed on barbiturates; he pointed to the fact that not only were there high levels of secobarbital found in his blood but that Williams had an enlarged heart. Also, there was pronounced anterior lividity and Tardieu-like hemorrhaging, his body having been found an estimated twelve hours after his death; he was crouched on his knees and had slumped forward between his bed and a bedside table. As a matter of conjecture, it is possible that Williams, in choking on the battle cap, may at the same time have experienced heart failure.·

The press kept calling Dr. Gross for the toxicology report, and he kept saying the work was incomplete. Actually, distrustful of his own toxicology laboratory, he ordered the samples of a twenty-seven-year-old man, Piero Malandrino, who reputedly had fallen or jumped off a roof, sent to the New York lab and those of Williams to the toxicologist in Nassau County. He later explained that because of Williams's celebrity he wanted to be sure that his lab did not leak anything to the press. As a result of the confusion between the two toxicology reports, identified by different case numbers, the New York report was attributed to Williams; it claimed that there were traces of cocaine in his nostrils and, preposterously enough, that he had the liver of a young man. Six months later, however, after the press had lost interest, Dr. Gross quietly issued another report saying that Williams had swallowed enough barbiturates to cause his death.

2. Peter Hoffman, "The Last Days of Tennessee Williams," *New York*, 25 July 1983, p. 48. This is a largely accurate account of events during the years 1982 and 1983.

3. Edwin McDowell, "About Books and Authors," *New York Times Book Review*, 13 March 1983.

4. John Uecker to LL and Granger Carr, interview, 8 March 1983, New Orleans.

5. Jane Lawrence Smith to LL, interview, 16 November 1983, New York.

6. *New York Times*, 26 February 1983, p. 10.

7. John Uecker to LL, interview, 7 April 1995, New York.

8. Linda Winer, "On Stage," *USA Today*, 28 February 1983, p. 5D.

9. Mel Gussow, *New York Times*, 26 February 1983.

10. T. E. Kalem, "The Laureate of the Outcast," *Time*, 7 March 1983, p. 88.

11. Gene Ruffins, Larry Nathanson, and Doug Frienden, "Torment of Tennessee Williams," *New York Post*, 26 February 1983, p. 5.

12. Ibid.

13. Ibid.

14. Hume Cronyn reading a message from Elia Kazan at a tribute held in New York at the Shubert Theatre on 25 March 1983.

15. Herbert Mitgang, "Eloquence at Williams Memorial Is His Own," *New York Times*, 26 March 1983, p. 28.

16. Rex Reed, "Tennessee Williams Turns Sixty," *Esquire*, September 1971, p. 220.

17. Anonymous letter, *New York*, 15 August 1983, p. 7.

18. David Richards, "Tennessee's Shallows," *Washington Post*, 5 June 1987, p. B6.

19. Jere Real, "Down in Virginia on a Visit," *The Advocate*, 15 September 1983, pp. 42–44.

20. Don Lee Keith, "Phoenix Rising from a Stoned Age?" *After Dark*, August 1971, p. 32.

21. Stanley Kunitz, "The Poet's Quest for the Father," *New York Times Book Review*, 22 February 1987, p. 37.

22. Bernard Winer, "A Good Year for Fascinating, Maddening Tennessee Williams," *San Francisco Chronicle Datebook*, 18 January 1976, p. 13.

23. Robert Berkvist, "Broadway Discovers Tennessee Williams," *New York Times*, 21 December 1975, p. 5.

24. Richard Freeman Leavitt, "Ave Atque Vale!" (private publication), August 1983, p. 11.

25. Rob Rains, *Miami Herald*, 6 March 1983.

26. Glenna Syse, *Chicago Sun-Times* (reprinted in *San Francisco Examiner*, 6 March 1983).

27. Dan Sullivan, *Los Angeles Times* (reprinted in *San Francisco Chronicle Datebook*, c. 6 March 1983.

28. Christopher Flanders, the Christ figure, to the dying Flora Goforth in *The Milk Train Doesn't Stop Here Anymore.*

1. The Family

1. Edwina Dakin Williams's memorabilia, as well as her voluminous correspondence, are housed in the Harry Ransom Humanities Research Center at the University of Texas in Austin (hereinafter: HRC), and are a part of the Tennessee Williams archives.
2. Dennis Brown, "Miss Edwina Under Glass," *St. Louisan*, March 1977, pp. 59–63.
3. The spelling Daykin was a further adaptation of the Norman-English Dakyn as it appears on the family coat of arms. As far as the genealogy has been traced, the first American Dakin lived in Concord, Massachusetts, before 1650, after which members of the family moved to New York State. During the American Revolution, a branch of the family emigrated to Canada as Tories, or King's Loyalists, and settled in Digby, Nova Scotia.
4. Edwina Dakin Williams, with Lucy Freeman, *Remember Me to Tom* (New York: Putnam, 1963), pp. 182–183 (hereinafter: EDW, *Tom*).
5. William Otte was also born in Hanover, Germany, and sailed to the United States in 1857. He first lived in Cincinnati and after that in Richmond, Indiana, finally settling in Marysville, where in 1871 he and his brother joined in a family business that continued until 1976. *Marysville Journal-Tribune*, 2 July 1976, p. 1.
6. Rose, the flower, and Stella, the star, were to become favorite images of Tennessee Williams.
7. In a letter to LL, 1 July 1987, and in a subsequent conversation, Dakin Williams said that his grandmother, given her sturdy, determined nature, could have made the decision not to have any more children. She was always the stronger, exhibiting a German stoicism in all things. He also felt that they may not have been able to have more children. "Grand and Grandfather always slept in the same bed (not twin beds!). And I would infer from that they did have sex together but considered it a very private matter between themselves."
8. EDW, *Tom*, p. 164.
9. Ibid., p. 167. Mrs. Williams described the institute as having "a high-sounding name for a boarding school for a few little girls from Mississippi" and Shelbyville as a lovely town "located not far from Nashville . . . with wide streets, on both sides of which spacious residences were set back in the midst of lawns filled with old forest trees" (p. 161).
10. The Williams family library, Washington University, St. Louis, Missouri. No. 111, McNamara, Mrs. Miles McNamara: *Prince Coastwind's Victory, or The Fairy Bride of Croton Lake.*
11. EDW, *Tom*, p. 170.
12. Ibid., p. 169.
13. Ibid., p. 173.
14. WED, *Miami Gazette* (Waynesville, Ohio), December 1905.
15. Melissa S. Whyte to TW, 1948. Another neighbor, Katherine Searcy, was quoted by Mrs. Douglas Bateman, director, Lowndes County Library System, Columbus Public Library, in a letter to LL, 26 February 1986: "I recall Miss Edwina singing in our church choir every Sunday. She was a pretty person, quite a lady. Her mother played the organ. The Dakin family was very charming and good looking. I shall never forget that Father Dakin literally prayed me back to life at my bedside when I was nine years old. I became gravely ill, and I remember his kind face and gentle manner and how he held my hand and prayed."
16. EDW maintained that a relative, Elijah Sabin, was disqualified as acceptable lineage because he was a Quaker and would not have fought in the Revolution. While it is true that Quakers did not take up arms, the DAR ruled that if they had furnished food and other comfort to the Colonial army, they qualified as proper references. Sabin is, in fact, in the DAR lineage books.
17. Dr. William J. MacArthur, Jr., "Knoxville: Crossroads of the New South (1890–1918)," McClung Historical Collection, Knox County Library System, Knoxville, Tennessee.
18. WDW to LL, interview, 13 April 1985, Collinsville, Illinois.
19. Ibid.

20. EDW, *Tom*, p. 185.
21. Ibid., p. 186.

2. A Mother Is Born

1. Edwina Dakin Williams, with Lucy Freeman, *Remember Me to Tom* (New York: Putnam, 1963), p. 186 (hereinafter: EDW, *Tom*).
2. EDW to WDW, letter, 1 June 1973, Dakin Williams collection.
3. EDW, *Tom*, p. 186.
4. T. E. Kalem, *Time*, 9 March 1962, p. 56.
5. One hundred and eighty-six of these books were housed in the Special Collections Library of Washington University, St. Louis, c. 1986. In a note to LL, Allean Hale contends, "To judge from the books in his library, the Reverend Dakin was more metaphysical and largely interested in theological questions like 'transfiguration.' In 1933 he sent Tom a book called *The Ascent of the Soul* with the inscription 'May he read, mark, learn and inwardly digest the thoughts of this book,' such thoughts as, 'Evil works misery and virtue leads to happiness beyond the grave as well as here. Seed sown on the earth may grow to its harvest in the ages that lie beyond.' "

Hale points out, "Tennessee Williams continually used Christian symbols in his writings and almost always punished his 'wrongdoers'—in many of his plays with crucifixion. Like many other Romantic writers, he was always 'hounded by Heaven' and in his search for God. This was particularly exemplified in *The Night of the Iguana*, which prompted some critics to label him a religious writer."

In the spring of 1989, Theodore Mann, the director of New York's Circle in the Square, was rehearsing *Iguana* in Moscow "when he realized that God and religion were going to play a major role in the Soviet production. . . . Mr. Mann realized that Williams's strong religious undertow was sweeping the members of the cast away, moving them even to the point of tears" (Celestine Bohlen, " 'Night of the Iguana' Treks to Moscow," *New York Times*, 6 August 1989).
6. EDW, *Tom*, p. 25.
7. See the "God and Mama" speech Shannon makes in the hammock in *The Night of the Iguana*.
8. EDW, *Tom*, p. 26.
9. EDW scrapbook, unidentified news article, HRC.
10. Louise Davis, *Nashville Tennessean Magazine*, March 3, 10, 1957.
11. Claiborne, Tate & Cowan, Knoxville, letter, 6 November 1913, Dakin Williams collection: "Mr. C.C. Williams was connected with us in the capacity of traveling salesman for about five years in the Mississippi and Alabama territory, having resigned his position with us. We take pleasure in recommending him to any one desiring a number one good salesman. He is a hard worker, thoroughly reliable and has splendid ability as a salesman. We feel we cannot recommend him too highly as he gave us entire satisfaction."
12. EDW, *Tom*, p. 14.
13. Ibid., p. 20.
14. Ibid., p. 19.
15. Louise Davis, "That Baby Doll Man," *The Nashville Tennessean*, 10 March 1957, p. 14.
16. Robert Rice, *New York Post Daily Magazine*, section II; article 4, 24 April 1958, p. M2; included in a series of eleven articles, 21 April through 2 May 1958, entitled "A Man Named Tennessee."
17. Ibid. This was a scene that Williams used forty years later in *Cat on a Hot Tin Roof.*
18. Ibid.
19. Louise Davis, "Nashville Was a 'Streetcar Named Happiness,' " *The Nashville Tennessean*, p. 13.
20. Alida Clark Heidelberg to LL, telephone interview, 29 August 1986.
21. EDW, *Tom*, p. 23.
22. Ibid., p. 25.
23. Ibid., p. 23.
24. Tennessee Williams, *Memoirs* (Garden City, N.Y.: Doubleday, 1975), pp. 11–12 (hereinafter: TW, *Memoirs*).

25. EDW, *Tom*, p. 19.

26. Ibid., p. 25.

27. Senator John S. Williams to EW, letter, 13 March 1918, McClung Historical Collection, Knoxville, Tennessee.

28. EW to RIW and TW, letter, n.d., c. spring 1918, McClung Collection.

29. TW to LL, interview, 22 February 1977, San Francisco.

3. Saint Louis

1. Tennessee Williams, *Memoirs* (Garden City, N.Y.: Doubleday, 1975), p. 13 (hereinafter: TW, *Memoirs*).

2. EDW as told to WDW, reported by WDW in a letter to LL, 1 June 1973.

3. Edwina Dakin Williams, with Lucy Freeman, *Remember Me to Tom* (New York: Putnam, 1963), p. 34 (hereinafter: EDW, *Tom*.)

4. Tennessee Williams, *The Glass Menagerie*, act II, sc. 7, Dramatists Play Service acting edition, p. 50.

5. TW, *Memoirs*, p. 13.

6. EDW, *Tom*, p. 35.

7. Ibid., p. 28. Both Williams and his mother asserted that the Westminster Place apartment was the setting for *The Glass Menagerie*, and while there were fragmentary impressions stored in seven-year-old Tom's memory, an apartment on Enright Avenue in University City occupied by the Williams family for nearly ten years during the Depression was the more likely setting. Myths persist, however, and the Westminster building was eventually renamed the Glass Menagerie Apartments.

8. Ibid., p. 30.

9. Lincoln Barnett, "Tennessee Williams," *Life*, 16 February 1948.

10. TW, *Memoirs*, p. 13.

11. Virginia Irwin, interview with TW, *St. Louis Post-Dispatch*, 22 December 1947.

12. Louise Davis, "Tennessee Was Music to Williams' Ears," *The Nashville Tennessean*, 27 March 1983, p. 1F.

13. Linton Weeks, *Clarksdale & Coahoma County: A History* (Clarksdale, Miss.: Carnegie Public Library, 1982), p. 112.

14. Blanche Cutrer's grandson, the Reverend John Cutrer Smith, described her as having "violet blue eyes, very fair skin and chestnut hair. She had a violent temper and, having been raised on a plantation, would chide her Negro servants in a way that ordinarily they would just quit anyone else's service. But she believed in live-and-let-live and never interfered with their privacy, while at the same time she was close to them personally and protective" (letter to LL, 4 December 1986).

15. Pauline Alston Clark to LL, letter, 15 December 1986: "In those days we did not have any apartments here, and those without homes rented rooms and ate in boardinghouses. This applied especially to young men who came to Clarksdale to buy cotton. A boardinghouse run by Mrs. Wingfield was really an attractive place with excellent food, good silver, linen and china."

16. Alida Clark Heidelberg to LL, telephone interview, 29 August 1986.

17. Pauline Alston Clark to LL, letter, 15 December 1986.

18. TW, "de preachuh's Boy," HRC.

19. WED to RIW, undated postcard, HRC.

20. EW to TW, letter, n.d., HRC.

21. RIW to EDW, letter, 24 February 1922, HRC. There was evidence that Tom did use the books Grand bought, for his name is written on the flyleaves, and the bindings are soiled and worn. It can be conjectured that Tom discovered in this encyclopedia some of the themes that were to be found in his writings.

22. TW, *Memoirs*, p. 13.

23. Ibid., p. 15.

24. EDW to TW, postcard, 11 July 1922, Dakin Williams collection.

25. Jane Bruce to LL, interview, 2 May 1985, New York.

26. WDW to LL, letter, 1 July 1987.

27. Jane Bruce to LL, interview, 2 May 1985.

28. TW, "Rainbows Comic Paper," n.d., c. 1920–1921, Dakin Williams collection.

29. "The Resemblance Between a Violin Case and a Coffin," in Tennessee Williams, *Collected Stories* (New York: New Directions, 1985), pp. 270–282.

30. "Recuerdo," in Tennessee Williams, *In the Winter of Cities* (New York: New Directions, 1952), p. 76.

4. The Writin' Son

1. Walter Dakin Williams and Shepherd Mead, *Tennessee Williams, An Intimate Biography* (New York: Arbor House, 1983), p. 23.

2. TW, "Isolated," file of *The Junior Life*, Ben Blewett Junior High School, vol. 1, H-30, November 1924, State Historical Society Library of Missouri, Columbia. Another of his earliest publications, to date untraced, was allegedly "A Ghost [or Great] Tale Told at Katrina's Party."

3. Benjamin Nelson, *Tennessee Williams, The Man and His Work* (New York: Ivan Obolensky, Inc., 1961), p. 15.

4. Edwina Dakin Williams, with Lucy Freeman, *Remember Me to Tom* (New York: Putnam, 1963), p. 39 (hereinafter: EDW, *Tom*).

5. Allean Hale, "Every Good Boy Does Fine" (a story describing St. Louis in the late 1920s, M.A. thesis, Writers Workshop, University of Iowa, 1962).

6. "The Resemblance Between a Violin Case and a Coffin," in Tennessee Williams, *Collected Stories* (New York: New Directions, 1985), p. 273.

7. Margaret Brownlow to LL, interview, 21 April 1985, Knoxville, Tennessee.

8. Tennessee Williams, *Memoirs* (Garden City, N.Y.: Doubleday, 1975), p. 117 (hereinafter: TW, *Memoirs*).

9. Ibid.

10. Ibid., p. 118.

11. Unknown correspondent to Margaret Tappan Thomas, letter, 1 October 1925, HRC.

12. TW, *Memoirs*, p. 15.

13. Esmeralda Mayes Treen to Allean Hale, interview, 2 June 1985, Brookfield, Wisconsin.

14. Esmeralda Mayes Treen to LL, letter, 9 September 1985.

15. TW, *Memoirs*, p. 29.

16. Ibid., p. 15.

17. Ibid., p. 18.

18. EDW, *Tom*, p. 44.

19. TW, *Memoirs*, p. 18.

20. EDW, *Tom*, p. 45.

21. RIW to Williams family, letter, 4 January 1926, HRC.

22. TW to WED, letter, n.d., HRC.

23. RIW to Williams family, letter, 10 January 1926, HRC.

24. Dan H. Buie to RIW, letter, 7 January 1926, HRC, enclosed in letter to "Mother & Dad," January 18, 1926.

25. RIW to EDW, letter, 28 February 1926, HRC.

26. RIW to ROD, letter, March 1926, HRC.

27. RIW to WED, letter, 5 April 1926, HRC.

28. RIW to CCW, letter, 18 March 1926, HRC.

29. Walter Dakin Williams, *The Bar Bizarre* (St. Louis: Sunrise Publishing Co., 1980), pp. 90–91.

30. RIW to TW, letter, n.d., 1926, HRC.

31. Allean Hale, *Petticoat Pioneer* (St. Paul: North Central, 1968), pp. 156–157.

5. University City

1. Mary Leslie Newton to RIW, letter, 16 July 1926, HRC.
2. Tennessee Williams, *Memoirs* (Garden City, N.Y.: Doubleday, 1975), p. 17 (hereinafter: TW, *Memoirs*).
3. Robert Rice, "A Man Named Tennessee," *New York Post*, 27 April 1958, p. 12.
4. TW, *Memoirs*, pp. 17–18.
5. RIW to TW, letter, 25 May 1927, HRC.
6. WED to TW, letter, 12 April 1927, Dakin Williams collection.
7. Edwina Dakin Williams, with Lucy Freeman, *Remember Me to Tom* (New York: Putnam, 1963), pp. 48–49 (hereinafter: EDW, *Tom*).
8. "The Vengeance of Nitocris," in Tennessee Williams, *Collected Stories* (New York: New Directions, 1985), pp. 1–12.
9. Esmeralda Mayes Treen to Allean Hale, interview, 2 June 1985, Brookfield, Wisconsin.
10. TW, *Memoirs*, p. 18. Williams would use this episode again in a play, *A Lovely Sunday for Creve Coeur* (New York: New Directions, 1980), pp. 51–52, in which an offstage character named Hathaway James suffered a problem of premature ejaculation, which ruined his romantic relationship with the play's central character, Dorothea; possibly Williams's rationalization for his failed affair with Hazel Kramer.
11. TW, "His Father's House," HRC.
12. RIW to EDW, letter, 18 April 1927, HRC.
13. RIW to EDW, letter, 13 May 1927, HRC.
14. EDW, *Tom*, p. 54.
15. Ibid., p. 55.
16. IWB to RIW, letter, 14 November 1927, HRC.
17. RIW, Knoxville trip diary, 14 November through 20 December 1927, HRC. All subsequent diary entries pertaining to this trip are from this source.
18. EDW, *Tom*, p. 55.
19. Esmeralda Mayes Treen to Allean Hale, interview, 2 June 1985.
20. TW, *Memoirs*, pp. 118–119.
21. Ibid.
22. EDW, *Tom*, p. 56.
23. Pauline Alston Clark to LL, letter, 15 December 1986.
24. TW to EDW, letter, n.d., c. 2 July 1928, HRC.
25. WED to ROD, letter, 3 July 1928, HRC.
26. TW to WED, letter, postmarked 31 January 1929, Dakin Williams collection.
27. TW to EDW, letter, n.d., c. 8 July 1928, HRC.
28. TW to "Dear Family," letter, n.d., HRC.
29. TW, *Memoirs*, p. 20.
30. TW to "Dear Family," letter, n.d., c. 13 July 1928, HRC.
31. WED to ROD, letter, postmarked 13 July 1928, HRC.
32. TW to Hazel Kramer, letter, n.d., Dakin Williams collection.
33. TW to EDW, letter, 19 July 1928, HRC.
34. TW, *Memoirs*, p. 20.
35. TW to CCW, postcard, postmarked 4 August 1928, HRC.
36. TW to EDW, letter, 5 August 1928, HRC.
37. TW to Williams family, letter, n.d., c. 10 August 1928, HRC.
38. TW, *Memoirs*, p. 21.
39. TW, written with poem "Cacti" (1939, Taos), "The strangers pass me in the night . . ." (1928, Amsterdam), HRC.
40. TW, *Memoirs*, p. 22.
41. TW, "Williams' Wells of Violence," *New York Times*, 8 March 1959. (Foreword to *Sweet Bird of Youth*.)
42. TW to WED, letter in an envelope postmarked 31 January 1929, Dakin Williams collection.

43. TW to WED, letter, n.d., c. November 1928, Dakin Williams collection. In this letter, Williams told his grandfather that "economics is a subject I just started this term and it interests me a great deal." It appears, however, that he did not complete either economics or sociology, although he was sufficiently absorbed to warn his grandfather about the fluctuations on the stock market: "My economics teacher was saying yesterday that periods of great 'inflation' were often followed by panics and that people should invest very cautiously."
44. TW to WED, letter, 13 March 1929, HRC.
45. Park Austin Philippi, interview with Allean Hale, 28 April 1988, St. Louis.
46. Walter Dakin Williams and Shepherd Mead, *Tennessee Williams, An Intimate Biography* (New York: Arbor House, 1983), p. 27; based on a letter of TW to WED, c. November 1928, Dakin Williams collection.
47. Esmeralda Mayes Treen to Allean Hale, interview, 2 June 1985.
48. TW to WED, letter, n.d., c. September–October 1928, Dakin Williams collection.
49. TW to WED, letter, n.d., c. November 1928, HRC.
50. RIW to EDW, letter, n.d., HRC.
51. TW to WED, letter, n.d., HRC.
52. WDW to LL, interview, 2 October 1984, New York.
53. EDW, *Tom*, p. 60.
54. TW to WED, letter, n.d., HRC.

6. The New Terrain

1. In 1821, the town of Columbia was settled by landowners from Kentucky and Virginia who had traveled northwest into Boone County. By 1839, they had established the first state university in the West. The six classic columns symbolically fronting Francis Quadrangle are the remnants of the original Academic Hall.
2. *Bulletin of the American Association of University Professors*, 16, no. 2 (February 1930).
3. Tennessee Williams, *Memoirs* (Garden City, N.Y.: Doubleday, 1975), p. 24 (hereinafter: TW, *Memoirs*).
4. Harold Edmund Carroll lived at Miss Effie's boardinghouse in the fall of 1929. He was from Brookfield, a small town near Kansas City.
5. Although Mrs. Williams identified the article (EDW, *Tom*, p. 51) as having appeared in "the university paper," there is no record of it; however, the Columbia *Missourian* reprinted it in the issue of 9 December 1984, pp. 10–11.
6. TW, *Memoirs*, p. 25.
7. Edwina Dakin Williams, with Lucy Freeman, *Remember Me to Tom* (New York: Putnam, 1963), pp. 52–53 (hereinafter: EDW, *Tom*).
8. TW to Dakins, letter, "Nov. '29," Dakin Williams collection.
9. TW to RIW, letter, "Oct. '29," Dakin Williams collection.
10. TW, *Memoirs*, pp. 26–27.
11. Allean Hale, "Tennessee Williams at Missouri," *Missouri Alumnus*, January–February 1986.
12. Andrea Herman, "Tennessee Talks of Ol' Mizzou," *American*, 19 December 1961, sec. 2, p. 9.
13. Hale, "Tennessee Williams at Missouri."
14. Herman, "Tennessee Talks."
15. Such an incident is related in *Memoirs*, describing a "kangaroo court" in the spring term of 1931, when an ATO member he calls Melmoth (after Oscar Wilde's alias) is expelled from the fraternity. In the unpublished manuscript of the memoirs, he identifies Melmoth as a member of the music faculty who did, in fact, go on leave from the university in 1931. But, since he returned to the faculty in 1932, it is unlikely the incident actually occurred.
16. Several biographers have concluded from the adventures described in *Memoirs* that Williams had his first homosexual experience while at Missouri. However, his own journal entries

clearly refute this, and he may have used Smitty as a generic name for several fraternity brothers whom he found attractive. Also, his unpublished memoirs—although Williams identifies Smitty as a specific roommate—interviews with classmates, and careful research into Williams's papers of the period indicate that he invented the happenings in which Smitty was involved. As an example, the frustrated boy-with-boy affair he describes as taking place around "Crazy Night" turns up later as fiction in a story of that title, where the sexual encounter is with a girl.

17. "The Important Thing," in Tennessee Williams, *Collected Stories* (New York: New Directions, 1985), p. 165.

18. TW to EDW, letter, "May 1930," HRC.

19. TW to WED, letter, 16 June 1930, HRC.

20. EDW to WED, letter, 23 June 1930, Dakin Williams collection.

21. TW, *Memoirs*, p. 28.

22. Esmeralda Mayes Treen to LL, letter, 1 February 1988.

23. "The Important Thing," *Collected Stories*, p. 166.

24. TW to Eugene B. Griesman, special to the *San Francisco Chronicle*, 28 February 1983, p. 2.

25. Esmeralda Mayes Treen to LL, letter, 9 September 1985. In this period, Tom also made the acquaintance of Sarah Guitar, a librarian at the State Historical Society, located on campus but independent of the university library. Of French descent, she was about thirty-seven years old and close to Tom for about a year. Her friend Sara Saper, an instructor of English at the university and a judge for the Mahan Essay Contest and for the Dramatic Arts Contest, remembered Tom as being shy and lonely. Saper said that Guitar years later maintained that she was Tennessee's model for Blanche in *A Streetcar Named Desire*. Sara Saper Gauldin to Allean Hale, 6 August 1994.

26. Harold A. Mitchell to LL, letter, 18 February 1986.

27. Harold A. Mitchell to LL, interview, 9 July 1986, San Francisco.

28. Mitchell to LL, letter, 18 February 1986.

29. Mrs. William (Edna Don Carlos) Watson to LL, interview, 10 July 1987, Media, Pennsylvania.

30. Mitchell to LL, letter, 18 February 1986.

31. Mitchell to LL, interview, 9 July 1986.

32. TW to RIW, letter, 22 January 1931, HRC.

33. EDW, *Tom*, p. 57.

34. TW, *Memoirs*, p. 35.

35. TW, *Hot Milk at Three in the Morning*, original ms. in University of Missouri library, Columbia, Missouri; also a Williams-authorized copy at HRC.

36. TW to RIW, letter, n.d., c. December 1931, HRC.

37. TW to CCW, letter, 29 January 1932, HRC.

38. TW to EDW, letter, 5 March 1932, HRC.

39. Bill Bell to TW, letter, 28 December 1958, HRC.

40. Griesman, *San Francisco Chronicle*, 28 February 1983.

41. TW to EDW, letter, 5 March 1932, HRC.

42. Henry Allen Moe memorandum in the Hart Crane file of the Guggenheim Foundation (New York).

43. "Big Black: A Mississippi Idyll," *Collected Stories*, pp. 26–31. Although the black population of Columbia during the antebellum period had made up half of the city's inhabitants, at the time Williams arrived, Negroes composed less than 10 percent. As recently as 1923, there had been a lynching, when the fourteen-year-old daughter of a university professor identified a black school janitor as having attempted to molest her. On a Saturday night at midnight, while law officers looked on, a mob of more than five hundred townspeople and students dragged the janitor to the Stewart Road bridge and hanged him there. Williams would have heard about this incident and many other injustices, and though he was a southern traditionalist, he was always openly opposed to racial persecution and discrimination.

44. RIW to TW, letter, 2 April 1932, Dakin Williams collection.
45. TW, *Memoirs*, pp. 35–36.

7. The Celotex Interior

1. Edwina Dakin Williams, with Lucy Freeman, *Remember Me to Tom* (New York: Putnam, 1963), p. 62 (hereinafter: EDW, *Tom*).
2. Ibid.
3. Nancy M. Tischler, *Tennessee Williams: Rebellious Puritan* (New York: Citadel Press, 1965), p. 38.
4. Ibid.
5. TW to Anna Jean O'Donnell, collection of Ms. Jerry Miller.
6. Anna Jean O'Donnell to TW, letter, 28 June 1932, Dakin Williams collection.
7. TW to WED, letter, n.d., summer 1932, Dakin Williams collection.
8. TW to *The Link*, 19 August 1932, HRC.
9. Tennessee Williams, *Memoirs* (Garden City, N.Y.: Doubleday, 1975), p. 16 (hereinafter: TW, *Memoirs*).
10. Ibid.
11. Ibid.
12. EDW, *Tom*, pp. 64–65.
13. Ibid.
14. Cardinal Le Gros to TW, letter, 9 November 1932, HRC.
15. Robert L. Ramsay to TW, letter, 10 December 1932, HRC.
16. Walter Dakin Williams and Shepherd Mead, *Tennessee Williams, An Intimate Biography* (New York: Arbor House, 1983), pp. 35–36.
17. WDW to LL, letter, 27 July 1987.
18. TW, *Memoirs*, p. 37.
19. TW to Harriet Monroe, note, 11 March 1933, HRC.
20. William A. Martin to TW, letter, 20 July 1933, HRC.
21. TW to Dakins, letter, 28 December 1933, HRC.
22. WDW to LL, interview, 2 October 1984, New York.
23. J. Louis Stoll to TW, letter, 31 January 1934, Dakin Williams collection.
24. TW, *Memoirs*, pp. 119–120. Williams was always vehemently opposed to the suggestion that there was anything physical in his relationship with Rose, and he went so far as to fire a director of *The Two-Character Play* when the brother and sister were merely touching each other.
25. Ibid.
26. TW to *Story* editor, letter, 7 January 1934, HRC.
27. TW, *Memoirs*, p. 37.
28. TW to WED, letter, 19 June 1934, HRC.
29. WDW and Mead, *Tennessee Williams*, pp. 43–44.
30. TW, unpublished memoirs (private collection), p. 197.
31. Robert Rice, "A Man Named Tennessee," *New York Post*, 27 April 1958, p. 12.
32. Postscript to "The Accent of a Coming Foot," HRC.
33. TW, *Memoirs*, p. 39.
34. EDW, *Tom*, p. 70.
35. Hazel Kramer to TW, letter, 6 April 1935, Dakin Williams collection.
36. TW, *Memoirs*, p. 39.
37. TW, "The Man in the Overstuffed Chair," *Antaeus* 45/46 (Spring/Summer 1982): 284; also in Tennessee Williams, *Collected Stories* (New York: New Directions, 1985), p. vii.
38. EDW, *Tom*, pp. 68–69.
39. CCW to TW, letter, 21 May 1935, Dakin Williams collection.
40. WDW to LL, letter, 16 August 1984.
41. TW, *Memoirs*, p. 40.

42. Ibid., p. 42.
43. TW, "Grand," Tennessee Williams, in *The Knightly Quest and Other Stories* (New York: New Directions, 1966), p. 177.
44. TW to WDW, letter, 25 June 1935, HRC.
45. TW, *Memoirs*, p. 41.

8. Blue Devils

1. TW to Dakins, letter, 1 September 1935, HRC.
2. TW, "Return to Dust," c. September 1938, p. 1, HRC.
3. TW, "Preface to My Poems," *Five Young American Poets*, 3d series (New York: New Directions, 1944); and *Where I Live, Selected Essays*, eds. Day and Woods (New York: New Directions, 1978), pp. 2–3.
4. CMMc to LL, interview, 27 August 1983, New York.
5. TW, "Preface to My Poems."
6. Nancy M. Tischler, *Tennessee Williams: Rebellious Puritan* (New York: Citadel Press, 1965), p. 44.
7. CMMc to LL, interview, 27 August 1983.
8. Ibid.
9. John Rood to TW, letter, 22 September 1935, HRC.
10. TW to Dakins, letter, 6 August 1936, HRC.
11. TW, "Return to Dust," pp. 2, 3.
12. Ibid., pp. 3, 4.
13. Writing in *Playbill*, Rebecca Morehouse gave some insight as to what majesty Alla Nazimova invested in her performances and what it was that so impressed the young Gene O'Neill and Tom Williams:

> Nazimova, a Russian born at Yalta on the Black Sea, was strikingly theatrical. Five-foot-three, she could look taller or shorter, beautiful or plain, for the stage. "As I think, so I am," she said. She had "a fascinating voice, blue-black hair, large dark eyes and white skin," wrote Ward Morehouse. . . .
>
> Schooled at Stanislavsky's Moscow Art Theatre, she came here with a soon-impoverished troupe which acted in Russian in a Lower East Side stable. In five months she learned English; within a decade she was the leading Ibsen actress. Extolled in plays by O'Neill and Chekhov, Ibsen remained her idol. She did *Hedda Gabler, A Doll's House, The Master Builder, The Wild Duck* and *Little Eyolf*.
>
> Her exoticism noticed by Hollywood, she became a silent film star at $14,000 a week, [discovered and] acted with Rudolph Valentino in *Camille*. The swimming pool of her sprawling Spanish villa (known later as The Garden of Allah, the famous bungalow-hotel) had the shape of the Black Sea; Tallulah Bankhead swam nude in it.

Nazimova died in 1945 at the age of sixty-six.
14. Mary Bragiotti, "Away from It All," *New York Post*, 12 December 1947.
15. Louis Sheaffer, *O'Neill: Son and Playwright*, vol. 1 (Boston: Little, Brown, 1968), pp. 121–122.
16. Tennessee Williams's journals are at the Harry Ransom Humanities Research Center at the University of Texas in Austin and in various private collections. They are excerpted in this volume to correspond as closely as possible with the actual time and events and places and persons as they occurred in his life and career.
17. TW to registrar, University of Missouri, unmailed or draft of letter, 2 March 1936, Dakin Williams collection.
18. "Gift of an Apple" was first published in Tennessee Williams, *Collected Stories* (New York: New Directions, 1985), p. 63. It is notable for the fact that it reflects a degree of sophistication

not found in his journals or other writings at that time except for "Ten Minute Stop" (p. 54). Both stories appear to have been inspired by hearsay or vicarious experiences in Memphis, and they possibly were written there during the summer of 1935.

19. Edwina Dakin Williams, with Lucy Freeman, *Remember Me to Tom* (New York: Putnam, 1963), pp. 79–80 (hereinafter: EDW, *Tom*); TW letter to Dakins, 12 March 1936, HRC.

20. EDW, *Tom*, p. 68.

21. TW to John Rood, unmailed letter, n.d., HRC.

22. IWB to TW, letter, 24 May 1936, HRC.

23. TW to Harriet Monroe, letter, 27 March 1936, HRC.

24. "Sand," *Collected Stories*, p. 49.

25. TW to *Story* magazine, unmailed letter, April 1936, HRC.

26. Wilbur L. Schramm to TW, letter, 4 April 1936, HRC.

27. CMMc to LL, interview, 27 August 1983.

28. Mary Gaylord Cobb to TW, letter, 21 April 1936, HRC.

29. EDW to Dakins, letter, n.d., HRC.

30. Wilbur L. Schramm to TW, letter, 3 May 1936, HRC.

31. Anatole Broyard, in "The Combustible Lawrence, Still Smoldering," *New York Times Book Review*, 8 November 1987, p. 14, defines qualities that would have excited the mind and emotions of Tom Williams:

> Yet Lawrence was so modern that we're still misreading him. His yearning for blood-brotherhood, for example, suggests not closet homosexuality, but loneliness. One of his favorite themes was "the isolation of personality." He was the first modern novelist to realize that men and women cannot solve one another's loneliness. . . . Nothing is enough, apparently, to prevent the kind of loneliness we have taught ourselves to feel.
>
> Also, for Lawrence another man, a friend, was a defense against the apocalypse-or-nothing of contemporary heterosexual love. To him, men were like mountaineers roped to keep one another from falling into the abyss of sexuality and love.

32. TW to Wilbur L. Schramm, letter, possibly unmailed, n.d., HRC.

33. TW to Dakins, letter, 30 August 1936, HRC.

34. EDW to Dakins, letter, 26 August 1936, HRC.

35. C. W. Lamke to TW, letter, 22 June 1936, HRC.

36. Medical dictionaries relate baleful *blue devils* to "the blues," a commonplace name tending to belittle painful periods of clinical mental depression, often accompanied by psychosomatic illnesses and apparitions seen during delirium tremens. In the United States, *blue devils* is a colloquialism dating to the late 1700s and throughout the 1800s. Thomas Jefferson and Herman Melville both spoke of blue devils. During the Great Depression of the 1930s, many of the major jazz innovators played in a traveling band called the Oklahoma City Blue Devils.

It is possible that Tom Williams heard the authentic blues music of its originator, W. C. Handy, who was a resident in Clarksdale, Mississippi, during Tom's childhood years 1916–1918 and especially at the most impressionable period of his young life, 1920–1921. Allean Hale notes: "By the time Handy first came to Clarksdale in 1902, the city was already noted for music by black musicians and itinerant minstrels, but Handy seems to have introduced what came to be called Boogie Woogie and the Blues. Like other blacks, he lived across the tracks near the local red light district and often played in the houses of prostitution there . . . but his Knights of Pythias band became so famous in the region that it was in constant demand for local events, dancehalls, political rallies and white folks' parties." Regardless of what Edwina Williams and Mrs. Dakin thought of music of this kind, it is most likely Tom and his grandfather heard Handy's blues at the gambling club Tennessee Williams would call the Moon Lake Casino and at the city's vaudeville house. Later, in his *Blue Mountain Ballads*, Williams wrote lyrics for "Gold Tooth Blues," "Kitchen Door Blues," and "Lonesome Man," among others.

37. TW, foreword to Oliver Evans, *Young Man With a Screwdriver* (University of Nebraska Press, 1950).

38. Scott Russell Sanders, "Audubon the Writer: Celebrity in Buckskin," *New York Times Book Review*, 19 October 1986, pp. 1, 46.

39. TW, "Concerning Eugene O'Neill," Center Theatre Group souvenir program for *More Stately Mansions*, 1967.

9. Blue Roses

1. Tennessee Williams, *27 Wagons Full of Cotton and Other One-Act Plays* (New York: New Directions, 1945), p. ix.

2. TW to WED, letter, n.d., HRC.

3. EDW to Dakins, letter, 24 September 1936, HRC.

4. RIW to WED, letter, 30 September 1936, HRC.

5. Tennessee Williams, *Memoirs* (Garden City, N.Y.: Doubleday, 1975), p. 122 (hereinafter: TW, *Memoirs*).

6. EDW to Dakins, letter, 9 October 1936, HRC.

7. TW, *Memoirs*, p. 121.

8. Ibid., p. 116.

9. CMMc to LL, interview, 27 August 1983, New York.

10. Edwina Dakin Williams, with Lucy Freeman, *Remember Me to Tom* (New York: Putnam, 1963), p. 87.

11. CMMc to LL, interview, 27 August 1983.

12. William Jay Smith, *Army Brat* (New York: Persea Books, 1980), pp. 190–191.

13. TW, *Memoirs*, p. 121.

14. William Jay Smith, entry in *Dictionary of Literary Biography, Documentary Series, An Illustrated Chronicle*, vol. 4 (Detroit: Gale Research, 1984), p. 27.

15. Louis Sheaffer, Eugene O'Neill's biographer, in a letter to LL, 22 July 1987, wrote: "It seemed to me that at times in the school essay [HRC] he was just making with words, but he also gets off some apt observations, as for instance when he calls O'Neill 'the poet of the inarticulate,' " but he was probably "too conscious of the surface novelties in O'Neill—the masks, the asides, the unusual length of certain of his plays, but later on he properly concentrates on the intensity of feeling, the passion . . . and could have been talking about himself when he talked of O'Neill's passion and loneliness."

16. TW to Dakins, letter, n.d., mid-October 1936, Dakin Williams collection.

17. TW, *27 Wagons Full of Cotton and Other One-Act Plays*, pp. viii–xi.

18. Robert Rice, "A Man Named Tennessee," *New York Post*, 29 April 1958, p. M2.

19. Anne H. Jennings (actress, reviewer, and eventual friend of TW), in unidentified newspaper, HRC.

20. Frederick Lewis Allen, *Since Yesterday, The Nineteen Thirties in America* (New York: Bantam, 1965), pp. 188–192. In addition to Allen's excellent summary of the 1930s, a more recent publication, Robert S. McElvaine, *The Great Depression, America 1929–1941* (New York: Times Books, 1984), is highly recommended both as reading and for research.

21. Washington University *STUDE—*, n.d., HRC.

22. EDW to Dakins, letter, 17 November 1936, HRC.

23. TW, *27 Wagons Full of Cotton and Other One-Act Plays*, pp. ix, x. Drama critic Burns Mantle, in *Best Plays 1935–36* (New York: Dodd, Mead, 1935), p. 14, summarized the play as "a reflection of the 'Miracle of Verdun' in that it relates the protest against war of soldiers killed in battle. A burial detail lays six cadavers in a trench (the same being the orchestra pit in the theatre) and is about to cover them with earth when the six rise in their burial clothes and refuse to be buried. Neither pleas nor high commands can alter their determination. When their women-folk are summoned to beg them, for the sake of peace and harmony now that they are dead, they still refuse. At the

play's end they are crawling over the trench to begin a march across the world that shall, by inference, voice the protest of all dead men killed in war against the foolishness of war."

24. Sinclair Lewis, in accepting his Nobel Prize in 1930, praised O'Neill and may have had a direct influence on the award's being given for the first time to an American playwright. See Croswell Bowen, *The Curse of the Misbegotten* (New York: McGraw-Hill, 1959), p. 251.

25. EW to CCW, letter, 16 November 1936, HRC.

26. EDW to Dakins, letter, 17 November 1936, HRC.

27. RIW to Dakins, letter, 18 November 1936, HRC.

28. Jack Pickering, *The Eliot*, 4, no. 2 (November 1936). *The Eliot* was named after the founder of Washington University, William Greenleaf Eliot, who was the grandfather of poet T. S. Eliot. In the years between 1932 and 1935, when Tom Williams was working at the shoe factory and living in the cramped apartment at 6254 Enright, he would slip his poetry under the office door of the magazine. In November and December of 1936, *The Eliot* published Williams's poems "Sonnet for Pygmalion," "Changeling," and "No Shaken Seas."

29. EDW to Dakins, letter, 1 December 1936, HRC.

30. EDW to Dakins, letter, 6 December 1936, HRC.

31. TW, *Memoirs*, p. 124.

32. EDW to ROD, letter, 12 December 1936, HRC.

33. WDW to LL, interview, 15 April 1985, St. Louis.

34. EDW to Dakins, letter, n.d., c. 21 December 1936, HRC.

35. RIW to ROD, letter, 29 December 1936, HRC.

36. RIW to EDW, letter, 24 December 1936, HRC.

10. Elegy for Rose

1. Robert Rice, "A Man Named Tennessee," *New York Post* Daily Magazine, 29 April 1958, Article VIII, p. M2.

2. RIW to WDW, letter, 1 January 1937, HRC.

3. RIW to EDW and CCW, letter, 2 January 1937, HRC.

4. EW to CCW, letter, 3 January 1937, HRC.

5. IWB to "Dearest Family," letter, 4 January 1937, HRC.

6. EDW to Dakins, letter, 13 January 1937, HRC.

7. EW to EDW, letter, 14 January 1937, HRC.

8. EW to CCW, letter, 26 January 1937, HRC.

9. IWB to CCW, letter, 23 February 1937, HRC.

10. EDW to Dakins, letter, 25 January 1937, HRC.

11. Tennessee Williams, *Memoirs* (Garden City, N.Y.: Doubleday, 1975), pp. 121–122.

12. EDW to Dakins, letter, "Feb. '37," HRC.

13. Rice, "A Man Named Tennessee," p. M2.

14. *The Eliot*, May 1937.

15. IWB to EDW, letter, 2 March 1937, HRC.

16. EW to EDW, letter, 2 March 1937, HRC.

17. William Jay Smith, *Army Brat* (New York: Persea Books, 1980), p. 186.

18. CMMc to LL, interview, 27 August 1983, New York.

19. Rice, "A Man Named Tennessee," p. M2.

20. Reed Hynds, review in *St. Louis Star-Times*, 19 March 1937, HRC.

21. *St. Louis Star-Times* interview, c. March 1937, HRC.

22. Colvin McPherson, review in *St. Louis Post-Dispatch*, 19 March 1937.

23. Rice, "A Man Named Tennessee," p. M2.

24. Nancy M. Tischler, *Tennessee Williams: Rebellious Puritan* (New York: Citadel Press, 1965), p. 48.

25. CMMc to LL, interview, 27 August 1983.

26. Hazel Kramer to TW, letter, 29 March 1937, Dakin Williams collection.

27. IWB to TW, letter, 24 March 1937, HRC.
28. Smith, *Army Brat*, p. 193.
29. TW to Willard Holland, letter, n.d., c. 15 April 1937, HRC.
30. Ibid.
31. The first appearance of Thomas Lanier Williams in *Poetry* magazine, June 1937, included the poems "The Shuttle," "This Hour," and "My Love Was Light."
32. EDW to Dakins, letter, 11 May 1937, HRC.
33. Unpublished poem, "St. Louis, 1937," HRC.

11. The Literary Factory

1. EDW to Dakins, letter, 17 May 1937, HRC.
2. EDW to Dakins, letter, 26 May 1937, HRC.
3. Robert Rice, "A Man Named Tennessee," *New York Post*, 28 April 1958, p. M2.
4. William G. B. Carson to Andreas Brown, letter, 19 July 1961, HRC.
5. Walter Dakin Williams and Shepherd Mead, *Tennessee Williams, An Intimate Biography* (New York: Arbor House, 1983), p. 57.
6. Ibid.
7. Martyl Schweig Langsdorf to LL, letter, 2 August 1983.
8. William Jay Smith, *Army Brat* (New York: Persea Books, 1980), pp. 193–194.
9. Washington University transcript, dated 10 September 1937, forwarded to registrar of the University of Iowa, HRC.
10. EDW to Dakins, letter, 3 July 1937, HRC.
11. CCW to ROD, letter, 6 July 1937, HRC.
12. TW, "Return to Dust," c. September 1938, p. 4, HRC.
13. CMMc to LL, interview, 27 August 1983, New York.
14. Rice, "A Man Named Tennessee," p. M2.
15. CMMc to LL, interview.
16. WDW to LL, interview, 2 October 1984, New York.
17. WDW and Mead, *Tennessee Williams*, p. 63.
18. WDW to LL, letter, 16 August 1984.
19. EDW to Dakins, letter, postmarked 3 August 1937, HRC.
20. Farmington medical report, 31 July 1937, Dakin Williams collection.
21. IWB to CCW, letter, 7 August 1937, in Edwina Dakin Williams, with Lucy Freeman, *Remember Me to Tom* (New York: Putnam, 1963), pp. 87–88.
22. *The Eliot*, June 1937.
23. EDW to Dakins, letter, n.d., c. 20 September 1937, HRC.

12. Iowa

1. Willard Holland to TW, letter, postmarked 26 September 1937, Dakin Williams collection.
2. TW to EDW, letter, n.d., in Edwina Dakin Williams, with Lucy Freeman, *Remember Me to Tom* (New York: Putnam, 1963), p. 90 (hereinafter: EDW, *Tom*).
3. TW to EDW, letter, n.d., HRC.
4. TW to EDW, letter, n.d., in EDW, *Tom*, p. 92.
5. TW to Willard Holland, letter, n.d., c. October 1937, Harriet Holland Brandt collection.
6. TW, preface to Marian Gallaway, *Constructing a Play* (New York: Prentice Hall, Inc., 1950), p. vii. Ultimately, Gallaway became head of the theatre department at the University of Alabama. She and Willard Holland were among the first who tried in vain to make Williams more conscious of play construction.
7. Phil Graves, *Daily Iowan* and *Des Moines Register*, c. July 1967.
8. Norman Felton to Clay Harshbarger, letter, 10 October 1980, reprinted in 1984 Iowa festival souvenir program, article entitled "Tennessee's Year at Iowa, 1937–38," by Charles Calmer.

9. Thomas D. Pawley to LL, letter, 13 February 1986. Pawley went on from Iowa to distinguish himself as a professor of speech and drama at Lincoln University in Jefferson City, Missouri.
10. Winston Barclay, University of Iowa Center for the Arts News Service, press release, 1 June 1984, HRC.
11. TW to EDW, letter, n.d., in EDW, *Tom*, p. 90.
12. P. A. M. Stewart to LL, letter, 17 June 1985. Mrs. Stewart said, "My father never had a brain tumor of any kind. He never had periods of mental lapse. He was never sent to a psychopathic ward for any reason. He was a genius with an interest in everything, but particularly in drawing the best work out of every student."

In 1950, Mabie suffered a stroke that partially disabled him, but it did not prevent him from overseeing his department until his death in 1956.

13. Ibid.
14. Olga Becker to TW, letter, 22 September 1937, HRC.
15. EDW to Dakins, letter, postmarked 5 October 1937, HRC.
16. TW to EDW, letter, n.d., HRC.
17. TW to EDW, postcard, 24 October 1937, Dakin Williams collection.
18. *The Eliot*, October 1937.
19. CMMc to TW, letter, n.d., c. September/October 1937, written from Hotel Pieroni, Boston, Dakin Williams collection.
20. TW to WED, letter, 18 November 1937, HRC.
21. TW to Willard Holland, letter, n.d., c. November 1937, Harriett Holland Brandt collection.
22. Robert Rice, "A Man Named Tennessee," *New York Post*, 29 April 1958, p. M2.
23. TW to Reed Hynds, unmailed letter, c. November 1937, Dakin Williams collection.
24. EDW to Dakins, letter, 1 January 1938, HRC.
25. Dr. C. C. Ault, summary, 16 December 1937, Farmington, Missouri, regarding Williams, Rose I., case no. 9014, Dakin Williams collection.
26. EDW to Dakins, letter, 1 January 1938, HRC.
27. TW to Willard Holland, letter fragment, n.d., Dakin Williams collection.

13. The Island of My Self

1. EDW to Dakins, letter, 1 January 1938, HRC.
2. TW to Dakins, letter, 2 January 1938, Dakin Williams collection.
3. Tennessee Williams, *Memoirs* (Garden City, N.Y.: Doubleday, 1975), pp. 44–45 (hereinafter: TW, *Memoirs*).
4. TW to Colvin McPherson, unmailed letter, n.d., HRC.
5. TW to Dakins, letter, n.d., HRC.
6. TW to EDW, letter, n.d., HRC.
7. Jack Gurney, "Williams' Little-Known Stint at Iowa Recalled," *Sarasota Herald-Tribune*, 6 March 1983.
8. TW to EDW, letter, n.d., HRC.
9. Charles Calmer's "Tennessee's Year at Iowa, 1937–38" (in 1984 Iowa festival souvenir program), p. 18.
10. Phil Graves, "In 1937—Tennessee Williams at U. of I.," *Des Moines Register*, 23 June 1968, p. 2T.
11. Winston Barclay, University of Iowa Center for the Arts News Service, press release, 1 June 1984.
12. Ibid.
13. John M. Pickering to TW, postcard, 29 January 1938, Dakin Williams collection.
14. TW to John Pickering, letter, 25 February 1938, HRC.
15. EDW to Dakins, letter, 17 Jan. 1938, HRC.
16. RIW to EDW, letter, dated erroneously 13 February 1937, Dakin Williams collection.
17. TW to EDW, letter, n.d., HRC.
18. Virginia Conkle to LL, letter, 10 December 1984.

19. TW to EDW, letter, n.d., HRC.
20. TW to EDW, letter, 25 April 1938, Dakin Williams collection.
21. TW to EDW, letter, n.d., HRC.
22. TW to EDW, letter, n.d., HRC.
23. EDW to ROD, letter, 16 March 1938, HRC.
24. EDW to Dakins, letter, 28 April 1938, HRC.
25. TW to EDW, letter, n.d., HRC.
26. EDW to Dakins, letter, 26 March 1938, HRC.
27. EDW to Dakins, letter, 9 April 1938, HRC.
28. Excerpted from an original draft, with later comment by TW, "This was based on an incident involving my sister," HRC. There is extant an unpublished revised version in which his anger tends to mar the lyrical beauty of this short six-page piece.
29. TW to EDW, letter, 4 April 1938, Dakin Williams collection.
30. TW, *Memoirs*, p. 46; Williams appears to have confused *Henry IV, Part I* with another play, *Richard of Bordeaux*, in which he would have enacted a similar role but of which there is no record at the university.
31. Marian Gallaway to Andreas Brown, letter, n.d., HRC.
32. TW, *Memoirs*, p. 47.
33. TW, unfinished poem, HRC.
34. EDW to Dakins, letter, n.d., c. 28 April 1938, HRC.
35. TW to EDW, letter, n.d., c. May 1938, HRC.
36. EDW to Dakins, letters, 10 and 11 May 1938, HRC.
37. TW, *Memoirs*, p. 49.
38. Truman Slitor to LL, letter, 11 April 1986.
39. Ibid.
40. Robert Leo Quinn to LL, letter, 1 August 1985.
41. TW to EDW, postcard, postmarked 1 June 1938, Dakin Williams collection.
42. TW to EDW, letter, n.d., c. 15 May 1938, HRC.
43. TW to CMMc, unmailed partial letter, n.d., Dakin Williams collection.
44. TW to Willard Holland, unmailed letter, n.d., HRC.
45. TW to EDW, letter, n.d., c. July 1938, HRC.
46. Tennessee Williams, *Orpheus Descending with Battle of Angels* (New York: New Directions, 1955), p. vii.
47. Milton Lomask to LL, letter, 9 December 1984.
48. TW to EDW, letter, n.d., HRC.
49. TW to EDW, letter, n.d., HRC.
50. Ibid.
51. TW to E. C. Mabie, letter, 8 August 1938, HRC.
52. TW to EDW, letter, n.d., c. 8 August 1938, HRC.
53. Milton Lomask to LL, letter, 4 December 1984.
54. EDW to ROD, letter, 15 August 1938, HRC.
55. Milton Lomask to LL, letter, 4 December 1984.
56. Sam Halley, Jr., to LL, telephone interview, 23 June 1985.
57. Wesley Gore to LL, letter, 6 August 1985.
58. EDW to ROD, letter, n.d., HRC.
59. TW, "Return to Dust," 1938, HRC.
60. TW, written on 42 Aberdeen Place stationery, c. 15 October 1938, HRC.
61. EDW to Dakins, letter, 28 September 1938, HRC.
62. TW, *Memoirs*, p. 123.
63. TW to CMMc, letter fragment, n.d., Dakin Williams collection.
64. William Jay Smith, *Army Brat* (New York: Persea Books, 1980), p. 192.
65. EDW to Dakins, letter, 19 December 1938, HRC.
66. EDW to ROD, letter, 9 December 1938, HRC.
67. TW to EDW, postcard, 29 December 1938, HRC.

68. ROD to EDW, letter, postmarked 10 January 1939, HRC.
69. EDW to TW, letter, 31 December 1938, HRC.

14. Vieux Carré

1. Tennessee Williams, *Vieux Carré* play (New York: New Directions, 1979), p. 4.
2. *People* magazine, "Tennessee Williams Stalks the Sweet Bird of His Youth in New Orleans," 14 February 1977, p. 50.
3. Edwina Dakin Williams, with Lucy Freeman, *Remember Me to Tom* (New York: Putnam, 1963), p. 103.
4. TW to Eric Paulsen, WWL-TV interview, 5 March 1982, New Orleans.
5. TW to EDW, letter, 2 January 1939, HRC.
6. "The Angel in the Alcove," in Tennessee Williams, *One Arm and Other Stories* (New York: New Directions, 1967), p. 141.
7. TW to EDW, letter, postmarked 9 January 1939, HRC.
8. Jon Nordheimer, "Louisiana Indictments: Only the Names Change," *New York Times*, 3 March 1985, p. 20.
9. EDW to Dakins, letter, 9 February 1939, HRC.
10. TW to EDW, letter, 2 January 1939, HRC.
11. TW to EDW, letter, n.d., c. 22 January 1939, Dakin Williams collection.
12. TW to EDW, letter, 25 January 1939, HRC.
13. TW to EDW, letter, n.d., c. 22 January 1939, Dakin Williams collection.
14. TW to EDW, letter, n.d., HRC.
15. Willard Holland to TW, letter, n.d., HRC.
16. Robert Rice, "A Man Named Tennessee," *New York Post*, 30 April 1958, p. M2.
17. Tennessee Williams, *In the Winter of Cities* (New York: New Directions, 1956), pp. 111–112.
18. TW to EDW, postcard, 18 February 1939, Dakin Williams collection.

15. West by Southwest

1. TW to EDW, letter, 21 February 1939, HRC.
2. Edwina Dakin Williams, with Lucy Freeman, *Remember Me to Tom* (New York: Putnam, 1963), pp. 103–104.
3. EDW to Dakins, letter, 26 February 1939, HRC.
4. TW, letter draft, n.d., Dakin Williams collection.
5. TW to CCW, letter, n.d., c. 1 March 1939, HRC.
6. TW to EDW, letter, 1 March 1939, HRC.
7. EDW to TW, letter, 26 February 1939, HRC.
8. T. E. Kalem, "Angel of the Odd," *Time* (cover story), 9 March 1962, p. 56.
9. Jim Parrott, "Tennessee Travels to Taos," *Tennessee Williams Literary Journal*, Spring 1989, p. 9.
10. EDW to Dakins, letter, 8 March 1939, HRC.
11. TW to EDW, letter, n.d., c. 8 March 1939, HRC.
12. TW to Anne and Blandford ("B.J.") Jennings, unmailed letter, c. 16 March 1939, HRC.
13. TW to CCW, letter, n.d., HRC.
14. TW to unknown correspondent (probably in New Orleans and possibly Frank Bunce), letter fragment, n.d., HRC.
15. EDW to TW and TW to EDW, letters, n.d., HRC.
16. EDW to TW, letter, n.d., HRC.
17. TW to EDW, letter, n.d., HRC.
18. TW to EDW, letter, n.d. (probably 21 March 1939), HRC.
19. EDW to TW, letter, 23 March 1939, HRC.
20. EDW to Dakins, letter, 23 March 1939, HRC.
21. CCW to TW, letter, 31 March 1939, HRC.

22. Molly Day Thacher to TW, letter, 20 March 1939, HRC.

23. TW to ROD, postcard, 10 April 1939, HRC.

24. Frieda Fishbein to TW, letter, 23 March 1939, Dakin Williams collection.

25. AW to TW, letter, 1 April 1939, HRC.

26. Max Wilk, *Mr. Williams and Miss Wood* (New York: Dramatists play service, 1990), p. 130.

27. Sam Webb to CCW, letter, 1 April 1939, HRC.

28. CCW to TW, letter, 17 April 1939, Dakin Williams collection.

29. Tennessee Williams, *Memoirs* (Garden City, N.Y.: Doubleday, 1975), p. 5 (hereinafter: TW, *Memoirs*).

30. AW to TW, letter, 13 April 1939, HRC.

31. TW to AW, postcard, postmarked 21 April 1939, HRC.

32. TW, *Memoirs*, p. 5.

33. AW to TW, letter, 28 April 1939, HRC.

34. Robert Rice, "A Man Named Tennessee," *New York Post*, 30 April 1958, p. M2.

35. TW to AW, letter, 5 May 1939, HRC.

36. TW to EDW, letter, n.d., HRC.

37. TW to EDW, letter, n.d., HRC.

38. TW to ROD, letter, n.d., Dakin Williams collection; and postcard, 21 May 1939, HRC.

39. TW to CCW via EDW, postcard, 3 May 1939, HRC.

40. Charlotte Chandler, *The Ultimate Seduction* (Garden City, N.Y.: Doubleday, 1984), p. 334.

41. TW to AW, letter, 5 May 1939, HRC.

42. AW to TW, letter, 22 May 1939, HRC.

43. TW to AW, letter, "June 1939," HRC.

44. AW to TW, letter, 20 June 1939, HRC. *Story* was founded in 1931 by Whit Burnett and his wife, Martha Foley, when they were newspaper correspondents in Vienna. Eventually, they moved the publication to New York. After their divorce in 1942, Burnett continued the magazine with his second wife, Hallie. *Story* was under continual financial pressure and published sporadically through 1971.

45. Don Lee Keith, *New Orleans Courier*, 26 January–2 February 1978, p. 4.

46. Paul Moor, *Harper's*, July 1948, p. 65.

47. Nancy M. Tischler, *Rebellious Puritan* (New York: Citadel Press, 1965), p. 63.

48. TW, "The Field of Blue Children," *Story*, September–October 1939, pp. 62–72; also in Tennessee Williams, *One Arm and Other Stories* (New York: New Directions, 1967), pp. 153–166, and in Tennessee Williams, *Collected Stories* (New York: New Directions, 1985), pp. 70–78.

49. TW to AW, letter, n.d., HRC.

50. TW to EDW, postcard, postmarked 6 July 1939, Dakin Williams collection.

51. TW to AW, letter, 16 July 1939, HRC.

52. AW to TW, letter, 24 July 1939, HRC.

53. TW, *Memoirs*, pp. 6, 7.

54. Jim Parrott, "Tennessee Travels to Taos," *Tennessee Williams Literary Journal*, Spring 1989, pp. 10–11.

55. AW to TW, letter, 24 July 1939, HRC.

56. AW to TW, letter, 11 July 1939, HRC.

57. TW to AW, letter, 16 July 1939, HRC.

58. TW to AW, letter, 30 July 1939, HRC.

59. TW to Frieda Lawrence, letter, dated in error "July 29, 1938" [1939], HRC.

60. W. Ed. Campbell to Jimmie Fidler, note, 5 July 1939, Dakin Williams collection.

61. TW to EDW, letter, n.d., HRC.

62. EDW to ROD, postscript on undated letter from TW, HRC.

63. Sam Webb to C. C. Williams, letter, 31 July 1939, HRC.

64. TW to CCW, letter, n.d., HRC.

16. Orpheus Ascending

1. Tennessee Williams, *Memoirs* (Garden City, N.Y.: Doubleday, 1975), p. 6 (hereinafter: TW, *Memoirs*).
2. TW to EDW, letter, n.d., HRC.
3. TW to AW, letter, 7 August 1939, HRC.
4. TW to EDW, letter, n.d., HRC.
5. Jim Parrott, "Tennessee Travels to Taos," *Tennessee Williams Literary Journal*, Spring 1989, pp. 11, 12.
6. TW to EDW, letter, n.d., c. mid-August 1939, HRC.
7. TW to EDW, letter, n.d., c. 26 August 1939, HRC.
8. TW to AW, letter, n.d., HRC.
9. TW to EDW, letter, n.d., HRC.
10. TW, fragment, HRC.
11. TW to EDW, letter, n.d., HRC.
12. TW to AW, letter, n.d., c. 24 August 1939, HRC.
13. "Cried the Fox," in Tennessee Williams, *In the Winter of Cities* (New York: New Directions, 1956), p. 16.
14. TW to EDW, postcard, postmarked 25 August 1939, HRC.
15. TW to AW, letter, 24 August 1939, HRC.
16. TW to AW, postcard, postmarked 28 August 1939, HRC.
17. EDW to ROD, letter, n.d., HRC.
18. TW to AW, letter, 11 September 1939, HRC.
19. James Parrott to TW, letter, 14 September 1939, Dakin Williams collection.
20. TW, *Memoirs*, p. 10.
21. Ibid.
22. TW to Williamses, letter, n.d., c. late September 1939, HRC.
23. TW to Dakins, letter, postmarked 2 October 1939, HRC.
24. TW to EDW, letter, 15 October 1939, HRC.
25. TW to AW, note, n.d., his first known use of "Tenn. Wms.," HRC.
26. EDW to ROD, letter, n.d., HRC.
27. TW to Molly Day Thacher, letter, n.d., HRC.
28. TW to AW, letter, n.d., HRC.
29. AW to TW, letter, 8 November 1939, HRC.
30. TW to AW, letter, n.d., HRC.
31. TW to AW, letter, n.d., HRC.
32. TW to AW, letter, 11 November 1939, HRC.
33. Willard Holland to TW, letter, 9 November 1939, Dakin Williams collection.
34. James Parrott to TW, letter, n.d., Dakin Williams collection.
35. TW to AW, letter, 30 November 1939, HRC.
36. TW to AW, letter, n.d., c. mid-December 1939, HRC.
37. TW to Dakins, letter, n.d., c. 6 December 1939, HRC.
38. EDW to ROD, letter, n.d., HRC.
39. Anne Bretzfelder Post to LL, interview, 6 December 1983, New York.
40. TW to AW, letter, n.d., HRC.

17. Broadway

1. TW to Dakins, postcard, postmarked 8 January 1940, HRC.
2. TW to EDW, postcard, in Richard Freeman Leavitt, *The World of Tennessee Williams* (New York: Putnam, 1978), p. 41.
3. Harold Clurman, *The Fervent Years* (New York: Harcourt Brace Jovanovich, 1975), p. 269.
4. TW to Dakins, letter, 19 January 1940, HRC.
5. TW to EDW, letter, n.d., c. January 1940, HRC.

6. TW to William Liebling, letter, misdated "11-19-40," HRC.

7. TW to LL, interview, 24 October 1978, San Francisco.

8. TW to AW, letter, n.d., HRC.

9. TW to AW, letter, n.d., HRC.

10. *The Long Goodbye*, in Tennessee Williams, *27 Wagons Full of Cotton and Other Plays* (New York: New Directions, 1966), p. 178.

11. Anne Bretzfelder Post to LL, interview, 2 October 1985, New York.

12. Gilbert Maxwell, *Tennessee Williams and Friends* (Cleveland: World Publishing, 1965), pp. 43–44.

13. Clifford Odets turned thirty-four in 1940, and after a number of successes *(Waiting for Lefty, Awake and Sing!, Paradise Lost, Golden Boy, Rocket to the Moon)*, he was plagued by self-doubt and wrote in his journal in capital letters, "this fear of not writing a play." He also noted that "when a play is coming alive in me, the journal is going dead in me," a parallel within Williams's experience *(The Time Is Ripe: The 1940 Journal of Clifford Odets* [New York: Grove Press, 1988]).

14. Anne Bretzfelder Post to LL, interview, 2 October 1985, New York.

15. Fleet Munson to AW, letter, 14 February 1940.

16. TW to EDW, postcard, postmarked 17 March 1940, HRC.

17. TW to AW, letter, n.d., HRC.

18. *Portrait of a Madonna* in TW, *27 Wagons Full of Cotton and Other Plays*, p. 89.

19. TW to AW, letter, n.d., HRC.

20. TW to EDW, letter, n.d., HRC.

21. Ibid.

22. TW to Bertha Case, letter, n.d., HRC.

23. AW to TW, letter, 19 April 1940, Dakin Williams collection.

24. TW to "Dear Folks," letter, n.d., HRC.

25. William Saroyan to TW, letter (from San Francisco), 10 June 1940, Jordan Massee collection.

26. EDW to TW, letter, n.d., HRC.

27. TW to Bertha Case, letter, n.d., HRC.

28. Celeste Holm to LL, interview, 16 August 1983, New York.

29. Tennessee Williams, *Memoirs* (Garden City, N.Y.: Doubleday, 1975), pp. 52–53.

18. The Broken World

1. Tennessee Williams, *Memoirs* (Garden City, N.Y.: Doubleday, 1975), p. 69 (hereinafter: TW, *Memoirs*).

2. Michiko Kakutani, "I Keep Writing, Sometimes I Am Pleased," *New York Times*, 13 August 1981, p. C-17.

3. TW to Bertha Case, letter, n.d., HRC.

4. TW to Bertha Case, letter, n.d., HRC.

5. Joseph Hazan to Robert Butman, letter, 30 October 1984, Robert Butman collection.

6. TW, *Memoirs*, p. 54.

7. TW to Bertha Case, letter, n.d., HRC.

8. Richard Freeman Leavitt, *The World of Tennessee Williams* (New York: Putnam, 1978), p. 43.

9. TW to EDW, letter, in Edwina Dakin Williams, with Lucy Freeman, *Remember Me to Tom* (New York: Putnam, 1963), p. 117.

10. *Tennessee Williams' Letters to Donald Windham—1940–1965*, ed. and with comments by Donald Windham (New York: Holt, Rinehart and Winston, 1977), pp. 9, 10.

11. TW, *Memoirs*, p. 55.

12. Ibid., pp. 55–56.

13. TW to Joseph Hazan, letter, n.d., HRC.

14. TW to Joseph Hazan, letter, n.d., HRC.

15. TW to AW, letter, n.d., HRC.

16. AW to TW, letter, 14 August 1940, HRC.

17. CMMc to LL, interview, 27 August 1983, New York.

18. TW to Joseph Hazan, letter, n.d., HRC.

19. TW to Kip Kiernan, letter, n.d., HRC.

20. TW to Bennett Cerf, letter, 28 August 1940, Columbia University, Rare Book and Manuscripts, Butler Library.

21. TW, *Memoirs*, p. 58.

22. TW to Joseph Hazan, letter, 3 September 1940, HRC.

23. TW, *Memoirs*, p. 58.

24. Mike Steen, *A Look at Tennessee Williams* (New York: Hawthorn Books, 1969), p. 144.

25. Paul Bowles, *Without Stopping* (New York: Ecco Press, 1972), p. 229.

26. TW, *Memoirs*, p. 59.

27. TW to Bennett Cerf, letter, "12 or 13" September 1940, Columbia University, Special Collections, Butler Library.

28. "The Night of the Iguana," in Tennessee Williams, *One Arm* (New York: New Directions, 1967), p. 170. A more detailed account of Williams's first Mexican adventure, called "A Summer of Discovery," appeared in the *New York Herald Tribune*, Sunday, 24 December 1961, prior to the opening of his play *The Night of the Iguana*, and was reprinted in a book of selected essays: Tennessee Williams, *Where I Live*, eds. Christine R. Day and Bob Woods (New York: New Directions, 1978), pp. 137–147. Although a more restrained and romantic description, devoid of the sensual experience, the essay is remarkable if only for the accuracy of Williams's memory and, as always, its vivid re-creation of time and place.

29. TW to Joseph Hazan, letter, n.d., HRC. In an article in the January 1972 issue of *Harper's Bazaar*, Williams gave a more detailed and charitable picture of the writer as speaking with "a cool, cultivated voice explaining how things had gone with 'the American Way.' . . ." On the strength of "rum-cocos . . . he started talking to me like a guru . . . passionately concerned with social-political problems and the intolerable inequities with which the Americans were diseased." He remembered the writer saying, "Humanity is nailed to the two-armed cross of cupidity and stupidity [by which] he meant the cupidity of the profiteer-imperialists and the stupidity of their victims."

30. TW to Joseph Hazan, letter, "24–25" September 1940, HRC.

31. TW to Joseph Hazan, letter, n.d., HRC.

32. Ibid., postscript.

33. Miscellaneous "Reflections" evidently intended for a sequel edition of *Memoirs*. Many such gleanings, like his unmailed letters, were scattered among his writings and, subsequently, to the winds.

19. *Battle of Angels*

1. *Battle of Angels* was first published by James Laughlin in the spring of 1945 in a little magazine, *Pharos*, and was distributed by New Directions; it contained an introduction by Williams, "The History of a Play (With Parentheses)," and a "Note on 'Battle of Angels' " by Margaret Webster. A later edition, *Orpheus Descending and Battle of Angels*, was published by New Directions in 1958, with an introduction by Williams, "The Past, the Present and the Perhaps." Subsequently in 1974, Dramatists Play Service issued an acting text of *Battle of Angels*, a version revised by Tennessee Williams.

2. "The History of a Play," in Tennessee Williams, *Battle of Angels*, *Pharos* 1 (Spring 1945): 117.

3. TW to Bennett Cerf, letter, 10 October 1940, HRC.

4. Roberta Barrett to TW, letter, 26 September 1940, HRC.

5. Roberta Barrett to TW, letter, 10 October 1940, HRC.

6. TW to Roberta Barrett, postcard, 24 October 1940, HRC.

7. EDW to Dakins and WED, letter, 25 October 1940, HRC.

8. Mark Barron, "Newest Find on Broadway Is a Mississippi Playwright Named Tennessee Williams," *The Commercial Appeal*, 24 November 1940, p. 14.

9. Nancy M. Tischler, *The Rebellious Puritan* (New York: Citadel Press, 1965), p. 73.

10. Lawrence Langner, *The Magic Curtain* (New York: Dutton, 1951), p. 332.

11. Margaret Webster, *Don't Put Your Daughter on the Stage* (New York: Alfred A. Knopf, 1972), p. 69.

12. Williams later said, "Miriam Hopkins could have been an Amanda to rival even Laurette Taylor" (TW to LL, interview, 24 October 1978, San Francisco). Williams was also attracted to the actress because of her love of literature and her ability to recite by heart the poems of Byron, Rossetti, and William Cullen Bryant's "Thanatopsis." Her adopted son said, "What I remember as I was growing up was Mother's huge collection of books. She was curious by nature and an avid reader" (Michael Hopkins to LL, telephone interview, 7 February 1986).

13. Webster, *Don't Put Your Daughter on the Stage*, pp. 65–69.

14. TW, "The History of a Play," p. 115.

15. Wesley Addy to LL, interview, 16 August 1983, New York.

16. CMMc to LL, interview, 27 August 1983, New York.

17. Elaine Steinbeck to LL, interview, 13 June 1985, New York.

18. Webster, *Don't Put Your Daughter on the Stage*, p. 71.

19. TW, "The History of a Play," p. 120.

20. Elaine Steinbeck to LL, interview, 13 June 1985.

21. William Jay Smith, entry in *Dictionary of Literary Biography, Documentary Series, An Illustrated Chronicle*, vol. 4 (Detroit: Gale Research, 1984), p. 29.

22. Max Wilk, *Mr. Williams and Miss Wood* (New York: Dramatists Play Service, 1990).

23. "The History of a Play," in Tennessee Williams, *Battle of Angels*, *Pharos* 1 (Spring 1945): 115–116.

24. Edwina Dakin Williams, with Lucy Freeman, *Remember Me to Tom* (New York: Putnam, 1963), pp. 120–121 (hereinafter: EDW, *Tom*).

25. Alexander Williams, "Battle of Angels," *Boston Herald*, 31 December 1940, p. 10.

26. "Wilbur Theatre: 'Battle of Angels,' " *Boston Globe*, 31 December 1940, p. 7.

27. Libby, *Variety*, 1 January 1941, p. 45.

28. *St. Louis Star-Times*, 7 January 1941.

29. UPI release, *St. Louis Star-Times*, 8 January 1941.

30. William Hughes to LL, interview, 31 October 1985, New York.

31. TW to Joseph Hazan, letter, n.d., c. January 1941, HRC.

32. UPI release, *St. Louis Star-Times*, 8 January 1941.

33. The American Theatre Society (the Theatre Guild, Inc.) letter to Guild subscribers, 20 January 1941.

34. Wilk, *Mr. Williams and Miss Wood*.

35. Tennessee Williams, *Memoirs* (Garden City, N.Y.: Doubleday, 1975), p. 62 (hereinafter: TW, *Memoirs*).

36. Marjory Adams, *Boston Globe*, 17 September 1945.

37. Frank Rich, "In London, Taking Williams Seriously," *New York Times*, 15 December 1988, p. C15.

38. Webster, *Don't Put Your Daughter on the Stage*, p. 74.

39. Elliot Norton, " 'Battle of Angels' a Defeat, but No Disaster," *Boston Post*, 12 January 1941.

40. TW to EDW, letter, 6 January 1941, HRC.

41. Jordan Massee to LL, telephone interview, 13 March 1986.

42. Gilbert Maxwell, *Tennessee Williams and Friends* (Cleveland and New York: World Publishing, 1965), pp. 38–40.

43. Margaret Webster to TW, letter, n.d., in EDW, *Tom*, p. 124.

44. TW to AW, note, 5 February 1941, Dakin Williams collection.

45. TW to Jo Healy, letter, n.d., Columbia University, Special Collections, Butler Library.

46. TW to "Dear Folks," letter, postmarked 12 February 1941, HRC.

47. TW, *Memoirs*, pp. 63–65.

48. EDW, *Tom*, p. 127.

49. TW to Lawrence Langner, uncompleted and unmailed letter, n.d., c. February–March 1941, HRC.

50. *The Case of the Crushed Petunias*, in Tennessee Williams, *American Blues, Five Short Plays* (New York: Dramatists Play Service), pp. 22–32.
51. AW to TW, letter, 27 February 1941, HRC.
52. TW to AW, letter, 27 February 1941, HRC.
53. AW to TW, letter, 8 March 1941, HRC.
54. AW to TW, letter, 12 March 1941, HRC.
55. TW to AW, letter, n.d., c. 15 March 1941, HRC.
56. TW to EDW, letter, n.d., in EDW, *Tom*, p. 128.
57. Luise M. Sillcox to TW, wire, 2 April 1941, HRC.
58. TW to AW, letter, 11 April 1941, HRC.

20. A Reckless Voyager

1. Tennessee Williams, *Memoirs* (Garden City, N.Y.: Doubleday, 1975), p. 74 (hereinafter: TW, *Memoirs*).
2. TW to AW, letter, n.d., c. 15 April 1941, HRC.
3. AW to TW, letter, 18 April 1941, HRC.
4. CMMc to LL, interview, 27 August 1983, New York.
5. TW, *Memoirs*, p. 69.
6. PB to LL, interview, 9 March 1986, Ocean City, New Jersey.
7. PB to Jordan Massee, letter, n.d., c. June 1941, Jordan Massee collection.
8. PB to LL, interview, 13 March 1986, Ocean City, New Jersey.
9. PB to Jordan Massee, letter, 9 July 1941, Jordan Massee collection.
10. PB to LL, interview, 13 March 1986.
   In *Memoirs*, Williams confused his departure for Provincetown the previous summer (1940) with the occasion this time, when in fact Paul Bigelow accompanied him to the train station for his trip to Gloucester.
11. TW to AW, letter, 2 July 1941, HRC.
12. Martin Gabel to AW, letter, 9 July 1941, private collection.
13. AW to TW, letter, 11 July 1941, HRC.
14. TW to EDW, letter, 6 July 1941, Dakin Williams collection.
15. TW to PB, letter, postmarked 25 July 1941, Paul Bigelow collection.
16. Donald Spoto, *The Kindness of Strangers* (Boston: Little, Brown, 1985), p. 81.
17. Poem in Paul Bigelow collection (revised and published in Tennessee Williams, *Androgyne, Mon Amour* [New York: New Directions, 1977], pp. 86–87).
18. AW to TW, letter, 16 August 1941, HRC.
19. TW to AW, letter, n.d., HRC.
20. TW to PB, letter, postmarked 27 August 1941, Paul Bigelow collection.
21. TW to AW, letter, 7 September 1941, HRC. In this letter, Williams also mentioned that an unnamed one-act he had written had been compared to William Saroyan's *The Beautiful People*, and he commented, "I suppose it is inevitable that some people will say I imitate Saroyan in spite of the fact that most of these one-acts were written before any of his plays were produced and I certainly did not have access to his unpublished manuscripts." From this point on, Williams regarded Saroyan with increasing disdain and envy.

21. New Orleans Revisited

1. TW to "Dear Folks," note, 16 September 1941, Dakin Williams collection.
2. AW to TW, letter, 22 September 1941, HRC.
3. Edwina Dakin Williams, with Lucy Freeman, *Remember Me to Tom* (New York: Putnam, 1963), pp. 129–130 (hereinafter: EDW, *Tom*).
4. TW to AW, letter, n.d., c. 24 September 1941, HRC.
5. TW to PB, letter, 25 September 1941, Paul Bigelow collection.
6. TW to PB, letter, postmarked 15 September 1941, Jordan Massee collection.

7. TW to PB, letter, 30 December 1941, Jordan Massee collection.
8. TW to EDW, letter, n.d., Dakin Williams collection.
9. WED to TW, letter, 3 October 1941, HRC.
10. In an author's note, written in September 1941, Williams described the action of the play, set in Vence, where Lawrence died, as imaginary. "Not long before Lawrence's death an exhibition was held of his paintings in London. Primitive in technique and boldly sensual in matter, this exhibition created a little tempest. The pictures were seized and would have been burned if the authorities had not been restrained by an injunction. At the time, Lawrence's great study of sexual passion, 'Lady Chatterley's Lover,' was likewise under the censor's ban, as much of his work had been in the past.

"Lawrence felt the mystery and power of sex, as the primal life urge, and was the lifelong adversary of those who wanted to keep the subject locked away in the cellars of prudery. Much of his work is chaotic and distorted by tangent obsessions, such as his insistence upon the woman's subservience to the male, but all in all his work is probably the greatest modern monument to the dark roots of creation."
11. TW to Lawrence Langner, unmailed letter, n.d., HRC.
12. TW to AW, letter, "Oct. 1941," HRC.
13. TW to PB, letter, 11 October 1941, Paul Bigelow collection.
14. EDW, *Tom*, p. 103.
15. TW to EDW, letter, 23 October 1941, Dakin Williams collection.
16. AW to TW, letter, 18 October 1941, HRC.
17. TW to AW, letter, 21 October 1941, HRC.
18. TW to PB, letter, postmarked 23 October 1941, Paul Bigelow collection.
19. TW to PB, letter, postmarked 3 November 1941, Paul Bigelow collection.
20. AW to TW, letter, 8 November 1941, HRC.
21. TW to AW, letter, 13 November 1941, HRC.
22. TW to William Saroyan, letter, n.d., c. November 1941, Fred Todd collection.
23. William Saroyan to TW, letter, 23 November 1941, Jordan Massee collection.
24. AW to TW, letter, 19 November 1941, HRC.
25. TW to AW, letter, n.d., HRC.
26. TW to EDW, letter, 17 December 1941, Dakin Williams collection.
27. TW to AW, letter, "rec'd" 24 December 1941, HRC.
28. AW to TW, note, 23 December 1941, HRC.

22. At Liberty

1. TW to PB, letter, postmarked 5 January 1942, Paul Bigelow collection.
2. TW to AW, letter, 6 January 1942, HRC.
3. AW to TW, letter, 9 January 1942, HRC.
4. Edwina Dakin Williams, with Lucy Freeman, *Remember Me to Tom* (New York: Putnam, 1963), p. 130.
5. Fred Melton to Richard Freeman Leavitt, interview, 8 April 1986, Fort Lauderdale.
6. TW to EDW, letter, n.d., Dakin Williams collection.
7. TW to AW, letter, received 30 July 1942, HRC.
8. TW to EDW, letter, received 30 July 1942, HRC.
9. TW to Erwin Piscator, unmailed letter, 2 February 1942, Dakin Williams collection.
10. TW to "Dear Folks," letter, n.d., c. February 1942, Dakin Williams collection.
11. Harold Norse, "Of Time and Tennessee Williams," *The Advocate*, 2 October 1984, p. 38.
12. Tennessee Williams, *Memoirs* (Garden City, N.Y.: Doubleday, 1975), pp. 70–71.
13. TW to "Dear Folks," letter, 6 March 1942, Dakin Williams collection.
14. WDW to LL, interview, 14 April 1986, New York.
15. Anne Bretzfelder Post to LL, interview, 2 October 1985, New York.
16. William F. McDermott, *Cleveland Plain Dealer*, 10 October 1943.
17. *The Purification*, in Tennessee Williams, *27 Wagons Full of Cotton and Other Plays* (New York: New Directions, 1945), pp. 29–62.

18. AW to TW, letter, 6 April 1942, HRC.

19. TW to AW, letter, n.d., c. April 1942, HRC.

20. Robert Lewis, *Slings and Arrows* (New York: Stein and Day, 1984), p. 132.

21. Patricia Bosworth, *Montgomery Clift* (New York: Harcourt Brace Jovanovich, 1978), p. 79.

22. TW to PB, letter, postmarked 15 May 1942, Paul Bigelow collection.

23. TW to AW, letter, n.d., c. May 1942, HRC.

24. Ibid.

25. TW to PB, letter, postmarked 5 June 1942, Paul Bigelow collection.

26. PB to Jordan Massee, letter, n.d., Jordan Massee collection.

27. PB to LL, interview, 30 April 1986, Ocean City, New Jersey.

28. TW to Andrew Lyndon, letter, 28 September 1943, Andrew Lyndon collection.

29. PB to LL, interview, 30 April 1986.

30. Ibid.

31. Ibid.

32. David Merrick to TW, letter, 14 June 1942, in Edwina Dakin Williams, with Lucy Freeman, *Remember Me to Tom* (New York: Putnam, 1963), p. 130.

33. AW to TW, letter, 15 June 1942, HRC.

34. PB to Jordan Massee, letter, n.d., Jordan Massee collection.

35. AW to PB, letter, 4 July 1942, Paul Bigelow collection.

36. TW to AW, letter, received 30 July 1942, HRC.

37. PB to Jordan Massee, letter, 30 July 1942, Jordan Massee collection.

38. TW to AW, letter, 21 July 1942, HRC.

39. TW to Mary Hunter, letter, 1 August 1942, HRC. Ultimately, the composite title, *Dragon Country*, was used for a collection of later plays published by New Directions in 1970.

40. Horton Foote, "Sometimes the One-Act Play Says It All," *New York Times*, 4 May 1986, p. 7.

41. AW to TW, letter, 5 August 1942, HRC.

42. PB to Jordan Massee, letter, 8 August 1942, Jordan Massee collection.

43. PB to Jordan Massee, letter, 13 June 1942, Jordan Massee collection.

44. PB to Jordan Massee, letter, postmarked 8 August 1942, Jordan Massee collection.

23. One Hand in Space

1. TW to Andrew Lyndon, letter, n.d., Andrew Lyndon collection.

2. TW to PB, letter, postmarked 19 August 1942, Paul Bigelow collection.

3. EDW to TW, letter, 10 August 1942, HRC.

4. TW to PB, letter, postmarked 25 August 1942, Paul Bigelow collection.

5. TW to AW, letter, n.d., HRC.

6. TW to PB, letter, 10 September 1942, Paul Bigelow collection.

7. AW to PB, letter, 4 September 1942, Paul Bigelow collection.

8. TW to PB, letter, 10 September 1942, Paul Bigelow collection.

9. TW to AW, letter, received 4 September 1942, HRC.

10. PB to Jordan Massee, letter, 10 October 1942, Jordan Massee collection.

11. TW to AW, letter, 4 September 1942, HRC.

12. TW to PB, letters, 22 September and 1 October 1942, Paul Bigelow collection.

13. TW to PB, letter, 7 October 1942, Paul Bigelow collection.

14. TW to PB, letter, n.d., Paul Bigelow collection.

15. AW to TW, letter, 5 October 1942, HRC.

16. TW to AW, letter, n.d., c. October 1942, HRC.

17. TW to PB, letter, postmarked 17 October 1942, Paul Bigelow collection.

18. Early *You Touched Me!* manuscript, Columbia University, Special Collections, Butler Library.

19. E. Graydon Carter, "James Laughlin's Newest Direction Is Looking Back," *Avenue*, December–January 1985, p. 136.

20. Helen Sheehy, *Margo, the Life and Theatre of Margo Jones* (Dallas: Southern Methodist University Press, 1989), pp. 46, 47, and 51.

21. PB to LL, interview, 30 July 1983, Margate, New Jersey.
22. TW to family, letter, 6 December 1942, Dakin Williams collection.

24. "If You Breathe, It Breaks"

1. TW to family, letter, 24 December 1942, Dakin Williams collection.
2. TW to James Laughlin, letter, 31 January 1943, Laughlin collection.
3. Philip Horton, *Hart Crane, the Life of an American Poet* (New York: Viking Press, Compass Books, 1937), pp. 227–228.
4. James Laughlin to TW, letter, 20 January 1943, HRC.
5. EDW to TW, letter, 20 January 1943, Dakin Williams collection.
6. TW to EDW, letter, 25 January 1943, Dakin Williams collection.
7. Elliot S. Valenstein, *Great and Desperate Cures: The Rise and Decline of Psychosurgery and Other Radical Treatments for Mental Illness* (New York: Basic Books, 1986), p. 149.
8. "Where Masters Mingle," *Daily Texan*, 11 February 1987, p. 16.
9. PB to LL, interview, 30 April 1986, Ocean City, New Jersey.
10. Audrey Wood took Williams to the Chekhov play, "thinking this would cheer him; it was the production of *Three Sisters* with Katharine Cornell, Judith Anderson and Ruth Gordon." Tennessee's Iowa classmate, Walter Fleischmann, renamed actor Anthony Dexter, joined them and recalled, "It was a depressing night. Tom had his cataract problem, he had not yet had the success he had expected, and he was a most unhappy sight to see. But he showed no sign of self-pity. He was his usual half-laughing self" (Donald Spoto, *The Kindness of Strangers* [Boston: Little, Brown, 1985], p. 93).
11. TW to Andrew Lyndon, letter, n.d., HRC.
12. Charlotte Chandler, *The Ultimate Seduction* (Garden City, N.Y.: Doubleday, 1984), p. 334.
13. TW to family, letter, n.d., HRC.
14. Ibid.
15. Tennessee Williams, *Memoirs* (Garden City, N.Y.: Doubleday, 1975), p. 70.
16. Gilbert Maxwell, *Tennessee Williams and Friends* (Cleveland and New York: World Publishing, 1965), pp. 65–66.
17. Sandy Campbell, *"B, Twenty-nine Letters from Coconut Grove"* (Verona, Italy: 1974), p. 8.
18. *Tennessee Williams' Letters to Donald Windham—1940–1945*, ed. and with comments by Donald Windham (New York: Holt, Rinehart and Winston, 1977), pp. 56–57.
19. TW to PB, unmailed letter, n.d., c. April 1943, Dakin Williams collection.
20. Ibid.
21. Ibid.
22. TW to James Laughlin, letter, "April 1943," HRC.
23. TW to AW, letter, 7 April 1943, HRC.
24. TW, *Daughter of Revolution (A Dramatic Portrait of an American Mother)*, "Notes on Play and Production," March 1943, HRC.

25. "Metro Goldmine Mayer"

1. TW to family, letter, postmarked 8 May 1943, HRC.
2. "The Summer Belvedere," in Tennessee Williams, *In the Winter of Cities* (New York: New Directions, 1956), p. 45.
3. EDW to TW, letter, n.d., c. 18 May 1943, HRC.
4. David Greggory to LL, interview, 30 June 1986, Santa Monica.
5. AW to TW, letter, 18 May 1943, HRC.
6. Ronald Haver, *David O. Selznick's Hollywood* (New York: Bonanza Books, 1985), p. 87.
7. TW to AW, letter, received 23 May 1943, HRC.
8. TW to PB, letter, 23 May 1943, Paul Bigelow collection.
9. Jonathan Fryer, *Isherwood* (Garden City, N.Y.: Doubleday, 1977), p. 214.
10. TW to AW, letter, received 23 May 1943, HRC.

11. TW to Christopher Isherwood, letter, n.d., HRC.

12. Ibid.

13. Stephen Spender, "Issyvoo's Conversion," *The New York Review of Books*, 14 August 1980, p. 18.

14. Armistead Maupin, "The First Couple," *Village Voice*, 2 July 1985, p. 18.

15. David Greggory to LL, interview, 30 June 1986.

16. AW to TW, letter, 26 May 1943, HRC.

17. PB to LL, interview, 19 August 1986, New York.

18. David Greggory to LL, interview, 30 June 1986.

19. TW to AW, letter, 31 May 1943, HRC.

20. AW to TW, letter, 18 May 1943, HRC.

21. EDW to TW, letter, 22 June 1943, HRC.

22. EDW to TW, letter, n.d., HRC.

23. WED to TW, letter, 19 June 1943, HRC.

24. TW to AW, letter, 18 June 1943, HRC.

25. TW to AW, letter, received 15 June 1943, HRC.

26. TW to AW, 18 June 1943, HRC.

27. David Greggory to LL, interview, 30 June 1986.

28. TW to AW, letter, 28 June 1943, HRC.

29. TW to AW, letter, 31 May 1943, HRC.

30. TW to AW, letter, 29 June 1943, HRC.

31. David Greggory to LL, interview, 30 June 1986, Santa Monica.

32. AW to TW, letter, 7 July 1943, HRC.

33. RIW to TW, letter (from state hospital, Farmington, Missouri), 8 July 1943, HRC.

34. Tennessee Williams, *Collected Stories* (New York: New Directions, 1986), pp. 112, 119.

35. TW to family, letter, 20 July 1943, Dakin Williams collection.

36. TW, "Provisional Film Story Treatment," June 1943, HRC.

37. AW to TW, letter, 14 June 1943, HRC.

38. TW to AW, letter, 18 June 1943, HRC.

39. Louise Davis, "Nashville Was a Streetcar Named Happiness," *Nashville Tennessean Magazine*, 10 March 1957, p. 13.

40. TW to AW, letter, 18 June 1943, HRC.

41. TW to AW, letter, 15 July 1943, HRC.

42. TW to AW, letter, 9 July 1943, HRC.

43. TW to AW, letter, 29 June 1943, HRC.

44. TW to AW, letter, 9 July 1943, HRC.

45. Horton Foote to LL, interview, 17 February 1989, New York.

46. AW to TW, letter, 15 July 1943, HRC.

47. EDW to TW, letter, 25 July 1943, HRC.

48. TW to AW, letter, 9 July 1943, HRC.

49. TW to AW, letter, received 28 June 1943, HRC.

50. TW to PB, letter, 15 July 1943, Paul Bigelow collection.

51. TW to Katherine Anne Porter, letter, 22 June 1943, McKeldin Library, University of Maryland, College Park.

52. TW to Katherine Anne Porter, letter, 30 July 1943, McKeldin Library.

53. Laurie Johnston, *New York Times*, 19 September 1980, p. 34.

54. TW to AW, letter, 2 August 1943, HRC.

26. Hollywood Lost

1. TW to AW, letter, received 11 August 1943, HRC.

2. William Liebling to TW, letter, 10 August 1943, HRC.

3. TW to EDW, letter, 24 August 1943, Dakin Williams collection.

4. Harriett Holland Brandt to LL, letter, 11 August 1985.

5. AW to TW, letter, 30 August 1943, HRC.

6. Margo Jones to Hallie Flanagan, letter, n.d., c. 15 August 1943.

7. "Cortege," in Tennessee Williams, *In the Winter of Cities* (New York: New Directions, 1956), p. 49.

8. Jane Lawrence Smith to LL, interviews, 16 November 1983 and 21 May 1986, New York.

9. Ibid.

10. AW to TW, letter, 16 October 1943, HRC.

11. TW to AW, letter, 21 October 1943, HRC.

12. TW to AW, letter, 14 September 1943, HRC.

13. "Angel in the Alcove," in Tennessee Williams, *One Arm and Other Stories* (New York: New Directions, 1948), pp. 143–144; later, in 1977, it was adapted and incorporated into a full-length play, *Vieux Carré*, along with another short story, "I Never Get Dressed Until After Dark on Sundays."

14. TW, early draft of "The Mattress by the Tomato Patch," dated "Santa Monica, September 1943," HRC.

15. TW to AW, letter, 21 October 1943, HRC.

16. David Greggory to LL, interview, 30 June 1986, New York City.

17. TW to AW, letter, 15 November 1943, HRC.

18. David Greggory to LL, interview, 30 June 1986.

19. TW to AW, letter, 30 November 1943, HRC.

20. WDW to TW, letter, 3 December 1943, Dakin Williams collection.

21. TW to Tony Smith, letter, n.d., HRC.

27. "The Leaf on a Windowsill"

1. "Grand," in Tennessee Williams, *Collected Stories* (New York: New Directions, 1985), pp. 385–387.

2. TW to Mary Hunter, letter, 27 December 1943, HRC.

3. TW, "The Man in the Overstuffed Chair," *Antaeus* 45/46 (Spring/Summer 1982): 281–291; also in *Collected Stories*, pp. ix–xii.

4. TW, "Grand," pp. 379–381; "Grand," *Esquire*, November 1966, pp. 136, 162.

5. TW, "The Man in the Overstuffed Chair," p. xii.

6. *Grand* was privately printed in 1964 by House of Books; it also appeared in *Esquire*, November 1966; in *The Knightly Quest and Other Stories* (New York: New Directions, 1966); and in *Collected Stories*.

7. TW to AW, letter, 16 January 1944, HRC.

8. TW, "Oriflamme," *Collected Stories*, p. 128. As Allean Hale has pointed out, the emphasis is on dying and on the color red—the red dress and the red blood. Intermixed are memories of adolescent dances and the panicked flight up Art Hill, relating to Rose—memories of hysterical flight applying to his own experience, as well. Further, working at Famous-Barr department store is Williams's substitute for the shoe factory. In this story, he has tied together three real-life happenings with the feeling of being imprisoned in St. Louis.

9. TW, "The Vine," *Collected Stories*, p. 142.

10. TW, "Homage to Ophelia," foreword to *You Touched Me!*, unpublished, St. Louis, January 1944, HRC.

11. James Laughlin to Felicia Geffen, executive secretary of the American Academy and Institute of Arts and Letters, letter, 14 February 1944, American Academy and Institute of Arts and Letters archives, New York.

12. TW to James Laughlin, letter, n.d., Laughlin collection.

13. Tennessee Williams, *Memoirs* (Garden City, N.Y.: Doubleday, 1975), pp. 59–60 (hereinafter: TW, *Memoirs*).

14. "Death is High," in Tennessee Williams, *In the Winter of Cities* (New York: New Directions, 1956), p. 117.

15. Walter Damrosch to TW, letter, 22 March 1944, American Academy and Institute of Arts and Letters archives.

16. TW to Walter Damrosch, letter, 24 March 1944, American Academy and Institute of Arts and Letters archives.

17. TW to James Laughlin, letter, April 1944, Laughlin collection.

18. TW to AW, letter, 4 March 1944, HRC.

19. TW to AW, wire, 14 June 1944, HRC.

20. AW's secretary to TW, letter, 5 July 1944, HRC.

21. Tony Smith to TW, unmailed letter, n.d., c. summer 1944, collection of Jane Lawrence Smith.

22. TW to AW, wire, 25 July 1944, HRC.

23. Dorothy J. Farnan, *Auden in Love* (New York: Simon and Schuster, 1984), pp. 108–109.

24. TW, *Memoirs*, pp. 83–84.

25. Bill Cannastra to TW, letter, n.d., HRC.

26. Farnan, *Auden in Love*, pp. 108–109.

27. Harold Norse, *City Magazine*, San Francisco, 7 October 1975, p. 13.

28. Chicago, Chicago

1. Ward Morehouse, *Matinee Tomorrow* (New York: Whittlesey House, McGraw-Hill, 1947).

2. George Jean Nathan, *The Theatre Book of the Year 1945–46* (New York: Alfred A. Knopf, 1946).

3. Marguerite Courtney, *Laurette* (New York: Atheneum, 1968), p. 393.

4. Helen Ormsbee, *New York Herald Tribune*, 22 April 1945.

5. Courtney, *Laurette*, p. 394.

6. Rosamond Gilder, *Theatre Arts*, June 1945, p. 329.

7. Horton Foote to LL, interview, 17 February 1989, New York.

8. TW to Margo Jones, letter, 18 October 1944, HRC.

9. TW to James Laughlin, letter, n.d., Laughlin collection.

10. Margo Jones, *Theatre in the Round* (New York: Rinehart & Company, 1951), pp. 56–57.

11. TW to WED, letter, 3 November 1944, Dakin Williams collection.

12. Mike Steen, *A Look at Tennessee Williams* (New York: Hawthorn Books, 1969), p. 96.

13. Helen Sheehy, *Margo, the Life and Theatre of Margo Jones* (Dallas: Southern Methodist University Press, 1989), p. 72.

14. TW to EDW, letter, n.d., c. November–December 1944, Dakin Williams collection.

15. Tennessee Williams, *Memoirs* (Garden City, N.Y.: Doubleday, 1975), p. 82 (hereinafter: TW, *Memoirs*).

16. Paul Bowles, *Without Stopping* (New York: Ecco Press, 1985), p. 256.

17. Jane Lawrence Smith to LL, interview, 2 May 1986, New York.

18. Courtney, *Laurette*, pp. 399–400.

19. Claudia Cassidy, *Chicago Tribune*, 19 September 1948.

20. Courtney, *Laurette*, p. 398.

21. TW, *Memoirs*, p. 81.

22. Courtney, *Laurette*, p. 398.

23. *Tennessee Williams' Letters to Donald Windham—1940–1965*, ed. and with comments by Donald Windham (New York: Holt, Rinehart and Winston, 1977), p. 155.

24. Jo Mielziner, *Designing for the Theatre* (New York: Bramhall House, 1965), pp. 12, 124.

25. Sheehy, *Margo*, pp. 80–81.

26. Ashton Stevens, "Excursions in Stageland," *Chicago Herald-American*.

27. Steen, *A Look at Tennessee Williams*, p. 145.

28. EDW to WED, letter, 25 December 1944, Dakin Williams collection.

29. Courtney, *Laurette*, p. 401.

30. Mielziner, *Designing for the Theatre*, p. 126.

31. Edwina Dakin Williams, with Lucy Freeman, *Remember Me to Tom* (New York: Putnam, 1963), p. 146 (hereinafter: EDW, *Tom*).

32. Donald Windham, *As if . . .* (Verona: Sandy Campbell, 1985), p. 39.

33. Frank Rich, "A Short Day's Journey to Eugene O'Neill's Childhood Home," *New York Times*, 6 August 1981, p. C15.
34. Nancy M. Tischler, *Tennessee Williams: Rebellious Puritan* (New York: Citadel, 1965), pp. 110–111.
35. TW, *Memoirs*, p. 85.
36. Max Wilk, *Mr. Williams and Miss Wood* (New York: Dramatists Play Service, 1990).
37. EDW, *Tom*, p. 150.
38. AW to TW, wire, 28 December 1944, HRC.
39. Steen, *A Look at Tennessee Williams*, pp. 96–97.
40. Courtney, *Laurette*, p. 396.
41. TW to LL, interview, 23 August 1976, San Francisco.

29. *The Glass Menagerie*

1. Claudia Cassidy, "On the Aisle," *Chicago Tribune*, 3 December 1961, pp. 9–10.
2. TW to EDW, letter, n.d., HRC.
3. Ashton Stevens, *Chicago Herald-American*, 10 December 1946.
4. Marguerite Courtney, *Laurette* (New York: Atheneum, 1968), pp. 404–405, 406.
5. Paul Wagman, *St. Louis Post-Dispatch*, 30 May 1974, p. 3-F.
6. WDW, "My Brother's Keeper," unpublished manuscript, p. 69, Dakin Williams collection.
7. Tennessee Williams, *Memoirs* (Garden City, N.Y.: Doubleday, 1975), pp. 86–87.
8. Courtney, *Laurette*, pp. 403–404.
9. Eddie Dowling to Jack Barefield, letters, 8 August 1968 and 17 March 1971. In all probability, Dowling's enmity became hatred when Audrey Wood gave Irene Mayer Selznick the rights to produce *A Streetcar Named Desire*. Referring to Laura and Blanche, he wrote Barefield that Tennessee Williams "went off with this beautiful sister into Cheap Clap Trap Melodrama aided and abetted by Mr. Kazan. And the strange Audrey Wood. Poor Williams, who could have gone into immortality with Shelley, Keats, Bacon, Goldsmith & Shaw, if he could have kept out of the pig sty." Jack Barefield collection.
10. Eddie Dowling to Jack Barefield, letter, 28 March 1968.
11. TW to Jo Mielziner, letter, n.d., HRC.
12. TW to AW, letter, 7 February 1945, HRC.
13. TW to AW, letter, n.d., HRC.
14. Ibid.
15. Helen Hayes, with Sandford Dody, *On Reflection* (New York: Evans, 1968), pp. 123–124.
16. Helen Hayes to LL, telephone interview, 19 June 1990.
17. Helen Hayes, with Katherine Hatch, *My Life in Three Acts* (New York: Harcourt Brace Jovanovich, 1990), pp. 164–165.
18. TW to AW, letter, 15 February 1945, HRC.
19. Anne Edwards, *A Remarkable Woman: A Biography of Katharine Hepburn* (New York: William Morrow, 1985), p. 305.
20. Max Wilk, *Mr. Williams and Miss Wood* (New York: Dramatists Play Service, 1990).
21. Ibid.
22. Norman Felton to Clay Harshbarger, letter, 10 October (c. 1980), University of Iowa.
23. Lawrence Christon, "Passion Spurs His Work," *San Francisco Chronicle Datebook*, 18 May 1986, p. 43.
24. TW to AW, letter, n.d., HRC.
25. AW to TW, letter, 15 February 1945, HRC.
26. AW to TW, telegram, 22 February 1945, HRC.
27. AW to TW, letter, 15 February 1945, HRC.
28. AW to TW, telegram, 27 February 1945, HRC.
29. TW to AW, letter, 15 February 1945, HRC.
30. TW to EDW, letter, n.d., HRC.

31. TW, introduction to William Inge, *The Dark at the Top of the Stairs* (New York: Random House, 1958), p. x.

32. AW to TW, letter, 6 March 1945, HRC.

33. TW to AW, letter, 8 March 1945, HRC.

34. TW to Guthrie McClintic, letter, 7 March 1945, Richard Stoddard collection.

35. William Liebling to TW, telegram, 15 March 1945, HRC.

36. TW to DW, letter fragment, n.d., HRC.

37. TW to AW, letter, 23 March 1945, HRC.

38. TW to Bennett Cerf, letter, 30 March 1945, Columbia University, Special Collections, Butler Library.

39. Bennett Cerf to TW, letter, 2 April 1945, Columbia University, Butler Library.

40. Wilk, *Mr. Williams and Miss Wood.*

41. Courtney, *Laurette*, p. 412.

42. Ibid., pp. 412–413.

30. *"En Avant!"*

1. Charlotte Chandler, *The Ultimate Seduction* (Garden City, N.Y.: Doubleday, 1984), pp. 334–335.

2. Laurette Taylor to Dwight Taylor, letter, 27 May 1945, Dwight Taylor collection.

3. George Jean Nathan, quoted in *P.M.* magazine section, 6 May 1945, pp. 6–7.

4. Louis Kronenberger, "A Triumph for Miss Taylor," *P.M.*, 2 April 1945.

5. Otis L. Guernsey, Jr., "The Theater at Its Best," *New York Herald Tribune*, 2 April 1945.

6. Lewis Nichols, "The Glass Menagerie," *New York Times*, 2 April 1945.

7. Ray Falk, "People Line Up for Tickets to Tennessee Williams' Play," *St. Louis Star-Times*, 6 April 1945, p. 10.

8. "The Winner," *Time*, 23 April 1945, p. 88.

9. "Bang-Bang Plays Disgust, Fascinate 'Glass' Author," *Portland Oregonian*, March 1946.

10. "On a Streetcar Named Success," *New York Times*, 30 November 1947, pp. 1, 3; also in Tennessee Williams, *Where I Live: Selected Essays* (New York: New Directions, 1978), p. 17.

11. EDW to CCW, letter, 23 April 1945, HRC.

12. Williams, *Where I Live*, p. 17.

13. Robert van Gelder, "Playwright with a Good Conceit," *New York Times*, 22 April 1945.

14. TW to Guthrie McClintic and Katharine Cornell, "Friday," n.d., Richard Stoddard collection.

15. TW to Guthrie McClintic, wire, 9 June 1945, Richard Stoddard collection.

16. TW to Guthrie McClintic, letter, 14 June 1945, Richard Stoddard collection.

17. TW to AW, letter, 20 June 1945, HRC.

18. Benedict Nightingale, "This 'Menagerie' Is Much Too Cozy," *New York Times*, 11 December 1983, pp. 3, 14.

19. Interview with Vivien Goldsmith, *London Evening Standard*, 8 June 1977.

20. Arthur Miller, *Timebends* (New York: Grove Press, 1987), p. 244.

21. I am especially indebted to the following authors as well as to the many who have written with keen insight, although often divergently, about *The Glass Menagerie*:

Bigsby, C. W. E., ed. *A Critical Introduction to Twentieth-Century American Drama*, vol. 2 (New York: Cambridge University Press, 1984).

Bloom, Harold, ed. *Tennessee Williams's "The Glass Menagerie": Modern Critical Interpretations* (New York: Chelsea House, 1988).

Bloom, Harold, ed. *Tennessee Williams: Modern Critical Views* (New York: Chelsea House, 1987): See Thomas L. King, "Irony and Distance in The Glass Menagerie," p. 85.

Nelson, Benjamin. *Tennessee Williams: The Man and His Work* (New York: Obolensky, 1961): See "The Play Is Memory," p. 97.

Stanton, Stephen S., ed. *Tennessee Williams: A Collection of Critical Essays* (Englewood Cliffs, N.J.:

Prentice-Hall, 1977): See Thomas P. Adler, "The Search for God in the Plays of Tennessee Williams," p. 138.

Stern, Stewart. *No Tricks in My Pocket: Paul Newman Directs* (New York: Grove Press, 1989).

Tharpe, Jac, ed. *Tennessee Williams: 13 Essays*, selected from *Tennessee Williams: A Tribute* (Oxford University Press of Mississippi, 1980): See Judith J. Thompson, "Symbol, Myth, and Ritual in *The Glass Menagerie, The Rose Tattoo* and *Orpheus Descending,*" p. 139.

Tischler, Nancy M. *Tennessee Williams: Rebellious Puritan* (New York: Citadel, 1965).

Photograph Credits

ILLUSTRATIONS: 1: Special Collections, University of Tennessee in Knoxville; 2: Courtesy of the Middle Georgia Archives, Washington Memorial Library, Macon, GA; 3, 11, 15: Special Collections, Butler Library, Columbia University, NYC; 4, 5, 10, 24, 28, 56, 60, 78, 84, 85: Dakin Williams Family Collection, Collinsville, IL; 6, 7, 8, 9, 13, 14, 21, 22, 23, 25, 26, 32, 36, 37, 40, 41, 42, 45, 46, 52, 53, 54, 55, 59, 61, 62, 63, 66, 67, 68, 74, 81, 83, 86, 87, 88: Picture Collection, Harry Ransom Humanities Research Center, University of Texas at Austin, Permission of the estate of Tennessee Williams; 53: Permission of the Witter Bynner Foundation for Poetry in Santa Fe, NM; 16, 57: Lyle Leverich, Kentfield, CA; 17: Missouri Historical Society, St. Louis, MO; 19, 29, 30, 38: Allean Hale, Urbana, IL; 12, 18, 20, 27, 31: Theatre Collection, Harvard University, Cambridge, MA; 33, 35: University Archives, Washington University, University City, St. Louis, MO; 34: Courtesy of William J. Smith; 39: Courtesy of The International Shoe Company, St. Louis, MO; 43: Courtesy of Harriet Holland Brandt; 44: Estate of Marion Black Vaccaro; 47: Courtesy of Milton Lomask; 48, 50: Kent Collection, University of Iowa Archives, Iowa City, Iowa; 49: Courtesy of Truman Slitor; 51: Historic New Orleans Collection; 58: Courtesy of Joe Hazan; 64, 65: The Billy Rose Theatre Collection, New York Public Library at Lincoln Center, Astor and Tilden Foundations; 69, 70, 71, 79: Collection of Jordan Massee, Macon, GA; 72: Courtesy of James Laughlin, New Directions, NYC; 73: DeGolyer Library, Southern Methodist University, Dallas, TX; 75, 76, 77: Cinemabilia, NYC; 80: Courtesy of Jane Lawrence Smith, NYC; 82: William Inge Collection, Independence Community College, Independence, KN; 89, 90, 91, 92: *Stage Magazine* Archives, NYC; 93, 94: *Theatre Arts Magazine* Archives (March 1952), NYC; 95: Wide World Photos, NYC; 96: Bettmann/UPI Archive, NYC.

Acknowledgments

I gratefully acknowledge the assistance of Kay Bost, Donald Bowden, Deborah Brown, Virginia Spencer Carr, Barbara S. Cook, Bernard R. Crystal, Rudolph Ellenbogen, Tom Erhardt, Peter Harvey, Jay Laughlin, James B. Lloyd, Richard Loiselle, Jean T. Lyndon, Peter MacGlashan, John T. Magill, Melissa Miller, Jeanne T. Newlin, Harry Olmstead, Sally Polhemus, Peer Edwin Ravnan, Earl M. Rogers, Steven Schwartz, Bob and Linda Shaw, Betty Travitsky, Ruth C. Tripp, Robert and Elmerline Vancore, Janice Weir, Dakin and Joyce Williams, and, especially, Allean Hale and Ann N. Paterra.

Richard Freeman Leavitt

Index